BRITISH HIT ALBUMS

- PAUL GAMBACCINI -
- TIM RICE - JONATHAN RICE -

5

GRR Editorial Associate: TONY BROWN

GUINNESS PUBLISHING

The three authors would like to thank Alan Jones and Graham Walker for their contributions to this edition.

Special thanks, too, to Eileen Heinink and Jan Rice. We also want to thank *New Musical Express* and *CIN* for their charts and many record company press offices for their patient help.

Picture Acknowledgements:
Hulton Picture Company; London Features International; Redferns; Rex Features.

Editor:
David Roberts
Deputy Editor:
Paola Simoneschi
Picture Research:
Image Select
Page Make-up:
Mandy Ward
Illustrations:
Carol Wright

GRR Publications Ltd 1992

First edition 1983, reprinted once
Second edition 1986
Third edition 1988
Fourth edition 1990
Fifth edition 1992

Published in Great Britain by Guinness Publishing Ltd, 33 London Road, Enfield, Middlesex

Typeset in Bembo by Ace Filmsetting Ltd, Frome, Somerset

Printed and bound in Great Britain by The Bath Press, Bath

A catalogue record for this book is available from the British LIbrary
ISBN 0-85112-967-6

INTRODUCTION

This is where it's at. Or, to be slightly more expansive: now, more than ever, this is where *you're* at. This book was originally conceived as a companion to the definitive guide to what record buyers were purchasing, *The Guinness Book of British Hit Singles.* In the early 90s we unexpectedly find ourselves in what might be considered reversed circumstances. It is this book, *British Hit Albums,* that now most accurately reflects what people are paying and putting down pieces of plastic for.

This is not to say that *British Hit Singles* is passé, though we admit to dark nights of the soul when we feared that might prove the case. The unprecedented sales of the latest edition of that title prove that memories associated to individual songs are as strong as ever. But the fact is that more people are now buying albums than singles, and the albums they are acquiring have little to do with what singles are being bought.

It is commonly assumed that dance music has dominated the singles chart for some time. Excepting the number one position, which has almost always been occupied by a mass appeal act, this is true. Yet anyone looking at the Top Twenty of the 1991 year-end best-selling albums chart would search in vain for dance acts. Only *The Immaculate Collection* by Madonna could be considered a dance album and she, of course, is a transcendent star who appeals to many audiences. Dance music may have dominated the airwaves of Britain's pop music stations, but it is not a style that has interested the general public.

It is also worth noting a disparity between the British album chart and another list, its American counterpart. In a staggering example of how musical taste has fragmented – not just between audiences but between countries – the top four UK albums of 1991 were nowhere to be found in the Billboard Top 100 of the year, and vice versa. The quintessential quartet of Simply Red, Eurythmics, Queen and Tina Turner were conspicuously absent from the US best sellers, and the fab four of the States, Mariah Carey, Garth Brooks, the Black Crowes and C&C Music Factory, were lacking on the list in the mother country.

There is some pleasure to be drawn from these facts, for two reasons. First, they show that even the best-educated and most experienced pundits are helpless in predicting the future when that future is in the hands of a public that doesn't care what they think. Almost any critic with a functioning brain forecast in the 1980s that technological innovations such as MTV would make it possible for everyone in the world to see and hear the same music at the same time. International taste would therefore grow more uniform. As events transpired, videos, a proliferation of radio and television stations and a burgeoning club culture made it possible for consumers to hear and see more different kinds of music. They expressed their preferences in geographically localized as well as stylistically fragmented ways.

Secondly, the two-year period since the last edition of this book proves that record companies cannot dictate popular taste, no matter how much manipulation they attempt. Despite great effort expended on its behalf, rave music did not export, just as punk failed to sell overseas in the late 70s. Similarly, the American labels releasing the works of Candyman, Firehouse, Travis Tritt and Yanni may have been delighted by their showings in the annual Billboard summaries, but might find British counterparts breaking into cold sweats trying to remember in what styles these acts perform.

4

The public wants what it likes, regardless of what it is expected to like. The three most eagerly awaited albums of autumn 1991 were the new works by Dire Straits, Michael Jackson and U2. These artists all rank highly in our lifetime achievement tables. At least one of the releases received enthusiastic reviews. Yet these three highly publicized and widely advertised discs spent a total of two weeks at number one. They were not failures, all finishing in the Top Twenty of the year, but the public preferred other releases, particularly *Stars* by Simply Red, a far less ballyhooed set that didn't even contain a top five single at that time.

What is it, then, that the British *have* chosen in the past two years? Certainly the fondness for Greatest Hits albums persists, with compilations by the Carpenters, Eurythmics, Elton John, Madonna, Queen, Jimmy Somerville, Status Quo, Tina Turner and Paul Young all placing in the year-end Top Twenty. The public still likes to reward both the persistent artist who is slow to find an audience, like 1990 breakout star Michael Bolton and 1991's long-time-coming group R.E.M., and the act to whom it takes a fancy on first release, such as Seal or Beverley Craven. In the past two years classical music has increased its market share, thanks to the popularity of Luciano Pavarotti, his fellow tenors José Carreras and Placido Domingo, and Nigel Kennedy. As *The Economist* showed in figures printed in late 1991, this is a British phenomenon, with the classical music slice of the pie actually shrinking in some European countries.

What typifies the hit album of 1990–91 is this: it is enjoyed by an adult audience. The cessation of the Stock–Aitken–Waterman domination of the charts has meant there has been nothing near a repetition of the circumstances of 1988–89, when Kylie Minogue and Jason Donovan had the year's best-selling albums with their first efforts. Donovan, of course, found an upmarket project in the successful revival of *Joseph and the Amazing Technicolor Dreamcoat*, but there was no album in the year-end Top Ten of either 1990 or 1991 that could be remotely considered to be targeted at the youth market.

Although they cannot control what buyers are choosing, record companies should at least be grateful that their worst-case nightmare, that the rock generation would stop buying music when it grew up, has not come to pass. Indeed, as adults they are buying in volume. An end to recession should mean they buy in even higher numbers to produce even larger sales figures. But that would be a prediction, and we have already said that in the case of popular music the future cannot be foretold. With a sigh of relief, we remember that the tools of our trade are yesterday's charts and not crystal balls.

Since our last edition the Compact Disc has continued to increase its market share at the expense of the vinyl LP. It has also resisted the advance of Digital Audio Tape. But though CD seems to have seen off the challenge of DAT, it is coming under fresh attack from the Mini Disc and the Digital Compact Cassette. Which form will be preferred when we next meet in these pages? What a relief it is to be able to say it's up to you.

5

Paul Gambaccini

Tim Rice

1958

In 1948 CBS introduced the long-playing microgroove recording to America. It was devised by Peter Goldmark who, it is said, had had enough of getting up several times during one piece of music to change several 78s. He thought there had to be a market for a single disc that could contain an entire symphony or sonata.

The eighteen albums that hit the chart in the last eight weeks of 1958, the first weeks of *Melody Maker*'s Top Ten chart (the first LP chart published in the UK), demonstrated that Goldmark's invention had other applications. None of the eighteen best-sellers was a classical orchestral performance! Thirteen were by adult male performers with wide audience appeal and five were of show business origin – that is, stage, screen or television.

The soundtrack to 'South Pacific' was number one for each of the eight weeks, a prelude to its equally total domination of the 1959 lists. The man with the most LPs to chart was Frank Sinatra, who touched the Top Ten four times. Elvis Presley had the most total weeks on chart, that is to say a sum of the runs of each of his hit LPs. Both 'Elvis' Golden Records' and 'King Creole' were on every one of the eight charts.

The other artists who contributed to the all-male domain were Perry Como, Russ Conway, Mario Lanza, the American satirist Tom Lehrer, and Johnny Mathis. Perhaps Lanza was the closest to what Goldmark had in mind: one side of his disc was the soundtrack to the film about the classical tenor Enrico Caruso, 'The Great Caruso'.

1959

It can be whispered in reverent awe or shouted from the rooftops, but the achievement is so great that it cannot be conveyed in casual conversation: the original soundtrack to the film 'South Pacific' was at number one for the entire year 1959. This family favourite led the list for every one of the 52 weeks, a feat which has never been matched, though later discs would surpass it in sales. 'South Pacific' boasted a wide range of memorable music, from the love ballad

'Some Enchanted Evening' (an American number one for Perry Como) to the novelty tune 'Happy Talk' (eventually a UK number one for Captain Sensible).

Film soundtracks were still the leading money-spinners in the LP market of 1959. The form was only a decade old, and soundtracks, Broadway cast performances and classical works were still the most logical initial uses of Peter Goldmark's invention, requiring the additional space a long player could provide. The movie versions of 'Gigi' and 'The King And I' were notable winners in 1959, as was the New York stage production of 'West Side Story'.

Rock-and-roll vocalists, previously content with singles, made further inroads into the album field, but Frank Sinatra still scored the most weeks on chart for a solo singer. Elvis Presley was a close second, registering an impressive success with 'Elvis' Golden Records'. The chart appearance of two LPs by Cliff Richard was the best 1959 showing by a young Briton.

'Curtain Up!', a compilation of stars from the London Palladium hosted by Bruce Forsyth, enjoyed a 13-week run, but the most impressive performance by a show business star was that of Peter Sellers, who spent 32 weeks in the Top Ten with two solo LPs and a further five with his colleagues the Goons.

1 9 6 0

'South Pacific' dominated the album charts one more time in 1960, though not to the extent it had in 1959. It was in the best-sellers for every one of the 53 charts of the year, the only title to achieve that run, but it did occasionally let other discs take the top spot. Number one on the very first *Record Retailer* album chart, that of 10 March, was 'The Explosive Freddy Cannon', which fell in fragments the following week after giving Cannon the distinction of being the first rock-and-roll singer to have a number one LP in the UK. Even the second, Elvis Presley, who had been a more likely contender for that honour, only managed one week at the summit, scoring with 'Elvis Is Back'. The other disc to interrupt the 'South Pacific' streak was 'Down Drury Lane To Memory Lane', a nostalgic effort by the studio group 101 Strings.

Rock-and-roll made great progress in the long playing market in 1960. The previous year only four rockers had charted in the entire 12 months. This time five of the top six acts were rock stars, though the majority of chart artists were still not of this nature. Presley pipped Peter Sellers as the individual with most weeks on the chart, though Sellers would have ranked above Presley if the computation included his additional appearances with the Goons and Sophia Loren, not, one must add, on the same disc.

American guitarist Duane Eddy's surprisingly strong showing in fourth place should not be overlooked.

1 9 6 1

Commercial success does not guarantee artistic immortality, as the George Mitchell Minstrels have proved. Their 'Black And White Minstrel Show' was an enormous success on television, record and stage, but an entire generation has grown up in, shall we say, the dark about their achievements.

'The Black And White Minstrel Show' was the only album to stay in the chart for the whole of 1961. It accumulated seven weeks at number one in four separate visits, while 'Another Black And White Minstrel Show' had a single mighty eight-week run at the top. Mass audiences loved the old-time performances of The Minstrels, many of whom blacked up to sing vintage popular songs. It was the dated nature of their material, as well as increased sophistication concerning racial matters, which spelled an end to large scale interest in the group in the late sixties.

Elvis Presley was the outstanding artist for the second consecutive year, enjoying 22 weeks at number one with the soundtrack to 'GI Blues'. The granddaddy of film favourites, 'South Pacific', put in a final nine weeks at the peak before retiring. It was a bumper year for original cast recordings of stage musicals, with a strong emphasis on the London stage. 'Oliver', 'Sound of Music' and 'Stop the World I Want To Get Off' all had lengthy runs with British rosters. The year saw hit honours for the well-remembered 'Beyond The Fringe' and the completely forgotten 'King Kong'. Even the London cast of 'Bye Bye Birdie' flew out of the wings and into the charts.

Frank Sinatra continued his series of fine years, entering the Top

Twenty with seven titles on four different labels. Cliff Richard had three new top two successes and one happy hangover from 1960, 'Me And My Shadows'. '21 Today' was his first number one, though his mates beat him to the top by six weeks with their debut disc 'The Shadows'.

1 9 6 2

Elvis Presley and the George Mitchell Minstrels overachieved again in 1962. The King of rock and roll notched up 18 weeks at number one with his 'Blue Hawaii' soundtrack, more time at the top than any other long player that year, and he ruled the roost for six more weeks with 'Pot Luck'. The Minstrels led the list with their new release, 'On Stage With The George Mitchell Minstrels', and then encored with their 1960 issue, the original 'Black And White Minstrel Show'. Their three albums tallied a total of 109 weeks in the chart, the first time any act had hit the century.

Compared to these two artists the rest of the field failed to flame, though 'South Pacific' again managed to appear in every one of the 52 charts. The new film sensation was 'West Side Story', surpassing its significant stage sales to pace the pack for 12 weeks. Four other multi-media successes were the soundtrack to 'It's Trad Dad', the original cast album of the London production *Blitz*, and two Dorothy Provine sets inspired by her television series 'The Roaring 20s'. Further evidence of the taste for trad was the appearance of a budget album, 'The Best of Ball, Barber and Bilk' at number one for two weeks. Chris Barber and Acker Bilk had appeared together on two fast-selling packages in 1961, sans Kenny Ball.

9

The Shadows achieved the fabulous feat of nabbing their second number one with their second effort, 'Out Of The Shadows'. They shared credit on Cliff Richard's table-topping 'The Young Ones'. Cliff managed to top the Shads in weeks on chart thanks to his subsequent release, the literally timed and titled '32 Minutes And 17 Seconds'.

1 9 6 3

Beatlemania spread like a flash fire in 1963, and the album chart showed its effects. The Fab Four's 'Please Please Me' seized the top spot on 11 May and held it for 30 consecutive weeks, to be replaced only by 'With the Beatles', which kept clear for a further 21. The Liverpudlians had come from nowhere to hold the premier position for one week shy of a full year. It was nothing short of a musical revolution: from their arrival until 1968, only one non-rock album would have a look in at number one. A field that had been the domain of the soundtrack and cast album overnight became ruled by rock. It was hard to believe that 1963 had begun with 'The Black and White Minstrel Show' still in the lead. With a couple of notable exceptions, the film and stage market dried up.

Cliff Richard was the weeks on chart champ this time, his total fed by three new successes. The second highest figures were achieved equally by Elvis Presley and Buddy Holly. The Pelvis began twitching in anxiety as the soundtracks to three bad films did progressively worse. Holly, dead for four years, had always been a strong album seller, but really surged in 1963 when the poignantly-titled collection 'Reminiscing' joined the list of his other posthumous bestsellers.

Frank Ifield proved a one-year though not a one-hit wonder, reaching number three with two releases. He never came close again. Frank Sinatra rebounded with three top tenners, including a team-up with Count Basie that went to number two.

1 9 6 4

The Beatles and Rolling Stones monopolized the number one position during 1964, making it the purest year for rock music in terms of holding the top spot. The only 12 weeks John, Paul, George and Ringo were not ahead with either 'With The Beatles', 'A Hard Day's Night' or 'Beatles For Sale', their chief competition was in front with the debut disc 'The Rolling Stones'. The fresh triumphs of 'A Hard Day's Night' and 'Beatles For Sale' gave the Beatles four number ones in four releases, a 100 per cent success ratio they maintained through all of their 11 official outings, though two other issues, a compilation and the 'Yellow Submarine' soundtrack on which they played only a part, fell short of the top. No other act has hit number one every time with as many records.

The Fab Four's quartet of hit LPs gave them 104 weeks on chart, the first time a century had been achieved by a rock act. But even they were outdistanced by Jim Reeves. The American country singer had enjoyed two big albums to accompany his two strong singles in the first half of the year. After he died in a plane crash in July, nine further packages made the chart, six in a four-week period. Gentleman Jim accumulated 115 weeks on chart in all, a record that would stand until 1968.

Third in the weeks on chart category was Roy Orbison, who enjoyed the distinction of seeing his 'In Dreams' set on every chart of the year, a feat attained for the second consecutive year by 'West Side Story'. Cliff Richard had only one new album, below average for his early years, and Elvis Presley slipped seriously as none of his three long players reached the top three.

1 9 6 5

For the three middle years of the sixties only the Beatles, Rolling Stones, Bob Dylan and 'The Sound Of Music' reached number one, trading off in a seemingly endless sequence. The first three were the rock artists who came to represent the spirit of the decade, while the last was a show business phenomenon that came, saw, conquered, and wouldn't go away.

The Beatles began the year on top with 'Beatles For Sale' and ended it there with 'Rubber Soul', having spent much of the summer there as well with 'Help'. Bob Dylan had the second highest total of chart-toppers, two, succeeding 'The Freewheelin' Bob Dylan' with his own 'Bringing It All Back Home', but his most impressive statistic was his 112 weeks on chart. Much of his back catalogue charted in late 1964 and 1965. Though primarily considered an album artist, he also logged five top thirty singles in 1965, his peak year.

Dylan's dear friend Joan Baez shared his success, with three charters to follow her 1964 debut. Her winners included 'Joan Baez', 'Joan Baez No. 5' and 'Farewell Angelina', but no sign of Joan Baez Nos. 2, 3 or 4.

Though Miss Baez was the front-running credited female vocalist, Julie Andrews accounted for the greatest grosses with her soundtracks. 'Mary Poppins' spent the most weeks on chart of any 1965 title, 50, and 'The Sound Of Music' began a run to rival that of 'South Pacific', accumulating its first 20 weeks at number one.

Sir Winston Churchill, who had died early in the year, had a posthumous Top Ten LP, 'The Voice Of Sir Winston Churchill'.

1 9 6 6

Cash register tills were still alive to 'The Sound Of Music' in 1966. If the Beatles or Rolling Stones didn't have a new album, the star soundtrack of the Sixties kept the number one position warm. It followed 'Rubber Soul' and preceded 'Aftermath'; it moved back in the aftermath of 'Aftermath' and before 'Revolver'. When the latter Beatles album had shot its bolt, Julie Andrews and company skipped back to the top for the last three months of the year.

'The Sound Of Music' was the only album to spend all of 1966 in the best sellers. It was as big an international phenomenon as a UK success. *Time* reported that it had sold seven million copies by Christmas, outmoving all other stage or screen sets, even the legendary 'South Pacific'.

The musical version of the Von Trapp family story was a timely purchase in any season, not linked to fad or fashion. The Beatles' unprecedented popularity, on the other hand, had made every one of their new discs an immediate must purchase. A short period of colossal concentrated sale would then be followed by a chart decline. Hence 'Revolver', a summer number one, was almost gone by Christmas. Parlophone, wanting a Beatles product for the major marketing month of the year, issued 'A Collection Of Beatles Oldies' in December. However, the fans weren't fooled. It peaked at seven, a commercial miscalculation.

The Beach Boys spent more weeks on the chart than anyone in 1966, with five long players accumulating 95 weeks between them. This success reflected their four consecutive top three singles. One album, the classic 'Pet Sounds', did much better in Britain than America, reaching number two.

The other album artist of note was Herb Alpert, who garnered 89 weeks, but while his Tijuana Brass LPs loitered on the list they did not reach the highest chart positions.

1 9 6 7

History remembers 1967 as the year of flower power and psychedelia. The only real evidence of this in the upper echelons of the LP charts was the tremendous success of the Beatles' landmark 'Sergeant Pepper's Lonely Hearts Club Band' and the considerable achievement of 'Are You Experienced?' by the Jimi Hendrix Experience.

'Sergeant Pepper', chosen the best rock album of all time in two international critics' polls, spent exactly half the year at number one. The other 26 weeks were divided between the recurrent 'The Sound of Music' and the first-time sets by the distinctly unpsychedelic Monkees. In a year when they had six hit singles and a cult television show, the 'fabricated four' reached the top with 'The Monkees' and 'More Of The Monkees'.

13

With only those four albums going all the way in 1967, it was a major achievement to get to number two. Hendrix and band did. Cream did respectably but not quite as well, earning Top Ten placings with their first two cartons of 'Fresh Cream' and 'Disraeli Gears'. The Rolling Stones surprisingly peaked at three with 'Between The Buttons'.

It was a fine year for easy listening and soul. In addition to 'Best Of The Beach Boys', records that rode the roster for all 52 weeks included the soundtracks of 'The Sound Of Music' and 'Dr Zhivago' and 'Going Places' by Herb Alpert and the Tijuana Brass. Alpert led overall by a toot with 101 weeks on chart, though the Beach Boys were a close second with 97. Tom Jones had three Top Ten issues and the Dubliners, Irish singers enjoying a year of British popularity, had two.

This was the best year on record for Geno Washington, an outstanding live soul attraction. Otis Redding and the Four Tops also had strong chart performances, but they would do even better in 1968.

1 9 6 8

The album chart lost its sense of discipline in 1968. In previous years the number of different artists who had reached number one, not counting performers on film soundtracks, could be counted on the fingers of a sawmill operator's hand. This time no fewer than a dozen different acts went all the way, with occasional further appearances by 'The Sound Of Music'.

The nature of the chart-toppers changed, too. Recently the number one spot had been the property of the world's outstanding rock talents. In 1968 Val Doonican, Tom Jones and Andy Williams managed to head the hordes. The Small Faces and Scott Walker enjoyed their only number one LPs, and Simon and Garfunkel their first. The Four Tops, Otis Redding, and Diana Ross and the Supremes broke the all-white stranglehold on the top spot. The only black faces to have been there before were the made-up ones of the George Mitchell Minstrels. Sadly, Redding's number one was achieved posthumously. Four albums charted after his death, two studio sets, a compilation, and a live LP.

For the fifth time in six seasons, the Fab Four had the Christmas number one, this year with the double disc 'The Beatles', often referred to as 'The White Album'. The Rolling Stones could reach no higher than three for the second straight year. Bob Dylan, on the other hand, had a marvellous comeback from his motorcycle mishap, spending 13 weeks at number one with 'John Wesley Harding'.

Tom Jones had 135 weeks on the chart, the highest total yet achieved in any calendar year. Otis Redding also broke the previous high, set by another aeroplane casualty, Jim Reeves, by tallying 121 weeks. In the How Great Thou Were department, Elvis Presley only had one week on the chart in 1968, as did the George Mitchell Minstrels. Even the Mothers of Invention did better than both of them put together.

1 9 6 9

For the third time the Beatles began and ended a year with different albums at number one. Their double LP 'The Beatles' ushered 1969 in and 'Abbey Road' showed it out. The 11 straight weeks the latter disc spent on top just before Christmas was the longest consecutive stint by any record since 'Sergeant Pepper'. 'Abbey Road' returned in the last week of the year, marking the fifth occasion in 1969 when a former number one encored at that position. This statistic demonstrates the instability of the chart during these 12 months.

Familiar faces atop the heap included Bob Dylan, who successfully flirted with country music in 'Nashville Skyline', the Rolling Stones, who managed a week out front with 'Let It Bleed', and Elvis Presley, who scored a glorious comeback with 'From Elvis In Memphis'. Other rock luminaries who led the list included Cream, whose farewell set 'Goodbye' had three separate appearances at number one, the Moody Blues, who scored the first of their three toppers, and Jethro Tull, making their only standout stint with 'Stand Up'.

But one cannot overlook the achievement of the easy listening mogul Ray Conniff, who spent three weeks ahead of the herd without the benefit of a hit single. Jim Reeves astonished all by registering the only number one of his career five years after his death. It should be noted, however, that his 'According To My Heart' was a budget album.

15

'Best of the Seekers' bested all competition on five separate occasions. The Australians had the most weeks on chart with a comparatively feeble total of 66, three ahead of Simon and Garfunkel, who tallied their total without the benefit of a new release.

One LP most chartologists might not have remembered as a number one which did get there was 'Diana Ross And The Supremes Join The Temptations'. One LP most chartologists might have thought of as a number one which did not get there was the Who's rock opera 'Tommy', which had to settle for the second spot.

1 9 7 0

Simon and Garfunkel were the mighty men of the new decade's first year. Britain's bestselling album of the seventies, 'Bridge Over Troubled Water', dominated the chart, spending 23 weeks at number one. The closest competitors, 'Abbey Road' and 'Led Zeppelin III', managed five weeks each. The S&G catalogue also sold handsomely in the wake of 'Water', giving the duo an astonishing 167 weeks on the chart in a single year, easily smashing Tom Jones' record of 135.

With the exception of the compilations 'Motown Chartbusters Vol 3 & 4' and the Christmas number one, 'Andy Williams' Greatest Hits', every chart-topper was by a rock artist. The Beatles began their break-up year with 'Abbey Road' and parted with their spring smash 'Let It Be'. Fab Four fans obviously didn't want to say goodbye, buying enough various Beatle albums to give the group 122 weeks in the chart, the highest total of any year in their career. In parallel fashion, the greatest American star of the sixties, Bob Dylan, also had his last two number one LPs in 1970, 'Self Portrait' and 'New Morning'.

It was a banner year for what was then called progressive music. The Moody Blues had a number one and an admirable 115 weeks on the chart. Led Zeppelin flew over all followers with both 'II' and 'III'. Pink Floyd exploded with a real mother, 'Atom Heart Mother', and Black Sabbath won hosannas for heavy metal with their powerful 'Paranoid'.

16

The outstanding performance by an artist in a supporting role was by Johnny Cash. Though he did not get to number one, the former Sun star did notch up 125 weeks on the chart as four albums entered on the heels of his phenomenally successful 'Johnny Cash At San Quentin'.

1 9 7 1

'Bridge Over Troubled Water' was the outstanding album of yet another year, accumulating 17 weeks at number one, more than any other title. It was the only LP to appear on every one of the year's weekly tabulations.

Simon and Garfunkel works spent a total of 102 weeks on the chart during 1971, a sum exceeded only by the product of the prolific Andy Williams. The long-time hitmaker was at the peak of his career courtesy of his popular television series, and two different titles, 'Greatest Hits' and 'Home Loving Man', reached number one for him during the 12-month period. No other artist had more than one chart-topper this year, although three lots of uncredited session singers and instrumentalists did go all the way with budget compilations of cover versions. If anyone was involved with more than one of these productions, they have wisely remained silent.

Two ex-Beatles fronted the flock with solo albums, Paul McCartney with 'Ram' and John Lennon with 'Imagine', though additional credits were given to Linda McCartney and the Plastic Ono Band, respectively. 'Sticky Fingers', the Rolling Stones' first effort on their eponymous label, gave them a one-for-one record. They continued their 100 per cent performance until their 1974 issue, 'It's Only Rock And Roll', only hit number two. The Stones' competitors for the title of the World's Greatest Live Rock and Roll Band, the Who, scored their only chart-topper ever, 'Who's Next', while after a year of dominating the singles scene T. Rex managed an album number one in 'Electric Warrior'. Other acts enjoying outstanding years included Led Zeppelin, Rod Stewart, James Taylor, and the veteran Frank Sinatra. Only the 'My Way' man and Elvis Presley were still going strong from the original crew of 1958.

1 9 7 2

Marc Bolan and a load of other people dominated the album charts in 1972. The T. Rex phenomenon was merely one aspect of genuine fan fervour. The appearance of five Various Artist LPs at number one was a triumph of marketing.

The year began with 'Electric Warrior' retaining the top spot. In May a double re-issue, 'My People Were Fair'/'Prophets Seers And Sages', grabbed the glory for a week, bearing the original label credit of Tyrannosaurus Rex. That an artist's old material released under an obsolete name could get to number one indicated the frenzied following T. Rex had at the time. The following set, 'Bolan Boogie', also went all the way.

Bolan's boys were one of four attractions to spend between 80 and 90 weeks on the chart in 1972. Cat Stevens did best with 89 in a year when no one hit the century.

Rod Stewart had his second good year as 'Never A Dull Moment' went to number one and 'Every Picture Tells A Story' continued a long run. These were the first two of six consecutive toppers by the leader of the Faces. That group's 'A Nod's As Good As A Wink' reached the second slot in 1972, narrowly missing an unusual double for Stewart. No artist had ever scored number ones as a soloist and a group member in the same year, though Cliff Richard had made it on his own and with the Shadows backing him. Paul Simon came close, touching the top with his solo debut in 1972, but 'Bridge Over Troubled Water' had, by then, finished making occasional appearances at number one.

Outside of the 'Concert For Bangladesh' triple album, the Various Artists compilations that led the list for 27 weeks, over half the year, were assembled by marketing firms for television advertising. This innovation in merchandising started a packaging trend that has stayed strong ever since. Sales of this type of disc generally offered no indication of how popular taste in music was changing, as success was attributable to the impact of the commercial rather than the music itself.

1 9 7 3

David Bowie and Max Bygraves have never shared the concert stage, but they certainly were together in the 1973 album charts. The innovatory space rocker had six hit LPs that year, the singalong star five. Two of Bowie's efforts, 'Aladdin Sane' and 'Pin Ups', were number ones, while the resuscitated 'Hunky Dory' soared to three. Bygraves scored three Top Ten entries with his everybody-join-in approach to medleys of old favourites.

'The Rise And Fall Of Ziggy Stardust And The Spiders From Mars' had broken Bowie big in '72. Now he ruled the album chart, accumulating an unprecedented 182 weeks on the list during '73 with the six different titles. This sum shattered the mark of 167 weeks set by Simon and Garfunkel in 1970. Ironically, the defunct duo still managed to total 104 weeks in 1973, three years after their break-up, with the potent pairing of 'Greatest Hits' and 'Bridge Over Troubled Water'.

The siblings from the States, the Carpenters, managed 88 weeks in the list to tie Max Bygraves for third, though the positions reached were less impressive. Elton John and Slade both achieved two number ones, Gilbert O'Sullivan his only one and Roxy Music their first. Rod Stewart nabbed one as a soloist and another as a member of the Faces, completing the odd double that had eluded him in 1972.

Perhaps the most telling statistic of the year is that twenty different albums reached number one. This new high suggested that even the outstanding artists were not dominating the charts as firmly as in the Sixties, and that marketing departments had learned how to achieve great sales in a limited time period.

1 9 7 4

Two artists who were already strong in 1973, the Carpenters and Elton John, surged in 1974. Richard and Karen accumulated 17 weeks at number one in four summit visits with 'The Singles 1969–73', the highest total since 'Bridge Over Troubled Water'. The bespectacled pianist, who had scored two number ones the previous 12 months, bagged another brace this time, reigning with 'Caribou' and the Christmas number one 'Elton John's Greatest Hits'.

Another keyboard wizard did a double. For the second successive year the previously unknown feat of hitting the heights both as a soloist and a group member was achieved. Rick Wakeman's last album with Yes, 'Tales From Topographic Oceans' was the year's first number one. That spring the synthesizer star topped the table again with his own 'Journey To The Centre Of The Earth'.

19

Dramatic evidence that the album and singles charts had grown far apart was offered in September. Mike Oldfield held the first two long player disc positions with his new release, 'Hergest Ridge', and his 1973 classic, 'Tubular Bells'. Simultaneously the Osmonds were at one and two in the seven-inch stakes with their own 'Love Me For A Reason' and Donny and Marie's 'I'm Leaving It (All) Up To You'. Oldfield and Osmonds – two more contrasting acts could hardly be imagined.

David Bowie narrowly nudged the Carpenters in the weeks on chart table in 1974, 107 to 106. In the process he picked up his third career number one, 'Diamond Dogs'.

The Beatles were close behind with 104, thanks to the year-long persistence of their 1973 compilations, '1962–66' and '1967–70'. Paul McCartney was doubtless more pleased by the seven-week tenure at the top by Wings' 'Band On The Run'.

1975

The album and singles charts showed greater similarities in 1975 than in the immediate past. The three best-selling singles of the year were by the Bay City Rollers, Rod Stewart and the Stylistics, and all three artists also achieved number one LPs. 'Best Of The Stylistics' spent more weeks in the Top Ten than any other disc, a statistic that startles until one recalls it benefited from a mighty marketing campaign that included considerable television advertising.

Other greatest hits albums that went to the summit courtesy of blurbs on the box included anthologies by Perry Como, Engelbert Humperdinck, Tom Jones and Jim Reeves; mass appeal singers logically benefited most from mass advertising. The one collection that went to number one naturally as a result of the artist's current popularity rather than artificial stimulus was 'Elton John's Greatest Hits'. By landing the laurels for the last five weeks of 1974 and the first five of 1975, the Pinner prodigy matched the Stylistics' ten weeks over two calendar years. Elton was out front on his own with his total of 105 weeks on the chart, approached only by the slow-to-fade Simon and Garfunkel, whose back catalogue stayed around for one hundred more seven-day spells.

The year ended with Queen's 'A Night At The Opera' ruling. It included the Christmas number one single, 'Bohemian Rhapsody'. Status Quo, Led Zeppelin and Pink Floyd all lent the number one spot a heavier touch during the course of '75. Max Boyce translated his Welsh superstardom into disc sales with the first ever comedy number one.

1976

Beware of Greeks bearing gift tokens. There must have been a lot of them about in 1976, because Demis Roussos came from out of the Aegean blue to spend more weeks in the album chart than any other artist. The man-mountain scaled the survey with two top five entries, 'Happy to Be' and 'Forever And Ever', in reaching his total of 84 weeks, one more than Queen, two more than John Denver, and three more than Pink Floyd. Roussos also topped the singles chart with his 'Roussos Phenomenon' EP, the first time an Extended Play disc triumphed in that table.

The low magnitude of the leading weeks on chart total suggests that no artist stood out as David Bowie had only recently. This was indeed the case, as only Led Zeppelin zapped two number ones in 1976, both of which stayed on top for only one week. Were there a trend it would appear to have been in Greatest Hits compilations, with number one packages coming from Perry Como, Roy Orbison, Slim Whitman, Abba, the Beach Boys, and Glen Campbell. The legendary guitar star Bert Weedon actually made it all the way with a set of other people's hits. This information should not suggest that Weedon, Whitman, Como, Campbell or even the Beach Boys were enjoying a renaissance in singles sales, merely that television advertising of the Greatest Hits LP had reached the peak of its success. Only the 11 weeks spent at number one by 'Abba's Greatest Hits', the highest sum of list leading weeks in 1976, reflected fame on forty-five. Indeed, the SuperSwedes were enjoying their best year on the singles chart.

'Rock Follies' and 'Stupidity' (by Dr Feelgood) both reached the top without benefit of a hit single. For 'Rock Follies' the feat was doubly distinctive: the Andy Mackay–Howard Schuman score was the first television soundtrack ever to top the album chart.

1 9 7 7

Marketing was the main matter when it came to getting to number one in 1977. Clever campaigns, with a heavy emphasis on television advertising, succeeded in helping several artists who had gone cold back to glory.

Slim Whitman, who had registered one hit single in 20 years, was once again brilliantly promoted to the premier long player position by United Artists marketing. The Beatles had their first weeks of supremacy since 'Let It Be' with an extremely after-the-fact live album. Connie Francis and Bread, both of whom had fallen flat for some time, had number one compilations. The roll call of artists who vaulted to Valhalla with TV anthologies reads like a Hall of Fame: Johnny Mathis, Elvis Presley, Cliff Richard, Diana Ross and the Supremes, the Shadows, and Frank Sinatra. By its very nature this plethora of platters could only be issued once, so 1977 was the peak of this kind of catalogue culling.

Abba were on top for a total of 10 weeks, more than any other act or compilation. The Sex Pistols made history with their debut disc, 'Never Mind The Bollocks Here's The Sex Pistols', number one for two weeks in November despite some retail reluctance to display the provocative title. It was the first New Wave number one.

Pink Floyd bested Abba for most weeks on chart, 108 to 106, on the basis of their new number two, 'Animals', and their still-selling back list. In the year of his death Elvis Presley accumulated 95 weeks with an unprecedented eighteen titles, almost all re-entries.

1 9 7 8

Two film soundtracks proved it was still possible for albums to achieve lengthy runs at number one, television advertising campaigns and a diverging market notwithstanding. 'Saturday Night Fever' stayed on top for 18 weeks, the longest uninterrupted reign since that of 'Sergeant Pepper's Lonely Hearts Club Band', and indeed there were fewer number one LPs in 1978, eight, than in any year since 1967, the time of the classic Beatles release.

'Grease' was the other movie megahit, spending 13 weeks atop the greasy pole. Since John Travolta starred in both films, one might assume he was on the number one for 31 weeks of the year, the most by any artist since the cast of 'The Sound of Music' achieved the same figure in 1966. But though Travolta was shown on the cover of 'Fever', earning a royalty, he did not figure in the music. The Bee Gees, whose tunes dominated the motion picture, did not appear on the screen. The real winner was the Robert Stigwood Organisation, which issued both films and discs.

Boney M, who enjoyed a pair of chart topping singles in 1978, also enjoyed their most successful LP, 'Nightflight To Venus'. Abba earned seven more number one weeks with 'The Album' and managed 112 weeks on chart during the year, clearly outdistancing all competition. Fleetwood Mac's 'Rumours', America's top record of 1977, finally managed seven days at the summit in Britain.

1979

Nineteen different albums played musical chairs with the number one position in 1979, more than twice the total of toppers the previous year. No piece of product could compete with RSO's 1978 soundtracks in terms of length of stay there. 'The Best Disco Album In The World', a Warner Brothers compilation released at the height of the disco craze and supported by television advertising, managed the longest stint, six weeks. Indeed, Warners as a company may have been the sales star of the year, managing to place three consecutive number ones at the top in their first week of release. Certainly the artists involved – Led Zeppelin, Gary Numan and Boney M – could not have been appealing to the same buyers.

The real star performers of 1979 were Abba, Blondie and the Electric Light Orchestra. The first two names each achieved two number ones, spending totals of seven and five weeks ahead respectively. Gary Numan did nab one winner under his own name and another in his group identity, Tubeway Army, but each of those only stayed in the lead for one week.

23

ELO's mark of merit was the 112 weeks spent on the chart by their various albums, including the number one 'Discovery'. The Jeff Lynne-led ensemble had their finest 12 months, enjoying four Top Ten singles as well. The only act to approach ELO in weeks on chart was Blondie with an exact century; Earth Wind and Fire trailed in third with 68.

'Bat Out Of Hell' by Meat Loaf and Jeff Wayne's 'War Of The Worlds' each spent the entire year on the chart as they headed for two of the longest runs in recent times. Neither album ever reached number one, but both ultimately outsold almost every disc that did in 1979.

1980

Twenty-three different albums led the list at some point during 1980, the most in any single year to date. The number one position was like New England's fabled weather: if you didn't like it, you could stick around for an hour and it would change. Johnny Mathis,

Genesis and Rose Royce appeared in quick succession, and if the rapid variation from easy listening to rock to soul wasn't enough for the catholic consumer, Sky followed with a kind of classical and pop hybrid that was impossible to categorize.

With more number one albums in a year than David Bowie has had images in a career, staying in front for even a month was an achievement. The Pretenders made it with their eponymous debut disc, and Roxy Music were champs for four weeks in two stints with 'Flesh And Blood'. The star performers of the year were Police and Abba. The Bleach Boys had their second number one LP, 'Zenyatta Mondatta', and scored 116 on chart in total, far in front of the 70-week sum of runner-up AC/DC. The Scandinavian sensations once again had chart-toppers early and late in a year, registering in January with 'Greatest Hits Volume 2' and beginning a nine-week rule in November with 'Super Trouper'.

An extremely odd circumstance characterized the spring. For the entire season, albums had two-week runs at number one and were then replaced. Seven LPs were in the spring string. The previous record for consecutive two-week reigns had been a mere two, so this development was certainly curious if ultimately unimportant.

24

1 9 8 1

To find the top album artists of 1981 one didn't have to look far beyond the letter 'A' in alphabetical browser bins. Abba began and ended the year at number one with 'Super Trouper' and 'The Visitors', extending their string of chart-topping LPs to seven. Adam and the Ants were the breakout act of the year, accumulating 12 weeks at the very top with 'Kings Of The Wild Frontier', the longest leading stint. 'Kings' was also one of five long players to stay the course for the entire year. It was joined by previous Adam material and the end-of-year release 'Prince Charming' to give the Ants 87 weeks on the chart, a total topped only by Barry Manilow. The American balladeer bettered the Ant total by five weeks. Personal appearances and heavy promotion gave him a career peak in Britain several years after he had done his best at home.

One had to look hard to find evidence of the growth of technopop, the synthesized sound making great inroads in the singles market.

'Dare' by the Human League was the nation's best-seller for one week, but this was before the fourth single from the set, 'Don't You Want Me', became the year's Christmas number one and propelled its parent back up the charts in 1982. Ultravox, important pioneers of technopop, re-entered for another 48 weeks with 'Vienna' on the strength of the single of the same name.

There were oddities, as always. 'The Royal Wedding' of Prince Charles to Lady Diana Spencer was number one for a fortnight, twice as long as Motorhead managed with their equally live 'No Sleep Till Hammersmith', but the Royals never challenged the heavy metal merchants to a battle of the bands.

1982

'Remember my name', Irene Cara advised in the title tune of the film 'Fame', 'I'm gonna live forever.' Well, almost. 'Fame' itself proved to be more enduring than any of the young people in it.

When the BBC began broadcasting the American television series 'Fame', a spin-off from the Alan Parker movie, Cara's original version of the song, a US hit in 1980, zoomed to the top of the UK singles chart. It was actually only the beginning of a phenomenon.

BBC Records' 'The Kids From Fame' television cast collection proceeded to lead the list itself. Fuelled by two Top Ten singles, this album sold over 850,000 copies by December, surpassing even the previous year's 'Royal Wedding' to become the BBC's best-selling long player.

RCA had leased the album because BBC1 could only plug vinyl with the BBC label, and they needed to establish the singing actors as a recording act. Mission accomplished, RCA issued a second TV platter, 'The Kids From Fame Again', and this also made the top three.

The sales success of the 'Kids From Fame' was peculiar to Britain. In contrast, the only LP that outsold theirs in the UK in 1982 was by a worldwide star. 'Love Songs' by Barbra Streisand was the year's best seller. That it did so well was perhaps surprising, since it was a make-do collection with only two new songs assembled in lieu of new product.

ABC distinguished themselves by spending their first-ever week on the chart at number one with 'The Lexicon Of Love'. The debut marked another first, the initial joint number one on the album chart. 'The Lexicon Of Love' shared the spotlight with – yes – 'Fame'.

1983

Two of the greatest stars of the early Seventies stood out this year, but whereas one, David Bowie, had already set album chart standards, Michael Jackson had previously been best known as a singles artist. He managed to reach number five in 1979 with 'Off The Wall', his solo album start on Epic, but nothing prepared the world for what happened in 1983.

'Thriller' first entered the sweepstakes in December 1982, but by the end of its first month of release had only climbed to fifteen. It was only with the release of the second single from the set, 'Billie Jean', that the platter peaked. It went all the way three times for a total of seven weeks and was the year's best-seller. Michael enjoyed three further weeks at number one when Motown's repackaged '18 Greatest Hits' proved popular during the summer. The llama lover totalled 123 weeks on chart.

This year, however, David Bowie achieved a total eclipse of the chart, setting a new mark with 198. This staggering sum beat his old record of 182, established a full decade earlier in 1973. Nearly all his success this year came in the wake of 'Let's Dance', which entered at number one. Thirteen Bowie titles in all appeared in the fifty-three charts of 1983. Ten Bowie albums were in the week of 16 July, the year's greatest monopoly.

Phil Collins racked up 78 weeks on chart on his own and also did very well with Genesis. Meat Loaf followed closely with 76. Mighty sales figures were accumulated by Paul Young and Lionel Richie. Richard Clayderman, the French pianist cleverly promoted in both print and television, enjoyed two of the year's Top 100 and amassed 66 weeks on chart. He was far and away 1983's most successful instrumentalist.

Thirteen of the year's twenty top albums were by groups. Culture Club were number one for five weeks with 'Colour By Numbers' and Men at Work toiled the same time at the top with 'Business As Usual'. Duran Duran only managed one week ahead of the field with 'Seven And The Ragged Tiger' but did stockpile 105 weeks on chart, more than any group save Dire Straits, who garnered 107 without issuing any new material. Twenty-three different titles reached number one during 1983, more than in any previous calendar year.

Bonnie Tyler was the only female artist to spend even a single week ahead of the field, though Alison 'Alf' Moyet was the featured vocalist with two-week champs Yazoo. Barbra Streisand was the woman winner in weeks on chart with 57, but most of these were the final flings of 1982's list leader, 'Love Songs'. The most noteworthy variety of female achievement from a chart-watcher's point of view was the faddish popularity of a new form – the workout album. Two of the year's Top 100 were of this sort, 'Jane Fonda's Workout Record' and Felicity Kendal's 'Shape Up And Dance (Volume 1)'. Jackie Genova also charted with an exercise exemplar.

1984

The face that dominated music advertising on television in George Orwell's dreaded year turned out not to be Big Brother but a pig. The porker was the meaty mascot of the EMI/Virgin anthologies 'Now That's What I Call Music'. The first 'Now' ended 1983 and began 1984 at number one. The second moved into the sty in the sky in April and the third checked in during August. The three double albums spent a total of 15 of the year's 52 weeks on top, more than any individual act managed to achieve. 'Now 4' did well enough in its mere month of release to be one of 1984's Top Ten but was kept out of number one by CBS/WEA's even more lucrative imitative compilation 'The Hits Album/The Hits Tape'.

Television advertising also played a prominent part in the success of the longest-running number one of the year, the late Bob Marley and the Wailers' 'Legend' (12 weeks). The top-selling album of 1984 was 'Can't Slow Down' by Lionel Richie. Though it was only number one for a fortnight it was near the top most of the year. The Motown marvel was one of an astonishing seven albums to stay on the chart for the entire year along with 'Can't Slow Down', Michael Jackson's 'Thriller', Paul Young's 'No Parlez', Meat Loaf's 'Bat Out

Of Hell', Queen's 'Greatest Hits' and U2's 'Live – Under A Blood Red Sky'.

Billy Joel had the most albums on chart in a single week, six. Nik Kershaw managed two of the year's Top Fifty, Elton John two of the Top 100. Michael Jackson also had a brace of best-sellers, 'Off The Wall' continuing its revival. Jackson wound up the year's number two week-wise, with 107 seven-day spells. However, combining the runs of his solo albums and the weeks in residence of Michael Jackson Plus the Jackson Five's '18 Greatest Hits' gave a total of 136. Dire Straits, who accumulated 116 weeks, still enough to place them in the all-time Top Ten for most in a single year, were the year's top weekly act.

Other groups with noteworthy performances included U2, who totalled an even 100 weeks on chart; Queen, who had two of the year's Top Fifty; and Wham!, whose 'Make It Big' was one of the year's Top Five. The Smiths scored two Top Tens on the independent Rough Trade label and 'Welcome To The Pleasuredome' by Frankie Goes To Hollywood gave ZTT its first week at number one.

28

It was not a great year for female soloists. None reached number one, though women did make the top spot as members of Eurythmics and the Thompson Twins. Sade had the biggest seller by a woman, 'Diamond Life', while Elaine Paige had two of the year's Top 100. Barbra Streisand accumulated 67 weeks on chart to lead the ladies. Instrumentalists fared poorly. Richard Clayderman was the only non-vocalist in the year's Top 100. The independent compilation company Street Sounds attained fifteen charters during the year. The devotional artist Bryn Yemm had three new albums in, more than any other British act. 1984 was itself a star. It was the first year to have three hit LPs named after it.

1 9 8 5

The long distance runner wasn't lonely in 1985. Nine albums remained on the chart for the entire fifty-two weeks, and four acts accumulated totals in excess of one hundred weeks on chart. Astonishing records were set. After a series of UK stadium dates Bruce Springsteen placed his entire catalogue of seven albums in the Top Fifty. Never before had an artist with that large a body of work got the lot that high. Springsteen finished the year with a total of 177 weeks on chart, the third best figure ever. 'Born In The U.S.A.' was one of the nine discs that saw the year through. It wound up the number four seller of 1985. Competing with The Boss for the title of Male Artist of the Year, Phil Collins finished with fewer weeks on chart, a still spectacular 131, but managed to nab the number two spot of the year-end tabulation with 'No Jacket Required'.

Madonna was clearly the female artist of 1985; her 'Like A Virgin' (the third best-selling set of the year) and her retitled first album both entered the Top Fifty. As noteworthy as her *own* success was the extremely strong showing by female artists in general. Seven of the year's top twenty were either by female soloists or outfits with female vocalists. Sade's two albums both finished in the Top Twenty.

Dire Straits and U2 vied for Group of Year honours. Mark Knopfler's lot put in a special claim with the year's number one, 'Brothers In Arms'. 1985 was the third successive year in which Dire Straits exceeded 100 weeks on chart, a feat previously performed only by Simon and Garfunkel. During the three-year period 1983–85, Mark's men leapt from 33rd to 8th on the all-time list. Despite their achievements they were slightly pipped in weeks on chart by U2, 168 to 158. The Irish band were also on a prolonged hot streak, having vaulted from 20 to 375 weeks on chart in three years.

29

Richard Clayderman retained his laurels as leading solo instrumentalist, but James Last bounced back as the top orchestra. It was also a good year for what might be called up-market material, with Andrew Lloyd Webber's 'Requiem', Leonard Bernstein's operatic version of 'West Side Story' and the Anderson/Rice/Ulvaeus 'Chess' all in 1985's Top 100.

The most successful broadcasting and charity event of all time, Live Aid, achieved another distinction as the single happening that has most influenced the album chart. In the 27 July chart nine albums by acts in the concert re-entered the Top 100, four after a long absence, and twenty-one previously peaked packages suddenly surged.

The craze of 1984, the TV compilations of recent and current hits, abated only slightly, with three EMI/Virgin 'Now' packages in the year-end Top Ten and two CBS/WEA 'Hits' collections in the Top Twenty.

Meat Loaf's 'Bat Out Of Hell' finally fell from favour but still managed to add 31 weeks on chart to equal *The Sound Of Music* as the all-time longest-running chart LP.

1 9 8 6

Were there a pinball machine of the album chart it would have tilted this year as Dire Straits amassed an unprecedented 217 listed weeks, an average of over four placings per week.

That 'Brothers In Arms' was the year's number two in sales, slipping down just one place from 1985's top spot, was remarkable enough. That Mark Knopfler's band was so popular that a substantial part of Dire Straits' back catalogue resided in the best sellers was astounding.

There was another artist, however, who accounted for three of the Top 100 of 1986. Madonna sold stacks of all three of her releases, and 'True Blue' was the year's number one. All told she spent 125 weeks on chart, by far the highest figure ever achieved by a woman. 1985 debutante Whitney Houston's first album was 1986's number five set of the year.

In the rich-get-richer category old friends Phil Collins and Queen excelled themselves, Collins moving up to third in the annual weeks on chart listing. Though his total fell from 131 to 113 he made amends by sharing Genesis' 28 weeks. Queen broke through the century mark for the first time while staying in the Top Ten artists list for the third consecutive year. Paul Simon's 'Graceland' was the year's number four.

Madonna and Collins were the only two solo artists in the year-end weeks on chart Top Ten. The LP list seemed the province of the big groups in 1986, with Simple Minds enjoying their biggest year and U2 finishing in the charmed circle for the fourth year in succession, even though they had no new issues. Talking Heads put in their finest career outing, while A-Ha and Five Star cut impressive figures in their first full year of activity. The 'Now' and 'Hits' series stayed strong.

1987

Whatever you thought of the charts in 1987, you had to agree it was a 'Bad' year. Lightning struck a second time for Michael Jackson as he once again achieved a year-end number one. The main difference was that whereas the champ of 1983, 'Thriller', had started slowly in 1982 and grown gradually, 'Bad' was a massive number one in its first week and retained its edge to finish several lengths in front. The new set was only the second package in history to debut at number one in both the UK and US charts. The first was another of this year's giants, 'Whitney', which wound up at number three for 1987.

'Bad', in contrast, seemed to pose no threat to 'Thriller', far and away the most successful LP ever released. Its global sales at about forty million were well ahead of the immediate runners-up, including 'Rumours' by Fleetwood Mac, but that 1977 phenomenon had its own reason to celebrate ten years later. During the course of 1987 it overtook 'Bat Out Of Hell' to become the longest-runner in chart chronicles.

The reappearance of 'Rumours' can be largely attributed to the continued growth of the compact disc market which gave a new lease of life to many classic albums. Collectors who already had black vinyl copies bought CD versions for their superior sound. The Beatles benefited most clearly from this. All of their original studio sets were issued on CD in 1987, and all charted. The 20th anniversary of 'Sergeant Pepper's Lonely Hearts Club Band' attracted massive media attention and boosted the classic package back to the Top Three.

Though Madonna did not have one of the year's Top Ten sellers she was the most charted artist of 1987, her albums making 127 appearances. This tally exceeded the record for a female artist she herself set only the previous year.

U2 and Queen followed the champ with 126 and 117 weeks respectively, both continuing their lengthy run of strong showings and improving on their fine 1986 figures. Dire Straits did well, too, their 84 weeks giving them a career total of exactly 900, the top total of acts still recording.

'The Phantom Of The Opera' made history by becoming the first original cast recording to top the UK chart. In this respect 'My Fair

Lady' may have been unlucky. In the very first chart of 1958 and peaking at number two, it may have been a number one had its earlier sales been tabulated.

1988

For the sixth consecutive year the three acts with the most weeks on chart totalled at least 100. Seven of 1988's ten top stars had been in the charmed circle before, six of them the previous year. Michael Jackson, who paced the pack with 114 weeks, was returning to the leaders for the first time since 1988.

Jacko's joyride came courtesy of 'Bad', on the chart all year, and a variety of back items including 'Thriller' and Motown repackages. In his case the progress from one year to the next looked like a week-to-week sequence, with 1987's number one slipping two places to number three on the 1988 year end tally. 'Bad' was constantly in the public eye thanks to Jackson's personal appearances at open air venues and a steady stream of hit singles. The promotion paid off. Britain was the one major country where 'Bad' outsold 'Thriller', and the artist topped the table of weeks on chart for the first time.

The second place finishers on both the sales and weeks on chart list were vinyl veterans. Cliff Richard, who had the year's number one single, 'Mistletoe And Wine', also had the runner-up album, 'Private Collection'. It was the first time he had finished in the top two in both chart categories. Fleetwood Mac, who had undergone a telephone book's worth of personnel changes since their album chart breakthrough in 1968, scored their first annual century with 107 weeks, second only to Jackson. They, too, were helped by touring, and scored two of the year's 30 best sellers, 'Tango In The Night' and 'Greatest Hits'. The Pet Shop Boys were the third act to accumulate 100 weeks on chart, doing best with 'Introspective'.

In addition to the two groups mentioned above, U2, Dire Straits, Whitney Houston and Luther Vandross repeated in the year's Top Ten acts. Whitney now had 200 weeks on chart with only two albums for an astonishing average of 100 weeks per release. This was still unlikely to impress U2 and Dire Straits, who continued their winning ways and seemed to guarantee they would finish ahead of Queen as the top album acts of the Eighties.

The most amazing achievement by a new artist belonged to Kylie Minogue. Before January 1988 she had never released an album in Britain. At the end of the year she had the top title of the twelve months, 'Kylie'. This was the first time a solo artist had scored the year's top seller with a debut disc. The teen market didn't just support Stock-Aitken-Waterman acts. The fresh-faced trio Bros wound up at number four with their debut issue, 'Push'. Another new act who came in the Top Ten sellers in famous fashion was Tracy Chapman, whose career took off after she appeared before a live global television audience at the Nelson Mandela Birthday Concert.

Compilations took up so many of the top positions in the album chart that the industry decided they would be segregated in future and have their own list in 1989. This meant that the performance of the 'Now That's What I Call Music' series in placing editions 11, 12 and 13 in the year-end top fifteen would never be repeated. Even compilation soundtracks like the phenomenal 'Dirty Dancing' would be separated out. As the year ended observers wondered if new artists would actually benefit from the new order, in which product by individual acts would overnight chart higher than it would have in 1988. Would the illusion of success become a reality?

33

1 9 8 9

The cosy feeling old friends gave the album chart in 1988 was displaced by the excitement of new acquaintances a year later. Jason Donovan, a co-star of Kylie Minogue on television's soap opera 'Neighbours', repeated his fellow Australian's feat of having the best selling LP of the year with a premiere performance. His 'Ten Good Reasons' outshone even Simply Red's long-burning 'A New Flame'.

The continued shift in sales from singles to albums was dramatically underscored this year when four LPs but no 45s sold over a million copies. Including sales in all configurations, the year's number one single, 'Ride On Time' by Black Box, managed 849,116 units. 'Ten Good Reasons' shifted 1,450,500. Indeed, the seven top albums of the year outsold every single. It was thus important financially as well as for image that the young Stock-Aitken-Waterman favourites did well on both sides. Kylie and Jason were each in the 1989 Top

Ten on both charts, with Miss Minogue enjoying the year's number six album, 'Enjoy Yourself'.

Kylie was one of eight acts to finish in the year's Top Ten acts who had not been in the previous list. Recalling that in 1988 only four names were non-repeaters gives an indication of the progress of new talent in 1989. Guns N' Roses made the most impressive showing, leading the lot with 85 weeks on chart. This figure, achieved by 'Appetite For Destruction' and 'GN'R Lies', was admittedly below the century, the first time since 1982 that the year's top tally was short of 100. Nonetheless it was a major achievement for a heavy metal act. Strong sellers in this genre usually open strong and fade quickly.

Erasure finished second in the weeks-on-chart sweepstakes, moving up from fourth the year before. Third in the table was what might be called a veteran newcomer, Gloria Estefan. In a masterful piece of public relations her group Miami Sound Machine groomed her as its focal point and then gave her joint and finally sole billing. The strategy succeeded spectacularly with the year's number four seller 'Anything For You' by Gloria Estefan and Miami Sound Machine, and the number five, 'Cuts Both Ways', credited merely to Gloria Estefan.

34

Another notable newcomer to the top acts list was the Scottish band Deacon Blue, who finished fourth. Bobby Brown, 1989's top singles star, made his album table bow at number ten. The late Roy Orbison experienced a phenomenal posthumous comeback, appearing in the Top Ten acts list for the first time since 1964. A quarter of a century was by far the longest gap between visits to this charmed circle.

The fastest selling work in 1989 was released late in the year. Phil Collins' '. . . But Seriously' managed to chalk up sales of over one million in only six weeks, beginning a long run at number one and setting itself up for continued chart domination in early 1990. Here was a case where the change of decades would be bridged by a single strong record. This had not been the case when the Seventies met the Eighties, when Greatest Hits acts by Abba and Rod Stewart took turns at the top. The *South Pacific* film soundtrack had welded 1959 and 1960 together, and the Beatles' 'Abbey Road' had both seen out 1969 and welcomed 1970. '. . . But Seriously' now joined these giants.

1990

Classic stars and classical music dominated 1990. Phil Collins spent a further ten weeks at number one at the beginning of the year with his late 1989 smash . . . *But Seriously*. Its total of 15 weeks at the top was the thirteenth longest run at number one in chart history. . . . *But Seriously* remained on the register all year long and wound up 1990's best seller. Collins had another of the year's Top Ten, *Serious Hits Live*, and discs by the singing drummer from Genesis spent more weeks on chart (85) than those of any other artist.

Collins was the outstanding male star to have dominated the field. Elton John was the only other artist to have two of the year's ten best sellers. His *Very Best of Elton John* and *Sleeping With The Past* were both number ones, making him the only act to have two chart toppers in 1990

Luciano Pavarotti followed with 1⅓ number ones, pacing the pack with his own *Essential Pavarotti* and as one of the 'three tenors' *In Concert*. José Carreras and Placido Domingo joined the inimitable Italian on the latter live recording. It was the first time three chart acts had joined forces to achieve a number one album as a trio. Jazzmen Kenny Ball, Chris Barber and Acker Bilk had gone to the top in 1962, but this was before Ball had charted on his own. By beating *In Concert* to number one with his own compilation, Luciano Pavarotti became the first classical artist to achieve a number one.

The top instrumentalist of the year was Nigel Kennedy, whose performance of Vivaldi's *Four Seasons* gave him the year's twelfth best seller and was the main factor in his finishing fourth on the Most Weeks On Chart list. His total of 66 was the highest ever by a classical artist.

The year's standout female star, Madonna, added to her historic achievements. Her *Immaculate Collection* was 1990's number two in sales. By leading the list for the last six weeks of the year, she took her career total to 16 weeks in pole position, overtaking Barbra Streisand as the woman with the most weeks at number one. Various Madonna titles accumulated 53 weeks on chart to regain for her the distinction as most charted woman that she had last enjoyed in 1987. Tina Turner shared her weeks on chart total, thanks to the long-running *Foreign Affair*, but trailed her in sales.

UB40 were the group with most weeks on chart, due in large measure to *Labour Of Love II*, but they were surpassed in sales by the Carpenters. Richard and Karen's *Only Yesterday* was one of the year's ten best sellers. The success of this catalogue promotion surprised the music business, especially since much of the material had been included in the 1974 number one *The Singles 1969–73*. The seven-week list-leading leasehold of *Only Yesterday* moved the Carpenters to a tie with Cliff Richard for eighth position on the Most Weeks At Number One list.

David Bowie also made noteworthy career progress. *ChangesBowie* was his seventh album to enter the chart at number one. Nobody else has debuted at the top as often. Bowie moved into a three-way tie for fifth in the Most Number One Albums category.

Special note should be taken of the achievement of Michael Bolton, whose *Soul Provider* never got higher than number four in any weekly chart, yet finished fifth for the year. In contrast, Prince was number one first week out with *Graffiti Bridge*, yet didn't even finish in the top 75 sellers of 1991. The American number one of the year, MC Hammer's *Please Hammer Don't Hurt 'Em*, was Britain's number 36, as good evidence as any that the massive sales enjoyed by rap artists in the US were not being duplicated in the UK.

1991

The brightest stars this year were the ones in the title of Simply Red's album, the best seller of the year and their fourth top two hit in as many releases. As exciting as the achievements of Mick Hucknall's group were, with *Stars* enjoying a long Top Five run and returning to number one as *A New Flame* had done two years earlier, Simply Red could not be said to have loomed large over the year. No act did. The weeks on chart winner for 1991, Michael Bolton, amassed the lowest total, 63, since Elvis Presley triumphed with 51 in 1960.

Whereas both Phil Collins and Elton John had each scored two of the year's Top Ten sellers in 1990, no artist achieved the feat in the following 12 months. Queen came closest, with three out of the Top Forty. Even before Freddie Mercury's death the quartet had tallied two number ones this calendar year, making them the only act to have more than one. *Innuendo* led the list for a fortnight in February and *Greatest Hits II* debuted at number one in November. The double gave Queen a career total of eight number ones, the third highest total in history, tying them with Abba and Led Zeppelin behind the Beatles (12) and the Rolling Stones (9).

Greatest Hits II returned to the top after Mercury passed away and stayed there through the holidays for a total of five weeks as head of the hits. It was the second highest figure for the year, Eurythmics' *Greatest Hits* having been number one for ten weeks. The latter disc was the year's best seller until the holiday period, when it was finally eclipsed by *Stars*.

Simply Red, Eurythmics and Queen had 1991's best sellers, but other groups merited attention. Roxette had most weeks on chart by a duo or group (62), just one shy of Michael Bolton's winning figure. After their first half dozen chart albums peaked short of the Top Ten, R.E.M. got lucky with number seven, going all the way with *Out Of Time* and winding up with one of the Top Ten of the year. The Doors broke on through with four items when Oliver Stone's film biography of Jim Morrison was released.

37

The year's greatest chart disappointments were also most registered by groups. Simple Minds and U2 broke their strings of consecutive number one releases at four and three, respectively. Dire Straits opened at number one with *On Every Street*, but its solitary seven days at the summit were a fleeting moment compared to the 14 weeks their preceding studio set, *Brothers In Arms*, had enjoyed.

The only one of 1990's Top Ten to repeat in '91 was Madonna's *Immaculate Collection*. She again accumulated the Most Weeks On Chart By A Female Artist. However, in a reversal of their 1990 two-woman race, Tina Turner outsold her, with *Simply The Best* finishing the year at number four, the best showing by any soloist. Cher was also in the year-end Top Ten. She nabbed the first number one of her 26-year chart career, *Love Hurts*.

The memory of the slow start by *Thriller* warns one from hasty judgment of Michael Jackson's work, but it certainly appeared from its first five weeks on the market that *Dangerous* was truly in peril compared to its immediate predecessors. After debuting at number one the set made way for the return of Queen's *Greatest Hits II*. By Christmas Jackson had the odd distinction of also being outsold by another Michael – Crawford.

No instrumentalists were in the year-end Top Fifty. Luciano Pavarotti was there with *Essential Pavarotti II* and as part of the 'three tenors' *In Concert*. For the second consecutive year Michael Bolton had one of the year's Top Ten sellers without ever getting to number one. Proving that there are always new records to be set, *Circle Of One* by Oleta Adams was the first album to re-enter the chart at number one.

If ever a week went by without a chart being compiled, the previous week's chart was used again for the purposes of all the statistics and information contained in this book. The dates used throughout correspond to the **Saturday ending the week** in which the chart was published. So, for example, Abba's *Waterloo* album entered the chart in the week ending 8 June 1974, making their first day of chart action 2 June 1974.

The charts used in compiling this book are:

8 Nov 58 First album chart published by *Melody Maker*. It is a Top Ten.

27 Jun 59 Newspaper strike. No chart published until 8 August, so the 20 June chart is repeated throughout.

12 Mar 60 First *Record Retailer* published, a Top 20. We have taken our information from the *Record Retailer* from this date onwards, although the *Melody Maker* chart continued.

14 Apr 66 Chart becomes a Top 30.

8 Dec 66 Chart becomes a Top 40.

12 Feb 69 Chart drops back to a Top 15.

8 Mar 69 Incorrect chart published. Correct chart calculated by back-tracking from following week's listings.

11 Jun 69 Chart becomes a Top 20 again.

25 Jun 69 Chart becomes a Top 40 again.

9 Aug 69 Chart is a Top 32 (!) for this one week only.

11 Oct 69 Chart drops back to a Top 25.

8 Nov 69 Chart varies from a Top 20 to a Top 24 until 24 Jan 70.

31 Jan 70 Chart lists from 47 to 77 albums each week until 9 Jan 71.

9 Jan 71 *Record Retailer* becomes *Record And Tape Retailer*.

16 Jan 71 Chart stabilizes as a Top 50.

6 Feb 71 Postal strike means no chart published until 3 Apr 71. 30 Jan chart repeated throughout.

7 Aug 71 The Full Price chart (the one we've been using) is combined with the previously separate Budget chart. This means there is a sudden influx of budget label albums onto the chart.

8 Jan 72 Chart reverts to a full price chart only, so the budget albums disappear as suddenly as they appeared.

18 Mar 72   *Record And Tape Retailer* becomes *Music Week.*

13 Jan 73   Chart is a Top 24 for this week only.

5 Jan 74   Chart is a Top 42 for this week only.

5 Jul 75   Chart becomes a Top 60.

14 Jan 78   Chart is a Top 30 for this week only.

2 Dec 78   Chart becomes a Top 75.

13 Oct 79   Two consecutive weeks' charts published simultaneously as a result of speedy new chart compilation system which enables *Music Week* to catch up a week. Until this date, the publication of the chart had been more than a week after the survey period. Both charts of this date are included in our calculations.

8 Aug 81   Chart becomes a Top 100.

14 Jan 89   Chart splits in two, and becomes a Top 75 'Artist Albums' and a Top 20 'Compilation Albums'. For this book, the 'Artist Albums' chart is considered the main chart, but we record separately the activities of the 'Compilations' chart.

40

HIT ALBUMS
ALPHABETICALLY BY ARTIST

The information given in this part of the book is as follows:

DATE the album first hit the chart, the album **TITLE**, **LABEL**, **CATALOGUE NUMBER**, the **HIGHEST POSITION** it reached on the chart, and the **TOTAL WEEKS** it remained on the chart. Number One albums are highlighted with a **STAR** ★ and Top 10 albums with a **DOT** ●. A **DAGGER** † indicates the album is still on the chart on 28 December 1991, the final chart included in our calculations for this edition.

For the purposes of this book, an album is considered a re-issue if it hits the chart for a second time with a new catalogue number. From the time when albums began to be produced in both mono and stereo versions (around 1966), we list only the stereo catalogue number. Cassette sales, and since the mid-80s CD sales, have become rapidly more significant in the compilation of the albums charts, but we have for consistency's sake listed only the 33⅓ rpm record catalogue number.

THE
ARTISTS

Freddie Mercury (1946–1991), lead singer of Queen the fifth most successful act in album chart history.

Describing a recording act in one sentence is often fraught with danger, but we have attempted to do so above each act's list of hits. Although we are aware that many of the 'vocalists' thus described also play an instrument, we have only mentioned this fact where the artist's instrumental skills were an important factor in the album's success.

a

AARONSON – *See HAGAR, SCHON, AARONSON, SHRIEVE*

ABBA
Sweden/Norway, male/female vocal/instrumental group   *506 wks*

8 Jun 74	**WATERLOO** *Epic EPC 80179*	28	2 wks
31 Jan 76	**ABBA** *Epic EPC 80835*	13	10 wks
10 Apr 76	★ **GREATEST HITS** *Epic EPC 69218*	1	130 wks
27 Nov 76	★ **ARRIVAL** *Epic EPC 86108*	1	92 wks
4 Feb 78	★ **THE ALBUM** *Epic EPC 86052*	1	61 wks
19 May 79	★ **VOULEZ-VOUS** *Epic EPC 86086*	1	43 wks
10 Nov 79	★ **GREATEST HITS VOL.2** *Epic EPC 10017*	1	63 wks
22 Nov 80	★ **SUPER TROUPER** *Epic EPC 10022*	1	43 wks
19 Dec 81	★ **THE VISITORS** *Epic EPC 10032*	1	21 wks
20 Nov 82	★ **THE SINGLES – THE FIRST TEN YEARS** *Epic ABBA 10*	1	22 wks
19 Nov 83	**THANK YOU FOR THE MUSIC** *Epic EPC 10043*	17	12 wks
19 Nov 88	**ABSOLUTE ABBA** *Telstar STAR 2329*	70	7 wks

Russ ABBOT *UK, male vocalist*   *16 wks*

5 Nov 83	**RUSS ABBOT'S MADHOUSE** *Ronco RTL 2096*	41	7 wks
23 Nov 85	**I LOVE A PARTY** *K-Tel ONE 1313*	12	9 wks

Gregory ABBOTT *US, male vocalist*   *5 wks*

10 Jan 87	**SHAKE YOU DOWN** *CBS 450061–1*	53	5 wks

ABC *UK, male vocal/instrumental group*   *90 wks*

3 Jul 82	★ **THE LEXICON OF LOVE** *Neutron NTRS 1*	1	50 wks
26 Nov 83	**BEAUTY STAB** *Neutron NTRL 2*	12	13 wks
26 Oct 85	**HOW TO BE A ZILLIONAIRE** *Neutron NTRH 3*	28	3 wks
24 Oct 87	● **ALPHABET CITY** *Neutron NTRH 4*	7	10 wks
28 Oct 89	**UP** *Neutron 838646 1*	58	1 wk
21 Apr 90	● **ABSOLUTELY** *Neutron 8429671*	7	12 wks
24 Aug 91	**ABRACADABRA** *Parlophone PCS 7355*	50	1 wk

Group was UK/US, male/female for third album.

Paula ABDUL *US, female vocalist*   *50 wks*

15 Apr 89	● **FOREVER YOUR GIRL** *Siren SRNLP 19*	3	39 wks
10 Nov 90	**SHUT UP AND DANCE (THE DANCE MIXES)**		
	Virgin America VUSLP 28	40	2 wks
27 Jul 91	● **SPELLBOUND** *Virgin America VUSLP 33*	4	9 wks

Father ABRAHAM and the SMURFS
Holland, male vocalist as himself and Smurfs　　　　　*11 wks*

| 25 Nov 78 | **FATHER ABRAHAM IN SMURFLAND** *Decca SMURF 1* | 19 | 11 wks |

A.B.'S *Japan, instrumental group*　　　　　*2 wks*

| 14 Apr 84 | **DEJA VU** *Street Sounds XKHAN 503* | 80 | 2 wks |

ACADEMY of ANCIENT MUSIC conducted by Christopher HOGWOOD *UK, male conductor/*
instrumentalist – harpsichord, UK chamber orchestra　　　　　*2 wks*

| 16 Mar 85 | **THE FOUR SEASONS (VIVALDI)** *L'Oiseau Lyre 4101261* | 85 | 2 wks |

ACADEMY OF ST MARTIN IN THE FIELDS – *See Neville MARRINER and the ACADEMY OF ST MARTIN IN THE FIELDS*

ACCEPT *Germany, male vocal/instrumental group*　　　　　*5 wks*

7 May 83	**RESTLESS AND WILD** *Heavy Metal Worldwide HMILP 6*	98	2 wks
30 Mar 85	**METAL HEART** *Portrait PRT 26358*	50	1 wk
15 Feb 86	**KAIZOKU-BAN** *Portrait PRT 5916*	91	1 wk
3 May 86	**RUSSIAN ROULETTE** *Portrait PRT 26893*	80	1 wk

AC/DC *Australia/UK, male vocal/instrumental group*　　　　　*236 wks*

5 Nov 77	**LET THERE BE ROCK** *Atlantic K 50366*	17	5 wks
20 May 78	**POWERAGE** *Atlantic K 50483*	26	9 wks
28 Oct 78	**IF YOU WANT BLOOD YOU'VE GOT IT** *Atlantic K 50532*	13	58 wks
18 Aug 79	● **HIGHWAY TO HELL** *Atlantic K 50628*	8	32 wks
9 Aug 80	★ **BACK IN BLACK** *Atlantic K 50735*	1	40 wks
5 Dec 81	● **FOR THOSE ABOUT TO ROCK** *Atlantic K 50851*	3	29 wks
3 Sep 83	● **FLICK OF THE SWITCH** *Atlantic 78-0100-1*	4	9 wks
13 Jul 85	● **FLY ON THE WALL** *Atlantic 781263*	7	10 wks
7 Jun 86	**WHO MADE WHO** *Atlantic WX 57*	11	12 wks
13 Feb 88	● **BLOW UP YOUR VIDEO** *Atlantic WX 144*	2	14 wks
6 Oct 90	● **THE RAZOR'S EDGE** *Atco WX 364*	4	18 wks

43

a

Bryan ADAMS
Canada, male vocalist/instrumentalist – guitar　　　　　*156 wks*

2 Mar 85	● **RECKLESS** *A&M AMA 5013*	7	111 wks
24 Aug 85	**YOU WANT IT, YOU GOT IT** *A&M AMLH 64864*	78	5 wks
15 Mar 86	**CUTS LIKE A KNIFE** *A&M AMLH 64919*	21	6 wks
11 Apr 87	● **INTO THE FIRE** *A&M AMA 3907*	10	21 wks
5 Oct 91	★ **WAKING UP THE NEIGHBOURS** *A&M 3971641*	1†	13 wks

Oleta ADAMS *US, female vocalist/instrumentalist – piano*　　　　　*26 wks*

| 26 May 90 | ★ **CIRCLE OF ONE** *Fontana 8427441* | 1 | 26 wks |

Cliff ADAMS SINGERS *UK, male/female vocal group*　　　　　*20 wks*

| 16 Apr 60 | **SING SOMETHING SIMPLE** *Pye MPL 28013* | 15 | 4 wks |
| 24 Nov 62 | **SING SOMETHING SIMPLE** *Pye Golden Guinea GGL 0150* | 15 | 2 wks |

A-Ha is the only act to start its chart career with three number twos.

The dance styles of **Paula Abdul** dominated music video choreography in the late 80s and early 90s.

Vermine In Ermine star **Marc Almond** poses with roses.

20 Nov 76	**SING SOMETHING SIMPLE '76**		
	Warwick WW 5016/17	23	8 wks
25 Dec 82	**SING SOMETHING SIMPLE** *Ronco RTD 2087*	39	6 wks

All the identically titled albums are different.

ADAMSKI *UK, male multi-instrumentalist/producer*   *16 wks*

9 Dec 89	**LIVE AND DIRECT** *MCA MCL 1900*	65	1 wk
13 Oct 90	● **DOCTOR ADAMSKI'S MUSICAL PHARMACY**		
	MCA MCG 6107	8	5 wks

King Sunny ADE and his AFRICAN BEATS
Nigeria, male vocalist and male vocal/instrumental group   *1 wk*

| 9 Jul 83 | **SYNCHRO SYSTEM** *Island ILPS 9737* .... | 93 | 1 wk |

ADEVA *US, female vocalist*   *24 wks*

| 9 Sep 89 | ● **ADEVA** *Cooltempo ICTLP 13* .... | 6 | 24 wks |

ADICTS *UK, male vocal/instrumental group*   *1 wk*

| 4 Dec 82 | **SOUND OF MUSIC** *Razor RAZ 2* .... | 99 | 1 wk |

ADVENTURES *UK, male/female vocal/instrumental group*   *11 wks*

| 21 May 88 | **THE SEA OF LOVE** *Elektra EKT 45* .... | 30 | 10 wks |
| 17 Mar 90 | **TRADING SECRETS WITH THE MOON** *Elektra EKT 63* | 64 | 1wk |

ADVERTS *UK, male/female vocal/instrumental group*   *1 wk*

| 11 Mar 78 | **CROSSING THE RED SEA WITH THE ADVERTS** | | |
| | *Bright BRL 201* .... | 38 | 1 wk |

AEROSMITH *US, male vocal/instrumental group*   *38 wks*

| 5 Sep 87 | **PERMANENT VACATION** *Geffen WX 126* .... | 37 | 14 wks |
| 23 Sep 89 | ● **PUMP** *Geffen WX 304* .... | 3 | 24 wks |

AFTER THE FIRE *UK, male vocal/instrumental group*   *4 wks*

13 Oct 79	**LASER LOVE** *CBS 83795*.........................	57	1 wk
1 Nov 80	**80 F** *Epic EPC 84545*	69	1 wk
3 Apr 82	**BATTERIES NOT INCLUDED** *CBS 85566*	82	2 wks

AFRICAN BEATS – *See King Sunny ADE and his AFRICAN BEATS*

A-HA *Norway, male vocal/instrumental group*   *136 wks*

9 Nov 85	● **HUNTING HIGH AND LOW** *Warner Bros. WX 30*	2	77 wks
18 Oct 86	● **SCOUNDREL DAYS** *Warner Bros. WX 62*	2	29 wks
14 May 88	● **STAY ON THESE ROADS** *Warner Bros. WX 166*	2	19 wks
2 Nov 90	**EAST OF THE SUN WEST OF THE MOON**		
	Warner Bros. WX 378	12	4 wks
16 Nov 91	**HEADLINES AND DEADLINES – THE HITS OF A-HA**		
	Warner Bros. WX 450	12†	7 wks

45

a

ALARM *UK, male vocal/instrumental group* — 29 wks

25 Feb 84	●	DECLARATION *IRS IRSA 7044*	....	6	11 wks
26 Oct 85		STRENGTH *IRS MIRF 1004*	....	18	6 wks
14 Nov 87		EYE OF THE HURRICANE *IRS MIRG 1023*	....	23	4 wks
5 Nov 88		ELECTRIC FOLKLORE LIVE *IRS MIRMC 5001*	......	62	2 wks
30 Sep 89		CHANGE *IRS EIRSAX 1020*	....	13	3 wks
24 Nov 90		STANDARDS *IRS EIRSA 1043*	....	47	1 wk
4 May 91		RAW *IRS EIRSA 1055*	....	33	2 wks

JOHN ALDISS – *See LONDON PHILHARMONIC CHOIR*

ALEXANDER BROTHERS *UK, male vocal duo* — 1 wk

10 Dec 66	THESE ARE MY MOUNTAINS *Pye GGL 0375*	....	29	1 wk

ALLEN – *See FOSTER and ALLEN*

ALIEN SEX FIEND
UK, male/female vocal/instrumental group — 1 wk

12 Oct 85	MAXIMUM SECURITY *Anagram GRAM 24*	....	100	1 wk

ALL ABOUT EVE
UK, male/female vocal/instrumental group — 36 wks

27 Feb 88	●	ALL ABOUT EVE *Mercury MERH 119*	....	7	29 wks
28 Oct 89	●	SCARLET AND OTHER STORIES *Mercury 838965 1*	...	9	4 wks
7 Sep 91		TOUCHED BY JESUS *Vertigo 510461*	....	17	3 wks

Patrick ALLEN – *See Kevin PEEK and Rick WAKEMAN*

Mose ALLISON *US, male vocalist/instrumentalist – piano* — 1 wk

4 Jun 66	MOSE ALIVE *Atlantic 587–007*	....	30	1 wk

ALLMAN BROTHERS BAND
US, male vocal/instrumental group — 4 wks

6 Oct 73	BROTHERS AND SISTERS *Warner Bros. K 47507*	......	42	3 wks
6 Mar 76	THE ROAD GOES ON FOREVER *Capricorn 2637 101*	...	54	1 wk

ALMIGHTY *UK, male vocal/instrumental group* — 5 wks

20 Oct 90	BLOOD FIRE AND LIVE *Polydor 8471071*	....	62	1 wk
30 Mar 91	SOUL DESTRUCTION *Polydor 8479611*	....	22	4 wks

Marc ALMOND *UK, male vocalist* — 14 wks

10 Nov 84	VERMIN IN ERMINE *Some Bizzare BIZL 8*	....	36	2 wks
5 Oct 85	STORIES OF JOHNNY *Some Bizzare FAITH 1*	....	22	3 wks
18 Apr 87	MOTHER FIST AND HER FIVE DAUGHTERS			
	Some Bizzare FAITH 2	....	41	2 wks
8 Oct 88	THE STARS WE ARE *Parlophone PCS 7324*	....	41	5 wks
16 Jun 90	ENCHANTED *Some Bizzare PCS 7344*	....	52	1 wk
26 Oct 91	TENEMENT SYMPHONY *Some Bizzare WX 442*	....	48	1 wk

Vermin In Ermine *and* Mother Fist and Her Five Daughters *credited to Marc Almond and the Willing Sinners – UK, male/female vocal/instrumental group. See also Marc and the Mambas.*

Herb ALPERT and the TIJUANA BRASS
US, male band leader/instrumentalist – trumpet   *312 wks*

29 Jan	66	● GOING PLACES *Pye NPL 28065*	4	138 wks
23 Apr	66	● WHIPPED CREAM AND OTHER DELIGHTS		
		Pye NPL 28058	2	42 wks
28 May	66	WHAT NOW MY LOVE *Pye NPL 28077*	18	17 wks
11 Feb	67	● S.R.O. *Pye NSPL 28088*	5	26 wks
15 Jul	67	SOUNDS LIKE *A & M AMLS 900*	21	10 wks
3 Feb	68	NINTH *A & M AMLS 905*	26	9 wks
29 Jun	68	● BEAT OF THE BRASS *A & M AMLS 916*	4	21 wks
9 Aug	69	WARM *A & M AMLS 937*	30	4 wks
14 Mar	70	THE BRASS ARE COMIN' *A & M AMLS 962*	40	1 wk
30 May	70	● GREATEST HITS *A & M AMLS 980*	8	27 wks
27 Jun	70	DOWN MEXICO WAY *A & M AMLS 974*	64	1 wk
13 Nov	71	AMERICA *A & M AMLB 1000*	45	1 wk
12 Nov	77	40 GREATEST *K-Tel NE 1005*	45	2 wks
17 Nov	79	RISE *A & M AMLH 64790*	37	7 wks
4 Apr	87	KEEP YOUR EYE ON ME *Breakout AMA 5125*	79	3 wks
28 Sep	91	THE VERY BEST OF HERB ALPERT *A & M 3971651* ..	34	3 wks

Last three hits credit only Herb Alpert. On 29 Jun 67 Going Places and What Now My Love changed labels and numbers to A & M AMLS 965 and AMLS 977 respectively.

ALTERED IMAGES
UK, male/female vocal/instrumental group   *40 wks*

19 Sep	81	HAPPY BIRTHDAY *Epic EPC 84893*	26	21 wks
15 May	82	PINKY BLUE *Epic EPC 85665*	12	10 wks
25 Jun	83	BITE *Epic EPC 25413*	16	9 wks

AMAZULU *UK, female vocal group*   *1 wk*

6 Dec	88	AMAZULU *Island ILPS 9851*	97	1 wk

AMEN CORNER *UK, male vocal/instrumental group*   *8 wks*

30 Mar	68	ROUND AMEN CORNER *Deram SML 1021*	26	7 wks
1 Nov	69	EXPLOSIVE COMPANY *Immediate IMSP 023*	19	1 wk

AMERICA *US, male vocal/instrumental group*   *22 wks*

22 Jan	72	AMERICA *Warner Bros. K 46093*	14	13 wks
9 Dec	72	HOMECOMING *Warner Bros. K 46180*	21	5 wks
10 Nov	73	HAT TRICK *Warner Bros. K 56016*	41	3 wks
7 Feb	76	HISTORY – AMERICA'S GREATEST HITS		
		Warner Bros. K 56169	60	1 wk

AND WHY NOT *UK, male vocal group*   *3 wks*

10 Mar	90	MOVE YOUR SKIN *Island ILPS 9935*	24	3 wks

Ian ANDERSON *UK, male vocalist/instrumentalist – flute*   *1 wk*

26 Nov	83	WALK INTO LIGHT *Chrysalis CDL 1443*	78	1 wk

Jon ANDERSON *UK, male vocalist*   *19 wks*

24 Jul	76	● OLIAS OF SUNHILLOW *Atlantic K 50261*	8	10 wks

47

a

15 Nov 80	**SONG OF SEVEN** *Atlantic K 50756*	38	3 wks
5 Jun 82	**ANIMATION** *Polydor POLD 5044*	43	6 wks

See also Jon and Vangelis; Anderson Bruford Wakeman Howe.

Laurie ANDERSON
US, female vocalist/multi-instrumentalist 8 wks

1 May 82	**BIG SCIENCE** *Warner Bros. K 57002*	29	6 wks
10 Mar 84	**MISTER HEARTBREAK** *Warner Bros. 92–5077–1*	93	2 wks

Lynn ANDERSON *US, female vocalist* 1 wk

17 Apr 71	**ROSE GARDEN** *CBS 64333*	45	1 wk

Moira ANDERSON *UK, female vocalist* 1 wk

20 Jun 70	**THESE ARE MY SONGS** *Decca SKL 5016*	50	1 wk

See also Harry Secombe and Moira Anderson.

ANDERSON BRUFORD WAKEMAN HOWE
UK, male vocal/instrumental group 6 wks

8 Jul 89	**ANDERSON BRUFORD WAKEMAN HOWE** *Arista 209970*	14	6 wks

See also Jon Anderson; Rick Wakeman; Steve Howe.

48

a

Julie ANDREWS *UK, female vocalist* 5 wks

16 Jul 83	**LOVE ME TENDER** *Peach River JULIE 1*	63	5 wks

ANGELIC UPSTARTS
UK, male vocal/instrumental group 20 wks

18 Aug 79	**TEENAGE WARNING** *Warner Bros. K 50634*	29	7 wks
12 Apr 80	**WE'VE GOTTA GET OUT OF THIS PLACE** *Warner Bros. K 56806*	54	3 wks
7 Jun 81	**2,000,000 VOICES** *Zonophone ZONO 104*	32	3 wks
26 Sep 81	**ANGELIC UPSTARTS** *Zonophone ZEM 102*	27	7 wks

ANIMAL NIGHTLIFE
UK, male vocal/instrumental group 6 wks

24 Aug 85	**SHANGRI-LA** *Island ILPS 9830*	36	6 wks

ANIMALS *UK, male vocal/instrumental group* 86 wks

14 Nov 64	● **THE ANIMALS** *Columbia 33SX 1669*	6	20 wks
22 May 65	● **ANIMAL TRACKS** *Columbia 33SX 1708*	6	26 wks
16 Apr 66	● **MOST OF THE ANIMALS** *Columbia 33SX 6035*	4	20 wks
28 May 66	● **ANIMALISMS** *Decca LK 4797*	4	17 wks
25 Sep 71	**MOST OF THE ANIMALS** (re-issue) *MFP 5218*	18	3 wks

ANNIHILATOR *UK, male vocal/instrumental group* 1 wk

11 Aug 90	**NEVER NEVERLAND** *Road Runner RR 93741*	48	1 wk

Adam ANT *UK, male vocalist* 142 wks

15 Nov 80	★ **KINGS OF THE WILD FRONTIER** CBS 84549	1	66 wks
17 Jan 81	**DIRK WEARS WHITE SOX** Do It RIDE 3	16	29 wks
14 Nov 81	● **PRINCE CHARMING** CBS 85268	2	21 wks
23 Oct 82	● **FRIEND OR FOE** CBS 25040	5	12 wks
19 Nov 83	**STRIP** CBS 25705	20	8 wks
14 Sep 85	**VIVE LE ROCK** CBS 26583	42	3 wks
24 Mar 90	**MANNERS AND PHYSIQUE** MCA MCG 6068	19	3 wks

All the albums up to and including Prince Charming *credited to Adam and the Ants – UK, male vocal/instrumental group.*

ANTHRAX *US, male vocal/instrumental group* 19 wks

18 Apr 87	**AMONG THE LIVING** Island ILPS 9865	18	5 wks
24 Sep 88	**STATE OF EUPHORIA** Island ILPS 9916	12	4 wks
8 Sep 90	**PERSISTENCE OF TIME** Island ILPS 9967	13	5 wks
20 Jul 91	**ATTACK OF THE KILLER B'S** Island ILPS 9980	13	5 wks

ANTI-NOWHERE LEAGUE
UK, male vocal/instrumental group 12 wks

22 May 82	**WE ARE ... THE LEAGUE** WXYZ LMNOP 1	24	11 wks
5 Nov 83	**LIVE IN YUGOSLAVIA** I.D. NOSE 3	88	1 wk

ANTI-PASTI *UK, male vocal/instrumental group* 7 wks

15 Aug 81	**THE LAST CALL** Rondelet ABOUT 5	31	7 wks

ANTS – *See Adam ANT*

Carmine APPICE – *See Jeff BECK, Tim BOGERT and Carmine APPICE*

Kim APPLEBY *UK, female vocalist* 13 wks

8 Dec 90	**KIM APPLEBY** Parlophone PCS 7348	23	13 wks

See also Mel and Kim.

APRIL WINE *Canada, male vocal/instrumental group* 8 wks

15 Mar 80	**HARDER ... FASTER** Capitol EST 12013	34	5 wks
24 Jan 81	**THE NATURE OF THE BEAST** Capitol EST 12125 ...	48	3 wks

ARCADIA *UK, male vocal/instrumental group* 10 wks

7 Dec 85	**SO RED THE ROSE** Parlophone Odeon PCSD 101	30	10 wks

ARGENT *UK, male vocal/instrumental group* 9 wks

29 Apr 72	**ALL TOGETHER NOW** Epic EPC 64962	13	8 wks
31 Mar 73	**IN DEEP** Epic EPC 65475	49	1 wk

Joan ARMATRADING *UK, female vocalist* 187 wks

4 Sep 76	**JOAN ARMATRADING** A & M AMLH 64588	12	27 wks
1 Oct 77	● **SHOW SOME EMOTION** A & M AMLH 68433	6	11 wks
14 Oct 78	**TO THE LIMIT** A & M AMLH 64732	13	10 wks

24 May 80	● ME MYSELF I *A & M AMLH 64809*	5	23 wks
12 Sep 81	● WALK UNDER LADDERS *A & M AMLH 64876*	6	29 wks
12 Mar 83	● THE KEY *A & M AMLX 64912*	10	14 wks
26 Nov 83	TRACK RECORD *A & M JA 2001*	18	32 wks
16 Feb 85	SECRET SECRETS *A & M AMA 5040*	14	12 wks
24 May 86	SLEIGHT OF HAND *A & M AMA 5130*	34	6 wks
16 Jul 88	THE SHOUTING STAGE *A & M AMA 5211*	28	10 wks
16 Jun 90	HEARTS AND FLOWERS *A & M 3952981*	29	4 wks
16 Mar 91	● THE VERY BEST OF JOAN ARMATRADING		
	A & M 3971221	9	9 wks

ARMOURY SHOW *UK, male vocal/instrumental group*   *1 wk*

21 Sep 85	WAITING FOR THE FLOODS *Parlophone ARM 1*	57	1 wk

Louis ARMSTRONG
US, male band leader vocalist/instrumentalist – trumpet/cornet   *14 wks*

22 Oct 60	SATCHMO PLAYS KING OLIVER		
	Audio Fidelity AFLP 1930	20	1 wk
28 Oct 61	JAZZ CLASSICS *Ace of Hearts AH 7*	20	1 wk
27 Jun 64	HELLO DOLLY *London HAR 8190*	11	6 wks
16 Nov 68	WHAT A WONDERFUL WORLD *Stateside SSL 10247* ..	37	3 wks
20 Feb 82	THE VERY BEST OF LOUIS ARMSTRONG		
	Warwick WW 5112	30	3 wks

Steve ARRINGTON *US, male vocalist*   *11 wks*

13 Apr 85	DANCIN' IN THE KEY OF LIFE *Atlantic 781245*	41	11 wks

Davey ARTHUR – *See FUREYS and Davey ARTHUR*

50

a

ART OF NOISE *UK, male/female instrumental duo*   *37 wks*

3 Nov 84	(WHO'S AFRAID OF) THE ART OF NOISE		
	ZTT ZTTIQ 2	27	17 wks
26 Apr 86	IN VISIBLE SILENCE *Chrysalis WOL 2*	18	15 wks
10 Oct 87	IN NO SENSE/NONSENSE *China WOL 4*	55	2 wks
3 Dec 88	THE BEST OF THE ART OF NOISE *China 837 367 1* ...	55	3 wks

Act was a group for first two albums.

ASAP *UK, male vocal/instrumental group*   *1 wk*

4 Nov 89	SILVER AND GOLD *EMI EMC 3566*	70	1 wk

ASHFORD and SIMPSON *US, male/female vocal duo*   *6 wks*

16 Feb 85	SOLID *Capitol SASH 1*	42	6 wks

ASIA *UK, male vocal/instrumental group*   *50 wks*

10 Apr 82	ASIA *Geffen GEF 85577*	11	38 wks
20 Aug 83	● ALPHA *Geffen GEF 25508*	5	11 wks
14 Dec 85	ASTRA *Geffen GEF 26413*	68	1 wk

ASSOCIATES *UK, male vocal/instrumental group*   *28 wks*

22 May 82	● SULK *Associates ASCL 1*	10	20 wks

| 16 Feb 85 | **PERHAPS** *WEA WX 9* | 23 | 7 wks |
| 31 Mar 90 | **WILD AND LONELY** *Circa CIRCA 11* | 71 | 1 wk |

Duo for the first album.

Rick ASTLEY *UK, male vocalist*   *62 wks*

28 Nov 87	★ **WHENEVER YOU NEED SOMEBODY**		
	RCA PL 71529	1	34 wks
10 Dec 88	● **HOLD ME IN YOUR ARMS** *RCA PL 71932*	8	19 wks
2 Mar 91	● **FREE** *RCA PL 74896*	9	9 wks

ASWAD *UK, male vocal/instrumental group*   *52 wks*

24 Jul 82	**NOT SATISFIED** *CBS 85666*	50	6 wks
10 Dec 83	**LIVE AND DIRECT** *Island IMA 6*	57	16 wks
3 Nov 84	**REBEL SOULS** *Island ILPS 9780*	48	2 wks
28 Jun 86	**TO THE TOP** *Simba SIMBALP 2*	71	3 wks
9 Apr 88	● **DISTANT THUNDER** *Mango ILPS 9895*	10	15 wks
3 Dec 88	**RENAISSANCE** *Stylus SMR 866*	52	8 wks
22 Sep 90	**TOO WICKED** *Mango MLPS 1054*	51	2 wks

ATHLETICO SPIZZ 80 *UK, male vocal/instrumental group*   *5 wks*

| 26 Jul 80 | **DO A RUNNER** *A & M AMLE 68514* | 27 | 5 wks |

Chet ATKINS *US, male instrumentalist – guitar*   *5 wks*

18 Mar 61	**THE OTHER CHET ATKINS** *RCA RD 27194*	20	1 wk
17 Jun 61	**CHET ATKINS' WORKSHOP** *RCA RD 27214*	19	1 wk
30 Feb 63	**CARIBBEAN GUITAR** *RCA RD 7519*	17	3 wks

Chet ATKINS and Mark KNOPFLER
US/UK, male vocal/instrumental duo   *6 wks*

| 24 Nov 90 | **NECK AND NECK** *CBS 4674351* | 41 | 6 wks |

See also Chet Atkins; Mark Knopfler.

Rowan ATKINSON *UK, male comedian*   *9 wks*

| 7 Feb 81 | **LIVE IN BELFAST** *Arista SPART 1150* | 44 | 9 wks |

ATLANTIC STARR
US, male/female vocal/instrumental group   *15 wks*

| 15 Jun 85 | **AS THE BAND TURNS** *A & M AMA 5019* | 64 | 3 wks |
| 11 Jul 87 | **ALL IN THE NAME OF LOVE** *WEA WX 115* | 48 | 12 wks |

ATOMIC ROOSTER *UK, male vocal/instrumental group*   *13 wks*

13 Jun 70	**ATOMIC ROOSTER** *B & C CAS 1010*	49	1 wk
16 Jan 71	**DEATH WALKS BEHIND YOU**		
	Charisma CAS 1026	12	8 wks
21 Aug 71	**IN HEARING OF ATOMIC ROOSTER**		
	Pegasus PEG 1	18	4 wks

ATTRACTIONS – *See Elvis COSTELLO and the ATTRACTIONS*

AU PAIRS *UK, female/male vocal/instrumental group* *10 wks*

6 Jun 81	**PLAYING WITH A DIFFERENT SEX** *Human HUMAN 1*	33	7 wks
4 Sep 82	**SENSE AND SENSUALITY** *Kamera KAM 010*	79	3 wks

Brian AUGER TRINITY – *See Julie DRISCOLL and the Brian AUGER TRINITY*

Patti AUSTIN *US, female vocalist* *1 wk*

26 Sep 81	**EVERY HOME SHOULD HAVE ONE** *Quest K 56931* ...	99	1 wk

AVERAGE WHITE BAND
UK, male vocal/instrumental group *47 wks*

1 Mar 75 ●	**AVERAGE WHITE BAND** *Atlantic K 50058*	6	14 wks
5 Jul 75	**CUT THE CAKE** *Atlantic K 50146*	28	4 wks
31 Jul 76	**SOUL SEARCHING TIME** *Atlantic K 50272*	60	1 wk
10 Mar 79	**I FEEL NO FRET** *RCA XL 13063*	15	15 wks
31 May 80	**SHINE** *RCA XL 13123*	14	13 wks

Roy AYERS *US, male vocalist/instrumentalist – vibraphone* *2 wks*

26 Oct 85	**YOU MIGHT BE SURPRISED** *CBS 26653*	91	2 wks

Pam AYRES *UK, female vocalist* *29 wks*

27 Mar 76	**SOME OF ME POEMS AND SONGS** *Galaxy GAL 6003* ..	13	23 wks
11 Dec 76	**SOME MORE OF ME POEMS AND SONGS**		
	Galaxy GAL 6010	23	6 wks

Charles AZNAVOUR *France, male vocalist* *21 wks*

29 Jun 74	**AZNAVOUR SINGS AZNAVOUR VOL. 3** *Barclay 80472* .	23	7 wks
7 Sep 74 ●	**A TAPESTRY OF DREAMS** *Barclay 90003*	9	13 wks
2 Aug 80	**HIS GREATEST LOVE SONGS** *K-Tel NE 1078*	73	1 wk

AZTEC CAMERA *UK, male vocal/instrumental group* *74 wks*

23 Apr 83	**HIGH LAND HARD RAIN** *Rough Trade ROUGH 47*	22	18 wks
29 Sep 84	**KNIFE** *WEA WX 8*	14	6 wks
21 Nov 87 ●	**LOVE** *WEA WX 128*	10	43 wks
16 Jun 90	**STRAY** *WEA WX 350*	22	7 wks

Derek B *UK, male rapper* *9 wks*

28 May 88	**BULLET FROM A GUN** *Tuff Audio DRKLP 1*	11	9 wks

Eric B. and RAKIM *US, male vocal/instrumental duo* *9 wks*

12 Sep 87	**PAID IN FULL** *Fourth & Broadway BRLP 514*	85	4 wks

| 6 Aug 88 | **FOLLOW THE LEADER** *MCA MCG 6031* .... | 25 | 4 wks |
| 7 Jul 90 | **LET THE RHYTHM HIT 'EM** *MCA MCG 6097* .... | 58 | 1 wk |

B BOYS *US, male vocal/instrumental group*   *1 wk*

| 28 Jan 84 | **CUTTIN' HERBIE** *Streetwave X KHAN 501* .... | 90 | 1 wk |

BACCARA *Spain, female vocal duo*   *6 wks*

| 4 Mar 78 | **BACCARA** *RCA PL 28316* .... | 26 | 6 wks |

Burt BACHARACH *US, orchestra and chorus*   *43 wks*

22 May 65	● **HIT MAKER – BURT BACHARACH** *London HAR 8233* .	3	18 wks
28 Nov 70	**REACH OUT** *A & M AMLS 908*	52	3 wks
3 Apr 71	● **PORTRAIT IN MUSIC** *A & M AMLS 2010*	5	22 wks

BACHELORS *Ireland, male vocal group*   *103 wks*

27 Jun 64	● **THE BACHELORS AND 16 GREAT SONGS**		
	Decca LK 4614	2	44 wks
9 Oct 65	**MORE GREAT SONG HITS FROM THE BACHELORS**		
	Decca LK 4721	15	6 wks
9 Jul 66	**HITS OF THE SIXTIES** *Decca TXL 102*	12	9 wks
5 Nov 66	**BACHELORS' GIRLS** *Decca LK 4827*	24	8 wks
1 Jul 67	**GOLDEN ALL TIME HITS** *Decca SKL 4849*	19	7 wks
14 Jun 69	● **WORLD OF THE BACHELORS** *Decca SPA 2*	8	18 wks
23 Aug 69	**WORLD OF THE BACHELORS VOL. 2** *Decca SPA 22* ..	11	7 wks
22 Dec 79	**25 GOLDEN GREATS** *Warwick WW 5068*	38	4 wks

53

b

BACHMAN-TURNER OVERDRIVE
Canada, male vocal/instrumental group   *13 wks*

| 14 Dec 74 | **NOT FRAGILE** *Mercury 9100 007* .... | 12 | 13 wks |

BAD COMPANY *UK, male vocal/instrumental group*   *87 wks*

15 Jun 74	● **BAD COMPANY** *Island ILPS 9279*	3	25 wks
12 Apr 75	● **STRAIGHT SHOOTER** *Island ILPS 9304*	3	27 wks
21 Feb 76	● **RUN WITH THE PACK** *Island ILPS 9346*	4	12 wks
19 Mar 77	**BURNIN' SKY** *Island ILPS 9441*	17	8 wks
17 Mar 79	● **DESOLATION ANGELS** *Swansong SSK 59408*	10	9 wks
28 Aug 82	**ROUGH DIAMONDS** *Swansong SSK 59419*	15	6 wks

BAD ENGLISH *UK/US, male vocal/instrumental group*   *2 wks*

| 16 Sep 89 | **BAD ENGLISH** *Epic 4634471* .... | 74 | 1 wk |
| 19 Oct 91 | **BACKLASH** *Epic 4685691* .... | 64 | 1 wk |

BAD MANNERS *UK, male vocal/instrumental group*   *44 wks*

26 Apr 80	**SKA 'N' B** *Magnet MAG 5033*	34	13 wks
29 Nov 80	**LOONEE TUNES** *Magnet MAG 5038*	36	12 wks
24 Oct 81	**GOSH IT'S BAD MANNERS** *Magnet MAGL 5043*	18	12 wks
27 Nov 82	**FORGING AHEAD** *Magnet MAGL 5050*	78	1 wk
7 May 83	**THE HEIGHT OF BAD MANNERS** *Telstar STAR 2229* ..	23	6 wks

Barclay James Harvest, chart regulars at home and major stars in Germany.

Everything by the **Bangles** lasted half a year on the chart, even though it included 'Eternal Flame'.

BAD NEWS *UK, male vocal group* 1 *wk*

24 Oct 87   **BAD NEWS** *EMI EMC 3535* 69   1 wk

BAD SEEDS – *See Nick CAVE featuring the BAD SEEDS*

Angelo BADALAMENTI *Italy, male arranger* 25 *wks*

17 Nov 90   **MUSIC FROM 'TWIN PEAKS'** *Warner Bros. 7599263161* . 27   25 wks

BADLANDS *UK, male vocal/instrumental group* 3 *wks*

24 Jun 89   **BADLANDS** *WEA 7819661* 39   2 wks
22 Jun 91   **VOODOO HIGHWAY** *Atlantic 7567822511* 74   1 wk

Joan BAEZ *US, female vocalist* 88 *wks*

18 Jul   64 ● **JOAN BAEZ IN CONCERT VOL. 2** *Fontana TFL 6033* ...   8   19 wks
15 May 65 ● **JOAN BAEZ NO. 5** *Fontana TFL 6043*   3   27 wks
19 Jun 65 ● **JOAN BAEZ** *Fontana TFL 6002*   9   13 wks
27 Nov 65 ● **FAREWELL ANGELINA** *Fontana TFL 6058*   5   23 wks
19 Jul   69   **JOAN BAEZ ON VANGUARD** *Vanguard SVXL 100* 15   5 wks
 3 Apr 71   **FIRST TEN YEARS** *Vanguard 6635 003* 41   1 wk

Philip BAILEY *US, male vocalist* 17 *wks*

30 Mar 85   **CHINESE WALL** *CBS 26161* 29   17 wks

Anita BAKER *US, female vocalist* 76 *wks*

 3 May 86   **RAPTURE** *Elektra EKT 37* 13   47 wks
29 Oct 88 ● **GIVING YOU THE BEST THAT I GOT** *Elektra EKT 49* .   9   20 wks
14 Jul   90 ● **COMPOSITIONS** *Elektra EKT 72*   7   9 wks

BAKER-GURVITZ ARMY
UK, male vocal/instrumental group 5 *wks*

22 Feb 75   **BAKER-GURVITZ ARMY** *Vertigo 9103 201* 22   5 wks
See also Ginger Baker's Air Force.

Ginger BAKER'S AIR FORCE
UK, male vocal/instrumental group 1 *wk*

13 Jun 70   **GINGER BAKER'S AIR FORCE** *Polydor 266 2001* 37   1 wk
See also Baker-Gurvitz Army.

BALAAM AND THE ANGEL
UK, male/vocal instrumental group 2 *wks*

16 Aug 86   **THE GREATEST STORY EVER TOLD** *Virgin V 2377* .. 67   2 wks

Kenny BALL *UK, male vocalist/instrumentalist – trumpet* 26 *wks*

 7 Sep 63 ● **KENNY BALL'S GOLDEN HITS**
                   Pye Golden Guinea GGL 0209   4   26 wks
See also Kenny Ball, Chris Barber and Acker Bilk.

55

b

Kenny BALL, Chris BARBER and Acker BILK

UK, male jazz band leaders/vocalists/instrumentalists – trumpet,
trombone and clarinet respectively   *24 wks*

25 Aug 62 ★ **BEST OF BALL, BARBER AND BILK**			
Pye Golden Guinea GGL 0131	**1**	24 wks

See also Kenny Ball; Chris Barber; Mr Acker Bilk.

BANANARAMA *UK, female vocal group*   *96 wks*

19 Mar 83 ● **DEEP SEA SKIVING** *London RAMA 1*	**7**	16 wks
28 Apr 84 **BANANARAMA** *London RAMA 2*	**16**	11 wks
19 Jul 86 **TRUE CONFESSIONS** *London RAMA 3*	**46**	5 wks
19 Sep 87 **WOW!** *London RAMA 4*	**27**	26 wks
22 Oct 88 ● **THE GREATEST HITS COLLECTION** *London RAMA 5* .	**3**	37 wks
25 May 91 **POP LIFE** *London 8282461*	**42**	1 wk

BAND *Canada/US, male vocal/instrumental group*   *18 wks*

31 Jan 70 **THE BAND** *Capitol EST 132*	**25**	11 wks
3 Oct 70 **STAGE FRIGHT** *Capitol EA SW 425*	**15**	6 wks
27 Nov 71 **CAHOOTS** *Capitol EA–ST 651*	**41**	1 wk

BANDERAS *UK, female vocal/instrumental duo*   *3 wks*

13 Apr 91 **RIPE** *London 8282471*	**40**	3 wks

BANGLES *US, female vocal/instrumental group*   *93 wks*

16 Mar 85 **ALL OVER THE PLACE** *CBS 26015*	**86**	1 wk
15 Mar 86 ● **DIFFERENT LIGHT** *CBS 26659*	**3**	47 wks
10 Dec 88 ● **EVERYTHING** *CBS 4629791*	**5**	26 wks
9 Jun 90 ● **GREATEST HITS** *CBS 4667691*	**4**	19 wks

Tony BANKS *UK, male instrumentalist – keyboards*   *7 wks*

20 Oct 79 **A CURIOUS FEELING** *Charisma CAS 1148*	**21**	5 wks
25 Jun 83 **THE FUGITIVE** *Charisma TBLP 1*	**50**	2 wks

BANSHEES – *See SIOUXSIE and the BANSHEES*

Chris BARBER *UK, male vocalist/instrumentalist – trombone*   *3 wks*

24 Sep 60 **CHRIS BARBER BAND BOX NO. 2** *Columbia 33SCX 3277*	**17**	1 wk
5 Nov 60 **ELITE SYNCOPATIONS** *Columbia 33SX 1245*	**18**	1 wk
12 Nov 60 **BEST OF CHRIS BARBER** *Ace Of Clubs ACL 1037*	**17**	1 wk

See also Chris Barber and Acker Bilk; Kenny Ball, Chris Barber and Acker Bilk.

Chris BARBER and Acker BILK *UK, male band*

leaders/vocalists/instrumentalists – trombone and clarinet   *61 wks*

27 May 61 ● **BEST OF BARBER AND BILK VOL. 1** *Pye GGL 0075* ...	**4**	43 wks
11 Nov 61 ● **BEST OF BARBER AND BILK VOL. 2** *Pye GGL 0096* ...	**8**	18 wks

See also Chris Barber; Mr Acker Bilk.

BARCLAY JAMES HARVEST
UK, male vocal/instrumental group   *42 wks*

14 Dec 74	**BARCLAY JAMES HARVEST LIVE** *Polydor 2683 052* ...	40	2 wks
18 Oct 75	**TIME HONOURED GHOST** *Polydor 2383 361*	32	3 wks
23 Oct 76	**OCTOBERON** *Polydor 2442 144*	19	4 wks
1 Oct 77	**GONE TO EARTH** *Polydor 2442 148*	30	7 wks
21 Oct 78	**BARCLAY JAMES HARVEST XII** *Polydor POLD 5006* ..	31	2 wks
23 May 81	**TURN OF THE TIDE** *Polydor POLD 5040*	55	2 wks
24 Jul 82	**A CONCERT FOR THE PEOPLE (BERLIN)**		
	Polydor POLD 5052	15	11 wks
28 May 83	**RING OF CHANGES** *Polydor POLH 3*	36	4 wks
14 Apr 84	**VICTIMS OF CIRCUMSTANCE** *Polydor POLD 5135*	33	6 wks
14 Feb 87	**FACE TO FACE** *Polydor POLD 5209*	65	1 wk

Daniel BARENBOIM – *See John WILLIAMS and Daniel BARENBOIM*

Syd BARRETT   *UK, male vocalist/instrumentalist – guitar*   *1 wk*

7 Feb 70	**MADCAP LAUGHS** *Harvest SHVL 765*	40	1 wk

Wild Willy BARRETT – *See John OTWAY and Wild Willy BARRETT*

BARRON KNIGHTS   *UK, male vocal/instrumental group*   *22 wks*

2 Dec 78	**NIGHT GALLERY** *Epic EPC 83221*	15	13 wks
1 Dec 79	**TEACH THE WORLD TO LAUGH** *Epic EPC 83891*	51	4 wks
13 Dec 80	**JUST A GIGGLE** *Epic EPC 84550*	45	5 wks

57

b

John BARRY   *UK, male arranger/conductor*   *17 wks*

29 Jan 72	**THE PERSUADERS** *CBS 64816*	18	9 wks
20 Apr 91	**DANCES WITH WOLVES (film soundtrack)**		
	Epic 4675911	45	8 wks

---

BASIA   *Poland, female vocalist*   *4 wks*

13 Feb 88	**TIME AND TIDE** *Portrait 4502631*	61	3 wks
3 Mar 90	**LONDON WARSAW NEW YORK** *Epic 4632821*	68	1 wk

---

Count BASIE   *US, male orchestra leader/instrumentalist – piano*   *1 wk*

16 Apr 60	**CHAIRMAN OF THE BOARD** *Columbia 33SX 1209*	17	1 wk

See also Frank Sinatra and Count Basie.

Toni BASIL   *US, female vocalist*   *16 wks*

6 Feb 82	**WORD OF MOUTH** *Radialchoice BASIL 1*	15	16 wks

---

Shirley BASSEY   *UK, female vocalist*   *266 wks*

28 Jan 61	**FABULOUS SHIRLEY BASSEY** *Columbia 33SX 1178* ...	12	2 wks
25 Feb 61	● **SHIRLEY** *Columbia 33SX 1286*	9	10 wks
17 Feb 62	**SHIRLEY BASSEY** *Columbia 33SX 1382*	14	11 wks
15 Dec 62	**LET'S FACE THE MUSIC** *Columbia 33SX 1454*	12	7 wks
4 Dec 65	**SHIRLEY BASSEY AT THE PIGALLE**		
	Columbia 33SX 1787	16	7 wks
27 Aug 66	**I'VE GOT A SONG FOR YOU** *United Artists ULP 1142* ...	26	1 wk
17 Feb 68	**TWELVE OF THOSE SONGS** *Columbia SCX 6204*	38	3 wks

7 Dec 68	**GOLDEN HITS OF SHIRLEY BASSEY**	
	Columbia SCX 6294	28 40 wks
11 Jul 70	**LIVE AT THE TALK OF THE TOWN**	
	United Artists UAS 29095	38 6 wks
29 Aug 70	● **SOMETHING** United Artists UAS 29100	5 28 wks
15 May 71	● **SOMETHING ELSE** United Artists UAG 29149	7 9 wks
2 Oct 71	**BIG SPENDER** Sunset SLS 50262	27 8 wks
30 Oct 71	**IT'S MAGIC** Starline SRS 5082	32 1 wk
6 Nov 71	**THE FABULOUS SHIRLEY BASSEY** MFP 1398	48 1 wk
4 Dec 71	**WHAT NOW MY LOVE** MFP 5230	17 5 wks
8 Jan 72	**THE SHIRLEY BASSEY COLLECTION**	
	United Artists UAD 60013/4	37 1 wk
19 Feb 72	**I CAPRICORN** United Artists UAS 29246	13 11 wks
29 Nov 72	**AND I LOVE YOU SO** United Artists UAS 29385	24 9 wks
2 Jun 73	● **NEVER NEVER NEVER** United Artists UAG 29471	10 10 wks
15 Mar 75	● **THE SHIRLEY BASSEY SINGLES ALBUM**	
	United Artists UAS 29728	2 23 wks
1 Nov 75	**GOOD, BAD BUT BEAUTIFUL** United Artists UAS 29881	13 7 wks
15 May 76	**LOVE, LIFE AND FEELINGS** United Artists UAS 29944 ..	13 5 wks
4 Dec 76	**THOUGHTS OF LOVE** United Artists UAS 30011	15 9 wks
25 Jun 77	**YOU TAKE MY HEART AWAY** United Artists UAS 30037	34 5 wks
4 Nov 78	● **25TH ANNIVERSARY ALBUM**	
	United Artists SBTV 601 4748	3 12 wks
12 May 79	**THE MAGIC IS YOU** United Artists UATV 30230	40 5 wks
17 Jul 82	**LOVE SONGS** Applause APKL 1163	48 5 wks
20 Oct 84	**I AM WHAT I AM** Towerbell TOWLP 7	25 18 wks
18 May 91	**KEEP THE MUSIC PLAYING** Dino DINTV 21	25 7 wks

Let's Face The Music has credit 'with The Nelson Riddle Orchestra'.

BASS-O-MATIC   UK, male multi-instrumentalist   2 wks

13 Oct 90	**SET THE CONTROLS FOR THE HEART OF THE BASS**	
	Virgin V 2641	57 2 wks

Mike BATT – See Justin Hayward, Mike Batt and the London Philharmonic Orchestra

BAUHAUS   UK, male vocal/instrumental group   24 wks

15 Nov 80	**IN THE FLAT FIELD** 4AD CAD 13	72 1 wk
24 Oct 81	**MASK** Beggars Banquet BEGA 29	30 5 wks
30 Oct 82	● **THE SKY'S GONE OUT** Beggars Banquet BEGA 42	4 6 wks
23 Jul 83	**BURNING FROM THE INSIDE** Beggars Banquet BEGA 45	13 10 wks
30 Nov 85	**1979–1983** Beggars Banquet BEGA 64	36 2 wks

BAY CITY ROLLERS   UK, male vocal/instrumental group   127 wks

12 Oct 74	★ **ROLLIN'** Bell BELLS 244	1 62 wks
3 May 75	**ONCE UPON A STAR** Bell SYBEL 8001	1 37 wks
13 Dec 75	● **WOULDN'T YOU LIKE IT** Bell SYBEL 8002	3 12 wks
25 Sep 76	● **DEDICATION** Bell SYBEL 8005	4 12 wks
13 Aug 77	**IT'S A GAME** Arista SPARTY 1009	18 4 wks

BBC SYMPHONY ORCHESTRA, SINGERS and CHORUS   UK, orchestra/choir and audience   6 wks

4 Oct 69	**LAST NIGHT OF THE PROMS** Philips SFM 23033	36 1 wk
11 Dec 82	**HIGHLIGHTS – LAST NIGHT OF THE PROMS '82**	
	K-Tel NE 1198	69 5 wks

Last Night Of The Proms was conducted by Colin Davis and Highlights – Last Night Of The Proms '82 by James Loughran.

BBC WELSH CHORUS – See Aled JONES

BEACH BOYS   US, male vocal/instrumental group   547 wks

25 Sep 65	**SURFIN' USA** Capitol T 1890	17 7 wks

19 Feb	66	●	**BEACH BOYS PARTY** *Capitol T 2398*	3	14 wks
16 Apr	66	●	**BEACH BOYS TODAY** *Capitol T 2269*	6	25 wks
9 Jul	66	●	**PET SOUNDS** *Capitol T 2458*	2	39 wks
16 Jul	66	●	**SUMMER DAYS** *Capitol T 2354*	4	22 wks
12 Nov	66	●	**BEST OF THE BEACH BOYS** *Capitol T 20865*	2	142 wks
11 Mar	67		**SURFER GIRL** *Capitol T 1981*	13	14 wks
21 Oct	67	●	**BEST OF THE BEACH BOYS VOL. 2** *Capitol ST 20956* ..	3	39 wks
18 Nov	67	●	**SMILEY SMILE** *Capitol ST 9001*	9	8 wks
16 Mar	68	●	**WILD HONEY** *Capitol ST 2859*	7	15 wks
21 Sep	68		**FRIENDS** *Capitol ST 2895*	13	8 wks
23 Nov	68	●	**BEST OF THE BEACH BOYS VOL. 3** *Capitol ST 21142* ..	9	12 wks
29 Mar	69	●	**20/20** *Capitol EST 133*	3	10 wks
19 Sep	70	●	**GREATEST HITS** *Capitol ST 21628*	5	30 wks
5 Dec	70		**SUNFLOWER** *Stateside SSL 8251*	29	6 wks
27 Nov	71		**SURF'S UP** *Stateside SLS 10313*	15	7 wks
24 Jun	72		**CARL AND THE PASSIONS/SO TOUGH**		
			Reprise K 44184	25	1 wk
17 Feb	73		**HOLLAND** *Reprise K 54008*	20	7 wks
10 Jul	76	★	**20 GOLDEN GREATS** *Capitol EMTV 1*	1	86 wks
24 Jul	76		**15 BIG ONES** *Reprise K 54079*	31	3 wks
7 May	77		**THE BEACH BOYS LOVE YOU** *Brother/Reprise K 54087* .	28	1 wk
21 Apr	79		**LA (LIGHT ALBUM)** *Caribou CRB 86081*	32	6 wks
12 Apr	80		**KEEPING THE SUMMER ALIVE** *Caribou CRB 86109* ...	54	3 wks
30 Jul	83	★	**THE VERY BEST OF THE BEACH BOYS**		
			Capitol BBTV 1867193	1	17 wks
22 Jun	85		**THE BEACH BOYS** *Caribou CRB 26378*	60	2 wks
23 Jun	90	●	**SUMMER DREAMS** *Capitol EMTVD 51*	2	23 wks

BEAKY – *See Dave DEE, DOZY, BEAKY, MICK and TICH*

BEASTIE BOYS *US, male vocal group* 42 wks

31 Jan	87	●	**LICENCE TO ILL** *Def Jam 450062*	7	40 wks
5 Aug	89		**PAUL'S BOUTIQUE** *Capitol EST 2102*	44	2 wks

b

BEAT *UK, male vocal/instrumental group* 69 wks

31 May	80	●	**JUST CAN'T STOP IT** *Go-Feet BEAT 001*	3	32 wks
16 May	81	●	**WHA'PPEN** *Go-Feet BEAT 3*	3	18 wks
9 Oct	82		**SPECIAL BEAT SERVICE** *Go-Feet BEAT 5*	21	6 wks
11 Jun	83	●	**WHAT IS BEAT? (THE BEST OF THE BEAT)**		
			Go-Feet BEAT 6	10	13 wks

BEATLES *UK, male vocal/instrumental group* 1082 wks

6 Apr	63	★	**PLEASE PLEASE ME** *Parlophone PMC 1202*	1	70 wks
30 Nov	63	★	**WITH THE BEATLES** *Parlophone PMC 1206*	1	51 wks
18 Jul	64	★	**A HARD DAY'S NIGHT** *Parlophone PMC 1230*	1	38 wks
12 Dec	64	★	**BEATLES FOR SALE** *Parlophone PMC 1240*	1	46 wks
14 Aug	65	★	**HELP** *Parlophone PMC 1255*	1	37 wks
11 Dec	65	★	**RUBBER SOUL** *Parlophone PMC 1267*	1	42 wks
13 Aug	66	★	**REVOLVER** *Parlophone PMC 7009*	1	34 wks
10 Dec	66	●	**A COLLECTION OF BEATLES OLDIES**		
			Parlophone PMC 7016	7	34 wks
3 Jun	67	★	**SERGEANT PEPPER'S LONELY HEARTS CLUB BAND**		
			Parlophone PCS 7027	1	148 wks
13 Jan	68		**MAGICAL MYSTERY TOUR** (import)		
			Capitol SMAL 2835	31	2 wks
7 Dec	68	●	**THE BEATLES** *Apple PCS 7067/8*	1	22 wks
1 Feb	69	●	**YELLOW SUBMARINE** *Apple PCS 7070*	3	10 wks
4 Oct	69	★	**ABBEY ROAD** *Apple PCS 7088*	1	81 wks
23 May	70	★	**LET IT BE** *Apple PXS 1*	1	59 wks
16 Jan	71		**A HARD DAY'S NIGHT** (re-issue) *Parlophone PCS 3058* .	30	1 wk
24 Jul	71		**HELP** (re-issue) *Parlophone PCS 3071*	33	2 wks
5 May	73	●	**THE BEATLES 1967–1970** *Apple PCSP 718*	2	113 wks
5 May	73	●	**THE BEATLES 1962–1966** *Apple PCSP 717*	3	148 wks

25 Jun 76	**ROCK 'N' ROLL MUSIC** *Parlophone PCSP 719*	**11** 15 wks
21 Aug 76	**THE BEATLES TAPES** *Polydor 2683 068*	**45** 1 wk
21 May 77 ★	**THE BEATLES AT THE HOLLYWOOD BOWL**	
	Parlophone EMTV 4	**1** 17 wks
17 Dec 77 ●	**LOVE SONGS** *Parlophone PCSP 721*	**7** 17 wks
3 Nov 79	**RARITIES** *Parlophone PCM 1001*	**71** 1 wk
15 Nov 80	**BEATLES BALLADS** *Parlophone PCS 7214*	**17** 16 wks
30 Oct 82 ●	**20 GREATEST HITS** *Parlophone PCTC 260*	**10** 30 wks
7 Mar 87	**PLEASE PLEASE ME** (re-issue)	
	Parlophone CDP 746 435–2	**32** 4 wks
7 Mar 87	**WITH THE BEATLES** (re-issue)	
	Parlophone CDP 746 436–2	**40** 2 wks
7 Mar 87	**A HARD DAY'S NIGHT** (2nd re-issue)	
	Parlophone CDP 746 437–2	**30** 4 wks
7 Mar 87	**BEATLES FOR SALE** (re-issue)	
	Parlophone CDP 746 438–2	**45** 2 wks
9 May 87	**HELP** (2nd re-issue) *Parlophone CDP 746 439–2*	**61** 2 wks
9 May 87	**RUBBER SOUL** (re-issue)	
	Parlophone CDP 746 440–2	**60** 3 wks
9 May 87	**REVOLVER** (re-issue)	
	Parlophone CDP 746 441–2	**55** 5 wks
6 Jun 87 ●	**SERGEANT PEPPER'S LONELY HEARTS CLUB BAND**	
	(re-issue) *Parlophone CDP 746 442–2*	**3** 16 wks
5 Sep 87	**THE BEATLES** (re-issue) *Parlophone CDS 746 443–9*	**18** 2 wks
5 Sep 87	**YELLOW SUBMARINE** (re-issue)	
	Parlophone CDP 746 445–2	**60** 1 wk
3 Oct 87	**MAGICAL MYSTERY TOUR** (re-issue)	
	Parlophone PCTC 255	**52** 1 wk
31 Oct 87	**ABBEY ROAD** (re-issue) *Parlophone CDP 746 446–2*	**30** 2 wks
31 Oct 87	**LET IT BE** (re-issue) *Parlophone CDP 746 447–2*	**50** 1 wk
19 Mar 88	**PAST MASTERS VOLUME 1** *Parlophone CDBPM 1*	**49** 1 wk
19 Mar 88	**PAST MASTERS VOLUME 2** *Parlophone CDBPM 2*	**46** 1 wk

60

Yellow Submarine *featured several tracks by the George Martin Orchestra. The albums recharted in 1987 after being made available as compact discs. The label numbers are the CD catalogue numbers of these re-issues.*

b

BEATMASTERS UK, *male/female instrumental group* *10 wks*

1 Jul 89	**ANYWAYAWANNA** *Rhythm King LEFTLP 10*	**30** 10 wks

BEATS INTERNATIONAL
UK, *male/female vocal/instrumental group* *14 wks*

14 Apr 90	**LET THEM EAT BINGO** *Go Beat 8421961*	**17** 14 wks

BEAUTIFUL SOUTH
UK, *male vocal/instrumental group* *45 wks*

4 Nov 89 ●	**WELCOME TO THE BEAUTIFUL SOUTH**	
	Go! Discs AGOLP 16	**2** 23 wks
10 Nov 90 ●	**CHOKE** *Go! Discs 8282331*	**2** 22 wks

BE-BOP DELUXE UK, *male vocal/instrumental group* *28 wks*

31 Jan 76	**SUNBURST FINISH** *Harvest SHSP 4053*	**17** 12 wks
25 Sep 76	**MODERN MUSIC** *Harvest SHSP 4058*	**12** 6 wks
6 Aug 77 ●	**LIVE! IN THE AIR AGE** *Harvest SHVL 816*	**10** 5 wks
25 Feb 78	**DRASTIC PLASTIC** *Harvest SHSP 4091*	**22** 5 wks

Jeff BECK UK, *male vocal/instrumentalist – guitar* *11 wks*

13 Sep 69	**BECK-OLA** *Columbia SCX 6351*	**39** 1 wk
24 Jul 76	**WIRED** *CBS 86012*	**38** 5 wks

Forget the jet lag, **Count Basie** goes to a Leicester Square rehearsal after a morning arrival from America.

The **Beautiful South** find as ugly a location as possible.

19 Jul 80	**THERE AND BACK** *Epic EPC 83288*	38	4 wks
17 Aug 85	**FLASH** *Epic EPC 26112*	83	1 wk

See also Jeff Beck, Tim Bogert and Carmine Appice.

Jeff BECK, Tim BOGERT and Carmine APPICE
UK/US, male vocal/instrumental group   *3 wks*

28 Apr 73	**JEFF BECK, TIM BOGERT & CARMINE APPICE** *Epic EPC 65455*	28	3 wks

See also Jeff Beck.

BEE GEES   *UK/Australia, male vocal/instrumental group*   *213 wks*

12 Aug 67	● **BEE GEES FIRST** *Polydor 583–012*	8	26 wks
24 Feb 68	**HORIZONTAL** *Polydor 582–020*	16	15 wks
28 Sep 68	● **IDEA** *Polydor 583–036*	4	18 wks
5 Apr 69	● **ODESSA** *Polydor 583–049/50*	10	1 wk
8 Nov 69	● **BEST OF THE BEE GEES** *Polydor 583–063*	7	22 wks
9 May 70	**CUCUMBER CASTLE** *Polydor 2383–010*	57	2 wks
17 Feb 79	★ **SPIRITS HAVING FLOWN** *RSO RSBG 001*	1	33 wks
10 Nov 79	● **BEE GEES GREATEST** *RSO RSDX 001*	6	25 wks
7 Nov 81	**LIVING EYES** *RSO RSBG 002*	73	8 wks
3 Oct 87	● **E.S.P.** *Warner Bros. WX 83*	5	24 wks
29 Apr 89	**ONE** *Warner Bros. WX 252*	29	3 wks
17 Nov 90	● **THE VERY BEST OF THE BEE GEES** *Polydor 8473391*	8	31 wks
6 Apr 91	**HIGH CIVILISATION** *Warner Bros. WX 417*	24	5 wks

All albums from Cucumber Castle onwards group were UK only.

Sir Thomas BEECHAM   *UK, conductor*   *2 wks*

26 Mar 60	**CARMEN** *HMV ALP 1762/4*	18	2 wks

Full credit on sleeve reads 'Orchestre National de la Radio Diffusion Francaise, conducted by Sir Thomas Beecham'.

BELL BIV DEVOE   *US, male vocal group*   *5 wks*

1 Sep 90	**POISON** *MCA MCG 6094*	35	5 wks

BELLAMY BROTHERS   *US, male vocal duo*   *6 wks*

19 Jun 76	**BELLAMY BROTHERS** *Warner Bros. K 56242*	21	6 wks

Regina BELLE   *US, female vocalist*   *5 wks*

1 Aug 87	**ALL BY MYSELF** *CBS 450 998–1*	53	4 wks
16 Sep 89	**STAY WITH ME** *CBS 465132 1*	62	1 wk

BELLE STARS   *UK, female vocal/instrumental group*   *12 wks*

5 Feb 83	**THE BELLE STARS** *Stiff SEEZ 45*	15	12 wks

Pierre BELMONDE
France, male instrumentalist – panpipes   *10 wks*

7 Jun 80	**THEMES FOR DREAMS** *K-Tel ONE 1077*	13	10 wks

BELMONTS – *See DION and the BELMONTS*

BELOVED *UK, male vocal/instrumental duo* 16 wks

3 Mar 90	**HAPPINESS** *East West WX 299*	14	14 wks
1 Dec 90	**BLISSED OUT** *East West WX 383*	38	2 wks

Pat BENATAR *US, female vocalist* 83 wks

25 Jul 81	**PRECIOUS TIME** *Chrysalis CHR 1346*	30	7 wks
13 Nov 82	**GET NERVOUS** *Chrysalis CHR 1396*	73	6 wks
15 Oct 83	**LIVE FROM EARTH** *Chrysalis CHR 1451*	60	5 wks
17 Nov 84	**TROPICO** *Chrysalis CHR 1471*	31	25 wks
24 Aug 85	**IN THE HEAT OF THE NIGHT** *Chrysalis CHR 1236*	98	1 wk
7 Dec 85	**SEVEN THE HARD WAY** *Chrysalis CHR 1507*	69	4 wks
7 Nov 87 ●	**BEST SHOTS** *Chrysalis PATV 1*	6	19 wks
16 Jul 88	**WIDE AWAKE IN DREAMLAND** *Chrysalis CDL 1628*	11	13 wks
4 May 91	**TRUE LOVE** *Chrysalis CHR 1805*	40	3 wks

Cliff BENNETT and the REBEL ROUSERS
UK, male vocal/instrumental group 3 wks

22 Oct 66	**DRIVIN' ME WILD** *MFP 1121*	25	3 wks

Tony BENNETT *US, male vocalist* 63 wks

29 May 65	**I LEFT MY HEART IN SAN FRANCISCO** *CBS BPG 62201*	13	14 wks
19 Feb 66 ●	**A STRING OF TONY'S HITS** *CBS DP 66010*	9	13 wks
10 Jun 67	**TONY'S GREATEST HITS** *CBS SBPG 62821*	14	24 wks
23 Sep 67	**TONY MAKES IT HAPPEN** *CBS SBPG 63055*	31	3 wks
23 Mar 68	**FOR ONCE IN MY LIFE** *CBS SBPG 63166*	29	5 wks
26 Feb 77	**THE VERY BEST OF TONY BENNETT – 20 GREATEST HITS** *Warwick PA 5021*	23	4 wks

63

b

George BENSON *US, male vocalist/instrumentalist – guitar* 262 wks

19 Mar 77	**IN FLIGHT** *Warner Bros. K 56237*	19	23 wks
18 Feb 78	**WEEKEND IN L.A.** *Warner Bros. K 66074*	47	1 wk
24 Mar 79	**LIVING INSIDE YOUR LOVE** *Warner Bros. K 66085*	24	14 wks
26 Jul 80 ●	**GIVE ME THE NIGHT** *Warner Bros. K 56823*	3	40 wks
14 Nov 81	**GEORGE BENSON COLLECTION** *Warner Bros. K 66107*	19	35 wks
11 Jun 83 ●	**IN YOUR EYES** *Warner Bros. 92–3744–1*	3	53 wks
26 Jan 85 ●	**20/20** *Warner Bros. 92–5178–1*	9	19 wks
19 Oct 85 ★	**THE LOVE SONGS** *K-Tel NE 1308*	1	27 wks
6 Sep 86	**WHILE THE CITY SLEEPS...** *Warner Bros. WX 55*	13	27 wks
10 Sep 88	**TWICE THE LOVE** *Warner Bros. WX 160*	16	10 wks
8 Jul 89	**TENDERLY** *Warner Bros. WX 263*	52	3 wks
26 Oct 91	**MIDNIGHT MOODS – THE LOVE COLLECTION** *Telstar STAR 2450*	25†	10 wks

See also George Benson and Earl Klugh.

George BENSON and Earl KLUGH
US, male instrumental duo – guitars 6 wks

11 Jul 87	**COLLABORATION** *Warner Bros. WX 91*	47	6 wks

See also George Benson.

BERLIN US, male/female vocal/instrumental group

11 wks

17 Jan 87	**COUNT THREE AND PRAY** Mercury MER 101	32	11 wks

BERLIN PHILHARMONIC ORCHESTRA – See Herbert VON KARAJAN

Leonard BERNSTEIN US, male conductor

2 wks

10 Feb 90	**BERNSTEIN IN BERLIN – BEETHOVEN'S 9TH** Deutsche Grammophon	54	2 wks

Leonard BERNSTEIN'S WEST SIDE STORY – See Studio Cast Recordings

Shelley BERMAN US, male vocalist – comedian

4 wks

19 Nov 60	**INSIDE SHELLEY BERMAN** Capitol CLP 1300	12	4 wks

Chuck BERRY US, male vocalist/instrumentalist – guitar

53 wks

25 May 63	**CHUCK BERRY** Pye International NPL 28024	12	16 wks
5 Oct 63	● **CHUCK BERRY ON STAGE** Pye International NPL 28027 .	6	11 wks
7 Dec 63	● **MORE CHUCK BERRY** Pye International NPL 28028	9	8 wks
30 May 64	● **HIS LATEST AND GREATEST** Pye NPL 28037	8	7 wks
3 Oct 64	**YOU NEVER CAN TELL** Pye NPL 29039	18	2 wks
12 Feb 77	● **MOTORVATIN'** Chess 9288 690	7	9 wks

64

b

Mike BERRY UK, male vocalist

3 wks

24 Jan 81	**THE SUNSHINE OF YOUR SMILE** Polydor 2383 592 ...	63	3 wks

Nick BERRY UK, male vocalist

1 wk

20 Dec 86	**NICK BERRY** BBC REB 618	99	1 wk

BEVERLEY-PHILLIPS ORCHESTRA
UK, orchestra

9 wks

9 Oct 76	**GOLD ON SILVER** Warwick WW 5018	22	9 wks

Frankie BEVERLY – See MAZE featuring Frankie BEVERLY

B-52s US, male/female vocal/instrumental group

60 wks

4 Aug 79	**B-52s** Island ILPS 9580	22	12 wks
13 Sep 80	**WILD PLANET** Island ILPS 9622	18	4 wks
11 Jul 81	**THE PARTY MIX ALBUM** Island IPM 1001	36	5 wks
27 Feb 82	**MESOPOTAMIA** EMI ISSP 4006	18	6 wks
21 May 83	**WHAMMY!** Island ILPS 9759	33	4 wks
8 Aug 87	**BOUNCING OFF THE SATELLITES** Island ILPS 9871 ..	74	2 wks
29 Jul 89	● **COSMIC THING** Reprise WX 283	8	27 wks

BIBLE UK, male vocal/instrumental group

2 wks

2 Jan 88	**EUREKA** Cooltempo CHR 1646	71	1 wk
7 Oct 89	**THE BIBLE** Ensign CHEN 12	67	1 wk

BIG AUDIO DYNAMITE

UK, male vocal/instrumental group   *43 wks*

16 Nov 85	**THIS IS BIG AUDIO DYNAMITE** CBS 26714	27	27 wks
8 Nov 86	**No. 10 UPPING STREET** CBS 450 137–1	11	8 wks
9 Jul 88	**TIGHTEN UP VOL. 88** CBS 4611991	33	3 wks
16 Sep 89	**MEGATOP PHOENIX** CBS 4657901	26	3 wks
2 Nov 90	**KOOL-AID** CBS 4674661	55	1 wk
17 Aug 91	**THE GLOBE** Columbia 4677061	63	1 wk

BIG BEN BANJO BAND *UK, male instrumental group*   *1 wk*

17 Dec 60	**MORE MINSTREL MELODIES** Columbia 33SX 1254	20	1 wk

BIG COUNTRY *UK, male vocal/instrumental group*   *142 wks*

6 Aug 83	● **THE CROSSING** Mercury MERH 27	3	80 wks
27 Oct 84	★ **STEELTOWN** Mercury MERH 49	1	21 wks
12 Jul 86	● **THE SEER** Mercury MERH 87	2	16 wks
8 Oct 88	● **PEACE IN OUR TIME** Mercury MERH 130	9	6 wks
26 May 90	● **THROUGH A BIG COUNTRY – GREATEST HITS**		
	Mercury 8460221	2	17 wks
28 Sep 91	**NO PLACE LIKE HOME** Vertigo 5102301	28	2 wks

BIG DADDY KANE *US, male vocalist*   *3 wks*

30 Sep 89	**IT'S A BIG DADDY THING** Cold Chillin' WX 305	37	3 wks

BIG DISH *UK, male vocal/instrumental group*   *3 wks*

11 Oct 86	**SWIMMER** Virgin V 2374	85	1 wk
23 Feb 91	**SATELLITES** East West WX 400	43	2 wks

BIG FUN *UK, male vocal group*   *11 wks*

12 May 90	● **A POCKETFUL OF DREAMS** Jive FUN 1	7	11 wks

BIG ROLL BAND – *See Zoot MONEY and the BIG ROLL BAND*

BIG SOUND – *See Simon DUPREE and the BIG SOUND*

Mr. Acker BILK

UK, male band leader, vocalist/instrumentalist – clarinet   *76 wks*

19 Mar 60	● **SEVEN AGES OF ACKER** Columbia 33SX 1205	6	6 wks
9 Apr 60	**ACKER BILK'S OMNIBUS** Pye NJL 22	14	3 wks
4 Mar 61	**ACKER** Columbia 33SX 1248	17	1 wk
1 Apr 61	**GOLDEN TREASURY OF BILK** Columbia 33SX 1304 ...	11	6 wks
26 May 62	● **STRANGER ON THE SHORE** Columbia 33SX 1407	6	28 wks
4 May 63	**A TASTE OF HONEY** Columbia 33SX 1493	17	4 wks
9 Oct 76	**THE ONE FOR ME** Pye NSPX 41052	38	6 wks
4 Jun 77	● **SHEER MAGIC** Warwick WW 5028	5	8 wks
11 Nov 78	**EVERGREEN** Warwick PW 5045	17	14 wks

See also Kenny Ball, Chris Barber and Acker Bilk; Chris Barber and Acker Bilk.

65

b

BIRDLAND UK, male vocal/instrumental group   1 wk

2 Mar 91 **BIRDLAND** Lazy LAZY 25 . . . . **44** 1 wk

BIRTHDAY PARTY
Australia, male vocal/instrumental group   3 wks

24 Jul 82 **JUNKYARD** 4AD CAD 207 . . . . **73** 3 wks

Stephen BISHOP US, male instrumentalist – piano   3 wks

1 Apr 72 **GRIEG AND SCHUMANN PIANO CONCERTOS**
               Philips 6500 166 . . . . **34** 3 wks

BLACK UK, male vocalist/instrumentalist, Colin Vearncombe   29 wks

26 Sep 87 ● **WONDERFUL LIFE** A & M AMA 5165 . . . . **3**   23 wks
29 Oct 88 **COMEDY** A & M AMA 5222 . . . . **32**   4 wks
1 Jun 91 **BLACK** A & M 3971261 . . . . **42**   2 wks

Cilla BLACK UK, female vocalist   61 wks

13 Feb 65 ● **CILLA** Parlophone PMC 1243 . . . . **5**   11 wks
14 May 66 ● **CILLA SINGS A RAINBOW** Parlophone PMC 7004 . . . . . . **4**   15 wks
13 Apr 68 ● **SHER-OO** Parlophone PCS 7041 . . . . **7**   11 wks
30 Nov 68 **BEST OF CILLA BLACK** Parlophone PCS 7065 . . . . **21**   11 wks
25 Jul 70 **SWEET INSPIRATION** Parlophone PCS 7103 . . . . **42**   4 wks
29 Jan 83 **THE VERY BEST OF CILLA BLACK** Parlophone EMTV 38 **20**   9 wks

BLACK BOX Italy, male/female vocal/instrumental group   30 wks

5 May 90 **DREAMLAND** deConstruction PL 74572 . . . . **16**   30 wks

BLACK CROWES US, male vocal/instrumental group   7 wks

24 Aug 91 **SHAKE YOUR MONEY MAKER** Def American 8425151 . . **36**   7 wks

BLACK LACE UK, male vocal/instrumental group   26 wks

8 Dec 84 ● **PARTY PARTY – 16 GREAT PARTY ICEBREAKERS**
               Telstar STAR 2250 . . . . **4**   14 wks
7 Dec 85 **PARTY PARTY 2** Telstar STAR 2266 . . . . **18**   6 wks
6 Dec 86 **PARTY CRAZY** Telstar STAR 2288 . . . . **58**   6 wks

BLACK, ROCK and RON US, male rap group   1 wk

22 Apr 89 **STOP THE WORLD** Supreme SU 5 . . . . **72**   1 wk

BLACK SABBATH UK/US, male vocal/instrumental group   209 wks

7 Mar 70 ● **BLACK SABBATH** Vertigo VO 6 . . . . **8**   42 wks
26 Sep 70 ★ **PARANOID** Vertigo 6360 011 . . . . **1**   27 wks
21 Aug 71 ● **MASTER OF REALITY** Vertigo 6360 050 . . . . **5**   13 wks
30 Sep 72 ● **BLACK SABBATH VOL. 4** Vertigo 6360 071 . . . . **8**   10 wks
8 Dec 73 ● **SABBATH BLOODY SABBATH** WWA WWA 005 . . . . . **4**   11 wks
27 Sep 75 ● **SABOTAGE** NEMS 9119 001 . . . . **7**   7 wks

7 Feb 76	**WE SOLD OUR SOUL FOR ROCK 'N' ROLL**		
	NEMS 6641 335	35	5 wks
6 Nov 76	**TECHNICAL ECSTASY** *Vertigo 9102 750*	13	6 wks
14 Oct 78	**NEVER SAY DIE** *Vertigo 9102 751*	12	6 wks
26 Apr 80	● **HEAVEN AND HELL** *Vertigo 9102 752*	9	22 wks
5 Jul 80	● **BLACK SABBATH LIVE AT LAST** *NEMS BS 001*	5	15 wks
27 Sep 80	**PARANOID (re-issue)** *NEMS NEL 6003*	54	2 wks
14 Nov 81	**MOB RULES** *Mercury 6V02119*	12	14 wks
22 Jan 83	**LIVE EVIL** *Vertigo SAB 10*	13	11 wks
24 Sep 83	● **BORN AGAIN** *Vertigo VERL 8*	4	7 wks
1 Mar 86	**SEVENTH STAR** *Vertigo VERH 29*	27	5 wks
28 Nov 87	**THE ETERNAL IDOL** *Vertigo VERH 51*	66	1 wk
29 Apr 89	**HEADLESS CROSS** *IRS EIRSA 1002*	31	2 wks
1 Sep 90	**TYR** *IRS EIRSA 1038*	24	3 wks

Seventh Star *credits Black Sabbath featuring Tony Iommi.*

BLACK UHURU
Jamaica, male/female vocal/instrumental group   *22 wks*

13 Jun 81	**RED** *Island ILPS 9625*	28	13 wks
22 Aug 81	**BLACK UHURU** *Virgin VX 1004*	81	2 wks
19 Jun 82	**CHILL OUT** *Island ILPS 9701*	38	6 wks
25 Aug 84	**ANTHEM** *Island ILPS 9773*	90	1 wk

Band of the BLACK WATCH *UK, military band*   *13 wks*

7 Feb 76	**SCOTCH ON THE ROCKS** *Spark SRLM 503*	11	13 wks

BLACK WIDOW *UK, male vocal/instrumental group*   *2 wks*

4 Apr 70	**SACRIFICE** *CBS 63948*	32	2 wks

67

b

BLACKFOOT *US, male vocal/instrumental group*   *22 wks*

18 Jul 81	**MARAUDER** *Atco K 50799*	38	12 wks
11 Sep 82	**HIGHWAY SONG – BLACKFOOT LIVE** *Atco K 50910* .	14	6 wks
21 May 83	**SIOGO** *Atco 79-0080-1*	28	3 wks
29 Sep 84	**VERTICAL SMILES** *Atco 790218*	82	1 wk

BLACKHEARTS – *See Joan JETT and the BLACKHEARTS*

Ritchie BLACKMORE'S RAINBOW – *See RAINBOW*

Howard BLAKE conducting the SINFONIA OF LONDON *UK, conductor and orchestra*   *12 wks*

22 Dec 84	**THE SNOWMAN** *CBS 71116*	54	12 wks

Narration by Bernard Cribbins.

BLANCMANGE *UK, male vocal/instrumental duo*   *57 wks*

9 Oct 82	**HAPPY FAMILIES** *London SH 8552*	30	38 wks
26 May 84	● **MANGE TOUT** *London SH 8554*	8	17 wks
26 Oct 85	**BELIEVE YOU ME** *London LONLP 10*	54	2 wks

BLIND FAITH *UK, male vocal/instrumental group*   *10 wks*

13 Sep 69	★ **BLIND FAITH** *Polydor 583-059*	1	10 wks

BLITZ *UK, male vocal/instrumental group*   *3 wks*

6 Nov 82	**VOICE OF A GENERATION**	*No Future PUNK 1*	27	3 wks

BLIZZARD OF OZ – *See Ozzy OSBOURNE*

BLOCKHEADS – *See Ian DURY and the BLOCKHEADS*

BLODWYN PIG *UK, male vocal/instrumental group*   *11 wks*

16 Aug 69	● **AHEAD RINGS OUT**	*Island ILPS 9101*	9	4 wks
23 Apr 70	● **GETTING TO THIS**	*Island ILPS 9122*	8	7 wks

BLONDIE *US/UK, female/male vocal/instrumental group*   *266 wks*

4 Mar 78	● **PLASTIC LETTERS**	*Chrysalis CHR 1166*	10	54 wks
23 Sep 78	★ **PARALLEL LINES**	*Chrysalis CDL 1192*	1	105 wks
10 Mar 79	**BLONDIE**	*Chrysalis CHR 1165*	75	1 wk
13 Oct 79	★ **EAT TO THE BEAT**	*Chrysalis CDL 1225*	1	38 wks
29 Nov 80	● **AUTOAMERICAN**	*Chrysalis CDL 1290*	3	16 wks
31 Oct 81	● **BEST OF BLONDIE**	*Chrysalis CDLTV 1*	4	40 wks
5 Jun 82	● **THE HUNTER**	*Chrysalis CDL 1384*	9	12 wks

See also Deborah Harry and Blondie.

BLOOD SWEAT AND TEARS
US/Canada, male vocal/instrumental group   *21 wks*

68

b

13 Jul 68	**CHILD IS FATHER TO THE MAN**	*CBS 63296*	40	1 wk
12 Apr 69	**BLOOD SWEAT AND TEARS**	*CBS 63504*	15	8 wks
8 Aug 70	**BLOOD SWEAT AND TEARS 3**	*CBS 64024*	14	12 wks

BLOW MONKEYS *UK, male vocal/instrumental group*   *27 wks*

19 Apr 86	**ANIMAL MAGIC**	*RCA PL 70910*	21	8 wks
25 Apr 87	**SHE WAS ONLY A GROCER'S DAUGHTER**			
	RCA PL 71245		20	8 wks
11 Feb 89	**WHOOPS! THERE GOES THE NEIGHBOURHOOD**			
	RCA PL 71858		46	2 wks
26 Aug 89	● **CHOICES**	*RCA PL 74191*	5	9 wks

BLUE AEROPLANES
UK, male/female vocal/instrumental group   *4 wks*

24 Feb 90	**SWAGGER**	*Ensign CHEN 13*	54	1 wk
17 Aug 91	**BEATSONGS**	*Ensign CHEN 21*	33	3 wks

BLUE MURDER *US, male vocal/instrumental group*   *3 wks*

6 May 89	**BLUE MURDER**	*Geffen WX 245*	45	3 wks

BLUE NILE *UK, male vocal/instrumental group*   *6 wks*

19 May 84	**A WALK ACROSS THE ROOFTOPS**	*Linn LKH 1*	80	2 wks
21 Oct 89	**HATS**	*Linn LKH 2*	12	4 wks

BLUE OYSTER CULT
US, male vocal/instrumental group   *40 wks*

3 Jul 76	**AGENTS OF FORTUNE** CBS 81385	26	10 wks
4 Feb 78	**SPECTRES** CBS 86050	60	1 wk
28 Oct 78	**SOME ENCHANTED EVENING** CBS 86074	18	4 wks
18 Aug 79	**MIRRORS** CBS 86087	46	5 wks
19 Jul 80	**CULTOSAURUS ERECTUS** CBS 86120	12	7 wks
25 Jul 81	**FIRE OF UNKNOWN ORIGIN** CBS 85137	29	7 wks
22 May 82	**EXTRATERRESTRIAL LIVE** CBS 22203	39	5 wks
19 Nov 83	**THE REVOLUTION BY NIGHT** CBS 25686	95	1 wk

BLUE PEARL   *UK/US, male/female vocal/instrumental group*   *2 wks*

| 1 Dec 90 | **NAKED** Big Life BLR LP4 .... | 58 | 2 wks |

BLUE RONDO A LA TURK
UK, male vocal/instrumental group   *2 wks*

| 6 Nov 82 | **CHEWING THE FAT** Diable Noir V 2240 .... | 80 | 2 wks |

BLUEBELLS   *UK, male vocal/instrumental group*   *10 wks*

| 11 Aug 84 | **SISTERS** London LONLP 1 .... | 22 | 10 wks |

BLUES BAND   *UK, male vocal/instrumental group*   *18 wks*

8 Mar 80	**OFFICIAL BOOTLEG ALBUM** Arista BBBP 101	40	9 wks
18 Oct 80	**READY** Arista BB 2	36	6 wks
17 Oct 81	**ITCHY FEET** Arista BB 3	60	3 wks

69

b

BLUR   *UK, male vocal/instrumental group*   *6 wks*

| 7 Sep 91 | ● **LEISURE** Food FOODLP 6 .... | 7 | 6 wks |

BODINES   *UK, male vocal/instrumental group*   *1 wk*

| 29 Aug 87 | **PLAYED** Pop BODL 2001 .... | 94 | 1 wk |

Tim BOGERT – *See Jeff BECK, Tim BOGERT and Carmine APPICE*

Marc BOLAN – *See T. REX*

BOLSHOI   *UK, male vocal/instrumental group*   *1 wk*

| 3 Oct 87 | **LINDY'S PARTY** Beggars Banquet BEGA 86 .... | 100 | 1 wk |

Michael BOLTON   *US, male vocalist*   *110 wks*

17 Mar 90	● **SOUL PROVIDER** CBS 4653431	4	72 wks
11 Aug 90	**THE HUNGER** CBS 4601631	44	5 wks
18 May 91	● **TIME LOVE AND TENDERNESS** Columbia 4678121	2†	33 wks

BOMB THE BASS   *UK, male producer, Tim Simenon*   *14 wks*

| 22 Oct 88 | **INTO THE DRAGON** Rhythm King DOOD 1 .... | 18 | 10 wks |
| 31 Aug 91 | **UNKNOWN TERRITORY** Rhythm King 4687740 .... | 19 | 4 wks |

BOMBALURINA featuring Timmy MALLETT
UK, male vocalist   *5 wks*

15 Dec 90	**HUGGIN' AN' A KISSIN'** *Polydor 8476481*	55	5 wks

BON JOVI *US, male vocal/instrumental group*   *148 wks*

28 Apr 84	**BON JOVI** *Vertigo VERL 14*	71	3 wks
11 May 85	**7800° FAHRENHEIT** *Vertigo VERL 24*	28	12 wks
20 Sep 86	● **SLIPPERY WHEN WET** *Vertigo VERH 38*	6	93 wks
1 Oct 88	★ **NEW JERSEY** *Vertigo VERH 62*	1	40 wks

See also Jon Bon Jovi.

Jon BON JOVI *US, male vocalist*   *23 wks*

25 Aug 90	● **BLAZE OF GLORY/YOUNG GUNS II** *Vertigo 8464731* ..	2	23 wks

See also Bon Jovi.

Graham BOND *UK, male vocalist/instrumentalist – keyboards* *2 wks*

20 Jun 70	**SOLID BOND** *Warner Bros. WS 3001*	40	2 wks

Gary U.S. BONDS *US, male vocalist*   *8 wks*

22 Aug 81	**DEDICATION** *EMI America AML 3017*	43	3 wks
10 Jul 82	**ON THE LINE** *EMI America AML 3022*	55	5 wks

70

b

BONEY M
Jamaica/Montserrat/Antilles, male/female vocal group   *130 wks*

23 Apr 77	**TAKE THE HEAT OFF ME** *Atlantic K 50314*	40	15 wks
6 Aug 77	**LOVE FOR SALE** *Atlantic K 50385*	60	1 wk
29 Jul 78	★ **NIGHT FLIGHT TO VENUS** *Atlantic/Hansa K 50498*	1	65 wks
29 Sep 79	★ **OCEANS OF FANTASY** *Atlantic/Hansa K 50610*	1	18 wks
12 Apr 80	★ **THE MAGIC OF BONEY M** *Atlantic/Hansa BMTV 1*	1	26 wks
6 Sep 86	**THE BEST OF 10 YEARS** *Stylus SMR 621*	35	5 wks

BONFIRE *Germany, male vocal/instrumental group*   *1 wk*

21 Oct 89	**POINT BLANK** *MSA ZL 74249*	74	1 wk

Graham BONNET *UK, male vocalist*   *3 wks*

7 Nov 81	**LINE UP** *Mercury 6302151*	62	3 wks

BONNIE – *See DELANEY and BONNIE and FRIENDS*

BONZO DOG DOO-DAH BAND
UK, male vocal/instrumental group   *4 wks*

18 Jan 69	**DOUGHNUT IN GRANNY'S GREENHOUSE** *Liberty LBS 83158*	40	1 wk
30 Aug 69	**TADPOLES** *Liberty LBS 83257*	36	1 wk
22 Jun 74	**THE HISTORY OF THE BONZOS** *United Artists UAD 60071*	41	2 wks

Bon Jovi reached new chart heights with each of their first four albums.

Blackfoot do a bad Kiss impersonation.

Betty BOO   *UK, female vocalist*   *24 wks*

22 Sep	90	● **BOOMANIA** *Rhythm King LEFTLP 12*	**4**	24 wks

BOOGIE DOWN PRODUCTIONS   *US, male rapper*   *9 wks*

18 Jan	88	**BY ALL MEANS NECESSARY** *Jive HIP 63*	**38**	3 wks
22 Jul	89	**GHETTO MUSIC** *Jive HIP 80*	**32**	4 wks
25 Aug	90	**EDUTAINMENT** *Jive HIP 100*	**52**	2 wks

BOOKER T. and the MG'S   *US, male instrumental group*   *5 wks*

25 Jul	64	**GREEN ONIONS** *London HAK 8182*	**11**	4 wks
11 Jul	70	**McLEMORE AVENUE** *Stax SXATS 1031*	**70**	1 wk

BOOMTOWN RATS   *Ireland, male vocal/instrumental group*   *93 wks*

17 Sep	77	**BOOMTOWN RATS** *Ensign ENVY 1*	**18**	11 wks
8 Jul	78	● **TONIC FOR THE TROOPS** *Ensign ENVY 3*	**8**	44 wks
3 Nov	79	● **THE FINE ART OF SURFACING** *Ensign ENROX 11*	**7**	26 wks
24 Jan	81	● **MONDO BONGO** *Mercury 6359 042*	**6**	7 wks
3 Apr	82	**V DEEP** *Mercury 6359 082*	**64**	5 wks

Pat BOONE   *US, male vocalist*   *12 wks*

72

b

22 Nov	58	● **STARDUST** *London HAD 2127*	**10**	1 wk
28 May	60	**HYMNS WE HAVE LOVED** *London HAD 2228*	**12**	2 wks
25 Jun	60	**HYMNS WE LOVE** *London HAD 2092*	**14**	1 wk
24 Apr	76	**PAT BOONE ORIGINALS** *ABC ABSD 301*	**16**	8 wks

BOOTZILLA ORCHESTRA – *See Malcolm McLAREN*

BOO-YAA T.R.I.B.E.   *US, male rap group*   *1 wk*

14 Apr	90	**NEW FUNKY NATION** *Fourth + Broadway*	**74**	1 wk

BOSTON   *US, male vocal/instrumental group*   *43 wks*

5 Feb	77	**BOSTON** *Epic EPC 81611*	**11**	20 wks
9 Sep	78	● **DON'T LOOK BACK** *Epic EPC 86057*	**9**	10 wks
4 Apr	81	**BOSTON** *Epic EPC 32038*	**58**	2 wks
18 Oct	86	**THIRD STAGE** *MCA MCG 6017*	**37**	11 wks

The two eponymous albums are different.

Judy BOUCHER   *UK, female vocalist*   *1 wk*

25 Apr	87	**CAN'T BE WITH YOU TONIGHT** *Orbitone OLP 024* ...	**95**	1 wk

BOW WOW WOW
UK, female/male vocal/instrumental group   *38 wks*

24 Oct	81	**SEE JUNGLE! SEE JUNGLE! GO JOIN YOUR GANG**		
		YEAH CITY ALL OVER! GO APE CRAZY		
		RCA RCALP 0027 3000	**26**	32 wks
7 Aug	82	**I WANT CANDY** *EMI EMC 3416*	**26**	6 wks

David BOWIE *UK, male vocalist*   *869 wks*

1 Jul	72	● **THE RISE AND FALL OF ZIGGY STARDUST AND THE**			
		SPIDERS FROM MARS *RCA Victor SF 8287*	5	106 wks
23 Sep	72	● **HUNKY DORY** *RCA Victor SF 8244*	3	69 wks
29 Nov	72	**SPACE ODDITY** *RCA Victor LSP 4813*	17	37 wks
29 Nov	72	**THE MAN WHO SOLD THE WORLD**		
		RCA Victor LSP 4816	26	22 wks
5 May	73	★ **ALADDIN SANE** *RCA Victor RS 1001*	1	47 wks
3 Nov	73	★ **PIN-UPS** *RCA Victor RS 1003*	1	21 wks
8 Jun	74	★ **DIAMOND DOGS** *RCA Victor APLI 0576*	1	17 wks
16 Nov	74	● **DAVID LIVE** *RCA Victor APL 1*	2	12 wks
5 Apr	75	● **YOUNG AMERICANS** *RCA Victor RS 1006*	2	12 wks
7 Feb	76	● **STATION TO STATION** *RCA Victor APLI 1327*	5	16 wks
12 Jun	76	● **CHANGESONEBOWIE** *RCA Victor RS 1055*	2	28 wks
29 Jan	77	● **LOW** *RCA Victor PL 12030*	2	18 wks
29 Oct	77	● **HEROES** *RCA Victor PL 12522*	3	18 wks
14 Oct	78	● **STAGE** *RCA Victor PL 02913*	5	10 wks
9 Jun	79	● **LODGER** *RCA BOW LP 1*	4	17 wks
27 Sep	80	★ **SCARY MONSTERS AND SUPER CREEPS**		
		RCA BOW LP 2	1	32 wks
10 Jan	81	● **VERY BEST OF DAVID BOWIE** *K-Tel NE 1111*	3	20 wks
17 Jan	81	**HUNKY DORY (re-issue)** *RCA International INTS 5064* ..	32	51 wks
31 Jan	81	**THE RISE AND FALL OF ZIGGY STARDUST AND THE**		
		SPIDERS FROM MARS (re-issue)		
		RCA International INTS 5063	33	62 wks
28 Nov	81	**CHANGESTWOBOWIE** *RCA BOW LP 3*	24	17 wks
6 Mar	82	**ALADDIN SANE (re-issue)**		
		RCA International INTS 5067	49	24 wks
14 Jan	83	**RARE** *RCA PL 45406*	34	11 wks
23 Apr	83	★ **LETS DANCE** *EMI America AML 3029*	1	56 wks
30 Apr	83	**PIN-UPS (re-issue)** *RCA International INTS 5236*	57	15 wks
30 Apr	83	**THE MAN WHO SOLD THE WORLD (2nd re-issue)**		
		RCA International INTS 5237	64	8 wks
14 May	83	**DIAMOND DOGS (re-issue)** *RCA International INTS 5068*	60	14 wks
11 Jun	83	**HEROES (re-issue)** *RCA International INTS 5066*	75	8 wks
11 Jun	83	**LOW (re-issue)** *RCA International INTS 5065*	85	5 wks
20 Aug	83	**GOLDEN YEARS** *RCA BOWLP 4*	33	5 wks
5 Nov	83	**ZIGGY STARDUST – THE MOTION PICTURE**		
		RCA PL 84862	17	6 wks
28 Apr	84	**FAME AND FASHION (ALL TIME GREATEST HITS)**		
		RCA PL 84919	40	6 wks
19 May	84	**LOVE YOU TILL TUESDAY** *Deram BOWIE 1*	53	4 wks
6 Oct	84	★ **TONIGHT** *EMI America DB 1*	1	19 wks
2 May	87	● **NEVER LET ME DOWN** *EMI America AMLS 3117*	6	16 wks
24 Mar	90	★ **CHANGESBOWIE** *EMI DBTV 1*	1	26 wks
14 Apr	90	**HUNKY DORY (2nd re-issue)** *EMI EMC 3572*	39	2 wks
14 Apr	90	**THE MAN WHO SOLD THE WORLD (2nd re-issue)**		
		EMC 3573	66	1 wk
14 Apr	90	**SPACE ODDITY (2nd re-issue)** *EMI EMC 3571*	64	1 wk
23 Jun	90	**THE RISE AND FALL OF ZIGGY STARDUST AND THE**		
		SPIDERS FROM MARS (2nd re-issue) *EMC 3577*	25	4 wks
28 Jul	90	**ALADDIN SANE (2nd re-issue)** *EMI EMC 3579*	43	1 wk
28 Jul	90	**PIN-UPS (re-issue)** *EMI EMC 3580*	52	1 wk
27 Oct	90	**DIAMOND DOGS (2nd re-issue)** *EMI EMC 3584*	67	1 wk
4 May	91	**YOUNG AMERICANS (2nd re-issue)** *EMI EMD 1021* ...	54	1 wk
4 May	91	**STATION TO STATION (2nd re-issue)** *EMI EMD 1020* .	57	1 wk
7 Sep	91	**LOW (2nd re-issue)** *EMI EMD 1027*	64	1 wk

BOXCAR WILLIE *US, male vocalist*   *12 wks*

31 May	80	● **KING OF THE ROAD** *Warwick WW 5084*	5	12 wks

Max BOYCE *UK, male vocalist/comedian*   *105 wks*

5 Jul	75	**LIVE AT TREORCHY** *One Up OU 2033*	21	32 wks

1 Nov 75 ★	**WE ALL HAD DOCTORS' PAPERS** *EMI MB 101*	1	17 wks
20 Nov 76 ●	**THE INCREDIBLE PLAN** *EMI MB 102*	9	12 wks
7 Jan 78	**THE ROAD AND THE MILES** *EMI MB 103*	50	3 wks
11 Mar 78	**LIVE AT TREORCHY (re-issue)** *One Up OU 54043*	42	6 wks
27 May 78 ●	**I KNOW COS I WAS THERE** *EMI MAX 1001*	6	14 wks
13 Oct 79	**NOT THAT I'M BIASED** *EMI MAX 1002*	27	13 wks
15 Nov 80	**ME AND BILLY WILLIAMS** *EMI MAX 1003*	37	8 wks

BOY GEORGE *UK, male vocalist* *6 wks*

27 Jun 87	**SOLD** *Virgin V 2430*	29	6 wks

See also Jesus Loves You

BOY MEETS GIRL *US, male/female vocal/instrumental duo* *1 wk*

4 Feb 89	**REEL LIFE** *RCA PL 88414*	74	1 wk

BOYS *UK, male vocal/instrumental group* *1 wk*

1 Oct 77	**THE BOYS** *NEMS NEL 6001*	50	1 wk

Paul BRADY *Ireland, male vocalist/instrumentalist – guitar* *1 wk*

6 Apr 91	**TRICK OR TREAT** *Fontana 8484541*	62	1 wk

Billy BRAGG *UK, male vocalist* *77 wks*

21 Jan 84	**LIFE'S A RIOT WITH SPY VS SPY**		
	Go! Discs UTILITY UTIL 1	30	30 wks
20 Oct 84	**BREWING UP WITH BILLY BRAGG**		
	Go! Discs AGOLP 4	16	21 wks
4 Oct 86 ●	**TALKING WITH THE TAXMAN ABOUT POETRY**		
	Go! Discs AGOLP 6	8	8 wks
13 Jun 87	**BACK TO BASICS** *Go! Discs AGOLP 8*	37	4 wks
1 Oct 88	**WORKERS PLAYTIME** *Go! Discs AGOLP 15*	17	4 wks
12 May 90	**THE INTERNATIONALE** *Utility UTIL 11*	34	4 wks
28 Sep 91 ●	**DON'T TRY THIS AT HOME** *Go! Discs 8282791*	8	6 wks

Wilfred BRAMBELL and Harry H. CORBETT
UK, male comic duo *34 wks*

23 Mar 63 ●	**STEPTOE AND SON** *Pye NPL 18081*	4	28 wks
11 Mar 64	**STEPTOE AND SON** *Pye GGL 0217*	14	5 wks
14 Mar 64	**MORE JUNK** *Pye NPL 18090*	19	1 wk

First two albums are different.

BRAND X *UK, male vocal/instrumental group* *6 wks*

21 May 77	**MOROCCAN ROLL** *Charisma CAS 1126*	37	5 wks
11 Sep 82	**IS THERE ANYTHING ABOUT?** *CBS 85967*	93	1 wk

Laura BRANIGAN *US, female vocalist* *18 wks*

18 Aug 84	**SELF CONTROL** *Atlantic 780147*	16	14 wks
24 Aug 85	**HOLD ME** *Atlantic 78–1265-1*	64	4 wks

BRASS CONSTRUCTION
US, male vocal/instrumental group   *12 wks*

20 Mar 76	● **BRASS CONSTRUCTION** *United Artists UAS 29923*	**9**	11 wks
30 Jun 84	**RENEGADES** *Capitol EJ 24 0160*	**94**	1 wk

BREAD   *US, male vocal/instrumental group*   *179 wks*

26 Sep 70	**ON THE WATERS** *Elektra 2469–005*	**34**	5 wks
18 Mar 72	● **BABY I'M A WANT-YOU** *Elektra K 42100*	**9**	19 wks
28 Oct 72	● **BEST OF BREAD** *Elektra K 42115*	**7**	100 wks
27 Jul 74	**THE BEST OF BREAD VOL. 2** *Elektra K 42161*	**48**	1 wk
29 Jan 77	**LOST WITHOUT YOUR LOVE** *Elektra K 52044*	**17**	6 wks
5 Nov 77	★ **THE SOUND OF BREAD** *Elektra K 52062*	**1**	46 wks
28 Nov 87	**THE VERY BEST OF BREAD** *Telstar STAR 2303*	**84**	2 wks

BREAK MACHINE   *US, male vocal/dance group*   *16 wks*

9 Jun 84	**BREAK MACHINE** *Record Shack SOHO LP 3*	**17**	16 wks

BREATHE   *UK, male vocal/instrumental group*   *5 wks*

8 Oct 88	**ALL THAT JAZZ** *Siren SRNLP 12*	**22**	5 wks

BREEDERS   *US, female/male vocal/instrumental group*   *3 wks*

9 Jun 90	**POD** *4AD CAD 0006*	**22**	3 wks

Adrian BRETT   *UK, male instrumentalist – flute*   *11 wks*

10 Nov 79	**ECHOES OF GOLD** *Warwick WW 5062*	**19**	11 wks

Paul BRETT   *UK, male instrumentalist – guitar*   *7 wks*

19 Jul 80	**ROMANTIC GUITAR** *K-Tel ONE 1079*	**24**	7 wks

Edie BRICKELL and the NEW BOHEMIANS
US, female/male vocal/instrumental group   *18 wks*

4 Feb 89	**SHOOTING RUBBERBANDS AT THE STARS**		
	Geffen WX 215	**25**	17 wks
10 Nov 90	**GHOST OF A DOG** *Geffen WX 386*	**63**	1 wk

BRIGHOUSE AND RASTRICK BRASS BAND
UK, male brass band   *11 wks*

28 Jan 78	● **FLORAL DANCE** *Logo 1001*	**10**	11 wks

Sarah BRIGHTMAN   *UK, female vocalist*   *2 wks*

17 Jun 89	**THE SONGS THAT GOT AWAY** *Really Useful 839116 1* ..	**48**	2 wks

See also Andrew Lloyd Webber.

BRILLIANT   *UK, male/female vocal/instrumental group*   *1 wk*

20 Sep 86	**KISS THE LIPS OF LIFE** *Food BRILL 1*	**83**	1 wk

75

b

Johnny BRISTOL   *US, male vocalist*   *7 wks*

| 5 Oct 74 | **HANG ON IN THERE BABY** *MGM 2315 303* .... | 12 | 7 wks |

June BRONHILL and Thomas ROUND
Australia/UK, female/male vocal duo   *1 wk*

| 18 Jun 60 | **LILAC TIME** *HMV CLP 1248* .... | 17 | 1 wk |

BRONSKI BEAT   *UK, male vocal/instrumental group*   *65 wks*

20 Oct 84	● **THE AGE OF CONSENT** *Forbidden Fruit BITLP 1*	4	53 wks
21 Sep 85	**HUNDREDS AND THOUSANDS** *Forbidden Fruit BITLP 2*	24	6 wks
10 May 86	**TRUTH DARE DOUBLE DARE** *Forbidden Fruit BITLP 3* .	18	6 wks

Elkie BROOKS   *UK, female vocalist*   *208 wks*

18 Jun 77	**TWO DAYS AWAY** *A&M AMLH 68409*	16	20 wks
13 May 78	**SHOOTING STAR** *A&M AMLH 64695*	20	13 wks
13 Oct 79	**LIVE AND LEARN** *A&M AMLH 68509*	34	6 wks
14 Nov 81	● **PEARLS** *A&M ELK 1981*	2	79 wks
13 Nov 82	● **PEARLS II** *A&M ELK 1982*	5	25 wks
14 Jul 84	**MINUTES** *A&M AML 68565*	35	7 wks
8 Dec 84	**SCREEN GEMS** *EMI SCREEN 1*	35	11 wks
6 Dec 86	● **NO MORE THE FOOL** *Legend LMA 1*	5	23 wks
27 Dec 86	● **THE VERY BEST OF ELKIE BROOKS** *Telstar STAR 2284*	10	18 wks
11 Jun 88	**BOOKBINDER'S KID** *Legend LMA 3*	57	3 wks
18 Nov 89	**INSPIRATIONS** *Telstar STAR 2354*	58	3 wks

76

b

Nigel BROOKS SINGERS
UK, male/female vocal choir   *17 wks*

| 29 Nov 75 | ● **SONGS OF JOY** *K-Tel NE 706* .... | 5 | 16 wks |
| 5 Jun 76 | **20 ALL TIME EUROVISION FAVOURITES** *K-Tel NE 712* .... | 44 | 1 wk |

BROS   *UK, male vocal/instrumental duo*   *69 wks*

9 Apr 88	● **PUSH** *CBS 460629 1*	2	54 wks
28 Oct 89	● **THE TIME** *CBS 465918 1*	4	13 wks
12 Oct 91	**CHANGING FACES** *Columbia 4688171*	18	2 wks

Act was a group for first album.

BROTHER BEYOND   *UK, male vocal/instrumental group*   *24 wks*

| 26 Nov 88 | ● **GET EVEN** *Parlophone PCS 7327* .... | 9 | 23 wks |
| 25 Nov 89 | **TRUST** *Parlophone PCS 7337* .... | 60 | 1 wk |

BROTHERHOOD OF MAN
UK, male/female vocal group   *40 wks*

24 Apr 76	**LOVE AND KISSES FROM** *Pye NSPL 18490*	20	8 wks
12 Aug 78	**B FOR BROTHERHOOD** *Pye NSPL 18567*	18	9 wks
7 Oct 78	● **BROTHERHOOD OF MAN** *K-Tel BML 7980*	6	15 wks
29 Nov 80	**SING 20 NUMBER ONE HITS** *Warwick WW 5087*	14	8 wks

BROTHERS JOHNSON
US, male vocal/instrumental duo   *22 wks*

19 Aug 78	**BLAM!!** *A & M AMLH 64714*	48	8 wks
23 Feb 80	**LIGHT UP THE NIGHT** *A & M AMLK 63716*	22	12 wks
18 Jul 81	**WINNERS** *A & M AMLK 63724*	42	2 wks

Edgar BROUGHTON BAND
UK, male vocal/instrumental group   *6 wks*

20 Jun 70	**SING BROTHER SING** *Harvest SHVL 772*	18	4 wks
5 Jun 71	**THE EDGAR BROUGHTON BAND**		
	Harvest SHVL 791	28	2 wks

Crazy World Of Arthur BROWN
UK, male vocal/instrumental group   *16 wks*

6 Jul 68	● **CRAZY WORLD OF ARTHUR BROWN** *Track 612005* .	2	16 wks

Bobby BROWN *US, male vocalist*   *57 wks*

28 Jan 89	● **DON'T BE CRUEL** *MCA MCF 3425*	3	41 wks
5 Aug 89	**KING OF STAGE** *MCA MCL 1886*	40	6 wks
2 Dec 89	**DANCE! ... YA KNOW IT!** *MCA MCG 6074*	26	10 wks

Dennis BROWN *Jamaica, male vocalist*   *6 wks*

26 Jun 82	**LOVE HAS FOUND ITS WAY** *A & M AMLH 64886*	72	6 wks

77

b

James BROWN *US, male vocalist*   *36 wks*

18 Oct 86	**GRAVITY** *Scotti Bros. SCT 57108*	85	3 wks
2 Jan 88	**BEST OF JAMES BROWN – GODFATHER OF SOUL**		
	K-Tel NE 1376	17	21 wks
25 Jun 88	**I'M REAL** *Scotti Brothers POLD 5230*	27	5 wks
16 Nov 91	**SEX MACHINE – THE VERY BEST OF JAMES BROWN**		
	Polydor 8458281	19†	7 wks

Joe BROWN *UK, male vocalist/instrumentalist – guitar*   *47 wks*

1 Sep 62	● **A PICTURE OF YOU** *Pye Golden Guinea GGL 0146*	3	39 wks
25 May 63	**JOE BROWN – LIVE** *Piccadilly NPL 38006*	14	8 wks

Sam BROWN *UK, female vocalist*   *30 wks*

11 Mar 89	● **STOP** *A & M AMA 5195*	4	18 wks
14 Apr 90	**APRIL MOON** *A & M AMA 9014*	38	12 wks

Jackson BROWNE *US, male vocalist*   *33 wks*

4 Dec 76	**THE PRETENDER** *Asylum K 53048*	26	5 wks
21 Jan 78	**RUNNING ON EMPTY** *Asylum K 53070*	28	7 wks
12 Jul 80	**HOLD OUT** *Asylum K 52226*	44	5 wks
13 Aug 83	**LAWYERS IN LOVE** *Asylum 96–0268–1*	37	7 wks
8 Mar 86	**LIVES IN THE BALANCE** *Asylum EKT 31*	36	7 wks
17 Jun 89	**WORLD IN MOTION** *Elektra EKT 50*	39	2 wks

It's ironic that the deeply religious **Pat Boone**, a secular singles star, should have half his album hits be hymns.

The first hit by **Sam Brown** stopped one short of father Joe's chart debut.

Dave BRUBECK QUARTET
US, male instrumental group   *17 wks*

25 Jun 60	**TIME OUT** *Fontana TFL 5085*	11	1 wk
7 Apr 62	**TIME FURTHER OUT** *Fontana TFL 5161*	12	16 wks

Second album just credited to Dave Brubeck.

Jack BRUCE *UK, male vocalist/instrumentalist – bass*   *9 wks*

27 Sep 69	● **SONGS FOR A TAILOR** *Polydor 583–058*	6	9 wks

BRUFORD – *See ANDERSON BRUFORD WAKEMAN HOWE*

Peabo BRYSON and Roberta FLACK
US, male/female vocal duo   *10 wks*

17 Sep 83	**BORN TO LOVE** *Capitol EST 7122841*	15	10 wks

See also Roberta Flack.

BUCKS FIZZ *UK, male/female vocal group*   *80 wks*

8 Aug 81	**BUCKS FIZZ** *RCA RCALP 5050*	14	28 wks
18 May 82	● **ARE YOU READY?** *RCA RCALP 8000*	10	23 wks
19 Mar 83	**HAND CUT** *RCA RCALP 6100*	17	13 wks
3 Dec 83	**GREATEST HITS** *RCA RCA PL 70022*	25	13 wks
24 Nov 84	**I HEAR TALK** *RCA PL 70397*	66	2 wks
13 Dec 86	**THE WRITING ON THE WALL** *Polydor POHL 30*	89	1 wk

79

b

Harold BUDD/Liz FRASER/Robin GUTHRIE/ Simon RAYMOND
UK, male/female vocal/instrumental group   *2 wks*

22 Nov 86	**THE MOON AND THE MELODIES** *4AD CAD 611*	46	2 wks

---

BUDGIE *UK, male vocal/instrumental group*   *10 wks*

8 Jun 74	**IN FOR THE KILL** *MCA MCF 2546*	29	3 wks
27 Sep 75	**BANDOLIER** *MCA MCF 2723*	36	4 wks
31 Oct 81	**NIGHT FLIGHT** *RCA RCALP 6003*	68	2 wks
23 Oct 82	**DELIVER US FROM EVIL** *RCA RCALP 6054*	62	1 wk

---

BUGGLES *UK, male vocal/instrumental duo*   *6 wks*

16 Feb 80	**THE AGE OF PLASTIC** *Island ILPS 9585*	27	6 wks

BUNNYMEN – *See ECHO and the BUNNYMEN*

Eric BURDON and WAR
UK, male vocalist and US, male vocal/instrumental group   *2 wks*

3 Oct 70	**ERIC BURDON DECLARES WAR** *Polydor 2310–041*	50	2 wks

Jean-Jacques BURNEL
UK, male vocalist/instrumentalist – bass guitar   *5 wks*

21 Apr 79	**EUROMAN COMETH** *United Artists UAG 30214*	**40**	5 wks

See also Dave Greenfield and Jean-Jacques Burnel.

Kate BUSH *UK, female vocalist*   *253 wks*

11 Mar 78	● **THE KICK INSIDE** *EMI EMC 3223*	**3**	70 wks
25 Nov 78	● **LIONHEART** *EMI EMA 787*	**6**	36 wks
20 Sep 80	★ **NEVER FOR EVER** *EMI EMA 7964*	**1**	23 wks
25 Sep 82	● **THE DREAMING** *EMI EMC 3419*	**3**	9 wks
28 Sep 85	★ **HOUNDS OF LOVE** *EMI KAB 1*	**1**	51 wks
22 Nov 86	★ **THE WHOLE STORY** *EMI KBTV 1*	**1**	44 wks
28 Oct 89	● **THE SENSUAL WORLD** *EMI EMD 1010*	**2**	20 wks

Jonathan BUTLER
South Africa, male vocalist/instrumentalist – guitar   *14 wks*

12 Sep 87	**JONATHAN BUTLER** *Jive HIP 46*	**12**	11 wks
4 Feb 89	**MORE THAN FRIENDS** *Jive HIP 70*	**29**	3 wks

BUTTHOLE SURFERS
UK, male vocal/instrumental group   *1 wk*

16 Mar 91	**PIOUHGD** *Rough Trade R 20812601*	**68**	1 wk

80

b

BUZZCOCKS *UK, male vocal/instrumental group*   *23 wks*

25 Mar 78	**ANOTHER MUSIC IN A DIFFERENT KITCHEN**		
	United Artists UAG 30159	**15**	11 wks
7 Oct 78	**LOVE BITES** *United Artists UAG 30184*	**13**	9 wks
6 Oct 79	**A DIFFERENT KIND OF TENSION**		
	United Artists UAG 30260	**26**	3 wks

BY ALL MEANS *US, male/female vocal group*   *1 wk*

16 Jul 88	**BY ALL MEANS** *Fourth & Broadway BRLP 520*	**80**	1 wk

Max BYGRAVES *UK, male vocalist*   *176 wks*

23 Sep 72	● **SING ALONG WITH MAX** *Pye NSPL 18361*	**4**	44 wks
2 Dec 72	**SING ALONG WITH MAX VOL. 2** *Pye NSPL 18383*	**11**	23 wks
5 May 73	● **SINGALONGAMAX VOL. 3** *Pye NSPL 18401*	**5**	30 wks
29 Sep 73	● **SINGALONGAMAX VOL. 4** *Pye NSPL 18410*	**7**	12 wks
15 Dec 73	**SINGALONGPARTY SONG** *Pye NSPL 18419*	**15**	6 wks
12 Oct 74	**YOU MAKE ME FEEL LIKE SINGING A SONG**		
	Pye NSPL 18436	**39**	3 wks
7 Dec 74	**SINGALONGAXMAS** *Pye NSPL 18439*	**21**	6 wks
13 Nov 76	● **100 GOLDEN GREATS** *Ronco RTDX 2019*	**3**	21 wks
28 Oct 78	**LINGALONGAMAX** *Ronco RPL 2033*	**39**	5 wks
16 Dec 78	**THE SONG AND DANCE MEN** *Pye NSPL 18574*	**67**	1 wk
19 Aug 89	● **SINGALONGAWARYEARS** *Parkfield Music PMLP 5001* ..	**5**	19 wks
25 Nov 89	**SINGALONGAWARYEARS VOLUME 2**		
	Parkfield Music PMLP 5006	**33**	6 wks

Charlie BYRD – *See Stan GETZ and Charlie BYRD*

Donald BYRD US, male vocalist/instrumentalist – trumpet   3 wks

10 Oct 81	**LOVE BYRD** Elektra K 52301	70	3 wks

BYRDS US, male vocal/instrumental group   42 wks

28 Aug 65 ●	**MR. TAMBOURINE MAN** CBS BPG 62571	7	12 wks
9 Apr 66	**TURN, TURN, TURN** CBS BPG 62652	11	5 wks
1 Oct 66	**5TH DIMENSION** CBS BPG 62783	27	2 wks
22 Apr 67	**YOUNGER THAN YESTERDAY** CBS SBPG 62988 ...	37	4 wks
4 May 68	**THE NOTORIOUS BYRD BROTHERS** CBS 63169	12	11 wks
24 May 69	**DR. BYRDS AND MR. HYDE** CBS 63545	15	1 wk
14 Feb 70	**BALLAD OF EASY RIDER** CBS 63795	41	1 wk
28 Nov 70	**UNTITLED** CBS 66253	11	4 wks
14 Apr 73	**BYRDS** Asylum SYLA 8754	31	1 wk
19 May 73	**HISTORY OF THE BYRDS** CBS 68242	47	1 wk

David BYRNE UK, male vocalist   2 wks

21 Oct 89	**REI MOMO** Warner Bros. WX 319	52	2 wks

C

C&C MUSIC FACTORY US, male production duo   13 wks

9 Feb 91 ●	**GONNA MAKE YOU SWEAT** Columbia 4678141	8	13 wks

Montserrat CABALLE – See Freddie MERCURY and Montserrat CABALLE

CABARET VOLTAIRE UK, male vocal/instrumental group 11 wks

26 Jun 82	**2 X 45** Rough Trade ROUGH 42	98	1 wk
13 Aug 83	**THE CRACKDOWN** Some Bizzare CV 1	31	5 wks
10 Nov 84	**MICRO-PHONIES** Some Bizzare CV 2	69	1 wk
3 Aug 85	**DRINKING GASOLINE** Some Bizzare CVM 1	71	2 wks
26 Oct 85	**THE COVENANT, THE SWORD AND THE ARM OF THE**		
	LORD Some Bizzare CV 3	57	2 wks

CACTUS WORLD NEWS
Ireland, male vocal/instrumental group   2 wks

24 May 86	**URBAN BEACHES** MCA MCG 6005	56	2 wks

J.J. CALE US, male vocalist/instrumentalist – guitar   22 wks

2 Oct 76	**TROUBADOUR** Island ISA 5011	53	1 wk
25 Aug 79	**5** Shelter ISA 5018	40	6 wks
21 Feb 81	**SHADES** Shelter ISA 5021	44	7 wks
20 Mar 82	**GRASSHOPPER** Shelter IFA 5022	36	5 wks
24 Sep 83	**#8** Mercury MERL 22	47	3 wks

John CALE – See Lou REED and John CALE

Maria CALLAS *Greece, female vocalist*　　　7 wks

| 20 Jun 87 | THE MARIA CALLAS COLLECTION *Stylus SMR 732* .. | 50 | 7 wks |

CAMEL *UK, male vocal/instrumental group*　　47 wks

24 May 75	THE SNOW GOOSE *Decca SKL 5207*	22	13 wks
17 Apr 76	MOON MADNESS *Decca TXS 115*	15	6 wks
17 Sep 77	RAIN DANCES *Decca TXS 124*	20	8 wks
14 Oct 78	BREATHLESS *Decca TXS 132*	26	1 wk
27 Oct 79	I CAN SEE YOUR HOUSE FROM HERE *Decca TXS 137*	45	3 wks
31 Jan 81	NUDE *Decca SKL 5323*	34	7 wks
15 May 82	THE SINGLE FACTOR *Decca SKL 5328*	57	5 wks
21 Apr 84	STATIONARY TRAVELLER *Decca SKL 5334*	57	4 wks

CAMEO *US, male vocal/instrumental group*　　47 wks

10 Aug 85	SINGLE LIFE *Club JABH 11*	66	12 wks
18 Oct 86 ●	WORD UP *Club JABH 19*	7	34 wks
26 Nov 88	MACHISMO *Club 836002 1*	86	1 wk

Glen CAMPBELL *US, male vocalist*　　183 wks

31 Jan 70	GLEN CAMPBELL LIVE *Capitol SB 21444*	16	14 wks
30 May 70	TRY A LITTLE KINDNESS *Capitol ESW 389*	37	10 wks
12 Dec 70	THE GLEN CAMPBELL ALBUM *Capitol ST 22493*	16	5 wks
27 Nov 71 ●	GREATEST HITS *Capitol ST 21885*	8	113 wks
25 Oct 75	RHINESTONE COWBOY *Capitol E-SW 11430*	38	9 wks
20 Nov 76 ★	20 GOLDEN GREATS *Capitol EMTV 2*	1	27 wks
23 Apr 77	SOUTHERN NIGHTS *Capitol E-ST 11601*	51	1 wk
22 Jul 89	THE COMPLETE GLEN CAMPBELL *Stylus SMR 979* ..	47	4 wks

See also Bobbie Gentry and Glen Campbell.

82

C

CANNED HEAT *US, male vocal/instrumental group*　　40 wks

29 Jun 68 ●	BOOGIE WITH CANNED HEAT *Liberty LBL 83103*	5	21 wks
14 Feb 70 ●	CANNED HEAT COOKBOOK *Liberty LBS 83303*	8	12 wks
4 Jul 70	CANNED HEAT '70 CONCERT *Liberty LBS 83333*	15	3 wks
10 Oct 70	FUTURE BLUES *Liberty LBS 83364*	27	4 wks

Freddy CANNON *US, male vocalist*　　11 wks

| 27 Feb 60 ★ | THE EXPLOSIVE FREDDY CANNON *Top Rank 25/108* . | 1 | 11 wks |

CAPTAIN SENSIBLE *UK, male vocalist*　　3 wks

| 11 Sep 82 | WOMEN AND CAPTAIN FIRST *A&M AMLH 68548* .. | 64 | 3 wks |

CAPTAIN and TENNILLE
US, male instrumentalist – keyboards and female vocalist　　6 wks

| 22 Mar 80 | MAKE YOUR MOVE *Casablanca CAL 2060* | 33 | 6 wks |

CAPTAIN BEEFHEART and his MAGIC BAND
US, male vocal/instrumental group　　16 wks

| 6 Dec 69 | TROUT MASK REPLICA *Straight STS 1053* | 21 | 1 wk |

23 Jan 71	**LICK MY DECALS OFF BABY** *Straight STS 1063*	**20**	10 wks
29 May 71	**MIRROR MAN** *Buddah 2365 002*	**49**	1 wk
19 Feb 72	**THE SPOTLIGHT KID** *Reprise K 44162*	**44**	2 wks
18 Sep 82	**ICE CREAM FOR CROW** *Virgin V 2337*	**90**	2 wks

CARAVAN UK, male vocal/instrumental group · 2 wks

| 30 Aug 75 | **CUNNING STUNTS** *Decca SKL 5210* .... | **50** | 1 wk |
| 15 May 76 | **BLIND DOG AT ST. DUNSTAN'S** *BTM BTM 1007* ..... | **53** | 1 wk |

Mariah CAREY US, female vocalist · 46 wks

| 15 Sep 90 | ● **MARIAH CAREY** *CBS 4668151* .... | **6** | 36 wks |
| 26 Oct 91 | ● **EMOTIONS** *Columbia 4688511* .... | **10†** | 10 wks |

Belinda CARLISLE US, female vocalist · 103 wks

2 Jan 88	● **HEAVEN ON EARTH** *Virgin V 2496*	**4**	54 wks
4 Nov 89	● **RUNAWAY HORSES** *Virgin V 2599*	**4**	39 wks
26 Oct 91	● **LIVE YOUR LIFE BE FREE** *V 2680*	**7†**	10 wks

CARMEL UK, female/male vocal/instrumental group · 11 wks

1 Oct 83	**CARMEL** *Red Flame RFM 9*	**94**	2 wks
24 Mar 84	**THE DRUM IS EVERYTHING** *London SH 8555*	**19**	8 wks
27 Sep 86	**THE FALLING** *London LONLP 17*	**88**	1 wk

Eric CARMEN US, male vocalist · 1 wk

| 15 May 76 | **ERIC CARMEN** *Arista ARTY 120* .... | **58** | 1 wk |

83

C

Kim CARNES US, female vocalist · 16 wks

| 20 Jun 81 | **MISTAKEN IDENTITY** *EMI America AML 3018* .... | **26** | 16 wks |

CARPENTERS US, male/female vocal/instrumental duo · 546 wks

23 Jan 71	**CLOSE TO YOU** *A&M AMLS 998*	**23**	82 wks
30 Oct 71	**THE CARPENTERS** *A&M AMLS 63502*	**12**	36 wks
15 Apr 72	**TICKET TO RIDE** *A&M AMLS 64342*	**20**	3 wks
23 Sep 72	**A SONG FOR YOU** *A&M AMLS 63511*	**13**	37 wks
7 Jul 73	● **NOW AND THEN** *A&M AMLH 63519*	**2**	65 wks
26 Jan 74	★ **THE SINGLES 1969-1973** *A&M AMLH 63601*	**1**	125 wks
28 Jun 75	★ **HORIZON** *A&M AMLK 64530*	**1**	27 wks
23 Aug 75	**TICKET TO RIDE (re-issue)** *Hamlet AMLP 8001*	**35**	2 wks
3 Jul 76	● **A KIND OF HUSH** *A&M AMLK 64581*	**3**	15 wks
8 Jan 77	**LIVE AT THE PALLADIUM** *A&M AMLS 68403*	**28**	3 wks
8 Oct 77	**PASSAGE** *A&M AMLK 64703*	**12**	12 wks
2 Dec 78	● **THE SINGLES 1974-1978** *A&M AMLT 19748*	**2**	27 wks
27 Jun 81	**MADE IN AMERICA** *A&M AMLK 63723*	**12**	10 wks
15 Oct 83	● **VOICE OF THE HEART** *A&M AMLX 64954*	**6**	19 wks
20 Oct 84	● **YESTERDAY ONCE MORE** *EMI/A&M SING 1*	**10**	26 wks
13 Jan 90	**LOVELINES** *A&M AMA 3931*	**73**	1 wk
31 Mar 90	★ **ONLY YESTERDAY** *A&M AMA 1990*	**1**	56 wks

Vikki CARR US, female vocalist · 12 wks

| 22 Jul 67 | **WAY OF TODAY** *Liberty SLBY 1331* .... | **31** | 2 wks |
| 12 Aug 67 | **IT MUST BE HIM** *Liberty LBS 83037* .... | **12** | 10 wks |

José CARRERAS *Spain, male vocalist*   *22 wks*

1 Oct 88	JOSE CARRERAS COLLECTION *Stylus SMR 860*	90	4 wks
23 Dec 89	JOSE CARRERAS SINGS ANDREW LLOYD WEBBER		
	WEA WX 325	42	6 wks
23 Feb 91	THE ESSENTIAL JOSE CARRERAS *Philips 4326921*	24	9 wks
6 Apr 91	HOLLYWOOD GOLDEN CLASSICS *East West WX 416* .	47	3 wks

See also Luciano Pavarotti, Placido Domingo and José Carreras.

Jasper CARROTT *UK, male comedian*   *66 wks*

18 Oct 75	● RABBITS ON AND ON *DJM DJLPS 462*	10	7 wks
6 Nov 76	CARROTT IN NOTTS *DJM DJF 20482*	56	1 wk
25 Nov 78	THE BEST OF JASPER CARROTT *DJM DJF 20549*	38	13 wks
20 Oct 79	THE UNRECORDED JASPER CARROTT		
	DJM DJF 20560	19	15 wks
19 Sep 81	BEAT THE CARROTT *DJM DJF 20575*	13	16 wks
25 Dec 82	CARROTT'S LIB *DJM DJF 20580*	80	3 wks
19 Nov 83	THE STUN (CARROTT TELLS ALL) *DJF 20582*	57	8 wks
7 Feb 87	COSMIC CARROTT *Portrait LAUGH 1*	66	3 wks

CARS *US, male vocal/instrumental group*   *72 wks*

2 Dec 78	CARS *Elektra K 52088*	29	15 wks
7 Jul 79	CANDY-O *Elektra K 52148*	30	6 wks
6 Oct 84	HEARTBEAT CITY *Elektra 960296*	25	30 wks
9 Nov 85	THE CARS GREATEST HITS *Elektra EKT 25*	27	19 wks
5 Sep 87	DOOR TO DOOR *Elektra EKT 42*	72	2 wks

84

c

CARTER – THE UNSTOPPABLE SEX MACHINE
UK, male vocal/instrumental duo   *14 wks*

2 Mar 91	● 30 SOMETHING *Rough Trade R 20112702*	8	9 wks
21 Sep 91	101 DAMNATIONS *Big Cat ABB 101*	29	5 wks

Johnny CASH *US, male vocalist*   *285 wks*

23 Jul 66	EVERYBODY LOVES A NUT *CBS BPG 62717*	28	1 wk
4 May 68	FROM SEA TO SHINING SEA *CBS 62972*	40	1 wk
6 Jul 68	OLD GOLDEN THROAT *CBS 63316*	37	2 wks
24 Aug 68	● FOLSOM PRISON *CBS 63308*	8	53 wks
23 Aug 69	● JOHNNY CASH AT SAN QUENTIN *CBS 63629*	2	114 wks
4 Oct 69	GREATEST HITS VOL. 1 *CBS 63062*	23	25 wks
7 Mar 70	● HELLO I'M JOHNNY CASH *CBS 63796*	6	16 wks
15 Aug 70	● WORLD OF JOHNNY CASH *CBS 66237*	5	31 wks
12 Dec 70	THE JOHNNY CASH SHOW *CBS 64089*	18	6 wks
18 Sep 71	MAN IN BLACK *CBS 64331*	18	7 wks
13 Nov 71	JOHNNY CASH *Hallmark SHM 739*	43	2 wks
20 May 72	● A THING CALLED LOVE *CBS 64898*	8	11 wks
14 Oct 72	STAR PORTRAIT *CBS 67201*	16	7 wks
10 Jul 76	ONE PIECE AT A TIME *CBS 81416*	49	3 wks
9 Oct 76	THE BEST OF JOHNNY CASH *CBS 10000*	48	2 wks
2 Sep 78	ITCHY FEET *CBS 10009*	36	4 wks

CASHFLOW *US, male vocal/instrumental group*   *3 wks*

28 Jun 86	CASHFLOW *Club JABH 17*	33	3 wks

CASHMERE *US, male vocal/instrumental group*   *5 wks*

2 Mar 85	CASHMERE *Fourth & Broadway BRLP 503*	63	5 wks

In America the Go-Go's got to number one with *Beauty and the Beat*, but Britain has preferred the group's lead singer **Belinda Carlisle** on her own.

Nick Cave is shown Seedless.

David CASSIDY *US, male vocalist*   *94 wks*

20 May 72	● CHERISH *Bell BELLS 210*	2	43 wks
24 Feb 73	● ROCK ME BABY *Bell BELLS 218*	2	20 wks
24 Nov 73	★ DREAMS ARE NOTHIN' MORE THAN WISHES *Bell BELLS 231*	1	13 wks
3 Aug 74	● CASSIDY LIVE *Bell BELLS 243*	9	7 wks
9 Aug 75	THE HIGHER THEY CLIMB *RCA Victor RS 1012*	22	5 wks
8 Jun 85	ROMANCE *Arista 206 983*	20	6 wks

Nick CAVE featuring the BAD SEEDS
Australia, male vocalist with male vocal/instrumental group   *7 wks*

2 Jun 84	FROM HER TO ETERNITY *Mute STUMM 17*	40	3 wks
15 Jun 85	THE FIRST BORN IS DEAD *Mute STUMM 21*	53	1 wk
30 Aug 86	KICKING AGAINST THE PRICKS *Mute STUMM 28* ...	89	1 wk
1 Oct 88	TENDER PREY *Mute STUMM 52*	67	1 wk
28 Apr 90	THE GOOD SON *Mute STUMM 76*	47	1 wk

CAVEMAN *UK, male rap duo*   *2 wks*

| 13 Apr 91 | POSITIVE REACTION   *Profile FILER 406* .... | 43 | 2 wks |

C.C.S. *UK, male vocal/instrumental group*   *5 wks*

| 8 Apr 72 | C.C.S.   *RAK SRAK 503* .... | 23 | 5 wks |

CENTRAL LINE *UK, male vocal/instrumental group*   *5 wks*

| 13 Feb 82 | BREAKING POINT   *Mercury MERA 001* .... | 64 | 5 wks |

CERRONE *France, male producer/multi-instrumentalist*   *1 wk*

| 30 Sep 78 | SUPERNATURE   *Atlantic K 50431* .... | 60 | 1 wk |

A CERTAIN RATIO *UK, male vocal/instrumental group*   *3 wks*

| 30 Jan 82 | SEXTET   *Factory FACT 55* .... | 53 | 3 wks |

Peter CETERA *US, male vocalist*   *4 wks*

| 13 Sep 86 | SOLITUDE/SOLITAIRE   *Full Moon 925474–1* .... | 56 | 4 wks |

Richard CHAMBERLAIN *US, male vocalist*   *8 wks*

| 16 Mar 63 | ● RICHARD CHAMBERLAIN SINGS   *MGM C 923* ...... | 8 | 8 wks |

CHAMELEONS *UK, male vocal/instrumental group*   *4 wks*

| 25 May 85 | WHAT DOES ANYTHING MEAN? BASICALLY
Statik STAT LP 22 .... | 60 | 2 wks |
| 20 Sep 86 | STRANGE TIMES   *Geffen 924 119–1* .... | 44 | 2 wks |

CHAMPAIGN *US, male/female vocal/instrumental group*   *4 wks*

| 27 Jun 81 | HOW 'BOUT US   *CBS 84927* .... | 38 | 4 wks |

CHANGE US, male/female vocal/instrumental group   23 wks

19 May 84	**CHANGE OF HEART** WEA WX 5	34	17 wks
27 Apr 85	**TURN ON THE RADIO** Cooltempo CHR 1504	39	6 wks

Michael CHAPMAN UK, male vocalist   1 wk

21 Mar 70	**FULLY QUALIFIED SURVIVOR** Harvest SHVL 764	45	1 wk

Tracy CHAPMAN US, female vocalist   91 wks

21 May 88	★ **TRACY CHAPMAN** Elektra EKT 44	1	75 wks
14 Oct 89	★ **CROSSROADS** Elektra EKT 61	1	16 wks

CHAPTERHOUSE UK, male vocal/instrumental group   3 wks

11 May 91	**WHIRLPOOL** Dedicated DEDLP 001	23	3 wks

CHAQUITO ORCHESTRA
UK, orchestra arranged and conducted by Johnny Gregory   2 wks

24 Feb 68	**THIS IS CHAQUITO** Fontana SFXL 50	36	1 wk
4 Mar 72	**THRILLER THEMES** Philips 6308 087	48	1 wk

First album credited to Chaquito and Quedo Brass.

CHARGE GBH UK, male vocal/instrumental group   6 wks

14 Aug 82	**CITY BABY ATTACKED BY RATS** Clay CLAYLP 4	17	6 wks

87

c

CHARLATANS UK, male vocal/instrumental group   17 wks

20 Oct 90	★ **SOME FRIENDLY** Situation Two SITU 30	1	17 wks

CHARLENE US, female vocalist   4 wks

17 Jul 82	**I'VE NEVER BEEN TO ME** Motown STML 12171	43	4 wks

Ray CHARLES US, male vocalist/instrumentalist – piano   42 wks

28 Jul 62	● **MODERN SOUNDS IN COUNTRY AND WESTERN MUSIC** HMV CLP 1580	6	16 wks
23 Feb 63	**MODERN SOUNDS IN COUNTRY AND WESTERN MUSIC VOL. 2** HMV CLP 1613	15	5 wks
20 Jul 63	**GREATEST HITS** HMV CLP 1626	16	5 wks
5 Oct 68	**GREATEST HITS VOL. 2** Stateside SSL 10241	24	8 wks
19 Jul 80	**HEART TO HEART – 20 HOT HITS** London RAY TV 1	29	5 wks
24 Mar 90	**THE COLLECTION** Arcade RCLP 101	36	3 wks

Tina CHARLES UK, female vocalist   7 wks

3 Dec 77	**HEART 'N' SOUL** CBS 82180	35	7 wks

CHAS and DAVE UK, male vocal/instrumental duo   96 wks

5 Dec 81	**CHAS AND DAVE'S CHRISTMAS JAMBOREE BAG** Warwick WW 5166	25	15 wks

17 Apr 82	**MUSTN'T GRUMBLE** *Rockney 909*	35	11 wks
8 Jan 83	**JOB LOT** *Rockney ROC 910*	59	15 wks
15 Oct 83	● **CHAS AND DAVE'S KNEES UP – JAMBOREE BAG NO 2**		
	Rockney ROC 911	7	17 wks
11 Aug 84	**WELL PLEASED** *Rockney ROC 912*	27	10 wks
17 Nov 84	**CHAS AND DAVE'S GREATEST HITS** *Rockney ROC 913*	16	10 wks
15 Dec 84	**CHAS AND DAVE'S CHRISTMAS JAMBOREE BAG**		
	(re-issue) *Rockney ROCM 001*	87	1 wk
9 Nov 85	**JAMBOREE BAG NUMBER 3** *Rockney ROC 914*	15	13 wks
13 Dec 86	**CHAS AND DAVE'S CHRISTMAS CAROL ALBUM**		
	Telstar STAR 2293	37	4 wks

CHEAP TRICK *US, male vocal/instrumental group* *15 wks*

24 Feb 79	**CHEAP TRICK AT BUDOKAN** *Epic EPC 86083*	29	9 wks
6 Oct 79	**DREAM POLICE** *Epic EPC 83522*	41	5 wks
5 Jun 82	**ONE ON ONE** *Epic EPC 85740*	95	1 wk

CHECK 1-2 – *See Craig McLACHLAN and CHECK 1-2*

Chubby CHECKER *US, male vocalist* *7 wks*

27 Jan 62	**TWIST WITH CHUBBY CHECKER** *Columbia 33SX 1315*	13	4 wks
3 Mar 62	**FOR TWISTERS ONLY** *Columbia 33SX 1341*	17	3 wks

CHER *US, female vocalist* *151 wks*

2 Oct 65	● **ALL I REALLY WANT TO DO** *Liberty LBY 3058*	7	9 wks
7 May 66	**SONNY SIDE OF CHER** *Liberty LBY 3072*	11	11 wks
16 Jan 88	**CHER** *Geffen WX 132*	26	22 wks
22 Jul 89	● **HEART OF STONE** *Geffen WX 262*	7	82 wks
29 Jun 91	★ **LOVE HURTS** *Geffen GEF 24427*	1†	27 wks

See also Sonny and Cher.

CHERELLE *US, female vocalist* *9 wks*

25 Jan 86	**HIGH PRIORITY** *Tabu TBU 26699*	17	9 wks

Neneh CHERRY *US, female vocalist* *42 wks*

17 Jun 89	● **RAW LIKE SUSHI** *Circa CIRCA 8*	2	42 wks

CHIC *US, male/female vocal/instrumental group* *44 wks*

3 Feb 79	● **C'EST CHIC** *Atlantic K 50565*	2	24 wks
18 Aug 79	**RISQUE** *Atlantic K 50634*	29	12 wks
15 Dec 79	**THE BEST OF CHIC** *Atlantic K 50686*	30	8 wks

See also Chic and Sister Sledge; Compilation Albums – Dino.

CHIC and SISTER SLEDGE
US, male/female vocal/instrumental group and female vocal group *3 wks*

5 Dec 87	**FREAK OUT** *Telstar STAR 2319*	72	3 wks

See also Chic; Sister Sledge.

CHICAGO *US, male vocal/instrumental group* *106 wks*

27 Sep 69	● **CHICAGO TRANSIT AUTHORITY** *CBS 66221*	9	14 wks

China Crisis had a chart crisis after 1985.

Neneh Cherry is shown in raw fashions five years before her chart debut.

4 Apr 70	● CHICAGO CBS 66233	6	27 wks
3 Apr 71	CHICAGO 3 CBS 66260	31	1 wk
30 Sep 72	CHICAGO 5 CBS 69108	24	2 wks
23 Oct 76	CHICAGO X CBS 86010	21	11 wks
2 Oct 82	CHICAGO 16 Full Moon K 99235	44	9 wks
4 Dec 82	LOVE SONGS TV Records TVA 6	42	8 wks
1 Dec 84	CHICAGO 17 Full Moon 925060	24	20 wks
25 Nov 89	THE HEART OF CHICAGO Reprise WX 328	15	14 wks

First album credited to Chicago Transit Authority.

CHICKEN SHACK
UK, male/female vocal/instrumental group   *9 wks*

22 Jul 68	40 BLUE FINGERS FRESHLY PACKED Blue Horizon 7-63203	12	8 wks
15 Feb 69	● OK KEN? Blue Horizon 7-63209	9	1 wk

CHIEFTAINS – *See James GALWAY and the CHIEFTAINS; Van MORRISON*

Toni CHILDS   *US, female vocalist*   *1 wk*

29 Apr 89	UNION A&M AMA 5175	73	1 wk

CHIMES   *UK, male/female vocal/instrumental group*   *19 wks*

23 Jun 90	THE CHIMES CBS 4664811	17	19 wks

90

c

CHINA CRISIS   *UK, male vocal/instrumental group*   *68 wks*

20 Nov 82	DIFFICULT SHAPES AND PASSIVE RHYTHMS Virgin V 2243	21	18 wks
12 Nov 83	WORKING WITH FIRE AND STEEL – POSSIBLE POP SONGS VOL 2 Virgin V 2286	20	16 wks
11 May 85	● FLAUNT THE IMPERFECTION Virgin V 2342	9	22 wks
6 Dec 86	WHAT PRICE PARADISE Virgin V 2410	63	6 wks
13 May 89	DIARY OF A HOLLOW HORSE Virgin V 2567	58	2 wks
15 Sep 90	CHINA CRISIS COLLECTION Virgin V 2613	32	4 wks

CHORDS   *UK, male vocal/instrumental group*   *3 wks*

24 May 80	SO FAR AWAY Polydor POLS 1019	30	3 wks

CHRISTIANS   *UK, male vocal/instrumental group*   *85 wks*

31 Oct 87	● THE CHRISTIANS Island ILPS 9876	2	68 wks
27 Jan 90	★ COLOUR Island ILPS 9948	1	17 wks

Tony CHRISTIE   *UK, male vocalist*   *10 wks*

24 Jul 71	I DID WHAT I DID FOR MARIA MCA MKPS 2016	37	1 wk
17 Feb 73	WITH LOVING FEELING MCA MUPS 468	19	2 wks
31 May 75	TONY CHRISTIE – LIVE MCA MCF 2703	33	3 wks
6 Nov 76	BEST OF TONY CHRISTIE MCA MCF 2769	28	4 wks

CHRON GEN   *UK, male vocal/instrumental group*   *3 wks*

3 Apr 82	CHRONIC GENERATION Secret SEC 3	53	3 wks

Sir Winston CHURCHILL *UK, male statesman*   *8 wks*

13 Feb 65	● THE VOICE OF CHURCHILL *Decca LXT 6200*	6	8 wks

CICCONE YOUTH
US, male/female vocal/instrumental group   *1 wk*

4 Feb 89	THE WHITEY ALBUM *Blast First BFFP 28*	63	1 wk

See also Sonic Youth – they are the same band.

CINDERELLA *US, male vocal/instrumental group*   *8 wks*

23 Jul 88	LONG COLD WINTER *Vertigo VERH 59*	30	6 wks
1 Dec 90	HEARTBREAK STATION *Vertigo 8480181*	36	2 wks

CITY BEAT BAND – *See PRINCE CHARLES and the CITY BEAT BAND*

Gary CLAIL ON-U SOUND SYSTEM
UK, male vocalist/producer   *2 wks*

4 May 91	EMOTIONAL HOOLIGAN *Perfecto PL 74965*	35	2 wks

CLANCY BROTHERS and Tommy MAKEM
Ireland, male vocal/instrumental group and male vocalist   *5 wks*

16 Apr 66	ISN'T IT GRAND BOYS *CBS BPG 62674*	22	5 wks

CLANNAD *Ireland, male/female vocal/instrumental group*   *123 wks*

2 Apr 83	MAGICAL RING *RCA RCALP 6072*	26	21 wks
12 May 84	LEGEND (MUSIC FROM ROBIN OF SHERWOOD)		
	RCA PL 70188	15	40 wks
2 Jun 84	MAGICAL RING (re-issue) *RCA PL 70003*	91	1 wk
26 Oct 85	MACALLA *RCA PL 70894*	33	24 wks
7 Nov 87	SIRIUS *RCA PL 71513*	34	4 wks
11 Feb 89	ATLANTIC REALM *BBC REB 727*	41	3 wks
6 May 89	● PASTPRESENT *RCA PL 74074*	5	23 wks
20 Oct 90	ANAM *RCA PL 74762*	14	7 wks

Eric CLAPTON *UK, male vocalist/instrumentalist – guitar*   *240 wks*

5 Sep 70	ERIC CLAPTON *Polydor 2383-021*	17	8 wks
26 Aug 72	HISTORY OF ERIC CLAPTON *Polydor 2659 2478 027* ..	20	6 wks
24 Aug 74	● 461 OCEAN BOULEVARD *RSO 2479 118*	3	19 wks
12 Apr 75	THERE'S ONE IN EVERY CROWD *RSO 2479 132*	15	8 wks
13 Sep 75	E.C. WAS HERE *RSO 2394 160*	14	6 wks
11 Sep 76	● NO REASON TO CRY *RSO 2479 179*	8	7 wks
26 Nov 77	SLOWHAND *RSO 2479 201*	23	13 wks
9 Dec 78	BACKLESS *RSO RSD 5001*	18	12 wks
10 May 80	● JUST ONE NIGHT *RSO RSDX 2*	3	12 wks
7 Mar 81	ANOTHER TICKET *RSO RSD 5008*	18	8 wks
24 Apr 82	TIME PIECES – THE BEST OF ERIC CLAPTON		
	RSO RSD 5010	20	13 wks
19 Feb 83	MONEY & CIGARETTES *Duck W 3773*	13	17 wks
9 Jun 84	BACKTRACKIN' *Starblend ERIC 1*	29	16 wks
23 Mar 85	● BEHIND THE SUN *Duck 92-5166-1*	8	14 wks
6 Dec 86	● AUGUST *Duck WX 71*	3	42 wks
18 Nov 89	● JOURNEYMAN *Duck WX 322*	2	32 wks
26 Oct 91	24 NIGHTS *Duck WX 373*	17	7 wks

See also Eric Clapton and Cream; John Mayall and Eric Clapton.

91

C

Eric CLAPTON and CREAM UK, male vocalist/
instrumentalist – guitar and male vocal/instrumental group   96 wks

26 Sep 87	● THE CREAM OF ERIC CLAPTON			
	Polydor ECTV 1	....	3	96 wks

See also Eric Clapton; Cream.

Petula CLARK UK, female vocalist   43 wks

30 Jul 66	I COULDN'T LIVE WITHOUT YOUR LOVE			
	Pye NPL 18148	....	11	10 wks
4 Feb 67	HIT PARADE Pye NPL 18159	....	18	13 wks
18 Feb 67	COLOUR MY WORLD Pye NSPL 18171	....	16	9 wks
7 Oct 67	THESE ARE MY SONGS Pye NSPL 18197	....	38	3 wks
6 Apr 68	THE OTHER MAN'S GRASS IS ALWAYS GREENER			
	Pye NSPL 18211	....	37	1 wk
5 Feb 77	20 ALL TIME GREATEST K-Tel NE 945	....	18	7 wks

Dave CLARK FIVE UK, male vocal/instrumental group   26 wks

18 Apr 64	● A SESSION WITH THE DAVE CLARK FIVE			
	Columbia 33SX 1598	....	3	8 wks
14 Aug 65	● CATCH US IF YOU CAN Columbia 33SX 1756	....	8	8 wks
4 Mar 78	● 25 THUMPING GREAT HITS Polydor POLTV 7	....	7	10 wks

Louis CLARK – See ROYAL PHILHARMONIC ORCHESTRA

John Cooper CLARKE UK, male vocalist   9 wks

19 Apr 80	SNAP CRACKLE AND BOP Epic EPC 84083	....	26	7 wks
5 Jun 82	ZIP STYLE METHOD Epic EPC 85667	....	97	2 wks

Stanley CLARKE US, male vocal/instrumentalist – bass   2 wks

12 Jul 80	ROCKS PEBBLES AND SAND Epic EPC 84342	....	42	2 wks

CLASH UK, male vocal/instrumental group   107 wks

30 Apr 77	CLASH CBS 82000	....	12	16 wks
25 Nov 78	● GIVE 'EM ENOUGH ROPE CBS 82431	....	2	14 wks
22 Dec 79	● LONDON CALLING CBS CLASH 3	....	9	20 wks
20 Dec 80	SANDINISTA CBS FSLN 1	....	19	9 wks
22 May 82	● COMBAT ROCK CBS FMLN 2	....	2	23 wks
16 Nov 85	CUT THE CRAP CBS 26601	....	16	3 wks
2 Apr 88	● THE STORY OF THE CLASH CBS 460244 1	....	7	20 wks
16 Nov 91	THE SINGLES Columbia 4689461	....	68	2 wks

CLASSIX NOUVEAUX
UK, male vocal/instrumental group   6 wks

30 May 81	NIGHT PEOPLE Liberty LBG 30325	....	66	2 wks
24 Apr 82	LA VERITE Liberty LBG 30346	....	44	4 wks

Richard CLAYDERMAN
France, male instrumentalist – piano   180 wks

13 Nov 82	● RICHARD CLAYDERMAN Decca SKL 5329	....	2	64 wks

8 Oct 83	**THE MUSIC OF RICHARD CLAYDERMAN**		
	Decca SKL 5333	21	28 wks
24 Nov 84	**THE MUSIC OF LOVE** *Decca SKL 5340*	28	21 wks
1 Dec 84	**CHRISTMAS** *Decca SKL 5337*	53	5 wks
23 Nov 85	**THE CLASSIC TOUCH** *Decca SKL 5343*	17	18 wks
22 Nov 86	**HOLLYWOOD AND BROADWAY** *Decca SKL 5344*	28	9 wks
28 Nov 87	**SONGS OF LOVE** *Decca SKL 5345*	19	13 wks
3 Dec 88	**A LITTLE NIGHT MUSIC** *Decca Delphine 8281251*	52	5 wks
25 Nov 89	**THE LOVE SONGS OF ANDREW LLOYD WEBBER**		
	Decca Delphine 8281751	18	10 wks
24 Nov 90	**MY CLASSIC COLLECTION** *Decca Delphine 8282281*	29	7 wks

The Classic Touch *and* My Classic Collection *are credited to Richard Clayderman with the Royal Philharmonic Orchestra. See also Richard Clayderman and James Last; Royal Philharmonic Orchestra.*

Richard CLAYDERMAN and James LAST
France, male instrumentalist – piano and Germany, orchestra leader　　　*8 wks*

9 Nov 91	**TOGETHER AT LAST** *Delphine/Polydor 5115251*	14†	8 wks

See also Richard Clayderman; James Last.

CLAYTOWN TROUPE　*UK, male vocal/instrumental group*　　*1 wk*

21 Oct 89	**THROUGH THE VEIL** *Island ILPS 9933*	72	1 wk

CLIMAX BLUES BAND　*UK, male vocal/instrumental group*　　*1 wk*

13 Nov 76	**GOLD PLATED** *BTM 1009*	56	1 wk

CLIMIE FISHER　*UK, male vocal/instrumental duo*　　*38 wks*

13 Feb 88	**EVERYTHING** *EMI EMC 3538*	14	36 wks
21 Oct 89	**COMING IN FOR THE KILL** *EMI EMC 3565*	35	2 wks

Patsy CLINE　*US, female vocalist*　　*14 wks*

19 Jan 91	**SWEET DREAMS** *MCA MCG 6003*	18	10 wks
19 Jan 91	**DREAMING** *Platinum Music PLAT 303*	55	4 wks

Luis COBOS　*Spain, male orchestra leader*　　*1 wk*

21 Apr 90	**OPERA EXTRAVAGANZA** *Epic MOOD 12*	72	1 wk

Eddie COCHRAN　*US, male vocalist/instrumentalist – guitar*　　*47 wks*

30 Jul 60	**SINGING TO MY BABY** *London HAU 2093*	19	1 wk
1 Oct 60 ●	**EDDIE COCHRAN MEMORIAL ALBUM**		
	London HAG 2267	9	12 wks
12 Jan 63	**CHERISHED MEMORIES** *Liberty LBY 1109*	15	3 wks
20 Apr 63	**EDDIE COCHRAN MEMORIAL ALBUM**		
	(re-issue) *Liberty LBY 1127*	11	18 wks
19 Oct 63	**SINGING TO MY BABY (re-issue)** *Liberty LBY 1158*	20	1 wk
9 May 70	**VERY BEST OF EDDIE COCHRAN** *Liberty LBS 83337* ..	34	3 wks
18 Aug 79	**THE EDDIE COCHRAN SINGLES ALBUM**		
	United Artists UAK 30244	39	6 wks
16 Apr 88	**C'MON EVERYBODY** *Liberty ECR 1*	53	3 wks

Brenda COCHRANE　*Ireland, female vocalist*　　*14 wks*

14 Apr 90	**THE VOICE** *Polydor 8431411*	23	11 wks
6 Apr 91	**IN DREAMS** *Polydor 8490341*	55	3 wks

93

C

The **Cocteau Twins** were neither related nor a duo.

The Frenchman **Richard Clayderman** enjoys a trip to Beverly Hills.

Love songs by Lionel Richie (second from left) provided most of the **Commodores'** greatest hits.

Joe COCKER UK, male vocalist   13 wks

26 Sep 70	**MAD DOGS AND ENIGLISHMEN** A & M AMLS 6002 ..	16	8 wks
6 May 72	**JOE COCKER/WITH A LITTLE HELP FROM MY**		
	FRIENDS Double Back TOOFA 1/2	29	4 wks
30 Jun 84	**A CIVILISED MAN** Capitol EJ 24 0139 1	100	1 wk

COCKNEY REBEL – See Steve HARLEY and COCKNEY REBEL

COCKNEY REJECTS UK, male vocal/instrumental group   17 wks

15 Mar 80	**GREATEST HITS VOL. 1** Zonophone ZONO 101	22	11 wks
25 Oct 80	**GREATEST HITS VOL. 2** Zonophone ZONO 102	23	3 wks
18 Apr 81	**GREATEST HITS VOL. 3 (LIVE AND LOUD)**		
	Zonophone ZEM 101	27	3 wks

COCONUTS – See Kid CREOLE and the COCONUTS

COCTEAU TWINS UK, male/female vocal group   39 wks

29 Oct 83	**HEAD OVER HEELS** 4AD CAD 313	51	15 wks
24 Nov 84	**TREASURE** 4AD CAD 412	29	8 wks
26 Apr 86	● **VICTORIALAND** 4AD CAD 602	10	7 wks
1 Oct 88	**BLUE BELL KNOLL** 4AD CAD 807	15	4 wks
22 Sep 90	● **HEAVEN OR LAS VEGAS** 4AD CAD 0012	7	5 wks

Leonard COHEN Canada, male vocalist   143 wks

31 Aug 68	**SONGS OF LEONARD COHEN** CBS 63241	13	71 wks
3 May 69	● **SONGS FROM A ROOM** CBS 63587	2	26 wks
24 Apr 71	● **SONGS OF LOVE AND HATE** CBS 69004	4	18 wks
28 Sep 74	**NEW SKIN FOR THE OLD CEREMONY** CBS 69087 ...	24	3 wks
10 Dec 77	**DEATH OF A LADIES' MAN** CBS 86042	35	5 wks
16 Feb 85	**VARIOUS POSITIONS** CBS 26222	52	6 wks
27 Feb 88	**I'M YOUR MAN** CBS 460642 1	48	13 wks
6 Aug 88	**GREATEST HITS** CBS 32644	99	1 wk

95

c

Marc COHN UK, male vocalist/instrumentalist – piano   15 wks

29 Jun 91	**MARC COHN** Atlantic 7567821781	27†	15 wks

COLDCUT UK, male production duo   4 wks

29 Apr 89	**WHAT'S THAT NOISE** Ahead Of Our Time CCUTLP 1 ...	20	4 wks

Lloyd COLE and the COMMOTIONS
UK, male vocalist and male vocal/instrumental group   84 wks

20 Oct 84	**RATTLESNAKES** Polydor LCLP 1	13	30 wks
30 Nov 85	● **EASY PIECES** Polydor LCLP 2	5	18 wks
7 Nov 87	● **MAINSTREAM** Polydor LCLP 3	9	20 wks
8 Apr 89	**1984–1989** Polydor 837736 1	14	7 wks
3 Mar 90	**LLOYD COLE** Polydor 8419071	11	6 wks
28 Sep 91	**DON'T GET WEIRD ON ME BABE** Polydor 5110931	21	3 wks

Last two albums were recorded by Lloyd Cole as a solo artist.

Nat 'King' COLE US, male vocalist   115 wks

19 Aug 61	**STRING ALONG WITH NAT 'KING' COLE**		
	Encore ENC 102	12	9 wks

Nat 'King' COLE and Dean MARTIN

US, male vocalists   1 wk

Nat 'King' COLE and the George SHEARING QUINTET *US, male vocalist and UK/US instrumental group*

7 wks

Natalie COLE *US, female vocalist*

31 wks

Dave and Ansil COLLINS *Jamaica, male vocal duo*

2 wks

Judy COLLINS *US, female vocalist*

18 wks

Phil COLLINS *UK, male vocalist/instrumentalist – drums*

730 wks

Willie COLLINS *US, male vocalist*

1 wk

COLOR ME BADD *US, male vocal group*

19 wks

The legendary **Sam Cooke** only hit the UK album chart twenty-two years after his death, when 'Wonderful World' was used in a jeans commercial. **Natalie Cole** had her greatest success when her tribute to father Nat, *Unforgettable*, went to number one in America in 1991.

Before they charted at home **Camel** loped in the US list with *Mirage*.

COLOSSEUM UK, male vocal/instrumental group   14 wks

17 May 69	**COLOSSEUM** Fontana S 5510	15	1 wk
22 Nov 69	**VALENTYNE SUITE** Vertigo VO 1	15	2 wks
5 Dec 70	**DAUGHTER OF TIME** Vertigo 6360 017	23	5 wks
26 Jun 71	**COLOSSEUM LIVE** Bronze ICD 1	17	6 wks

COLOURBOX UK, male vocal/instrumental group   2 wks

24 Aug 85	**COLOURBOX** 4AD CAD 508	67	2 wks

COLOUR FIELD UK, male vocal/instrumental group   8 wks

4 May 85	**VIRGINS AND PHILISTINES** Chrysalis CHR 1480	12	7 wks
4 Apr 87	**DECEPTION** Chrysalis CDL 1546	95	1 wk

Alice COLTRANE – See Carlos SANTANA and Alice COLTRANE

COMETS – See Bill HALEY and his COMETS

COMIC RELIEF UK, charity ensemble of comedians   8 wks

10 May 86	● **UTTERLY UTTERLY LIVE!** WEA WX 51	10	8 wks

COMMITMENTS

98

Ireland, male/female vocal/instrumental group   10 wks

C

26 Oct 91	● **THE COMMITMENTS (film soundtrack)** MCA MCA 10286	4†	10 wks

COMMODORES US/UK, male vocal/instrumental group   126 wks

13 May 78	**LIVE** Motown TMSP 6007	60	1 wk
10 Jun 78	● **NATURAL HIGH** Motown STML 12087	8	23 wks
2 Dec 78	**GREATEST HITS** Motown STML 12100	19	16 wks
18 Aug 79	**MIDNIGHT MAGIC** Motown STMA 8032	15	25 wks
28 Jun 80	**HEROES** Motown STMA 8034	50	5 wks
18 Jul 81	**IN THE POCKET** Motown STML 12156	69	5 wks
14 Aug 82	● **LOVE SONGS** K-Tel NE 1171	5	28 wks
23 Feb 85	**NIGHTSHIFT** Motown ZL 72343	13	10 wks
9 Nov 85	**THE VERY BEST OF THE COMMODORES**		
	Telstar STAR 2249	25	13 wks

Group were US only for first seven albums.

COMMOTIONS – See Lloyd COLE and the COMMOTIONS

COMMUNARDS UK, male vocal/instrumental duo   74 wks

2 Aug 86	● **COMMUNARDS** London LONLP 18	7	45 wks
17 Oct 87	● **RED** London LONLP 39	4	29 wks

Perry COMO US, male vocalist   191 wks

8 Nov 58	● **DEAR PERRY** RCA RD 27078	6	5 wks
31 Jan 59	● **COMO'S GOLDEN RECORDS** RCA RD 27100	4	5 wks
10 Apr 71	**IT'S IMPOSSIBLE** RCA Victor SF 8175	13	13 wks
7 Jul 73	★ **AND I LOVE YOU SO** RCA Victor SF 8360	1	109 wks
24 Aug 74	**PERRY** RCA Victor APLI 0585	26	3 wks
19 Apr 75	**MEMORIES ARE MADE OF HITS** RCA Victor RS 1005 ..	14	16 wks

| 25 Oct 75 | ★ **40 GREATEST HITS** *K-Tel NE 700* .... | **1** | 34 wks |
| 3 Dec 83 | **FOR THE GOOD TIMES** *Telstar STAR 2235* .... | **41** | 6 wks |

COMPILATION ALBUMS – *See VARIOUS ARTISTS*

COMSAT ANGELS *UK, male vocal/instrumental group*   *9 wks*

5 Sep 81	**SLEEP NO MORE** *Polydor POLS 1038*	**51**	5 wks
18 Sep 82	**FICTION** *Polydor POLS 1075*	**94**	2 wks
8 Oct 83	**LAND** *Jive HIP 8*	**91**	2 wks

Harry CONNICK Jr
US, male vocalist/instrumentalist – piano   *56 wks*

| 22 Sep 90 | ● **WE ARE IN LOVE** *CBS 4667361* .... | **7** | 46 wks |
| 26 Oct 91 | **BLUE LIGHT RED LIGHT** *Columbia 4690871* .... | **16†** | 10 wks |

Ray CONNIFF *US, male orchestra leader*   *96 wks*

28 May 60	**IT'S THE TALK OF THE TOWN** *Philips BBL 7354*	**15**	1 wk
25 Jun 60	**S'AWFUL NICE** *Philips BBL 7281*	**13**	1 wk
26 Nov 60	● **HI-FI COMPANION ALBUM** *Philips BET 101*	**3**	44 wks
20 May 61	**MEMORIES ARE MADE OF THIS** *Philips BBL 7439*	**14**	4 wks
29 Dec 62	**WE WISH YOU A MERRY CHRISTMAS** *CBS BPG 62092*	**12**	1 wk
29 Dec 62	**'S WONDERFUL 'S MARVELLOUS** *CBS DPG 66001* ..	**18**	3 wks
16 Apr 66	**HI-FI COMPANION ALBUM (re-issue)** *CBS DP 66011* .	**24**	4 wks
9 Sep 67	**SOMEWHERE MY LOVE** *CBS SBPG 62740*	**34**	3 wks
21 Jun 69	★ **HIS ORCHESTRA, HIS CHORUS, HIS SINGERS, HIS SOUND** *CBS SPR 27*	**1**	16 wks
23 May 70	**BRIDGE OVER TROUBLED WATER** *CBS 64020*	**30**	14 wks
12 Jun 71	**LOVE STORY** *CBS 64294*	**34**	1 wk
19 Feb 72	**I'D LIKE TO TEACH THE WORLD TO SING** *CBS 64449*	**17**	4 wks

99

C

Billy CONNOLLY *UK, male vocalist*   *108 wks*

20 Jul 74	● **SOLO CONCERT** *Transatlantic TRA 279*	**8**	33 wks
18 Jan 75	● **COP YER WHACK OF THIS** *Polydor 2383 310*	**10**	29 wks
20 Sep 75	**WORDS AND MUSIC** *Transatlantic TRA SAM 32*	**34**	10 wks
6 Dec 75	● **GET RIGHT INTAE HIM** *Polydor 2383 368*	**6**	14 wks
11 Dec 76	**ATLANTIC BRIDGE** *Polydor 2383 419*	**20**	9 wks
28 Jan 78	**RAW MEAT FOR THE BALCONY** *Polydor 2383 463*	**57**	3 wks
5 Dec 81	**PICK OF BILLY CONNOLLY** *Polydor POLTV 15*	**23**	8 wks
5 Dec 87	**BILLY AND ALBERT** *10 DIX 65*	**81**	2 wks

Russ CONWAY *UK, male instrumentalist – piano*   *69 wks*

22 Nov 58	● **PACK UP YOUR TROUBLES** *Columbia 33SX 1120*	**9**	5 wks
2 May 59	● **SONGS TO SING IN YOUR BATH** *Columbia 33SX 1149* .	**8**	10 wks
19 Sep 59	● **FAMILY FAVOURITES** *Columbia 33SX 1169*	**3**	16 wks
19 Dec 59	● **TIME TO CELEBRATE** *Columbia 33SX 1197*	**3**	7 wks
26 Mar 60	● **MY CONCERTO FOR YOU** *Columbia 33SX 1214*	**5**	17 wks
17 Dec 60	● **PARTY TIME** *Columbia 33SX 1279*	**7**	11 wks
23 Apr 77	**RUSS CONWAY PRESENTS 24 PIANO GREATS** *Ronco RTL 2022*	**25**	3 wks

Ry COODER *US, male vocalist/instrumentalist – guitar*   *30 wks*

11 Aug 79	**BOP TILL YOU DROP** *Warner Bros. K 56691*	**36**	9 wks
18 Oct 80	**BORDER LINE** *Warner Bros. K 56864*	**35**	6 wks
24 Apr 82	**THE SLIDE AREA** *Warner Bros. K 56976*	**18**	12 wks
14 Nov 87	**GET RHYTHM** *Warner Bros. WX 121*	**75**	3 wks

Peter COOK and Dudley MOORE
UK, male comedy duo   *34 wks*

21 May 66	**ONCE MOORE WITH COOK** *Decca LK 4785*	**25**	1 wk
18 Sep 76	**DEREK AND CLIVE LIVE** *Island ILPS 9434*	**12**	25 wks
24 Dec 77	**COME AGAIN** *Virgin V 2094*	**18**	8 wks

See also Dudley Moore.

Sam COOKE   *US, male vocalist*   *27 wks*

26 Apr 86	● **THE MAN AND HIS MUSIC** *RCA PL 87127*	**8**	27 wks

COOKIE CREW   *UK, female vocal duo*   *4 wks*

6 May 89	**BORN THIS WAY!** *London 828134 1*	**24**	4 wks

Rita COOLIDGE   *US, female vocalist*   *40 wks*

6 Aug 77	● **ANYTIME ANYWHERE** *A & M AMLH 64616*	**6**	28 wks
8 Jul 78	**LOVE ME AGAIN** *A & M AMLH 64699*	**51**	1 wk
14 Mar 81	● **VERY BEST OF** *A & M AMLH 68520*	**6**	11 wks

See also Kris Kristofferson and Rita Coolidge.

COOL NOTES   *UK, male/female vocal/instrumental group*   *2 wks*

9 Nov 85	**HAVE A GOOD FOREVER** *Abstract Dance ADLP 1*	**66**	2 wks

Alice COOPER   *US, male vocalist*   *122 wks*

5 Feb 72	**KILLER** *Warner Bros. K 56005*	**27**	18 wks
22 Jul 72	● **SCHOOL'S OUT** *Warner Bros. K 56007*	**4**	20 wks
9 Sep 72	**LOVE IT TO DEATH** *Warner Bros. K 46177*	**28**	7 wks
24 Mar 73	★ **BILLION DOLLAR BABIES** *Warner Bros. K 56013*	**1**	23 wks
12 Jan 74	**MUSCLE OF LOVE** *Warner Bros. K 56018*	**34**	4 wks
15 Mar 75	**WELCOME TO MY NIGHTMARE** *Anchor ANCL 2011* ..	**19**	8 wks
24 Jul 76	**ALICE COOPER GOES TO HELL** *Warner Bros. K 56171* .	**23**	7 wks
28 May 77	**LACE AND WHISKY** *Warner Bros. K 56365*	**33**	3 wks
23 Dec 78	**FROM THE INSIDE** *Warner Bros. K 56577*	**68**	3 wks
17 May 80	**FLUSH THE FASHION** *Warner Bros. K 56805*	**56**	3 wks
12 Sep 81	**SPECIAL FORCES** *Warner Bros. K 56927*	**96**	1 wk
12 Nov 83	**DADA** *Warner Bros. 92–3969–1*	**93**	1 wk
1 Nov 86	**CONSTRICTOR** *MCA MCF 3341*	**41**	2 wks
7 Nov 87	**RAISE YOUR FIST AND YELL** *MCA MCF 3392*	**48**	3 wks
26 Aug 89	● **TRASH** *Epic 465130 1*	**2**	12 wks
13 Jul 91	● **HEY STOOPID** *Epic 4684161*	**4**	7 wks

Alice Cooper was US, male vocal/instrumental group for first five albums.

Julian COPE   *UK, male vocalist*   *24 wks*

3 Mar 84	**WORLD SHUT YOUR MOUTH** *Mercury MERL 37*	**40**	4 wks
24 Nov 84	**FRIED** *Mercury MERL 48*	**87**	1 wk
14 Mar 87	**SAINT JULIAN** *Island ILPS 9861*	**11**	10 wks
29 Oct 88	**MY NATION UNDERGROUND** *Island ILPS 9918*	**42**	2 wks
16 Mar 91	**PEGGY SUICIDE** *Island ILPSD 9977*	**23**	7 wks

Harry H. CORBETT – *See Wilfred BRAMBELL and Harry H. CORBETT*

Hugh CORNWELL *UK, male vocalist* — 1 wk

18 Jun 88	**WOLF** *Virgin V 2420*	98	1 wk

CORRIES *UK, male vocal/instrumental duo* — 5 wks

9 May 70	**SCOTTISH LOVE SONGS** *Fontana 6309–004*	46	4 wks
16 Sep 72	**SOUND OF PIBROCH** *Columbia SCX 6511*	39	1 wk

Elvis COSTELLO and the ATTRACTIONS
UK, male vocalist and male vocal/instrumental group — 182 wks

6 Aug 77	**MY AIM IS TRUE** *Stiff SEEZ 3*	14	12 wks
1 Apr 78	● **THIS YEAR'S MODEL** *Radar RAD 3*	4	14 wks
20 Jan 79	● **ARMED FORCES** *Radar RAD 14*	2	28 wks
23 Feb 80	● **GET HAPPY** *F-Beat XXLP 1*	2	14 wks
31 Jan 81	● **TRUST** *F-Beat XXLP 11*	9	7 wks
31 Oct 81	● **ALMOST BLUE** *F-Beat XXLP 13*	7	18 wks
10 Jul 82	● **IMPERIAL BEDROOM** *F-Beat XXLP 17*	6	12 wks
6 Aug 83	● **PUNCH THE CLOCK** *F-Beat XXLP 19*	3	13 wks
7 Jul 84	● **GOODBYE CRUEL WORLD** *F-Beat ZL 70317*	10	10 wks
20 Apr 85	● **THE BEST OF ELVIS COSTELLO – THE MAN** *Telstar STAR 2247*	8	17 wks
1 May 86	**KING OF AMERICA** *F-Beat ZL 70496*	11	9 wks
27 Sep 86	**BLOOD AND CHOCOLATE** *Imp XFIEND 80*	16	5 wks
18 Feb 89	● **SPIKE** *Warner Bros. WX 238*	5	16 wks
28 Oct 89	**GIRLS GIRLS GIRLS** *Demon DFIEND 160*	67	1 wk
25 May 91	● **MIGHTY LIKE A ROSE** *Warner Bros. WX 419*	5	6 wks

My Aim Is True, This Year's Model, Trust *and* The Best of Elvis Costello – The Man *are credited to* Elvis Costello *only.* King of America *credited to* Costello Show – Elvis *and a US backing band.*

101

C

John COUGAR – *See John Cougar MELLENCAMP*

Phil COULTER
Ireland, male orchestra leader/instrumentalist – piano — 15 wks

13 Oct 84	**SEA OF TRANQUILLITY** *K-Tel Ireland KLP 185*	46	14 wks
18 May 85	**PHIL COULTER'S IRELAND** *K-Tel ONE 1296*	86	1 wk

David COVERDALE *UK, male vocalist* — 1 wk

27 Feb 82	**NORTHWINDS** *Purple TTS 3513*	78	1 wk

COWBOY JUNKIES
US, male/female vocal/instrumental group — 4 wks

24 Mar 90	**THE CAUTION HORSES** *RCA PL 90450*	33	4 wks

CRAMPS *US, male/female vocal/instrumental group* — 13 wks

25 Jun 83	**OFF THE BONE** *Illegal ILP 012*	44	4 wks
26 Nov 83	**SMELL OF FEMALE** *Big Beat NED 6*	74	2 wks
1 Mar 86	**A DATE WITH ELVIS** *Big Beat WIKA 46*	34	6 wks
24 Feb 90	**STAY SICK!** *Enigma ENVLP 1001*	62	1 wk

CRANES *UK, male vocal/instrumental group* — 1 wk

28 Sep 91	**WINGS OF JOY** *Dedicated DEDLP 003*	52	1 wk

CRASS *UK, male vocal/instrumental group* *2 wks*

28 Aug 82 **CHRIST THE ALBUM** *Crass BOLLOX 2U2* .... 26 2 wks

Beverley CRAVEN
UK, female vocalist/instrumentalist – piano *33 wks*

2 Mar 91 ● **BEVERLEY CRAVEN** *Columbia 4670531* .... 3† 33 wks

Michael CRAWFORD *UK, male vocalist* *28 wks*

28 Nov 87 **SONGS FROM THE STAGE AND SCREEN**
　　　　　　　Telstar STAR 2308 .... 12 13 wks
2 Dec 89 **WITH LOVE** *Telstar STAR 2340* .... 31 7 wks
9 Nov 91 ● **PERFORMS ANDREW LLOYD WEBBER**
　　　　　　　Telstar STAR 2544 .... 3† 8 wks

Songs From The Stage And Screen *credits the London Symphony Orchestra. See also the London Symphony Orchestra.*

Randy CRAWFORD *US, female vocalist* *138 wks*

28 Jun 80 ● **NOW WE MAY BEGIN** *Warner Bros. K 56791* .... 10 16 wks
16 May 81 ● **SECRET COMBINATION** *Warner Bros. K 56904* .... 2 60 wks
12 Jun 82 ● **WINDSONG** *Warner Bros. K 57011* .... 7 17 wks
22 Oct 83 **NIGHTLINE** *Warner Bros. 92–3976–1* .... 37 4 wks
13 Oct 84 ● **MISS RANDY CRAWFORD – THE GREATEST HITS**
　　　　　　　K-Tel NE 1281 .... 10 17 wks
28 Jun 86 **ABSTRACT EMOTIONS** *Warner Bros. WX 46* .... 14 10 wks
10 Oct 87 **THE LOVE SONGS** *Telstar STAR 2299* .... 27 13 wks
21 Oct 89 **RICH AND POOR** *Warner Bros. WX 308* .... 63 1 wk

Robert CRAY BAND *US, male vocal/instrumental group* *48 wks*

12 Oct 85 **FALSE ACCUSATIONS** *Demon FIEND 43* .... 68 1 wk
15 Nov 86 **STRONG PERSUADER** *Mercury MERH 97* .... 34 28 wks
3 Sep 88 **DON'T BE AFRAID OF THE DARK** *Mercury MERH 129* . 13 12 wks
22 Sep 90 **MIDNIGHT STROLL** *Mercury 8466521* .... 19 7 wks

CRAZY HORSE – *See Neil YOUNG*

CRAZY WORLD – *See Crazy World of Arthur BROWN*

CREAM *UK, male vocal/instrumental group* *182 wks*

24 Dec 66 ● **FRESH CREAM** *Reaction 593–001* .... 6 17 wks
18 Nov 67 ● **DISRAELI GEARS** *Reaction 594–003* .... 5 42 wks
17 Aug 68 ● **WHEELS OF FIRE (double)** *Polydor 583–031/2* .... 3 26 wks
17 Aug 68 ● **WHEELS OF FIRE (single)** *Polydor 583–033* .... 7 13 wks
8 Feb 69 ● **FRESH CREAM (re-issue)** *Reaction 594–001* .... 7 2 wks
15 Mar 69 ★ **GOODBYE** *Polydor 583–053* .... 1 28 wks
8 Nov 69 ● **BEST OF CREAM** *Polydor 583–060* .... 6 34 wks
4 Jul 70 ● **LIVE CREAM** *Polydor 2383–016* .... 4 15 wks
24 Jun 72 **LIVE CREAM VOL. 2** *Polydor 2383 119* .... 15 5 wks

See also Eric Clapton and Cream.

CREATURES *UK, male/female vocal/instrumental duo* *9 wks*

28 May 83 **FEAST** *Wonderland SHELP 1* .... 17 9 wks

The **Cramps** keep a date with the photographer in 1979.

Culture Club attend the *TV Times* awards in February 1984.

Crosby, Stills, Nash and Young line up as (from left) Stephen Stills, David Crosby, Graham Nash and Neil Young.

CREEDENCE CLEARWATER REVIVAL
US, male vocal/instrumental group   *65 wks*

24 Jan 70	**GREEN RIVER** *Liberty LBS 83273*	20	6 wks
28 Mar 70 ●	**WILLY AND THE POOR BOYS** *Liberty LBS 83338*	10	24 wks
2 May 70	**BAYOU COUNTRY** *Liberty LBS 83261*	62	1 wk
12 Sep 70 ★	**COSMO'S FACTORY** *Liberty LBS 83388*	1	15 wks
23 Jan 71	**PENDULUM** *Liberty LBG 83400*	23	12 wks
30 Jun 79	**GREATEST HITS** *Fantasy FT 558*	35	5 wks
19 Oct 85	**THE CREEDENCE COLLECTION** *Impression IMDP 3* ..	68	2 wks

CREME – *See GODLEY and CREME*

Kid CREOLE and the COCONUTS
US, male/female vocal/instrumental group   *54 wks*

22 May 82 ●	**TROPICAL GANGSTERS** *Ze ILPS 7016*	3	40 wks
26 Jun 82	**FRESH FRUIT IN FOREIGN PLACES** *Ze ILPS 7014* ...	99	1 wk
17 Sep 83	**DOPPELGANGER** *Island ILPS 9743*	21	6 wks
15 Sep 84	**CRE-OLE** *Island IMA 13*	21	7 wks

Bernard CRIBBINS – *See Howard BLAKE conducting the SINFONIA OF LONDON*

CRICKETS *US, male vocal/instrumental group*   *7 wks*

25 Mar 61	**IN STYLE WITH THE CRICKETS** *Coral LVA 9142*	13	7 wks

See also Buddy Holly and the Crickets; Bobby Vee and the Crickets.

Bing CROSBY *US, male vocalist*   *42 wks*

8 Oct 60 ●	**JOIN BING AND SING ALONG** *Warner Brothers WM 4021*	7	11 wks
21 Dec 74	**WHITE CHRISTMAS** *MCA MCF 2568*	45	3 wks
20 Sep 75	**THAT'S WHAT LIFE IS ALL ABOUT**		
	United Artists UAG 2973	28	6 wks
5 Nov 77	**THE BEST OF BING** *MCA MCF 2540*	41	7 wks
5 Nov 77 ●	**LIVE AT THE LONDON PALLADIUM** *K-Tel NE 951* ..	9	2 wks
17 Dec 77	**SEASONS** *Polydor 2442 151*	25	7 wks
5 May 79	**SONGS OF A LIFETIME** *Philips 6641 923*	29	3 wks
14 Dec 91	**CHRISTMAS WITH BING CROSBY** *Telstar STAR 2468*	66†	3 wks

Dave CROSBY *US, male vocalist*   *7 wks*

24 Apr 71	**IF ONLY I COULD REMEMBER MY NAME**		
	Atlantic 2401-005	12	7 wks

See also Crosby, Stills and Nash; Crosby, Stills, Nash and Young; Graham Nash and David Crosby.

CROSBY, STILLS and NASH
US/UK, male vocal/instrumental group   *14 wks*

23 Aug 69	**CROSBY STILLS AND NASH** *Atlantic 588–189*	25	5 wks
9 Jul 77	**CSN** *Atlantic K 50369*	23	9 wks

See also Dave Crosby; Crosby, Stills, Nash and Young; Graham Nash; Stephen Stills.

CROSBY, STILLS, NASH and YOUNG
US/UK/Canada, male vocal/instrumental group   *79 wks*

30 May 70 ●	**DEJA VU** *Atlantic 2401-001*	5	61 wks
22 May 71 ●	**FOUR-WAY STREET** *Atlantic 2956 004*	5	12 wks

21 Sep 74   **SO FAR** *Atlantic K 50023* ....   **25**   6 wks

See also Dave Crosby; Crosby, Stills and Nash; Graham Nash; Stephen Stills; Neil Young.

CROSS *UK/US, male vocal/instrumental group*   *2 wks*

6 Feb 88   **SHOVE IT** *Virgin V 2477* ....   **58**   2 wks

Christopher CROSS *US, male vocalist*   *93 wks*

21 Feb 81   **CHRISTOPHER CROSS** *Warner Bros. K 56789* ....   **14**   77 wks
19 Feb 83 ● **ANOTHER PAGE** *Warner Bros. W 3757* ....   **4**   16 wks

CROWDED HOUSE
Australia/New Zealand, male vocal/instrumental group   *4 wks*

13 Jul 91   **WOODFACE** *Capitol EST 2144* ....   **34**   4 wks

CROWN HEIGHTS AFFAIR
US, male vocal/instrumental group   *3 wks*

23 Sep 78   **DREAM WORLD** *Philips 6372 754* ....   **40**   3 wks

CRUSADERS *US, male vocal/instrumental group*   *30 wks*

21 Jul 79 ● **STREET LIFE** *MCA MCF 3008* ....   **10**   16 wks
19 Jul 80   **RHAPSODY AND BLUE** *MCA MCG 4010* ....   **40**   5 wks
12 Sep 81   **STANDING TALL** *MCA MCF 3122* ....   **47**   5 wks
7 Apr 84   **GHETTO BLASTER** *MCA MCF 3176* ....   **46**   4 wks

105

C

Bobby CRUSH *UK, male instrumentalist – piano*   *12 wks*

29 Nov 72   **BOBBY CRUSH** *Philips 6308 135* ....   **15**   7 wks
18 Dec 82   **THE BOBBY CRUSH INCREDIBLE DOUBLE DECKER**
          PARTY *Warwick WW 5126/7* ....   **53**   5 wks

CUDDLES – *See Keith HARRIS, ORVILLE and CUDDLES*

CULT *UK, male vocal/instrumental group*   *75 wks*

18 Jun 83   **SOUTHERN DEATH CULT** *Beggars Banquet BEGA 46* ...   **43**   3 wks
8 Sep 84   **DREAMTIME** *Beggars Banquet BEGA 57* ....   **21**   8 wks
26 Oct 85 ● **LOVE** *Beggars Banquet BEGA 65* ....   **4**   22 wks
18 Apr 87 ● **ELECTRIC** *Beggars Banquet BEGA 80* ....   **4**   27 wks
22 Apr 89 ● **SONIC TEMPLE** *Beggars Banquet BEGA 98* ....   **3**   11 wks
5 Oct 91 ● **CEREMONY** *Beggars Banquet BEGA 122* ....   **9**   4 wks

First album credited to Southern Death Cult.

CULT JAM – *See LISA LISA and CULT JAM with FULL FORCE*

CULTURE *Jamaica, male vocal/instrumental group*   *1 wk*

1 Apr 78   **TWO SEVENS CLASH** *Lightning LIP 1* ....   **60**   1 wk

CULTURE CLUB *UK, male vocal/instrumental group*   *144 wks*

16 Oct 82 ● **KISSING TO BE CLEVER** *Virgin V 2232* ....   **5**   59 wks
22 Oct 83 ★ **COLOUR BY NUMBERS** *Virgin V 2285* ....   **1**   56 wks

3 Nov 84 ● **WAKING UP WITH THE HOUSE ON FIRE**			
Virgin V 2330		2	13 wks
12 Apr 86 ● **FROM LUXURY TO HEARTACHE** *Virgin V 2380*		10	6 wks
18 Apr 87 ● **THIS TIME** *Virgin VTV 1*		8	10 wks

CURE   *UK, male vocal/instrumental group*   *176 wks*

2 Jun 79	**THREE IMAGINARY BOYS** *Fiction FIX 001*	44	3 wks
3 May 80	**17 SECONDS** *Fiction FIX 004*	20	10 wks
25 Apr 81	**FAITH** *Fiction FIX 6*	14	8 wks
15 May 82 ●	**PORNOGRAPHY** *Fiction FIX D7*	8	9 wks
3 Sep 83	**BOYS DON'T CRY** *Fiction SPELP 26*	71	7 wks
24 Dec 83	**JAPANESE WHISPERS** *Fiction FIXM 8*	26	14 wks
12 May 84 ●	**THE TOP** *Fiction FIXS 9*	10	10 wks
3 Nov 84	**CONCERT – THE CURE LIVE** *Fiction FIXH 10*	26	4 wks
7 Sep 85 ●	**THE HEAD ON THE DOOR** *Fiction FIXH 11*	7	13 wks
31 May 86 ●	**STANDING ON A BEACH – THE SINGLES**		
	Fiction FIXH 12	4	35 wks
6 Jun 87 ●	**KISS ME KISS ME KISS ME** *Fiction FIXH 13*	6	15 wks
13 May 89 ●	**DISINTEGRATION** *Fiction FIXH 14*	3	26 wks
17 Nov 90 ●	**MIXED UP** *Fiction 8470991*	8	17 wks
6 Apr 91 ●	**ENTREAT** *Fiction FIXH 17*	10	5 wks

The compact disc version of FIXH 12 was titled Staring At The Sea.

CURIOSITY KILLED THE CAT
UK, male vocal/instrumental group   *27 wks*

9 May 87 ★	**KEEP YOUR DISTANCE** *Mercury CATLP 1*	1	24 wks
4 Oct 89	**GET AHEAD** *Mercury 842010 1*	29	3 wks

106

d

CURVED AIR   *UK, male/female vocal/instrumental group*   *32 wks*

5 Dec 70 ●	**AIR CONDITIONING** *Warner Bros. WSX 3012*	8	21 wks
9 Oct 71	**CURVED AIR** *Warner Bros. K 46092*	11	6 wks
13 May 72	**PHANTASMAGORIA** *Reprise K 46158*	20	5 wks

Adge CUTLER and the WURZELS
UK, male vocal/instrumental group   *4 wks*

11 Mar 67	**ADGE CUTLER AND THE WURZELS**		
	Columbia SX 6126	38	4 wks

See also the Wurzels.

CUTTING CREW   *UK/Canada, male vocal/instrumental group*   *6 wks*

29 Nov 86	**BROADCAST** *Siren SIRENLP 7*	41	6 wks

Holger CZUKAY – *See David SYLVIAN and Holger CZUKAY*

d

Heavy D and the BOYZ
US, male vocal/instrumental group   *3 wks*

10 Aug 91	**A PEACEFUL JOURNEY** *MCA MCA 10289*	40	3 wks

D. MOB *UK, male producer, Danny D*   *11 wks*

11 Nov 89	**A LITTLE BIT OF THIS A LITTLE BIT OF THAT**		
	FFRR 8281591	46	11 wks

DAINTEES – *See Martin STEPHENSON and the DAINTEES*

DAKOTAS – *See Billy J. KRAMER and the DAKOTAS*

DALEK I *UK, male vocal/instrumental group*   *2 wks*

9 Aug 80	**COMPASS KUMPAS** *Backdoor OPEN 1*	54	2 wks

DALI'S CAR *UK, male vocal/instrumental duo*   *1 wk*

1 Dec 84	**THE WAKING HOUR** *Paradox DOXLP 1*	84	1 wk

Roger DALTREY *UK, male vocalist*   *24 wks*

26 Jul 75	**RIDE A ROCK HORSE** *Polydor 2660 111*	14	10 wks
4 Jul 77	**ONE OF THE BOYS** *Polydor 2442 146*	45	1 wk
23 Aug 80	**McVICAR (film soundtrack)** *Polydor POLD 5034*	39	11 wks
2 Nov 85	**UNDER A RAGING MOON** *10 DIX 17*	52	2 wks

Glen DALY *UK, male vocalist*   *2 wks*

20 Nov 71	**GLASGOW NIGHT OUT** *Golden Guinea GGL 0479*	28	2 wks

107

d

DAMNED *UK, male vocal/instrumental group*   *54 wks*

12 Mar 77	**DAMNED DAMNED DAMNED** *Stiff SEEZ 1*	36	10 wks
17 Nov 79	**MACHINE GUN ETIQUETTE** *Chiswick CWK 3011*	31	5 wks
29 Nov 80	**THE BLACK ALBUM** *Chiswick CWK 3015*	29	3 wks
28 Nov 81	**BEST OF** *Chiswick DAM 1*	43	12 wks
23 Oct 82	**STRAWBERRIES** *Bronze BRON 542*	15	4 wks
27 Jul 85	**PHANTASMAGORIA** *MCA MCF 3275*	11	17 wks
13 Dec 86	**ANYTHING** *MCA MCG 6015*	40	2 wks
12 Dec 87	**LIGHT AT THE END OF THE TUNNEL**		
	MCA MCSP 312	87	1 wk

Vic DAMONE *US, male vocalist*   *8 wks*

25 Apr 81	**NOW!** *RCA INTS 5080*	28	7 wks
2 Apr 83	**VIC DAMONE SINGS THE GREAT SONGS** *CBS 32261* .	87	1 wk

DANA *Ireland, female vocalist*   *2 wks*

3 Jan 81	**EVERYTHING IS BEAUTIFUL** *Warwick WW 5099*	43	2 wks

Suzanne DANDO *UK, female exercise instructor*   *1 wk*

17 Mar 84	**SHAPE UP AND DANCE WITH SUZANNE DANDO**		
	Lifestyle LEG 21	87	1 wk

Charlie DANIELS BAND
US, male vocal/instrumental group   *1 wk*

10 Nov 79	**MILLION MILE REFLECTIONS** *Epic EPC 83446*	74	1 wk

Doris Day didn't have her day in the album chart until years after her singles successes.

Roger Daltrey is shown, uncharacteristically, playing guitar.

DANNY WILSON *UK, male vocal/instrumental group* *11 wks*

30 Apr	88	**MEET DANNY WILSON** *Virgin V 2419*	65	5 wks
29 Jul	89	**BEEBOP MOPTOP** *Virgin V 2594*	24	5 wks
31 Aug	91	**SWEET DANNY WILSON** *Virgin V 2669*	54	1 wk

DANSE SOCIETY *UK, male vocal/instrumental group* *4 wks*

| 11 Feb | 84 | **HEAVEN IS WAITING** *Society 205 972* .... | 39 | 4 wks |

Stephen DANTE *UK, male vocalist* *1 wk*

| 3 Sep | 88 | **FIND OUT** *Cooltempo CTLP 6* .... | 87 | 1 wk |

Terence Trent D'ARBY *US, male vocalist* *70 wks*

| 25 Jul | 87 | ★ **INTRODUCING THE HARDLINE ACCORDING TO** **TERENCE TRENT D'ARBY** *CBS 450 911-1* .... | 1 | 65 wks |
| 4 Nov | 89 | **NEITHER FISH NOR FLESH** *CBS 4658091* .... | 12 | 5 wks |

DARE *UK, male vocal/instrumental group* *1 wk*

| 14 Sep | 91 | **BLOOD FROM STONE** *A & M 3953601* .... | 48 | 1 wk |

Bobby DARIN *US, male vocalist* *15 wks*

19 Mar	60	● **THIS IS DARIN** *London HA 2235*	4	8 wks
9 Apr	60	**THAT'S ALL** *London HAE 2172*	15	1 wk
5 Oct	85	**THE LEGEND OF BOBBY DARIN – HIS GREATEST** **HITS** *Stylus SMR 8504*	39	6 wks

109

d

DARLING BUDS *UK, male/female vocal/instrumental group* *3 wks*

| 18 Feb | 89 | **POP SAID** *Epic 462894 1* .... | 23 | 3 wks |

DARTS *UK, male/female vocal/instrumental group* *57 wks*

3 Dec	77	● **DARTS** *Magnet MAG 5020*	9	22 wks
3 Jun	78	**EVERYONE PLAYS DARTS** *Magnet MAG 5022*	12	18 wks
18 Nov	78	● **AMAZING DARTS** *K-Tel/Magnet DLP 7981*	8	13 wks
6 Oct	79	**DART ATTACK** *Magnet MAG 5030*	38	4 wks

F.R. DAVID *France, male vocalist* *6 wks*

| 7 May | 83 | **WORDS** *Carrere CAL 145* .... | 46 | 6 wks |

Windsor DAVIES – *See Don ESTELLE and Windsor DAVIES*

Colin DAVIS – *See BBC SYMPHONY ORCHESTRA*

Carl DAVIS and the ROYAL LIVERPOOL PHILHARMONIC ORCHESTRA
US, male conductor and orchestra *4 wks*

| 19 Oct | 91 | **PAUL McCARTNEY'S LIVERPOOL ORATORIO** *EMI Classics PAUL 1* .... | 36 | 4 wks |

Miles DAVIS *US, male instrumentalist – trumpet*   *6 wks*

11 Jul 70	**BITCHES BREW** *CBS 66236*	71	1 wk
15 Jun 85	**YOU'RE UNDER ARREST** *CBS 26447*	88	1 wk
18 Oct 86	**TUTU** *Warner Bros. 925490 1*	74	2 wks
3 Jun 89	**AMANDLA** *Warner Bros. WX 250*	49	2 wks

Sammy DAVIS Jr *US, male vocalist*   *1 wk*

13 Apr 63	**SAMMY DAVIS JR. AT THE COCONUT GROVE** *Reprise R 6063/2*	19	1 wk

Spencer DAVIS GROUP
UK, male vocal/instrumental group   *47 wks*

8 Jan 66	● **THEIR 1ST LP** *Fontana TL 5242*	6	9 wks
22 Jan 66	● **THE 2ND LP** *Fontana TL 5295*	3	18 wks
11 Sep 66	● **AUTUMN '66** *Fontana TL 5359*	4	20 wks

DAWN *US, male/female vocal group*   *2 wks*

4 May 74	**GOLDEN RIBBONS** *Bell BELLS 236*	46	2 wks

Doris DAY *US, female vocalist*   *20 wks*

110

6 Jan 79	**20 GOLDEN GREATS** *Warwick PR 5053*	12	11 wks
11 Nov 89	**A PORTRAIT OF DORIS DAY** *Stylus SMR 984*	32	9 wks

d

Taylor DAYNE *US, female vocalist*   *17 wks*

5 Mar 88	**TELL IT TO MY HEART** *Arista 208898*	24	17 wks

Chris DE BURGH *Ireland, male vocalist*   *238 wks*

12 Sep 81	**BEST MOVES** *A & M AMLH 68532*	65	4 wks
9 Oct 82	**THE GETAWAY** *A & M AMLH 68549*	30	16 wks
19 May 84	**MAN ON THE LINE** *A & M AMLX 65002*	11	24 wks
29 Dec 84	● **THE VERY BEST OF CHRIS DE BURGH** *Telstar STAR 2248*	6	70 wks
24 Aug 85	**SPANISH TRAIN AND OTHER STORIES** *A & M AMLH 68343*	78	3 wks
7 Jun 86	● **INTO THE LIGHT** *A & M AM 5121*	2	59 wks
4 Oct 86	**CRUSADER** *A & M AMLH 64746*	72	1 wk
15 Oct 88	★ **FLYING COLOURS** *A & M AMA 5224*	1	30 wks
4 Nov 89	● **FROM A SPARK TO A FLAME – THE VERY BEST OF CHRIS DE BURGH** *A & M CDBLP 100*	4	25 wks
22 Sep 90	**HIGH ON EMOTION – LIVE FROM DUBLIN** *A & M 3970861*	15	6 wks

DE LA SOUL *US, male rap/sampling group*   *68 wks*

25 Mar 89	**3 FEET HIGH AND RISING** *Big Life DLSLP 1*	13	57 wks
25 May 91	● **DE LA SOUL IS DEAD** *Big Life BLRLP 8*	7	11 wks

Waldo DE LOS RIOS *Argentina, orchestra*   *26 wks*

1 May 71	● **SYMPHONIES FOR THE SEVENTIES** *A & M AMLS 2014*	6	26 wks

Sacha Distel was the top charting French male vocalist until overtaken by Charles Aznavour.

This young man with a horn is all-time jazz great **Miles Davis**.

Manitas DE PLATA *Spain, male instrumentalist – guitar* *1 wk*

29 Jul	67	**FLAMENCO GUITAR** *Philips SBL 7786*	**40**	1 wk

DEACON BLUE *UK, male/female vocal/instrumental group* *162 wks*

6 Jun	87	**RAINTOWN** *CBS 4505491*	**14**	77 wks
15 Apr	89	★ **WHEN THE WORLD KNOWS YOUR NAME**		
		CBS 4633211	**1**	54 wks
22 Sep	90	● **OOH LAS VEGAS** *CBS 4672421*	**3**	8 wks
15 Jun	91	● **FELLOW HOODLUMS** *Columbia 4685501*	**2**	23 wks

DEAD KENNEDYS *US, male vocal/instrumental group* *8 wks*

13 Sep	80	**FRESH FRUIT FOR ROTTING VEGETABLES**		
		Cherry Red BRED 10	**33**	6 wks
4 Jul	87	**GIVE ME CONVENIENCE** *Alternative Tentacles VIRUS 5* .	**84**	2 wks

DEAD OR ALIVE *UK, male vocal/instrumental group* *22 wks*

28 Apr	84	**SOPHISTICATED BOOM BOOM** *Epic EPC 25835*	**29**	3 wks
25 May	85	● **YOUTHQUAKE** *Epic EPC 26420*	**9**	15 wks
14 Feb	87	**MAD, BAD AND DANGEROUS TO KNOW**		
		Epic 450 257-1	**27**	4 wks

DEAN – *See JAN and DEAN*

Hazell DEAN *UK, female vocalist* *3 wks*

22 Oct	88	**ALWAYS** *EMI EMC 3546*	**38**	3 wks

DeBARGE *US, male/female vocal group* *2 wks*

25 May	85	**RHYTHM OF THE NIGHT** *Gordy ZL 72340*	**94**	2 wks

Kiki DEE *UK, female vocalist* *9 wks*

26 Mar	77	**KIKI DEE** *Rocket ROLA 3*	**24**	5 wks
18 Jul	81	**PERFECT TIMING** *Ariola ARL 5050*	**47**	4 wks

Dave DEE, DOZY, BEAKY, MICK and TICH
UK, male vocal/instrumental group *15 wks*

2 Jul	66	**DAVE DEE, DOZY, BEAKY, MICK AND TICH**		
		Fontana STL 5350	**11**	10 wks
7 Jan	67	**IF MUSIC BE THE FOOD OF LOVE . . . PREPARE FOR**		
		INDIGESTION *Fontana STL 5388*	**27**	5 wks

DEEE-LITE *US, male/female vocal/instrumental group* *18 wks*

8 Sep	90	**WORLD CLIQUE** *Elektra EKT 77*	**14**	18 wks

DEEP PURPLE *UK, male vocal/instrumental group* *271 wks*

24 Jan	70	**CONCERTO FOR GROUP AND ORCHESTRA**		
		Harvest SHVL 767	**26**	4 wks

20 Jun	70	● DEEP PURPLE IN ROCK *Harvest SHVL 777*	4	68 wks
18 Sep	71	★ FIREBALL *Harvest SHVL 793*	1	25 wks
15 Apr	72	★ MACHINE HEAD *Purple TPSA 7504*	1	24 wks
6 Jan	73	MADE IN JAPAN *Purple TPSP 351*	16	14 wks
17 Feb	73	● WHO DO WE THINK WE ARE *Purple TPSA 7508*	4	11 wks
2 Mar	74	● BURN *Purple TPA 3505*	3	21 wks
23 Nov	74	● STORM BRINGER *Purple TPS 3508*	6	12 wks
5 Jul	75	24 CARAT PURPLE *Purple TPSM 2002*	14	17 wks
22 Nov	75	COME TASTE THE BAND *Purple TPSA 7515*	19	4 wks
27 Nov	76	DEEP PURPLE LIVE *Purple TPSA 7517*	12	6 wks
21 Apr	79	THE MARK II PURPLE SINGLES *Purple TPS 3514*	24	6 wks
19 Jul	80	★ DEEPEST PURPLE *Harvest EMTV 25*	1	15 wks
13 Dec	80	IN CONCERT *Harvest SHDW 4121/4122*	30	8 wks
4 Sep	82	DEEP PURPLE LIVE IN LONDON *Harvest SHSP 4124* .	23	5 wks
10 Nov	84	● PERFECT STRANGERS *Polydor POLH 16*	5	15 wks
29 Jun	85	THE ANTHOLOGY *Harvest PUR 1*	50	3 wks
24 Jan	87	● THE HOUSE OF BLUE LIGHT *Polydor POLH 32*	10	9 wks
16 Jul	88	NOBODY'S PERFECT *Polydor PODV 10*	38	2 wks
2 Nov	90	SLAVES AND MASTERS *RCA PL 90535*	45	2 wks

DEF LEPPARD *UK, male vocal/instrumental group*   *122 wks*

22 Mar	80	ON THROUGH THE NIGHT *Vertigo 9102 040*	15	8 wks
25 Jul	81	HIGH 'N' DRY *Vertigo 6359 045*	26	8 wks
12 Mar	83	PYROMANIA *Vertigo VERS 2*	18	8 wks
29 Aug	87	★ HYSTERIA *Bludgeon Riffola HYSLP 1*	1	98 wks

DEFINITION OF SOUND *US, male rap group*   *4 wks*

29 Jun	91	LOVE AND LIFE *Circa CIRCA 14*	38	3 wks

Desmond DEKKER *Jamaica, male vocalist*   *4 wks*

5 Jul	69	THIS IS DESMOND DEKKER *Trojan TTL 4*	27	4 wks

DEL AMITRI *UK, male vocal/instrumental group*   *44 wks*

24 Feb	90	● WAKING HOURS *A & M AMA 9006*	6	44 wks

DELANEY and BONNIE and FRIENDS
US/UK, male/female vocal/instrumental group   *3 wks*

6 Jun	70	ON TOUR *Atlantic 2400–013*	39	3 wks

DEMON *UK, male vocal/instrumental group*   *5 wks*

14 Aug	82	THE UNEXPECTED GUEST *Carrere CAL 139*	47	3 wks
2 Jul	83	THE PLAGUE *Clay CLAY LP 6*	73	2 wks

Cathy DENNIS *UK, female vocalist*   *21 wks*

10 Aug	91	● MOVE TO THIS *Polydor 8495031*	3†	21 wks

Sandy DENNY *UK, female vocalist*   *2 wks*

2 Oct	71	THE NORTH STAR GRASSMAN AND THE RAVENS *Island ILPS 9165*	31	2 wks

113

d

John DENVER *US, male vocalist* *204 wks*

2 Jun 73	**POEMS, PRAYERS AND PROMISES**		
	RCA SF 8219	19	5 wks
23 Jun 73	**RHYMES AND REASONS** *RCA Victor SF 8348*	21	5 wks
30 Mar 74	● **THE BEST OF JOHN DENVER** *RCA Victor APL1 0374*	7	69 wks
7 Sep 74	● **BACK HOME AGAIN** *RCA Victor APL1 0548*	3	29 wks
22 Mar 75	**AN EVENING WITH JOHN DENVER**		
	RCA Victor LSA 3211/12	31	4 wks
11 Oct 75	**WIND SONG** *RCA Victor APL1 1183*	14	21 wks
15 May 76	● **LIVE IN LONDON** *RCA Victor RS 1050*	2	29 wks
4 Sep 76	● **SPIRIT** *RCA Victor APL1 1694*	9	11 wks
19 Mar 77	● **BEST OF JOHN DENVER VOL. 2** *RCA Victor PL 42120*	9	9 wks
11 Feb 78	**I WANT TO LIVE** *RCA PL 12561*	25	5 wks
21 Apr 79	**JOHN DENVER** *RCA Victor PL 13075*	68	1 wk
22 Oct 83	**IT'S ABOUT TIME** *RCA RCALP 6087*	90	2 wks
1 Dec 84	**JOHN DENVER COLLECTION** *Telstar STAR 2253*	20	11 wks
23 Aug 86	**ONE WORLD** *RCA PL 85811*	91	3 wks

See also Placido Domingo and John Denver.

Karl DENVER *UK, male vocalist* *27 wks*

23 Dec 61	● **WIMOWEH** *Ace Of Clubs ACL 1098*	7	27 wks

DEPECHE MODE *UK, male vocal/instrumental group* *142 wks*

14 Nov 81	● **SPEAK AND SPELL** *Mute STUMM 5*	10	33 wks
9 Oct 82	● **A BROKEN FRAME** *Mute STUMM 9*	8	11 wks
3 Sep 83	● **CONSTRUCTION TIME AGAIN** *Mute STUMM 13*	6	12 wks
6 Sep 84	● **SOME GREAT REWARD** *Mute STUMM 19*	5	12 wks
26 Oct 85	● **THE SINGLES 81–85** *Mute MUTEL 1*	6	22 wks
29 Mar 86	● **BLACK CELEBRATION** *Mute STUMM 26*	4	11 wks
10 Oct 87	● **MUSIC FOR THE MASSES** *Mute STUMM 47*	10	4 wks
25 Mar 89	● **101** *Mute STUMM 101*	5	8 wks
31 Mar 90	● **VIOLATOR** *Mute STUMM 64*	2	29 wks

DEREK AND CLIVE – *See Peter COOK and Dudley MOORE*

DEREK and the DOMINOES
UK/US, male vocal/instrumental group *1 wk*

24 Mar 73	**IN CONCERT** *RSO 2659 020*	36	1 wk

DESTROYERS – *See George THOROGOOD and the DESTROYERS*

DETROIT SPINNERS *US, male vocal group* *3 wks*

14 May 77	**DETROIT SPINNERS' SMASH HITS** *Atlantic K 50363*	37	3 wks

Sidney DEVINE *UK, male vocalist* *11 wks*

10 Apr 76	**DOUBLE DEVINE** *Philips 6625 019*	14	10 wks
11 Dec 76	**DEVINE TIME** *Philips 6308 283*	49	1 wk

DEVO *US, male vocal/instrumental group* *22 wks*

16 Sep 78	**Q: ARE WE NOT MEN? A: NO WE ARE DEVO!**		
	Virgin V 2106	12	7 wks
23 Jun 79	**DUTY NOW FOR THE FUTURE** *Virgin V 2125*	49	6 wks
24 May 80	**FREEDOM OF CHOICE** *Virgin V 2162*	47	5 wks
5 Sep 81	**NEW TRADITIONALISTS** *Virgin V 2191*	50	4 wks

114

d

Howard DEVOTO   *UK, male vocalist*   *2 wks*

6 Aug 83	JERKY VERSIONS OF THE DREAM	*Virgin V 2272*	....	57	2 wks

DEXY'S MIDNIGHT RUNNERS
UK, male/female vocal/instrumental group   *78 wks*

26 Jul	80	● SEARCHING FOR THE YOUNG SOUL REBELS			
		Parlophone PCS 7213	6	10 wks
7 Aug	82	● TOO-RYE-AY *Mercury MERS 5*	2	46 wks
26 Mar	83	GENO *EMI EMS 1007*	79	2 wks
21 Sep	85	DON'T STAND ME DOWN *Mercury MERH 56*	22	6 wks
8 Jun	91	THE VERY BEST OF DEXY'S MIDNIGHT RUNNERS		
		Mercury 8464601	12	14 wks

Group was all male for first album.

Neil DIAMOND   *US, male vocalist*   *481 wks*

3 Apr	71	TAP ROOT MANUSCRIPT *Uni UNLS 117*	19	12 wks
3 Apr	71	GOLD *Uni UNLS 116*	23	11 wks
11 Dec	71	STONES *Uni UNLS 121*	18	14 wks
5 Aug	72	● MOODS *Uni UNLS 128*	7	19 wks
12 Jan	74	HOT AUGUST NIGHT *Uni ULD 1*	32	2 wks
16 Feb	74	JONATHAN LIVINGSTON SEAGULL *CBS 69047*	35	1 wk
9 Mar	74	RAINBOW *MCA MCF 2529*	39	5 wks
29 Jul	74	HIS 12 GREATEST HITS *MCA MCF 2550*	13	78 wks
9 Nov	74	SERENADE *CBS 69067*	11	14 wks
10 Jul	76	● BEAUTIFUL NOISE *CBS 86004*	10	26 wks
12 Mar	77	● LOVE AT THE GREEK *CBS 95001*	3	32 wks
6 Aug	77	HOT AUGUST NIGHT (re-issue) *MCA MCSP 255*	60	1 wk
17 Dec	77	I'M GLAD YOU'RE HERE WITH ME TONIGHT		
		CBS 86044	16	12 wks
25 Nov	78	● 20 GOLDEN GREATS *MCA EMTV 14*	2	26 wks
6 Jan	79	YOU DON'T BRING ME FLOWERS *CBS 86077*	15	23 wks
19 Jan	80	SEPTEMBER MORN *CBS 86096*	14	11 wks
22 Nov	80	● THE JAZZ SINGER (film soundtrack) *Capitol EAST 12120*	3	110 wks
28 Feb	81	LOVE SONGS *MCA MCF 3092*	43	6 wks
5 Dec	81	THE WAY TO THE SKY *CBS 85343*	39	13 wks
19 Jun	82	12 GREATEST HITS VOL. 2 *CBS 85844*	32	8 wks
13 Nov	82	HEARTLIGHT *CBS 25073*	43	10 wks
10 Dec	83	THE VERY BEST OF NEIL DIAMOND *K-Tel NE 1265* .	33	11 wks
28 Jul	84	● PRIMITIVE *CBS 86306*	7	10 wks
24 May	86	HEADED FOR THE FUTURE *CBS 26952*	36	8 wks
28 Nov	87	HOT AUGUST NIGHT 2 *CBS 460 408–1*	74	4 wks
25 Feb	89	THE BEST YEARS OF OUR LIVES *CBS 463201 1*	42	6 wks
9 Nov	91	LOVESCAPE *Columbia 4688901*	36†	8 wks

115

d

DIAMOND HEAD   *UK, male vocal/instrumental group*   *9 wks*

23 Oct	82	BORROWED TIME *MCA DH 1001*	24	5 wks
24 Sep	83	CANTERBURY *MCA DH 1002*	32	4 wks

DICKIES   *US, male vocal/instrumental group*   *19 wks*

17 Feb	79	THE INCREDIBLE SHRINKING DICKIES		
		A & M AMLE 64742	18	17 wks
24 Nov	79	DAWN OF THE DICKIES *A & M AMLE 68510*	60	2 wks

Bruce DICKINSON   *UK, male vocalist*   *9 wks*

19 May 90	TATTOOED MILLIONAIRE *EMI EMC 3574*	14	9 wks

Barbara DICKSON *UK, female vocalist* *126 wks*

18 Jun	77	**MORNING COMES QUICKLY** *RSO 2394 188*	58	1 wk
12 Apr	80	● **THE BARBARA DICKSON ALBUM** *Epic EPC 84088* ...	7	12 wks
16 May	81	**YOU KNOW IT'S ME** *Epic EPC 84551*	39	6 wks
6 Feb	82	● **ALL FOR A SONG** *Epic 10030*	3	38 wks
24 Sep	83	**TELL ME IT'S NOT TRUE** *Legacy LLM 101*	100	1 wk
23 Jun	84	**HEARTBEATS** *Epic EPC 25706*	21	8 wks
12 Jan	85	● **THE BARBARA DICKSON SONGBOOK** *K-Tel NE 1287*	5	19 wks
23 Nov	85	**GOLD** *K-Tel ONE 1312*	11	18 wks
15 Nov	86	**THE VERY BEST OF BARBARA DICKSON** *Telstar STAR 2276*	78	8 wks
29 Nov	86	**THE RIGHT MOMENT** *K-Tel ONE 1335*	39	8 wks
6 May	89	**COMING ALIVE AGAIN** *Telstar STAR 2349*	30	7 wks

Tell Me It's Not True *is a mini-album featuring songs from the musical* Blood Brothers.

Bo DIDDLEY *US, male vocalist/instrumentalist – guitar* *16 wks*

5 Oct	63	**BO DIDDLEY** *Pye International NPL 28026*	11	8 wks
9 Oct	63	**BO DIDDLEY IS A GUNSLINGER** *Pye NJL 33*	20	1 wk
30 Nov	63	**BO DIDDLEY RIDES AGAIN** *Pye International NPL 28029*	19	1 wk
15 Feb	64	**BO DIDDLEY'S BEACH PARTY** *Pye NPL 28032*	13	6 wks

DIESEL PARK WEST *UK, male vocal/instrumental group* *2 wks*

11 Feb	89	**SHAKESPEARE ALABAMA** *Food FOODLP 2*	55	2 wks

DIFFORD and TILBROOK
UK, male vocal/instrumental duo *3 wks*

14 Jul	84	**DIFFORD AND TILBROOK** *A&M AMLX 64985*	47	3 wks

DIGITAL UNDERGROUND
US, male vocal/instrumental group *2 wks*

7 Apr	90	**SEX PACKETS** *BCM BCM 377LP*	59	1 wk
30 Jun	90	**DOWUTCHYALIKE/PACKET MAN** *BCM BCM 463X* .	59	1 wk

Richard DIMBLEBY *UK, male broadcaster* *5 wks*

4 Jun	66	**VOICE OF RICHARD DIMBLEBY** *MFP 1087*	14	5 wks

DINOSAUR JR *US, male vocalist* *2 wks*

2 Mar	91	**GREEN MIND** *blanco y negro BYN 24*	36	2 wks

DIO *UK/US, male vocal/instrumental group* *48 wks*

11 Jun	83	**HOLY DIVER** *Vertigo VERS 5*	13	15 wks
21 Jul	84	● **THE LAST IN LINE** *Vertigo VERL 16*	4	14 wks
7 Sep	85	● **SACRED HEART** *Vertigo VERH 30*	4	6 wks
5 Jul	86	**INTERMISSION** *Vertigo VERB 40*	22	5 wks
22 Aug	87	● **DREAM EVIL** *Vertigo VERH 46*	8	5 wks
26 May	90	**LOCK UP THE WOLVES** *Vertigo 8460331*	28	3 wks

DION and the BELMONTS *US, male vocal group* *5 wks*

12 Apr	80	**20 GOLDEN GREATS** *K-Tel NE 1057*	31	5 wks

DIRE STRAITS UK, male vocal/instrumental group   1030 wks

22 Jul	78 ●	DIRE STRAITS *Vertigo 9102 021*	5	130 wks
23 Jun	79 ●	COMMUNIQUE *Vertigo 9102 031*	5	32 wks
25 Oct	80 ●	MAKIN' MOVIES *Vertigo 6359 034*	4	249 wks
2 Oct	82 ★	LOVE OVER GOLD *Vertigo 6359 109*	1	198 wks
24 Mar	84 ●	ALCHEMY – DIRE STRAITS LIVE *Vertigo VERY 11*	3	163 wks
25 May	85 ★	BROTHERS IN ARMS *Vertigo VERH 25*	1	195 wks
29 Oct	88 ★	MONEY FOR NOTHING *Vertigo VERH 64*	1	48 wks
21 Sep	91 ★	ON EVERY STREET *Vertigo 5101601*	1†	15 wks

DISCHARGE UK, male vocal/instrumental group   5 wks

15 May 82	HEAR NOTHING, SEE NOTHING, SAY NOTHING *Clay CLAYLP 3*	40	5 wks

DISCIPLES OF SOUL – *See LITTLE STEVEN*

Sacha DISTEL France, male vocalist   14 wks

2 May 70	SACHA DISTEL *Warner Bros. WS 3003*	21	14 wks

DIVINYLS Australia, male/female vocal/instrumental duo   1 wk

20 Jul 91	DIVINYLS *Virgin America VUSLP 30*	59	1 wk

117

d

DJ JAZZY JEFF and FRESH PRINCE
US, male rap duo   4 wks

28 Feb 87	ROCK THE HOUSE *Champion CHAMP 1004*	97	1 wk
21 May 88	HE'S THE DJ, I'M THE RAPPER *Jive HIP 61*	68	2 wks
14 Sep 91	HOMEBASE *Jive HIP 116*	69	1 wk

DOCTOR and the MEDICS
UK, male/female vocal/instrumental group   3 wks

21 Jun 86	LAUGHING AT THE PIECES *MCA MIRG 1010*	25	3 wks

DR. FEELGOOD UK, male vocal/instrumental group   33 wks

18 Oct 75	MALPRACTICE *United Artists UAS 29880*	17	6 wks
2 Oct 76 ★	STUPIDITY *United Artists UAS 29990*	1	9 wks
4 Jun 77 ●	SNEAKIN' SUSPICION *United Artists UAS 30075*	10	6 wks
8 Oct 77	BE SEEING YOU *United Artists UAS 30123*	55	3 wks
7 Oct 78	PRIVATE PRACTICE *United Artists UAG 30184*	41	5 wks
2 Jun 79	AS IT HAPPENS *United Artists UAK 30239*	42	4 wks

DR. HOOK US, male vocal/instrumental group   130 wks

25 Jun 76 ●	A LITTLE BIT MORE *Capitol E-ST 23795*	5	42 wks
29 Oct 77	MAKING LOVE AND MUSIC *Capitol EST 11632*	39	4 wks
27 Oct 79	PLEASURE AND PAIN *Capitol EAST 11859*	47	6 wks
17 Nov 79	SOMETIMES YOU WIN *Capitol EST 12018*	14	44 wks
29 Nov 80	RISING *Mercury 6302 076*	44	5 wks
6 Dec 80 ●	DR. HOOK'S GREATEST HITS *Capitol EST 26037*	2	28 wks
14 Nov 81	DR. HOOK LIVE IN THE UK *Capitol EST 26706*	90	1 wk

Ken DODD UK, *male vocalist*   36 wks

25 Dec 65	●	**TEARS OF HAPPINESS** *Columbia 33SX 1793*	6	12 wks
23 Jul 66		**HITS FOR NOW AND ALWAYS** *Columbia SX 6060*	14	11 wks
14 Jan 67		**FOR SOMEONE SPECIAL** *Columbia SCX 6224*	40	1 wk
29 Nov 80	●	**20 GOLDEN GREATS OF KEN DODD** *Warwick WW 5098*	8	12 wks

DOGS D'AMOUR UK, *male vocal/instrumental group*   11 wks

22 Oct 88	**IN THE DYNAMITE JET SALOON** *China WOL 8*	97	1 wk
25 Mar 89	**A GRAVEYARD OF EMPTY BOTTLES** *China 8390740* .	16	4 wks
30 Sep 89	**ERROL FLYNN** *China 8397001*	22	3 wks
6 Oct 90	**STRAIGHT** *China 8437961*	32	2 wks
7 Sep 91	**DOG'S HITS AND THE BOOTLEG ALBUM** *China WOL 1020*	58	1 wk

DOKKEN US, *male vocal/instrumental group*   1 wk

21 Nov 87	**BACK FOR THE ATTACK** *Elektra EKT 43*	96	1 wk

Thomas DOLBY
UK, male vocalist/instrumentalist – keyboards   27 wks

22 May 82	**THE GOLDEN AGE OF WIRELESS** *Venice In Peril VIP 1001*	65	10 wks
18 Feb 84	**THE FLAT EARTH** *Parlophone Odeon PCS 2400341*	14	14 wks
7 May 88	**ALIENS ATE MY BUICK** *Manhattan MTL 1020*	30	3 wks

DOLLAR UK, *male/female vocal duo*   28 wks

15 Sep 79	**SHOOTING STARS** *Carrere CAL 111*	36	8 wks
24 Apr 82	**THE VERY BEST OF DOLLAR** *Carrere CAL 3001*	31	9 wks
30 Oct 82	**THE DOLLAR ALBUM** *WEA DTV 1*	18	11 wks

Placido DOMINGO Spain, *male vocalist*   52 wks

21 May 83	**MY LIFE FOR A SONG** *CBS 73683*	31	8 wks
27 Dec 86	**PLACIDO DOMINGO COLLECTION** *Stylus SMR 625* ..	30	14 wks
23 Apr 88	**GREATEST LOVE SONGS** *CBS 44701*	63	2 wks
17 Jun 89	**GOYA...A LIFE IN A SONG** *CBS 463294 1*	36	4 wks
17 Jun 89	**THE ESSENTIAL DOMINGO** *Deutsche Grammophon PDTV 1*	20	8 wks
24 Nov 90	**BE MY LOVE...AN ALBUM OF LOVE** *EMI EMTV 54* .	14	12 wks
7 Dec 91	**THE BROADWAY I LOVE** *East West 9031755901*	45†	4 wks

See also Placido Domingo and John Denver; Andrew Lloyd Webber; Luciano Pavarotti, Placido Domingo and José Carreras.

Placido DOMINGO and John DENVER
Spain/US, male vocal duo   21 wks

28 Nov 81	**PERHAPS LOVE** *CBS 73592*	17	21 wks

See also Placido Domingo; John Denver.

Fats DOMINO US, *male vocalist/instrumentalist – piano*   1 wk

16 May 70	**VERY BEST OF FATS DOMINO** *Liberty LBS 83331*	56	1 wk

DOMINOES – *See DEREK and the DOMINOES*

Lonnie DONEGAN UK, *male vocalist*　　29 wks

1 Sep 62 ● **GOLDEN AGE OF DONEGAN**		
Pye Golden Guinea GGL 0135	3	23 wks
9 Feb 63 **GOLDEN AGE OF DONEGAN VOL. 2**		
Pye Golden Guinea GGL 0170	15	3 wks
25 Feb 78 **PUTTING ON THE STYLE** *Chrysalis CHR 1158*	51	3 wks

DONOVAN UK, *male vocalist*　　73 wks

5 Jun 65 ● **WHAT'S BIN DID AND WHAT'S BIN HID**		
Pye NPL 18117	3	16 wks
6 Nov 65 **FAIRY TALE** *Pye NPL 18128*	20	2 wks
8 Jul 67 **SUNSHINE SUPERMAN** *Pye NPL 18181*	25	7 wks
14 Oct 67 ● **UNIVERSAL SOLDIER** *Marble Arch MAL 718*	5	18 wks
11 May 68 **A GIFT FROM A FLOWER TO A GARDEN**		
Pye NSPL 20000	13	14 wks
12 Sep 70 **OPEN ROAD** *Dawn DNLS 3009*	30	4 wks
24 Mar 73 **COSMIC WHEELS** *Epic EPC 65450*	15	12 wks

Jason DONOVAN Australia, *male vocalist*　　94 wks

13 May 89 ★ **TEN GOOD REASONS** *PWL HF 7*	1	54 wks
9 Jun 90 ● **BETWEEN THE LINES** *PWL HF 14*	2	26 wks
28 Sep 91 ● **GREATEST HITS** *PWL HF 20*	9†	14 wks

See also Stage Cast Recordings – Joseph And The Amazing Technicolour Dreamcoat.

119

d

DOOBIE BROTHERS US, *male vocal/instrumental group*　　30 wks

30 Mar 74 **WHAT WERE ONCE VICES ARE NOW HABITS**		
Warner Bros. K 56206	19	10 wks
17 May 75 **STAMPEDE** *Warner Bros. K 56094*	14	11 wks
10 Apr 76 **TAKIN' IT TO THE STREETS** *Warner Bros. K 56196*	42	2 wks
17 Sep 77 **LIVING ON THE FAULT LINE** *Warner Bros. K 56383*	25	5 wks
11 Oct 80 **ONE STEP CLOSER** *Warner Bros. K 56824*	53	2 wks

DOOLEYS UK, *male/female vocal/instrumental group*　　27 wks

30 Jun 79 ● **THE BEST OF THE DOOLEYS** *GTO GTTV 038*	6	21 wks
3 Nov 79 **THE CHOSEN FEW** *GTO GTLP 040*	56	4 wks
25 Oct 80 **FULL HOUSE** *GTO GTTV 050*	54	2 wks

Val DOONICAN Ireland, *male vocalist*　　170 wks

12 Dec 64 ● **LUCKY 13 SHADES OF VAL DOONICAN**		
Decca LK 4648	2	27 wks
3 Dec 66 ● **GENTLE SHADES OF VAL DOONICAN**		
Decca LK 4831	5	52 wks
2 Dec 67 ★ **VAL DOONICAN ROCKS BUT GENTLY**		
Pye NSPL 18204	1	23 wks
30 Nov 68 ● **VAL** *Pye NSPL 18236*	6	11 wks
14 Jun 69 ● **WORLD OF VAL DOONICAN** *Decca SPA 3*	2	31 wks
13 Dec 69 **SOUNDS GENTLE** *Pye NSPL 18321*	22	9 wks
19 Dec 70 **THE MAGIC OF VAL DOONICAN** *Philips 6642 003*	34	3 wks
27 Nov 71 **THIS IS VAL DOONICAN** *Philips 6382 017*	40	1 wk
22 Feb 75 **I LOVE COUNTRY MUSIC** *Philips 9299261*	37	2 wks
21 May 77 **SOME OF MY BEST FRIENDS ARE SONGS**		
Philips 6641 607	29	5 wks
24 Mar 90 **SONGS FROM MY SKETCH BOOK** *Parkfield PMLP 5014*	33	6 wks

The costumes reveal it's the late 70s, the peak period for **Earth Wind and Fire**.

Jason Donovan is shown in his amazing technicolour dreamshirt.

DOORS *US, male vocal/instrumental group* *84 wks*

28 Sep 68	**WAITING FOR THE SUN** *Elektra EKS7 4024*	16	10 wks
11 Apr 70	**MORRISON HOTEL** *Elektra EKS 75007*	12	8 wks
26 Sep 70	**ABSOLUTELY LIVE** *Elektra 2665 002*	69	1 wk
31 Jul 71	**L.A. WOMAN** *Elektra K 42090*	28	4 wks
1 Apr 72	**WEIRD SCENES INSIDE THE GOLD MINE**		
	Elektra K 62009	50	1 wk
29 Oct 83	**ALIVE, SHE CRIED** *Elektra 96-0269-1*	36	5 wks
4 Jul 87	**LIVE AT THE HOLLYWOOD BOWL** *Elektra EKT 40* ..	51	3 wks
6 Apr 91	**THE DOORS (soundtrack)** *Elektra EKT 85*	11	17 wks
20 Apr 91	**BEST OF THE DOORS** *Elektra EKT 21*	17	18 wks
20 Apr 91	**THE DOORS** *Elektra K 42012*	43	12 wks
1 Jun 91	**IN CONCERT** *Elektra EKT 88*	24	5 wks

Lee DORSEY *US, male vocalist* *4 wks*

17 Dec 66	**NEW LEE DORSEY** *Stateside SSL 10192*	34	4 wks

DOUBLE *Switzerland, male vocal/instrumental duo* *4 wks*

8 Mar 86	**BLUE** *Polydor POLD 5187*	69	4 wks

DOUBLE TROUBLE *UK, male production duo* *1 wk*

4 Aug 90	**AS ONE** *Desire LULP 6*	73	1 wk

DOUBLE TROUBLE – *See Stevie Ray VAUGHAN and DOUBLE TROUBLE*

Craig DOUGLAS *UK, male vocalist* *2 wks*

6 Aug 60	**CRAIG DOUGLAS** *Top Rank BUY 049*	17	2 wks

Will DOWNING *US, male vocalist* *28 wks*

26 Mar 88	**WILL DOWNING** *Fourth & Broadway BRLP 518*	20	23 wks
18 Nov 89	**COME TOGETHER AS ONE** *Fourth & Broadway BRLP 538*	36	2 wks
6 Apr 91	**A DREAM FULFILLED** *Fourth & Broadway BRLP 565*	43	3 wks

DOZY – *See Dave DEE, DOZY, BEAKY, MICK and TICH*

DREAD ZEPPELIN *UK, male vocal/instrumental group* *2 wks*

11 Aug 90	**UN-LED-ED** *IRS EIRSA 1042*	71	2 wks

DREAM ACADEMY
UK, male/female vocal/instrumental group *2 wks*

12 Oct 85	**THE DREAM ACADEMY** *blanco y negro BYN 6*	58	2 wks

DREAM WARRIORS *Canada, male rap group* *7 wks*

16 Feb 91	**AND NOW THE LEGACY BEGINS**		
	Fourth & Broadway BRLP 560	18	7 wks

DREAMERS – *See FREDDIE and the DREAMERS*

121

d

DRIFTERS US, male vocal group — 65 wks

18 May 68	**GOLDEN HITS**	Atlantic 588–103		27	7 wks
10 Jun 72	**GOLDEN HITS**	Atlantic K 40018		26	8 wks
8 Nov 75	● **24 ORIGINAL HITS**	Atlantic K 60106		2	34 wks
13 Dec 75	**LOVE GAMES**	Bell BELLS 246		51	1 wk
18 Oct 86	**THE VERY BEST OF THE DRIFTERS**	Telstar STAR 2280		24	15 wks

See also Ben E. King and the Drifters.

Julie DRISCOLL and the Brian AUGER TRINITY UK, female/male vocal/instrumental group — 13 wks

8 Jun 68	**OPEN**	Marmalade 608–002		12	13 wks

D-TRAIN US, male vocalist/multi-instrumentalist, Hubert Eaves — 4 wks

8 May 82	**D-TRAIN**	Epic EPC 85683		72	4 wks

DUBLINERS Ireland, male vocal/instrumental group — 88 wks

13 May 67	● **A DROP OF THE HARD STUFF**	Major Minor MMLP 3		5	41 wks
9 Sep 67	**BEST OF THE DUBLINERS**	Transatlantic TRA 158		25	11 wks
7 Oct 67	● **MORE OF THE HARD STUFF**	Major Minor MMLP 5		8	23 wks
2 Mar 68	**DRINKIN' AND COURTIN'**	Major Minor SMLP 14		31	3 wks
25 Apr 87	**THE DUBLINERS 25 YEARS CELEBRATION**	Stylus SMR 731		43	10 wks

Stephen 'Tin Tin' DUFFY UK, male vocalist — 7 wks

20 Apr 85	**THE UPS AND DOWNS**	10 DIX 5		35	7 wks

George DUKE US, male vocalist/instrumentalist – keyboards — 4 wks

26 Jul 80	**BRAZILIAN LOVE AFFAIR**	Epic EPC 84311		33	4 wks

DUKES – See Steve EARLE

Candy DULFER Holland, female instrumentalist – saxophone — 9 wks

18 Aug 90	**SAXUALITY**	RCA PL 74661		27	9 wks

Simon DUPREE and the BIG SOUND
UK, male vocal/instrumental group — 1 wk

13 Aug 67	**WITHOUT RESERVATIONS**	Parlophone PCS 7029		39	1 wk

DURAN DURAN UK, male vocal/instrumental group — 345 wks

27 Jun 81	● **DURAN DURAN**	EMI EMC 3372		3	118 wks
22 May 82	● **RIO**	EMI EMC 3411		2	109 wks
3 Dec 83	★ **SEVEN AND THE RAGGED TIGER**	EMI DD 1		1	47 wks
24 Nov 84	● **ARENA**	Parlophone DD 2		6	31 wks
6 Dec 86	**NOTORIOUS**	EMI DDN 331		16	16 wks
29 Oct 88	**BIG THING**	EMI DDB 33		15	5 wks
25 Nov 89	● **DECADE**	EMI DDX 10		5	15 wks

1 Sep 90 ● **LIBERTY** *Parlophone PCSD 112* .... 8 4 wks

Group were UK/US on last hit and were billed as Duranduran on EMI DDB 33.

Deanna DURBIN *Canada, female vocalist* 4 wks

30 Jan 82 **THE BEST OF DEANNA DURBIN**
MCA International MCL 1634 .... 84 4 wks

Ian DURY and the BLOCKHEADS

UK, male vocal/instrumental group 118 wks

22 Oct 77 ● **NEW BOOTS AND PANTIES!!** *Stiff SEEZ 4* .... 5 90 wks
2 Jun 79 ● **DO IT YOURSELF** *Stiff SEEZ 14* .... 2 18 wks
6 Dec 80 **LAUGHTER** *Stiff SEEZ 30* .... 48 4 wks
10 Oct 81 **LORD UPMINSTER** *Polydor POLD 5042* .... 53 4 wks
4 Feb 84 **4,000 WEEKS HOLIDAY** *Polydor POLD 5112* .... 54 2 wks

4,000 Weeks Holiday credits the Music Students – UK, male vocal/instrumental group.

Bob DYLAN *US, male vocalist* 560 wks

23 May 64 ★ **THE FREEWHEELIN' BOB DYLAN** *CBS BPG 62193* .. 1 49 wks
11 Jul 64 ● **THE TIMES THEY ARE A-CHANGIN'** *CBS BPG 62251* 4 20 wks
21 Nov 64 ● **ANOTHER SIDE OF BOB DYLAN** *CBS BPG 62429* .... 8 19 wks
8 May 65 **BOB DYLAN** *CBS BPG 62022* .... 13 6 wks
15 May 65 ★ **BRINGING IT ALL BACK HOME** *CBS BPG 62515* ..... 1 29 wks
9 Oct 65 ● **HIGHWAY 61 REVISITED** *CBS BPG 62572* .... 4 15 wks
20 Aug 66 ● **BLONDE ON BLONDE** *CBS DDP 66012* .... 3 15 wks
14 Jan 67 ● **GREATEST HITS** *CBS SBPG 62847* .... 6 82 wks
2 Mar 68 ● **JOHN WESLEY HARDING** *CBS SBPG 63252* .... 1 29 wks
17 May 69 ★ **NASHVILLE SKYLINE** *CBS 63601* .... 1 42 wks
11 Jul 70 ★ **SELF PORTRAIT** *CBS 66250* .... 1 15 wks
28 Nov 70 ★ **NEW MORNING** *CBS 69001* .... 1 18 wks
25 Dec 71 **MORE BOB DYLAN GREATEST HITS** *CBS 67238/9* ... 12 15 wks
29 Sep 73 **PAT GARRETT AND BILLY THE KID (film soundtrack)**
CBS 69042 .... 29 11 wks
23 Feb 74 ● **PLANET WAVES** *Island ILPS 9261* .... 7 8 wks
13 Jul 74 ● **BEFORE THE FLOOD** *Asylum IDBD 1* .... 8 7 wks
15 Feb 75 ● **BLOOD ON THE TRACKS** *CBS 69097* .... 4 16 wks
26 Jul 75 ● **THE BASEMENT TAPES** *CBS 88147* .... 8 10 wks
31 Jan 76 ● **DESIRE** *CBS 86003* .... 3 35 wks
9 Oct 76 ● **HARD RAIN** *CBS 86016* .... 3 7 wks
1 Jul 78 ● **STREET LEGAL** *CBS 86067* .... 2 20 wks
26 May 79 ● **BOB DYLAN AT BUDOKAN** *CBS 96004* .... 4 19 wks
8 Sep 79 ● **SLOW TRAIN COMING** *CBS 86095* .... 2 13 wks
28 Jun 80 ● **SAVED** *CBS 86113* .... 3 8 wks
29 Aug 81 ● **SHOT OF LOVE** *CBS 85178* .... 6 8 wks
12 Nov 83 ● **INFIDELS** *CBS 25539* .... 9 12 wks
15 Dec 84 **REAL LIVE** *CBS 26334* .... 54 2 wks
22 Jun 85 **EMPIRE BURLESQUE** *CBS 86313* .... 11 6 wks
2 Aug 86 **KNOCKED OUT LOADED** *CBS 86326* .... 35 5 wks
23 Apr 88 **GREATEST HITS** *CBS 460907 1* .... 99 1 wk
25 Jun 88 **DOWN IN THE GROOVE** *CBS 460267 1* .... 32 3 wks
14 Oct 89 ● **OH MERCY** *CBS 465800 1* .... 6 7 wks
22 Sep 90 **UNDER THE RED SKY** *CBS 4671881* .... 13 3 wks
13 Apr 91 **THE BOOTLEG SERIES VOLS 1–3** *Columbia 4680861* ... 32 5 wks

The two Greatest Hits collections are different. See also Bob Dylan and the Grateful Dead.

Bob DYLAN and the GRATEFUL DEAD

US, male vocalist and vocal/instrumental group 3 wks

18 Feb 89 **DYLAN AND THE DEAD** *CBS 463381 1* .... 38 3 wks

See also Bob Dylan; Grateful Dead.

123

d

e

E STREET BAND – *See Bruce* SPRINGSTEEN

EAGLES *US, male vocal/instrumental group*   *284 wks*

27 Apr 74	**ON THE BORDER** *Asylum SYL 9016*	28	9 wks
12 Jul 75	● **ONE OF THESE NIGHTS** *Asylum SYLA 8759*	8	40 wks
12 Jul 75	**DESPERADO** *Asylum SYLL 9011*	39	9 wks
6 Mar 76	● **THEIR GREATEST HITS 1971–1975** *Asylum K 53017*	2	77 wks
25 Dec 76	● **HOTEL CALIFORNIA** *Asylum K 53051*	2	63 wks
13 Oct 79	● **THE LONG RUN** *Asylum K 52181*	4	16 wks
22 Nov 80	**LIVE** *Asylum K 62032*	24	13 wks
18 May 85	● **BEST OF THE EAGLES** *Asylum EKT 5*	8	57 wks

Steve EARLE and the DUKES
US, male vocal/instrumental group   *15 wks*

4 Jul 87	**EXIT 0** *MCA MCF 3379*	77	2 wks
19 Nov 88	**COPPERHEAD ROAD** *MCA MCF 3426*	44	8 wks
7 Jul 90	**THE HARD WAY** *MCA MCG 6095*	22	4 wks
19 Oct 91	**SHUT UP AND DIE LIKE AN AVIATOR** *MCA MCA 10315*	62	1 wk

Copperhead Road *credits Steve Earle alone.*

EARTH WIND AND FIRE
US, male vocal/instrumental group   *154 wks*

21 Jan 78	**ALL 'N' ALL** *CBS 86051*	13	23 wks
16 Dec 78	● **THE BEST OF EARTH WIND AND FIRE VOL. 1** *CBS 83284*	6	42 wks
23 Jun 79	● **I AM** *CBS 86084*	5	41 wks
1 Nov 80	● **FACES** *CBS 88498*	10	6 wks
14 Nov 81	**RAISE** *CBS 85272*	14	22 wks
19 Feb 83	**POWERLIGHT** *CBS 25120*	22	7 wks
10 May 86	● **THE COLLECTION** *K-Tel NE 1322*	5	13 wks

EASTERHOUSE *UK, male vocal/instrumental group*   *1 wk*

28 Jun 86	**CONTENDERS** *Rough Trade ROUGH 94*	91	1 wk

EAST OF EDEN *UK, male vocal/instrumental group*   *2 wks*

14 Mar 70	**SNAFU** *Deram SML 1050*	29	2 wks

Sheena EASTON *UK, female vocalist*   *37 wks*

31 Jan 81	**TAKE MY TIME** *EMI EMC 3354*	17	19 wks
3 Oct 81	**YOU COULD HAVE BEEN WITH ME** *EMI EMC 3378* .	33	6 wks
25 Sep 82	**MADNESS, MONEY AND MUSIC** *EMI EMC 3414*	44	4 wks
15 Oct 83	**BEST KEPT SECRET** *EMI EMC 1077951*	99	1 wk
4 Mar 89	**THE LOVER IN ME** *MCA MCG 6036*	30	7 wks

Clint EASTWOOD and General SAINT
Jamaica, male vocal duo   *3 wks*

6 Feb 82	**TWO BAD DJ** *Greensleeves GREL 24*	99	2 wks

28 May 83   **STOP THAT TRAIN** *Greensleeves GREL 53* .... **98** 1 wk

Hubert EAVES – *See D-TRAIN*

ECHO and the BUNNYMEN
UK, male vocal/instrumental group   *89 wks*

26 Jul 80	**CROCODILES** *Korova KODE 1*	**17**	6 wks
6 Jun 81	● **HEAVEN UP HERE** *Korova KODE 3*	**10**	16 wks
12 Feb 83	● **PORCUPINE** *Korova KODE 6*	**2**	17 wks
12 May 84	● **OCEAN RAIN** *Korova KODE 8*	**4**	26 wks
23 Nov 85	● **SONGS TO LEARN & SING** *Korova KODE 13*	**6**	15 wks
18 Jul 87	● **ECHO AND THE BUNNYMEN** *WEA WX 108*	**4**	9 wks

EDDIE and the HOT RODS
UK, male vocal/instrumental group   *5 wks*

18 Dec 76	**TEENAGE DEPRESSION** *Island ILPS 9457*	**43**	1 wk
3 Dec 77	**LIFE ON THE LINE** *Island ILPS 9509*	**27**	3 wks
24 Mar 79	**THRILLER** *Island ILPS 9563*	**50**	1 wk

Duane EDDY *US, male instrumentalist – guitar*   *88 wks*

6 Jun 59	● **HAVE TWANGY GUITAR WILL TRAVEL** *London HAW 2160*	**6**	3 wks
31 Oct 59	● **SPECIALLY FOR YOU** *London HAW 2191*	**6**	8 wks
19 Mar 60	● **THE TWANG'S THE THANG** *London HAW 2236*	**2**	25 wks
26 Nov 60	**SONGS OF OUR HERITAGE** *London HAW 2285*	**13**	5 wks
1 Apr 61	● **A MILLION DOLLARS' WORTH OF TWANG** *London HAW 2325*	**5**	19 wks
9 Jun 62	**A MILLION DOLLARS' WORTH OF TWANG VOL. 2** *London HAW 2435*	**18**	1 wk
21 Jul 62	● **TWISTIN' AND TWANGIN'** *RCA RD 27264*	**8**	12 wks
8 Dec 62	**TWANGY GUITAR – SILKY STRINGS** *RCA RD 7510* .	**13**	11 wks
16 Mar 63	**DANCE WITH THE GUITAR MAN** *RCA RD 7545*	**14**	4 wks

EDMONTON SYMPHONY ORCHESTRA – *See PROCOL HARUM*

Dave EDMUNDS *UK, male vocalist/instrumentalist – guitar*   *21 wks*

23 Jun 79	**REPEAT WHEN NECESSARY** *Swansong SSK 59409*	**39**	12 wks
18 Apr 81	**TWANGIN'** *Swansong SSK 59411*	**37**	4 wks
3 Apr 82	**DE7** *Arista SPART 1184*	**60**	3 wks
30 Apr 83	**INFORMATION** *Arista 205 348*	**92**	2 wks

Dennis EDWARDS *US, male vocalist*   *1 wk*

14 Apr 84	**DON'T LOOK ANY FURTHER** *Gordy ZL 72148*	**91**	1 wk

EEK-A-MOUSE *Jamaica, male vocalist*   *3 wks*

14 Aug 82	**SKIDIP** *Greensleeves GREL 41*	**61**	3 wks

801 *UK, male vocal/instrumental group*   *2 wks*

20 Nov 76	**801 LIVE** *Island ILPS 9444*	**52**	2 wks

808 STATE *UK, male instrumental group*   *15 wks*

16 Dec 89	**NINETY** *ZTT ZTT 2*	**57**	5 wks
16 Mar 91	● **EX:EL** *ZTT ZTT 6*	**4**	10 wks

125

e

EIGHTH WONDER
UK, male/female vocal/instrumental group   *4 wks*

| 23 Jul | 88 | **FEARLESS** CBS 460628 1 .... | 47 | 4 wks |

ELECTRIBE 101
UK/Germany, male/female vocal/instrumental group   *4 wks*

| 20 Oct | 90 | **ELECTRIBAL MEMORIES** Mercury 8429651 .... | 26 | 3 wks |

ELECTRIC LIGHT ORCHESTRA
UK, male vocal/instrumental group   *370 wks*

12 Aug	72	**ELECTRIC LIGHT ORCHESTRA** Harvest SHVL 797 ...	32	4 wks
31 Mar	73	**ELO 2** Harvest SHVL 806	35	1 wk
11 Dec	76	● **A NEW WORLD RECORD** United Artists UAG 30017 ...	6	100 wks
12 Nov	77	● **OUT OF THE BLUE** United Artists UAR 100	4	108 wks
6 Jan	79	**THREE LIGHT YEARS** Jet JET BX 1	38	9 wks
16 Jun	79	★ **DISCOVERY** Jet JET LX 500	1	46 wks
1 Dec	79	● **ELO'S GREATEST HITS** Jet JET LX 525	7	18 wks
8 Aug	81	★ **TIME** Jet JETLP 236	1	32 wks
2 Jul	83	● **SECRET MESSAGES** Jet JET LX 527	4	15 wks
15 Mar	86	● **BALANCE OF POWER** Epic EPC 26467	9	12 wks
16 Dec	89	**THE GREATEST HITS** Telstar STAR 2370	23	21 wks
1 Jun	91	**ELECTRIC LIGHT ORCHESTRA PART 2** Telstar STAR 2503	34	4 wks

A New World Record *changed to* JET LP 200 *and* Out Of The Blue *changed label number to* JET DP 400 *during their chart runs.* The Greatest Hits *was also issued under the title* The Very Best of Electric Light Orchestra, *with the same track listings and catalogue number. Last album credited to ELO Part 2.*

ELECTRIC SUN – *See Uli Jon ROTH and ELECTRIC SUN*

ELECTRIC WIND ENSEMBLE
UK, male instrumental group   *9 wks*

| 18 Feb | 84 | **HAUNTING MELODIES** Nouveau Music NML 1007 ...... | 28 | 9 wks |

ELECTRONIC *UK, male vocal/instrumental duo*   *16 wks*

| 8 Jun | 91 | ● **ELECTRONIC** Factory FACT 290 .... | 2 | 16 wks |

Danny ELFMAN *US, male orchestra leader*   *6 wks*

| 12 Aug | 89 | **BATMAN** Warner Bros. WX 287 .... | 45 | 6 wks |

Duke ELLINGTON *US, orchestra*   *2 wks*

| 8 Apr | 61 | **NUT CRACKER SUITE** Philips BBL 7418 .... | 11 | 2 wks |

Ben ELTON *UK, male comedian*   *2 wks*

| 14 Nov | 87 | **MOTORMOUTH** Mercury BENLP 1 .... | 86 | 2 wks |

EMERSON, LAKE and PALMER
UK, male instrumental group   *135 wks*

| 5 Dec | 70 | ● **EMERSON, LAKE AND PALMER** Island ILPS 9132 .... | 4 | 28 wks |

19 Jun 71 ★ **TARKUS** *Island ILPS 9155*	**1**	17 wks
4 Dec 71 ● **PICTURES AT AN EXHIBITION** *Island HELP 1*	**3**	5 wks
8 Jul 72 ● **TRILOGY** *Island ILPS 9186*	**2**	29 wks
22 Dec 73 ● **BRAIN SALAD SURGERY** *Manticore K 53501*	**2**	17 wks
24 Aug 74 ● **WELCOME BACK MY FRIENDS TO THE SHOW THAT NEVER ENDS – LADIES AND GENTLEMEN: EMERSON, LAKE AND PALMER** *Manticore K 63500*	**5**	5 wks
9 Apr 77 ● **WORKS** *Atlantic K 80009*	**9**	25 wks
10 Dec 77 **WORKS VOL. 2** *Atlantic K 50422*	**20**	5 wks
9 Dec 78 **LOVE BEACH** *Atlantic K 50552*	**48**	4 wks

See also Greg Lake; Emerson, Lake and Powell.

EMERSON, LAKE and POWELL
UK, male vocal/instrumental group   *5 wks*

14 Jun 86 **EMERSON, LAKE AND POWELL** *Polydor POLD 5191* ..	**35**	5 wks

See also Greg Lake; Cozy Powell; Emerson, Lake and Palmer.

EMF *UK, male vocal/instrumental group*   *19 wks*

18 May 91 ● **SCHUBERT DIP** *Parlophone PCS 7353*	**3**	19 wks

---

An EMOTIONAL FISH *UK, male vocal/instrumental group*   *3 wks*

25 Aug 90 **AN EMOTIONAL FISH** *East West WX 359*	**40**	3 wks

---

EN VOGUE *US, female vocal group*   *13 wks*

2 Jun 90 **BORN TO SING** *Atlantic 7567820841*	**23**	13 wks

---

ENERGY ORCHARD *Ireland, male vocal/instrumental group*   *2 wks*

12 May 90 **ENERGY ORCHARD** *MCA MCG 6083*	**52**	2 wks

---

ENGLAND FOOTBALL WORLD CUP SQUAD *UK, male football team vocalists*   *18 wks*

16 May 70 ● **THE WORLD BEATERS SING THE WORLD BEATERS** *Pye NSPL 18337*	**4**	8 wks
15 May 82 **THIS TIME** *K-Tel NE 1169*	**37**	10 wks

ENGLISH CHAMBER ORCHESTRA – *See John WILLIAMS with the ENGLISH CHAMBER ORCHESTRA; Nigel KENNEDY; Andrew LLOYD WEBBER; Kiri TE KANAWA*

ENIGMA *UK, male vocal/instrumental group*   *3 wks*

5 Sep 81 **AIN'T NO STOPPIN'** *Creole CRX 1*	**80**	3 wks

---

ENIGMA *Romania, male producer*   *46 wks*

22 Dec 90 ★ **MCMXC AD** *Virgin International MCVIR 11*	**1†**	46 wks

---

Brian ENO *UK, male instrumentalist – keyboards*   *4 wks*

9 Mar 74 **HERE COME THE WARM JETS** *Island ILPS 9268*	**26**	2 wks
21 Oct 78 **MUSIC FOR FILMS** *Polydor 2310 623*	**55**	1 wk

127

e

He's worked with Bowie, Roxy Music and U2, but **Brian Eno** has also charted with a series of his own distinctive projects.

Ben Elton exhibits his album title's facial feature while simultaneously endorsing environment-friendly washing up liquid.

8 May 82   **AMBIENT FOUR ON LAND**   *EG EGED 20* ....   **93**   1 wk
See also Brian Eno and David Byrne.

Brian ENO and David BYRNE
UK, male instrumentalist – keyboards and UK, male vocalist   *8 wks*

21 Feb 81   **MY LIFE IN THE BUSH OF GHOSTS**   *Polydor EGLP 48* ..   **29**   8 wks
See also Brian Eno.

ENUFF Z'NUFF   *US, male vocal/instrumental group*   *1 wk*

13 Apr 91   **STRENGTH**   *Atco 7567916381* ....   **56**   1 wk

ENYA   *Ireland, female vocalist*   *74 wks*

6 Jun 87   **ENYA**   *BBC REB 605* ....   **69**   4 wks
15 Oct 88 ● **WATERMARK**   *WEA WX 199* ....   **5**   63 wks
16 Nov 91 ★ **SHEPHERD MOONS**   *WEA WX 431* ....   **1†**   7 wks

EPMD   *US, male rap duo*   *1 wk*

16 Feb 91   **BUSINESS AS USUAL**   *Def Jam 4676971* ....   **69**   1 wk

EQUALS   *UK, male vocal/instrumental group*   *10 wks*

18 Nov 67 ● **UNEQUALLED EQUALS**   *President PTL 1006* ....   **10**   9 wks
9 Mar 68   **EQUALS EXPLOSION**   *President PTLS 1015* ....   **32**   1 wk

ERASURE   *UK, male vocal/instrumental duo*   *250 wks*

14 Jun 86   **WONDERLAND**   *Mute STUMM 25* ....   **71**   7 wks
11 Apr 87 ● **THE CIRCUS**   *Mute STUMM 35* ....   **6**   107 wks
30 Apr 88 ★ **THE INNOCENTS**   *Mute STUMM 55* ....   **1**   78 wks
28 Oct 89 ★ **WILD!**   *Mute STUMM 75* ....   **1**   48 wks
26 Oct 91 ★ **CHORUS**   *Mute STUMM 95* ....   **1†**   10 wks

David ESSEX   *UK, male vocalist*   *148 wks*

24 Nov 73 ● **ROCK ON**   *CBS 65823* ....   **7**   22 wks
19 Oct 74 ● **DAVID ESSEX**   *CBS 69088* ....   **2**   24 wks
27 Sep 75 ● **ALL THE FUN OF THE FAIR**   *CBS 69160* ....   **3**   20 wks
5 Jun 76   **ON TOUR**   *CBS 95000* ....   **51**   1 wk
30 Oct 76   **OUT ON THE STREET**   *CBS 86017* ....   **31**   9 wks
8 Oct 77   **GOLD AND IVORY**   *CBS 86038* ....   **29**   4 wks
6 Jan 79   **DAVID ESSEX ALBUM**   *CBS 10011* ....   **29**   7 wks
31 Mar 79   **IMPERIAL WIZARD**   *Mercury 9109 616* ....   **12**   9 wks
12 Jun 80   **HOT LOVE**   *Mercury 6359 017* ....   **75**   1 wk
19 Jun 82   **STAGE-STRUCK**   *Mercury MERS 4* ....   **31**   15 wks
27 Nov 82   **THE VERY BEST OF DAVID ESSEX**   *TV Records TVA 4* .   **37**   11 wks
15 Oct 83   **MUTINY**   *Mercury MERH 30* ....   **39**   4 wks
17 Dec 83   **THE WHISPER**   *Mercury MERH 34* ....   **67**   6 wks
6 Dec 86   **CENTRE STAGE**   *K-Tel ONE 1333* ....   **82**   4 wks
19 Oct 91   **HIS GREATEST HITS**   *Mercury 5103081* ....   **13†**   11 wks

*Mutiny is a studio recording of a musical that was not staged until 1985. Both this album and the eventual stage
production starred David Essex and Frank Finlay.*

Gloria ESTEFAN *US, female vocalist* *154 wks*

19 Nov 88	★ **ANYTHING FOR YOU** *Epic 4631251*	1	54 wks
5 Aug 89	★ **CUTS BOTH WAYS** *Epic 4651451*	1	64 wks
16 Feb 91	● **INTO THE LIGHT** *Epic 4677821*	2	36 wks

First album credits the Miami Sound Machine – US, male instrumental group.

Don ESTELLE and Windsor DAVIES
UK, male vocal duo *8 wks*

10 Jan 76	● **SING LOFTY** *EMI EMC 3102*	10	8 wks

Melissa ETHERIDGE *US, female vocalist* *1 wk*

30 Sep 89	**BRAVE AND CRAZY** *Island ILPS 9939*	63	1 wk

EUROPE *Sweden, male vocal/instrumental group* *43 wks*

22 Nov 86	● **THE FINAL COUNTDOWN** *Epic EPC 26808*	9	37 wks
17 Sep 88	**OUT OF THIS WORLD** *Epic 4624491*	12	5 wks
19 Oct 91	**PRISONERS IN PARADISE** *Epic 4687551*	61	1 wk

EUROPEANS *UK, male vocal/instrumental group* *1 wk*

11 Feb 84	**LIVE** *A&M SCOT 1*	100	1 wk

EURYTHMICS *UK, female/male vocal/instrumental group* *367 wks*

12 Feb 83	● **SWEET DREAMS (ARE MADE OF THIS)** *RCA RCALP 6063*	3	60 wks
26 Nov 83	★ **TOUCH** *RCA PL 70109*	1	48 wks
9 Jun 84	**TOUCH DANCE** *RCA PG 70354*	31	5 wks
24 Nov 84	**1984 (FOR THE LOVE OF BIG BROTHER)** *Virgin V 1984*	23	17 wks
11 May 85	● **BE YOURSELF TONIGHT** *RCA PL 70711*	3	80 wks
12 Jul 86	● **REVENGE** *RCA PL 71050*	3	52 wks
21 Nov 87	● **SAVAGE** *RCA PL 71555*	7	33 wks
23 Sep 89	★ **WE TOO ARE ONE** *RCA PL 74251*	1	32 wks
30 Mar 91	★ **GREATEST HITS** *RCA PL 74856*	1†	40 wks

Phil EVERLY *US, male vocalist* *1 wk*

7 May 83	**PHIL EVERLY** *Capitol EST 27670*	61	1 wk

See also the Everly Brothers.

EVERLY BROTHERS *US, male vocal duo* *118 wks*

2 Jul 60	● **IT'S EVERLY TIME** *Warner Bros. WM 4006*	2	23 wks
15 Oct 60	● **FABULOUS STYLE OF THE EVERLY BROTHERS** *London HAA 2266*	4	11 wks
4 Mar 61	● **A DATE WITH THE EVERLY BROTHERS** *Warner Bros. WM 4028*	3	14 wks
21 Jul 62	**INSTANT PARTY** *Warner Bros. WM 4061*	20	1 wk
12 Sep 70	● **ORIGINAL GREATEST HITS** *CBS 66255*	7	16 wks
8 Jun 74	**THE VERY BEST OF THE EVERLY BROTHERS** *Warner Bros. K 46008*	43	1 wk
29 Nov 75	● **WALK RIGHT BACK WITH THE EVERLYS** *Warner Bros. K 56118*	10	10 wks
9 Apr 77	**LIVING LEGENDS** *Warwick WW 5027*	12	10 wks

The **Exploited** kept punk alive in the early 80s.

Marianne Faithfull had things her way in June 1965.

The initial success of **EMF** (led by James Aitken) was unbelievable.

18 Dec 82	**LOVE HURTS** *K-Tel NE 1197*	**31**	22 wks
7 Jan 84	**EVERLY BROTHERS REUNION CONCERT**		
	Impression IMDP 1	**47**	6 wks
3 Nov 84	**THE EVERLY BROTHERS** *Mercury MERH 44*	**36**	4 wks

See also Phil Everly.

EVERYTHING BUT THE GIRL
UK, male/female vocal/instrumental group   *64 wks*

16 Jun 84	**EDEN** *blanco y negro BYN 2*	**14**	22 wks
27 Apr 85	● **LOVE NOT MONEY** *blanco y negro BYN 3*	**10**	9 wks
6 Sep 86	**BABY THE STARS SHINE BRIGHT**		
	blanco y negro BYN 9	**22**	9 wks
12 Mar 88	**IDLEWILD** *blanco y negro BYN 14*	**13**	9 wks
6 Aug 88	**IDLEWILD (re-issue)** *blanco y negro BYN 16*	**21**	6 wks
17 Feb 90	● **THE LANGUAGE OF LOVE** *blanco y negro BYN 21*	**10**	6 wks
5 Oct 91	**WORLDWIDE** *blanco y negro BYN 25*	**29**	3 wks

EXODUS   *US, male vocal/instrumental group*   *1 wk*

11 Feb 89	**FABULOUS DISASTER** *Music For Nations MFN 90*	**67**	1 wk

EXPLOITED   *UK, male vocal/instrumental group*   *26 wks*

16 May 81	**PUNK'S NOT DEAD** *Secret SEC 1*	**20**	11 wks
14 Nov 81	**EXPLOITED LIVE** *Superville EXPLP 2001*	**52**	3 wks
19 Jun 82	**TROOPS OF TOMORROW** *Secret SEC 8*	**17**	12 wks

132

EXTREME   *US, male vocal/instrumental group*   *31 wks*

1 Jun 91	**EXTREME II PORNOGRAFFITI** *A & M 3953131*	**12†**	31 wks

f

FAB   *UK, male producer*   *3 wks*

10 Nov 90	**POWER THEMES 90** *Telstar STAR 2430*	**53**	3 wks

FACES   *UK, male vocal/instrumental group*   *56 wks*

4 Apr 70	**FIRST STEP** *Warner Bros. WS 3000*	**45**	1 wk
8 May 71	**LONG PLAYER** *Warner Bros. W 3011*	**31**	7 wks
25 Dec 71	● **A NOD'S AS GOOD AS A WINK...TO A BLIND HORSE**		
	Warner Bros. K 56006	**2**	22 wks
21 Apr 73	★ **OOH-LA-LA** *Warner Bros. K 56011*	**1**	13 wks
26 Jan 74	● **OVERTURE AND BEGINNERS** *Mercury 9100 001*	**3**	7 wks
21 May 77	**THE BEST OF THE FACES** *Riva RVLP 3*	**24**	6 wks

Overture And Beginners credited to Rod Stewart and the Faces. See also Rod Stewart.

Donald FAGEN   *US, male vocalist*   *16 wks*

20 Oct 82	**THE NIGHTFLY** *Warner Bros. 923696*	**44**	16 wks

FAIRGROUND ATTRACTION
UK, male/female vocal/instrumental group   *54 wks*

28 May 88 ●	**THE FIRST OF A MILLION KISSES**	*RCA PL 71696*	2	52 wks
30 Jun 90	**AY FOND KISS**	*RCA PL 74596*	55	2 wks

Group were male only on last album.

FAIRPORT CONVENTION
UK, male/female vocal/instrumental group   *41 wks*

2 Aug 69	**UNHALFBRICKING**	*Island ILPS 9102*	12	8 wks
17 Jan 70	**LIEGE AND LIEF**	*Island ILPS 9115*	17	15 wks
18 Jul 70	**FULL HOUSE**	*Island ILPS 9130*	13	11 wks
3 Jul 71 ●	**ANGEL DELIGHT**	*Island ILPS 9162*	8	5 wks
12 Jul 75	**RISING FOR THE MOON**	*Island ILPS 9313*	52	1 wk
28 Jan 89	**RED AND GOLD**	*New Routes RUE 002*	74	1 wk

FAITH BROTHERS   *UK, male vocal/instrumental group*   *1 wk*

9 Nov 85	**EVENTIDE**	*Siren SIRENLP 1*	66	1 wk

FAITH NO MORE   *US, male vocal/instrumental group*   *37 wks*

17 Feb 90	**THE REAL THING**	*Slash 8281541*	30	33 wks
16 Feb 91	**LIVE AT THE BRIXTON ACADEMY**	*Slash 8282381*	20	4 wks

Adam FAITH   *UK, male vocalist*   *44 wks*

19 Nov 60 ●	**ADAM**	*Parlophone PMC 1128*	6	36 wks
11 Feb 61	**BEAT GIRL (film soundtrack)**	*Columbia 33SX 1225*	11	3 wks
24 Mar 62	**ADAM FAITH**	*Parlophone PMC 1162*	20	1 wk
25 Sep 65	**FAITH ALIVE**	*Parlophone PMC 1249*	19	1 wk
19 Dec 81	**20 GOLDEN GREATS**	*Warwick WW 5113*	61	3 wks

Marianne FAITHFULL   *UK, female vocalist*   *19 wks*

5 Jun 65	**COME MY WAY**	*Decca LK 4688*	12	7 wks
5 Jun 65	**MARIANNE FAITHFULL**	*Decca LK 4689*	15	2 wks
24 Nov 79	**BROKEN ENGLISH**	*Island M1*	57	3 wks
17 Oct 81	**DANGEROUS ACQUAINTANCES**	*Island ILPS 9648* ...	45	4 wks
26 Mar 83	**A CHILD'S ADVENTURE**	*Island ILPS 9734*	99	1 wk
8 Aug 87	**STRANGE WEATHER**	*Island ILPS 9874*	78	2 wks

FALCO   *Austria, male vocalist*   *15 wks*

26 Apr 86	**FALCO 3**	*A & M AMA 5105*	32	15 wks

FALL   *UK, male vocal/instrumental group*   *25 wks*

20 Mar 82	**HEX ENDUCTION HOUR**	*Kamera KAM 005*	71	3 wks
20 Oct 84	**THE WONDERFUL AND FRIGHTENING WORLD OF ...**			
		Beggars Banquet BEGA 58	62	2 wks
5 Oct 85	**THE NATION'S SAVING GRACE**			
		Beggars Banquet BEGA 67	54	2 wks
11 Oct 86	**BEND SINISTER**	*Beggars Banquet BEGA 75*	36	3 wks
12 Mar 88	**THE FRENZ EXPERIMENT**	*Beggars Banquet BEGA 91* ...	19	4 wks
12 Nov 88	**I AM KURIOUS, ORANJ**	*Beggars Banquet BEGA 96*	54	2 wks

133

8 Jul	89	**SEMINAL LIVE** *Beggars Banquet BBL 102*	40	2 wks
3 Mar	90	**EXTRICATE** *Cog Sinister 8422041*	31	3 wks
15 Sep	90	**458489** *Beggars Banquet BEGA 111*	44	2 wks
4 May	91	**SHIFT WORK** *Cog Sinister 8485941*	17	2 wks

Agnetha FALTSKOG *Sweden, female vocalist*   *17 wks*

11 Jun	83	**WRAP YOUR ARMS AROUND ME** *Epic EPC 25505* ...	18	13 wks
4 May	85	**EYES OF A WOMAN** *Epic EPC 26446*	38	3 wks
12 Mar	88	**I STAND ALONE** *WEA WX 150*	72	1 wk

Georgie FAME *UK, male vocalist*   *72 wks*

17 Oct	64	**FAME AT LAST** *Columbia 33SX 1638*	15	8 wks
14 May	66	● **SWEET THINGS** *Columbia SX 6043*	6	22 wks
15 Oct	66	● **SOUND VENTURE** *Columbia SX 6076*	9	9 wks
11 Mar	67	**HALL OF FAME** *Columbia SX 6120*	12	18 wks
1 Jul	67	**TWO FACES OF FAME** *CBS SBPG 63018*	22	15 wks

FAMILY *UK, male vocal/instrumental group*   *41 wks*

10 Aug	68	**MUSIC IN THE DOLLS HOUSE** *Reprise RLP 6312*	35	3 wks
22 Mar	69	● **FAMILY ENTERTAINMENT** *Reprise RSLP 6340*	6	3 wks
7 Feb	70	● **A SONG FOR ME** *Reprise RSLP 9001*	4	13 wks
28 Nov	70	● **ANYWAY** *Reprise RSX 9005*	7	7 wks
20 Nov	71	**FEARLESS** *Reprise K 54003*	14	2 wks
30 Sep	72	**BANDSTAND** *Reprise K 54006*	15	10 wks
29 Sep	73	**IT'S ONLY A MOVIE** *Raft RA 58501*	30	3 wks

134

f

FAMILY STAND *US, male/female vocal/instrumental group*   *3 wks*

19 May	90	**CHAIN** *Atlantic WX 349*	52	3 wks

FAMILY STONE – *See SLY and the FAMILY STONE*

Chris FARLOWE *UK, male vocalist*   *3 wks*

2 Apr	66	**14 THINGS TO THINK ABOUT** *Immediate IMLP 005*	19	1 wk
10 Dec	66	**THE ART OF CHRIS FARLOWE** *Immediate IMLP 006* ...	37	2 wks

FARM *UK, male vocal/instrumental group*   *17 wks*

16 Mar	91	★ **SPARTACUS** *Produce MILKLP 1*	1	17 wks

FARMERS BOYS *UK, male vocal/instrumental group*   *1 wk*

29 Oct	83	**GET OUT AND WALK** *EMI EMC 1077991*	49	1 wk

John FARNHAM *Australia, male vocalist*   *9 wks*

11 Jul	87	**WHISPERING JACK** *RCA PL 71224*	35	9 wks

FARRAR – *See MARVIN, WELCH and FARRAR*

FASHION *UK, male vocal/instrumental group*   *17 wks*

3 Jul	82	● **FABRIQUE** *Arista SPART 1185*	10	16 wks
16 Jun	84	**TWILIGHT OF IDOLS** *De Stijl EPC 25909*	69	1 wk

This foursome was in **Fashion** in 1982.

Ella Fitzgerald shows incomparable style.

FASTER PUSSYCAT US, male vocal/instrumental group   2 wks

16 Sep 89	**WAKE ME WHEN IT'S OVER** Elektra EKT 64	35	2 wks

FASTWAY UK, male vocal/instrumental group   2 wks

30 Apr 83	**FASTWAY** CBS 25359	43	2 wks

FAT BOYS US, male rap group   5 wks

3 Oct 87	**CRUSHIN'** Urban URBLP 3	49	4 wks
30 Jul 88	**COMING BACK HARD AGAIN** Urban URBLP 13	98	1 wk

FAT LADY SINGS UK, male vocal/instrumental group   1 wk

18 May 91	**TWIST** East West WX 418	50	1 wk

FAT LARRY'S BAND US, male vocal/instrumental group   4 wks

9 Oct 82	**BREAKIN' OUT** Virgin V 2229	58	4 wks

FATBACK BAND US, male vocal/instrumental group   7 wks

6 Mar 76	**RAISING HELL** Polydor 2391 203	19	6 wks
4 Jul 87	**FATBACK LIVE** Start STL 12	80	1 wk

FBI – See Redhead KINGPIN and the FBI

136

f

Phil FEARON and GALAXY
UK, male/female vocal/instrumental group   9 wks

25 Aug 84	● **PHIL FEARON AND GALAXY** Ensign ENCL 2	8	8 wks
14 Feb 85	**THIS KIND OF LOVE** Ensign ENCL 4	98	1 wk

Wilton FELDER US, male instrumentalist – tenor sax   3 wks

23 Feb 85	**SECRETS** MCA MCF 3237	77	3 wks

Also featuring Bobby Womack and introducing Alltrina Grayson.

Jose FELICIANO US, male vocalist/instrumentalist – guitar   40 wks

2 Nov 68	● **FELICIANO** RCA Victor SF 7946	6	36 wks
29 Nov 69	**JOSE FELICIANO** RCA Victor SF 8044	29	2 wks
14 Feb 70	**10 TO 23** RCA SF 7946	38	1 wk
22 Aug 70	**FIREWORKS** RCA SF 8124	65	1 wk

Julie FELIX US, female vocalist   4 wks

11 Sep 66	**CHANGES** Fontana TL 5368	27	4 wks

Bryan FERRY UK, male vocalist   154 wks

3 Nov 73	● **THESE FOOLISH THINGS** Island ILPS 9249	5	42 wks
20 Jul 74	● **ANOTHER TIME, ANOTHER PLACE** Island ILPS 9284	4	25 wks

2 Oct 76	**LET'S STICK TOGETHER** *Island ILPSX 1*	19	5 wks
5 Mar 77	● **IN YOUR MIND** *Polydor 2302 055*	5	17 wks
30 Sep 78	**THE BRIDE STRIPPED BARE** *Polydor POLD 5003*	13	5 wks
15 Jun 85	★ **BOYS AND GIRLS** *EG EGLP 62*	1	44 wks
14 Nov 87	● **BETE NOIRE** *Virgin V 2474*	9	16 wks

See also Bryan Ferry and Roxy Music.

Bryan FERRY and ROXY MUSIC
UK, male vocal/instrumental group　　　　　　　　*104 wks*

26 Apr 86	★ **STREET LIFE – 20 GREAT HITS** *EG EGTV 1*	1	77 wks
19 Nov 88	● **THE ULTIMATE COLLECTION** *EG EGTV 2*	6	27 wks

See also Bryan Ferry; Roxy Music.

Brad FIDEL *Germany, male arranger*　　　　　*7 wks*

31 Aug 91	**TERMINATOR 2** *Vareses Sarabande VS 5335*	26	7 wks

Gracie FIELDS *UK, female vocalist*　　　　　*3 wks*

20 Dec 75	**THE GOLDEN YEARS** *Warwick WW 5007*	48	3 wks

FIELDS OF THE NEPHILIM
UK, male vocal/instrumental group　　　　　　*9 wks*

30 May 87	**DAWNRAZOR** *Situation 2 SITU 18*	62	2 wks
17 Sep 88	**THE NEPHILIM** *Situation 2 SITU 22*	14	3 wks
6 Oct 90	**ELIZIUM** *Beggars Banquet BEGA 115*	22	2 wks
6 Apr 91	**EARTH INFERNO** *Beggars Banquet BEGA 120*	39	2 wks

137

f

52ND STREET *UK, male/female vocal/instrumental group*　　*1 wk*

19 Apr 86	**CHILDREN OF THE NIGHT** *10 DIX 25*	71	1 wk

FINE YOUNG CANNIBALS
UK, male vocal/instrumental group　　　　　　*94 wks*

21 Dec 85	**FINE YOUNG CANNIBALS** *London LONLP 16*	11	25 wks
18 Feb 89	★ **THE RAW AND THE COOKED** *London 8280691*	1	68 wks
15 Dec 90	**FYC** *London 8282211*	61	1 wk

FYC, a remix album of The Raw and the Cooked, credited to FYC.

FIRM *UK, male vocal/instrumental group*　　　　*8 wks*

2 Mar 85	**THE FIRM** *Atlantic 78–1239–1*	15	5 wks
5 Apr 86	**MEAN BUSINESS** *Atlantic WX 35*	46	3 wks

FIRST CIRCLE *US, male vocal/instrumental group*　　*2 wks*

2 May 87	**BOYS' NIGHT OUT** *EMI America AML 3118*	70	2 wks

FISCHER-Z *UK, male vocal/instrumental group*　　*1 wk*

23 Jun 79	**WORD SALAD** *United Artists UAG 30232*	66	1 wk

FISH UK, male vocalist   9 wks

| 10 Feb 90 ● | VIGIL IN A WILDERNESS OF MIRRORS EMI EMD 1015 | 5 | 6 wks |
| 9 Nov 91 | INTERNAL EXILE Polydor 5110491 .... | 21 | 3 wks |

FISHBONE US, male vocal/instrumental group   1 wk

| 13 Jul 91 | THE REALITY OF MY SURROUNDINGS | | |
| | Columbia 4676151 .... | 75 | 1 wk |

Ella FITZGERALD US, female vocalist   23 wks

11 Jun 60	ELLA SINGS GERSHWIN Brunswick LA 8648	13	3 wks
18 Jun 60	ELLA AT THE OPERA HOUSE Columbia 3SX 10126	16	1 wk
23 Jul 60	ELLA SINGS GERSHWIN VOL. 5 HMV CLP 1353	18	2 wks
10 May 80	THE INCOMPARABLE ELLA Polydor POLTV 9	40	7 wks
27 Feb 88	A PORTRAIT OF ELLA FITZGERALD Stylus SMR 847 .	42	10 wks

FIVE PENNY PIECE
UK, male/female vocal/instrumental group   6 wks

| 24 Mar 73 | MAKING TRACKS Columbia SCX 6536 .... | 37 | 1 wk |
| 3 Jul 76 ● | KING COTTON EMI EMC 3129 .... | 9 | 5 wks |

138

f

FIVE STAR UK, male/female vocal group   153 wks

3 Aug 85	LUXURY OF LIFE Tent PL 70735	12	70 wks
30 Aug 86 ★	SILK AND STEEL Tent PL 71100	1	58 wks
26 Sep 87 ●	BETWEEN THE LINES Tent PL 71505	7	17 wks
27 Aug 88	ROCK THE WORLD Tent PL 71747	17	5 wks
21 Oct 89	GREATEST HITS Tent PL 74080	53	3 wks

FIVE THIRTY UK, male vocal/instrumental group   1 wk

| 31 Aug 91 | BED East West WX 530 .... | 57 | 1 wk |

FIXX UK, male vocal/instrumental group   7 wks

| 22 May 82 | SHUTTERED ROOM MCA FX 1001 .... | 54 | 6 wks |
| 21 May 83 | REACH THE BEACH MCA FX 1002 .... | 91 | 1 wk |

Roberta FLACK US, female vocalist   18 wks

15 Jul 72	FIRST TAKE Atlantic K 40040	47	2 wks
13 Oct 73	KILLING ME SOFTLY Atlantic K 50021	40	2 wks
31 Mar 84	GREATEST HITS K-Tel NE 1269	35	14 wks

See also Roberta Flack and Donny Hathaway; Peabo Bryson and Roberta Flack.

Roberta FLACK and Donny HATHAWAY
US, female/male vocal duo   7 wks

| 7 Jun 80 | ROBERTA FLACK AND DONNY HATHAWAY | | |
| | Atlantic K 50696 .... | 31 | 7 wks |

See also Roberta Flack.

FLASH AND THE PAN
Australia, male vocal/instrumental group   *2 wks*

16 Jul 83 **PAN-ORAMA** *Easy Beat EASLP 100* . . . . **69** 2 wks

FLEETWOOD MAC
UK/US, male/female vocal/instrumental group   *765 wks*

2 Mar 68	● **FLEETWOOD MAC** *Blue Horizon BPG 7–63200*	**4**	37 wks
7 Sep 68	● **MR. WONDERFUL** *Blue Horizon 7–63205*	**10**	11 wks
30 Aug 69	**PIOUS BIRD OF GOOD OMEN** *Blue Horizon 7–63215*	**18**	4 wks
4 Oct 69	● **THEN PLAY ON** *Reprise RSLP 9000*	**6**	11 wks
10 Oct 70	**KILN HOUSE** *Reprise RSLP 9004*	**39**	2 wks
19 Feb 72	**GREATEST HITS** *CBS 6901*	**36**	12 wks
6 Nov 76	**FLEETWOOD MAC** *Reprise K 54043*	**23**	20 wks
26 Feb 77	★ **RUMOURS** *Warner Bros. K 56344*	**1**	443 wks
27 Oct 79	★ **TUSK** *Warner Bros. K 66088*	**1**	26 wks
13 Dec 80	**FLEETWOOD MAC LIVE** *Warner Bros. K 66097*	**31**	9 wks
10 Jul 82	● **MIRAGE** *Warner Bros. K 56592*	**5**	39 wks
25 Apr 87	★ **TANGO IN THE NIGHT** *Warner Bros. WX 65*	**1**	99 wks
3 Dec 88	● **GREATEST HITS** *Warner Bros. WX 221*	**3**	31 wks
21 Apr 90	★ **BEHIND THE MASK** *Warner Bros. WX 335*	**1**	21 wks

Group were UK and male only for first 6 albums. All the above albums are different, although some are identically titled.

Berni FLINT *UK, male vocalist*   *6 wks*

2 Jul 77 **I DON'T WANT TO PUT A HOLD ON YOU**
            EMI EMC 3184 . . . . **37** 6 wks

FLOATERS *US, male vocal/instrumental group*   *8 wks*

20 Aug 77 **FLOATERS** *ABC ABCL 5229* . . . . **17** 8 wks

FLOCK *UK, male vocal/instrumental group*   *2 wks*

2 May 70 **FLOCK** *CBS 63733* . . . . **59** 2 wks

A FLOCK OF SEAGULLS
UK, male vocal/instrumental group   *59 wks*

17 Apr 82	**A FLOCK OF SEAGULLS** *Jive HOP 201*	**32**	44 wks
7 May 83	**LISTEN** *Jive HIP 4*	**16**	10 wks
1 Sep 84	**THE STORY OF A YOUNG HEART** *Jive HIP 14*	**30**	5 wks

FLOWERED UP *UK, male vocal/instrumental group*   *3 wks*

7 Sep 91 **A LIFE WITH BRIAN** *London 8282441* . . . . **23** 3 wks

Eddie FLOYD *US, male vocalist*   *5 wks*

29 Apr 67 **KNOCK ON WOOD** *Stax 589–006* . . . . **36** 5 wks

A FLUX OF PINK INDIANS
UK, male vocal/instrumental group   *2 wks*

5 Feb 83 **STRIVE TO SURVIVE CAUSING LEAST SUFFERING
            POSSIBLE** *Spiderleg SDL 8* . . . . **79** 2 wks

FLYING LIZARDS UK, male/female vocal/instrumental group 3 wks

16 Feb 80	**FLYING LIZARDS** *Virgin V 2150*	**60**	3 wks

FLYING PICKETS UK, male vocal group 22 wks

17 Dec 83	**LIVE AT THE ALBANY EMPIRE** *AVM AVMLP 0001* ...	**48**	11 wks
9 Jun 84	**LOST BOYS** *10 DIX 4*	**11**	11 wks

FM UK, male vocal/instrumental group 3 wks

20 Sep 86	**INDISCREET** *Portrait PRT 26827*	**76**	1 wk
14 Oct 89	**TOUGH IT OUT** *Epic 465589 1*	**34**	2 wks

FOCUS Holland, male instrumental group 65 wks

11 Nov 72	● **MOVING WAVES** *Polydor 2931 002*	**2**	34 wks
2 Dec 72	● **FOCUS 3** *Polydor 2383 016*	**6**	15 wks
20 Oct 73	**FOCUS AT THE RAINBOW** *Polydor 2442 118*	**23**	5 wks
25 May 74	**HAMBURGER CONCERTO** *Polydor 2442 124*	**20**	5 wks
9 Aug 75	**FOCUS** *Polydor 2384 070*	**23**	6 wks

Dan FOGELBERG US, male vocalist 3 wks

29 Mar 80	**PHOENIX** *Epic EPC 83317*	**42**	3 wks

140

f

John FOGERTY US, male vocalist/instrumentalist – guitar 11 wks

16 Feb 85	**CENTERFIELD** *Warner Bros. 92–5203–1*	**48**	11 wks

Ellen FOLEY US, female vocalist 3 wks

17 Nov 79	**NIGHT OUT** *Epic EPC 83718*	**68**	1 wk
4 Apr 81	**SPIRIT OF ST. LOUIS** *Epic EPC 84809*	**57**	2 wks

Jane FONDA US, female exercise instructor 51 wks

29 Jan 83	● **JANE FONDA'S WORKOUT RECORD** *CBS 88581*	**7**	47 wks
22 Sep 84	**JANE FONDA'S WORKOUT RECORD: NEW AND IMPROVED** *CBS 88640*	**60**	4 wks

Wayne FONTANA and the MINDBENDERS
UK, male vocalist and male vocal/instrumental group 1 wk

20 Feb 65	**WAYNE FONTANA AND THE MINDBENDERS** *Fontana TL 5230*	**18**	1 wk

See also the Mindbenders.

Steve FORBERT US, male vocalist 3 wks

9 Jun 79	**ALIVE ON ARRIVAL** *Epic EPC 83308*	**56**	1 wk
24 Nov 79	**JACK RABBIT SLIM** *Epic EPC 83879*	**54**	2 wks

Clinton FORD *UK, male vocalist*   *4 wks*

26 May 62	**CLINTON FORD** *Oriole PS 40021*	16	4 wks

Lita FORD *UK, female vocalist*   *2 wks*

26 May 84	**DANCIN' ON THE EDGE** *Vertigo VERL 13*	96	1 wk
23 Jun 90	**STILETTO** *RCA PL 82090*	66	1 wk

Julia FORDHAM *UK, female vocalist*   *30 wks*

18 Jun 88	**JULIA FORDHAM** *Circa CIRCA 4*	20	22 wks
21 Oct 89	**PORCELAIN** *Circa CIRCA 10*	13	5 wks
2 Nov 91	**SWEPT** *Circa CIRCA 18*	33	3 wks

FOREIGNER *UK/US, male vocal/instrumental group*   *118 wks*

26 Aug 78	**DOUBLE VISION** *Atlantic K 50476*	32	5 wks
25 Jul 81	● **4** *Atlantic K 50796*	5	62 wks
18 Dec 82	**RECORDS** *Atlantic A 0999*	58	11 wks
22 Dec 84	★ **AGENT PROVOCATEUR** *Atlantic 78–1999–1*	1	32 wks
19 Dec 87	**INSIDE INFORMATION** *Atlantic WX 143*	64	7 wks
6 Jul 91	**UNUSUAL HEAT** *Atlantic WX 424*	56	1 wk

49ers *Italy, male producer*   *5 wks*

10 Mar 90	**THE 49ERS** *Fourth & Broadway BRLP 547*	51	5 wks

FOSTER and ALLEN *Ireland, male vocal duo*   *120 wks*

14 May 83	**MAGGIE** *Ritz RITZLP 0012*	72	6 wks
5 Nov 83	**I WILL LOVE YOU ALL OF MY LIFE** *Ritz RITZLP 0015*	71	6 wks
17 Nov 84	**THE VERY BEST OF FOSTER AND ALLEN** *Ritz RITZ LP TV 1*	18	18 wks
29 Mar 86	**AFTER ALL THESE YEARS** *Ritz RITZLP 0032*	82	2 wks
25 Oct 86	**REMINISCING** *Stylus SMR 623*	11	15 wks
27 Jun 87	**LOVE SONGS – THE VERY BEST OF FOSTER AND ALLEN VOL 2** *Ritz RITZLP 0036*	92	1 wk
10 Oct 87	**REFLECTIONS** *Stylus SMR 739*	16	16 wks
30 Apr 88	**REMEMBER YOU'RE MINE** *Stylus SMR 853*	16	15 wks
28 Oct 89	**THE MAGIC OF FOSTER AND ALLEN** *Stylus SMR 989* .	29	12 wks
9 Dec 89	**THE FOSTER AND ALLEN CHRISTMAS ALBUM** *Stylus SMR 995*	40	4 wks
10 Nov 90	**SOUVENIRS** *Telstar STAR 2457*	15	12 wks
8 Dec 90	**THE CHRISTMAS COLLECTION** *Telstar STAR 2459* ...	44	4 wks
2 Nov 91	**MEMORIES** *Telstar STAR 2527*	18†	9 wks

FOTHERINGAY *UK, male/female vocal/instrumental group*   *6 wks*

11 Jul 70	**FOTHERINGAY** *Island ILPS 9125*	18	6 wks

FOUR PENNIES *UK, male vocal/instrumental group*   *5 wks*

7 Nov 64	**TWO SIDES OF FOUR PENNIES** *Philips BL 7642*	13	5 wks

FOUR SEASONS *US, male vocal group*   *49 wks*

6 Jul 63	**SHERRY** *Stateside SL 10033*	20	1 wk

10 Apr 71	**EDIZIONE D'ORO** *Philips 6640–002*	11	7 wks
20 Nov 71	**THE BIG ONES** *Philips 6336–208*	37	1 wk
6 Mar 76	**THE FOUR SEASONS STORY** *Private Stock DAPS 1001* .	20	8 wks
6 Mar 76	**WHO LOVES YOU** *Warner Bros. K 56179*	12	17 wks
20 Nov 76	● **GREATEST HITS** *K-Tel NE 942*	4	6 wks
21 May 88	**THE COLLECTION** *Telstar STAR 2320*	38	9 wks

Last two albums credited to Frankie Valli and the Four Seasons.

4-SKINS *UK, male vocal/instrumental group* *4 wks*

17 Apr 82	**THE GOOD, THE BAD AND THE 4-SKINS**		
	Secret SEC 4	80	4 wks

FOUR TOPS *US, male vocal group* *239 wks*

19 Nov 66	● **FOUR TOPS ON TOP** *Tamla Motown TML 11037*	9	23 wks
11 Feb 67	● **FOUR TOPS LIVE!** *Tamla Motown STML 11041*	4	72 wks
25 Nov 67	● **REACH OUT** *Tamla Motown STML 11056*	4	34 wks
20 Jan 68	★ **GREATEST HITS** *Tamla Motown STML 11061*	1	67 wks
8 Feb 69	**YESTERDAY'S DREAMS** *Tamla Motown STML 11087* ...	37	1 wk
27 Jun 70	**STILL WATERS RUN DEEP**		
	Tamla Motown STML 11149	29	8 wks
27 Nov 71	**FOUR TOPS' GREATEST HITS VOL. 2**		
	Tamla Motown STML 11195	25	10 wks
10 Nov 73	**THE FOUR TOPS STORY 1964–72**		
	Tamla Motown TMSP 11241/2	35	5 wks
13 Feb 82	**THE BEST OF THE FOUR TOPS** *K-Tel NE 1160*	13	13 wks
8 Dec 90	**THEIR GREATEST HITS** *Telstar STAR 2437*	47	6 wks

See also Supremes and Four Tops.

142

f

FOX *UK, male/female vocal instrumental group* *8 wks*

17 May 75	● **FOX** *GTO GTLP 001*	7	8 wks

---

Samantha FOX *UK, female vocalist* *18 wks*

26 Jul 86	**TOUCH ME** *Jive HIP 39*	17	10 wks
1 Aug 87	**SAMANTHA FOX** *Jive HIP 48*	22	6 wks
18 Feb 89	**I WANNA HAVE SOME FUN** *Jive HIP 72*	46	2 wks

---

Bruce FOXTON *UK, male vocalist* *4 wks*

12 May 84	**TOUCH SENSITIVE** *Arista 206 251*	68	4 wks

---

John FOXX *UK, male vocalist* *17 wks*

2 Feb 80	**METAMATIX** *Metalbeat V 2146*	18	7 wks
3 Oct 81	**THE GARDEN** *Virgin V 2194*	24	6 wks
8 Oct 83	**THE GOLDEN SECTION** *Virgin V 2233*	27	3 wks
5 Oct 85	**IN MYSTERIOUS WAYS** *Virgin V 2355*	85	1 wk

---

FRAGGLES *UK/US, puppets* *4 wks*

21 Apr 84	**FRAGGLE ROCK** *RCA PL 70221*	38	4 wks

---

Peter FRAMPTON *UK, male vocalist/instrumentalist – guitar* *49 wks*

22 May 76	● **FRAMPTON COMES ALIVE**		
	A & M AMLM 63703	6	39 wks
18 Jun 77	**I'M IN YOU** *A & M AMLK 64039*	19	10 wks

Aretha Franklin displays stagewear ill-befitting the Queen of Soul.

Below: **The Four Seasons** took their name from a bowling alley cocktail lounge.

Bottom: **A Flock of Seagulls** flew away in 1984.

Connie FRANCIS *US, female vocalist* *26 wks*

26 Mar 60	**ROCK 'N' ROLL MILLION SELLERS** MGM C 804	12	1 wk
11 Feb 61	**CONNIE'S GREATEST HITS** MGM C 831	16	3 wks
18 Jun 77	★ **20 ALL TIME GREATS** Polydor 2391 290	1	22 wks

FRANKIE GOES TO HOLLYWOOD
UK, male vocal/instrumental group *71 wks*

10 Nov 84	★ **WELCOME TO THE PLEASUREDOME** ZTT ZTTIQ 1	1	58 wks
1 Nov 86	● **LIVERPOOL** ZTT ZTTIQ 8	5	13 wks

Aretha FRANKLIN *US, female vocalist* *58 wks*

12 Aug 67	**I NEVER LOVED A MAN** Atlantic 587-006	36	2 wks
13 Apr 68	**LADY SOUL** Atlantic 588-099	25	18 wks
14 Sep 68	● **ARETHA NOW** Atlantic 588-114	6	11 wks
18 Jan 86	**WHO'S ZOOMIN' WHO?** Arista 2072 02	49	12 wks
24 May 86	**THE FIRST LADY OF SOUL** Stylus SMR 8506	89	1 wk
8 Nov 86	**ARETHA** Arista 208 020	51	13 wks
3 Jun 89	**THROUGH THE STORM** Arista 209842	46	1 wk

Rodney FRANKLIN *US, male instrumentalist – piano* *2 wks*

24 May 80	**YOU'LL NEVER KNOW** CBS 83812	64	2 wks

Liz FRASER – *See Harold BUDD/Liz FRASER/Robin GUTHRIE/Simon RAYMOND*

144

f

FRAZIER CHORUS
UK, male/female vocal/instrumental group *2 wks*

20 May 89	**SUE** Virgin V 2578	56	1 wk
16 Mar 91	**RAY** Virgin VFC 2654	66	1 wk

FREDDIE and the DREAMERS
UK, male vocal/instrumental group *26 wks*

9 Nov 63	● **FREDDIE AND THE DREAMERS** Columbia 33SX 1577	5	26 wks

FREDERICK – *See NINA and FREDERICK*

FREE *UK, male vocal/instrumental group* *71 wks*

11 Jul 70	● **FIRE AND WATER** Island ILPS 9120	2	18 wks
23 Jan 71	**HIGHWAY** Island ILPS 9138	41	10 wks
26 Jun 71	● **FREE LIVE!** Island ILPS 9160	4	12 wks
17 Jun 72	● **FREE AT LAST** Island ILPS 9192	9	9 wks
3 Feb 73	● **HEARTBREAKER** Island ILPS 9217	9	7 wks
16 Mar 74	● **THE FREE STORY** Island ISLD 4	2	6 wks
2 Mar 91	● **THE BEST OF FREE – ALL RIGHT NOW** Island ILPTV 2	9	9 wks

FREEEZ *UK, male vocal/instrumental group* *18 wks*

7 Feb 81	**SOUTHERN FREEEZ** Beggars Banquet BEGA 22	17	15 wks
22 Oct 83	**GONNA GET YOU** Beggars Banquet BEGA 48	46	3 wks

FREHLEY'S COMET US, male vocal/instrumental group — 1 wk

18 Jun 88   **SECOND SIGHT** *Atlantic 781862 1* ....   **79**   1 wk

FRESH PRINCE – *See DJ JAZZY JEFF and FRESH PRINCE*

Glenn FREY US, male vocalist — 9 wks

6 Jul 85   **THE ALLNIGHTER** *MCA MCF 3277* ....   **31**   9 wks

FRIDA Norway, female vocalist — 8 wks

18 Sep 82   **SOMETHING'S GOING ON** *Epic EPC 85966* ....   **18**   7 wks
20 Oct 84   **SHINE** *Epic EPC 26178* ....   **67**   1 wk

Dean FRIEDMAN US, male vocalist — 14 wks

21 Oct 78   **WELL, WELL, SAID THE ROCKING CHAIR**
      Lifesong LSLP 6019 ....   **21**   14 wks

FRIENDS – *See DELANEY and BONNIE and FRIENDS*

FRIENDS – *See Richard HARVEY and FRIENDS*

FRIENDS – *See Brian MAY and FRIENDS*

Robert FRIPP UK, male vocalist/instrumentalist – guitar — 1 wk

12 May 79   **EXPOSURE** *Polydor EGLP 101* ....   **71**   1 wk

FRONT 242 US, male vocal/instrumental duo — 1 wk

2 Feb 91   **TYRANNY FOR YOU** *RRE RRE 011* ....   **49**   1 wk

FUGAZI UK, male vocal/instrumental group — 1 wk

21 Sep 91   **STEADY DIET OF NOTHING** *Dischord DISCHORD 60* ..   **63**   1 wk

FULL FORCE – *See LISA LISA and CULT JAM with FULL FORCE*

FUN BOY THREE UK, male vocal/instrumental group — 40 wks

20 Mar 82 ● **FUN BOY THREE** *Chrysalis CHR 1383* ....   **7**   20 wks
19 Feb 83   **WAITING** *Chrysalis CHR 1417* ....   **14**   20 wks

FUNK FEDERATION – *See Arlene PHILLIPS*

FUNKADELIC US, male vocal/instrumental group — 5 wks

23 Dec 78   **ONE NATION UNDER A GROOVE** *Warner Bros. K 56539*   **56**   5 wks

FUNKY BUNCH – *See MARKY MARK and the FUNKY BUNCH*

FUREYS and Davey ARTHUR
Ireland/UK, male vocal/instrumental group — 38 wks

8 May 82   **WHEN YOU WERE SWEET SIXTEEN**
      Ritz RITZLP 0004 ....   **99**   1 wk

145

f

Robert Fripp is shown in 1979, the
year of his chart exposure.

10 Nov 84	**GOLDEN DAYS** *K-Tel ONE 1283*	17	19 wks
26 Oct 85	**AT THE END OF THE DAY** *K-Tel ONE 1310*	35	11 wks
21 Nov 87	**FUREYS FINEST** *Telstar HSTAR 2311*	65	7 wks

FURIOUS FIVE – *See GRANDMASTER FLASH and the FURIOUS FIVE*

Billy FURY   *UK, male vocalist*   51 wks

4 Jun 60	**THE SOUND OF FURY** *Decca LF 1329*	18	2 wks
23 Sep 61	● **HALFWAY TO PARADISE** *Ace Of Clubs ACL 1083*	5	9 wks
11 May 63	● **BILLY** *Decca LK 4533*	6	21 wks
26 Oct 63	**WE WANT BILLY** *Decca LK 4548*	14	2 wks
19 Feb 83	**HIT PARADE** *Decca TAB 37*	44	15 wks
26 Mar 83	**THE ONE AND ONLY** *Polydor POLD 5069*	54	2 wks

FUZZBOX – *See WE'VE GOT A FUZZBOX AND WE'RE GONNA USE IT*

g

Kenny G   *US, male instrumentalist – saxophone*   17 wks

17 Mar 84	**G FORCE** *Arista 206 168*	56	5 wks
8 Aug 87	**DUOTONES** *Arista 207 792*	28	5 wks
14 Apr 90	**MONTAGE** *Arista 210621*	32	7 wks

Peter GABRIEL   *UK, male vocalist*   169 wks

12 Mar 77	● **PETER GABRIEL** *Charisma CDS 4006*	7	19 wks
17 Jun 78	● **PETER GABRIEL** *Charisma CDS 4013*	10	8 wks
7 Jun 80	★ **PETER GABRIEL** *Charisma CDS 4019*	1	18 wks
18 Sep 82	● **PETER GABRIEL** *Charisma PG 4*	6	16 wks
18 Jun 83	● **PETER GABRIEL PLAYS LIVE** *Charisma PGDL 1*	8	9 wks
30 Apr 85	**BIRDY – MUSIC FROM THE FILM** *Charisma CAS 1167*	51	3 wks
31 May 86	★ **SO** *Virgin PG 5*	1	76 wks
17 Jun 89	**PASSION** *Virgin RWLP 1*	29	5 wks
1 Dec 90	**SHAKING THE TREE – GOLDEN GREATS** *Virgin PGTV 6*	11	15 wks

First four albums are different.

GALAXY – *See Phil FEARON and GALAXY*

GALLAGHER and LYLE
UK, male vocal/instrumental duo   44 wks

| 28 Feb 76 | ● **BREAKAWAY** *A&M AMLH 68348* | 6 | 35 wks |
| 29 Jan 77 | **LOVE ON THE AIRWAYS** *A&M AMLH 64620* | 19 | 9 wks |

Rory GALLAGHER
UK, male vocalist/instrumentalist – guitar   43 wks

29 May 71	**RORY GALLAGHER** *Polydor 2383–044*	32	2 wks
4 Dec 71	**DEUCE** *Polydor 2383–076*	39	1 wk
20 May 72	● **LIVE IN EUROPE** *Polydor 2383 112*	9	15 wks
24 Feb 73	**BLUE PRINT** *Polydor 2383 189*	12	7 wks
17 Nov 73	**TATTOO** *Polydor 2383 230*	32	3 wks

147

g

27 Jul 74	**IRISH TOUR '74** *Polydor 2659 031*	36	2 wks
30 Oct 76	**CALLING CARD** *Chrysalis CHR 1124*	32	1 wk
22 Sep 79	**TOP PRIORITY** *Chrysalis CHR 1235*	56	4 wks
8 Nov 80	**STAGE STRUCK** *Chrysalis CHR 1280*	40	3 wks
8 May 82	**JINX** *Chrysalis CHR 1359*	68	5 wks

James GALWAY *UK, male instrumentalist – flute* *63 wks*

27 May 78	**THE MAGIC FLUTE OF JAMES GALWAY**		
	RCA Red Seal LRLI 5131	43	6 wks
1 Jul 78	**THE MAN WITH THE GOLDEN FLUTE**		
	RCA Red Seal LRLI 5127	52	3 wks
9 Sep 78 ●	**JAMES GALWAY PLAYS SONGS FOR ANNIE**		
	RCA Red Seal RL 25163	7	40 wks
15 Dec 79	**SONGS OF THE SEASHORE** *Solar RL 25253*	39	6 wks
18 Dec 82	**THE JAMES GALWAY COLLECTION**		
	Telstar STAR 2224	41	8 wks

See also James Galway and the Chieftains; James Galway and Henry Mancini; Cleo Laine and James Galway.

James GALWAY and Henry MANCINI with the NATIONAL PHILHARMONIC ORCHESTRA
UK, male instrumentalist – flute, US conductor with UK orchestra *6 wks*

| 8 Dec 84 | **IN THE PINK** *RCA Red Seal RL 85315* .... | 62 | 6 wks |

See also James Galway; Henry Mancini.

148

g

James GALWAY and the CHIEFTAINS
UK, male instrumentalist – flute with Ireland, male instrumental group *5 wks*

| 28 Mar 87 | **JAMES GALWAY AND THE CHIEFTAINS IN IRELAND** | | |
| | *RCA Red Seal RL 85798* .... | 32 | 5 wks |

See also James Galway; Van Morrison.

GANG OF FOUR *UK, male vocal/instrumental group* *9 wks*

13 Oct 79	**ENTERTAINMENT** *EMI EMC 3313*	45	3 wks
21 Mar 81	**SOLID GOLD** *EMI EMC 3364*	52	2 wks
29 May 82	**SONGS OF THE FREE** *EMI EMC 3412*	61	4 wks

GANG STARR *US, male rap group* *3 wks*

| 26 Jan 91 | **STEP IN THE ARENA** *Cooltempo ZCTLP 21* .... | 45 | 3 wks |

GAP BAND *US, male vocal/instrumental group* *3 wks*

| 7 Feb 87 | **GAP BAND 8** *Total Experience FL 89992* .... | 47 | 3 wks |

Art GARFUNKEL *US, male vocalist* *58 wks*

13 Oct 73	**ANGEL CLARE** *CBS 69021*	14	7 wks
1 Nov 75 ●	**BREAKAWAY** *CBS 86002*	7	10 wks
18 Mar 78	**WATER MARK** *CBS 86054*	25	5 wks
21 Apr 79 ●	**FATE FOR BREAKFAST** *CBS 86082*	2	20 wks
19 Sep 81	**SCISSORS CUT** *CBS 85259*	51	3 wks
17 Nov 84	**THE ART GARFUNKEL ALBUM** *CBS 10046*	12	13 wks

See also Simon and Garfunkel.

Judy GARLAND *US, female vocalist* 3 wks

| 3 Mar 62 | JUDY AT CARNEGIE HALL *Capitol W 1569* .... | 13 | 3 wks |

Errol GARNER *US, male instrumentalist – piano* 1 wk

| 14 Jul 62 | CLOSE UP IN SWING *Philips BBL 7579* .... | 20 | 1 wk |

David GATES *US, male vocalist* 4 wks

| 31 May 75 | NEVER LET HER GO *Elektra K 52012* .... | 32 | 1 wk |
| 29 Jul 78 | GOODBYE GIRL *Elektra K 52091* .... | 28 | 3 wks |

Marvin GAYE *US, male vocalist* 98 wks

16 Mar 68	GREATEST HITS *Tamla Motown STML 11065*	40	1 wk
10 Nov 73	LET'S GET IT ON *Tamla Motown STMA 8013*	39	1 wk
15 May 76	I WANT YOU *Tamla Motown STML 12025*	22	5 wks
30 Oct 76	THE BEST OF MARVIN GAYE *Tamla Motown STML 12042*	56	1 wk
28 Feb 81	IN OUR LIFETIME *Motown STML 12149*	48	4 wks
20 Nov 82 ●	MIDNIGHT LOVE *CBS 85977*	10	16 wks
12 Nov 83	GREATEST HITS *Telstar STAR 2234*	13	61 wks
15 Jun 85	DREAM OF A LIFETIME *CBS 26239*	46	4 wks
2 Nov 90	LOVE SONGS *Telstar STAR 2427*	39	5 wks

See also Marvin Gaye and Smokey Robinson; Marvin Gaye and Tammi Terrell; Diana Ross and Marvin Gaye.

Marvin GAYE and Smokey ROBINSON

US, male vocal duo 9 wks

| 12 Nov 88 | LOVE SONGS *Telstar STAR 2331* .... | 69 | 9 wks |

See also Marvin Gaye; Smokey Robinson.

Marvin GAYE and Tammi TERRELL

US, male/female vocal duo 4 wks

| 22 Aug 70 | GREATEST HITS *Tamla Motown STML 11153* .... | 60 | 4 wks |

See also Marvin Gaye.

GAYE BYKERS ON ACID

UK, male vocal/instrumental group 1 wk

| 14 Nov 87 | DRILL YOUR OWN HOLE *Virgin V 2478* .... | 95 | 1 wk |

Crystal GAYLE *US, female vocalist* 25 wks

21 Jan 78	WE MUST BELIEVE IN MAGIC *United Artists UAG 30108*	15	7 wks
23 Sep 78	WHEN I DREAM *United Artists UAG 30169*	25	8 wks
22 Mar 80 ●	THE CRYSTAL GAYLE SINGLES ALBUM		
	United Artists UAG 30287	7	10 wks

Gloria GAYNOR *US, female vocalist* 17 wks

8 Mar 75	NEVER CAN SAY GOODBYE *MGM 2315 321*	32	8 wks
24 Mar 79	LOVE TRACKS *Polydor 2391 385*	31	7 wks
16 Aug 86	THE POWER OF GLORIA GAYNOR *Stylus SMR 618* ..	81	2 wks

J. GEILS BAND US, male vocal/instrumental group — 15 wks

27 Feb 82	**FREEZE FRAME** EMI America AML 3020	12	15 wks

Bob GELDOF Ireland, male vocalist — 7 wks

6 Dec 86	**DEEP IN THE HEART OF NOWHERE** Mercury BOBLP 1	79	1 wk
4 Aug 90	**THE VEGETARIANS OF LOVE** Mercury 8462501	21	6 wks

GENE LOVES JEZEBEL
UK, male vocal/instrumental group — 5 wks

19 Jul 87	**DISCOVER** Beggars Banquet BEGA 73	32	4 wks
24 Oct 87	**HOUSE OF DOLLS** Beggars Banquet BEGA 87	81	1 wk

GENERATION X UK, male vocal/instrumental group — 9 wks

8 Apr 78	**GENERATION X** Chrysalis CHR 1169	29	4 wks
17 Feb 79	**VALLEY OF THE DOLLS** Chrysalis CHR 1193	51	5 wks

GENESIS UK, male vocal/instrumental group — 385 wks

14 Oct 72	**FOXTROT** Charisma CAS 1058	12	7 wks
11 Aug 73	● **GENESIS LIVE** Charisma CLASS 1	9	10 wks
20 Oct 73	● **SELLING ENGLAND BY THE POUND** Charisma CAS 1074	3	21 wks
11 May 74	**NURSERY CRYME** Charisma CAS 1052	39	1 wk
7 Dec 74	● **THE LAMB LIES DOWN ON BROADWAY** Charisma CGS 101	10	6 wks
28 Feb 76	● **A TRICK OF THE TAIL** Charisma CDS 4001	3	39 wks
15 Jan 77	● **WIND AND WUTHERING** Charisma CDS 4005	7	22 wks
29 Oct 77	● **SECONDS OUT** Charisma GE 2001	4	17 wks
15 Apr 78	● **AND THEN THERE WERE THREE** Charisma CDS 4010	3	32 wks
5 Apr 80	★ **DUKE** Charisma CBR 101	1	30 wks
26 Sep 81	★ **ABACAB** Charisma CBR 102	1	27 wks
12 Jun 82	● **3 SIDES LIVE** Charisma GE 2002	2	19 wks
15 Oct 83	★ **GENESIS** Charisma GENLP 1	1	51 wks
31 Mar 84	**NURSERY CRYME (re-issue)** Charisma CHC 22	68	1 wk
21 Apr 84	**TRESPASS** Charisma CHC 12	98	1 wk
21 Jun 86	★ **INVISIBLE TOUCH** Charisma GENLP 2	1	95 wks
23 Nov 91	★ **WE CAN'T DANCE** Virgin GENLP 3	1†	6 wks

Jackie GENOVA UK, female exercise instructor — 2 wks

21 May 83	**WORK THAT BODY** Island ILPS 9732	74	2 wks

Bobbie GENTRY US, female vocalist — 1 wk

25 Oct 69	**TOUCH 'EM WITH LOVE** Capitol EST 155	21	1 wk

See also Bobbie Gentry and Glen Campbell.

Bobbie GENTRY and Glen CAMPBELL
US, female/male vocal duo — 1 wk

28 Feb 70	**BOBBIE GENTRY AND GLEN CAMPBELL** Capitol ST 2928	50	1 wk

See also Bobbie Gentry; Glen Campbell.

Lowell GEORGE US, male vocalist/instrumentalist – guitar *1 wk*

21 Apr 79 **THANKS BUT I'LL EAT IT HERE** *Warner Bros. K 56487* . **71** 1 wk

Robin GEORGE UK, male vocal/instrumentalist – guitar *3 wks*

2 Mar 85 **DANGEROUS MUSIC** *Bronze BRON 554* . . . . **65** 3 wks

GEORGIA SATELLITES
US, male vocal/instrumental group *9 wks*

7 Feb 87 **GEORGIA SATELLITES** *Elektra 980 496–1* . . . . **52** 7 wks
2 Jul 88 **OPEN ALL NIGHT** *Elektra EKT 47* . . . . **39** 2 wks

GERRY and the PACEMAKERS
UK, male vocal/instrumental group *29 wks*

26 Oct 63 ● **HOW DO YOU LIKE IT?** *Columbia 33SX 1546* . . . . **2** 28 wks
6 Feb 65 **FERRY CROSS THE MERSEY** *Columbia 33SX 1676* . . . . **19** 1 wk

Stan GETZ and Charlie BYRD
US, male instrumental duo – saxophone and guitar *7 wks*

23 Feb 63 **JAZZ SAMBA** *Verve SULP 9013* . . . . **15** 7 wks

Andy GIBB UK, male vocalist *9 wks*

19 Aug 78 **SHADOW DANCING** *RSO RSS 0001* . . . . **15** 9 wks

Barry GIBB UK, male vocalist *2 wks*

20 Oct 84 **NOW VOYAGER** *Polydor POLH 14* . . . . **85** 2 wks

Steve GIBBONS BAND UK, male vocal/instrumental group *3 wks*

22 Oct 77 **CAUGHT IN THE ACT** *Polydor 2478 112* . . . . **22** 3 wks

Debbie GIBSON US, female vocalist *52 wks*

30 Jan 88 **OUT OF THE BLUE** *Atlantic WX 139* . . . . **28** 35 wks
11 Feb 89 ● **ELECTRIC YOUTH** *Atlantic WX 231* . . . . **8** 16 wks
30 Mar 91 **ANYTHING IS POSSIBLE** *Atlantic WX 399* . . . . **69** 1 wk

Don GIBSON US, male vocalist *10 wks*

22 Mar 80 **COUNTRY NUMBER ONE** *Warwick WW 5079* . . . . **13** 10 wks

GIBSON BROTHERS
Martinique, male vocal/instrumental group *3 wks*

30 Aug 80 **ON THE RIVIERA** *Island ILPS 9620* . . . . **50** 3 wks

151

g

Debbie Gibson came out of the blue in 1988.

Corner left: The **Gang of Four** provided chart entertainment in 1979.

Marvin Gaye emotes as an early 60s Tamla sex symbol.

GILLAN UK, male vocal/instrumental group　　　　　53 wks

17 Jul	76		**CHILD IN TIME**	*Polydor 2490 136*		55	1 wk
20 Oct	79		**MR. UNIVERSE**	*Acrobat ACRO 3*		11	6 wks
16 Aug	80	●	**GLORY ROAD**	*Virgin V 2171*		3	12 wks
25 Apr	81	●	**FUTURE SHOCK**	*Virgin VK 2196*		2	13 wks
7 Nov	81		**DOUBLE TROUBLE**	*Virgin VGD 3506*		12	15 wks
2 Oct	82		**MAGIC**	*Virgin V 2238*		17	6 wks

Child In Time *credited to Ian Gillan Band. See also Ian Gillan.*

Ian GILLAN UK, male vocalist　　　　　1 wk

28 Jul	90	**NAKED THUNDER**	*Teldec 9031718991*		63	1 wk

See also Gillan.

David GILMOUR UK, male instrumentalist – guitar　　　　　18 wks

10 Jun	78	**DAVID GILMOUR**	*Harvest SHVL 817*		17	9 wks
17 Mar	84	**ABOUT FACE**	*Harvest SHSP 2400791*		21	9 wks

Gordon GILTRAP UK, male instrumentalist – guitar　　　　　7 wks

18 Feb	78	**PERILOUS JOURNEY**	*Electric TRIX 4*		29	7 wks

GIPSY KINGS France, male vocal/instrumental group　　　　　49 wks

15 Apr	89	**GIPSY KINGS**	*Telstar STAR 2355*		16	29 wks
25 Nov	89	**MOSAIQUE**	*Telstar STAR 2398*		27	13 wks
13 Jul	91	**ESTE MUNDO**	*Columbia 4686481*		19	7 wks

153

g

GIRL UK, male vocal/instrumental group　　　　　6 wks

9 Feb	80	**SHEER GREED**	*Jet JETLP 224*		33	5 wks
23 Jan	82	**WASTED YOUTH**	*Jet JETLP 238*		92	1 wk

GIRLS AT OUR BEST
UK, male/female vocal/instrumental group　　　　　3 wks

7 Nov	81	**PLEASURE**	*Happy Birthday RVLP 1*		60	3 wks

GIRLSCHOOL UK, female vocal/instrumental group　　　　　23 wks

5 Jul	80		**DEMOLITION**	*Bronze BRON 525*		28	10 wks
25 Apr	81	●	**HIT 'N' RUN**	*Bronze BRON 534*		5	6 wks
12 Jun	82		**SCREAMING BLUE MURDER**	*Bronze BRON 541*		27	6 wks
12 Nov	83		**PLAY DIRTY**	*Bronze BRON 548*		66	1 wk

Gary GLITTER UK, male vocalist　　　　　92 wks

21 Oct	72	●	**GLITTER**	*Bell BELLS 216*		8	40 wks
16 Jun	73	●	**TOUCH ME**	*Bell BELLS 222*		2	33 wks
29 Jun	74	●	**REMEMBER ME THIS WAY**	*Bell BELLS 237*		5	14 wks
27 Mar	76		**GARY GLITTER'S GREATEST HITS**	*Bell BELLS 262*		33	5 wks

GLITTER BAND UK, male vocal/instrumental group　　　　　17 wks

14 Sep	74	**HEY**	*Bell BELLS 241*		13	12 wks

3 May 75	**ROCK 'N' ROLL DUDES** *Bell BELLS 253*	**17**	4 wks
19 Jun 76	**GREATEST HITS** *Bell BELLS 264*	**52**	1 wk

GLOVE *UK, male vocal/instrumental group*   *3 wks*

17 Sep 83	**BLUE SUNSHINE** *Wonderland SHELP 2*	**35**	3 wks

GO WEST *UK, male vocal/instrumental group*   *88 wks*

13 Apr 85 ●	**GO WEST/BANGS AND CRASHES**		
	Chrysalis CHR 1495	**8**	83 wks
6 Jun 87	**DANCING ON THE COUCH** *Chrysalis CDL 1550*	**19**	5 wks

Bangs and Crashes is an album of remixed versions of Go West tracks and some new material. From 31 May 1986 both records were available together as a double album.

GO-BETWEENS
Australia, male/female vocal/instrumental group   *2 wks*

13 Jun 87	**TALLULAH** *Beggars Banquet BEGA 81*	**91**	1 wk
10 Sep 88	**16 LOVERS LANE** *Beggars Banquet BEGA 95*	**81**	1 wk

GODFATHERS *UK, male vocal/instrumental group*   *3 wks*

13 Feb 88	**BIRTH SCHOOL WORK DEATH** *Epic 460263 1*	**80**	2 wks
20 May 89	**MORE SONGS ABOUT LOVE AND HATE**		
	Epic 463394 1	**49**	1 wk

GODLEY and CREME *UK, male vocal/instrumental duo*   *16 wks*

19 Nov 77	**CONSEQUENCES** *Mercury CONS 017*	**52**	1 wk
9 Sep 78	**L** *Mercury 9109 611*	**47**	2 wks
17 Oct 81	**ISMISM** *Polydor POLD 5043*	**29**	13 wks

Consequences credited to Kevin Godley and Lol Creme. See also 10 C.C. and Godley and Creme.

GO-GO'S *US, female vocal/instrumental group*   *3 wks*

21 Aug 82	**VACATION** *IRS SP 70031*	**75**	3 wks

Andrew GOLD *US, male vocalist/instrumentalist – piano*   *7 wks*

15 Apr 78	**ALL THIS AND HEAVEN TOO** *Asylum K 53072*	**31**	7 wks

GOLDEN EARRING *Holland, male vocal/instrumental group*   *4 wks*

2 Feb 74	**MOONTAN** *Track 2406 112*	**24**	4 wks

Glen GOLDSMITH *UK, male vocalist*   *9 wks*

23 Jul 88	**WHAT YOU SEE IS WHAT YOU GET** *RCA PL 71750* ...	**14**	9 wks

GOODBYE MR. MACKENZIE
UK, male/female vocal/instrumental group   *4 wks*

22 Apr 89	**GOOD DEEDS AND DIRTY RAGS** *Capitol EST 2089*	**26**	3 wks
16 Mar 91	**HAMMER AND TONGS** *Radioactive RAR 10227*	**61**	1 wk

GOODIES UK, male vocal group — 11 wks

8 Nov 75 **THE NEW GOODIES LP** Bradley's BRADL 1010 .... 25 11 wks

Benny GOODMAN US, male instrumentalist – clarinet — 1 wk

3 Apr 71 **BENNY GOODMAN TODAY** Decca DDS 3 .... 49 1 wk

Ron GOODWIN UK, orchestra — 1 wk

2 May 70 **LEGEND OF THE GLASS MOUNTAIN**
Studio Two TWO 220 .... 49 1 wk

GOOMBAY DANCE BAND
Germany/Montserrat, male/female vocal group — 9 wks

10 Apr 82 **SEVEN TEARS** Epic EPC 85702 .... 16 9 wks

GOONS UK, male comedy group — 31 wks

28 Nov 59 ● **BEST OF THE GOON SHOWS** Parlophone PMC 1108 .... 8 14 wks
17 Dec 60 **BEST OF THE GOON SHOWS VOL. 2**
Parlophone PMC 1129 .... 12 6 wks
4 Nov 72 ● **LAST GOON SHOW OF ALL**
BBC Radio Enterprises REB 142 .... 8 11 wks

GORDON – See PETER and GORDON

155

Martin L. GORE UK, male vocalist/instrumentalist – keyboards — 1 wk

g

24 Jun 89 **COUNTERFEIT E.P.** Mute STUMM 67 .... 51 1 wk

Jaki GRAHAM UK, female vocalist — 10 wks

14 Sep 85 **HEAVEN KNOWS** EMI JK 1 .... 48 5 wks
20 Sep 86 **BREAKING AWAY** EMI EMC 3514 .... 25 5 wks

GRAND PRIX UK, male vocal/instrumental group — 2 wks

18 Jun 83 **SAMURAI** Chrysalis CHR 1430 .... 65 2 wks

GRANDMASTER FLASH and the FURIOUS FIVE US, male vocalist and male vocal group — 20 wks

23 Oct 82 **THE MESSAGE** Sugar Hill SHLP 1007 .... 77 3 wks
23 Jun 84 **GREATEST MESSAGES** Sugar Hill SHLP 5552 .... 41 16 wks
23 Feb 85 **THEY SAID IT COULDN'T BE DONE** Elektra 9–60389–1 95 1 wk

GRANDMASTER MELLE MEL US, male vocalist — 5 wks

20 Oct 84 **WORK PARTY** Sugar Hill SHLP 5553 .... 45 5 wks

Amy GRANT US, female vocalist — 15 wks

22 Jun 91 **HEART IN MOTION** A&M 3953211 .... 25 15 wks

Jazz legend **Benny Goodman** charted late in life with a live album recorded in Sweden.

Not everyone in this line-up stayed with the **Hollies**.

David GRANT *UK, male vocalist*   *7 wks*

| 5 Nov 83 | **DAVID GRANT** *Chrysalis CHR 1448* .... | 32 | 6 wks |
| 18 May 85 | **HOPES AND DREAMS** *Chrysalis CHR 1483* .... | 96 | 1 wk |

Eddy GRANT *Guyana, male vocalist/multi-instrumentalist*   *47 wks*

30 May 81	**CAN'T GET ENOUGH** *Ice ICELP 21*	39	6 wks
27 Nov 82 ●	**KILLER ON THE RAMPAGE** *Ice ICELP 3023*	7	23 wks
17 Nov 84	**ALL THE HITS** *K-Tel NE 1284*	23	10 wks
1 Jul 89	**WALKING ON SUNSHINE (THE BEST OF EDDY GRANT)** *Parlophone PCSD 108*	20	8 wks

GRATEFUL DEAD *US, male vocal/instrumental group*   *9 wks*

19 Sep 70	**WORKINGMAN'S DEAD** *Warner Bros. WS 1869*	69	2 wks
3 Aug 74	**GRATEFUL DEAD FROM THE MARS HOTEL** *Atlantic K 59302*	47	1 wk
1 Nov 75	**BLUES FOR ALLAH** *United Artists UAS 29895*	45	1 wk
4 Sep 76	**STEAL YOUR FACE** *United Artists UAS 60131/2*	42	1 wk
20 Aug 77	**TERRAPIN STATION** *Arista SPARTY 1016*	30	1 wk
19 Sep 87	**IN THE DARK** *Arista 208 564*	57	3 wks

See also Bob Dylan and the Grateful Dead.

David GRAY and Tommy TYCHO
UK, male arrangers   *6 wks*

| 16 Oct 76 | **ARMCHAIR MELODIES** *K-Tel NE 927* .... | 21 | 6 wks |

Alltrina GRAYSON – *See Wilton FELDER*

GREAT WHITE *US, male vocal/instrumental group*   *1 wk*

| 9 Mar 91 | **HOOKED** *Capitol EST 2138* .... | 43 | 1 wk |

Al GREEN *US, male vocalist*   *23 wks*

| 26 Apr 75 | **AL GREEN'S GREATEST HITS** *London SHU 8481* ..... | 18 | 16 wks |
| 1 Oct 88 | **HI LIFE – THE BEST OF AL GREEN** *K-Tel NE 1420* .... | 34 | 7 wks |

Peter GREEN *UK, male vocalist/instrumentalist – guitar*   *17 wks*

| 9 Jul 79 | **IN THE SKIES** *Creole PULS 101* .... | 32 | 13 wks |
| 24 May 80 | **LITTLE DREAMER** *PUK PULS 102* .... | 34 | 4 wks |

GREEN ON RED *US, male vocal/instrumental group*   *1 wk*

| 26 Oct 85 | **NO FREE LUNCH** *Mercury MERM 78* .... | 99 | 1 wk |

Dave GREENFIELD and Jean-Jacques BURNEL
UK, male vocal/instrumental duo   *1 wk*

| 3 Dec 83 | **FIRE AND WATER** *Epic EPC 25707* .... | 94 | 1 wk |

See also Jean-Jacques Burnel.

GREENSLADE UK, male vocal/instrumental group   3 wks

14 Sep 74   **SPYGLASS GUEST** *Warner Bros. K 56055* . . . .   **34**   3 wks

Christina GREGG UK, female exercise instructor   1 wk

27 May 78   **MUSIC 'N' MOTION** *Warwick WW 5041* . . . .   **51**   1 wk

Nanci GRIFFITH US, female vocalist   9 wks

28 Mar 88   **LITTLE LOVE AFFAIRS** *MCA MCF 3413* . . . .   **78**   1 wk
23 Sep 89   **STORMS** *MCA MCG 6066* . . . .   **38**   3 wks
28 Sep 91   **LATE NIGHT GRANDE HOTEL** *MCA MCA 10306* . . . .   **40**   5 wks

GROUNDHOGS UK, male vocal/instrumental group   50 wks

 6 Jun 70 ● **THANK CHRIST FOR THE BOMB** *Liberty LBS 83295* . . .   **9**   13 wks
 3 Apr 71 ● **SPLIT** *Liberty LBG 83401* . . . .   **5**   27 wks
18 Mar 72 ● **WHO WILL SAVE THE WORLD**
            United Artists UAG 29237 . . . .   **8**   9 wks
13 Jul 74   **SOLID** *WWA WWA 004* . . . .   **31**   1 wk

Sir Charles GROVES/RPO & CHORUS/ Sarah WALKER
UK, male conductor, orchestra and female vocalist   4 wks

158

g

22 Sep 90   **MUSIC FOR THE LAST NIGHT OF THE PROMS**
            Cirrus TVLP 501 . . . .   **39**   4 wks

See also Royal Philharmonic Orchestra.

GTR UK, male vocal/instrumental group   4 wks

19 Jul 86   **GTR** *Arista 207 716* . . . .   **41**   4 wks

GUILDFORD CATHEDRAL CHOIR UK, choir   4 wks

10 Dec 66   **CHRISTMAS CAROLS FROM GUILDFORD CATHEDRAL**
            MFP 1104 . . . .   **24**   4 wks

Record credits Barry Rose as conductor.

GUN UK, male vocal/instrumental group   10 wks

22 Jul 89   **TAKING ON THE WORLD** *A & M AMA 7007* . . . .   **44**   10 wks

David GUNSON UK, male after dinner speaker   2 wks

25 Dec 82   **WHAT GOES UP MIGHT COME DOWN** *Big Ben BB 0012*   **92**   2 wks

GUNS N' ROSES US, male vocal/instrumental group   157 wks

 1 Aug 87 ● **APPETITE FOR DESTRUCTION** *Geffen WX 125* . . . . . .   **5**   90 wks
17 Dec 88   **G N' R LIES . . .** *Geffen WX 218* . . . .   **22**   39 wks
28 Sep 91 ● **USE YOUR ILLUSION I** *Geffen GEF 24415* . . . .   **2†**   14 wks
28 Sep 91 ★ **USE YOUR ILLUSION II** *Geffen GEF 24420* . . . .   **1†**   14 wks

GURU JOSH *UK, male producer*   *2 wks*

14 Jul 90   **INFINITY** *deConstruction PL 74701*   41   2 wks

G.U.S. (FOOTWEAR) BAND and the MORRISTOWN ORPHEUS CHOIR
UK, male instrumental group and male/female vocal group   *1 wk*

3 Oct 70   **LAND OF HOPE AND GLORY** *Columbia SCX 6406*   54   1 wk

Arlo GUTHRIE *US, male vocalist*   *1 wk*

7 Mar 70   **ALICE'S RESTAURANT** *Reprise RSLP 6267*   44   1 wk

Gwen GUTHRIE *US, female vocalist*   *14 wks*

23 Aug 86   **GOOD TO GO LOVER** *Boiling Point POLD 5201*   42   14 wks

Robin GUTHRIE – *See Harold BUDD/Liz FRASER/Robin GUTHRIE/Simon RAYMOND*

Buddy GUY *US, male vocalist/instrumentalist – guitar*   *5 wks*

22 Jun 91   **DAMN RIGHT I'VE GOT THE BLUES**
                Silvertone ORELP 516   43   5 wks

A GUY CALLED GERALD
UK, male multi-instrumentalist   *1 wk*

14 Apr 90   **AUTOMANIKK** *Subscape 4664821*   68   1 wk

GUYS 'N' DOLLS *UK, male/female vocal group*   *1 wk*

31 May 75   **GUYS 'N' DOLLS** *Magnet MAG 5005*   43   1 wk

GWENT CHORALE – *See Bryn YEMM*

159

h

h

Steve HACKETT
UK, male vocalist/instrumentalist – guitar   *38 wks*

1 Nov 75	**VOYAGE OF THE ACOLYTE** *Charisma CAS 1111*	26	4 wks
6 May 78	**PLEASE DON'T TOUCH** *Charisma CDS 4012*	38	5 wks
26 May 79	**SPECTRAL MORNINGS** *Charisma CDS 4017*	22	11 wks
21 Jun 80	● **DEFECTOR** *Charisma CDS 4018*	9	7 wks
29 Aug 81	**CURED** *Charisma CDS 4021*	15	5 wks
30 Apr 83	**HIGHLY STRUNG** *Charisma HACK 1*	16	3 wks
19 Nov 83	**BAY OF KINGS** *Lamborghini LMGLP 3000*	70	1 wk
22 Sep 84	**TILL WE HAVE FACES** *Lamborghini LMGLP 4000*	54	2 wks

Sammy HAGAR *US, male vocalist/instrumentalist – guitar* *19 wks*

29 Sep	79	**STREET MACHINE** *Capitol EST 11983*	38	4 wks
22 Mar	80	**LOUD AND CLEAR** *Capitol EST 25330*	12	8 wks
7 Jun	80	**DANGER ZONE** *Capitol EST 12069*	25	3 wks
13 Feb	82	**STANDING HAMPTON** *Geffen GEF 85456*	84	2 wks
4 Jul	87	**SAMMY HAGAR** *Geffen WX 114*	86	2 wks

See also Hagar, Schon, Aaronson, Shrieve.

HAGAR, SCHON, AARONSON, SHRIEVE
US, male vocal/instrumental group *1 wk*

19 May	84	**THROUGH THE FIRE** *Geffen GEF 25893*	92	1 wk

See also Sammy Hagar.

Paul HAIG *UK, male vocalist* *2 wks*

22 Oct	83	**RHYTHM OF LIFE** *Crepuscule ILPS 9742*	82	2 wks

HAIRCUT 100 *UK, male vocal/instrumental group* *34 wks*

6 Mar	82	● **PELICAN WEST** *Arista HCC 100*	2	34 wks

Bill HALEY and his COMETS
US, male vocal/instrumental group *5 wks*

18 May	68	**ROCK AROUND THE CLOCK** *Ace Of Hearts AH 13*	34	5 wks

160

h

HALF MAN HALF BISCUIT
UK, male vocal/instrumental group *14 wks*

8 Feb	86	**BACK IN THE DHSS** *Probe Plus PROBE 4*	59	14 wks

Daryl HALL *US, male vocalist* *5 wks*

23 Aug	86	**THREE HEARTS IN THE HAPPY ENDING MACHINE** *RCA PL 87196*	26	5 wks

See also Daryl Hall and John Oates.

Daryl HALL and John OATES *US, male vocal duo* *145 wks*

3 Jul	76	**HALL AND OATES** *RCA Victor APLI 1144*	56	1 wk
18 Sep	76	**BIGGER THAN BOTH OF US** *RCA Victor APLI 1467*	25	7 wks
15 Oct	77	**BEAUTY ON A BACK STREET** *RCA PL 12300*	40	2 wks
6 Feb	82	● **PRIVATE EYES** *RCA RCALP 6001*	8	21 wks
23 Oct	82	**H2O** *RCA RCALP 6056*	24	35 wks
29 Oct	83	**ROCK 'N' SOUL (PART 1)** *RCA PL 84858*	16	45 wks
27 Oct	84	**BIG BAM BOOM** *RCA PL 85309*	28	13 wks
28 Sep	85	**LIVE AT THE APOLLO WITH DAVID RUFFIN AND EDDIE KENDRICK** *RCA PL 87035*	32	5 wks
18 Jun	88	**OOH YEAH!** *RCA 208895*	52	3 wks
27 Oct	90	**CHANGE OF SEASON** *Arista 210548*	44	2 wks
19 Oct	91	● **THE BEST OF HALL AND OATES – LOOKING BACK** *Arista PL 90388*	9†	11 wks

See also Daryl Hall.

HALO JAMES *UK, male vocal/instrumental group*   *4 wks*

14 Apr 90 **WITNESS** *Epic 466761* 18   4 wks

HAMBURG STUDENTS' CHOIR
Germany, male vocal group   *6 wks*

17 Dec 60 **HARK THE HERALD ANGELS SING** *Pye GGL 0023* .. 11   6 wks

George HAMILTON IV *US, male vocalist*   *11 wks*

10 Apr 71 **CANADIAN PACIFIC** *RCA SF 8062* 45   1 wk
10 Feb 79 **REFLECTIONS** *Lotus WH 5008* 25   9 wks
13 Nov 82 **SONGS FOR A WINTER'S NIGHT** *Ronco RTL 2082* 94   1 wk

HAMMER – *See MC HAMMER*

Jan HAMMER *Czechoslovakia, male instrumentalist – keyboards*   *12 wks*

14 Nov 87 **ESCAPE FROM TV** *MCA MCF 3407* 34   12 wks

Herbie HANCOCK
US, male vocalist/instrumentalist – keyboards   *24 wks*

9 Sep 78 **SUNLIGHT** *CBS 82240* 27   6 wks
24 Feb 79 **FEETS DON'T FAIL ME NOW** *CBS 83491* 28   8 wks
27 Aug 83 **FUTURE SHOCK** *CBS 25540* 27   10 wks

161

h

Tony HANCOCK *UK, male comedian*   *42 wks*

9 Apr 60 ● **THIS IS HANCOCK** *Pye NPL 10845* 2   22 wks
12 Nov 60 **PIECES OF HANCOCK** *Pye NPL 18054* 17   2 wks
3 Mar 62 **HANCOCK** *Pye NPL 18068* 12   14 wks
14 Sep 63 **THIS IS HANCOCK (re-issue)**
            Pye Golden Guinea GGL 0206 16   4 wks

Vernon HANDLEY – *See Nigel KENNEDY*

Bo HANNSON *Sweden, multi-instrumentalist*   *2 wks*

18 Nov 72 **LORD OF THE RINGS** *Charisma CAS 1059* 34   2 wks

HANOI ROCKS *Finland/UK, male vocal/instrumental group*   *4 wks*

11 Jun 83 **BACK TO MYSTERY CITY** *Lick LICLP 1* 87   1 wk
20 Oct 84 **TWO STEPS FROM THE MOVE** *CBS 26066* 28   3 wks

John HANSON *UK, male vocalist*   *12 wks*

23 Apr 60 **THE STUDENT PRINCE** *Pye NPL 18046* 17   1 wk
2 Sep 61 ● **THE STUDENT PRINCE/VAGABOND KING**
            Pye GGL 0086 9   7 wks
10 Dec 77 **JOHN HANSON SINGS 20 SHOWTIME GREATS**
            K-Tel NE 1002 16   4 wks

HAPPY MONDAYS *UK, male vocal/instrumental group* *45 wks*

27 Jan	90	**BUMMED** *Factory FACT 220*	59	14 wks
17 Nov	90	● **PILLS 'N' THRILLS AND BELLYACHES**		
		Factory FACT 320	4	28 wks
12 Oct	91	**LIVE** *Factory FACT 322*	21	3 wks

HAPPY PIANO – *See Brian SMITH and his HAPPY PIANO*

Paul HARDCASTLE
UK, male producer/instrumentalist – synthesizer *5 wks*

30 Nov	85	**PAUL HARDCASTLE** *Chrysalis CHR 1517*	53	5 wks

Mike HARDING *UK, male comedian* *24 wks*

30 Aug	75	**MRS 'ARDIN'S KID** *Rubber RUB 011*	24	6 wks
10 Jul	76	**ONE MAN SHOW** *Philips 6625 022*	19	10 wks
11 Jun	77	**OLD FOUR EYES IS BACK** *Philips 6308 290*	31	6 wks
24 Jun	78	**CAPTAIN PARALYTIC AND THE BROWN ALE COWBOY**		
		Philips 6641 798	60	2 wks

HARDY – *See LAUREL and HARDY*

Steve HARLEY and COCKNEY REBEL
UK, male vocalist and male vocal/instrumental group *52 wks*

22 Jun	74	● **THE PSYCHOMODO** *EMI EMC 3033*	8	20 wks
22 Mar	75	● **THE BEST YEARS OF OUR LIVES** *EMI EMC 3068*	4	19 wks
14 Feb	76	**TIMELESS FLIGHT** *EMI EMA 775*	18	6 wks
27 Nov	76	**LOVE'S A PRIMA DONNA** *EMI EMC 3156*	28	3 wks
30 Jul	77	**FACE TO FACE – A LIVE RECORDING**		
		EMI EMSP 320	40	4 wks

First album credited to Cockney Rebel.

Roy HARPER *UK, male vocalist/instrumentalist – guitar* *5 wks*

9 Mar	74	**VALENTINE** *Harvest SHSP 4027*	27	1 wk
21 Jun	75	**H.Q.** *Harvest SHSP 4046*	31	2 wks
12 Mar	77	**BULLINAMINGVASE** *Harvest SHSP 4060*	25	2 wks

See also Roy Harper and Jimmy Page.

Roy HARPER and Jimmy PAGE
UK, male vocal/instrumental duo *4 wks*

16 Mar	85	**WHATEVER HAPPENED TO JUGULA?**		
		Beggars Banquet BEGA 60	44	4 wks

See also Roy Harper; Jimmy Page.

Anita HARRIS *UK, female vocalist* *5 wks*

27 Jan	68	**JUST LOVING YOU** *CBS SBPG 63182*	29	5 wks

Emmylou HARRIS *US, female vocalist* *29 wks*

14 Feb	76	**ELITE HOTEL** *Reprise K 54060*	17	11 wks
29 Jan	77	**LUXURY LINER** *Warner Bros. K 56344*	17	6 wks

4 Feb 78	**QUARTER MOON IN A TEN CENT TOWN**	
	Warner Bros. K 56433 40	5 wks
29 Mar 80	**HER BEST SONGS** K-Tel NE 1058 36	3 wks
14 Feb 81	**EVANGELINE** Warner Bros. K 56880 53	4 wks

See also Dolly Parton/Linda Ronstadt/Emmylou Harris.

Keith HARRIS, ORVILLE and CUDDLES
UK, male ventriloquist vocalist with dummies 1 wk

4 Jun 83	**AT THE END OF THE RAINBOW** BBC REH 465 92	1 wk

George HARRISON
UK, male vocalist/instrumentalist – guitar 76 wks

26 Dec 70	● **ALL THINGS MUST PASS** Apple STCH 639 4	24 wks
7 Jul 73	● **LIVING IN THE MATERIAL WORLD** Apple PAS 10006 2	12 wks
18 Oct 75	**EXTRA TEXTURE (READ ALL ABOUT IT)**	
	Apple PAS 10009 16	4 wks
18 Dec 76	**THIRTY THREE AND A THIRD** Dark Horse K 56319 ... 35	4 wks
17 Mar 79	**GEORGE HARRISON** Dark Horse K 56562 39	5 wks
13 Jun 81	**SOMEWHERE IN ENGLAND** Dark Horse K 56870 13	4 wks
14 Nov 87	● **CLOUD NINE** Dark Horse WX 123 10	23 wks

Jane HARRISON *UK, female operatic vocalist* 1 wk

4 Feb 89	**NEW DAY** Stylus SMR 869 70	1 wk

163

h

Debbie HARRY *US, female vocalist* 25 wks

8 Aug 81	● **KOO KOO** Chrysalis CHR 1347 6	7 wks
29 Nov 86	**ROCKBIRD** Chrysalis CHR 1540 31	11 wks
28 Oct 89	**DEF DUMB AND BLONDE** Chrysalis CHR 1650 12	7 wks

Act known as Deborah Harry on third album. See also Deborah Harry and Blondie.

Deborah HARRY and BLONDIE
US, female vocalist and UK/US, male/female vocal/instrumental group 26 wks

17 Dec 88	**ONCE MORE INTO THE BLEACH** Chrysalis CJB 2 50	4 wks
16 Mar 91	● **THE COMPLETE PICTURE – THE VERY BEST OF**	
	DEBORAH HARRY AND BLONDIE	
	Chrysalis CHR 1817 3	22 wks

See also Debbie Harry; Blondie.

Keef HARTLEY BAND *UK, male vocal/instrumental group* 3 wks

5 Sep 70	**THE TIME IS NEAR** Deram SML 1071 41	3 wks

Richard HARVEY and FRIENDS
UK, male instrumental group 1 wk

6 May 89	**EVENING FALLS** Telstar STAR 2350 72	1 wk

HATFIELD AND THE NORTH
UK, male/female vocal/instrumental group 1 wk

29 Mar 75	**ROTTERS CLUB** Virgin V 2030 43	1 wk

Donny HATHAWAY – *See Roberta FLACK and Donny HATHAWAY*

Chesney HAWKES *UK, male vocalist* *7 wks*

13 Apr 91	**BUDDY'S SONG** *Chrysalis CHR 1812*	18	7 wks

---

Ted HAWKINS *US, male vocalist/instrumentalist – guitar* *1 wk*

18 Apr 87	**HAPPY HOUR** *Windows On The World WOLP 2*	82	1 wk

---

HAWKWIND *UK, male vocal/instrumental group* *99 wks*

6 Nov 71	**IN SEARCH OF SPACE** *United Artists UAS 29202*	18	19 wks
23 Dec 72	**DOREMI FASOL LATIDO** *United Artists UAS 29364*	14	5 wks
2 Jun 73 ●	**SPACE RITUAL ALIVE** *United Artists UAD 60037/8*	9	5 wks
21 Sep 74	**HALL OF THE MOUNTAIN GRILL** *United Artists UAG 29672*	16	5 wks
31 May 75	**WARRIOR ON THE EDGE OF TIME** *United Artists UAG 29766*	13	7 wks
24 Apr 76	**ROAD HAWKS** *United Artists UAK 29919*	34	4 wks
18 Sep 76	**ASTONISHING SOUNDS, AMAZING MUSIC** *Charisma CDS 4004*	33	5 wks
9 Jul 77	**QUARK STRANGENESS AND CHARM** *Charisma CDS 4008*	30	6 wks
21 Oct 78	**25 YEARS ON** *Charisma CD 4014*	48	3 wks
30 Jun 79	**PXR 5** *Charisma CDS 4016*	59	5 wks
9 Aug 80	**LIVE 1979** *Bronze BRON 527*	15	7 wks
8 Nov 80	**LEVITATION** *Bronze BRON 530*	21	4 wks
24 Oct 81	**SONIC ATTACK** *RCA RCALP 5004*	19	5 wks
22 May 82	**CHURCH OF HAWKWIND** *RCA RCALP 9004*	26	6 wks
23 Oct 82	**CHOOSE YOUR MASQUES** *RCA RCALP 6055*	29	5 wks
5 Nov 83	**ZONES** *Flicknife SHARP 014*	57	2 wks
25 Feb 84	**HAWKWIND** *Liberty SLS 1972921*	75	1 wk
16 Nov 85	**CHRONICLE OF THE BLACK SWORD** *Flicknife SHARP 033*	65	2 wks
14 May 88	**THE XENON CODEX** *GWR GWLP 26*	79	2 wks
6 Oct 90	**SPACE BANDITS** *GWR GWLP 103*	70	1 wk

25 Years On *credited to Hawklords, a pseudonym for Hawkwind.*

Isaac HAYES *US, male vocalist/multi-instrumentalist* *14 wks*

18 Dec 71	**SHAFT** *Polydor 2659 007*	17	13 wks
12 Feb 72	**BLACK MOSES** *Stax 2628 004*	38	1 wk

---

HAYSI FANTAYZEE *UK, male/female vocal duo* *5 wks*

26 Feb 83	**BATTLE HYMNS FOR CHILDREN SINGING** *Regard RGLP 6000*	53	5 wks

---

Justin HAYWARD *UK, male vocalist* *10 wks*

5 Mar 77	**SONGWRITER** *Deram SDL 15*	28	5 wks
19 Jul 80	**NIGHT FLIGHT** *Decca TXS 138*	41	4 wks
19 Oct 85	**MOVING MOUNTAINS** *Towerbell TOWLP 15*	78	1 wk

See also Justin Hayward and John Lodge; Justin Hayward, Mike Batt and the London Philharmonic Orchestra.

Justin HAYWARD, Mike BATT and the LONDON PHILHARMONIC ORCHESTRA
UK, male vocalist, male producer and orchestra   *7 wks*

28 Oct 89	**CLASSIC BLUE** *Trax MODEM 1040*	47	7 wks

See also Justin Hayward; London Philharmonic Orchestra.

Justin HAYWARD and John LODGE
UK, male vocal/instrumental duo   *18 wks*

29 Mar 75	● **BLUE JAYS** *Threshold THS 12*	4	18 wks

See also Justin Hayward; John Lodge; Justin Hayward, Mike Batt and the London Philharmonic Orchestra.

Lee HAZLEWOOD – *See Nancy SINATRA and Lee HAZLEWOOD*

Jeff HEALEY BAND *US, male vocal/instrumental group*   *13 wks*

14 Jan 89	**SEE THE LIGHT** *Arista 209441*	58	7 wks
9 Jun 90	**HELL TO PAY** *Arista 210815*	18	6 wks

HEART *US, female/male vocal/instrumental group*   *135 wks*

22 Jan 77	**DREAMBOAT ANNIE** *Arista ARTY 139*	36	8 wks
23 Jul 77	**LITTLE QUEEN** *Portrait PRT 82075*	34	4 wks
19 Jun 82	**PRIVATE AUDITION** *Epic EPC 85792*	77	2 wks
26 Oct 85	**HEART** *Capitol EJ 24-0372-1*	19	43 wks
6 Jun 87	● **BAD ANIMALS** *Capitol ESTU 2032*	7	56 wks
14 Apr 90	● **BRIGADE** *Capitol ESTU 2121*	3	20 wks
28 Sep 91	**ROCK THE HOUSE 'LIVE'** *Capitol ESTU 2154*	45	2 wks

Heart changed label number during its chart run to Capitol LOVE 1.

165

h

HEARTBREAKERS *US, male vocal/instrumental group*   *1 wk*

5 Nov 77	**L.A.M.F.** *Track 2409 218*	55	1 wk

Ted HEATH AND HIS MUSIC
UK, conductor and orchestra   *5 wks*

21 Apr 62	**BIG BAND PERCUSSION** *Decca PFM 24004*	17	5 wks

HEATWAVE *UK/US, male vocal/instrumental group*   *27 wks*

11 Jun 77	**TOO HOT TO HANDLE** *GTO GTLP 013*	46	2 wks
6 May 78	**CENTRAL HEATING** *GTO GTLP 027*	26	15 wks
14 Feb 81	**CANDLES** *GTO GTLP 047*	29	9 wks
23 Feb 91	**GANGSTERS OF THE GROOVE** *Telstar STAR 2434*	56	1 wk

HEAVEN 17 *UK, male vocal/instrumental group*   *126 wks*

26 Sep 81	**PENTHOUSE AND PAVEMENT** *Virgin V 2208*	14	76 wks
7 May 83	● **THE LUXURY GAP** *Virgin V 2253*	4	36 wks
6 Oct 84	**HOW MEN ARE** *B.E.F. V 2326*	12	11 wks
12 Jul 86	**ENDLESS** *Virgin TCVB/CDV 2383*	70	2 wks
29 Nov 86	**PLEASURE ONE** *Virgin V 2400*	78	1 wk

Endless was available only on cassette and CD.

HEAVY PETTIN' UK, male vocal/instrumental group — 4 wks

29 Oct 83	LETTIN' LOOSE Polydor HEPLP 1	55	2 wks
13 Jul 85	ROCK AIN'T DEAD Polydor HEPLP 2	81	2 wks

HELLOWEEN Germany, male vocal/instrumental group — 9 wks

17 Sep 88	KEEPER OF THE SEVEN KEYS PART 2 Noise International NUK 117	24	5 wks
15 Apr 89	LIVE IN THE UK EMI EMC 3558	26	2 wks
23 Mar 91	PINK BUBBLES GO APE EMI EMC 3588	41	2 wks

Jimi HENDRIX US, male vocalist/instrumentalist – guitar — 209 wks

27 May 67	● ARE YOU EXPERIENCED Track 612-001	2	33 wks
16 Dec 67	● AXIS: BOLD AS LOVE Track 613-003	5	16 wks
27 Apr 68	● SMASH HITS Track 613-004	4	25 wks
16 Nov 68	● ELECTRIC LADYLAND Track 613-008/9	6	12 wks
4 Jul 70	● BAND OF GYPSIES Track 2406-001	6	30 wks
3 Apr 71	● CRY OF LOVE Track 2408-101	2	14 wks
28 Aug 71	● EXPERIENCE Ember NR 5057	9	6 wks
20 Nov 71	JIMI HENDRIX AT THE ISLE OF WIGHT Track 2302 016	17	2 wks
4 Dec 71	RAINBOW BRIDGE Reprise K 44159	16	8 wks
5 Feb 72	● HENDRIX IN THE WEST Polydor 2302 018	7	14 wks
11 Dec 72	WAR HEROES Polydor 2302 020	23	3 wks
21 Jul 73	SOUNDTRACK RECORDINGS FROM THE FILM 'JIMI HENDRIX' Warner Bros. K 64017	37	1 wk
29 Mar 75	JIMI HENDRIX Polydor 2343 080	35	4 wks
30 Aug 75	CRASH LANDING Polydor 2310 398	35	3 wks
29 Nov 75	MIDNIGHT LIGHTNING Polydor 2310 415	46	1 wk
14 Aug 82	THE JIMI HENDRIX CONCERTS CBS 88592	16	11 wks
19 Feb 83	THE SINGLES ALBUM Polydor PODV 6	77	4 wks
11 Mar 89	RADIO ONE Castle Collectors CCSLP 212	30	6 wks
2 Nov 90	● CORNERSTONES 1967–1970 Polydor 8472311	5	16 wks

See also Jimi Hendrix and Curtis Knight. Act billed as Jimi Hendrix Experience, US/UK, male vocal/ instrumental group, for first four hits.

Jimi HENDRIX and Curtis KNIGHT
US, male vocal/instrumental duo — 2 wks

18 May 68	GET THAT FEELING London HA 8349	39	2 wks

See also Jimi Hendrix.

Don HENLEY US, male vocalist — 27 wks

9 Mar 85	BUILDING THE PERFECT BEAST Geffen GEF 25939	14	11 wks
8 Jul 89	THE END OF INNOCENCE Geffen WX 253	17	16 wks

Band and Chorus of HER MAJESTY'S GUARDS DIVISION UK, military band — 4 wks

22 Nov 75	30 SMASH HITS OF THE WAR YEARS Warwick WW 5006	38	4 wks

HERD UK, male vocal/instrumental group — 1 wk

24 Feb 68	PARADISE LOST Fontana STL 5458	38	1 wk

A L P H A B E T I C A L L Y   B Y   A R T I S T

HERMAN'S HERMITS *UK, male vocal/instrumental group* 11 wks

18 Sep 65	**HERMAN'S HERMITS** *Columbia 33SX 1727*	16	2 wks
25 Sep 71	**THE MOST OF HERMAN'S HERMITS** *MFP 5216*	14	5 wks
8 Oct 77	**GREATEST HITS** *K-Tel NE 1001*	37	4 wks

Nick HEYWARD *UK, male vocalist* 13 wks

29 Oct 83	● **NORTH OF A MIRACLE** *Arista NORTH 1*	10	13 wks

HI JACK *US, male vocal group* 1 wk

19 Oct 91	**THE HORNS OF JERICHO** *Warner Bros. 7599263861*	54	1 wk

HI TENSION *UK, male vocal/instrumental group* 4 wks

6 Jan 79	**HI TENSION** *Island ILPS 9564*	74	4 wks

John HIATT *US, male vocalist* 1 wk

7 Jul 90	**STOLEN MOMENTS** *A & M 3953101*	72	1 wk

HIGH *UK, male vocal group* 2 wks

17 Nov 90	**SOMEWHERE SOON** *London 8282241*	59	2 wks

167

h

Benny HILL *UK, male vocalist* 8 wks

11 Dec 71	● **WORDS AND MUSIC** *Columbia SCX 6479*	9	8 wks

Vince HILL *UK, male vocalist* 10 wks

20 May 67	**EDELWEISS** *Columbia SCX 6141*	23	9 wks
29 Apr 78	**THAT LOVING FEELING** *K-Tel NE 1017*	51	1 wk

Steve HILLAGE *UK, male vocalist/instrumentalist – guitar* 41 wks

3 May 75	**FISH RISING** *Virgin V 2031*	33	3 wks
16 Oct 76	● **L** *Virgin V 2066*	10	12 wks
22 Oct 77	**MOTIVATION RADIO** *Virgin V 2777*	28	5 wks
29 Apr 78	**GREEN VIRGIN** *V 2098*	30	8 wks
17 Feb 79	**LIVE HERALD** *Virgin VGD 3502*	54	5 wks
5 May 79	**RAINBOW DOME MUSIC** *Virgin VR 1*	52	5 wks
27 Oct 79	**OPEN** *Virgin V 2135*	71	1 wk
5 Mar 83	**FOR TO NEXT** *Virgin V 2244*	48	2 wks

HIPSWAY *UK, male vocal/instrumental group* 23 wks

19 Apr 86	**HIPSWAY** *Mercury MERH 85*	42	23 wks

Roger HODGSON *UK, male vocalist* 4 wks

20 Oct 84	**IN THE EYE OF THE STORM** *A & M AMA 5004*	70	4 wks

Gerard HOFFNUNG *UK, male comedian*   *19 wks*

3 Sep 60 ● **AT THE OXFORD UNION** *Decca LF 1330*	**4**	19 wks

Susanna HOFFS *US, female vocalist*   *2 wks*

6 Apr 91 **WHEN YOU'RE A BOY** *Columbia 4672021*	**56**	2 wks

Christopher HOGWOOD – *See ACADEMY OF ANCIENT MUSIC conducted by Christopher HOGWOOD*

HOLE *US, male vocal/instrumental group*   *1 wk*

12 Oct 91 **PRETTY ON THE INSIDE** *City Slang E 04071*	**59**	1 wk

Billie HOLIDAY *US, female vocalist*   *10 wks*

16 Nov 85 **THE LEGEND OF BILLIE HOLIDAY** *MCA BHTV 1* ...	**60**	10 wks

Jools HOLLAND *UK, male vocalist/instrumentalist – piano*   *1 wk*

5 May 90 **WORLD OF HIS OWN** *IRS EIRSA 1018*	**71**	1 wk

168

h

HOLLIES *UK, male vocal/instrumental group*   *143 wks*

15 Feb 64 ● **STAY WITH THE HOLLIES** *Parlophone PMC 1220*	**2**	25 wks
2 Oct 65 ● **HOLLIES** *Parlophone PMC 1261*	**8**	14 wks
16 Jul 66 **WOULD YOU BELIEVE** *Parlophone PMC 7008*	**16**	8 wks
17 Dec 66 **FOR CERTAIN BECAUSE** *Parlophone PCS 17011*	**23**	7 wks
17 Jun 67 **EVOLUTION** *Parlophone PCS 7022*	**13**	10 wks
17 Aug 68 ★ **GREATEST HITS** *Parlophone PCS 7057*	**1**	27 wks
17 May 69 ● **HOLLIES SING DYLAN** *Parlophone PCS 7078*	**3**	7 wks
28 Nov 70 **CONFESSIONS OF THE MIND** *Parlophone PCS 7117*	**30**	5 wks
16 Mar 74 **HOLLIES** *Polydor 2383 262*	**38**	3 wks
19 Mar 77 ● **HOLLIES LIVE HITS** *Polydor 2383 428*	**4**	12 wks
22 Jul 78 ● **20 GOLDEN GREATS** *EMI EMTV 11*	**2**	20 wks
1 Oct 88 **ALL THE HITS AND MORE** *EMI EM 1301*	**51**	5 wks

The two albums titled Hollies *are different.*

Laurie HOLLOWAY – *See SOUTH BANK ORCHESTRA*

Buddy HOLLY and the CRICKETS
US, male vocalist, male vocal/instrumental group   *319 wks*

2 May 59 ● **BUDDY HOLLY STORY** *Coral LVA 9105*	**2**	156 wks
15 Oct 60 ● **BUDDY HOLLY STORY VOL. 2** *Coral LVA 9127*	**7**	14 wks
21 Oct 61 ● **THAT'LL BE THE DAY** *Ace Of Hearts AH 3*	**5**	14 wks
6 Apr 63 ● **REMINISCING** *Coral LVA 9212*	**2**	31 wks
13 Jun 64 ● **BUDDY HOLLY SHOWCASE** *Coral LVA 9222*	**3**	16 wks
26 Jun 65 **HOLLY IN THE HILLS** *Coral LVA 9227*	**13**	6 wks
15 Jul 67 ● **BUDDY HOLLY'S GREATEST HITS** *Ace Of Hearts AH 148*	**9**	40 wks
12 Apr 69 **GIANT** *MCA MUPS 371*	**13**	1 wk
21 Aug 71 **BUDDY HOLLY'S GREATEST HITS (re-issue)** *Coral CP 8*	**32**	6 wks
12 Jul 75 **BUDDY HOLLY'S GREATEST HITS (2nd re-issue)** *Coral CDLM 8007*	**42**	3 wks
11 Mar 78 ★ **20 GOLDEN GREATS** *MCA EMTV 8*	**1**	20 wks
8 Sep 84 **GREATEST HITS (3rd re-issue)** *MCA MCL 1618*	**100**	1 wk

18 Feb 89 ● **TRUE LOVE WAYS** *Telstar STAR 2339* . . . . 8 11 wks
Most albums feature the Crickets on at least some tracks. See also The Crickets.

John HOLT *Jamaica, male vocalist* 2 wks

1 Feb 75 **A THOUSAND VOLTS OF HOLT** *Trojan TRLS 75* . . . . . . 42 2 wks

HOME *UK, male vocal/instrumental group* 1 wk

11 Nov 72 **DREAMER** *CBS 67522* . . . . 41 1 wk

HONEYDRIPPERS
UK/US, male vocal/instrumental group 10 wks

1 Dec 84 **THE HONEYDRIPPERS VOLUME 1** *Es Paranza 790220* . 56 10 wks

John Lee HOOKER *US, male vocalist* 20 wks

4 Feb 67 **HOUSE OF THE BLUES** *Marble Arch MAL 663* . . . . 34 2 wks
11 Nov 89 **THE HEALER** *Silvertone ORELP 508* . . . . 63 8 wks
21 Sep 91 ● **MR LUCKY** *Silvertone ORELP 519* . . . . 3 10 wks

Mary HOPKIN *UK, female vocalist* 9 wks

1 Mar 69 ● **POSTCARD** *Apple SAPCOR 5* . . . . 3 9 wks

169

h

Bruce HORNSBY and the RANGE
US, male vocal/instrumental group 51 wks

13 Sep 86 **THE WAY IT IS** *RCA PL 89901* . . . . 16 26 wks
14 May 88 **SCENES FROM THE SOUTHSIDE** *RCA PL 86686* . . . . . 18 18 wks
30 Jun 90 **A NIGHT ON THE TOWN** *RCA PL 82041* . . . . 23 7 wks

HORSE *UK, male/female vocal/instrumental group* 2 wks

23 Jun 90 **THE SAME SKY** *Echo Chamber EST 2123* . . . . 44 2 wks

HORSLIPS *Ireland, male vocal/instrumental group* 3 wks

30 Apr 77 **THE BOOK OF INVASIONS – A CELTIC SYMPHONY**
DJM DJF 20498 . . . . 39 3 wks

HOT CHOCOLATE *UK, male vocal/instrumental group* 111 wks

15 Nov 75 **HOT CHOCOLATE** *RAK SRAK 516* . . . . 34 7 wks
7 Aug 76 **MAN TO MAN** *RAK SRAK 522* . . . . 32 7 wks
20 Nov 76 ● **GREATEST HITS** *RAK SRAK 524* . . . . 6 35 wks
8 Apr 78 **EVERY 1'S A WINNER** *RAK SRAK 531* . . . . 30 8 wks
15 Dec 79 ● **20 HOTTEST HITS** *RAK EMTV 22* . . . . 3 19 wks
25 Sep 82 **MYSTERY** *RAK SRAK 549* . . . . 24 7 wks
21 Feb 87 ★ **THE VERY BEST OF HOT CHOCOLATE**
RAK EMTV 42 . . . . 1 28 wks

HOT RODS – *See EDDIE and the HOT RODS*

HOTHOUSE FLOWERS
Ireland, male vocal/instrumental group   40 wks

18 Jun 88 ● **PEOPLE** London LONLP 58	2	19 wks
16 Jun 90 ● **HOME** London 8281971	5	21 wks

HOUND DOG and the MEGAMIXERS
UK, male producer   9 wks

1 Dec 90 **THE GREATEST EVER JUNIOR PARTY MEGAMIX**		
Pop & Arts PATLP 201	34	9 wks

HOUSE OF LOVE   *UK, male vocal/instrumental group*   11 wks

10 Mar 90 ● **HOUSE OF LOVE** Fontana 8422931	8	10 wks
10 Nov 90 **HOUSE OF LOVE** Fontana 8469781	49	1 wk

Identically titled albums are different.

HOUSEMARTINS   *UK, male vocal/instrumental group*   70 wks

5 Jul 86 ● **LONDON 0 HULL 4** Go! Discs AGOLP 7	3	41 wks
27 Dec 86 **HOUSEMARTINS' CHRISTMAS SINGLES BOX**		
Go! Discs GOD 816	84	1 wk
3 Oct 87 ● **THE PEOPLE WHO GRINNED THEMSELVES TO DEATH**		
Go! Discs AGOLP 9	9	18 wks
21 May 88 ● **NOW THAT'S WHAT I CALL QUITE GOOD!**		
Go! Discs AGOLP 11	8	10 wks

Whitney HOUSTON   *US, female vocalist*   249 wks

14 Dec 85 ● **WHITNEY HOUSTON** Arista 206978	2	119 wks
13 Jun 87 ★ **WHITNEY** Arista 208141	1	101 wks
17 Nov 90 ● **I'M YOUR BABY TONIGHT** Arista 211039	4	29 wks

Steve HOWE   *UK, male vocalist/instrumentalist – guitar*   6 wks

15 Nov 75 **BEGINNINGS** Atlantic K 50151	22	4 wks
24 Nov 79 **STEVE HOWE ALBUM** Atlantic K 50621	68	2 wks

See also Anderson Bruford Wakeman Howe.

HUDDERSFIELD CHORAL SOCIETY
UK, choir   14 wks

15 Mar 86 ● **THE HYMNS ALBUM** HMV EMTV 40	8	10 wks
13 Dec 86 **THE CAROLS ALBUM** EMI EMTV 43	29	4 wks

HUE AND CRY   *UK, male vocal/instrumental duo*   68 wks

7 Nov 87 **SEDUCED AND ABANDONED** Circa CIRCA 2	22	11 wks
10 Dec 88 ● **REMOTE/THE BITTER SUITE** Circa CIRCA 6	10	48 wks
29 Jun 91 ● **STARS CRASH DOWN** Circa CIRCA 15	10	9 wks

Remote re-entered the chart on 16 Dec 89 when it was made available with a free album The Bitter Suite.

Alan HULL   *UK, male vocalist*   3 wks

28 Jul 73 **PIPEDREAM** Charisma CAS 1069	29	3 wks

HUMAN LEAGUE
UK, male/female vocal/instrumental group　　　　　*181 wks*

31 May 80	**TRAVELOGUE** *Virgin V 2160*	16	42 wks
22 Aug 81	**REPRODUCTION** *Virgin V 2133*	49	23 wks
24 Oct 81	★ **DARE** *Virgin V 2192*	1	71 wks
19 May 84	● **HYSTERIA** *Virgin V 2315*	3	18 wks
20 Sept 86	● **CRASH** *Virgin V 2391*	7	6 wks
12 Nov 88	● **GREATEST HITS** *Virgin HLTV 1*	3	19 wks
22 Sep 90	**ROMANTIC?** *Virgin V 2624*	24	2 wks

HUMBLE PIE　*UK, male vocal/instrumental group*　　　*10 wks*

6 Sep 69	**AS SAFE AS YESTERDAY IS** *Immediate IMSP 025*	32	1 wk
22 Jan 72	**ROCKING AT THE FILLMORE** *A & M AMLH 63506*	32	2 wks
15 Apr 72	**SMOKIN'** *A & M AMLS 64342*	28	5 wks
7 Apr 73	**EAT IT** *A & M AMLS 6004*	34	2 wks

Engelbert HUMPERDINCK　*UK, male vocalist*　　*233 wks*

20 May 67	● **RELEASE ME** *Decca SKL 4868*	6	58 wks
25 Nov 67	● **THE LAST WALTZ** *Decca SKL 4901*	3	33 wks
3 Aug 68	● **A MAN WITHOUT LOVE** *Decca SKL 4939*	3	45 wks
1 Mar 69	● **ENGELBERT** *Decca SKL 4985*	3	8 wks
6 Dec 69	● **ENGELBERT HUMPERDINCK** *Decca SKL 5030*	5	23 wks
11 Jul 70	**WE MADE IT HAPPEN** *Decca SKL 5054*	17	11 wks
18 Sep 71	**ANOTHER TIME, ANOTHER PLACE** *Decca SKL 5097*	48	1 wk
26 Feb 72	**LIVE AT THE RIVIERA LAS VEGAS** *Decca TXS 105*	45	1 wk
21 Dec 74	★ **ENGELBERT HUMPERDINCK – HIS GREATEST HITS** *Decca SKL 5198*	1	34 wks
4 May 85	**GETTING SENTIMENTAL** *Telstar STAR 2254*	35	10 wks
4 Apr 87	**THE ENGELBERT HUMPERDINCK COLLECTION** *Telstar STAR 2294*	35	9 wks

171

h

Ian HUNTER　*UK, male vocalist*　　　*26 wks*

12 Apr 75	**IAN HUNTER** *CBS 80710*	21	15 wks
29 May 76	**ALL AMERICAN ALIEN BOY** *CBS 81310*	29	4 wks
5 May 79	**YOU'RE NEVER ALONE WITH A SCHIZOPHRENIC** *Chrysalis CHR 1214*	49	3 wks
26 Apr 80	**WELCOME TO THE CLUB** *Chrysalis CJT 6*	61	2 wks
29 Aug 81	**SHORT BACK AND SIDES** *Chrysalis CHR 1326*	79	2 wks

HURRAH!　*UK, male vocal/instrumental group*　　*1 wk*

28 Feb 87	**TELL GOD I'M HERE** *Kitchenware 208 201*	71	1 wk

HURRICANES – See *JOHNNY and the HURRICANES*

HÜSKER DÜ　*US, male vocal/instrumental group*　　*1 wk*

14 Feb 87	**WAREHOUSE: SONGS AND STORIES** *Warner Bros. 925 544–1*	72	1 wk

Phyllis HYMAN　*US, female vocalist*　　*1 wk*

20 Sep 86	**LIVING ALL ALONE** *Philadelphia International PHIL 4001*	**971** wk

i

ICE CUBE *US, male rapper*   *8 wks*

28 Jul	90	**AMERIKKKA'S MOST WANTED**			
		Fourth & Broadway BRLP 551	48	5 wks
9 Mar	91	**KILL AT WILL** *Fourth & Broadway BRLM 572*	66	3 wks

ICEHOUSE
Australia/New Zealand, male vocal/instrumental group   *7 wks*

| 5 Mar | 83 | **LOVE IN MOTION** *Chrysalis CHR 1390* .... | 64 | 6 wks |
| 2 Apr | 88 | **MAN OF COLOURS** *Chrysalis CHR 1592* .... | 93 | 1 wk |

ICE-T *US, male rapper*   *6 wks*

21 Oct	89	**THE ICEBERG/FREEDOM OF SPEECH**		
		Warner Bros. WX 316	42	2 wks
25 May	91	**O.G.: ORIGINAL GANGSTER** *Sire WX 412*	38	4 wks

ICICLE WORKS *UK, male vocal/instrumental group*   *18 wks*

31 Mar	84	**THE ICICLE WORKS** *Beggars Banquet BEGA 50*	24	6 wks
28 Sep	85	**THE SMALL PRICE OF A BICYCLE**		
		Beggars Banquet BEGA 61	55	3 wks
1 Mar	86	**SEVEN SINGLES DEEP** *Beggars Banquet BEGA 71*	52	2 wks
21 Mar	87	**IF YOU WANT TO DEFEAT YOUR ENEMY SING HIS SONG**		
		Beggars Banquet BEGA 78	28	4 wks
14 May	88	**BLIND** *Beggars Banquet IWA 2*	40	3 wks

Billy IDOL *UK, male vocalist*   *97 wks*

8 Jun	85	● **VITAL IDOL** *Chrysalis CUX 1502*	7	34 wks
28 Sep	85	**REBEL YELL** *Chrysalis CHR 1450*	36	11 wks
1 Nov	86	● **WHIPLASH SMILE** *Chrysalis CDL 1514*	8	20 wks
2 Jul	88	● **IDOL SONGS: 11 OF THE BEST** *Chrysalis BILIVD 1*	2	25 wks
12 May	90	**CHARMED LIFE** *Chrysalis CHR 1735*	15	7 wks

Frank IFIELD *UK, male vocalist*   *83 wks*

16 Feb	63	● **I'LL REMEMBER YOU** *Columbia 33SX 1467*	3	36 wks
21 Sep	63	● **BORN FREE** *Columbia 33SX 1462*	3	32 wks
28 Mar	64	● **BLUE SKIES** *Columbia 55SX 1588*	10	12 wks
19 Dec	64	● **GREATEST HITS** *Columbia 33SX 1633*	9	3 wks

Julio IGLESIAS *Spain, male vocalist*   *116 wks*

7 Nov	81	**DE NINA A MUJER** *CBS 85063*	43	5 wks
28 Nov	81	● **BEGIN THE BEGUINE** *CBS 85462*	5	28 wks
16 Oct	82	**AMOR** *CBS 25103*	14	14 wks
2 Jul	83	● **JULIO** *CBS 10038*	5	17 wks
1 Sep	84	**1100 BEL AIR PLACE** *CBS 86308*	14	14 wks
19 Oct	85	**LIBRA** *CBS 26623*	61	4 wks

3 Sep 88	**NON STOP** *CBS 460990 1*	33	14 wks
1 Dec 90	**STARRY NIGHT** *CBS 4672841*	27	20 wks

I-LEVEL   *UK, male vocal/instrumental group*   *4 wks*

9 Jul 83	**I-LEVEL** *Virgin V 2270*	50	4 wks

IMAGINATION   *UK, male vocal group*   *122 wks*

24 Oct 81	**BODY TALK** *R & B RBLP 1001*	20	53 wks
11 Sep 82 ●	**IN THE HEAT OF THE NIGHT** *R & B RBLP 1002*	7	29 wks
14 May 83 ●	**NIGHT DUBBING** *R & B RBDUB 1*	9	20 wks
12 Nov 83	**SCANDALOUS** *R & B RBLP 1004*	25	8 wks
12 Aug 89 ●	**IMAGINATION** *Stylus SMR 985*	7	12 wks

IMMACULATE FOOLS   *UK, male vocal/instrumental group*   *2 wks*

11 May 85	**HEARTS OF FORTUNE** *A & M AMA 5030*	65	2 wks

INCANTATION   *UK, male instrumental group*   *52 wks*

11 Dec 82 ●	**CACHARPAYA (PANPIPES OF THE ANDES)**		
	Beggars Banquet BEGA 39	9	26 wks
17 Dec 83	**DANCE OF THE FLAMES** *Beggars Banquet BEGA 49*	61	7 wks
28 Dec 85	**BEST OF INCANTATION – MUSIC FROM THE ANDES**		
	West Five CODA 19	28	19 wks

INCOGNITO   *France, male instrumental group*   *10 wks*

18 Apr 81	**JAZZ FUNK** *Ensign ENVY 504*	28	8 wks
27 Jul 91	**INSIDE LIFE** *Talkin Loud 8485461*	44	2 wks

INCREDIBLE STRING BAND
UK, male/female vocal/instrumental group   *36 wks*

21 Oct 67	**5,000 SPIRITS OR THE LAYERS OF THE ONION**		
	Elektra EUKS 257	26	4 wks
6 Apr 68 ●	**HANGMAN'S BEAUTIFUL DAUGHTER**		
	Elektra EVKS7 258	5	21 wks
20 Jul 68	**INCREDIBLE STRING BAND** *Elektra EKL 254*	34	3 wks
24 Jan 70	**CHANGING HORSES** *Elektra EKS 74057*	30	1 wk
9 May 70	**I LOOKED UP** *Elektra 2469–002*	30	4 wks
31 Oct 70	**U** *Elektra 2665–001*	34	2 wks
30 Oct 71	**LIQUID ACROBAT AS REGARDS THE AIR**		
	Island ILPS 9172	46	1 wk

INFA RIOT   *UK, male vocal/instrumental group*   *4 wks*

7 Aug 82	**STILL OUT OF ORDER** *Secret SEC 7*	42	4 wks

James INGRAM   *US, male vocalist*   *19 wks*

31 Mar 84	**IT'S YOUR NIGHT** *Qwest 9239701*	25	17 wks
30 Aug 86	**NEVER FELT SO GOOD** *Qwest WX 44*	72	2 wks

INNER CITY   *US, male/female vocal/instrumental duo*   *37 wks*

20 May 89 ●	**PARADISE** *10 DIX 81*	3	31 wks
10 Feb 90	**PARADISE REMIXED** *10 XID 81*	17	6 wks

INNOCENCE UK, male/female vocal/instrumental group 19 wks

10 Nov 90	**BELIEF** Cooltempo CTLP 20	24	19 wks

INSPIRAL CARPETS UK, male vocal/instrumental group 27 wks

5 May 90	● **LIFE** Cow DUNG 8	2	21 wks
4 May 91	● **THE BEAST INSIDE** Cow DUNG 14	5	6 wks

INSPIRATIONAL CHOIR US, male/female choir 4 wks

18 Jan 86	**SWEET INSPIRATION** Portrait PRT 10048	59	4 wks

INTI ILLIMANI-GUAMARY
Chile, male vocal/instrumental group – panpipes 7 wks

17 Dec 83	**THE FLIGHT OF THE CONDOR – ORIGINAL TV SOUNDTRACK** BBC REB 440	62	7 wks

INVISIBLE GIRLS – See Pauline MURRAY and the INVISIBLE GIRLS

INXS Australia, male vocal/instrumental group 164 wks

8 Feb 86	**LISTEN LIKE THIEVES** Mercury MERH 82	48	15 wks
28 Nov 87	● **KICK** Mercury MERH 114	9	99 wks
6 Oct 90	● **X** Mercury 8466681	2	43 wks
16 Nov 91	● **LIVE BABY LIVE** Mercury 5105801	8†	7 wks

Tony IOMMI – See BLACK SABBATH

IQ UK, male vocal/instrumental group 1 wk

22 Jun 85	**THE WAKE** Sahara SAH 136	72	1 wk

IRON MAIDEN UK, male vocal/instrumental group 170 wks

26 Apr 80	● **IRON MAIDEN** EMI EMC 3330	4	15 wks
28 Feb 81	**KILLERS** EMI EMC 3357	12	8 wks
10 Apr 82	★ **THE NUMBER OF THE BEAST** EMI EMC 3400	1	31 wks
28 May 83	● **PIECE OF MIND** EMI EMA 800	3	18 wks
15 Sep 84	● **POWERSLAVE** EMI POWER 1	2	13 wks
15 Jun 85	**IRON MAIDEN** (re-issue) Fame FA 41–3121–1	71	2 wks
26 Oct 85	● **LIVE AFTER DEATH** EMI RIP 1	2	14 wks
11 Oct 86	● **SOMEWHERE IN TIME** EMI EMC 3512	3	11 wks
20 Jun 87	**THE NUMBER OF THE BEAST** (re-issue) Fame FA 3178	98	1 wk
23 Apr 88	★ **SEVENTH SON OF A SEVENTH SON** EMI EMD 1006 .	1	18 wks
24 Feb 90	● **RUNNING FREE/SANCTUARY** EMI IRN 1	10	4 wks
3 Mar 90	● **WOMEN IN UNIFORM/TWILIGHT ZONE** EMI IRN 2	10	3 wks
10 Mar 90	● **PURGATORY/MAIDEN JAPAN** EMI IRN 3	5	3 wks
17 Mar 90	● **RUN TO THE HILLS/THE NUMBER OF THE BEAST** EMI IRN 4	3	2 wks
24 Mar 90	● **FLIGHT OF ICARUS/THE TROOPER** EMI IRN 5	7	2 wks
31 Mar 90	**2 MINUTES TO MIDNIGHT/ACES HIGH** EMI IRN 6 ..	11	2 wks
7 Apr 90	● **RUNNING FREE (LIVE)/RUN TO THE HILLS (LIVE)** EMI IRN 7	9	2 wks
14 Apr 90	● **WASTED YEARS/STRANGER IN A STRANGE LAND** EMI IRN 8	9	2 wks
21 Apr 90	● **CAN I PLAY WITH MADNESS/THE EVIL THAT MEN DO** EMI IRN 9	10	3 wks
28 Apr 90	**THE CLAIRVOYANT/INFINITE DREAMS (LIVE)** EMI IRN 10	11	2 wks
13 Oct 90	● **NO PRAYER FOR THE DYING** EMI EMD 1017	2	14 wks

Inspiral Carpets model a range of early 1990s trainers.

THE RAY COOPER APPRECIATION SOCIETY

Elton John shows his appreciation of his ace percussionist Ray Cooper.

Gregory ISAACS *Jamaica, male vocalist* 6 wks

12 Sep 81	**MORE GREGORY** *Charisma PREX 9*	93	1 wk
4 Sep 82	**NIGHT NURSE** *Island ILPS 9721*	32	5 wks

Chris ISAAK *US, male vocalist* 29 wks

26 Jan 91	● **WICKED GAME** *Reprise WX 406*	3	29 wks

ISLEY BROTHERS *US, male vocal/instrumental group* 24 wks

14 Dec 68	**THIS OLD HEART OF MINE** *Tamla Motown STML 11034* .	23	6 wks
14 Aug 76	**HARVEST FOR THE WORLD** *Epic EPC 81268*	50	5 wks
14 May 77	**GO FOR YOUR GUNS** *Epic EPC 86027*	46	2 wks
24 Jun 78	**SHOWDOWN** *Epic EPC 86039*	50	1 wk
5 Mar 88	**GREATEST HITS** *Telstar STAR 2306*	41	10 wks

IT BITES *UK, male vocal/instrumental group* 12 wks

6 Sep 86	**THE BIG LAD IN THE WINDMILL** *Virgin V 2378*	35	5 wks
2 Apr 88	**ONCE AROUND THE WORLD** *Virgin V 2456*	43	3 wks
24 Jun 89	**EAT ME IN ST. LOUIS** *Virgin V 2591*	40	3 wks
31 Aug 91	**THANK YOU AND GOODNIGHT** *Virgin VGD 24233* ...	59	1 wk

IT'S A BEAUTIFUL DAY
US, male/female vocal/instrumental group 3 wks

23 May 70	**IT'S A BEAUTIFUL DAY** *CBS 63722*	58	1 wk
18 Jul 70	**MARRYING MAIDEN** *CBS 66236*	45	2 wks

IT'S IMMATERIAL *UK, male vocal/instrumental group* 3 wks

27 Sep 86	**LIFE'S HARD AND THEN YOU DIE** *Siren SIRENLP 4* .	62	3 wks

j

j

Freddie JACKSON *US, male vocalist* 48 wks

18 May 85	**ROCK ME TONIGHT** *Capitol EJ 2440316–1*	27	22 wks
8 Nov 86	**JUST LIKE THE FIRST TIME** *Capitol EST 2023*	30	15 wks
30 Jul 88	**DON'T LET LOVE SLIP AWAY** *Capitol EST 2067*	24	9 wks
17 Nov 90	**DO ME AGAIN** *Capitol EST 2134*	48	2 wks

Janet JACKSON *US, female vocalist* 128 wks

5 Apr 86	● **CONTROL** *A & M AMA 5016*	8	72 wks
14 Nov 87	**CONTROL – THE REMIXES** *Breakout MIXLP 1*	20	14 wks
30 Sep 89	● **RHYTHM NATION 1814** *A & M AMA 3920*	4	42 wks

Jermaine JACKSON *US, male vocalist* — *12 wks*

| 31 May 80 | **LET'S GET SERIOUS** *Motown STML 12127* .... | 22 | 6 wks |
| 12 May 84 | **DYNAMITE** *Arista 206 317* .... | 57 | 6 wks |

See also Jacksons.

Joe JACKSON *UK, male vocalist* — *104 wks*

17 Mar 79	**LOOK SHARP** *A & M AMLH 64743*	40	11 wks
13 Oct 79	**I'M THE MAN** *A & M AMLH 64794*	12	16 wks
18 Oct 80	**BEAT CRAZY** *A & M AMLH 64837*	42	3 wks
4 Jul 81	**JUMPIN' JIVE** *A & M AMLH 68530*	14	14 wks
3 Jul 82	● **NIGHT AND DAY** *A & M AMLH 64906*	3	27 wks
7 Apr 84	**BODY AND SOUL** *A & M AMLX 65000*	14	14 wks
5 Apr 86	**BIG WORLD** *A & M JWA 3*	41	5 wks
7 May 88	**LIVE 1980–1986** *A & M AMA 6706*	66	2 wks
29 Apr 89	**BLAZE OF GLORY** *A & M AMA 5249*	36	3 wks
15 Sep 90	● **STEPPING OUT – THE VERY BEST OF JOE JACKSON** *A & M 3970521*	7	7 wks
11 May 91	**LAUGHTER AND LUST** *Virgin America VUSLP 34*	41	2 wks

Jumpin' Jive credited to Joe Jackson's Jumpin' Jive.

Michael JACKSON *US, male vocalist* — *538 wks*

3 Jun 72	**GOT TO BE THERE** *Tamla Motown STML 11205*	37	5 wks
13 Jan 73	**BEN** *Tamla Motown STML 11220*	17	7 wks
29 Sep 79	● **OFF THE WALL** *Epic EPC 83468*	5	173 wks
4 Jul 81	**BEST OF MICHAEL JACKSON** *Motown STMR 9009*	11	18 wks
18 Jul 81	**ONE DAY IN YOUR LIFE** *Motown STML 12158*	29	8 wks
11 Dec 82	★ **THRILLER** *Epic EPC 85930*	1	168 wks
12 Feb 83	**E.T. THE EXTRA TERRESTRIAL** *MCA 7000*	82	2 wks
3 Dec 83	**MICHAEL JACKSON 9 SINGLE PACK** *Epic MJ1*	66	3 wks
9 Jun 84	● **FAREWELL MY SUMMER LOVE** *Motown ZL 72227* ...	9	14 wks
12 Sep 87	★ **BAD** *Epic EPC 450 291–1*	1	109 wks
26 Dec 87	**THE MICHAEL JACKSON MIX** *Stylus SMR 745*	27	25 wks
30 Jul 88	**SOUVENIR SINGLES PACK** *Epic MJ 5*	91	1 wk
30 Nov 91	★ **DANGEROUS** *Epic 4658021*	1†	5 wks

See also the Jacksons; Diana Ross/Michael Jackson/Gladys Knight/Stevie Wonder.

177

j

Millie JACKSON *US, female vocalist* — *7 wks*

| 18 Feb 84 | **E.S.P.** *Sire 250382* .... | 59 | 5 wks |
| 6 Apr 85 | **LIVE AND UNCENSORED** *Important TADLP 001* ...... | 81 | 2 wks |

JACKSONS *US, male vocal group* — *140 wks*

21 Mar 70	**DIANA ROSS PRESENTS THE JACKSON FIVE** *Tamla Motown STML 11142*	16	4 wks
15 Aug 70	**ABC** *Tamla Motown STML 11153*	22	6 wks
7 Oct 72	**GREATEST HITS** *Tamla Motown STML 11212*	26	14 wks
18 Nov 72	**LOOKIN' THROUGH THE WINDOWS** *Tamla Motown STML 11214*	16	8 wks
16 Jul 77	**THE JACKSONS** *Epic EPC 86009*	54	1 wk
3 Dec 77	**GOIN' PLACES** *Epic EPC 86035*	45	1 wk
5 May 79	**DESTINY** *Epic EPC 83200*	33	7 wks
11 Oct 80	**TRIUMPH** *Epic EPC 86112*	13	16 wks
12 Dec 81	**THE JACKSONS** *Epic EPC 88562*	53	9 wks
9 Jul 83	★ **18 GREATEST HITS** *Telstar STAR 2232*	1	58 wks
21 Jul 84	● **VICTORY** *Epic EPC 86303*	3	13 wks
1 Jul 89	**2300 JACKSON ST** *Epic 463352 1*	39	3 wks

First four albums credited to Jackson Five. 18 Greatest Hits, credited to Michael Jackson plus the Jackson Five, contains hits by both acts. All other albums credited to the Jacksons. Jermaine Jackson appeared on the first four albums. See also Michael Jackson; Jermaine Jackson.

Mick JAGGER *UK, male vocalist* *16 wks*

16 Mar 85	● **SHE'S THE BOSS** *CBS 86310*	6	11 wks
26 Sep 87	**PRIMITIVE COOL** *CBS 460 123–1*	26	5 wks

JAM *UK, male vocal/instrumental group* *162 wks*

28 May 77	**IN THE CITY** *Polydor 2383 447*	20	18 wks
26 Nov 77	**THIS IS THE MODERN WORLD** *Polydor 2383 475*	22	5 wks
11 Nov 78	● **ALL MOD CONS** *Polydor POLD 5008*	6	17 wks
24 Nov 79	● **SETTING SONS** *Polydor POLD 5028*	4	19 wks
6 Dec 80	● **SOUND AFFECTS** *Polydor POLD 5035*	2	19 wks
20 Mar 82	★ **THE GIFT** *Polydor POLD 5055*	1	24 wks
18 Dec 82	● **DIG THE NEW BREED** *Polydor POLD 5075*	2	15 wks
27 Aug 83	**IN THE CITY (re-issue)** *Polydor SPELP 27*	100	1 wk
22 Oct 83	● **SNAP** *Polydor SNAP 1*	2	30 wks
13 Jul 91	● **GREATEST HITS** *Polydor 8495541*	2	14 wks

JAMES *UK, male vocal/instrumental group* *32 wks*

2 Aug 86	**STUTTER** *blanco y negro JIMLP 1*	68	2 wks
8 Oct 88	**STRIP MINE** *Sire JIMLP 2*	90	1 wk
16 Jun 90	● **GOLD MOTHER** *Fontana 8461891*	2	29 wks

Rick JAMES *US, male vocalist* *2 wks*

24 Jul 82	**THROWIN' DOWN** *Motown STML 12167*	93	2 wks

JAN and DEAN *US, male vocal duo* *2 wks*

12 Jul 80	**THE JAN AND DEAN STORY** *K-Tel NE 1084*	67	2 wks

JANE'S ADDICTION *US, male vocal/instrumental group* *2 wks*

8 Sep 90	**RITUAL DE LO HABITUAL** *Warner Bros. WX 306*	37	2 wks

JAPAN *UK, male vocal/instrumental group* *136 wks*

9 Feb 80	**QUIET LIFE** *Ariola Hansa AHAL 8011*	53	8 wks
15 Nov 80	**GENTLEMEN TAKE POLAROIDS** *Virgin V 2180*	45	10 wks
26 Sep 81	**ASSEMBLAGE** *Hansa HANLP 1*	26	46 wks
28 Nov 81	**TIN DRUM** *Virgin V 2209*	12	50 wks
18 Jun 83	● **OIL ON CANVAS** *Virgin VD 2513*	5	14 wks
8 Dec 84	**EXORCISING GHOSTS** *Virgin VGD 3510*	45	8 wks

Jeff JARRATT and Don REEDMAN
UK, male producers *8 wks*

22 Nov 80	**MASTERWORKS** *K-Tel ONE 1093*	39	8 wks

Jean-Michel JARRE *France, male instrumentalist/producer* *216 wks*

20 Aug 77	● **OXYGENE** *Polydor 2310 555*	2	24 wks
16 Dec 78	**EQUINOXE** *Polydor POLD 5007*	11	26 wks
6 Jun 81	● **MAGNETIC FIELDS** *Polydor POLS 1033*	6	17 wks
15 May 82	● **THE CONCERTS IN CHINA** *Polydor PODV 3*	6	17 wks
12 Nov 83	**THE ESSENTIAL JEAN MICHEL JARRE**		
	Polystar PROLP 3	14	29 wks

24 Nov 84	**ZOOLOOK** *Polydor POLH 15*	47	14 wks
12 Apr 86 ●	**RENDEZ-VOUS** *Polydor POLH 27*	9	37 wks
18 Jul 87	**IN CONCERT LYONS/HOUSTON** *Polydor POLH 36* ...	18	15 wks
8 Oct 88 ●	**REVOLUTIONS** *Polydor POLH 45*	2	13 wks
14 Oct 89	**JARRE LIVE** *Polydor 841258 1*	16	4 wks
23 Jun 90	**WAITING FOR COUSTEAU** *Dreyfus 8436141*	14	10 wks
26 Oct 91	**IMAGES – THE BEST OF JEAN-MICHEL JARRE** *Dreyfus 5113061*	14†	10 wks

Al JARREAU *US, male vocalist* — *37 wks*

5 Sep 81	**BREAKING AWAY** *Warner Bros. K 56917*	60	8 wks
30 Apr 83	**JARREAU** *WEA International U 0070*	39	18 wks
17 Nov 84	**HIGH CRIME** *WEA 250807*	81	1 wk
13 Sep 86	**L IS FOR LOVER** *WEA International 253 080-1*	45	10 wks

JEFFERSON AIRPLANE
US/UK, female/male vocal/instrumental group — *10 wks*

28 Jun 69	**BLESS ITS POINTED LITTLE HEAD** *RCA SF 8019*	38	1 wk
7 Mar 70	**VOLUNTEERS** *RCA SF 8076*	34	7 wks
2 Oct 71	**BARK** *Grunt FTR 1001*	42	1 wk
2 Sep 72	**LONG JOHN SILVER** *Grunt FTR 1007*	30	1 wk

See also Jefferson Starship; Starship – later incarnations of Jefferson Airplane.

JEFFERSON STARSHIP
US, male vocal/instrumental group — *13 wks*

| 31 Jul 76 | **SPITFIRE** *Grunt RFL 1557* .... | 30 | 2 wks |
| 9 Feb 80 | **FREEDOM AT POINT ZERO** *Grunt FL 13452* .... | 22 | 11 wks |

See also Jefferson Airplane; Starship.

JELLYBEAN *US, male instrumentalist/producer* — *35 wks*

| 31 Oct 87 | **JUST VISITING THIS PLANET** *Chrysalis CHR 1569* ..... | 15 | 28 wks |
| 3 Sep 88 | **ROCKS THE HOUSE!** *Chrysalis CJB 1* .... | 16 | 7 wks |

JESUS AND MARY CHAIN
UK, male vocal/instrumental group — *28 wks*

30 Nov 85	**PSYCHOCANDY** *blanco y negro BYN 7*	31	10 wks
12 Sep 87 ●	**DARKLANDS** *blanco y negro BYN 11*	5	7 wks
30 Apr 88 ●	**BARBED WIRE KISSES** *blanco y negro BYN 15*	9	7 wks
21 Oct 89	**AUTOMATIC** *blanco y negro BYN 20*	11	4 wks

JESUS JONES *UK, male vocal/instrumental group* — *27 wks*

| 14 Oct 89 | **LIQUIDIZER** *Food FOODLP 3* .... | 32 | 3 wks |
| 9 Feb 91 ★ | **DOUBT** *Food FOODLP 5* .... | 1 | 24 wks |

JESUS LOVES YOU *UK, male vocalist, Boy George* — *1 wk*

| 13 Apr 91 | **THE MARTYR MANTRAS** *More Protein CUMLP 1* ..... | 60 | 1 wk |

See also Boy George.

JETHRO TULL *UK, male vocal/instrumental group* — *229 wks*

| 2 Nov 68 ● | **THIS WAS** *Island ILPS 9085* .... | 10 | 22 wks |

179

j

Main picture: **Freddie Jackson** rocked the UK LP charts with the album titled after his first number one Black Music hit. Top right: The records of **Millie Jackson** were the most sexually explicit of all the chart Jacksons. Bottom right: **Joe Jackson** can't believe he's had more chart albums than any other Jackson, including Michael.

9 Aug 69	★ **STAND UP** *Island ILPS 9103*	1	29 wks
9 May 70	● **BENEFIT** *Island ILPS 9123*	3	13 wks
3 Apr 71	● **AQUALUNG** *Island ILPS 9145*	4	21 wks
18 Mar 72	● **THICK AS A BRICK** *Chrysalis CHR 1003*	5	14 wks
15 Jul 72	● **LIVING IN THE PAST** *Chrysalis CJT 1*	8	11 wks
28 Jul 73	**A PASSION PLAY** *Chrysalis CHR 1040*	13	8 wks
2 Nov 74	**WAR CHILD** *Chrysalis CHR 1067*	14	4 wks
27 Sep 75	**MINSTREL IN THE GALLERY** *Chrysalis CHR 1082*	20	6 wks
31 Jan 76	**M.U. THE BEST OF JETHRO TULL** *Chrysalis CHR 1078*	44	5 wks
15 May 76	**TOO OLD TO ROCK 'N' ROLL TOO YOUNG TO DIE** *Chrysalis CHR 1111*	25	10 wks
19 Feb 77	**SONGS FROM THE WOOD** *Chrysalis CHR 1132*	13	12 wks
29 Apr 78	**HEAVY HORSES** *Chrysalis CHR 1175*	20	10 wks
14 Oct 78	**LIVE BURSTING OUT** *Chrysalis CJT 4*	17	8 wks
6 Oct 79	**STORM WATCH** *Chrysalis CDL 1238*	27	4 wks
6 Sep 80	**A** *Chrysalis CDL 1301*	25	5 wks
17 Apr 82	**BROADSWORD AND THE BEAST** *Chrysalis CDL 1380*	27	19 wks
15 Sep 84	**UNDER WRAPS** *Chrysalis CDL 1461*	18	5 wks
2 Nov 85	**ORIGINAL MASTERS** *Chrysalis JTTV 1*	63	3 wks
19 Sep 87	**CREST OF A KNAVE** *Chrysalis CDL 1590*	19	10 wks
9 Jul 88	**20 YEARS OF JETHRO TULL** *Chrysalis TBOX 1*	78	1 wk
2 Sep 89	**ROCK ISLAND** *Chrysalis CHR 1708*	18	6 wks
14 Sep 91	**CATFISH RISING** *Chrysalis CHR 1886*	27	3 wks

JETS *UK, male vocal/instrumental group* — 6 wks

10 Apr 82	**100 PERCENT COTTON** *EMI EMC 3399*	30	6 wks

JETS *US, male/female vocal/instrumental group* — 4 wks

11 Apr 87	**CRUSH ON YOU** *MCA MCF 3312*	57	4 wks

181

j

Joan JETT and the BLACKHEARTS
US, female/male vocal/instrumental group — 7 wks

8 May 82	**I LOVE ROCK 'N' ROLL** *Epic EPC 85686*	25	7 wks

JIVE BUNNY and the MASTERMIXERS
UK, male production/mixing group — 29 wks

9 Dec 89	● **JIVE BUNNY – THE ALBUM** *Telstar STAR 2390*	2	22 wks
8 Dec 90	**IT'S PARTY TIME** *Telstar STAR 2449*	23	7 wks

JO BOXERS *UK, male vocal/instrumental group* — 5 wks

24 Sep 83	**LIKE GANGBUSTERS** *RCA BOXXLP 1*	18	5 wks

Billy JOEL *US, male vocalist* — 289 wks

25 Mar 78	**THE STRANGER** *CBS 82311*	25	40 wks
25 Nov 78	● **52ND STREET** *CBS 83181*	10	43 wks
22 Mar 80	● **GLASS HOUSES** *CBS 86108*	9	24 wks
10 Oct 81	**SONGS IN THE ATTIC** *CBS 85273*	57	3 wks
2 Oct 82	**NYLON CURTAIN** *CBS 85959*	27	8 wks
10 Sep 83	● **AN INNOCENT MAN** *CBS 25554*	2	94 wks
4 Feb 84	**COLD SPRING HARBOUR** *CBS 32400*	95	1 wk
23 Jun 84	**PIANO MAN** *CBS 32002*	98	1 wk
20 Jul 85	● **GREATEST HITS VOLUME I & VOLUME II** *CBS 88666*	7	39 wks
16 Aug 86	**THE BRIDGE** *CBS 86323*	38	10 wks
28 Nov 87	**KOHYEPT – LIVE IN LENINGRAD** *CBS 460 407-1*	92	1 wk
4 Nov 89	● **STORM FRONT** *CBS 4656581*	5	25 wks

Elton JOHN *UK, male vocalist/instrumentalist – piano* *709 wks*

23 May 70	**ELTON JOHN** *DJM DJLPS 406*	11 14 wks
16 Jan 71 ●	**TUMBLEWEED CONNECTION** *DJM DJLPS 410*	6 20 wks
1 May 71	**THE ELTON JOHN LIVE ALBUM 17-11-70**	
	DJM DJLPS 414	20 2 wks
20 May 72	**MADMAN ACROSS THE WATER** *DJM DJLPH 420* ...	41 2 wks
3 Jun 72 ●	**HONKY CHATEAU** *DJM DJLPH 423*	2 23 wks
10 Feb 73 ★	**DON'T SHOOT ME I'M ONLY THE PIANO PLAYER**	
	DJM DJLPH 427	1 42 wks
3 Nov 73 ★	**GOODBYE YELLOW BRICK ROAD** *DJM DJLPO 1001*	1 84 wks
13 Jul 74 ★	**CARIBOU** *DJM DJLPH 439*	1 18 wks
23 Nov 74 ★	**ELTON JOHN'S GREATEST HITS** *DJM DJLPH 442* ...	1 84 wks
7 Jun 75 ●	**CAPTAIN FANTASTIC AND THE BROWN DIRT**	
	COWBOY *DJM DJLPX 1*	2 24 wks
8 Nov 75 ●	**ROCK OF THE WESTIES** *DJM DJLPH 464*	5 12 wks
15 May 76 ●	**HERE AND THERE** *DJM DJLPH 473*	6 9 wks
6 Nov 76 ●	**BLUE MOVES** *Rocket ROSP 1*	3 15 wks
15 Oct 77 ●	**GREATEST HITS VOL. 2** *DJM DJH 20520*	6 24 wks
4 Nov 78 ●	**A SINGLE MAN** *Rocket TRAIN 1*	8 26 wks
20 Oct 79	**VICTIM OF LOVE** *Rocket HISPD 125*	41 3 wks
8 Mar 80	**LADY SAMANTHA** *DJM 22085*	56 2 wks
31 May 80	**21 AT 33** *Rocket HISPD 126*	12 13 wks
25 Oct 80	**THE VERY BEST OF ELTON JOHN** *K-Tel NE 1094*	24 13 wks
30 May 81	**THE FOX** *Rocket TRAIN 16*	12 12 wks
17 Apr 82	**JUMP UP** *Rocket HISPD 127*	13 12 wks
6 Nov 82	**LOVE SONGS** *TV Records TVA 3*	39 13 wks
11 Jun 83 ●	**TOO LOW FOR ZERO** *Rocket HISPD 24*	7 73 wks
30 Jun 84 ●	**BREAKING HEARTS** *Rocket HISPD 25*	2 23 wks
16 Nov 85 ●	**ICE ON FIRE** *Rocket HISPD 26*	3 23 wks
15 Nov 86	**LEATHER JACKETS** *Rocket EJLP 1*	24 9 wks
12 Sep 87	**LIVE IN AUSTRALIA** *Rocket EJBXL 1*	43 7 wks
16 Jul 88	**REG STRIKES BACK** *Rocket EJLP 3*	18 6 wks
23 Sep 89 ★	**SLEEPING WITH THE PAST** *Rocket 8388391*	1 42 wks
10 Nov 90 ★	**THE VERY BEST OF ELTON JOHN** *Rocket 8469471*	1† 59 wks

182

j

Live In Australia *credits Elton John and the Melbourne Symphony Orchestra. It reappeared in 1988 as EJLP 2;
EJBXL 1 was the original 'de luxe' version.*

JOHNNY HATES JAZZ
UK, male vocal/instrumental group *39 wks*

23 Jan 88 ★	**TURN BACK THE CLOCK** *Virgin V 2475*	1 39 wks

JOHNNY and the HURRICANES
US, male instrumental group *5 wks*

3 Dec 60	**STORMSVILLE** *London HAI 2269*	18 1 wk
1 Apr 61	**BIG SOUND OF JOHNNY AND THE HURRICANES**	
	London HAK 2322	14 4 wks

Holly JOHNSON *UK, male vocalist* *17 wks*

6 May 89 ★	**BLAST** *MCA MCG 6042*	1 17 wks

Linton Kwesi JOHNSON *Jamaica, male poet* *8 wks*

30 Jun 79	**FORCE OF VICTORY** *Island ILPS 9566*	66 1 wk
31 Oct 80	**BASS CULTURE** *Island ILPS 9605*	46 5 wks
10 Mar 84	**MAKING HISTORY** *Island ILPS 9770*	73 2 wks

Matt JOHNSON – *See The THE*

Paul JOHNSON   *UK, male vocalist*   *3 wks*

4 Jul	87	**PAUL JOHNSON** *CBS 450640 1*	**63**	2 wks
16 Sep	89	**PERSONAL** *CBS 463284 1*	**70**	1 wk

Al JOLSON   *US, male vocalist*   *11 wks*

14 Mar	81	**20 GOLDEN GREATS** *MCA MCTV 4*	**18**	7 wks
17 Dec	83	**THE AL JOLSON COLLECTION** *Ronco RON LP 5*	**67**	4 wks

JON and VANGELIS
UK, male vocalist and Greece, male instrumentalist – keyboards   *53 wks*

26 Jan	80	● **SHORT STORIES** *Polydor POLD 5030*	**4**	11 wks
11 Jul	81	● **THE FRIENDS OF MR. CAIRO** *Polydor POLD 5039*	**17**	8 wks
23 Jan	82	● **THE FRIENDS OF MR. CAIRO (re-issue)**		
		Polydor POLD 5053	**6**	15 wks
2 Jul	83	**PRIVATE COLLECTION** *Polydor POLH 4*	**22**	10 wks
11 Aug	84	**THE BEST OF JON AND VANGELIS** *Polydor POLH 6* ..	**42**	9 wks

See also Jon Anderson; Vangelis.

JONES – *See SMITH and JONES*

Aled JONES   *UK, male chorister*   *140 wks*

183

27 Apr	85	● **VOICES FROM THE HOLY LAND** *BBC REC 564*	**6**	43 wks
29 Jun	85	● **ALL THROUGH THE NIGHT** *BBC REH 569*	**2**	43 wks
23 Nov	85	**ALED JONES WITH THE BBC WELSH CHORUS**		
		10/BBC AJ 1	**11**	10 wks
22 Feb	86	**WHERE E'ER YOU WALK** *10 DIX 21*	**36**	6 wks
12 Jul	86	**PIE JESU** *10 AJ 2*	**25**	16 wks
29 Nov	86	**AN ALBUM OF HYMNS** *Telstar STAR 2272*	**18**	11 wks
14 Mar	87	**ALED (MUSIC FROM THE TV SERIES)** *10 AJ 3*	**52**	6 wks
5 Dec	87	**THE BEST OF ALED JONES** *10 AJ 5*	**59**	5 wks

j

First three albums credit the BBC Welsh Chorus.

Glenn JONES   *US, male vocalist*   *1 wk*

31 Oct	87	**GLENN JONES** *Jive HIP 51*	**62**	1 wk

Grace JONES   *US, female vocalist*   *80 wks*

30 Aug	80	**WARM LEATHERETTE** *Island ILPS 9592*	**45**	2 wks
23 May	81	**NIGHTCLUBBING** *Island ILPS 9624*	**35**	16 wks
20 Nov	82	**LIVING MY LIFE** *Island ILPS 9722*	**15**	22 wks
9 Nov	85	**SLAVE TO THE RHYTHM** *ZTT GRACE 1*	**12**	8 wks
14 Dec	85	● **ISLAND LIFE** *Island GJ 1*	**4**	30 wks
29 Nov	86	**INSIDE STORY** *Manhattan MTL 1007*	**61**	2 wks

Howard JONES   *UK, male vocalist*   *120 wks*

17 Mar	84	★ **HUMAN'S LIB** *WEA WX 1*	**1**	57 wks
8 Dec	84	**THE 12" ALBUM** *WEA WX 14*	**15**	33 wks
23 Mar	85	● **DREAM INTO ACTION** *WEA WX 15*	**2**	25 wks
25 Oct	86	● **ONE TO ONE** *WEA WX 68*	**10**	4 wks
1 Apr	89	**CROSS THAT LINE** *WEA WX 225*	**64**	1 wk

Jack JONES US, male vocalist   70 wks

29 Apr	72	● **A SONG FOR YOU** RCA Victor SF 8228	....	9	6 wks
3 Jun	72	● **BREAD WINNERS** RCA Victor SF 8280	....	7	36 wks
7 Apr	73	● **TOGETHER** RCA Victor SF 8342	....	8	10 wks
23 Feb	74	● **HARBOUR** RCA Victor APLI 0408	....	10	5 wks
19 Feb	77	**THE FULL LIFE** RCA Victor PL 12067	....	41	5 wks
21 May	77	● **ALL TO YOURSELF** RCA TVL 2	....	10	8 wks

Quincy JONES US, male arranger/instrumentalist – keyboards   41 wks

18 Apr	81	**THE DUDE** A & M AMLK 63721	....	19	25 wks
20 Mar	82	**THE BEST** A & M AMLH 68542	....	41	4 wks
20 Jan	90	**BACK ON THE BLOCK** Qwest WX 313	....	26	12 wks

Rickie Lee JONES US, female vocalist   39 wks

16 Jun	79	**RICKIE LEE JONES** Warner Bros. K 56628	....	18	19 wks
8 Aug	81	**PIRATES** Warner Bros. K 56816	....	37	11 wks
2 Jul	83	**GIRL AT HER VOLCANO** Warner Bros. 92–3805–1	......	51	3 wks
13 Oct	84	**THE MAGAZINE** Warner Bros. 925117	....	40	4 wks
7 Oct	89	**FLYING COWBOYS** Geffen WX 309	....	50	2 wks

Tammy JONES UK, female vocalist   5 wks

12 Jul	75	**LET ME TRY AGAIN** Epic EPC 80853	....	38	5 wks

184

j

Tom JONES UK, male vocalist   415 wks

5 Jun	65	**ALONG CAME JONES** Decca LK 6693	....	11	5 wks
8 Oct	66	**FROM THE HEART** Decca LK 4814	....	23	8 wks
8 Apr	67	● **GREEN GREEN GRASS OF HOME** Decca SKL 4855	....	3	49 wks
24 Jun	67	● **LIVE AT THE TALK OF THE TOWN** Decca SKL 4874	..	6	90 wks
30 Dec	67	● **13 SMASH HITS** Decca SKL 4909	....	5	49 wks
27 Jul	68	★ **DELILAH** Decca SKL 4946	....	1	29 wks
21 Dec	68	● **HELP YOURSELF** Decca SKL 4982	....	4	9 wks
28 Jun	69	● **THIS IS TOM JONES** Decca SKL 5007	....	2	20 wks
15 Nov	69	● **TOM JONES LIVE IN LAS VEGAS** Decca SKL 5032	.....	3	45 wks
25 Apr	70	● **TOM** Decca SKL 5045	....	4	18 wks
14 Nov	70	● **I WHO HAVE NOTHING** Decca SKL 5072	....	10	10 wks
29 May	71	● **SHE'S A LADY** Decca SKL 5089	....	9	7 wks
27 Nov	71	**LIVE AT CAESAR'S PALACE** Decca 1/1–1/2	....	27	5 wks
24 Jun	72	**CLOSE UP** Decca SKL 5132	....	17	4 wks
23 Jun	73	**THE BODY AND SOUL OF TOM JONES** Decca SKL 5162		31	1 wk
5 Jan	74	**GREATEST HITS** Decca SKL 5176	....	15	13 wks
22 Mar	75	★ **20 GREATEST HITS** Decca TJD 1/11/2	....	1	21 wks
7 Oct	78	**I'M COMING HOME** Lotus WH 5001	....	12	9 wks
16 May	87	**THE GREATEST HITS** Telstar STAR 2296	....	16	12 wks
13 May	89	**AT THIS MOMENT** Jive TOMTV 1	....	34	3 wks
8 Jul	89	**AFTER DARK** Stylus SMR 978	....	46	4 wks
6 Apr	91	**CARRYING A TORCH** Dover ADD 20	....	44	4 wks

Janis JOPLIN US, female vocalist   7 wks

17 Apr	71	**PEARL** CBS 64188	....	50	1 wk
22 Jul	72	**JANIS JOPLIN IN CONCERT** CBS 67241	....	30	6 wks

JOURNEY US, male vocal/instrumental group   30 wks

20 Mar	82	**ESCAPE** CBS 85138	....	32	16 wks

19 Feb 83	● **FRONTIERS** *CBS 25261*	....	6	8 wks
6 Aug 83	**EVOLUTION** *CBS 32342*	....	100	1 wk
24 May 86	**RAISED ON RADIO** *CBS 26902*	....	22	5 wks

JOY DIVISION *UK, male vocal/instrumental group* 29 wks

26 Jul 80	● **CLOSER** *Factory FACT 25*	....	6	8 wks
30 Aug 80	**UNKNOWN PLEASURES** *Factory FACT 10*	....	71	1 wk
17 Oct 81	● **STILL** *Factory FACT 40*	....	5	12 wks
23 Jul 88	● **1977–1980 SUBSTANCE** *Factory FAC 250*	....	7	8 wks

JUDAS PRIEST *UK, male vocal/instrumental group* 77 wks

14 May 77	**SIN AFTER SIN** *CBS 82008*	....	23	6 wks
25 Feb 78	**STAINED GLASS** *CBS 82430*	....	27	5 wks
11 Nov 78	**KILLING MACHINE** *CBS 83135*	....	32	9 wks
6 Oct 79	● **UNLEASHED IN THE EAST** *CBS 83852*	....	10	8 wks
19 Apr 80	● **BRITISH STEEL** *CBS 84160*	....	4	17 wks
7 Mar 81	**POINT OF ENTRY** *CBS 84834*	....	14	5 wks
17 Jul 82	**SCREAMING FOR VENGEANCE** *CBS 85941*	....	11	9 wks
28 Jan 84	**DEFENDERS OF THE FAITH** *CBS 25713*	....	19	5 wks
19 Apr 86	**TURBO** *CBS 26641*	....	33	4 wks
13 Jun 87	**PRIEST LIVE** *CBS 450 639–1*	....	47	2 wks
28 May 88	**RAM IT DOWN** *CBS 461108 1*	....	24	5 wks
22 Sep 90	**PAINKILLER** *CBS 4672901*	....	24	2 wks

JUDGE DREAD *UK, male vocalist* 14 wks

6 Dec 75	**BEDTIME STORIES** *Cactus CTLP 113*	....	26	12 wks
7 Mar 81	**40 BIG ONES** *Creole BIG 1*	....	51	2 wks

185

k

JUICY LUCY *UK, male vocal/instrumental group* 5 wks

18 Apr 70	**JUICY LUCY** *Vertigo VO 2*	....	41	4 wks
21 Nov 70	**LIE BACK AND ENJOY IT** *Vertigo 6360 014*	....	53	1 wk

JULUKA *South Africa, male/female vocal/instrumental group* 3 wks

23 Jul 83	**SCATTERLINGS** *Safari SHAKA 1*	....	50	3 wks

JUNGLE BROTHERS *US, male rap group* 3 wks

3 Feb 90	**DONE BY THE FORCES OF NATURE** *Eternal WX 332* .	41	3 wks

JUNIOR *UK, male vocalist* 14 wks

5 Jun 82	**JI** *Mercury MERS 3*	....	28	14 wks

k

Bert KAEMPFERT *Germany, orchestra* 104 wks

5 Mar 66	● **BYE BYE BLUES** *Polydor BM 84086*	....	4	22 wks

16 Apr 66	**BEST OF BERT KAEMPFERT** *Polydor 84–012*	27	1 wk
28 May 66	**SWINGING SAFARI** *Polydor LPHM 46–384*	20	15 wks
30 Jul 66	**STRANGERS IN THE NIGHT** *Polydor LPHM 84–053* ...	13	26 wks
4 Feb 67	**RELAXING SOUND OF BERT KAEMPFERT**		
	Polydor 583–501	33	3 wks
18 Feb 67	**BERT KAEMPFERT – BEST SELLER** *Polydor 583–551* .	25	18 wks
29 Apr 67	**HOLD ME** *Polydor 184–072*	36	5 wks
26 Aug 67	**KAEMPFERT SPECIAL** *Polydor 236–207*	24	5 wks
19 Jun 71	**ORANGE COLOURED SKY** *Polydor 2310–091*	49	1 wk
5 Jul 80	**SOUNDS SENSATIONAL** *Polydor POLTB 10*	17	8 wks

KAJAGOOGOO *UK, male vocal/instrumental group*   *23 wks*

30 Apr 83	● **WHITE FEATHERS** *EMI EMC 3433*	5	20 wks
26 May 84	**ISLANDS** *EMI KAJA 1*	35	3 wks

Nick KAMEN *UK, male vocalist*   *7 wks*

18 Apr 87	**NICK KAMEN** *WEA WX 84*	34	7 wks

KANE GANG *UK, male vocal/instrumental group*   *12 wks*

23 Feb 85	**THE BAD AND LOWDOWN WORLD OF THE KANE GANG**		
	Kitchenware KWLP 2	21	8 wks
8 Aug 87	**MIRACLE** *Kitchenware KWLP 7*	41	4 wks

Mick KARN *UK, male vocalist/instrumentalist – bass*   *4 wks*

20 Nov 82	**TITLES** *Virgin V 2249*	74	3 wks
28 Feb 87	**DREAMS OF REASON PRODUCE MONSTERS**		
	Virgin V 2389	89	1 wk

KATRINA and the WAVES
UK/US, female/male vocal/instrumental group   *7 wks*

8 Jun 85	**KATRINA AND THE WAVES** *Capitol KTW 1*	28	6 wks
10 May 86	**WAVES** *Capitol EST 2010*	70	1 wk

K.C. and the SUNSHINE BAND
US, male vocal/instrumental group   *17 wks*

30 Aug 75	**K.C. AND THE SUNSHINE BAND** *Jayboy JSL 9*	26	7 wks
1 Mar 80	● **GREATEST HITS** *TK TKR 83385*	10	6 wks
27 Aug 83	**ALL IN A NIGHT'S WORK** *Epic EPC 85847*	46	4 wks

KEEL *US, male vocal/instrumental group*   *2 wks*

17 May 86	**THE FINAL FRONTIER** *Vertigo VERH 33*	83	2 wks

Howard KEEL *US, male vocalist*   *36 wks*

14 Apr 84	● **AND I LOVE YOU SO** *Warwick WW 5137*	6	19 wks
9 Nov 85	**REMINISCING – THE HOWARD KEEL COLLECTION**		
	Telstar STAR 2259	20	12 wks
28 Mar 88	**JUST FOR YOU** *Telstar STAR 2318*	51	5 wks

Felicity KENDAL *UK, female exercise instructor*   *47 wks*

19 Jun 82   **SHAPE UP AND DANCE (VOL. 1)**   *Lifestyle LEG 1* ......   **29**   47 wks

Eddie KENDRICK – *See Daryl HALL and John OATES*

Brian KENNEDY *Ireland, male vocalist*   *1 wk*

31 Mar 90   **THE GREAT WAR OF WORDS**   *RCA PL 74475* ....   **64**   1 wk

Nigel KENNEDY *UK, male instrumentalist – violin*   *109 wks*

 1 Mar 86   **ELGAR VIOLIN CONCERTO**   *EMI EMX 4120581* ......   **97**   1 wk
 7 Oct 89 ● **VIVALDI: FOUR SEASONS**   *EMI NIGE 2* ....   **3**   81 wks
 5 May 90   **MENDELSSOHN/BRUCH/SCHUBERT** *HMV 7496631* .   **28**   15 wks
 6 Apr 91   **BRAHMS VIOLIN CONCERTO**   *EMI NIGE 3* ....   **16**   12 wks

Elgar Violin Concerto *was with the London Philharmonic Orchestra, conducted by Vernon Handley.* Vivaldi Four Seasons *was with the English Chamber Orchestra.* Mendelssohn/Bruch/Schubert *credits Jeffrey Tate and the English Chamber Orchestra. See also London Philharmonic Orchestra.*

KENNY *UK, male vocal/instrumental group*   *1 wk*

17 Jan 76   **THE SOUND OF SUPER K**   *RAK SRAK 518* ....   **56**   1 wk

Gerard KENNY *US, male vocalist*   *4 wks*

21 Jul 79   **MADE IT THROUGH THE RAIN**   *RCA Victor PL 25218* .   **19**   4 wks

187

k

Nik KERSHAW *UK, male vocalist*   *100 wks*

10 Mar 84 ● **HUMAN RACING**   *MCA MCF 3197* ....   **5**   61 wks
 1 Dec 84 ● **THE RIDDLE**   *MCA MCF 3245* ....   **8**   36 wks
 8 Nov 86   **RADIO MUSICOLA**   *MCA MCG 6016* ....   **47**   3 wks

Chaka KHAN *US, female vocalist*   *39 wks*

20 Oct 84   **I FEEL FOR YOU**   *Warner Bros. 925 162* ....   **15**   22 wks
 9 Aug 86   **DESTINY**   *Warner Bros. WX 45* ....   **77**   2 wks
 3 Jun 89   **LIFE IS A DANCE – THE REMIX PROJECT**
             Warner Bros. WX 268 ....   **14**   15 wks

See also Rufus and Chaka Khan.

Aram KHATCHATURIAN/VIENNA PHILMARONIC ORCHESTRA
Russia, male conductor/Austria, orchestra   *15 wks*

22 Jan 72   **SPARTACUS**   *Decca SXL 6000* ....   **16**   15 wks

KIDS FROM FAME
US, male/female vocal/instrumental group   *117 wks*

24 Jul 82 ★ **KIDS FROM FAME**   *BBC REP 447* ....   **1**   45 wks
16 Oct 82 ● **KIDS FROM FAME AGAIN**   *RCA RCALP 6057* ....   **2**   21 wks
26 Feb 83 ● **THE KIDS FROM FAME LIVE**   *BBC KIDLP 003* ....   **8**   28 wks
14 May 83   **THE KIDS FROM FAME SONGS**   *BBC KIDLP 004* .....   **14**   16 wks
20 Aug 83   **SING FOR YOU**   *BBC KIDLP 005* ....   **28**   7 wks

KILLING JOKE UK, male vocal/instrumental group   30 wks

25 Oct 80	**KILLING JOKE** Polydor EGMD 545	**39**	4 wks
20 Jun 81	**WHAT'S THIS FOR** Malicious Damage EGMD 550	**42**	4 wks
8 May 82	**REVELATIONS** Malicious Damage EGMD 3	**12**	6 wks
27 Nov 82	**'HA' – KILLING JOKE LIVE** EG EGMDT 4	**66**	2 wks
23 Jul 83	**FIRE DANCES** EG EGMD 5	**29**	3 wks
9 Mar 85	**NIGHT TIME** EG EGLP 61	**11**	9 wks
22 Nov 86	**BRIGHTER THAN A THOUSAND SUNS** EG EGLP 66	**54**	1 wk
9 Jul 88	**OUTSIDE THE GATE** EG EGLP 73	**92**	1 wk

KIM – *See MEL and KIM*

KIMERA with the LONDON SYMPHONY ORCHESTRA Korea, female vocalist with UK, orchestra   4 wks

26 Oct 85	**HITS ON OPERA** Stylus SMR 8505	**38**	4 wks

See also London Symphony Orchestra.

KING UK, male vocal/instrumental group   32 wks

9 Feb 85	● **STEPS IN TIME** CBS 26095	**6**	21 wks
23 Nov 85	**BITTER SWEET** CBS 86320	**16**	11 wks

B.B. KING US, male vocalist/instrumentalist – guitar   5 wks

25 Aug 79	**TAKE IT HOME** MCA MCF 3010	**60**	5 wks

Ben E. KING US, male vocalist   3 wks

1 Jul 67	**SPANISH HARLEM** Atlantic 590–001	**30**	3 wks

See also Ben E. King and the Drifters.

Ben E. KING and the DRIFTERS
US, male vocalist and male vocal group   24 wks

14 Mar 87	**STAND BY ME (THE ULTIMATE COLLECTION)** Atlantic WX 90	**14**	8 wks
20 Oct 90	**THE BEST OF BEN E. KING AND THE DRIFTERS** Telstar STAR 2373	**15**	16 wks

See also Ben E. King; Drifters.

Carole KING US, female vocalist/instrumentalist – piano   102 wks

24 Jul 71	● **TAPESTRY** A & M AMLS 2025	**4**	90 wks
15 Jan 72	**MUSIC** A & M AMLH 67013	**18**	10 wks
2 Dec 72	**RHYMES AND REASONS** Ode 77016	**40**	2 wks

Evelyn KING US, female vocalist   9 wks

11 Sep 82	**GET LOOSE** RCA RCALP 3093	**35**	9 wks

Mark KING UK, male vocalist/instrumentalist – bass   2 wks

21 Jul 84	**INFLUENCES** Polydor MKLP 1	**77**	2 wks

Solomon KING *US, male vocalist* *1 wk*

| 22 Jun 68 | **SHE WEARS MY RING** *Columbia SCX 6250* .... | 40 | 1 wk |

KING CRIMSON *UK, male vocal/instrumental group* *53 wks*

1 Nov 69 ●	**IN THE COURT OF THE CRIMSON KING**		
	Island ILPS 9111	5	18 wks
30 May 70 ●	**IN THE WAKE OF POSEIDON** *Island ILPS 9127*	4	13 wks
16 Jan 71	**LIZARD** *Island ILPS 9141*	30	1 wk
8 Jan 72	**ISLANDS** *Island ILPS 9175*	30	1 wk
7 Apr 73	**LARKS' TONGUES IN ASPIC** *Island ILPS 9230*	20	4 wks
13 Apr 74	**STARLESS AND BIBLE BLACK** *Island ILPS 9275*	28	2 wks
26 Oct 74	**RED** *Island ILPS 9308*	45	1 wk
10 Oct 81	**DISCIPLINE** *EG EGLP 49*	41	4 wks
26 Jun 82	**BEAT** *EG EGLP 51*	39	5 wks
31 Mar 84	**THREE OF A PERFECT PAIR** *EG EGLP 55*	30	4 wks

KING KURT *UK, male vocal/instrumental group* *5 wks*

| 10 Dec 83 | **OOH WALLAH WALLAH** *Stiff SEEZ 52* .... | 99 | 1 wk |
| 8 Mar 86 | **BIG COCK** *Stiff SEEZ 62* .... | 50 | 4 wks |

KINGDOM COME *US, male vocal/instrumental group* *10 wks*

| 28 Mar 88 | **KINGDOM COME** *Polydor KCLP 1* .... | 43 | 6 wks |
| 13 May 89 | **IN YOUR FACE** *Polydor 839192 1* .... | 25 | 4 wks |

KINGMAKER *UK, male vocal/instrumental group* *1 wk*

| 19 Oct 91 | **EAT YOURSELF WHOLE** *Scorch CHR 1878* .... | 69 | 1 wk |

Redhead KINGPIN and the FBI *US, male vocalist* *3 wks*

| 9 Sep 89 | **A SHADE OF RED** *10 DIX 85* .... | 35 | 3 wks |

The Choir of KING'S COLLEGE, CAMBRIDGE
UK, choir *3 wks*

| 11 Dec 71 | **THE WORLD OF CHRISTMAS** *Argo SPAA 104* .... | 38 | 3 wks |

KINGS OF SWING ORCHESTRA
Australia, orchestra *11 wks*

| 29 May 82 | **SWITCHED ON SWING** *K-Tel ONE 1166* .... | 28 | 11 wks |

KINGS X *US, male vocal/instrumental group* *2 wks*

| 1 Jul 89 | **GRETCHEN GOES TO NEBRASKA** *Atlantic WX 279* ... | 52 | 1 wk |
| 10 Nov 90 | **FAITH HOPE LOVE** *Megaforce 756821451* .... | 70 | 1 wk |

KINKS *UK, male vocal/instrumental group* *125 wks*

17 Oct 64 ●	**KINKS** *Pye NPL 18096*	3	25 wks
13 Mar 65 ●	**KINDA KINKS** *Pye NPL 18112*	3	15 wks
4 Dec 65 ●	**KINKS KONTROVERSY** *Pye NPL 18131*	9	12 wks

189

k

11 Sep 66	● **WELL RESPECTED KINKS** *Marble Arch MAL 612*	5	31 wks
5 Nov 66	**FACE TO FACE** *Pye NPL 18149*	12	11 wks
14 Oct 67	**SOMETHING ELSE** *Pye NSPL 18193*	35	2 wks
2 Dec 67	● **SUNNY AFTERNOON** *Marble Arch MAL 716*	9	11 wks
23 Oct 71	**GOLDEN HOUR OF THE KINKS** *Golden Hour GH 501* ..	21	4 wks
14 Oct 78	**20 GOLDEN GREATS** *Ronco RPL 2031*	19	6 wks
5 Nov 83	**KINKS GREATEST HITS – DEAD END STREET**		
	PRT KINK 1	96	1 wk
16 Sep 89	**THE ULTIMATE COLLECTION**		
	Castle Communications CTVLP 001	35	7 wks

Kathy KIRBY *UK, female vocalist* 8 wks

4 Jan 64	**16 HITS FROM STARS AND GARTERS**		
	Decca LK 5475	11	8 wks

KISS *US, male vocal/instrumental group* 62 wks

29 May 76	**DESTROYER** *Casablanca CBSP 4008*	22	5 wks
25 Jun 76	**ALIVE!** *Casablanca CBSP 401*	49	2 wks
17 Dec 77	**ALIVE** *Casablanca CALD 5004*	60	1 wk
7 Jul 79	**DYNASTY** *Casablanca CALH 2051*	50	6 wks
28 Jun 80	**UNMASKED** *Mercury 6302 032*	48	3 wks
5 Dec 81	**THE ELDER** *Casablanca 6302 163*	51	3 wks
26 Jun 82	**KILLERS** *Casablanca CANL 1*	42	6 wks
6 Nov 82	**CREATURES OF THE NIGHT** *Casablanca CANL 4* ...	22	4 wks
8 Oct 83	● **LICK IT UP** *Vertigo VERL 9*	7	7 wks
6 Oct 84	**ANIMALISE** *Vertigo VERL 18*	11	4 wks
5 Oct 85	**ASYLUM** *Vertigo VERH 32*	12	3 wks
7 Nov 87	● **CRAZY NIGHTS** *Vertigo VERH 49*	4	14 wks
10 Dec 88	**SMASHES, THRASHES AND HITS** *Vertigo 836759 1* ...	62	2 wks
4 Nov 89	**HOT IN THE SHADE** *Fontana 838913 1*	35	2 wks

190

k

KISSING THE PINK
UK, male/female vocal/instrumental group 5 wks

4 Jun 83	**NAKED** *Magnet KTPL 1001*	54	5 wks

KITCHENS OF DISTINCTION
UK, male vocal/instrumental group 1 wk

30 Mar 91	**STRANGE FREE WORLD** *One Little Indian TPLP 19*	45	1 wk

Eartha KITT *US, female vocalist* 1 wk

11 Feb 61	**REVISITED** *London HA 2296*	17	1 wk

KLEEER *US, male vocal/instrumental group* 1 wk

6 Jul 85	**SEEEKRET** *Atlantic 78–1254–1*	96	1 wk

KLF *UK, male multi-instrumental/production duo with guest vocalists* 28 wks

16 Mar 91	● **THE WHITE ROOM** *KLF Communications JAMSLP 6*	3†	28 wks

Earl KLUGH – *See George BENSON and Earl KLUGH*

KNACK *US, male vocal/instrumental group* — 2 wks

4 Aug 79	**GET THE KNACK** *Capitol EST 11948*	65	2 wks

Curtis KNIGHT – *See Jimi HENDRIX and Curtis KNIGHT*

Gladys KNIGHT and the PIPS
US, female vocalist/male vocal backing group — 105 wks

31 May 75	**I FEEL A SONG** *Buddah BDLP 4030*	20	15 wks
28 Feb 76	● **THE BEST OF GLADYS KNIGHT AND THE PIPS**		
	Buddah BDLH 5013	6	43 wks
16 Jul 77	**STILL TOGETHER** *Buddah BDLH 5014*	42	3 wks
12 Nov 77	● **30 GREATEST** *K-Tel NE 1004*	3	22 wks
4 Oct 80	**A TOUCH OF LOVE** *K-Tel NE 1090*	16	6 wks
4 Feb 84	**THE COLLECTION – 20 GREATEST HITS**		
	Starblend NITE 1	43	5 wks
27 Feb 88	**ALL OUR LOVE** *MCA MCF 3409*	80	1 wk
28 Oct 89	**THE SINGLES ALBUM** *Polygram GKTV 1*	13	10 wks

See also Diana Ross/Michael Jackson/Gladys Knight/Stevie Wonder.

KNIGHTSBRIDGE STRINGS *UK, male orchestra* — 1 wk

25 Jun 60	**STRING SWAY** *Top Rank BUY 017*	20	1 wk

David KNOPFLER
UK, male vocalist/instrumentalist – guitar — 1 wk

19 Nov 83	**RELEASE** *Peach River DAVID 1*	82	1 wk

Mark KNOPFLER *UK, male vocalist/instrumentalist – guitar* — 14 wks

16 Apr 83	**LOCAL HERO** *Vertigo VERL 4*	14	11 wks
20 Oct 84	**CAL – MUSIC FROM THE FILM** *Vertigo VERH 17*	65	3 wks

See also Chet Atkins and Mark Knopfler.

Frankie KNUCKLES *US, male producer* — 2 wks

17 Aug 91	**BEYOND THE MIX** *Virgin America VUSLP 6*	59	2 wks

John KONGOS
South Africa, male vocalist/multi-instrumentalist — 2 wks

15 Jan 72	**KONGOS** *Fly HIFLY 7*	29	2 wks

KOOL AND THE GANG
US, male vocal/instrumental group — 115 wks

21 Nov 81	● **SOMETHING SPECIAL** *De-Lite DSR 001*	10	20 wks
2 Oct 82	**AS ONE** *De-Lite DSR 3*	49	10 wks
7 May 83	● **TWICE AS KOOL** *De-Lite PROLP 2*	4	23 wks
14 Jan 84	**IN THE HEART** *De-Lite DSR 4*	18	23 wks
15 Dec 84	**EMERGENCY** *De-Lite DSR 6*	47	25 wks
12 Nov 88	**THE SINGLES COLLECTION** *De-Lite KGTV 1*	28	13 wks
27 Oct 90	**KOOL LOVE** *Telstar STAR 2435*	50	1 wk

KORGIS *UK, male vocal/instrumental duo* *4 wks*

26 Jul 80	**DUMB WAITERS** *Rialto TENOR 104*	**40**	4 wks

KRAFTWERK *Germany, male vocal/instrumental group* *71 wks*

17 May 75 ●	**AUTOBAHN** *Vertigo 6360 620*	**4**	18 wks
20 May 78 ●	**THE MAN-MACHINE** *Capitol EST 11728*	**9**	13 wks
23 May 81	**COMPUTER WORLD** *EMI EMC 3370*	**15**	22 wks
6 Feb 82	**TRANS-EUROPE EXPRESS** *Capitol EST 11603*	**49**	7 wks
22 Jun 85	**AUTOBAHN (re-issue)** *Parlophone AUTO 1*	**61**	3 wks
15 Nov 86	**ELECTRIC CAFE** *EMI EMD 1001*	**58**	2 wks
22 Jun 91	**THE MIX** *EMI EM 1408*	**15**	6 wks

Billy J. KRAMER and the DAKOTAS
UK, male vocalist, male instrumental backing group *17 wks*

16 Nov 63	**LISTEN TO BILLY J. KRAMER** *Parlophone PMC 1209* ...	**11**	17 wks

Lenny KRAVITZ *US, male vocalist* *30 wks*

26 May 90	**LET LOVE RULE** *Virgin America VUSLP 10*	**56**	4 wks
13 Apr 91 ●	**MAMA SAID** *Virgin America VUSLP 31*	**8**	26 wks

Kris KRISTOFFERSON and Rita COOLIDGE
US, male/female vocal duo *4 wks*

6 May 78	**NATURAL ACT** *A & M AMLH 64690*	**35**	4 wks

See also Rita Coolidge.

192

l

KROKUS *Switzerland/Malta, male vocal/instrumental group* *11 wks*

21 Feb 81	**HARDWARE** *Ariola ARL 5064*	**44**	4 wks
20 Feb 82	**ONE VICE AT A TIME** *Arista SPART 1189*	**28**	5 wks
16 Apr 83	**HEADHUNTER** *Arista 205 255*	**74**	2 wks

Charlie KUNZ *US, male instrumentalist – piano* *11 wks*

14 Jun 69 ●	**THE WORLD OF CHARLIE KUNZ** *Decca SPA 15*	**9**	11 wks

l

L.A. GUNS *US, male/female vocal/instrumental group* *4 wks*

5 Mar 88	**L.A. GUNS** *Vertigo VERH 55*	**73**	1 wk
30 Sep 89	**COCKED AND LOADED** *Vertigo 8385921*	**45**	2 wks
13 Jul 91	**HOLLYWOOD VAMPIRES** *Mercury 8496041*	**44**	1 wk

LA'S UK, male vocal/instrumental group
19 wks

13 Oct 90   **THE LA'S**   Go! Discs 8282021   ....   **30**   19 wks

Patti LaBELLE US, female vocalist
17 wks

24 May 86   **THE WINNER IN YOU**   MCA MCF 3319   ....   **30**   17 wks

LADYSMITH BLACK MAMBAZO
South Africa, male vocal group   **11 wks**

11 Apr 87   **SHAKA ZULU**   Warner Bros. WX 94   ....   **34**   11 wks

Cleo LAINE UK, female vocalist
1 wk

2 Dec 78   **CLEO**   Arcade ADEP 37   ....   **68**   1 wk
See also Cleo Laine and John Williams; Cleo Laine and James Galway.

Cleo LAINE and James GALWAY
UK, female vocalist and male instrumentalist – flute   **14 wks**

31 May 80   **SOMETIMES WHEN WE TOUCH**   RCA PL 25296   .....   **15**   14 wks
See also Cleo Laine; James Galway.

193

l

Cleo LAINE and John WILLIAMS
UK, female vocalist and male instrumentalist – guitar   **22 wks**

7 Jan 78   **BEST OF FRIENDS**   RCA RS 1094   ....   **18**   22 wks
See also Cleo Laine; John Williams.

Frankie LAINE US, male vocalist
29 wks

24 Jun 61   ● **HELL BENT FOR LEATHER**   Philips BBL 7468   ....   **7**   23 wks
24 Sep 77   ● **THE VERY BEST OF FRANKIE LAINE**   Warwick PR 5032   **7**   6 wks

Greg LAKE UK, male vocalist
3 wks

17 Oct 81   **GREG LAKE**   Chrysalis CHR 1357   ....   **62**   3 wks
See also Emerson, Lake and Palmer; Emerson, Lake and Powell.

Annabel LAMB UK, female vocalist
1 wk

28 Apr 84   **THE FLAME**   A&M AMLX 68564   ....   **84**   1 wk

LAMBRETTAS UK, male vocal/instrumental group
8 wks

5 Jul 80   **BEAT BOYS IN THE JET AGE**   Rocket TRAIN 10   ....   **28**   8 wks

LANDSCAPE UK, male vocal/instrumental group
12 wks

21 Mar 81   **FROM THE TEAROOMS OF MARS TO THE HELLHOLES OF URANUS**   RCA RCALP 5003   ....   **13**   12 wks

Ronnie LANE and the Band SLIM CHANCE

UK, male vocal/instrumental group   *1 wk*

17 Aug 74	**ANYMORE FOR ANYMORE**	*GM GML 1013*	48	1 wk

See also Pete Townshend and Ronnie Lane.

Thomas LANG *UK, male vocalist*   *1 wk*

20 Feb 88	**SCALLYWAG JAZ**	*Epic 450996 1*	92	1 wk

Mario LANZA *US, male vocalist*   *56 wks*

6 Dec 58 ●	**THE STUDENT PRINCE/THE GREAT CARUSO**			
	RCA RB 16113		4	21 wks
23 Jul 60 ●	**THE GREAT CARUSO** *RCA RB 16112*		3	15 wks
9 Jan 71	**HIS GREATEST HITS VOL. 1** *RCA LSB 4000*		39	1 wk
5 Sep 81	**THE LEGEND OF MARIO LANZA** *K-Tel NE 1110*		29	11 wks
14 Nov 87	**A PORTRAIT OF MARIO LANZA** *Stylus SMR 741*		49	8 wks

The Great Caruso side of the first album is a film soundtrack.

LARD *UK, male vocal/instrumental group*   *1 wk*

6 Oct 90	**THE LAST TEMPTATION**			
	Alternative Tentacles VIRUS 84		69	1 wk

194

James LAST *Germany, male orchestra leader*   *386 wks*

15 Apr 67 ●	**THIS IS JAMES LAST** *Polydor 104–678*		6	48 wks
22 Jul 67	**HAMMOND A-GO-GO** *Polydor 249–043*		27	10 wks
26 Aug 67	**NON-STOP DANCING** *Polydor 236–203*		35	1 wk
26 Aug 67	**LOVE THIS IS MY SONG** *Polydor 583–553*		32	2 wks
22 Jun 68	**JAMES LAST GOES POP** *Polydor 249–160*		32	3 wks
8 Feb 69	**DANCING '68 VOL. 1** *Polydor 249–216*		40	1 wk
31 May 69	**TRUMPET A-GO-GO** *Polydor 249–239*		13	1 wk
9 Aug 69	**NON-STOP DANCING '69** *Polydor 249–294*		26	1 wk
24 Jan 70	**NON-STOP DANCING '69/2** *Polydor 249/354*		27	3 wks
23 May 70	**NON-STOP EVERGREENS** *Polydor 249–370*		26	1 wk
11 Jul 70	**CLASSICS UP TO DATE** *Polydor 249–371*		44	1 wk
11 Jul 70	**NON-STOP DANCING '70** *Polydor 2371–04*		67	1 wk
24 Oct 70	**VERY BEST OF JAMES LAST** *Polydor 2371–054*		45	4 wks
8 May 71	**NON-STOP DANCING '71** *Polydor 2371–111*		21	4 wks
26 Jun 71	**SUMMER HAPPENING** *Polydor 2371–133*		38	1 wk
18 Sep 71	**BEACH PARTY 2** *Polydor 2371–211*		47	1 wk
2 Oct 71	**YESTERDAY'S MEMORIES** *Contour 2870–117*		17	14 wks
16 Oct 71	**NON-STOP DANCING 12** *Polydor 2371–141*		30	3 wks
19 Feb 72	**NON-STOP DANCING 13** *Polydor 2371–189*		32	2 wks
4 Mar 72	**POLKA PARTY** *Polydor 2371–190*		22	3 wks
29 Apr 72	**JAMES LAST IN CONCERT** *Polydor 2371–191*		13	6 wks
24 Jun 72	**VOODOO PARTY** *Polydor 2371–235*		45	1 wk
16 Sep 72	**CLASSICS UP TO DATE VOL. 2** *Polydor 184–061*		49	1 wk
30 Sep 72	**LOVE MUST BE THE REASON** *Polydor 2371–281*		32	2 wks
27 Jan 73	**THE MUSIC OF JAMES LAST** *Polydor 2683 010*		19	12 wks
24 Feb 73	**JAMES LAST IN RUSSIA** *Polydor 2371 293*		12	9 wks
24 Feb 73	**NON-STOP DANCING VOL. 14** *Polydor 2371–319*		27	3 wks
28 Jul 73	**OLE** *Polydor 2371 384*		24	5 wks
1 Sep 73	**NON-STOP DANCING VOL. 15** *Polydor 2371–376*		34	2 wks
20 Apr 74	**NON-STOP DANCING VOL. 16** *Polydor 2371–444*		43	2 wks
29 Jun 74	**IN CONCERT VOL. 2** *Polydor 2371–320*		49	1 wk
23 Nov 74	**GOLDEN MEMORIES** *Polydor 2371–472*		39	2 wks
26 Jul 75 ●	**TEN YEARS NON-STOP JUBILEE** *Polydor 2660–111*		5	16 wks
2 Aug 75	**VIOLINS IN LOVE** *K-Tel /*		60	1 wk
22 Nov 75 ●	**MAKE THE PARTY LAST** *Polydor 2371–612*		3	19 wks

8 May 76	**CLASSICS UP TO DATE VOL. 3** *2371–538*	54 1 wk
6 May 78	**EAST TO WEST** *Polydor 2630–092*	49 4 wks
14 Apr 79	● **LAST THE WHOLE NIGHT LONG** *Polydor PTD 001* ...	2 45 wks
23 Aug 80	**THE BEST FROM 150 GOLD RECORDS** *Polydor 2681 211*	56 3 wks
1 Nov 80	**CLASSICS FOR DREAMING** *Polydor POLTV 11*	12 18 wks
14 Feb 81	**ROSES FROM THE SOUTH** *Polydor 2372 051*	41 5 wks
21 Nov 81	**HANSIMANIA** *Polydor POLTV 14*	18 13 wks
28 Nov 81	**LAST FOREVER** *Polydor 2630 135*	88 2 wks
5 Mar 83	**BLUEBIRD** *Polydor POLD 5072*	57 3 wks
30 Apr 83	**THE BEST OF MY GOLD RECORDS** *Polydor PODV 7* ..	42 5 wks
30 Apr 83	**NON-STOP DANCING '83 – PARTY POWER**	
	Polydor POLD 5094	56 2 wks
3 Dec 83	**THE GREATEST SONGS OF THE BEATLES**	
	Polydor POLD 5119	52 8 wks
24 Mar 84	**THE ROSE OF TRALEE AND OTHER IRISH FAVOURITES**	
	Polydor POLD 5131	21 11 wks
13 Oct 84	**PARADISE** *Polydor POLD 5163*	74 2 wks
8 Dec 84	**JAMES LAST IN SCOTLAND** *Polydor POLD 5166*	68 9 wks
14 Sep 85	**LEAVE THE BEST TO LAST** *Polydor PROLP 7*	11 27 wks
18 Apr 87	**BY REQUEST** *Polydor POLH 34*	22 11 wks
26 Nov 88	**DANCE DANCE DANCE** *Polydor JLTV 1*	38 8 wks
14 Apr 90	**CLASSICS BY MOONLIGHT** *Polydor 8432181*	12 11 wks
15 Jun 91	● **POP SYMPHONIES** *Polydor 8494291*	10 11 wks

See also Richard Clayderman and James Last.

LATIN QUARTER   *UK, male/female vocal/instrumental group*   *3 wks*

1 Mar 86	**MODERN TIMES** *Rockin' Horse RHLP 1*	91 2 wks
6 Jun 87	**MICK AND CAROLINE** *Rockin' Horse 208 142*	96 1 wk

---

Cyndi LAUPER   *US, female vocalist*   *56 wks*

18 Feb 84	**SHE'S SO UNUSUAL** *Portrait PRT 25792*	16 32 wks
11 Oct 86	**TRUE COLORS** *Portrait PRT 26948*	25 12 wks
1 Jul 89	● **A NIGHT TO REMEMBER** *Epic 462499 1*	9 12 wks

---

LAUREL and HARDY   *UK/US, male comic duo*   *4 wks*

6 Dec 75	**THE GOLDEN AGE OF HOLLYWOOD COMEDY**	
	United Artists UAG 29676	55 4 wks

---

LAW   *UK/US, male vocal/instrumental duo*   *1 wk*

6 Apr 91	**THE LAW** *Atlantic 7567821951*	61 1 wk

---

Syd LAWRENCE   *UK, orchestra*   *9 wks*

8 Aug 70	**MORE MILLER AND OTHER BIG BAND MAGIC**	
	Philips 6642 001	14 4 wks
25 Dec 71	**SYD LAWRENCE WITH THE GLENN MILLER SOUND**	
	Fontana SFL 13178	31 2 wks
25 Dec 71	**MUSIC OF GLENN MILLER IN SUPER STEREO**	
	Philips 6641–017	43 2 wks
26 Feb 72	**SOMETHING OLD, SOMETHING NEW** *Philips 6308 090*	34 1 wk

---

Ronnie LAWS   *US, male vocalist/instrumentalist – saxophone*   *1 wk*

17 Oct 81	**SOLID GROUND** *Liberty LBG 30336*	100 1 wk

Doug LAZY *US, male vocalist*   *1 wk*

10 Mar 90	**DOUG LAZY GETTIN' CRAZY**	*Atlantic 7567820661*	....	65	1 wk

LEAGUE UNLIMITED ORCHESTRA
UK, male/female instrumental/vocal group   *52 wks*

17 Jul 82	● **LOVE AND DANCING**	*Virgin OVED 6*	....	3	52 wks

This album is a predominantly instrumental version of previously recorded Human League songs re-mixed by UK producer Martin Rushent.

LED ZEPPELIN *UK, male vocal/instrumental group*   *432 wks*

12 Apr 69	● **LED ZEPPELIN**	*Atlantic 588–171*	....	6	79 wks
8 Nov 69	★ **LED ZEPPELIN 2**	*Atlantic 588–198*	....	1	138 wks
7 Nov 70	★ **LED ZEPPELIN 3**	*Atlantic 2401–002*	....	1	40 wks
27 Nov 71	★ **FOUR SYMBOLS**	*Atlantic K 2401–012*	....	1	63 wks
14 Apr 73	★ **HOUSES OF THE HOLY**	*Atlantic K 50014*	....	1	13 wks
15 Mar 75	★ **PHYSICAL GRAFFITI**	*Swan Song SSK 89400*	....	1	27 wks
24 Apr 76	★ **PRESENCE**	*Swan Song SSK 59402*	....	1	14 wks
6 Nov 76	★ **THE SONG REMAINS THE SAME**	*Swan Song SSK 89402*		1	15 wks
8 Sep 79	★ **IN THROUGH THE OUT DOOR**	*Swan Song SSK 59410*	.	1	16 wks
4 Dec 82	● **CODA**	*Swan Song A 0051*	....	4	7 wks
27 Oct 90	● **REMASTERS**	*Atlantic ZEP 1*	....	10	18 wks
10 Nov 90	**LED ZEPPELIN**	*Atlantic 7567821441*	....	48	2 wks

Led Zeppelin 2 changed label/number to Atlantic K 40037, Four Symbols changed to Atlantic K 50008 during their runs. The fourth Led Zeppelin album appeared in the chart under various guises: The Fourth Led Zeppelin Album, Runes, The New Led Zeppelin Album, Led Zeppelin 4 and Four Symbols. The two Led Zeppelin albums are different. The 1990 entry was a boxed CD set of old and previously unreleased material.

196

l

LEE – *See PETERS and LEE*

Brenda LEE *US, female vocalist*   *57 wks*

24 Nov 62	**ALL THE WAY**	*Brunswick LAT 8383*	....	20	2 wks
16 Feb 63	**BRENDA – THAT'S ALL**	*Brunswick LAT 8516*	....	13	9 wks
13 Apr 63	● **ALL ALONE AM I**	*Brunswick LAT 8530*	....	8	20 wks
16 Jul 66	**BYE BYE BLUES**	*Brunswick LAT 8649*	....	21	2 wks
1 Nov 80	**LITTLE MISS DYNAMITE**	*Warwick WW 5083*	....	15	11 wks
7 Jan 84	**25TH ANNIVERSARY**	*MCA MCLD 609*	....	65	4 wks
30 Mar 85	**THE VERY BEST OF BRENDA LEE**	*MCA LETV 1*	....	16	9 wks

Peggy LEE *US, female vocalist*   *17 wks*

4 Jun 60	● **LATIN A LA LEE**	*Capitol T 1290*	....	8	15 wks
20 May 61	**BEST OF PEGGY LEE VOL. 2**	*Brunswick LAT 8355*	......	18	1 wk
21 Oct 61	**BLACK COFFEE**	*Ace of Hearts AH 5*	....	20	1 wk

See also Peggy Lee and George Shearing.

Peggy LEE and George SHEARING
US, female vocalist and UK, male instrumentalist – piano   *6 wks*

11 Jun 60	**BEAUTY AND THE BEAT**	*Capitol T 1219*	....	16	6 wks

See also Peggy Lee; Nat 'King' Cole and the George Shearing Quintet.

Raymond LEFEVRE *France, orchestra*   *9 wks*

7 Oct 67	● **RAYMOND LEFEVRE**	*Major Minor MMLP 4*	....	10	7 wks
17 Feb 68	**RAYMOND LEFEVRE VOL. 2**	*Major Minor SMLP 13*	....	37	2 wks

Tom LEHRER *US, male comic vocalist* 26 wks

8 Nov 58	● SONGS BY TOM LEHRER *Decca LF 1311*	7	19 wks
25 Jun 60	● AN EVENING WASTED WITH TOM LEHRER		
	Decca LK 4332	7	7 wks

John LENNON *UK, male vocalist* 297 wks

16 Jan 71	JOHN LENNON AND THE PLASTIC ONO BAND		
	Apple PCS 7124	11	11 wks
30 Oct 71	★ IMAGINE *Apple PAS 10004*	1	101 wks
14 Oct 72	SOMETIME IN NEW YORK CITY *Apple PCSP 716*	11	6 wks
8 Dec 73	MIND GAMES *Apple PCS 7165*	13	12 wks
19 Oct 74	● WALLS AND BRIDGES *Apple PCTC 253*	6	10 wks
8 Mar 75	● ROCK 'N' ROLL *Apple PCS 7169*	6	28 wks
8 Nov 75	● SHAVED FISH *Apple PCS 7173*	8	29 wks
22 Nov 80	★ DOUBLE FANTASY *Geffen K 99131*	1	36 wks
20 Nov 82	★ THE JOHN LENNON COLLECTION		
	Parlophone EMTV 37	1	42 wks
4 Feb 84	● MILK AND HONEY *Polydor POLH 5*	3	13 wks
8 Mar 86	LIVE IN NEW YORK CITY *Parlophone PCS 7031*	55	3 wks
22 Oct 88	IMAGINE – MUSIC FROM THE MOTION PICTURE		
	Parlophone PCSP 722	64	6 wks

Imagine *changed its label credit to Parlophone PAS 10004 between its initial chart run and later runs.* John Lennon and the Plastic Ono Band *is credited to John Lennon and the Plastic Ono Band.* Imagine *is credited to John Lennon and the Plastic Ono Band with the Flux Fiddlers.* Sometime In New York City *is credited to John and Yoko Lennon with the Plastic Ono Band and Elephant's Memory.* Double Fantasy *and* Milk And Honey *are credited to John Lennon and Yoko Ono.* Shaved Fish *and* The John Lennon Collection *are compilations and so have various credits.* Imagine – Music From The Motion Picture *includes tracks by the* Beatles. *See also Beatles; Yoko Ono.*

197

l

Julian LENNON *UK, male vocalist* 20 wks

3 Nov 84	VALOTTE *Charisma JLLP 1*	20	15 wks
5 Apr 86	THE SECRET VALUE OF DAYDREAMING		
	Charisma CAS 1171	93	1 wk
5 Oct 91	HELP YOURSELF *Virgin V 2668*	42	4 wks

Deke LEONARD *UK, male vocalist/instrumentalist – guitar* 1 wk

13 Apr 74	KAMIKAZE *United Artists UAG 29544*	50	1 wk

Paul LEONI *UK, male instrumentalist – pan flute* 19 wks

24 Sep 83	FLIGHTS OF FANCY *Nouveau Music NML 1002*	17	19 wks

LEVEL 42 *UK, male vocal/instrumental group* 223 wks

29 Aug 81	LEVEL 42 *Polydor POLS 1036*	20	18 wks
10 Apr 82	THE EARLY TAPES JULY–AUGUST 1980		
	Polydor POLS 1064	46	6 wks
18 Sep 82	THE PURSUIT OF ACCIDENTS *Polydor POLD 5067*	17	16 wks
3 Sep 83	● STANDING IN THE LIGHT *Polydor POLD 5110*	9	13 wks
13 Oct 84	TRUE COLOURS *Polydor POLH 10*	14	8 wks
6 Jul 85	A PHYSICAL PRESENCE *Polydor POLH 23*	28	5 wks
26 Oct 85	● WORLD MACHINE *Polydor POLH 25*	3	72 wks
28 Mar 87	● RUNNING IN THE FAMILY *Polydor POLH 42*	2	54 wks
1 Oct 88	● STARING AT THE SUN *Polydor POLH 50*	2	11 wks
18 Nov 89	● LEVEL BEST *Polydor LEVTV 1*	5	15 wks
14 Sep 91	● GUARANTEED *RCA PL 75005*	3	5 wks

A proud group leader stands in front of a
blow-up of the chart in which **Huey
Lewis and the News** first reached
number one in America.

LEVELLERS *UK, male vocal/instrumental group* *5 wks*

19 Oct 91   **LEVELLING THE LAND** *China WOL 1022* .... **14**   5 wks

LEVERT *UK, male vocal group* *1 wk*

29 Aug 87   **THE BIG THROWDOWN** *Atlantic 781773–1* .... **86**   1 wk

Huey LEWIS and the NEWS
US, male vocal/instrumental group *86 wks*

14 Sep 85   **SPORTS** *Chrysalis CHR 1412* .... **23**   24 wks
20 Sep 86 ● **FORE!** *Chrysalis CDL 1534* .... **8**   52 wks
6 Aug 88   **SMALL WORLD** *Chrysalis CDL 1622* .... **12**   8 wks
18 May 91   **HARD AT PLAY** *Chrysalis CHR 1847* .... **39**   2 wks

Jerry Lee LEWIS *US, male vocalist/instrumentalist – piano* *6 wks*

2 Jun 62   **JERRY LEE LEWIS VOL. 2** *London HA 2440* .... **14**   6 wks

Linda LEWIS *UK, female vocalist* *4 wks*

9 Aug 75   **NOT A LITTLE GIRL ANYMORE** *Arista ARTY 109* .... **40**   4 wks

Ramsey LEWIS TRIO *US, male instrumental trio* *4 wks*

21 May 66   **HANG ON RAMSEY** *Chess CRL 4520* .... **20**   4 wks

LFO *UK, male instrumental group* *2 wks*

3 Aug 91   **FREQUENCIES** *Warp WARPLP 3* .... **42**   2 wks

LIGHT OF THE WORLD *UK, male vocal/instrumental group* *1 wk*

24 Jan 81   **ROUND TRIP** *Ensign ENVY 14* .... **73**   1 wk

Gordon LIGHTFOOT *Canada, male vocalist* *2 wks*

20 May 72   **DON QUIXOTE** *Reprise K 44166* .... **44**   1 wk
17 Aug 74   **SUNDOWN** *Reprise K 54020* .... **45**   1 wk

LIGHTNING SEEDS *UK, male vocalist* *2 wks*

10 Feb 90   **CLOUDCUCKOOLAND** *Ghetto GHETT 3* .... **50**   2 wks

LIL LOUIS *US, male producer* *5 wks*

26 Aug 89   **FRENCH KISSES** *FFRR 828170 1* .... **35**   5 wks

LIMAHL *UK, male vocalist* *3 wks*

1 Dec 84   **DON'T SUPPOSE** *EMI PLML 1* .... **63**   3 wks

LINDISFARNE *UK, male vocal/instrumental group* *118 wks*

30 Oct 71	★ FOG ON THE TYNE *Charisma CAS 1050*	1	56 wks
15 Jan 72	● NICELY OUT OF TUNE *Charisma CAS 1025*	8	30 wks
30 Sep 72	● DINGLY DELL *Charisma CAS 1057*	5	10 wks
11 Aug 73	LINDISFARNE LIVE *Charisma CLASS 2*	25	6 wks
18 Oct 75	FINEST HOUR *Charisma CAS 1108*	55	1 wk
24 Jun 78	BACK AND FOURTH *Mercury 9109 609*	22	11 wks
9 Dec 78	MAGIC IN THE AIR *Mercury 6641 877*	71	1 wk
23 Oct 82	SLEEPLESS NIGHT *LMP GET 1*	59	3 wks

LINX *UK, male vocal/instrumental duo* *23 wks*

28 Mar 81	● INTUITION *Chrysalis CHR 1332*	8	19 wks
31 Oct 81	GO AHEAD *Chrysalis CHR 1358*	35	4 wks

LIQUID GOLD *UK, male/female vocal/instrumental group* *3 wks*

16 Aug 80	LIQUID GOLD *Polo POLP 101*	34	3 wks

LISA – *See WENDY and LISA*

LISA LISA and CULT JAM with FULL FORCE
US, female vocalist with two US, male vocal/instrumental groups *1 wk*

l

21 Sep 85	LISA LISA AND CULT JAM WITH FULL FORCE *CBS 26593*	96	1 wk

LITTLE ANGELS *UK, male vocal/instrumental group* *6 wks*

2 Mar 91	YOUNG GODS *Polydor 8478461*	17	6 wks

LITTLE FEAT *US, male vocal/instrumental group* *19 wks*

6 Dec 75	THE LAST RECORD ALBUM *Warner Bros. K 56156*	36	3 wks
21 May 77	● TIME LOVES A HERO *Warner Bros. K 56349*	8	11 wks
11 Mar 78	WAITING FOR COLUMBUS *Warner Bros. K 66075*	43	1 wk
1 Dec 79	DOWN ON THE FARM *Warner Bros. K 56667*	46	3 wks
8 Aug 81	HOY HOY *Warner Bros. K 666100*	76	1 wk

LITTLE STEVEN *US, male vocalist/instrumentalist – guitar* *4 wks*

6 Nov 82	MEN WITHOUT WOMEN *EMI America 3027*	73	2 wks
6 Jun 87	FREEDOM NO COMPROMISE *Manhattan MTL 1010*	52	2 wks

First album credited to Little Steven and the Disciples of Soul.

LIVING COLOR *US, male vocal/instrumental group* *19 wks*

15 Sep 90	TIME'S UP *Epic 4669201*	20	19 wks

LIVING IN A BOX *UK, male vocal/instrumental group* *35 wks*

9 May 87	LIVING IN A BOX *Chrysalis CDL 1547*	25	19 wks
8 Jul 89	GATECRASHING *Chrysalis CDI 1676*	21	16 wks

LL COOL J *US, male rapper* *25 wks*

15 Feb	86	**RADIO** *Def Jam DEF 26745*	....	71	1 wk
13 Jun	87	**BIGGER AND DEFFER** *Def Jam 450 515-1*	....	54	19 wks
8 Jul	89	**WALKING WITH A PANTHER** *Def Jam 465112 1*	......	43	3 wks
13 Oct	90	**MAMA SAID KNOCK YOU OUT** *Def Jam 4673151*	......	49	2 wks

Andrew LLOYD WEBBER
UK, male composer/producer *37 wks*

11 Feb	78	● **VARIATIONS** *MCA MCF 2824*	....	2	19 wks
23 Mar	85	● **REQUIEM** *HMV ALW 1*	....	4	18 wks

Variations *features cellist Julian Lloyd Webber.* Requiem *credits Placido Domingo, Sarah Brightman, Paul Miles-Kingston, Winchester Cathedral Choir and the English Chamber Orchestra conducted by Lorin Maazel.*

Julian LLOYD WEBBER *UK, male instrumentalist* *19 wks*

14 Sep	85	**PIECES** *Polydor PROLP 6*	....	59	5 wks
21 Feb	87	**ELGAR CELLO CONCERTO** *Philips 416 354-1*	....	94	1 wk
27 Oct	90	**LLOYD WEBBER PLAYS LLOYD WEBBER** *Philips 4322911*	....	15	13 wks

First two albums credit the London Symphony Orchestra, third credits the Royal Philharmonic Orchestra. See also the London Symphony Orchestra; Andrew Lloyd Webber; Royal Philharmonic Orchestra.

Los LOBOS *US, male vocal/instrumental group* *9 wks*

6 Apr	85	**HOW WILL THE WOLF SURVIVE?** *Slash SLMP 3*	....	77	6 wks
7 Feb	87	**BY THE LIGHT OF THE MOON** *Slash SLAP 13*	....	77	3 wks

l

Tone LOC *US, male rapper* *16 wks*

25 Mar	89	**LOC'ED AFTER DARK** *Delicious BRLP 526*	....	22	16 wks

Josef LOCKE *Ireland, male vocalist* *1 wk*

28 Jun	69	**THE WORLD OF JOSEF LOCKE TODAY** *Decca SPA 21*		29	1 wk

John LODGE *UK, male vocalist/instrumentalist – guitar* *2 wks*

19 Feb	77	**NATURAL AVENUE** *Decca TXS 120*	....	38	2 wks

See also Justin Hayward and John Lodge.

Nils LOFGREN *US, male vocalist/instrumentalist – guitar* *30 wks*

17 Apr	76	● **CRY TOUGH** *A & M AMLH 64573*	....	8	11 wks
26 Mar	77	**I CAME TO DANCE** *A & M AMLH 64628*	....	30	4 wks
5 Nov	77	**NIGHT AFTER NIGHT** *A & M AMLH 68439*	....	38	2 wks
26 Sep	81	**NIGHT FADES AWAY** *Backstreet MCF 3121*	....	50	3 wks
1 May	82	**A RHYTHM ROMANCE** *A & M AMLH 68543*	....	100	1 wk
6 Jul	85	**FLIP** *Towerbell TOWLP 11*	....	36	7 wks
5 Apr	86	**CODE OF THE ROAD** *Towerbell TOWDLP 17*	....	86	1 wk
27 Apr	91	**SILVER LINING** *Essential ESSLP 145*	....	61	1 wk

Johnny LOGAN *Ireland, male vocalist* *1 wk*

22 Aug	87	**HOLD ME NOW** *CBS 451 073-1*	....	83	1 wk

LONDON BOYS *UK, male vocal duo* *38 wks*

29 Jul 89 ● THE TWELVE COMMANDMENTS OF DANCE			
WEA WX 278	**2**	38 wks

LONDON PHILHARMONIC CHOIR *UK, choir* *20 wks*

3 Dec 60 ● THE MESSIAH *Pye Golden Guinea GGL 0062*	**10**	7 wks
13 Nov 76 ● SOUND OF GLORY *Arcade ADEP 25*	**10**	10 wks
13 Apr 91 PRAISE – 18 CHORAL MASTERPIECES		
Pop & Arts PATLP 301	**54**	3 wks

The Messiah *credits the London Orchestra conducted by Walter Susskind.* Sound Of Glory *credits the National Philharmonic Orchestra and conductor John Aldiss.* Praise *credits the National Philharmonic Orchestra.*

LONDON PHILHARMONIC ORCHESTRA
UK, orchestra *5 wks*

23 Apr 60 RAVEL'S BOLERO *London HAV 2189*	**15**	4 wks
8 Apr 61 VICTORY AT SEA *Pye GGL 0073*	**12**	1 wk

See also Nigel Kennedy; Ennio Morricone; Justin Hayward, Mike Batt and the London Philharmonic Orchestra.

LONDON SYMPHONY ORCHESTRA
UK, orchestra *173 wks*

18 Mar 72 TOP TV THEMES *Studio Two STWO 372*	**13**	7 wks
16 Dec 72 ● THE STRAUSS FAMILY *Polydor 2659 014*	**2**	21 wks
5 Jul 75 MUSIC FROM 'EDWARD VII' *Polydor 2659 041*	**52**	1 wk
21 Jan 78 STAR WARS (soundtrack) *20th Century BTD 541*	**21**	12 wks
8 Jul 78 ● CLASSIC ROCK *K-Tel ONE 1009*	**3**	39 wks
10 Feb 79 CLASSIC ROCK – THE SECOND MOVEMENT		
K-Tel NE 1039	**26**	8 wks
5 Jan 80 RHAPSODY IN BLACK *K-Tel ONE 1063*	**34**	5 wks
1 Aug 81 ● CLASSIC ROCK – ROCK CLASSICS *K-Tel ONE 1123*	**5**	23 wks
27 Nov 82 THE BEST OF CLASSIC ROCK *K-Tel ONE 1080*	**35**	11 wks
27 Aug 83 ROCK SYMPHONIES *K-Tel ONE 1243*	**40**	9 wks
16 Nov 85 THE POWER OF CLASSIC ROCK *Portrait PRT 10049* ..	**13**	15 wks
14 Nov 87 CLASSIC ROCK COUNTDOWN *CBS MOOD 3*	**32**	16 wks
18 Nov 89 CLASSIC ROCK – THE LIVING YEARS *CBS MOOD 9*	**51**	6 wks

The Strauss Family *was conducted by Cyril Ornadel. See also Michael Crawford; Kimera; Julian Lloyd Webber; Spike Milligan.*

LONDON WELSH MALE VOICE CHOIR
UK, male choir *10 wks*

5 Sep 81 SONGS OF THE VALLEYS *K-Tel NE 1117*	**61**	10 wks

LONDONBEAT *UK/US, male vocal/instrumental group* *6 wks*

13 Oct 90 IN THE BLOOD *AnXious ZL 74810*	**34**	6 wks

LONE JUSTICE *US, male/female vocal/instrumental group* *5 wks*

6 Jul 85 LONE JUSTICE *Geffen GEF 26288*	**49**	2 wks
8 Nov 86 SHELTER *Geffen WX 73*	**84**	3 wks

Lone Justice are best known now as the first success of singer Maria McKee.

Bert Kaempfert said bye-bye and then stayed around, even after his death in June 1980.

Kajagoogoo fell shy of the top ten after parting with lead singer Limahl (far right).

LONE STAR UK, male vocal/instrumental group   7 wks

2 Oct 76	**LONE STAR** Epic EPC 81545	47	1 wk
17 Sep 77	**FIRING ON ALL SIX** CBS 82213	36	6 wks

LONG RYDERS US, male vocal/instrumental group   1 wk

16 Nov 85	**STATE OF OUR UNION** Island ILPS 9802	66	1 wk

Joe LONGTHORNE UK, male vocalist – impersonator   26 wks

3 Dec 88	**THE JOE LONGTHORNE SONGBOOK**		
	Telstar STAR 2353	16	12 wks
29 Jul 89	**ESPECIALLY FOR YOU** Telstar STAR 2365	22	10 wks
9 Dec 89	**THE JOE LONGTHORNE CHRISTMAS ALBUM**		
	Telstar STAR 2385	44†	4 wks

LOOP UK, male vocal/instrumental group   2 wks

4 Feb 89	**FADE OUT** Chapter 22 CHAPLP 34	51	1 wk
3 Feb 90	**A GILDED ETERNITY** Situation Two SITU 27	39	1 wk

LOOSE ENDS UK, male/female vocal/instrumental group   39 wks

21 Apr 84	**A LITTLE SPICE** Virgin V 2301	46	9 wks
20 Apr 85	**SO WHERE ARE YOU?** Virgin V 2340	13	13 wks
18 Oct 86	**ZAGORA** Virgin V 2384	15	8 wks
2 Jul 88	**THE REAL CHUCKEEBOO** Virgin V 2528	52	4 wks
22 Sep 90	**LOOK HOW LONG** Ten DIX 94	19	5 wks

Trini LOPEZ US, male vocalist   42 wks

26 Oct 63	● **TRINI LOPEZ AT P.J.'S** Reprise R 6093	7	25 wks
25 Mar 67	● **TRINI LOPEZ IN LONDON** Reprise RSLP 6238	6	17 wks

Jeff LORBER US, male vocalist/instrumentalist – keyboards   2 wks

18 May 85	**STEP BY STEP** Club JABH 9	97	2 wks

Sophia LOREN – See Peter SELLERS and Sophia LOREN

Joe LOSS UK, orchestra   10 wks

30 Oct 71	**ALL-TIME PARTY HITS** MFP 5227	24	10 wks

See also the George Mitchell Minstrels.

LOTUS EATERS UK, male vocal/instrumental group   1 wk

16 Jun 84	**NO SENSE OF SIN** Sylvan 206 263	96	1 wk

James LOUGHRAN – See BBC SYMPHONY ORCHESTRA

Jacques LOUSSIER France, male instrumentalist – piano   3 wks

30 Mar 85	**THE BEST OF PLAY BACH** Start STL 1	58	3 wks

LOVE US, male vocal/instrumental group   8 wks

| 24 Feb 68 | **FOREVER CHANGES** Elektra EKS7 4013 .... | 24 | 6 wks |
| 16 May 70 | **OUT HERE** Harvest Show 3/4 .... | 29 | 2 wks |

Geoff LOVE UK, orchestra   28 wks

7 Aug 71	**BIG WAR MOVIE THEMES** MFP 5171	11	20 wks
21 Aug 71	**BIG WESTERN MOVIE THEMES** MFP 5204	38	3 wks
30 Oct 71	**BIG LOVE MOVIE THEMES** MFP 5221	28	5 wks

See also Manuel and his Music of the Mountains.

Monie LOVE UK, female rapper   3 wks

| 26 Oct 90 | **DOWN TO EARTH** Cooltempo CTLP 14 .... | 26 | 3 wks |

LOVE AND MONEY UK, male vocal/instrumental group   2 wks

| 29 Oct 88 | **STRANGE KIND OF LOVE** Fontana SFLP 7 .... | 71 | 1 wk |
| 3 Aug 91 | **DOGS IN THE TRAFFIC** Fontana 8489931 .... | 41 | 1 wk |

Lene LOVICH US, female vocalist   17 wks

| 17 Mar 79 | **STATELESS** Stiff SEEZ 7 .... | 35 | 11 wks |
| 2 Feb 80 | **FLEX** Stiff SEEZ 19 .... | 19 | 6 wks |

LOVIN' SPOONFUL
US/Canada, male vocal/instrumental group   11 wks

| 7 May 66 | ● **DAYDREAM** Pye NPL 28078 .... | 8 | 11 wks |

Nick LOWE UK, male vocalist   17 wks

11 Mar 78	**THE JESUS OF COOL** Radar RAD 1	22	9 wks
23 Jun 79	**LABOUR OF LUST** Radar RAD 21	43	6 wks
20 Feb 82	**NICK THE KNIFE** F.Beat XXLP 14	99	2 wks

LULU UK, female vocalist   6 wks

| 25 Sep 71 | **THE MOST OF LULU** MFP 5215 .... | 15 | 6 wks |

Bob LUMAN US, male vocalist   1 wk

| 14 Jan 61 | **LET'S THINK ABOUT LIVING** Warner Bros. WM 4025 .. | 18 | 1 wk |

LURKERS UK, male vocal/instrumental group   1 wk

| 1 Jul 78 | **FULHAM FALLOUT** Beggars Banquet BEGA 2 .... | 57 | 1 wk |

LYLE – See GALLAGHER and LYLE

Vera LYNN UK, female vocalist   15 wks

| 21 Nov 81 | **20 FAMILY FAVOURITES** EMI EMTV 28 .... | 25 | 12 wks |
| 9 Sep 89 | **WE'LL MEET AGAIN** Telstar STAR 2369 .... | 44 | 3 wks |

205

l

Jeff LYNNE *UK, male vocalist* 4 *wks*

4 Aug 90	**ARMCHAIR THEATRE** *Reprise WX 347*	24	4 wks

Philip LYNOTT *Ireland, male vocalist* 6 *wks*

26 Apr 80	**SOLO IN SOHO** *Vertigo 9102 038*	28	6 wks

See also Phil Lynott and Thin Lizzy.

Phil LYNOTT and THIN LIZZY
Ireland/UK/US, male vocal/instrumental group 10 *wks*

14 Nov 87	**SOLDIER OF FORTUNE – THE BEST OF PHIL LYNOTT AND THIN LIZZY** *Telstar STAR 2300*	55	10 wks

See also Philip Lynott; Thin Lizzy.

LYNYRD SKYNYRD *US, male vocal/instrumental group* 19 *wks*

3 May 75	**NUTHIN' FANCY** *MCA MCF 2700*	43	1 wk
28 Feb 76	**GIMME BACK MY BULLETS** *MCA MCF 2744*	34	5 wks
6 Nov 76	**ONE MORE FOR THE ROAD** *MCA MCPS 279*	17	4 wks
12 Nov 77	**STREET SURVIVORS** *MCA MCG 3525*	13	4 wks
4 Nov 78	**SKYNYRD'S FIRST AND LAST** *MCA MCG 3529*	50	1 wk
9 Feb 80	**GOLD AND PLATINUM** *MCA MCSP 308*	49	4 wks

206

m

m

Lorin **MAAZEL** – *See Andrew LLOYD WEBBER*

MAC BAND featuring the McCAMPBELL BROTHERS *US, male vocal group* 3 *wks*

20 Aug 88	**THE MAC BAND** *MCA MCC 6032*	61	3 wks

Frankie McBRIDE *Ireland, male vocalist* 3 *wks*

17 Feb 68	**FRANKIE McBRIDE** *Emerald SLD 28*	29	3 wks

MACC LADS *UK, male vocal/instrumental group* 1 *wk*

7 Oct 89	**FROM BEER TO ETERNITY** *Hectic House HHLP 12*	72	1 wk

McCAMPBELL BROTHERS – *See MAC BAND featuring the McCAMPBELL BROTHERS*

Paul McCARTNEY *UK, male vocalist/multi-instrumentalist* 516 *wks*

2 May 70	● **McCARTNEY** *Apple PCS 7102*	2	32 wks
5 Jun 71	★ **RAM** *Apple PAS 10003*	1	24 wks
18 Dec 71	**WILD LIFE** *Apple PCS 7142*	11	9 wks
19 May 73	● **RED ROSE SPEEDWAY** *Apple PCTC 251*	5	16 wks
15 Dec 73	★ **BAND ON THE RUN** *Apple PAS 10007*	1	124 wks

Date			Title	Pos	Wks
21 Jun	75	★	**VENUS AND MARS** *Apple PCTC 254*	1	29 wks
17 Apr	76	●	**WINGS AT THE SPEED OF SOUND** *Apple PAS 10010* ..	2	35 wks
15 Jan	77	●	**WINGS OVER AMERICA** *Parlophone PAS 720*	8	22 wks
15 Apr	78	●	**LONDON TOWN** *Parlophone PAS 10012*	4	23 wks
16 Dec	78	●	**WINGS GREATEST HITS** *Parlophone PCTC 256*	5	32 wks
23 Jun	79	●	**BACK TO THE EGG** *Parlophone PCTC 257*	6	15 wks
31 May	80	★	**McCARTNEY II** *Parlophone PCTC 258*	1	18 wks
7 Mar	81		**McCARTNEY INTERVIEW** *EMI CHAT 1*	34	4 wks
8 May	82	★	**TUG OF WAR** *Parlophone PCTC 259*	1	27 wks
12 Nov	83	●	**PIPES OF PEACE** *Parlophone PCTC 1652301*	4	23 wks
3 Nov	84	★	**GIVE MY REGARDS TO BROAD STREET** *Parlophone PCTC 2*	1	21 wks
13 Sep	86	●	**PRESS TO PLAY** *Parlophone PCSD 103*	8	6 wks
14 Nov	87	●	**ALL THE BEST!** *Parlophone PMTV 1*	2	21 wks
17 Jun	89	★	**FLOWERS IN THE DIRT** *Parlophone PCSD 106*	1	20 wks
17 Nov	90		**TRIPPING THE LIVE FANTASTIC** *Parlophone PCST 7346*	17	11 wks
1 Jun	91	●	**UNPLUGGED – THE OFFICIAL BOOTLEG** *Parlophone PCSD 116*	7	3 wks
12 Oct	91		**CHOBA B CCCP (THE RUSSIAN ALBUM)** *Parlophone CDPCSD 117*	63	1 wk

Ram *credited to Paul and Linda McCartney.* Red Rose Speedway *and* Band On The Run *credited to Paul McCartney and Wings.* Wild Life *and the five albums from* Venus and Mars *to* Wings Greatest Hits *inclusive credited to Wings. All other albums credited to Paul McCartney.*

Kirsty MacCOLL   *UK, female vocalist*   *20 wks*

20 May 89	**KITE** *Virgin KMLP 1*	34	12 wks
6 Jul 91	**ELECTRIC LANDLADY** *Virgin V 2663*	17	8 wks

Van McCOY and the SOUL CITY SYMPHONY
US, orchestra   *11 wks*

5 Jul 75	**DISCO BABY** *Avco 9109 004*	32	11 wks

207

m

George McCRAE   *US, male vocalist*   *29 wks*

3 Aug 74	**ROCK YOUR BABY** *Jayboy JSL 3*	13	28 wks
13 Sep 75	**GEORGE McCRAE** *Jayboy JSL 10*	54	1 wk

Ian McCULLOCH   *UK, male vocalist*   *3 wks*

7 Oct 89	**CANDLELAND** *WEA WX 303*	18	3 wks

Michael McDONALD   *US, male vocalist*   *39 wks*

22 Nov 86	●	**SWEET FREEDOM: BEST OF MICHAEL McDONALD** *Warner Bros. WX 67*	6	35 wks
26 May 90		**TAKE IT TO HEART** *Reprise WX 285*	35	4 wks

Bobby McFERRIN   *US, male vocalist*   *1 wk*

29 Oct 88	**SIMPLE PLEASURES** *Manhattan MTL 1018*	92	1 wk

Kate and Anna McGARRIGLE
Canada, female vocal duo   *4 wks*

26 Feb 77	**DANCER WITH BRUISED KNEES** *Warner Bros. K 56356*	35	4 wks

Ronnie Van Zant (right) died in the 1977 **Lynyrd Skynyrd** plane crash. Gary Rossington (left) survived to form the Rossington Collins Band.

Magnum are shown performing on Channel 4.

Mary MacGREGOR *US, female vocalist*   *1 wk*

23 Apr 77	**TORN BETWEEN TWO LOVERS**	
	Ariola America AAS 1504	59 1 wk

McGUINNESS FLINT *UK, male vocal/instrumental group*   *10 wks*

23 Jan 71	● **McGUINNESS FLINT** *Capitol EA–ST 22625*	9 10 wks

Maria McKEE *US, female vocalist*   *3 wks*

24 Jun 89	**MARIA McKEE** *Geffen WX 270*	49 3 wks

Kenneth McKELLAR *UK, male vocalist*   *10 wks*

28 Jun 69	**THE WORLD OF KENNETH McKELLAR** *Decca SPA 11*	27 7 wks
31 Jan 70	**ECCO DI NAPOLI** *Decca SKL 5018*	45 3 wks

Craig McLACHLAN and CHECK 1–2
Australia, male vocal/instrumental group   *11 wks*

21 Jul 90	● **CRAIG McLACHLAN AND CHECK 1–2** *Epic 4663471* ...	10 11 wks

Malcolm McLAREN *UK, male vocalist*   *40 wks*

4 Jun 83	**DUCK ROCK** *Charisma MMLP 1*	18 17 wks
26 May 84	**WOULD YA LIKE MORE SCRATCHIN'**	
	Charisma CLAM 1	44 4 wks
29 Dec 84	**FANS** *Charisma MMDL 2*	47 8 wks
15 Jul 89	**WALTZ DANCING** *Epic 460736 1*	30 11 wks

Would Ya Like More Scratchin' *is credited to Malcolm McLaren and the World's Famous Supreme Team Show.* Waltz Dancing *credits the Bootzilla Orchestra.*

Mahavishnu John McLAUGHLIN – *See Carlos SANTANA and Mahavishnu John McLAUGHLIN; MAHAVISHNU ORCHESTRA*

Don McLEAN *US, male vocalist*   *89 wks*

11 Mar 72	● **AMERICAN PIE** *United Artists UAS 29285*	3 54 wks
17 Jun 72	**TAPESTRY** *United Artists UAS 29350*	16 12 wks
24 Nov 73	**PLAYIN' FAVORITES** *United Artists UAG 29528*	42 2 wks
14 Jun 80	**CHAIN LIGHTNING** *EMI International INS 3025*	19 9 wks
27 Sep 80	● **THE VERY BEST OF DON McLEAN**	
	United Artists UAG 30314	4 12 wks

Rita MacNEIL *Canada, female vocalist*   *4 wks*

24 Nov 90	**REASON TO BELIEVE** *Polydor 8471061*	32 4 wks

Ralph McTELL *UK, male vocalist*   *17 wks*

18 Nov 72	**NOT TILL TOMORROW** *Reprise K 44210*	36 1 wk
2 Mar 74	**EASY** *Reprise K 54013*	31 4 wks
15 Feb 75	**STREETS** *Warner Bros. K 56105*	13 12 wks

Christine McVIE *UK, female vocalist*　　　　　*4 wks*

11 Feb 84	**CHRISTINE McVIE** *Warner Bros. 92 5059*	58	4 wks

David McWILLIAMS *UK, male vocalist*　　　　　*9 wks*

10 Jun 67	**DAVID McWILLIAMS SINGS** *Major Minor MMLP 2*	38	2 wks
4 Nov 67	**DAVID McWILLIAMS VOL. 2** *Major Minor MMLP 10*	23	6 wks
9 Mar 68	**DAVID McWILLIAMS VOL. 3** *Major Minor MMLP 11*	39	1 wk

MADNESS *UK, male vocal/instrumental group*　　　　　*300 wks*

3 Nov 79	● **ONE STEP BEYOND** *Stiff SEEZ 17*	2	78 wks
4 Oct 80	● **ABSOLUTELY** *Stiff SEEZ 29*	2	46 wks
10 Oct 81	● **MADNESS 7** *Stiff SEEZ 39*	5	29 wks
1 May 82	★ **COMPLETE MADNESS** *Stiff HIT-TV 1*	1	88 wks
13 Nov 82	● **THE RISE AND FALL** *Stiff SEEZ 46*	10	22 wks
3 Mar 84	● **KEEP MOVING** *Stiff SEEZ 53*	6	19 wks
12 Oct 85	**MAD NOT MAD** *Zarjazz JZLP 1*	16	9 wks
6 Dec 86	**UTTER MADNESS** *Zarjazz JZLP 2*	29	8 wks
7 May 88	**THE MADNESS** *Virgin V 2507*	65	1 wk

MADONNA *US, female vocalist*　　　　　*514 wks*

11 Feb 84	● **MADONNA/THE FIRST ALBUM** *Sire 923867*	6	123 wks
24 Nov 84	★ **LIKE A VIRGIN** *Sire 925157*	1	152 wks
12 Jul 86	★ **TRUE BLUE** *Sire WX 54*	1	81 wks
28 Nov 87	● **YOU CAN DANCE** *Sire WX 76*	5	14 wks
1 Apr 89	★ **LIKE A PRAYER** *Sire WX 239*	1	66 wks
2 Jun 90	● **I'M BREATHLESS** *Sire WX 351*	2	20 wks
24 Nov 90	★ **THE IMMACULATE COLLECTION** *Sire WX 370*	1†	58 wks

From 22 Aug 85 Madonna was repackaged and was available as The First Album *SIRE WX 22. Like A Virgin changed label number during its chart run to SIRE WX 20.*

MAGAZINE *UK, male vocal/instrumental group*　　　　　*24 wks*

24 Jun 78	**REAL LIFE** *Virgin V 2100*	29	8 wks
14 Apr 79	**SECONDHAND DAYLIGHT** *Virgin V 2121*	38	8 wks
10 May 80	**CORRECT USE OF SOAP** *Virgin V 2156*	28	4 wks
13 Dec 80	**PLAY** *Virgin V 2184*	69	1 wk
27 Jun 81	**MAGIC, MURDER AND THE WEATHER**		
	Virgin V 2200	39	3 wks

MAGIC BAND – *See CAPTAIN BEEFHEART and his MAGIC BAND*

MAGNA CARTA *UK, male vocal/instrumental group*　　　　　*2 wks*

8 Aug 70	**SEASONS** *Vertigo 6360 003*	55	2 wks

MAGNUM *UK, male vocal/instrumental group*　　　　　*44 wks*

16 Sep 78	**KINGDOM OF MADNESS** *Jet JETLP 210*	58	1 wk
19 Apr 80	**MARAUDER** *Jet JETLP 230*	34	5 wks
6 Mar 82	**CHASE THE DRAGON** *Jet JETLP 235*	17	7 wks
21 May 83	**THE ELEVENTH HOUR** *Jet JETLP 240*	38	4 wks
25 May 85	**ON A STORYTELLER'S NIGHT** *FM WKFM LP 34*	24	7 wks
4 Oct 86	**VIGILANTE** *Polydor POLD 5198*	24	5 wks
9 Apr 88	● **WINGS OF HEAVEN** *Polydor POLD 5221*	5	9 wks
21 Jul 90	● **GOODNIGHT L.A.** *Polydor 8435681*	9	5 wks
14 Sep 91	**THE SPIRIT** *Polydor 5111691*	50	1 wk

MAHAVISHNU ORCHESTRA
UK/US, male instrumental group   *5 wks*

31 Mar 73	**BIRDS OF FIRE** CBS 65321	20	5 wks

See also Carlos Santana and Mahavishnu John McLaughlin.

MAI TAI   *Holland, female vocal group*   *1 wk*

6 Jul 85	**HISTORY** Virgin V 2359	91	1 wk

MAJESTICS   *UK, male/female vocal group*   *4 wks*

4 Apr 87	**TUTTI FRUTTI** BBC REN 629	64	4 wks

Tommy MAKEM – *See CLANCY BROTHERS and Tommy MAKEM*

Timmy MALLET – *See BOMBALURINA featuring Timmy MALLETT*

Yngwie J. MALMSTEEN
Sweden, male instrumentalist – guitar   *10 wks*

21 May 88	**ODYSSEY** Polydor POLD 5224	27	7 wks
4 Nov 89	**TRIAL BY FIRE – LIVE IN LENINGRAD**		
	Polydor 839726 1	65	1 wk
28 Apr 90	**ECLIPSE** Polydor 8434611	43	2 wks

MAMA'S BOYS   *Ireland, male vocal/instrumental group*   *4 wks*

6 Apr 85	**POWER AND PASSION** Jive HIP 24	55	4 wks

MAMAS and PAPAS   *US, male/female vocal group*   *61 wks*

25 Jun 66	● **THE MAMAS AND PAPAS** RCA Victor RD 7803	3	18 wks
28 Jan 67	**CASS, JOHN, MICHELLE, DENNY**		
	RCA Victor SF 7639	24	6 wks
24 Jun 67	● **MAMAS AND PAPAS DELIVER** RCA Victor SF 7880	4	22 wks
26 Apr 69	● **HITS OF GOLD** Stateside S 5007	7	2 wks
18 Jun 77	● **THE BEST OF THE MAMAS AND PAPAS**		
	Arcade ADEP 30	6	13 wks

MAMBAS – *See MARC and the MAMBAS*

MAN   *UK, male vocal/instrumental group*   *11 wks*

20 Oct 73	**BACK INTO THE FUTURE** United Artists UAD 60053/4 ..	23	3 wks
25 May 74	**RHINOS WINOS AND LUNATICS**		
	United Artists UAG 29631	24	4 wks
11 Oct 75	**MAXIMUM DARKNESS** United Artists UAG 29872	25	2 wks
17 Apr 76	**WELSH CONNECTION** MCA MCF 2753	40	2 wks

MANCHESTER BOYS CHOIR   *UK, male choir*   *2 wks*

21 Dec 85	**THE NEW SOUND OF CHRISTMAS** K-Tel ONE 1314 .	80	2 wks

Henry MANCINI   *US, orchestra/chorus*   *8 wks*

16 Oct 76	**HENRY MANCINI** Arcade ADEP 24	26	8 wks

See also James Galway and Henry Mancini; Johnny Mathis and Henry Mancini; Luciano Pavarotti with the Henry Mancini Orchestra.

211

m

MANFRED MANN

South Africa/UK, male vocal/instrumental group   *72 wks*

19 Sep 64 ● **FIVE FACES OF MANFRED MANN** *HMV CLP 1731* ...	**3**	24 wks
23 Oct 65 ● **MANN MADE** *HMV CLP 1911*	**7**	11 wks
17 Sep 66 **MANN MADE HITS** *HMV CLP 3559*	**11**	18 wks
29 Oct 66 **AS IS** *Fontana TL 5377*	**22**	4 wks
21 Jan 67 **SOUL OF MANN** *HMV CSD 3594*	**40**	1 wk
15 Sep 79 ● **SEMI-DETACHED SUBURBAN** *EMI EMTV 19*	**9**	14 wks

See also Manfred Mann's Earth Band.

MANHATTAN TRANSFER

US, male/female vocal group   *85 wks*

12 Mar 77 **COMING OUT** *Atlantic K 50291*	**12**	20 wks
19 Mar 77 **MANHATTAN TRANSFER** *Atlantic K 50138*	**49**	7 wks
25 Feb 78 ● **PASTICHE** *Atlantic K 50444*	**10**	34 wks
11 Nov 78 ● **LIVE** *Atlantic K 50540*	**4**	17 wks
17 Nov 79 **EXTENSIONS** *Atlantic K 50674*	**63**	3 wks
18 Feb 84 **BODIES AND SOULS** *Atlantic 780104*	**53**	4 wks

MANHATTANS *US, male vocal group*   *3 wks*

14 Aug 76 **MANHATTANS** *CBS 81513*	**37**	3 wks

Barry MANILOW *US, male vocalist*   *321 wks*

23 Sep 78 **EVEN NOW** *Arista SPART 1047*	**12**	28 wks
3 Mar 79 ● **MANILOW MAGIC** *Arista ARTV 2*	**3**	151 wks
20 Oct 79 **ONE VOICE** *Arista SPART 1106*	**18**	7 wks
29 Nov 80 ● **BARRY** *Arista DLART 2*	**5**	34 wks
25 Apr 81 **GIFT SET** *Arista BOX 1*	**62**	1 wk
3 Oct 81 ● **IF I SHOULD LOVE AGAIN** *Arista BMAN 1*	**5**	26 wks
1 May 82 ★ **BARRY LIVE IN BRITAIN** *Arista ARTV 4*	**1**	23 wks
27 Nov 82 ● **I WANNA DO IT WITH YOU** *Arista BMAN 2*	**7**	9 wks
8 Oct 83 ● **A TOUCH MORE MAGIC** *Arista BMAN 3*	**10**	12 wks
1 Dec 84 **2.00 AM PARADISE CAFE** *Arista 206 496*	**28**	6 wks
16 Nov 85 **MANILOW** *RCA PL 87044*	**40**	6 wks
20 Feb 88 **SWING STREET** *Arista 208860*	**81**	1 wk
20 May 89 **SONGS TO MAKE THE WHOLE WORLD SING** *Arista 209927*	**20**	4 wks
17 Mar 90 **LIVE ON BROADWAY** *Arista 303785*	**19**	3 wks
30 Jun 90 **SONGS 1975–1990** *Arista 303868*	**13**	7 wks
2 Nov 91 **SHOWSTOPPERS** *Arista 212091*	**53**	3 wks

Roberto MANN *UK, male orchestra leader*   *9 wks*

9 Dec 67 **GREAT WALTZES** *Deram SML 1010*	**19**	9 wks

Shelley MANNE *US, male instrumentalist – drums*   *1 wk*

18 Jun 60 **MY FAIR LADY** *Vogue LAC 12100*	**20**	1 wk

Manfred MANN'S EARTH BAND

South Africa/UK, male vocal/instrumental group   *24 wks*

18 Sep 76 ● **THE ROARING SILENCE** *Bronze ILPS 9357*	**10**	9 wks
17 Jun 78 **WATCH** *Bronze BRON 507*	**33**	6 wks
24 Mar 79 **ANGEL STATION** *Bronze BRON 516*	**30**	8 wks

26 Feb 83 **SOMEWHERE IN AFRIKA** *Bronze BRON 543* .... **87** 1 wk

See also Manfred Mann.

MANOWAR *US, male vocal/instrumental group* *3 wks*

| 18 Feb 84 | **HAIL TO ENGLAND** *Music For Nations MFN 19* .... | **83** | 2 wks |
| 6 Oct 84 | **SIGN OF THE HAMMER** *10 DIX 10* .... | **73** | 1 wk |

MANTOVANI *UK, orchestra* *151 wks*

21 Feb 59	● **CONTINENTAL ENCORES** *Decca LK 4298*	**4**	12 wks
18 Feb 61	**CONCERT SPECTACULAR** *Decca LK 4377*	**16**	2 wks
16 Apr 66	● **MANTOVANI MAGIC** *Decca LK 7949*	**3**	15 wks
15 Oct 66	**MR MUSIC – MANTOVANI** *Decca LK 4809*	**24**	3 wks
14 Jan 67	● **MANTOVANI'S GOLDEN HITS** *Decca SKL 4818*	**10**	43 wks
30 Sep 67	**HOLLYWOOD** *Decca SKL 4887*	**37**	1 wk
14 Jun 69	● **THE WORLD OF MANTOVANI** *Decca SPA 1*	**6**	31 wks
4 Oct 69	● **THE WORLD OF MANTOVANI VOL. 2** *Decca SPA 36* ..	**4**	19 wks
16 May 70	**MANTOVANI TODAY** *Decca SKL 5003*	**16**	8 wks
26 Feb 72	**TO LOVERS EVERYWHERE** *Decca SKL 5112*	**44**	1 wk
3 Nov 79	● **20 GOLDEN GREATS** *Warwick WW 5067*	**9**	13 wks
16 Mar 85	**MANTOVANI MAGIC** *Telstar STAR 2237*	**52**	3 wks

Mantovani Magic on Telstar conducted by Roland Shaw.

MANTRONIX *Jamaica/US, male vocal/instrumental duo* *17 wks*

29 Mar 86	**THE ALBUM** *10 DIX 37*	**45**	3 wks
13 Dec 86	**MUSICAL MADNESS** *10 DIX 50*	**66**	3 wks
2 Apr 88	**IN FULL EFFECT** *10 DIX 74*	**39**	3 wks
17 Feb 90	**THIS SHOULD MOVE YA** *Capitol EST 2117*	**18**	6 wks
30 Mar 91	**THE INCREDIBLE SOUND MACHINE** *Capitol EST 2139*	**36**	2 wks

MANUEL and his MUSIC OF THE MOUNTAINS
UK, orchestra conductor Geoff Love *38 wks*

10 Sep 60	**MUSIC OF THE MOUNTAINS** *Columbia 33SX 1212*	**17**	1 wk
7 Aug 71	**THIS IS MANUEL** *Studio Two STWO 5*	**18**	19 wks
31 Jan 76	● **CARNIVAL** *Studio Two TWO 337*	**3**	18 wks

See also Geoff Love.

Phil MANZANERA *UK, male vocalist/instrumentalist – guitar* *1 wk*

| 24 May 75 | **DIAMOND HEAD** *Island ILPS 9315* .... | **40** | 1 wk |

MARC and the MAMBAS
UK, male/female vocal/instrumental group *9 wks*

| 16 Oct 82 | **UNTITLED** *Some Bizzare BZA 13* .... | **42** | 4 wks |
| 20 Aug 83 | **TORMENT AND TOREROS** *Some Bizzare BIZL 4* ...... | **28** | 5 wks |

See also Marc Almond.

MARILLION *UK, male vocal/instrumental group* *151 wks*

26 Mar 83	● **SCRIPT FOR A JESTER'S TEAR** *EMI EMC 3429*	**7**	31 wks
24 Mar 84	● **FUGAZI** *EMI EMC 2400851*	**5**	20 wks
17 Nov 84	● **REAL TO REEL** *EMI JEST 1*	**8**	21 wks
29 Jun 85	★ **MISPLACED CHILDHOOD** *EMI MRL 2*	**1**	41 wks
4 Jul 87	● **CLUTCHING AT STRAWS** *EMI EMD 1002*	**2**	15 wks

23 Jul	88	**B SIDES THEMSELVES** *EMI EMS 1295*	64	6 wks
10 Dec	88	**THE THIEVING MAGPIE** *EMI MARIL 1*	25	6 wks
7 Oct	89	● **SEASON'S END** *EMI EMD 1011 22*	7	4 wks
6 Jul	91	● **HOLIDAYS IN EDEN** *EMI EMD 1022*	7	7 wks

Yannis MARKOPOULOS *Greece, orchestra*   *8 wks*

26 Aug	78	**WHO PAYS THE FERRYMAN** *BBC REB 315*	22	8 wks

Marky MARK and the FUNKY BUNCH
US, male vocalist   *1 wk*

5 Oct	91	**MUSIC FOR THE PEOPLE** *Interscope 7567917371*	61	1 wk

Bob MARLEY and the WAILERS
Jamaica, male vocal/instrumental group   *294 wks*

4 Oct	75	**NATTY DREAD** *Island ILPS 9281*	43	5 wks
20 Dec	75	**LIVE** *Island ILPS 9376*	38	11 wks
8 May	76	**RASTAMAN VIBRATION** *Island ILPS 9383*	15	13 wks
11 Jun	77	● **EXODUS** *Island ILPS 9498*	8	56 wks
1 Apr	78	● **KAYA** *Island ILPS 9517*	4	24 wks
16 Dec	78	**BABYLON BY BUS** *Island ISLD 11*	40	11 wks
13 Oct	79	**SURVIVAL** *Island ILPS 9542*	20	6 wks
28 Jun	80	● **UPRISING** *Island ILPS 9596*	6	17 wks
28 May	83	● **CONFRONTATION** *Island ILPS 9760*	5	19 wks
19 May	84	★ **LEGEND** *Island BMW 1*	1	129 wks
28 Jul	86	**REBEL MUSIC** *Island ILPS 9843*	54	3 wks

Live *Island ILPS 9376* returned to the chart in 1981 under the title Live At The Lyceum.

214

m

Neville MARRINER and the ACADEMY OF ST MARTIN IN THE FIELDS
UK, male conductor with chamber orchestra   *6 wks*

6 Apr	85	**AMADEUS – ORIGINAL SOUNDTRACK** *London LONDP 6*	64	6 wks

Bernie MARSDEN *UK, male vocalist/instrumentalist – guitar*   *2 wks*

5 Sep	81	**LOOK AT ME NOW** *Parlophone PCF 7217*	71	2 wks

Lena MARTELL *UK, female vocalist*   *71 wks*

25 May	74	**THAT WONDERFUL SOUND OF LENA MARTELL** *Pye SPL 18427*	35	2 wks
8 Jan	77	**THE BEST OF LENA MARTELL** *Pye NSPL 18506*	13	16 wks
27 May	78	**THE LENA MARTELL COLLECTION** *Ronco RTL 2028* .	12	19 wks
20 Oct	79	● **LENA'S MUSIC ALBUM** *Pye N 123*	5	18 wks
19 Apr	80	● **BY REQUEST** *Ronco RTL 2046*	9	9 wks
29 Nov	80	**BEAUTIFUL SUNDAY** *Ronco RTL 2052*	23	7 wks

MARTHA and the MUFFINS
Canada, male/female vocal/instrumental group   *6 wks*

15 Mar	80	**METRO MUSIC** *DinDisc DID 1*	34	6 wks

MARTIKA *US, female vocalist*   *43 wks*

16 Sep 89	**MARTIKA** *CBS 463355 1*	11	37 wks
7 Sep 91	**MARTIKA'S KITCHEN** *Columbia 4671891*	15	6 wks

Dean MARTIN *US, male vocalist*   *24 wks*

13 May 61	**THIS TIME I'M SWINGING** *Capitol T 1442*	18	1 wk
25 Feb 67	**AT EASE WITH DEAN** *Reprise RSLP 6322*	35	1 wk
4 Nov 67	**WELCOME TO MY WORLD** *Philips DBL 001*	39	1 wk
12 Oct 68	**GREATEST HITS VOL. 1** *Reprise RSLP 6301*	40	1 wk
22 Feb 69	● **BEST OF DEAN MARTIN** *Capitol ST 21194*	9	1 wk
22 Feb 69	● **GENTLE ON MY MIND** *Reprise RSLP 6330*	9	8 wks
13 Nov 76	● **20 ORIGINAL DEAN MARTIN HITS** *Reprise K 54066* ...	7	11 wks

See also Nat 'King' Cole and Dean Martin.

George MARTIN ORCHESTRA – *See BEATLES*

Juan MARTIN and the ROYAL PHILHARMONIC ORCHESTRA
Spain, male instrumentalist – guitar with UK, orchestra   *9 wks*

11 Feb 84	**SERENADE** *K-Tel NE 1267*	21	9 wks

See also Royal Philharmonic Orchestra.

John MARTYN *UK, male vocalist/instrumentalist – guitar*   *23 wks*

4 Feb 78	**ONE WORLD** *Island ILPS 9492*	54	1 wk
1 Nov 80	**GRACE AND DANGER** *Island ILPS 9560*	54	2 wks
26 Sep 81	**GLORIOUS FOOL** *Geffen K 99178*	25	7 wks
4 Sep 82	**WELL KEPT SECRET** *WEA K 99255*	20	7 wks
17 Nov 84	**SAPPHIRE** *Island ILPS 9779*	57	2 wks
8 Mar 86	**PIECE BY PIECE** *Island ILPS 9807*	28	4 wks

Hank MARVIN *UK, male vocalist/instrumentalist – guitar*   *5 wks*

22 Nov 69	**HANK MARVIN** *Columbia SCX 6352*	14	2 wks
20 Mar 82	**WORDS AND MUSIC** *Polydor POLD 5054*	66	3 wks

See also Marvin, Welch and Farrar.

MARVIN, WELCH and FARRAR
UK, male vocal/instrumental group   *4 wks*

3 Apr 71	**MARVIN, WELCH AND FARRAR** *Regal Zonophone SRZA 8502*	30	4 wks

See also Hank Marvin.

MARY JANE GIRLS *US, female vocal group*   *9 wks*

28 May 83	**MARY JANE GIRLS** *Gordy STML 12189*	51	9 wks

MARY – *See PETER, PAUL and MARY*

Richard MARX *US, male vocalist*   *15 wks*

9 Apr 88	**RICHARD MARX** *Manhattan MTL 1017*	68	2 wks

20 May 89 ●	**REPEAT OFFENDER** *EMI-USA MTL 1043*	8	12 wks
16 Nov 91	**RUSH STREET** *Capitol ESTU 2158*	60	1 wk

MASSED WELSH CHOIRS UK, male voice choir — 7 wks

9 Aug 69 ●	**CYMANSA GANN** *BBC REC 53 M*	5	7 wks

MASSIVE UK, male vocal/instrumental group — 14 wks

20 Apr 91	**BLUE LINES** *Wild Bunch WBRLP 1*	13	14 wks

MASTERMIXERS – See JIVE BUNNY and the MASTERMIXERS

MATCHBOX UK, male vocal/instrumental group — 14 wks

2 Feb 80	**MATCHBOX** *Magnet MAG 5031*	44	5 wks
11 Oct 80	**MIDNITE DYNAMOS** *Magnet MAG 5036*	23	9 wks

Mireille MATHIEU France, female vocalist — 1 wk

2 Mar 68	**MIREILLE MATHIEU** *Columbia SCX 6210*	39	1 wk

Johnny MATHIS US, male vocalist — 193 wks

8 Nov 58 ●	**WARM** *Fontana TBA TFL 5015*	6	2 wks
24 Jan 59 ●	**SWING SOFTLY** *Fontana TBA TFL 5039*	10	1 wk
13 Feb 60 ●	**RIDE ON A RAINBOW** *Fontana TFL 5061*	10	2 wks
10 Dec 60 ●	**RHYTHMS AND BALLADS OF BROADWAY**		
	Fontana SET 101	6	10 wks
17 Jun 61	**I'LL BUY YOU A STAR** *Fontana TFL 5143*	18	1 wk
16 May 70	**RAINDROPS KEEP FALLING ON MY HEAD**		
	CBS 63587	23	10 wks
3 Apr 71	**LOVE STORY** *CBS 64334*	27	5 wks
9 Sep 72	**FIRST TIME EVER I SAW YOUR FACE**		
	CBS 64930	40	3 wks
16 Dec 72	**MAKE IT EASY ON YOURSELF** *CBS 65161*	49	1 wk
8 Mar 75	**I'M COMING HOME** *CBS 65690*	18	11 wks
5 Apr 75	**THE HEART OF A WOMAN** *CBS 80533*	39	2 wks
26 Jul 75	**WHEN WILL I SEE YOU AGAIN** *CBS 80738*	13	10 wks
3 Jul 76	**I ONLY HAVE EYES FOR YOU** *CBS 81329*	14	12 wks
19 Feb 77	**GREATEST HITS VOL. IV** *CBS 86022*	31	5 wks
18 Jun 77 ★	**THE JOHNNY MATHIS COLLECTION** *CBS 10003*	1	40 wks
17 Dec 77	**SWEET SURRENDER** *CBS 86036*	55	1 wk
29 Apr 78 ●	**YOU LIGHT UP MY LIFE** *CBS 86055*	3	19 wks
7 Apr 79	**THE BEST DAYS OF MY LIFE** *CBS 86080*	38	5 wks
3 Nov 79	**MATHIS MAGIC** *CBS 86103*	59	4 wks
8 Mar 80 ★	**TEARS AND LAUGHTER** *CBS 10019*	1	15 wks
12 Jul 80	**ALL FOR YOU** *CBS 86115*	20	8 wks
19 Sep 81 ●	**CELEBRATION** *CBS 10028*	9	16 wks
15 May 82	**FRIENDS IN LOVE** *CBS 85652*	34	7 wks
15 Sep 84	**A SPECIAL PART OF ME** *CBS 25475*	45	3 wks

See also Johnny Mathis and Natalie Cole; Johnny Mathis and Henry Mancini; Johnny Mathis and Deniece Williams.

Johnny MATHIS and Natalie COLE
US, male/female vocal duo — 16 wks

17 Sep 83 ●	**UNFORGETTABLE: A MUSICAL TRIBUTE TO NAT KING**		
	COLE *CBS 10042*	5	16 wks

See also Johnny Mathis; Natalie Cole.

Johnny MATHIS and Henry MANCINI
US, male vocalist with US, orchestra   8 wks

13 Dec 86   THE HOLLYWOOD MUSICALS   CBS 450 258-1   46   8 wks
See also Johnny Mathis; Henry Mancini.

Johnny MATHIS and Deniece WILLIAMS
US, male/female vocal duo   11 wks

26 Aug 78   THAT'S WHAT FRIENDS ARE FOR   CBS 86068   16   11 wks
See also Johnny Mathis; Deniece Williams.

MATT BIANCO   UK, male vocalist, Mark Riley   67 wks

8 Sep 84   WHOSE SIDE ARE YOU ON   WEA WX 7   35   39 wks
22 Mar 86   MATT BIANCO   WEA WX 35   26   13 wks
9 Jul 88   INDIGO   WEA WX 181   23   13 wks
2 Nov 90   THE BEST OF MATT BIANCO   East West WX 376   49   2 wks
For first album, act was a UK/Poland, male/female vocal/instrumental group.

MATTHEWS' SOUTHERN COMFORT
UK, male vocal/instrumental group   4 wks

25 Jul 70   SECOND SPRING   Uni UNLS 112   52   4 wks

MAX Q   Australia, male vocal/instrumental duo   1 wk

4 Nov 89   MAX Q   Mercury 838942 1   69   1 wk

Brian MAY and FRIENDS   UK, male vocalist/instrumentalist –
guitar, and UK/US, male instrumental group   4 wks

12 Nov 83   STAR FLEET PROJECT   EMI SFLT 1078061   35   4 wks

Simon MAY ORCHESTRA   UK, orchestra   7 wks

27 Sep 86   SIMON'S WAY   BBC REB 594   59   7 wks

John MAYALL   UK, male vocalist   97 wks

4 Mar 67 ● A HARD ROAD   Decca SKL 4853   10   19 wks
23 Sep 67 ● CRUSADE   Decca SKL 4890   8   14 wks
25 Nov 67   BLUES ALONE   Ace Of Clubs SCL 1243   24   5 wks
16 Mar 68   DIARY OF A BAND VOL. 1   Decca SKL 4918   27   9 wks
16 Mar 68   DIARY OF A BAND VOL. 2   Decca SKL 4919   28   5 wks
20 Jul 68 ● BARE WIRES   Decca SKL 4945   3   17 wks
18 Jan 69   BLUES FROM LAUREL CANYON   Decca SKL 4972   33   3 wks
23 Aug 69   LOOKING BACK   Decca SKL 5010   14   7 wks
15 Nov 69   TURNING POINT   Polydor 583-571   11   7 wks
11 Apr 70 ● EMPTY ROOMS   Polydor 583-580   9   8 wks
12 Dec 70   U.S.A. UNION   Polydor 2425-020   50   1 wk
26 Jun 71   BACK TO THE ROOTS   Polydor 2657-005   31   2 wks
First four Decca albums credited to John Mayall's Bluesbreakers. See also John Mayall and Eric Clapton.

217

m

John MAYALL and Eric CLAPTON
UK, male vocal/instrumental duo 17 wks

30 Jul	66	● **BLUES BREAKERS** *Decca LK 4804*	6	17 wks

See also John Mayall; Eric Clapton.

Curtis MAYFIELD *US, male vocalist* 2 wks

31 Mar 73	**SUPERFLY** *Buddah 2318 065*	26	2 wks

MAZE featuring Frankie BEVERLY
US, male vocalist and male vocal/instrumental group 25 wks

7 May 83	**WE ARE ONE** *Capitol EST 12262*	38	6 wks
9 Mar 85	**CAN'T STOP THE LOVE** *Capitol MAZE 1*	41	12 wks
27 Sep 86	**LIVE IN LOS ANGELES** *Capitol ESTSP 24*	70	2 wks
16 Sep 89	**SILKY SOUL** *Warner Bros. WX 301*	43	5 wks

MC HAMMER *US, male rapper* 64 wks

28 Jul 90	● **PLEASE HAMMER DON'T HURT 'EM**		
	Capitol EST 2120	8	59 wks
6 Apr 91	**LET'S GET IT STARTED** *Capitol EST 2140*	46	2 wks
2 Nov 91	**TOO LEGIT TO QUIT** *Capitol ESTP 26*	41	3 wks

Last album credited simply to Hammer.

218

m

MC TUNES *UK, male rapper* 3 wks

13 Oct 90	**THE NORTH AT ITS HEIGHTS** *ZTT ZTT 3*	26	3 wks

Vaughn MEADER *US, male comedian* 8 wks

29 Dec 62	**THE FIRST FAMILY** *London HAA 8048*	12	8 wks

MEAT LOAF *US, male vocalist* 548 wks

11 Mar 78	● **BAT OUT OF HELL** *Epic EPC 82419*	9	416 wks
12 Sep 81	★ **DEAD RINGER** *Epic EPC 83645*	1	46 wks
7 May 83	● **MIDNIGHT AT THE LOST AND FOUND**		
	Epic EPC 25243	7	23 wks
10 Nov 84	● **BAD ATTITUDE** *Arista 206 619*	8	16 wks
26 Jan 85	● **HITS OUT OF HELL** *Epic EPC 26156*	2	39 wks
11 Oct 86	**BLIND BEFORE I STOP** *Arista 207 741*	28	6 wks
7 Nov 87	**LIVE AT WEMBLEY** *RCA 208599*	60	2 wks

Hits Out of Hell was also released on Epic 4504471.

MECHANICS – *See MIKE and the MECHANICS*

Glenn MEDEIROS *US, male vocalist* 2 wks

8 Oct 88	**NOT ME** *London LONLP 68*	63	2 wks

MEDICS – *See DOCTOR and the MEDICS*

MEGACITY FOUR *UK, male vocal/instrumental group* 1 wk

17 Jun 89	**TRANZOPHOBIA** *Decoy DYL 3*	67	1 wk

MEGADETH US, male vocal/instrumental group *9 wks*

26 Mar 88	**SO FAR SO GOOD . . . SO WHAT!** *Capitol EST 2053*	18	5 wks
6 Oct 90	● **RUST IN PEACE** *Capitol EST 2132*	8	4 wks

MEL and KIM UK, female vocal duo *25 wks*

25 Apr 87	● **F.L.M.** *Supreme SU 2*	3	25 wks

See also Kim Appleby.

MELANIE US, female vocalist *69 wks*

19 Sep 70	● **CANDLES IN THE RAIN** *Buddah 2318–009*	5	27 wks
16 Jan 71	**LEFTOVER WINE** *Buddah 2318–011*	22	11 wks
29 May 71	● **GOOD BOOK** *Buddah 2322 001*	9	9 wks
8 Jan 72	**GATHER ME** *Buddah 2322 002*	14	14 wks
1 Apr 72	**GARDEN IN THE CITY** *Buddah 2318 054*	19	6 wks
7 Oct 72	**THE FOUR SIDES OF MELANIE** *Buddah 2659 013*	23	2 wks

MELBOURNE SYMPHONY ORCHESTRA – *See Elton JOHN*

John Cougar MELLENCAMP US, male vocalist *25 wks*

6 Nov 82	**AMERICAN FOOL** *Riva RVLP 16*	37	6 wks
3 Mar 84	**UH-HUH** *Riva RIVL 1*	92	1 wk
3 Oct 87	**THE LONESOME JUBILEE** *Mercury MERH 109*	31	12 wks
27 May 89	**BIG DADDY** *Mercury MERH 838220 1*	25	4 wks
19 Oct 91	**WHENEVER WE WANTED** *Mercury 5101511*	39	2 wks

American Fool credited to John Cougar.

MEN AT WORK Australia, male vocal/instrumental group *71 wks*

15 Jan 83	★ **BUSINESS AS USUAL** *Epic EPC 85669*	1	44 wks
30 Apr 83	● **CARGO** *Epic EPC 25372*	8	27 wks

MEN THEY COULDN'T HANG
UK, male vocal/instrumental group *9 wks*

27 Jul 85	**NIGHT OF A THOUSAND CANDLES** *Imp FIEND 50* ..	91	2 wks
8 Nov 86	**HOW GREEN IS THE VALLEY** *MCA MCF 3337*	68	2 wks
23 Apr 88	**WAITING FOR BONAPARTE** *Magnet MAGL 5075*	41	2 wks
6 May 89	**SILVER TOWN** *Silvertone ORELP 503*	39	2 wks
1 Sep 90	**THE DOMINO CLUB** *Silvertone ORELP 512*	53	1 wk

MEN WITHOUT HATS
Canada, male vocal/instrumental group *1 wk*

12 Nov 83	**RHYTHM OF YOUTH** *Statik STATLP 10*	96	1 wk

MEMBERS UK, male vocal/instrumental group *5 wks*

28 Apr 79	**AT THE CHELSEA NIGHTCLUB** *Virgin V 2120*	45	5 wks

Freddie MERCURY UK, male vocalist *23 wks*

11 May 85	● **MR BAD GUY** *CBS 86312*	6	23 wks

See also Freddie Mercury and Montserrat Caballe.

219

m

In 1991 **Metallica** entered both the UK and US album charts at number one.

New Kids on the Block and protégé Jay Stone (fourth from left) help celebrate the eighteenth birthday of Tiffany (far left).

Freddie MERCURY and Montserrat CABALLE
UK/Spain, male/female vocal duo   *4 wks*

| 22 Oct 88 | **BARCELONA** *Polydor POLH 44* .... | 25 | 4 wks |

See also Freddie Mercury.

MERLE and ROY *UK, female/male vocal/instrumental duo*   *5 wks*

| 26 Sep 87 | **REQUESTS** *Mynod Mawr RMBR 8713* .... | 74 | 5 wks |

MERSEYBEATS *UK, male vocal/instrumental group*   *9 wks*

| 20 Jun 64 | **THE MERSEYBEATS** *Fontana TL 5210* .... | 12 | 9 wks |

METALLICA *US/Denmark, male vocal/instrumental group*   *24 wks*

11 Aug 84	**RIDE THE LIGHTNING** *Music For Nations MFN 27*	87	2 wks
15 Mar 86	**MASTER OF PUPPETS** *Music For Nations MFN 60*	41	4 wks
17 Sep 88 ●	**...AND JUSTICE FOR ALL** *Vertigo VERH 61*	4	6 wks
19 May 90	**THE GOOD THE BAD AND THE LIVE** *Vertigo 8754871* .	56	1 wk
24 Aug 91 ★	**METALLICA** *Vertigo 5100221*	1	11 wks

METEORS *UK, male vocal/instrumental group*   *3 wks*

| 26 Feb 83 | **WRECKIN' CREW** *I.D. NOSE 1* .... | 53 | 3 wks |

MEZZOFORTE *Iceland, male instrumental group*   *10 wks*

| 5 Mar 83 | **SURPRISE SURPRISE** *Steinar STELP 02* .... | 23 | 9 wks |
| 2 Jul 83 | **CATCHING UP WITH MEZZOFORTE** *Steinar STELP 03* | 95 | 1 wk |

MG'S – *See Booker T. and the MG's*

MIAMI SOUND MACHINE – *See Gloria ESTEFAN*

George MICHAEL *UK, male vocalist*   *128 wks*

| 14 Nov 87 ★ | **FAITH** *Epic 4600001* .... | 1 | 72 wks |
| 15 Sep 90 ★ | **LISTEN WITHOUT PREJUDICE** *Epic 4672951* .... | 1 | 56 wks |

Keith MICHELL *Australia, male vocalist*   *12 wks*

| 9 Feb 80 | **CAPTAIN BEAKY AND HIS BAND** *Polydor 238 3462* ... | 28 | 12 wks |

MICK – *See Dave DEE, DOZY BEAKY, MICK and TICH*

Bette MIDLER *US, female vocalist*   *20 wks*

| 15 Jul 89 | **BEACHES** *Atlantic 7819931* .... | 21 | 9 wks |
| 13 Jul 91 ● | **SOME PEOPLE'S LIVES** *Atlantic 7567821291* .... | 5 | 11 wks |

MIDNIGHT OIL *Australia, male vocal/instrumental group*   *19 wks*

| 25 Jun 88 | **DIESEL AND DUST** *CBS 4600051* .... | 19 | 16 wks |
| 10 Mar 90 | **BLUE SKY MINING** *CBS 4656531* .... | 28 | 3 wks |

MIDNIGHT STAR
US, male/female vocal/instrumental group — *6 wks*

2 Feb	85	**PLANETARY INVASION**	*Solar MCF 3251*	....	85	2 wks
5 Jul	86	**HEADLINES**	*Solar MCF 3322*	....	42	4 wks

MIGHTY LEMON DROPS
UK, male vocal/instrumental group — *5 wks*

4 Oct	86	**HAPPY HEAD**	*Blue Guitar AZLP 1*	....	58	2 wks
27 Feb	88	**THE WORLD WITHOUT END**	*Blue Guitar AZLP 4*	....	34	3 wks

MIGHTY WAH *UK, male vocal/instrumental group* — *11 wks*

18 Jul	81	**NAH-POO = THE ART OF BLUFF**	*Eternal CLASSIC 1*	..	33	5 wks
4 Aug	84	**A WORD TO THE WISE GUY**	*Beggars Banquet BEGA 54*		28	6 wks

First album credited to Wah!

MIKE and the MECHANICS
UK, male vocal/instrumental group — *29 wks*

15 Mar	86	**MIKE AND THE MECHANICS**	*WEA WX 49*	....	78	3 wks
26 Nov	88	● **THE LIVING YEARS**	*WEA WX 203*	....	2	19 wks
27 Apr	91	**WORD OF MOUTH**	*Virgin V 2662*	....	11	7 wks

See also Mike Rutherford.

Buddy MILES – *See Carlos SANTANA and Buddy MILES*

222

m

John MILES *UK, male vocalist/multi-instrumentalist* — *25 wks*

27 Mar	76	● **REBEL**	*Decca SKL 5231*	....	9	10 wks
26 Feb	77	**STRANGER IN THE CITY**	*Decca TXS 118*	....	37	3 wks
1 Apr	78	**ZARAGON**	*Decca TXS 126*	....	43	5 wks
21 Apr	79	**MORE MILES PER HOUR**	*Decca TXS 135*	....	46	5 wks
29 Aug	81	**MILES HIGH**	*EMI EMC 3374*	....	96	2 wks

Paul MILES-KINGSTON – *See Andrew LLOYD WEBBER*

Frankie MILLER *UK, male vocalist* — *1 wk*

14 Apr	79	**FALLING IN LOVE**	*Chrysalis CHR 1220*	....	54	1 wk

Glenn MILLER *US, orchestra* — *68 wks*

28 Jan	61	● **GLENN MILLER PLAYS SELECTIONS FROM 'THE GLENN MILLER STORY' AND OTHER HITS** *RCA RD 27068 0023*	10	18 wks
5 Jul	69	● **THE BEST OF GLENN MILLER** *RCA International 1002*	5	14 wks
6 Sep	69	**NEARNESS OF YOU** *RCA International INTS 1019*	30	2 wks
25 Apr	70	**A MEMORIAL 1944–1969** *RCA GM 1*	18	17 wks
25 Dec	71	**THE REAL GLENN MILLER AND HIS ORCHESTRA PLAY THE ORIGINAL MUSIC OF THE FILM 'THE GLENN MILLER STORY' AND OTHER HITS** *RCA International INTS 1157*	28	2 wks
14 Feb	76	**A LEGENDARY PERFORMER** *RCA Victor DPM 2065* ..	41	5 wks
14 Feb	76	**A LEGENDARY PERFORMER VOL. 2** *RCA Victor CPL 11349*	53	2 wks

9 Apr 77 ● **THE UNFORGETTABLE GLENN MILLER**
RCA Victor TVL 1 .... **4** 8 wks

The Real Glenn Miller And His Orchestra Play . . . *is a re-titled re-issue of the first album.*

Steve MILLER BAND   *US, male vocal/instrumental group*   *50 wks*

12 Jun 76   **FLY LIKE AN EAGLE**   *Mercury 9286 177* .... **11** 17 wks
4 Jun 77   **BOOK OF DREAMS**   *Mercury 9286 456* .... **12** 12 wks
19 Jun 82 ● **ABRACADABRA**   *Mercury 6302 204* .... **10** 16 wks
7 May 83   **STEVE MILLER BAND LIVE!**   *Mercury MERL 18* .... **79** 2 wks
6 Oct 90   **THE BEST OF 1968–1973**   *Capitol EST 2133* .... **34** 3 wks

MILLICAN and NESBIT   *UK, male vocal duo*   *24 wks*

23 Mar 74 ● **MILLICAN AND NESBIT**   *Pye NSPL 18428* .... **3** 21 wks
4 Jan 75   **EVERYBODY KNOWS MILLICAN AND NESBIT**
Pye NSPL 18446 .... **23** 3 wks

Spike MILLIGAN   *UK, male comedian*   *5 wks*

25 Nov 61   **MILLIGAN PRESERVED**   *Parlophone PMC 1152* .... **11** 4 wks
18 Dec 76   **THE SNOW GOOSE**   *RCA RS 1088* .... **49** 1 wk

Second album credits the London Symphony Orchestra. See also Harry Secombe, Peter Sellers and Spike Milligan; London Symphony Orchestra.

MILLI VANILLI   *France/Germany, male vocal duo*   *24 wks*

21 Jan 89 ● **ALL OR NOTHING/2X2**   *Cooltempo CTLP 11* .... **6** 24 wks

All Or Nothing was repackaged and available with a free re-mix album, 2X2, from 16 Oct 89 onwards.

Mrs. MILLS   *UK, female instrumentalist – piano*   *13 wks*

10 Dec 66   **COME TO MY PARTY**   *Parlophone PMC 7010* .... **17** 7 wks
28 Dec 68   **MRS. MILLS' PARTY PIECES**   *Parlophone PCS 7066* ..... **32** 3 wks
13 Dec 69   **LET'S HAVE ANOTHER PARTY**   *Parlophone PCS 7035* . **23** 2 wks
6 Nov 71   **I'M MIGHTY GLAD**   *MFP 5225* .... **49** 1 wk

MILLTOWN BROTHERS
UK, male vocal/instrumental group   *5 wks*

23 Mar 91   **SLINKY**   *A & M 3953461* .... **27** 5 wks

MINDBENDERS   *UK, male vocal/instrumental group*   *4 wks*

25 Jun 66   **THE MINDBENDERS**   *Fontana TL 5324* .... **28** 4 wks

See also Wayne Fontana and the Mindbenders.

Zodiac MINDWARP and the LOVE REACTION
UK, male vocal/instrumental group   *5 wks*

5 Mar 88   **TATTOOED BEAT MESSIAH**   *Mercury ZODLP 1* .... **20** 5 wks

Liza MINNELLI   *US, female vocalist*   *26 wks*

7 Apr 73 ● **LIZA WITH A 'Z'**   *CBS 65212* .... **9** 15 wks

223

m

16 Jun	73	**THE SINGER** *CBS 65555*		**45**	1 wk
21 Oct	89	● **RESULTS** *Epic 465511 1*		**6**	10 wks

MINIPOPS *UK, male/female vocal group* 12 wks

26 Dec	81	**MINIPOPS** *K-Tel NE 1102*		**63**	7 wks
19 Feb	83	**WE'RE THE MINIPOPS** *K-Tel ONE 1187*		**54**	5 wks

Dannii MINOGUE *Australia, female vocalist* 18 wks

15 Jun	91	● **LOVE AND KISSES** *MCA MCA 10340*		**8†**	18 wks

Kylie MINOGUE *Australia, female vocalist* 130 wks

16 Jul	88	★ **KYLIE** *PWL HF 3*		**1**	67 wks
21 Oct	89	★ **ENJOY YOURSELF** *PWL HF 9*		**1**	33 wks
24 Nov	90	● **RHYTHM OF LOVE** *PWL HF 18*		**9**	22 wks
26 Oct	91	**LET'S GO TO IT** *PWL HF 21*		**15**	8 wks

MIRAGE *UK, male/female vocal/instrumental group* 33 wks

26 Dec	87	● **THE BEST OF MIRAGE JACK MIX '88** *Stylus SMR 746* ..		**7**	15 wks
25 Jun	88	● **JACK MIX IN FULL EFFECT** *Stylus SMR 856*		**7**	12 wks
7 Jan	89	**ROYAL MIX '89** *Stylus SMR 871*		**34**	6 wks

MISSION *UK, male vocal/instrumental group* 43 wks

22 Nov	86	**GOD'S OWN MEDICINE** *Mercury MERH 102*		**14**	20 wks
4 Jul	87	**THE FIRST CHAPTER** *Mercury MISH 1*		**35**	4 wks
12 Mar	88	● **LITTLE CHILDREN** *Mercury MISH 2*		**2**	9 wks
17 Feb	90	● **CARVED IN SAND** *Mercury 8422511*		**7**	8 wks
2 Nov	90	**GRAINS OF SAND** *Mercury 8469371*		**28**	2 wks

MR. BIG *US, male vocal/instrumental group* 3 wks

22 Jul	89	**MR. BIG** *Atlantic 781990 1*		**60**	1 wk
13 Apr	91	**LEAN INTO IT** *Atlantic 7567822091*		**52**	2 wks

MR. BUNGLE *US, male vocal/instrumental group* 1 wk

21 Sep	91	**MR BUNGLE** *London 8282671*		**57**	1 wk

MR. MISTER *US, male vocal/instrumental group* 24 wks

15 Feb	86	● **WELCOME TO THE REAL WORLD** *RCA PL 89647* ...		**6**	24 wks

Joni MITCHELL *Canada, female vocalist* 113 wks

6 Jun	70	● **LADIES OF THE CANYON** *Reprise RSLP 6376*		**8**	25 wks
24 Jul	71	● **BLUE** *Reprise K 44128*		**3**	18 wks
16 Mar	74	**COURT AND SPARK** *Asylum SYLA 8756*		**14**	11 wks
1 Feb	75	**MILES OF AISLES** *Asylum SYSP 902*		**34**	4 wks
27 Dec	75	**THE HISSING OF SUMMER LAWNS**			
		Asylum SYLA 8763		**14**	10 wks
11 Dec	76	**HEJIRA** *Asylum K 53063*		**11**	5 wks
21 Jan	78	**DON JUAN'S RECKLESS DAUGHTER**			
		Asylum K 63003		**20**	7 wks
14 Jul	79	**MINGUS** *Asylum K 53091*		**24**	7 wks

4 Oct 80	**SHADOWS AND LIGHT** *Elektra K 62030*	63	3 wks
4 Dec 82	**WILD THINGS RUN FAST** *Geffen GEF 25102*	32	8 wks
30 Nov 85	**DOG EAT DOG** *Geffen GEF 26455*	57	3 wks
2 Apr 88	**CHALK MARK IN A RAIN STORM** *Geffen WX 141*......	26	7 wks
9 Mar 91	**NIGHT RIDE HOME** *Geffen GEF 24302*	25	5 wks

George MITCHELL MINSTRELS
UK, male/female vocal group   *240 wks*

26 Nov 60	★ **THE BLACK AND WHITE MINSTREL SHOW** *HMV CLP 1399*	1	90 wks
21 Oct 61	★ **ANOTHER BLACK AND WHITE MINSTREL SHOW** *HMV CLP 1460*	1	64 wks
20 Oct 62	★ **ON STAGE WITH THE GEORGE MITCHELL MINSTRELS** *HMV CLP 1599*	1	26 wks
2 Nov 63	● **ON TOUR WITH THE GEORGE MITCHELL MINSTRELS** *HMV CLP 1667*	6	18 wks
12 Dec 64	● **SPOTLIGHT ON THE GEORGE MITCHELL MINSTRELS** *HMV CLP 1803*	6	7 wks
4 Dec 65	● **MAGIC OF THE MINSTRELS** *HMV CLP 1917*	9	7 wks
26 Nov 66	**HERE COME THE MINSTRELS** *HMV CLP 3579*	11	11 wks
16 Dec 67	**SHOWTIME** *HMV CSD 3642*	26	2 wks
14 Dec 68	**SING THE IRVING BERLIN SONGBOOK** *Columbia SCX 6267*	33	1 wk
19 Dec 70	**THE MAGIC OF CHRISTMAS** *Columbia SCX 6431*	32	4 wks
19 Nov 77	● **30 GOLDEN GREATS** *EMI EMTV 7*	10	10 wks

30 Golden Greats *also credits the Joe Loss Orchestra. See also Joe Loss.*

MOCK TURTLES   *UK, male/female vocal/instrumental group*   *4 wks*

25 May 91	**TURTLE SOUP** *Imaginary ILLUSION 012*	33	4 wks

225

m

MODERN EON   *UK, male vocal/instrumental group*   *1 wk*

13 Jun 81	**FICTION TALES** *DinDisc DID 11*	65	1 wk

MODERN LOVERS – *See Jonathan RICHMAN and the MODERN LOVERS*

MODERN ROMANCE   *UK, male vocal/instrumental group*   *13 wks*

16 Apr 83	**TRICK OF THE LIGHT** *WEA X 0127*	53	7 wks
3 Dec 83	**PARTY TONIGHT** *Ronco RON LP 3*	45	6 wks

MODERN TALKING   *Germany, male vocal/instrumental group*   *3 wks*

11 Oct 86	**READY FOR ROMANCE** *RCA PL 71133*	76	3 wks

MOLLY HATCHET   *US, male vocal/instrumental group*   *1 wk*

25 Jan 86	**DOUBLE TROUBLE – LIVE** *Epic EPC 88670*	94	1 wk

Zoot MONEY and the BIG ROLL BAND
UK, male vocalist and male instrumental backing group   *3 wks*

15 Oct 66	**ZOOT** *Columbia SX 6075*	23	3 wks

MONKEES *US/UK, male vocal/instrumental group*   *101 wks*

28 Jan	67 ★ THE MONKEES *RCA Victor SF 7844*	1	36 wks
15 Apr	67 ★ MORE OF THE MONKEES *RCA Victor SF 7868*	1	25 wks
8 Jul	67 ● HEADQUARTERS *RCA Victor SF 7886*	2	19 wks
13 Jan	68 ● PISCES, AQUARIUS, CAPRICORN & JONES LTD.		
	RCA Victor SF 7912	5	11 wks
28 Nov	81 THE MONKEES *Arista DARTY 12*	99	1 wk
15 Apr	89 HEY HEY IT'S THE MONKEES – GREATEST HITS		
	K-Tel NE 1432	12	9 wks

The two albums titled The Monkees *are different.*

MONOCHROME SET *UK, male vocal/instrumental group*   *4 wks*

3 May	80 STRANGE BOUTIQUE *Dindisc DID 4*	62	4 wks

Tony MONOPOLY *Australia, male vocalist*   *4 wks*

12 Jun	76 TONY MONOPOLY *BUK BULP 2000*	25	4 wks

Matt MONRO *UK, male vocalist*   *15 wks*

7 Aug	65 I HAVE DREAMED *Parlophone PMC 1250*	20	1 wk
17 Sep	66 THIS IS THE LIFE *Capitol T 2540*	25	2 wks
26 Aug	67 INVITATION TO THE MOVIES *Capitol ST 2730*	30	1 wk
15 Mar	80 ● HEARTBREAKERS *EMI EMTV 23*	5	11 wks

226

m

MONTROSE *US, male vocal/instrumental group*   *1 wk*

15 Jun	74 MONTROSE *Warner Bros. K 46276*	43	1 wk

MONTY PYTHON'S FLYING CIRCUS
UK, male comedy group   *33 wks*

30 Oct	71 ANOTHER MONTY PYTHON RECORD		
	Charisma CAS 1049	26	3 wks
27 Jan	73 MONTY PYTHON'S PREVIOUS ALBUM		
	Charisma CAS 1063	39	3 wks
23 Feb	74 MATCHING TIE AND HANDKERCHIEF		
	Charisma CAS 1080	49	2 wks
27 Jul	74 LIVE AT DRURY LANE *Charisma CLASS 4*	19	8 wks
9 Aug	75 MONTY PYTHON *Charisma CAS 1003*	45	4 wks
24 Nov	79 THE LIFE OF BRIAN *Warner Bros. K 56751*	63	3 wks
18 Oct	80 CONTRACTUAL OBLIGATION ALBUM		
	Charisma CAS 1152	13	8 wks
16 Nov	91 MONTY PYTHON SINGS *Virgin MONT 1*	62	2 wks

MOODY BLUES *UK, male vocal/instrumental group*   *310 wks*

27 Jan	68 DAYS OF FUTURE PASSED *Deram SML 707*	27	16 wks
3 Aug	68 ● IN SEARCH OF THE LOST CHORD *Deram SML 711* ...	5	32 wks
3 May	69 ★ ON THE THRESHOLD OF A DREAM *Deram SML 1035*	1	73 wks
6 Dec	69 ● TO OUR CHILDREN'S CHILDREN'S CHILDREN		
	Threshold THS 1	2	44 wks
15 Aug	70 ★ A QUESTION OF BALANCE *Threshold THS 3*	1	19 wks
7 Aug	71 ★ EVERY GOOD BOY DESERVES FAVOUR		
	Threshold THS 5	1	21 wks
2 Dec	72 ● SEVENTH SOJOURN *Threshold THS 7*	5	18 wks
16 Nov	74 THIS IS THE MOODY BLUES *Threshold MB 1/2*	14	18 wks
24 Jun	78 ● OCTAVE *Decca TXS 129*	6	18 wks

10 Nov 79	**OUT OF THIS WORLD** *K-Tel NE 1051*	15	10 wks
23 May 81	● **LONG DISTANCE VOYAGER** *Threshold TXS 139*	7	19 wks
10 Sep 83	**THE PRESENT** *Threshold TXS 140*	15	8 wks
10 May 86	**THE OTHER SIDE OF LIFE** *Threshold POLD 5190*	24	6 wks
25 Jun 88	**SUR LA MER** *Polydor POLH 43*	21	5 wks
20 Jan 90	**GREATEST HITS** *Threshold 8406591*	71	1 wk
13 Jul 91	**KEYS OF THE KINGDOM** *Threshold 8494331*	54	2 wks

Christy MOORE *Ireland, male vocalist*   *4 wks*

4 May 91	**SMOKE AND STRONG WHISKEY** *Newberry CM 21* ...	49	3 wks
21 Sep 91	**THE CHRISTY MOORE COLLECTION**		
	East West WX 434	69	1 wk

Dudley MOORE *UK, male instrumentalist – piano*   *19 wks*

4 Dec 65	**THE OTHER SIDE OF DUDLEY MOORE**		
	Decca LK 4732	11	9 wks
11 Jun 66	**GENUINE DUD** *Decca LK 4788*	13	10 wks

Second album credited to the Dudley Moore Trio. See also Peter Cook and Dudley Moore.

Gary MOORE *UK, male vocalist/instrumentalist – guitar*   *71 wks*

3 Feb 79	**BACK ON THE STREETS** *MCA MCF 2853*	70	1 wk
16 Oct 82	**CORRIDORS OF POWER** *Virgin V 2245*	30	6 wks
18 Feb 84	**VICTIMS OF THE FUTURE** *10 DIX 2*	12	7 wks
13 Oct 84	**WE WANT MOORE!** *10 GMDL 1*	32	3 wks
14 Sep 85	**RUN FOR COVER** *10 DIX 16*	12	8 wks
12 Jul 86	**ROCKIN' EVERY NIGHT** *10 XID 1*	99	1 wk
14 Mar 87	● **WILD FRONTIER** *10 DIX 56*	8	14 wks
11 Feb 89	**AFTER THE WAR** *Virgin V 2575*	23	5 wks
7 Apr 90	**STILL GOT THE BLUES** *Virgin V 2612*	13	26 wks

Patrick MORAZ
Switzerland, male instrumentalist – keyboards   *8 wks*

10 Apr 76	**PATRICK MORAZ** *Charisma CDS 4002*	28	7 wks
23 Jul 77	**OUT IN THE SUN** *Charisma CDS 4007*	44	1 wk

MORDRED *UK, male vocal/instrumental group*   *1 wk*

16 Feb 91	**IN THIS LIFE** *Noise International NO 1591*	70	1 wk

Giorgio MORODER – *See Philip OAKEY and Giorgio MORODER*

Joseph MOROVITZ– *See SOUTH BANK ORCHESTRA*

Ennio MORRICONE *Italy, orchestra*   *15 wks*

2 May 81	**THIS IS ENNIO MORRICONE** *EMI THIS 33*	23	5 wks
9 May 81	**CHI MAI** *BBC REH 414*	29	6 wks
7 Mar 87	**THE MISSION – ORIGINAL SOUNDTRACK**		
	Virgin V 2402	73	4 wks

The Mission credits the London Philharmonic Orchestra. See also London Philharmonic Orchestra.

Van MORRISON *UK, male vocalist*   *132 wks*

18 Apr 70	**MOONDANCE** *Warner Bros. WS 1835*	32	2 wks
11 Aug 73	**HARD NOSE THE HIGHWAY** *Warner Bros. K 46242*	22	3 wks
16 Nov 74	**VEEDON FLEECE** *Warner Bros. K 56068*	41	1 wk

227

m

7 May 77	**A PERIOD OF TRANSITION** *Warner Bros. K 56322*	23	5 wks
21 Oct 78	**WAVELENGTH** *Warner Bros. K 56526*	27	6 wks
8 Sep 79	**INTO THE MUSIC** *Vertigo 9120 852*	21	9 wks
20 Sep 80	**THE COMMON ONE** *Mercury 6302 021*	53	3 wks
27 Feb 82	**BEAUTIFUL VISION** *Mercury 6302 122*	31	14 wks
26 Mar 83	**INARTICULATE SPEECH OF THE HEART** *Mercury MERL 16*	14	8 wks
3 Mar 84	**LIVE AT THE GRAND OPERA HOUSE** *Mercury MERL 36*	47	4 wks
9 Feb 85	**A SENSE OF WONDER** *Mercury MERH 54*	25	5 wks
2 Aug 86	**NO GURU, NO METHOD, NO TEACHER** *Mercury MERH 94*	27	5 wks
19 Sep 87	**POETIC CHAMPIONS COMPOSE** *Mercury MERH 110* ..	26	6 wks
2 Jul 88	**IRISH HEARTBEAT** *Mercury MERH 124*	18	7 wks
10 Jun 89	**AVALON SUNSET** *Polydor 839262 1*	13	14 wks
7 Apr 90	● **THE BEST OF VAN MORRISON** *Polydor 8419701*	4	20 wks
20 Oct 90	● **ENLIGHTENMENT** *Polydor 8471001*	5	14 wks
21 Sep 91	● **HYMNS TO THE SILENCE** *Polydor 8490261*	5	6 wks

Irish Heartbeat credits The Chieftains, Ireland, male instrumental group. See also James Galway and the Chieftains.

MORRISSEY *UK, male vocalist* 28 wks

26 Mar 88	★ **VIVA HATE** *HMV CSD 3787*	1	20 wks
27 Oct 90	● **BONA DRAG** *HMV CLP 3788*	9	4 wks
16 Mar 91	● **KILL UNCLE** *HMV CSD 3789*	8	4 wks

MORRISSEY MULLEN
UK, male vocal/instrumental duo 11 wks

18 Jul 81	**BADNESS** *Beggars Banquet BEGA 27*	43	5 wks
3 Apr 82	**LIFE ON THE WIRE** *Beggars Banquet BEGA 33*	47	5 wks
23 Apr 83	**IT'S ABOUT TIME** *Beggars Banquet BEGA 44*	95	1 wk

MORRISTOWN ORPHEUS CHOIR – *See G.U.S. (FOOTWEAR) BAND and the MORRISTOWN ORPHEUS CHOIR*

MOTHERS OF INVENTION
US, male vocal/instrumental group 12 wks

29 Jun 68	**WE'RE ONLY IN IT FOR THE MONEY** *Verve SVLP 9199*	32	5 wks
28 Mar 70	**BURNT WEENY SANDWICH** *Reprise RSLP 6370*	17	3 wks
3 Oct 70	**WEASELS RIPPED MY FLESH** *Reprise RSLP 2028*	28	4 wks

MOTLEY CRUE *US, male vocal/instrumental group* 24 wks

13 Jul 85	**THEATRE OF PAIN** *Elektra EKT 8*	36	3 wks
30 May 87	**GIRLS GIRLS GIRLS** *Elektra EKT 39*	14	11 wks
16 Sep 89	● **DR. FEELGOOD** *Elektra EKT 59*	4	7 wks
19 Oct 91	**DECADE OF DECADENCE** *Elektra EKT 95*	20	3 wks

MOTORHEAD *UK, male vocal/instrumental group* 101 wks

24 Sep 77	**MOTORHEAD** *Chiswick WIK 2*	43	5 wks
24 Mar 79	**OVERKILL** *Bronze BRON 515*	24	11 wks
27 Oct 79	**BOMBER** *Bronze BRON 523*	12	13 wks
8 Dec 79	**ON PARADE** *United Artists LBR 1004*	65	2 wks
8 Nov 80	● **ACE OF SPADES** *Bronze BRON 531*	4	16 wks
27 Jun 81	★ **NO SLEEP TILL HAMMERSMITH** *Bronze BRON 535* ..	1	21 wks
17 Apr 82	● **IRONFIST** *Bronze BRNA 539*	6	9 wks
26 Feb 83	**WHAT'S WORDS WORTH** *Big Beat NED 2*	71	2 wks
4 Jun 83	**ANOTHER PERFECT DAY** *Bronze BRON 546*	20	4 wks

15 Sep 84	**NO REMORSE** *Bronze PROTV MOTOR 1*	14	6 wks
9 Aug 86	**ORGASMATRON** *GWR GWLP 1*	21	4 wks
5 Sep 87	**ROCK 'N' ROLL** *GWR GWLP 14*	34	3 wks
15 Oct 88	**NO SLEEP AT ALL** *GWR GWR 31*	79	1 wk
2 Feb 91	**1916** *Epic 4674811*	24	4 wks

MOTORS UK, male vocal/instrumental group   6 wks

| 15 Oct 77 | **THE MOTORS** *Virgin V 2089* .... | 46 | 5 wks |
| 3 Jun 78 | **APPROVED BY THE MOTORS** *Virgin V 2101* .... | 60 | 1 wk |

MOTT THE HOOPLE
UK, male vocal/instrumental group   32 wks

2 May 70	**MOTT THE HOOPLE** *Island ILPS 9108*	66	1 wk
17 Oct 70	**MAD SHADOWS** *Island ILPS 9119*	48	2 wks
17 Apr 71	**WILD LIFE** *Island ILPS 9144*	44	2 wks
23 Sep 72	**ALL THE YOUNG DUDES** *CBS 65184*	21	4 wks
11 Aug 73	● **MOTT** *CBS 69038*	7	15 wks
13 Apr 74	**THE HOOPLE** *CBS 69062*	11	5 wks
23 Nov 74	**LIVE** *CBS 69093*	32	2 wks
4 Oct 75	**DRIVE ON** *CBS 69154*	45	1 wk

MOUNTAIN US/Canada, male vocal/instrumental group   4 wks

| 5 Jun 71 | **NANTUCKET SLEIGHRIDE** *Island ILPS 9148* .... | 43 | 1 wk |
| 8 Jul 72 | **THE ROAD GOES EVER ON** *Island ILPS 9199* .... | 21 | 3 wks |

Nana MOUSKOURI Greece, female vocalist   208 wks

7 Jun 69	● **OVER AND OVER** *Fontana S 5511*	10	105 wks
4 Apr 70	● **THE EXQUISITE NANA MOUSKOURI**		
	Fontana STL 5536	10	25 wks
10 Oct 70	**RECITAL '70** *Fontana 6312 003*	68	1 wk
3 Apr 71	**TURN ON THE SUN** *Fontana 6312 008*	16	15 wks
29 Jul 72	**BRITISH CONCERT** *Fontana 6651 003*	29	11 wks
28 Apr 73	**SONGS FROM HER TV SERIES** *Fontana 6312 036*	29	11 wks
28 Sep 74	**SPOTLIGHT ON NANA MOUSKOURI**		
	Fontana 6641 197	38	6 wks
10 Jul 76	● **PASSPORT** *Philips 9101 061*	3	16 wks
22 Feb 86	**ALONE** *Philips PHH 3*	19	10 wks
8 Oct 88	**THE MAGIC OF NANA MOUSKOURI** *Philips NMTV 1* .	44	8 wks

MOVE UK, male vocal/instrumental group   9 wks

| 13 Apr 68 | **MOVE** *Regal Zonophone SLPZ 1002* .... | 15 | 9 wks |

Alison MOYET UK, female vocalist   142 wks

17 Nov 84	★ **ALF** *CBS 26229*	1	84 wks
18 Apr 87	● **RAINDANCING** *CBS 450 152-1*	2	52 wks
4 May 91	**HOODOO** *Columbia 4682721*	11	6 wks

MSG Germany/UK, male vocal/instrumental group   2 wks

| 24 Oct 87 | **PERFECT TIMING** *EMI EMC 3539* .... | 65 | 2 wks |

MSG is the Michael Schenker Group with Robin McAuley in place of Michael Schenker. See also Michael Schenker Group.

MTUME US, male/female vocal/instrumental group · 1 wk

6 Oct 84	**YOU, ME AND HE** Epic EPC 26077	85	1 wk

MUD UK, male vocal/instrumental group · 58 wks

28 Sep 74	● **MUD ROCK** RAK SRAK 508	8	35 wks
26 Jul 75	● **MUD ROCK VOL. 2** RAK SRAK 513	6	12 wks
1 Nov 75	**MUD'S GREATEST HITS** RAK SRAK 6755	25	6 wks
27 Dec 75	**USE YOUR IMAGINATION** Private Stock PVLP 1003	33	5 wks

MUDHONEY UK, male vocal/instrumental group · 2 wks

31 Aug 91	**EVERY GOOD BOY DESERVES FUDGE** Subpop SP 18160	34	2 wks

MUFFINS – See MARTHA and the MUFFINS

Gerry MULLIGAN and Ben WEBSTER
US, male instrumental duo – baritone and tenor sax · 1 wk

24 Sep 60	**GERRY MULLIGAN MEETS BEN WEBSTER** HMV CLP 1373	15	1 wk

MUNGO JERRY UK, male vocal/instrumental group · 14 wks

8 Aug 70	**MUNGO JERRY** Dawn DNLS 3008	13	6 wks
10 Apr 71	**ELECTRONICALLY TESTED** Dawn DNLS 3020	14	8 wks

MUPPETS US, puppets · 45 wks

11 Jun 77	★ **THE MUPPET SHOW** Pye NSPH 19	1	35 wks
25 Feb 78	**THE MUPPET SHOW VOL. 2** Pye NSPH 21	16	10 wks

Peter MURPHY UK, male vocalist · 1 wk

26 Jul 86	**SHOULD THE WORLD FAIL TO FALL APART** Beggars Banquet BEGA 69	82	1 wk

Anne MURRAY Canada, female vocalist · 10 wks

3 Oct 81	**VERY BEST OF ANNE MURRAY** Capitol EMTV 31	14	10 wks

Pauline MURRAY and the INVISIBLE GIRLS
UK, female vocalist with male vocal/instrumental group · 4 wks

11 Oct 80	**PAULINE MURRAY AND THE INVISIBLE GIRLS** Elusive 2394 227	25	4 wks

MUSIC OF THE MOUNTAINS – See MANUEL and his MUSIC OF THE MOUNTAINS

MUSICAL YOUTH UK, male vocal/instrumental group · 22 wks

4 Dec 82	**THE YOUTH OF TODAY** MCA YOULP 1	24	22 wks

MUSIC STUDENTS – *See Ian DURY*

MY BLOODY VALENTINE
UK, male/female vocal/instrumental group 2 wks

23 Nov 91 **LOVELESS** *Creation CRELP 060* .... 24 2 wks

Alannah MYLES *Canada, female vocalist* 21 wks

28 Apr 90 ● **ALANNAH MYLES** *Atlantic 7819561* .... 3 21 wks

n

NAPALM DEATH *UK, male vocal/instrumental group* 1 wk

15 Sep 90 **HARMONY OF CORRUPTION** *Earache MOSH 19* ..... 67 1 wk

NARADA *US, male vocalist/instrumentalist/producer* 5 wks

14 May 88 **DIVINE EMOTION** *Reprise WX 172* .... 60 5 wks

Graham NASH *UK, male vocalist* 8 wks

26 Jun 71 **SONGS FOR BEGINNERS** *Atlantic 2401–011* .... 13 8 wks
See also Crosby, Stills and Nash; Crosby, Stills, Nash and Young; Graham Nash and David Crosby.

Graham NASH and David CROSBY
UK/US, male vocal duo 5 wks

13 May 72 **GRAHAM NASH AND DAVID CROSBY** *Atlantic K 50011* 13 5 wks
See also Graham Nash; Dave Crosby.

Johnny NASH *US, male vocalist* 17 wks

5 Aug 72 **I CAN SEE CLEARLY NOW** *CBS 64860* .... 39 6 wks
10 Dec 77 **JOHNNY NASH COLLECTION** *Epic EPC 10008* .... 18 11 wks

NASH THE SLASH
Canada, male vocalist/multi-instrumentalist 1 wk

21 Feb 81 **CHILDREN OF THE NIGHT** *DinDisc DID 9* .... 61 1 wk

NATASHA *UK, female vocalist* 3 wks

9 Oct 82 **CAPTURED** *Towerbell TOWLP 2* .... 53 3 wks

In this photo Jonn of **Ned's Atomic Dustbin** bears an uncanny resemblance to Andrew Strong in *The Commitments*.

Ted Nugent is shown in 1976 displaying early signs of Cat Scratch Fever.

NATIONAL BRASS BAND UK, orchestra   10 wks

10 May 80   **GOLDEN MELODIES** K-Tel ONE 1075 ....   **15**   10 wks

NATIONAL PHILHARMONIC ORCHESTRA – See LONDON PHILHARMONIC
CHOIR; James GALWAY and Henry MANCINI

NAZARETH UK, male vocal/instrumental group   51 wks

26 May 73	**RAZAMANAZ** Mooncrest CREST 1	**11**	25 wks
24 Nov 73 ●	**LOUD 'N' PROUD** Mooncrest CREST 4	**10**	7 wks
18 May 74	**RAMPANT** Mooncrest CREST 15	**13**	3 wks
13 Dec 75	**GREATEST HITS** Mountain TOPS 108	**54**	1 wk
3 Feb 79	**NO MEAN CITY** Mountain TOPS 123	**34**	9 wks
28 Feb 81	**THE FOOL CIRCLE** NEMS NEL 6019	**60**	3 wks
3 Oct 81	**NAZARETH LIVE** NEMS NELD 102	**78**	3 wks

NED'S ATOMIC DUSTBIN
UK, male vocal/instrumental group   6 wks

9 Feb 91	**BITE (import)** Rough Trade Germany RTD 14011831	**72**	1 wk
13 Apr 91 ●	**GOD FODDER** Furtive 4681121	**4**	5 wks

Bill NELSON UK, male vocalist/multi-instrumentalist   21 wks

24 Feb 79	**SOUND ON SOUND** Harvest SHSP 4095	**33**	5 wks
23 May 81 ●	**QUIT DREAMING AND GET ON THE BEAM**		
	Mercury 6359 055	**7**	6 wks
3 Jul 82	**THE LOVE THAT WHIRLS (DIARY OF A THINKING**		
	HEART) Mercury WHIRL 3	**28**	4 wks
14 May 83	**CHIMERA** Mercury MERB 19	**30**	5 wks
3 May 86	**GETTING THE HOLY GHOST ACROSS**		
	Portrait PRT 26602	**91**	1 wk

First album credited to Bill Nelson's Red Noise – UK, male vocal/instrumental group.

Phyllis NELSON US, female vocalist   10 wks

20 Apr 85   **MOVE CLOSER** Carrere CAL 203 ....   **29**   10 wks

NENA Germany, female/male vocal/instrumental group   5 wks

24 Mar 84   **NENA** Epic EPC 25925 ....   **31**   5 wks

NESBIT – See MILLICAN and NESBIT

Robbie NEVIL US, male vocalist   1 wk

13 Jun 87   **C'EST LA VIE** Manhattan MTL 1006 ....   **93**   1 wk

Aaron NEVILLE – See Linda RONSTADT; NEVILLE BROTHERS

NEVILLE BROTHERS US, male vocal/instrumental group   3 wks

18 Aug 90   **BROTHER'S KEEPER** A & M 3953121 ....   **35**   3 wks

NEW BOHEMIANS – See Edie BRICKELL and the NEW BOHEMIANS

233

n

NEW FAST AUTOMATIC DAFFODILS
UK, male vocal/instrumental group   1 wk

| 17 Nov 90 | **PIGEON HOLE** *Play It Again Sam BIAS 185* .... | 49 | 1 wk |

NEW KIDS ON THE BLOCK   *US, male vocal group*   103 wks

9 Dec 89	● **HANGIN' TOUGH** CBS 4608741	2	41 wks
30 Jun 90	★ **STEP BY STEP** CBS 4666861	1	31 wks
2 Nov 90	● **NEW KIDS ON THE BLOCK** CBS 4675041	6	13 wks
15 Dec 90	**MERRY MERRY CHRISTMAS** CBS 4659071	13	5 wks
2 Mar 91	**NO MORE GAMES – THE REMIX ALBUM**		
	Columbia 4674941	15	11 wks
21 Dec 91	**H.I.T.S.** Columbia 4694381	50†	2 wks

NEW MODEL ARMY   *UK, male vocal/instrumental group*   18 wks

12 May 84	**VENGEANCE** Abstract ABT 008	73	5 wks
25 May 85	**NO REST FOR THE WICKED** EMI NMAL 1	22	3 wks
11 Oct 86	**THE GHOST OF CAIN** EMI EMC 3516	45	3 wks
18 Feb 89	**THUNDER AND CONSOLATION** EMI EMC 3552	20	3 wks
6 Oct 90	**IMPURITY** EMI EMC 3581	23	2 wks
22 Jun 91	**RAW MELODY MEN** EMI EMC 3595	43	2 wks

NEW MUSIK   *UK, male vocal/instrumental group*   11 wks

| 17 May 80 | **FROM A TO B** GTO GTLP 041 .... | 35 | 9 wks |
| 14 Mar 81 | **ANYWHERE** GTO GTLP 044 .... | 68 | 2 wks |

NEW ORDER   *UK, male/female vocal/instrumental group*   105 wks

28 Nov 81	**MOVEMENT** Factory FACT 50	30	10 wks
14 May 83	● **POWER, CORRUPTION AND LIES** Factory FACT 75 ..	4	29 wks
25 May 85	● **LOW-LIFE** Factory FACT 100	7	10 wks
11 Oct 86	● **BROTHERHOOD** Factory FACT 150	9	5 wks
29 Aug 87	● **SUBSTANCE** Factory FACT 200	3	37 wks
11 Feb 89	★ **TECHNIQUE** Factory FACT 275	1	14 wks

NEW POWER GENERATION – *See PRINCE*

NEW SEEKERS   *UK, male/female vocal/instrumental group*   49 wks

5 Feb 72	**NEW COLOURS** Polydor 2383 066	40	4 wks
1 Apr 72	● **WE'D LIKE TO TEACH THE WORLD TO SING**		
	Polydor 2883 103	2	25 wks
12 Aug 72	**NEVER ENDING SONG OF LOVE** Polydor 2383 126	35	4 wks
14 Oct 72	**CIRCLES** Polydor 2442 102	23	5 wks
21 Apr 73	**NOW** Polydor 2383 195	47	2 wks
30 Mar 74	**TOGETHER** Polydor 2383 264	12	9 wks

NEW WORLD THEATRE ORCHESTRA
UK, orchestra   1 wk

| 24 Dec 60 | **LET'S DANCE TO THE HITS OF THE 30'S AND 40'S** | | |
| | Pye Golden Guinea GGL 0026 .... | 20 | 1 wk |

NEWCLEUS   *US, male vocal/instrumental group*   2 wks

| 25 Aug 84 | **JAM ON REVENGE** Sunnyview SVLP 6600 .... | 84 | 2 wks |

Bob NEWHART *US, male comedian*　　　　　*37 wks*

1 Oct 60 ● **BUTTON-DOWN MIND OF BOB NEWHART**		
Warner Bros. WM 4010	2	37 wks

Anthony NEWLEY *UK, male vocalist*　　　　　*14 wks*

14 May 60 **LOVE IS A NOW AND THEN THING** *Decca LK 4343* ...	19	2 wks
8 Jul 61 ● **TONY** *Decca LK 4406*	5	12 wks

See also Anthony Newley, Peter Sellers, Joan Collins.

Anthony NEWLEY, Peter SELLERS, Joan COLLINS
UK, male/female comedians　　　　　*10 wks*

28 Sep 63 ● **FOOL BRITANNIA** *Ember CEL 902*	10	10 wks

See also Anthony Newley; Peter Sellers.

NEWS – *See Huey LEWIS and the NEWS*

Olivia NEWTON-JOHN *UK, female vocalist*　　　　　*93 wks*

2 Mar 74 **MUSIC MAKES MY DAY** *Pye NSPL 28186*	37	3 wks
29 Jun 74 **LONG LIVE LOVE** *EMI EMC 3028*	40	2 wks
26 Apr 75 **HAVE YOU NEVER BEEN MELLOW** *EMI EMC 3069* .	37	2 wks
29 May 76 **COME ON OVER** *EMI EMC 3124*	49	4 wks
27 Aug 77 **MAKING A GOOD THING BETTER** *EMI EMC 3192* ...	60	1 wk
21 Jan 78 **GREATEST HITS** *EMI EMA 785*	19	9 wks
9 Dec 78 **TOTALLY HOT** *EMI EMA 789*	30	9 wks
31 Oct 81 **PHYSICAL** *EMI EMC 3386*	11	22 wks
23 Oct 82 ● **GREATEST HITS** *EMI EMTV 36*	8	38 wks
8 Mar 86 **SOUL KISS** *Mercury MERH 77*	66	3 wks

NICE *UK, male instrumental group*　　　　　*38 wks*

13 Sep 69 ● **NICE** *Immediate IMSP 026*	3	6 wks
27 Jun 70 ● **FIVE BRIDGES** *Charisma CAS 1014*	2	21 wks
17 Apr 71 ● **ELEGY** *Charisma CAS 1030*	5	11 wks

Paul NICHOLAS *UK, male vocalist*　　　　　*8 wks*

29 Nov 86 **JUST GOOD FRIENDS** *K-Tel ONE 1334*	30	8 wks

Stevie NICKS *US, female vocalist*　　　　　*77 wks*

8 Aug 81 **BELLA DONNA** *WEA K 99169*	11	16 wks
2 Jul 83 **THE WILD HEART** *WEA 25-0071-1*	28	19 wks
14 Dec 85 **ROCK A LITTLE** *Modern PCS 7300*	30	22 wks
10 Jun 89 ● **THE OTHER SIDE OF THE MIRROR** *EMI EMD 1008* .	3	14 wks
14 Sep 91 **TIMESPACE – THE BEST OF STEVIE NICKS**		
EMI EMD 3595	15	6 wks

Hector NICOL *UK, male vocalist*　　　　　*1 wk*

28 Apr 84 **BRAVO JULIET** *Klub KLP 42*	92	1 wk

NICOLE *Germany, female vocalist*   2 wks

2 Oct 82	**A LITTLE PEACE** *CBS 85011*	85	2 wks

NILSSON *US, male vocalist*   43 wks

29 Jan 72	**THE POINT** *RCA Victor SF 8166*	46	1 wk
5 Feb 72 ●	**NILSSON SCHMILSSON** *RCA Victor SF 8242*	4	22 wks
19 Aug 72	**SON OF SCHMILSSON** *RCA Victor SF 8297*	41	1 wk
28 Jul 73	**A LITTLE TOUCH OF SCHMILSSON IN THE NIGHT** *RCA Victor SF 8371*	20	19 wks

NINA and FREDERICK *Denmark, female/male vocal duo*   6 wks

13 Feb 60 ●	**NINA AND FREDERICK** *Pye NPT 19023*	9	2 wks
29 Apr 61	**NINA AND FREDERICK** *Columbia COL 1314*	11	4 wks

These two albums, although identically named, are different.

9 BELOW ZERO *UK, male vocal/instrumental group*   12 wks

14 Mar 81	**DON'T POINT YOUR FINGER** *A & M AMLH 68521* ...	56	6 wks
20 Mar 82	**THIRD DEGREE** *A & M AMLH 68537*	38	6 wks

NINE INCH NAILS *UK, male vocal/instrumental group*   1 wk

12 Oct 91	**PRETTY HATE MACHINE** *TVT ILPS 9973*	67	1 wk

999 *UK, male vocal/instrumental group*   1 wk

25 Mar 78	**999** *United Artists UAG 30199*	53	1 wk

NIRVANA *US, male vocal/instrumental group*   13 wks

5 Oct 91	**NEVERMIND** *DGC DGC 24425*	33†	13 wks

NOLANS *Ireland, female vocal group*   84 wks

20 Jul 78 ●	**20 GIANT HITS** *Target TGS 502*	3	12 wks
19 Jan 80	**NOLANS** *Epic EPC 83892*	15	13 wks
25 Oct 80	**MAKING WAVES** *Epic EPC 10023*	11	33 wks
27 Mar 82 ●	**PORTRAIT** *Epic EPC 10033*	7	10 wks
20 Nov 82	**ALTOGETHER** *Epic EPC 10037*	52	8 wks
17 Nov 84	**GIRLS JUST WANNA HAVE FUN** *Towerbell TOWLP 10* .	39	8 wks

First album credited to Nolan Sisters.

NOMAD *UK, male/female vocal/instrumental duo*   2 wks

22 Jun 91	**CHANGING CABINS** *Rumour RULP 100*	48	2 wks

NORTHSIDE *UK, male vocal/instrumental group*   3 wks

29 Jun 91	**CHICKEN RHYTHMS** *Factory FACT 310*	19	3 wks

NOT THE 9 O'CLOCK NEWS CAST
UK/New Zealand, male/female TV cast   *51 wks*

8 Nov 80	● **NOT THE 9 O'CLOCK NEWS** *BBC REB 400*	5	23 wks
17 Oct 81	● **HEDGEHOG SANDWICH** *BBC REB 421*	5	24 wks
23 Oct 82	**THE MEMORY KINDA LINGERS** *BBC REF 453*	63	4 wks

NOTTING HILLBILLIES
UK, male vocal/instrumental group   *14 wks*

17 Mar 90	● **MISSING . . . PRESUMED HAVING A GOOD TIME** *Vertigo 8426711*	2	14 wks

NU SHOOZ   *US, male/female vocal duo*   *8 wks*

14 Jun 86	**POOLSIDE** *Atlantic WX 60*	32	8 wks

NUCLEAR ASSAULT   *US, male vocal/instrumental group*   *1 wk*

7 Oct 89	**HANDLE WITH CARE** *Under One Flag FLAG 35*	60	1 wk

NUCLEUS   *UK, male instrumental group*   *1 wk*

11 Jul 70	**ELASTIC ROCK** *Vertigo 6360 006*	46	1 wk

Ted NUGENT   *US, male vocalist/instrumentalist – guitar*   *14 wks*

4 Sep 76	**TED NUGENT** *Epic EPC 81268*	56	1 wk
30 Oct 76	**FREE FOR ALL** *Epic EPC 81397*	33	2 wks
2 Jul 77	**CAT SCRATCH FEVER** *Epic EPC 82010*	28	5 wks
11 Mar 78	**DOUBLE LIVE GONZO** *Epic EPC 88282*	47	2 wks
14 Jun 80	**SCREAM DREAM** *Epic EPC 86111*	37	3 wks
25 Apr 81	**IN 10 CITIES** *Epic EPC 84917*	75	1 wk

Gary NUMAN   *UK, male vocalist*   *136 wks*

9 Jun 79	★ **REPLICAS** *Beggars Banquet BEGA 7*	1	31 wks
25 Aug 79	**TUBEWAY ARMY** *Beggars Banquet BEGA 4*	14	10 wks
22 Sep 79	★ **THE PLEASURE PRINCIPLE** *Beggars Banquet BEGA 10* .	1	21 wks
13 Sep 80	★ **TELEKON** *Beggars Banquet BEGA 19*	1	11 wks
2 May 81	● **LIVING ORNAMENTS 1979–1980** *Beggars Banquet BOX 1*	2	4 wks
2 May 81	**LIVING ORNAMENTS 1979** *Beggars Banquet BEGA 24* ...	47	3 wks
2 May 81	**LIVING ORNAMENTS 1980** *Beggars Banquet BEGA 25* ...	39	3 wks
12 Sep 81	● **DANCE** *Beggars Banquet BEGA 28*	3	8 wks
18 Sep 82	● **I, ASSASSIN** *Beggars Banquet BEGA 40*	8	6 wks
27 Nov 82	**NEW MAN NUMAN – THE BEST OF GARY NUMAN** *TV Records TVA 7*	45	7 wks
24 Sep 83	**WARRIORS** *Beggars Banquet BEGA 47*	12	6 wks
6 Oct 84	**THE PLAN** *Beggars Banquet BEGA 55*	29	4 wks
24 Nov 84	**BERSERKER** *Numa NUMA 1001*	45	3 wks
13 Apr 85	**WHITE NOISE - LIVE** *Numa NUMAD 1002*	29	5 wks
28 Sep 85	**THE FURY** *Numa NUMA 1003*	24	5 wks
8 Nov 86	**STRANGE CHARM** *Numa NUMA 1005*	59	2 wks
3 Oct 87	**EXHIBITION** *Beggars Banquet BEGA 88*	43	3 wks
8 Oct 88	**METAL RHYTHM** *Illegal ILP 035*	48	2 wks
28 Oct 89	**SKIN MECHANIC** *IRS EIRSA 1019*	55	1 wk
30 Mar 91	**OUTLAND** *IRS EIRSA 1039*	39	1 wk

First two albums credited to Tubeway Army. The Plan is credited to Tubeway Army and Gary Numan. All other albums are credited to Gary Numan. Living Ornaments 1979–1980 is a boxed set of Living Ornaments 1979 and Living Ornaments 1980. See also Sharpe and Numan.

N.W.A. US, male rap group
6 wks

30 Sep 89	**STRAIGHT OUTTA COMPTON**			
	Fourth & Broadway BRLP 534	**41**	4 wks	
15 Jun 91	**EFIL4ZAGGIN** Fourth & Broadway BRLP 562	**25**	2 wks	

O

Philip OAKEY and Giorgio MORODER
UK/Italy, male vocal/instrumental duo   5 wks

10 Aug 85	**PHILIP OAKEY AND GIORGIO MORODER**		
	Virgin V 2351	**52**	5 wks

OASIS UK, male/female vocal group
14 wks

28 Apr 84	**OASIS** WEA WX 3	**23**	14 wks

John OATES – See Daryl HALL and John OATES

Billy OCEAN UK, male vocalist
119 wks

24 Nov 84	● **SUDDENLY** Jive JIP 12	**9**	59 wks
17 May 86	● **LOVE ZONE** Jive HIP 35	**2**	32 wks
19 Mar 88	● **TEAR DOWN THESE WALLS** Jive HIP 57	**3**	13 wks
28 Oct 89	● **GREATEST HITS** Jive BOTV 1	**4**	15 wks

Des O'CONNOR UK, male vocalist
41 wks

7 Dec 68	● **I PRETEND** Columbia SCX 6295	**8**	10 wks
5 Dec 70	**WITH LOVE** Columbia SCX 6417	**40**	4 wks
2 Dec 72	**SING A FAVOURITE SONG** Pye NSPL 18390	**25**	6 wks
2 Feb 80	**JUST FOR YOU** Warwick WW 5071	**17**	7 wks
13 Oct 84	**DES O'CONNOR NOW** Telstar STAR 2245	**24**	14 wks

Hazel O'CONNOR UK, female vocalist
45 wks

9 Aug 80	● **BREAKING GLASS (film soundtrack)**		
	A & M AMLH 64820	**5**	38 wks
12 Sep 81	**COVER PLUS** Albion ALB 108	**32**	7 wks

Sinéad O'CONNOR Ireland, female vocalist
71 wks

23 Jan 88	**THE LION AND THE COBRA** Ensign CHEN 7	**27**	20 wks
24 Mar 90	★ **I DO NOT WANT WHAT I HAVEN'T GOT**		
	Ensign CHEN 14	**1**	51 wks

Daniel O'DONNELL Ireland, male vocalist
36 wks

15 Oct 88	**FROM THE HEART** Telstar STAR 2327	**56**	12 wks

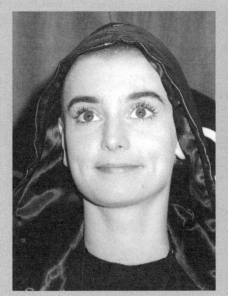

Top left: **Sinead O'Connor** attends the 1990 *Billboard* Music Awards. Top right: **Jeffrey Osborne** is shown at the 1991 Movie Awards at the Universal Amphitheatre. Above right: The engineer of *Abbey Road* and *Dark Side of the Moon* went on to give his name to the **Alan Parsons Project**, a creative collaboration with his partner Eric Woolfson. Above left: **Edith Piaf** entered the British album chart two dozen years after her death.

28 Oct 89	**THOUGHTS OF HOME** *Telstar STAR 2372*	**43**	10 wks
21 Apr 90	**FAVOURITES** *Ritz RITZLP 058*	**75**	1 wk
17 Nov 90	**THE LAST WALTZ** *Ritz RITZALP 058*	**53**	5 wks
9 Nov 91	**THE VERY BEST OF DANIEL O'DONNELL**		
	Ritz RITZBLD 700	**34†**	8 wks

ODYSSEY *US, male/female vocal group*   32 wks

16 Aug 80	**HANG TOGETHER** *RCA PL 13526*	**38**	3 wks
4 Jul 81	**I'VE GOT THE MELODY** *RCA RCALP 5028*	**29**	7 wks
3 Jul 82	**HAPPY TOGETHER** *RCA RCALP 6036*	**21**	9 wks
20 Nov 82	**THE MAGIC TOUCH OF ODYSSEY** *Telstar STAR 2223* .	**69**	5 wks
26 Sep 87	**THE GREATEST HITS** *Stylus SMR 735*	**26**	8 wks

Esther and Abi OFARIM *Israel, female/male vocal duo*   24 wks

| 24 Feb 68 | ● **2 IN 3** *Philips SBL 7825* .... | **6** | 20 wks |
| 12 Jul 69 | **OFARIM CONCERT – LIVE '69** *Philips XL 4* .... | **29** | 4 wks |

Mary O'HARA *UK, female vocalist/instrumentalist – harp*   12 wks

8 Apr 78	**MARY O'HARA AT THE ROYAL FESTIVAL HALL**		
	Chrysalis CHR 1159	**37**	3 wks
1 Dec 79	**TRANQUILLITY** *Warwick WW 5072*	**12**	9 wks

David OISTRACH – *See Herbert VON KARAJAN*

240

0

Mike OLDFIELD *UK, male multi-instrumentalist/vocalist*   473 wks

14 Jul 73	★ **TUBULAR BELLS** *Virgin V 2001*	**1**	264 wks
14 Sep 74	★ **HERGEST RIDGE** *Virgin V 2013*	**1**	17 wks
8 Feb 75	**THE ORCHESTRAL TUBULAR BELLS** *Virgin V 2026* .	**17**	7 wks
15 Nov 75	● **OMMADAWN** *Virgin V 2043*	**4**	23 wks
20 Nov 76	**BOXED** *Virgin V BOX 1*	**22**	13 wks
9 Dec 78	**INCANTATIONS** *Virgin VDT 101*	**14**	17 wks
11 Aug 79	**EXPOSED** *Virgin VD 2511*	**16**	9 wks
8 Dec 79	**PLATINUM** *Virgin V 2141*	**24**	9 wks
8 Nov 80	**QE 2** *Virgin V 2181*	**27**	12 wks
27 Mar 82	● **FIVE MILES OUT** *Virgin V 2222*	**7**	27 wks
4 Jun 83	● **CRISES** *Virgin V 2262*	**6**	29 wks
7 Jul 84	**DISCOVERY** *Virgin V 2308*	**15**	16 wks
15 Dec 84	**THE KILLING FIELDS** *Virgin V 2328*	**97**	1 wk
2 Nov 85	**THE COMPLETE MIKE OLDFIELD** *Virgin MOC 1*	**36**	17 wks
10 Oct 87	**ISLANDS** *Virgin V 2466*	**29**	5 wks
22 Jul 89	**EARTH MOVING** *Virgin V 2610*	**30**	5 wks
9 Jun 90	**AMAROK** *Virgin V 2640*	**49**	2 wks

The Orchestral Tubular Bells is with the Royal Philharmonic Orchestra. See also Royal Philharmonic Orchestra.

OMAR *UK, male vocalist*   10 wks

14 Jul 90	**THERE'S NOTHING LIKE THIS** *Kongo Dance KDLP 2* ..	**54**	4 wks
27 Jul 91	**THERE'S NOTHING LIKE THIS (re-issue)**		
	Talkin Loud 5100211	**19**	6 wks

ONE HUNDRED & ONE STRINGS
Germany, orchestra   35 wks

26 Sep 59	● **GYPSY CAMPFIRES** *Pye GGL 0009*	**9**	7 wks
26 Mar 60	**SOUL OF SPAIN** *Pye GGL 0017*	**17**	1 wk
16 Apr 60	● **GRAND CANYON SUITE** *Pye GGL 0048*	**10**	1 wk

27 Aug 60 ★ **DOWN DRURY LANE TO MEMORY LANE**
    Pye GGL 0061 . . . . **1**   21 wks
15 Oct 83 **MORNING, NOON AND NIGHT** *Ronco RTL 2094* . . . . . . **32**   5 wks
The orchestra was American based for last album.

ONE WORLD *UK, male vocal/instrumental group*   *3 wks*

9 Jun 90 **ONE WORLD ONE VOICE** *Virgin V 2632* . . . . **27**   3 wks

Alexander O'NEAL *US, male vocalist*   *140 wks*

1 Jun 85 **ALEXANDER O'NEAL** *Tabu TBU 26485* . . . . **19** 18 wks
8 Aug 87 ● **HEARSAY/ALL MIXED UP** *Tabu 4509361* . . . . **4** 103 wks
17 Dec 88 **MY GIFT TO YOU** *Tabu 463152 1* . . . . **53**   3 wks
2 Feb 91 ● **ALL TRUE MAN** *Tabu 4658821* . . . . **2** 16 wks
All Mixed Up, a re-mixed album of Hearsay, *was listed with* Hearsay *from 15 Jul 89.*

ONLY ONES *UK, male vocal/instrumental group*   *8 wks*

3 Jun 78 **THE ONLY ONES** *CBS 82830* . . . . **56**   1 wk
31 Mar 79 **EVEN SERPENTS SHINE** *CBS 83451* . . . . **42**   2 wks
3 May 80 **BABY'S GOT A GUN** *CBS 84089* . . . . **37**   5 wks

Yoko ONO *Japan, female vocalist*   *2 wks*

20 Jun 81 **SEASON OF GLASS** *Geffen K 99164* . . . . **47**   2 wks
See also John Lennon.

241

O

ONSLAUGHT *UK, male vocal/instrumental group*   *2 wks*

20 May 89 **IN SEARCH OF SANITY** *London 828142 1* . . . . **46**   2 wks

ORANGE JUICE *UK, male vocal/instrumental group*   *18 wks*

6 Mar 82 **YOU CAN'T HIDE YOUR LOVE FOREVER**
    Polydor POLS 1057 . . . . **21**   6 wks
20 Nov 82 **RIP IT UP** *Holden Caulfield Universal* *POLS 1076* . . . . **39**   8 wks
10 Mar 84 **TEXAS FEVER** *Polydor OJMLP 1* . . . . **34**   4 wks

ORB *UK, male producer*   *5 wks*

27 Apr 91 **ORB'S ADVENTURES BEYOND THE ULTRAWORLD**
    Big Life BLRDLP 5 . . . . **29**   5 wks

Roy ORBISON *US, male vocalist*   *218 wks*

8 Jun 63 **LONELY AND BLUE** *London HAU 2342* . . . . **15**   8 wks
29 Jun 63 **CRYING** *London HAU 2437* . . . . **17**   3 wks
30 Nov 63 ● **IN DREAMS** *London HAU 8108* . . . . **6** 57 wks
25 Jul 64 **EXCITING SOUNDS OF ROY ORBISON** *Ember NR 5013* **17**   2 wks
5 Dec 64 ● **OH PRETTY WOMAN** *London HAU 8207* . . . . **4** 16 wks
25 Sep 65 ● **THERE IS ONLY ONE ROY ORBISON**
    London HAU 8252 . . . . **10** 12 wks
26 Feb 66 **THE ORBISON WAY** *London HAU 8279* . . . . **11** 10 wks
24 Sep 66 **THE CLASSIC ROY ORBISON** *London HAU 8297* . . . . . **12**   8 wks
22 Jul 67 **ORBISONGS** *Monument SMO 5004* . . . . **40**   1 wk
30 Sep 67 **ROY ORBISON'S GREATEST HITS**
    Monument SMO 5007 . . . . **40**   1 wk

27 Jan 73	**ALL-TIME GREATEST HITS** *Monument MNT 67290*	39	3 wks
29 Nov 75	★ **THE BEST OF ROY ORBISON** *Arcade ADEP 19*	1	20 wks
18 Jul 81	**GOLDEN DAYS** *CBS 10026*	63	1 wk
4 Jul 87	**IN DREAMS: THE GREATEST HITS** *Virgin VGD 3514* .	86	2 wks
29 Oct 88	★ **THE LEGENDARY ROY ORBISON** *Telstar STAR 2330* .	1	38 wks
11 Feb 89	● **MYSTERY GIRL** *Virgin V 2576*	2	23 wks
25 Nov 89	**A BLACK AND WHITE NIGHT** *Virgin V 2601*	51	3 wks
2 Nov 90	**BALLADS** *Telstar STAR 2441*	38	10 wks

ORBITAL   *UK, male instrumental group*   2 wks

12 Oct 91	**ORBITAL** *ffrr 8282481*	71	1 wk

ORCHESTRAL MANOEUVRES IN THE DARK
UK, male vocal/instrumental duo   211 wks

1 Mar 80	**ORCHESTRAL MANOEUVRES IN THE DARK**		
	DinDisc DID 2	27	29 wks
1 Nov 80	● **ORGANISATION** *DinDisc DID 6*	6	25 wks
14 Nov 81	● **ARCHITECTURE AND MORALITY** *DinDisc DID 12* ..	3	39 wks
12 Mar 83	● **DAZZLE SHIPS** *Telegraph V 2261*	5	13 wks
12 May 84	● **JUNK CULTURE** *Virgin V 2310*	9	27 wks
29 Jun 85	**CRUSH** *Virgin V 2349*	13	12 wks
11 Oct 86	**THE PACIFIC AGE** *Virgin V 2398*	15	7 wks
12 Mar 88	● **THE BEST OF O.M.D.** *Virgin OMD 1*	2	32 wks
18 May 91	● **SUGAR TAX** *Virgin V 2648*	3	27 wks

L'ORCHESTRE ELECTRONIQUE
UK, male synthesized orchestra   1 wk

29 Oct 83	**SOUND WAVES** *Nouveau Musique NML 1005*	75	1 wk

ORCHESTRE NATIONALE DE LA RADIO DIFFUSION FRANÇAISE – *See Sir Thomas BEECHAM*

Cyril ORNADEL – *See LONDON SYMPHONY ORCHESTRA*

ORVILLE – *See Keith HARRIS, ORVILLE and CUDDLES*

Jeffrey OSBORNE   *US, male vocalist*   10 wks

5 May 84	**STAY WITH ME TONIGHT** *A & M AMLX 64940*	56	7 wks
13 Oct 84	**DON'T STOP** *A & M AMA 5017*	59	3 wks

Ozzy OSBOURNE   *UK, male vocalist*   57 wks

20 Sep 80	● **OZZY OSBOURNE'S BLIZZARD OF OZ**		
	Jet JETLP 234	7	8 wks
7 Nov 81	**DIARY OF A MADMAN** *Jet JETLP 237*	14	12 wks
27 Nov 82	**TALK OF THE DEVIL** *Jet JETDP 401*	21	6 wks
10 Dec 83	**BARK AT THE MOON** *Epic EPC 25739*	24	7 wks
22 Feb 86	● **THE ULTIMATE SIN** *Epic EPC 26404*	8	10 wks
23 May 87	**TRIBUTE** *Epic 450 475–1*	13	6 wks
22 Oct 88	**NO REST FOR THE WICKED** *Epic 462581 1*	23	4 wks
17 Mar 90	**JUST SAY OZZY** *Epic 4659401*	69	1 wk
19 Oct 91	**NO MORE TEARS** *Epic 4678591*	17	3 wks

Ozzy Osbourne's Blizzard Of Oz are a UK/US male vocal/instrumental group.

OSIBISA   *Ghana/Nigeria, male vocal/instrumental group*   17 wks

22 May 71	**OSIBISA** *MCA MDKS 8001*	11	10 wks
5 Feb 72	**WOYAYA** *MCA MDKS 8005*	11	7 wks

Donny OSMOND *US, male vocalist* *104 wks*

23 Sep	72	●	**PORTRAIT OF DONNY**	*MGM 2315 108*	....	5	43 wks
16 Dec	72	●	**TOO YOUNG**	*MGM 2315 113*	....	7	24 wks
26 May	73	●	**ALONE TOGETHER**	*MGM 2315 210*	....	6	19 wks
15 Dec	73	●	**A TIME FOR US**	*MGM 2315 273*	....	4	13 wks
8 Feb	75		**DONNY**	*MGM 2315 314*	....	16	4 wks
2 Oct	76		**DISCOTRAIN**	*Polydor 2391 226*	....	59	1 wk

See also Osmonds; Donny and Marie Osmond.

Donny and Marie OSMOND *US, male/female vocal duo* *19 wks*

2 Nov	74		**I'M LEAVING IT ALL UP TO YOU**	*MGM 2315 307*	.....	13	15 wks
26 Jul	75		**MAKE THE WORLD GO AWAY**	*MGM 2315 343*	......	30	3 wks
5 Jun	76		**DEEP PURPLE**	*Polydor 2391 220*	....	48	1 wk

See also Donny Osmond; Marie Osmond.

Little Jimmy OSMOND *US, male vocalist* *12 wks*

17 Feb	73	**KILLER JOE**	*MGM 2315 157*	....	20	12 wks

Marie OSMOND *US, female vocalist* *1 wk*

9 Feb	74	**PAPER ROSES**	*MGM 2315 262*	....	46	1 wk

See also Donny and Marie Osmond.

243

O

OSMONDS *US, male vocal/instrumental group* *103 wks*

18 Nov	72		**OSMONDS LIVE**	*MGM 2315 117*	....	13	22 wks
16 Dec	72	●	**CRAZY HORSES**	*MGM 2315 123*	....	9	19 wks
25 Aug	73	●	**THE PLAN**	*MGM 2315 251*	....	6	25 wks
17 Aug	74	●	**OUR BEST TO YOU**	*MGM 2315 300*	....	5	20 wks
7 Dec	74		**LOVE ME FOR A REASON**	*MGM 2315 312*	....	13	9 wks
14 Jun	75		**I'M STILL GONNA NEED YOU**	*MGM 2315 342*	....	19	7 wks
10 Jan	76		**AROUND THE WORLD – LIVE IN CONCERT**				
				MGM 2659 044	....	41	1 wk

See also Donny Osmond.

Gilbert O'SULLIVAN *UK, male vocalist* *195 wks*

25 Sep	71	●	**HIMSELF**	*MAM 501*	....	5	82 wks
18 Nov	72	★	**BACK TO FRONT**	*MAM 502*	....	1	64 wks
6 Oct	73	●	**I'M A WRITER NOT A FIGHTER**	*MAMS 505*	....	2	25 wks
26 Oct	74	●	**STRANGER IN MY OWN BACK YARD**				
				MAM MAMS 506	....	9	8 wks
18 Dec	76		**GREATEST HITS**	*MAM MAMA 2003*	....	13	11 wks
12 Sep	81		**20 GOLDEN GREATS**	*K-Tel NE 1133*	....	98	1 wk
11 May	91		**NOTHING BUT THE BEST**				
				Castle Communications CTVLP 107	....	50	4 wks

John OTWAY and Wild Willy BARRETT
UK, male vocal/instrumental duo *1 wk*

1 Jul	78	**DEEP AND MEANINGLESS**	*Polydor 2382 501*	....	44	1 wk

OVERLORD X UK, male rapper 1 wk

4 Feb 89	**WEAPON IS MY LYRIC** Mango Street ILPS 9924	68	1 wk

OZRIC TENTACLES UK, male vocal/instrumental group 1 wk

31 Aug 91	**STRANGEITUDE** Dovetail DOVELP 3	70	1 wk

P

PACEMAKERS – See GERRY and the PACEMAKERS

Jimmy PAGE UK, male instrumentalist – guitar 10 wks

27 Feb 82	**DEATHWISH II (film soundtrack)** Swansong SSK 59415 .	40	4 wks
2 Jul 88	**OUTRIDER** Geffen WX 155	27	6 wks

See also Roy Harper with Jimmy Page.

Elaine PAIGE UK, female vocalist 132 wks

1 May 82	**ELAINE PAIGE** WEA K 58385	56	6 wks
5 Nov 83 ●	**STAGES** K-Tel NE 1262	2	48 wks
20 Oct 84	**CINEMA** K-Tel NE 1282	12	25 wks
16 Nov 85 ●	**LOVE HURTS** WEA WX 28	8	20 wks
29 Nov 86	**CHRISTMAS** WEA WX 80	27	6 wks
5 Dec 87	**MEMORIES – THE BEST OF ELAINE PAIGE**		
	Telstar STAR 2313	14	15 wks
19 Nov 88	**THE QUEEN ALBUM** Siren SRNLP 22	51	8 wks
27 Apr 91	**LOVE CAN DO THAT** RCA PL 74932	36	4 wks

PALE FOUNTAINS UK, male vocal/instrumental group 3 wks

10 Mar 84	**PACIFIC STREET** Virgin V 2274	85	2 wks
16 Feb 85	**FROM ACROSS THE KITCHEN TABLE** Virgin V 2333 .	94	1 wk

PALE SAINTS UK, male/female vocal/instrumental group 2 wks

24 Feb 90	**THE COMFORTS OF MADNESS** 4AD CAD 0002	40	2 wks

PALLAS UK, male vocal/instrumental group 4 wks

25 Feb 84	**SENTINEL** Harvest SHSP 2400121	41	3 wks
22 Feb 86	**THE WEDGE** Harvest SHVL 850	70	1 wk

Robert PALMER UK, male vocalist 127 wks

6 Nov 76	**SOME PEOPLE CAN DO WHAT THEY LIKE**		
	Island ILPS 9420	46	1 wk
14 Jul 79	**SECRETS** Island ILPS 9544	54	4 wks
6 Sep 80	**CLUES** Island ILPS 9595	31	8 wks
3 Apr 82	**MAYBE IT'S LIVE** Island ILPS 9665	32	6 wks
23 Apr 83	**PRIDE** Island ILPS 9720	37	9 wks

16 Nov 85	● **RIPTIDE** *Island ILPS 9801*	**5**	37 wks
9 Jul 88	**HEAVY NOVA** *EMI EMD 1007*	**17**	25 wks
11 Nov 89	● **ADDICTIONS VOLUME 1** *Island ILPS 9944*	**7**	17 wks
17 Nov 90	**DON'T EXPLAIN** *EMI EMDX 1018*	**9**	20 wks

PAPAS – *See MAMAS and PAPAS*

Mica PARIS *UK, female vocalist* *35 wks*

3 Sep 88	● **SO GOOD** *Fourth & Broadway BRLP 525*	**6**	32 wks
27 Oct 90	**CONTRIBUTION** *Fourth & Broadway BRLP 558*	**26**	3 wks

PARIS ANGELS *Ireland, male vocal/instrumental duo* *2 wks*

17 Aug 91	**SUNDEW** *Virgin V 2667*	**37**	2 wks

Graham PARKER and the RUMOUR
UK, male vocal/instrumental group *35 wks*

27 Nov 76	**HEAT TREATMENT** *Vertigo 6360 137*	**52**	2 wks
12 Nov 77	**STICK TO ME** *Vertigo 9102 017*	**19**	4 wks
27 May 78	**PARKERILLA** *Vertigo 6641 797*	**14**	5 wks
7 Apr 79	**SQUEEZING OUT SPARKS** *Vertigo 9102 030*	**18**	8 wks
7 Jun 80	**THE UP ESCALATOR** *Stiff SEEZ 23*	**11**	10 wks
27 Mar 82	**ANOTHER GREY AREA** *RCA RCALP 6029*	**40**	6 wks

Another Grey Area credited to Graham Parker.

Ray PARKER Jr. *US, male vocalist* *7 wks*

10 Oct 87	**AFTER DARK** *WEA WX 122*	**40**	7 wks

John PARR *UK, male vocalist* *2 wks*

2 Nov 85	**JOHN PARR** *London LONLP 12*	**60**	2 wks

Alan PARSONS PROJECT
UK, male vocal/instrumental group *38 wks*

28 Aug 76	**TALES OF MYSTERY AND IMAGINATION** *Charisma CDS 4003*	**56**	1 wk
13 Aug 77	**I ROBOT** *Arista SPARTY 1016*	**30**	1 wk
10 Jun 78	**PYRAMID** *Arista SPART 1054*	**49**	4 wks
29 Sep 79	**EVE** *Arista SPARTY 1100*	**74**	1 wk
15 Nov 80	**THE TURN OF A FRIENDLY CARD** *Arista DLART 1* ..	**38**	4 wks
29 May 82	**EYE IN THE SKY** *Arista 204 666*	**27**	11 wks
26 Nov 83	**THE BEST OF THE ALAN PARSONS PROJECT** *Arista APP 1*	**99**	1 wk
3 Mar 84	**AMMONIA AVENUE** *Arista 206 100*	**24**	8 wks
23 Feb 85	**VULTURE CULTURE** *Arista 206 577*	**40**	5 wks
14 Feb 87	**GAUDI** *Arista 208 084*	**66**	2 wks

PARTISANS *UK, male vocal/instrumental group* *1 wk*

19 Feb 83	**THE PARTISANS** *No Future PUNK 4*	**94**	1 wk

Dolly PARTON US, female vocalist   13 wks

| 25 Nov 78 | **BOTH SIDES** Lotus WH 5006 | 45 | 12 wks |
| 7 Sep 85 | **GREATEST HITS** RCA PL 84422 | 74 | 1 wk |

See also Dolly Parton/Linda Ronstadt/Emmylou Harris.

Dolly PARTON/Linda RONSTADT/Emmylou HARRIS US, female vocal trio   4 wks

| 14 Mar 87 | **TRIO** Warner Bros. 925 491–1 | 60 | 4 wks |

See also Dolly Parton; Linda Ronstadt; Emmylou Harris.

PARTRIDGE FAMILY US, male/female vocal group   13 wks

8 Jan 72	**UP TO DATE** Bell SBLL 143	46	2 wks
22 Apr 72	**THE PARTRIDGE FAMILY SOUND MAGAZINE**		
	Bell BELLS 206	14	7 wks
30 Sep 72	**SHOPPING BAG** Bell BELLS 212	28	3 wks
9 Dec 72	**CHRISTMAS CARD** Bell BELLS 214	45	1 wk

PASADENAS UK, male vocal group   21 wks

| 22 Oct 88 | ● **TO WHOM IT MAY CONCERN** CBS 462877 1 | 3 | 21 wks |

246

p

PASSIONS UK, male/female vocal/instrumental group   1 wk

| 3 Oct 81 | **THIRTY THOUSAND FEET OVER CHINA** | | |
| | Polydor POLS 1041 | 92 | 1 wk |

PAUL – See PETER, PAUL and MARY

Luciano PAVAROTTI Italy, male vocalist   137 wks

15 May 82	**PAVAROTTI'S GREATEST HITS** Decca D 2362	95	1 wk
9 Aug 86	**THE PAVAROTTI COLLECTION** Stylus SMR 8617	12	34 wks
16 Jul 88	**THE NEW PAVAROTTI COLLECTION LIVE!**		
	Stylus SMR 857	63	8 wks
17 Mar 90	★ **THE ESSENTIAL PAVAROTTI** Decca 4302101	1†	70 wks
20 Jul 91	★ **ESSENTIAL PAVAROTTI II** Decca 4304701	1†	24 wks

See also Luciano Pavarotti, Placido Domingo and José Carreras; Luciano Pavarotti with the Henry Mancini Orchestra.

Luciano PAVAROTTI, Placido DOMINGO and José CARRERAS Italy/Spain, male tenors   63 wks

| 1 Sep 90 | ★ **IN CONCERT** Decca 4304331 | 1† | 63 wks |

See also Luciano Pavarotti; Placido Domingo; Jose Carreras.

Luciano PAVAROTTI with the Henry MANCINI ORCHESTRA Italy, male vocalist with US, conductor/orchestra   1 wk

| 30 Jun 84 | **MAMMA** Decca 411959 | 96 | 1 wk |

See also Luciano Pavarotti; Henry Mancini.

Tom PAXTON *US, male vocalist*   10 wks

13 Jun 70	**NO. 6** *Elektra 2469–003*	23	5 wks
3 Apr 71	**THE COMPLEAT TOM PAXTON** *Elektra EKD 2003*	18	4 wks
1 Jul 72	**PEACE WILL COME** *Reprise K 44182*	47	1 wk

David PEASTON *UK, male vocalist*   1 wk

| 26 Aug 89 | **INTRODUCING . . . DAVID PEASTON** *Geffen 924228 1* | 66 | 1 wk |

PEBBLES *US, female vocalist*   4 wks

| 14 May 88 | **PEBBLES** *MCA MCF 3418* .... | 56 | 4 wks |

PEDDLERS *UK, male vocal/instrumental group*   16 wks

| 16 Mar 68 | **FREE WHEELERS** *CBS SBPG 63183* .... | 27 | 13 wks |
| 7 Feb 70 | **BIRTHDAY** *CBS 63682* .... | 16 | 3 wks |

Kevin PEEK *UK, male instrumentalist – guitar*   2 wks

| 21 Mar 81 | **AWAKENING** *Ariola ARL 5065* .... | 52 | 2 wks |

See also Kevin Peek and Rick Wakeman.

Kevin PEEK and Rick WAKEMAN
UK, male instrumental duo – guitar and keyboards   6 wks

| 13 Oct 84 | **BEYOND THE PLANETS** *Telstar STAR 2244* .... | 64 | 6 wks |

Beyond the Planets also features Jeff Wayne with narration by Patrick Allen. See also Kevin Peek; Rick Wakeman; Jeff Wayne.

Teddy PENDERGRASS *US, male vocalist*   8 wks

| 21 May 88 | **JOY** *Elektra 960775 1* .... | 45 | 8 wks |

PENETRATION *UK, male/female vocal/instrumental group*   8 wks

| 28 Oct 78 | **MOVING TARGETS** *Virgin V 2109* .... | 22 | 4 wks |
| 6 Oct 79 | **COMING UP FOR AIR** *Virgin V 2131* .... | 36 | 4 wks |

PENGUIN CAFE ORCHESTRA
UK, male instrumental group   5 wks

| 4 Apr 87 | **SIGNS OF LIFE** *Edition EG EGED 50* .... | 49 | 5 wks |

PENTANGLE *UK, male/female vocal/instrumental group*   39 wks

15 Jun 68	**THE PENTANGLE** *Transatlantic TRA 162*	21	9 wks
1 Nov 69	● **BASKET OF LIGHT** *Transatlantic TRA 205*	5	28 wks
12 Dec 70	**CRUEL SISTER** *Transatlantic TRA 228*	51	2 wks

PEPA – *See SALT 'N' PEPA*

Most folksingers did best in the 60s, but **Tom Paxton** enjoyed consistent success in the early 70s.

PEPSI and SHIRLIE *UK, female vocal duo*   *2 wks*

7 Nov 87	**ALL RIGHT NOW**	*Polydor POLH 38*	69	2 wks

Carl PERKINS *US, male vocalist*   *3 wks*

15 Apr 78	**OL' BLUE SUEDES IS BACK**	*Jet UATV 30146*	38	3 wks

Steve PERRY *US, male vocalist*   *2 wks*

14 Jul 84	**STREET TALK**	*CBS 25967*	59	2 wks

PESTALOZZI CHILDREN'S CHOIR
International, male/female vocal group   *2 wks*

26 Dec 81	**SONGS OF JOY**	*K-Tel NE 1140*	65	2 wks

PET SHOP BOYS *UK, male vocal/instrumental duo*   *273 wks*

5 Apr 86	● **PLEASE**	*Parlophone PSB 1*	3	82 wks
29 Nov 86	**DISCO**	*EMI PRG 1001*	15	72 wks
19 Sep 87	● **PET SHOP BOYS ACTUALLY**	*Parlophone PCSD 104*	2	59 wks
22 Oct 88	● **INTROSPECTIVE**	*Parlophone PCS 7325*	2	39 wks
3 Nov 90	● **BEHAVIOUR**	*Parlophone PCSD 113*	2	14 wks
16 Nov 91	● **DISCOGRAPHY**	*Parlophone PMTV 3*	3†	7 wks

249

PETER and GORDON *UK, male vocal duo*   *1 wk*

p

20 Jun 64	**PETER AND GORDON**	*Columbia 33SX 1630*	18	1 wk

PETER, PAUL and MARY
US, male/female vocal/instrumental group   *26 wks*

4 Jan 64	**PETER PAUL AND MARY**	*Warner Bros. WM 4064*	18	1 wk
21 Mar 64	**IN THE WIND**	*Warner Bros. WM 8142*	11	19 wks
13 Feb 65	**IN CONCERT VOL. 1**	*Warner Bros. WM 8158*	20	2 wks
5 Sep 70	**TEN YEARS TOGETHER**	*Warner Bros. WS 2552*	60	4 wks

PETERS and LEE *UK, male/female vocal duo*   *166 wks*

30 Jun 73	★ **WE CAN MAKE IT**	*Philips 6308 165*	1	55 wks
22 Dec 73	● **BY YOUR SIDE**	*Philips 6308 192*	9	48 wks
21 Sep 74	● **RAINBOW**	*Philips 6308 208*	6	27 wks
4 Oct 75	● **FAVOURITES**	*Philips 9109 205*	2	32 wks
18 Dec 76	**INVITATION**	*Philips 9101 027*	44	4 wks

Tom PETTY and the HEARTBREAKERS
US, male vocal/instrumental group   *68 wks*

4 Jun 77	**TOM PETTY AND THE HEARTBREAKERS**			
	Shelter ISA 5014		24	12 wks
1 Jul 78	**YOU'RE GONNA GET IT**	*Island ISA 5017*	34	5 wks
17 Nov 79	**DAMN THE TORPEDOES**	*MCA MCF 3044*	57	4 wks
23 May 81	**HARD PROMISES**	*MCA MCF 3098*	32	5 wks
20 Nov 82	**LONG AFTER DARK**	*MCA MCF 3155*	45	4 wks
20 Apr 85	**SOUTHERN ACCENTS**	*MCA MCF 3260*	23	6 wks

2 May 87	LET ME UP (I'VE HAD ENOUGH)	MCA MCG 6014	...	59	2 wks
8 Jul 89	● FULL MOON FEVER	MCA MCG 6034	....	8	16 wks
20 Jul 91	● INTO THE GREAT WIDE OPEN	MCA MCA 10317	....	3	14 wks

Full Moon Fever *credited simply to Tom Petty.*

PhD *UK, male vocal/instrumental duo* — 8 wks

| 1 May 82 | PhD | WEA K 99150 | .... | 33 | 8 wks |

Barrington PHELOUNG *Australia, male conductor/arranger* — 22 wks

| 2 Mar 91 | ● INSPECTOR MORSE – MUSIC FROM THE TV SERIES | | | | |
| | *Virgin Television VTLP 2* | .... | 4 | 22 wks |

PHENOMENA *UK, male vocal/instrumental group* — 2 wks

| 6 Jul 85 | PHENOMENA | *Bronze PM 1* | .... | 63 | 2 wks |

Arlene PHILLIPS *UK, female exercise instructor* — 24 wks

| 28 Aug 82 | KEEP IN SHAPE SYSTEM | *Supershape SUP 01* | .... | 41 | 23 wks |
| 18 Feb 84 | KEEP IN SHAPE SYSTEM VOL. 2 | *Supershape SUP 2* | .... | 100 | 1 wk |

Keep In Shape System *features music by Funk Federation.*

PHOTOS *UK, male/female vocal/instrumental group* — 9 wks

| 21 Jun 80 | ● THE PHOTOS | *CBS PHOTO 5* | .... | 4 | 9 wks |

250

p

Edith PIAF *France, female vocalist* — 5 wks

| 26 Sep 87 | HEART AND SOUL | *Stylus SMR 736* | .... | 58 | 5 wks |

PIGBAG *UK, male instrumental group* — 14 wks

| 13 Mar 82 | DR HECKLE AND MR JIVE | *Y Y 17* | .... | 18 | 14 wks |

PILOT *UK, male vocal/instrumental group* — 1 wk

| 31 May 75 | SECOND FLIGHT | *EMI EMC 3075* | .... | 48 | 1 wk |

Courtney PINE *UK, male instrumentalist – saxophone* — 13 wks

| 25 Oct 86 | JOURNEY TO THE URGE WITHIN | *Island ILPS 9846* | .. | 39 | 11 wks |
| 6 Feb 88 | DESTINY'S SONGS | *Antilles AN 8275* | .... | 54 | 2 wks |

PINK FAIRIES *UK, male vocal/instrumental group* — 1 wk

| 29 Jul 72 | WHAT A BUNCH OF SWEETIES | *Polydor 2383 132* | ..... | 48 | 1 wk |

PINK FLOYD *UK, male vocal/instrumental group* — 746 wks

19 Aug 67	● PIPER AT THE GATES OF DAWN	*Columbia SCX 6157*	.	6	14 wks
13 Jul 68	● SAUCERFUL OF SECRETS	*Columbia SCX 6258*	....	9	11 wks
28 Jun 69	● MORE (film soundtrack)	*Columbia SCX 6346*	....	9	5 wks

15 Nov	69 ●	UMMAGUMMA *Harvest SHDW 1/2*	5	21 wks
24 Oct	70 ★	ATOM HEART MOTHER *Harvest SHVL 781*	1	23 wks
7 Aug	71	RELICS *Starline SRS 5071*	32	6 wks
20 Nov	71 ●	MEDDLE *Harvest SHVL 795*	3	82 wks
17 Jun	72 ●	OBSCURED BY CLOUDS (film soundtrack)		
		Harvest SHSP 4020	6	14 wks
31 Mar	73 ●	DARK SIDE OF THE MOON *Harvest SHVL 804* ...	2	301 wks
19 Jan	74	A NICE PAIR (double re-issue) *Harvest SHDW 403*	21	20 wks
27 Sep	75 ★	WISH YOU WERE HERE *Harvest SHVL 814*	1	84 wks
19 Feb	77 ●	ANIMALS *Harvest SHVL 815*	2	33 wks
8 Dec	79 ●	THE WALL *Harvest SHDW 411*	3	51 wks
5 Dec	81	A COLLECTION OF GREAT DANCE SONGS		
		Harvest SHVL 822	37	10 wks
2 Apr	83 ★	THE FINAL CUT *Harvest SHPF 1983*	1	25 wks
19 Sep	87 ●	A MOMENTARY LAPSE OF REASON		
		EMI EMD 1003	3	34 wks
3 Dec	88	DELICATE SOUND OF THUNDER *EMI EQ 5009*	11	12 wks

A Nice Pair *is a double re-issue of the first two albums.*

PIPS – *See Gladys KNIGHT and the PIPS*

PIRANHAS *UK, male vocal/instrumental group*   *3 wks*

20 Sep	80	PIRANHAS *Sire SRK 6098*	69	3 wks

---

PIRATES *UK, male vocal/instrumental group*   *3 wks*

19 Nov	77	OUT OF THEIR SKULLS *Warner Bros. K 56411*	57	3 wks

p

Gene PITNEY *US, male vocalist*   *73 wks*

11 Apr	64 ●	BLUE GENE *United Artists ULP 1061*	7	11 wks
6 Feb	65	GENE PITNEY'S BIG 16 *Stateside SL 10118*	12	6 wks
20 Mar	65	I'M GONNA BE STRONG *Stateside SL 10120*	15	2 wks
20 Nov	65	LOOKIN' THRU THE EYES OF LOVE *Stateside SL 10148*	15	5 wks
17 Sep	66	NOBODY NEEDS YOUR LOVE *Stateside SL 10183*	13	17 wks
4 Mar	67	YOUNG WARM AND WONDERFUL *Stateside SSL 10194*	39	1 wk
22 Apr	67	GENE PITNEY'S BIG SIXTEEN *Stateside SSL 10199*	40	1 wk
20 Sep	69 ●	BEST OF GENE PITNEY *Stateside SSL 10286*	8	9 wks
2 Oct	76 ●	HIS 20 GREATEST HITS *Arcade ADEP 22*	6	14 wks
20 Oct	90	BACKSTAGE – THE GREATEST HITS AND MORE		
		Polydor 8471191	17	7 wks

PIXIES *US, male/female vocal/instrumental group*   *22 wks*

29 Apr	89 ●	DOOLITTLE *4AD CAD 905*	8	9 wks
25 Aug	90 ●	BOSSANOVA *4AD CAD 0010*	3	8 wks
5 Oct	91 ●	TROMPE LE MONDE *4AD CAD 1014*	7	5 wks

---

Robert PLANT *UK, male vocalist*   *49 wks*

10 Jul	82 ●	PICTURES AT ELEVEN *Swansong SSK 59418*	2	15 wks
23 Jul	83 ●	THE PRINCIPLES OF MOMENTS *WEA 7901011*	7	14 wks
1 Jun	85	SHAKEN 'N' STIRRED *Es Paranza 79–0265-1*	19	4 wks
12 Feb	88 ●	NOW AND ZEN *Es Paranza WX 149*	10	7 wks
31 Mar	90	MANIC NIRVANA *Es Paranza WX 339*	15	9 wks

---

PLASMATICS *US, male/female vocal/instrumental group*   *3 wks*

11 Oct	80	NEW HOPE FOR THE WRETCHED *Stiff SEEZ 24*	55	3 wks

PLASTIC ONO BAND – *See John LENNON*

PLATTERS *US, male/female vocal group*   *13 wks*

8 Apr 78 ● **20 CLASSIC HITS** *Mercury 9100 049*	8	13 wks

PLAYERS ASSOCIATION
US, male/female vocal/instrumental group   *4 wks*

17 Mar 79 **TURN THE MUSIC UP** *Vanguard VSD 79421*	54	4 wks

PLAYN JAYN *UK, male vocal/instrumental group*   *1 wk*

1 Sep 84 **FRIDAY THE 13TH (AT THE MARQUEE CLUB)** *A & M JAYN 13*	93	1 wk

PM DAWN *US, male rap duo*   *8 wks*

14 Sep 91 ● **OF THE HEART OF THE SOUL AND OF THE CROSS** *Gee Street GEEA 7*	8	8 wks

POGUES *Ireland, male vocal/instrumental group*   *55 wks*

3 Nov 84 **RED ROSES FOR ME** *Stiff SEEZ 55*	89	1 wk
17 Aug 85 **RUM, SODOMY AND THE LASH** *Stiff SEEZ 58*	13	14 wks
30 Jan 88 ● **IF I SHOULD FALL FROM GRACE WITH GOD** *Stiff NYR 1*	3	16 wks
29 Jul 89 ● **PEACE AND LOVE** *WEA WX 247*	5	8 wks
13 Oct 90 **HELL'S DITCH** *Pogue Mahone WX 366*	12	5 wks
12 Oct 91 **BEST OF THE POGUES** *Pogue Mahone WX 430*	11†	11 wks

Group was male/female for first two albums.

POINTER SISTERS *US, female vocal group*   *88 wks*

29 Aug 81 **BLACK AND WHITE** *Planet K 52300*	21	13 wks
5 May 84 ● **BREAK OUT** *Planet PL 84705*	9	58 wks
27 Jul 85 **CONTACT** *Planet PL 85457*	34	7 wks
29 Jul 89 **JUMP – THE BEST OF THE POINTER SISTERS** *RCA PL 90319*	11	10 wks

POISON *US, male vocal/instrumental group*   *34 wks*

21 May 88 **OPEN UP AND SAY . . . AAH!** *Capitol EST 2059*	18	21 wks
21 Jul 90 ● **FLESH AND BLOOD** *Enigma EST 2126*	3	11 wks
14 Dec 91 **SWALLOW THIS LIVE** *Capitol ESTU 2159*	52	2 wks

POLECATS *UK, male vocal/instrumental group*   *2 wks*

4 Jul 81 **POLECATS** *Vertigo 6359 057*	28	2 wks

POLICE *UK, male vocal/instrumental group*   *328 wks*

21 Apr 79 ● **OUTLANDOS D'AMOUR** *A & M AMLH 68502*	6	96 wks
13 Oct 79 ★ **REGGATTA DE BLANC** *A & M AMLH 64792*	1	74 wks
11 Oct 80 ★ **ZENYATTA MONDATTA** *A & M AMLH 64831*	1	31 wks
10 Oct 81 ★ **GHOST IN THE MACHINE** *A & M AMLK 63730*	1	27 wks

25 Jun 83 ★ **SYNCHRONICITY** *A&M AMLX 63735*	**1**	48 wks
8 Nov 86 ★ **EVERY BREATH YOU TAKE – THE SINGLES**		
A&M EVERY 1	**1**	52 wks

Su POLLARD *UK, female vocalist*   *3 wks*

22 Nov 86	**SU** *K-Tel NE 1327*	**86**	3 wks

Iggy POP *US, male vocalist*   *26 wks*

9 Apr 77	**THE IDIOT** *RCA Victor PL 12275*	**30**	3 wks
4 Jun 77	**RAW POWER** *Embassy 31464*	**44**	2 wks
1 Oct 77	**LUST FOR LIFE** *RCA PL 12488*	**28**	5 wks
19 May 79	**NEW VALUES** *Arista SPART 1092*	**60**	4 wks
16 Feb 80	**SOLDIER** *Arista SPART 1117*	**62**	2 wks
11 Oct 86	**BLAH-BLAH-BLAH** *A&M AMA 5145*	**43**	7 wks
2 Jul 88	**INSTINCT** *A&M AMA 5198*	**61**	1 wk
21 Jul 90	**BRICK BY BRICK** *Virgin America VUSLP 19*	**50**	2 wks

Raw Power *credited to Iggy and the Stooges.*

POP WILL EAT ITSELF
UK, male vocal/instrumental group   *5 wks*

13 May 89	**THIS IS THE DAY, THIS IS THE HOUR** *RCA PL 74141*	**24**	2 wks
2 Nov 90	**CURE FOR SANITY** *RCA PL 74828*	**33**	3 wks

Nick PORTLOCK – *See ROYAL PHILHARMONIC ORCHESTRA*

253

p

Sandy POSEY *US, female vocalist*   *1 wk*

11 Mar 67	**BORN A WOMAN** *MGM MGMCS 8035*	**39**	1 wk

Frank POURCEL *France, male vocalist*   *7 wks*

20 Nov 71 ● **THIS IS POURCEL** *Studio Two STWO 7*	**8**	7 wks

Cozy POWELL *UK, male instrumentalist – drums*   *8 wks*

26 Jan 80	**OVER THE TOP** *Ariola ARL 5038*	**34**	3 wks
19 Sep 81	**TILT** *Polydor POLD 5047*	**58**	4 wks
28 May 83	**OCTOPUSS** *Polydor POLD 5093*	**86**	1 wk

See also Emerson, Lake and Powell.

Peter POWELL *UK, male exercise instructor*   *13 wks*

20 Mar 82 ● **KEEP FIT AND DANCE** *K-Tel NE 1167*	**9**	13 wks

POWER STATION *UK/US, male vocal/instrumental group*   *23 wks*

6 Apr 85	**THE POWER STATION** *Parlophone POST 1*	**12**	23 wks

PRAYING MANTIS *UK, male vocal/instrumental group*   *2 wks*

11 Apr 81	**TIME TELLS NO LIES** *Arista SPART 1153*	**60**	2 wks

PREFAB SPROUT UK, male/female vocal/instrumental group 87 wks

17 Mar 84	**SWOON** Kitchenware KWLP 1	22	7 wks
22 Jun 85	**STEVE McQUEEN** Kitchenware KWLP 3	21	35 wks
26 Mar 88	● **FROM LANGLEY PARK TO MEMPHIS**		
	Kitchenware KWLP 9	5	24 wks
1 Jul 89	**PROTEST SONGS** Kitchenware KWLP 4	18	4 wks
8 Sep 90	● **JORDAN: THE COMEBACK** Kitchenware KWLP 14	7	17 wks

Elvis PRESLEY US, male vocalist 1026 wks

8 Nov 58	● **ELVIS' GOLDEN RECORDS** RCA RB 16069	3	44 wks
8 Nov 58	● **KING CREOLE (film soundtrack)** RCA RD 27086	4	14 wks
4 Apr 59	● **ELVIS (ROCK 'N' ROLL NO. 1)** HMV CLP 1093	4	9 wks
8 Aug 59	● **A DATE WITH ELVIS** RCA RD 27128	4	15 wks
18 Jun 60	★ **ELVIS IS BACK** RCA RD 27171	1	27 wks
18 Jun 60	● **ELVIS' GOLDEN RECORDS VOL. 2** RCA RD 27159	4	20 wks
10 Dec 60	★ **G.I. BLUES (film soundtrack)** RCA RD 27192	1	55 wks
20 May 61	● **HIS HAND IN MINE** RCA RD 27211	3	25 wks
4 Nov 61	● **SOMETHING FOR EVERYBODY** RCA RD 27224	2	18 wks
9 Dec 61	★ **BLUE HAWAII (film soundtrack)** RCA RD 27238	1	65 wks
7 Jul 62	★ **POT LUCK** RCA RD 27265	1	25 wks
8 Dec 62	● **ROCK 'N' ROLL NO. 2** RCA RD 7528	3	17 wks
26 Jan 63	● **GIRLS! GIRLS! GIRLS! (film soundtrack)** RCA RD 7534	2	21 wks
11 May 63	**IT HAPPENED AT THE WORLD'S FAIR (film soundtrack)**		
	RCA RD 7565	4	21 wks
28 Dec 63	● **FUN IN ACAPULCO (film soundtrack)** RCA RD 7609	9	14 wks
11 Apr 64	● **ELVIS' GOLDEN RECORDS VOL. 3** RCA RD 7630	6	13 wks
4 Jul 64	● **KISSIN' COUSINS (film soundtrack)** RCA RD 7645	5	17 wks
9 Jan 65	**ROUSTABOUT (film soundtrack)** RCA RD 7678	12	4 wks
1 May 65	● **GIRL HAPPY (film soundtrack)** RCA RD 7714	8	18 wks
25 Sep 65	**FLAMING STAR AND SUMMER KISSES** RCA RD 7723	11	4 wks
4 Dec 65	● **ELVIS FOR EVERYBODY** RCA RD 7782	8	8 wks
15 Jan 66	**HAREM HOLIDAY (film soundtrack)** RCA RD 7767	11	5 wks
30 Apr 66	**FRANKIE AND JOHNNY (film soundtrack)**		
	RCA RD 7793	11	5 wks
6 Aug 66	● **PARADISE HAWAIIAN STYLE (film soundtrack)**		
	RCA Victor RD 7810	7	9 wks
26 Nov 66	**CALIFORNIA HOLIDAY (film soundtrack)**		
	RCA Victor RD 7820	17	6 wks
8 Apr 67	**HOW GREAT THOU ART** RCA Victor SF 7867	11	14 wks
2 Sep 67	**DOUBLE TROUBLE (film soundtrack)**		
	RCA Victor SF 7892	34	1 wk
20 Apr 68	**CLAMBAKE (film soundtrack)** RCA Victor SD 7917	39	1 wk
3 May 69	● **ELVIS – NBC TV SPECIAL** RCA RD 8011	2	26 wks
5 Jul 69	● **FLAMING STAR** RCA International INTS 1012	2	14 wks
23 Aug 69	★ **FROM ELVIS IN MEMPHIS** RCA SF 8029	1	13 wks
28 Feb 70	**PORTRAIT IN MUSIC (import)** RCA 558	36	1 wk
14 Mar 70	● **FROM MEMPHIS TO VEGAS – FROM VEGAS TO**		
	MEMPHIS RCA SF 8080/1	3	16 wks
1 Aug 70	● **ON STAGE** RCA SF 8128	2	18 wks
5 Dec 70	**ELVIS' GOLDEN RECORDS VOL. 1 (re-issue)**		
	RCA SF 8129	21	11 wks
12 Dec 70	**WORLDWIDE 50 GOLD AWARD HITS VOL. 1**		
	RCA LPM 6401	49	2 wks
30 Jan 71	**THAT'S THE WAY IT IS** RCA SF 8162	12	41 wks
10 Apr 71	● **ELVIS COUNTRY** RCA SF 8172	6	9 wks
24 Jul 71	● **LOVE LETTERS FROM ELVIS** RCA SF 8202	7	5 wks
7 Aug 71	● **C'MON EVERYBODY** RCA International INTS 1286	5	21 wks
7 Aug 71	**YOU'LL NEVER WALK ALONE** RCA Camden CDM 1088	20	4 wks
25 Sep 71	**ALMOST IN LOVE** RCA International INTS 1206	38	2 wks
4 Dec 71	● **ELVIS' CHRISTMAS ALBUM** RCA International INTS 1126	7	5 wks
18 Dec 71	**I GOT LUCKY** RCA International INTS 1322	26	3 wks
27 May 72	**ELVIS NOW** RCA Victor SF 8266	12	8 wks
3 Jun 72	**ROCK AND ROLL (re-issue of ROCK 'N' ROLL NO. 1)**		
	RCA Victor SF 8233	34	4 wks
3 Jun 72	**ELVIS FOR EVERYONE** RCA Victor SF 8232	48	1 wk

254

p

15 Jul	72	●	**ELVIS AT MADISON SQUARE GARDEN**		
			RCA Victor SF 8296	3	20 wks
12 Aug	72		**HE TOUCHED ME** *RCA Victor SF 8275*	38	3 wks
24 Feb	73		**ALOHA FROM HAWAII VIA SATELLITE**		
			RCA Victor DPS 2040	11	10 wks
15 Sep	73		**ELVIS** *RCA Victor SF 8378*	16	4 wks
2 Mar	74		**A LEGENDARY PERFORMER VOL. 1**		
			RCA Victor CPLI 0341	20	3 wks
25 May	74		**GOOD TIMES** *RCA Victor APLI 0475*	42	1 wk
7 Sep	74		**ELVIS PRESLEY LIVE ON STAGE IN MEMPHIS**		
			RCA Victor APLI 0606	44	1 wk
22 Feb	75		**PROMISED LAND** *RCA Victor APLI 0873*	21	4 wks
14 Jun	75		**TODAY** *RCA Victor RS 1011*	48	3 wks
5 Jul	75	★	**40 GREATEST HITS** *Arcade ADEP 12*	1	38 wks
6 Sep	75		**THE ELVIS PRESLEY SUN COLLECTION**		
			RCA Starcall HY 1001	16	13 wks
19 Jun	76		**FROM ELVIS PRESLEY BOULEVARD, MEMPHIS,**		
			TENNESSEE *RCA Victor RS 1060*	29	5 wks
19 Feb	77		**ELVIS IN DEMAND** *RCA Victor PL 42003*	12	11 wks
27 Aug	77	●	**MOODY BLUE** *RCA PL 12428*	3	15 wks
3 Sep	77	●	**WELCOME TO MY WORLD** *RCA PL 12274*	7	9 wks
3 Sep	77		**G.I. BLUES (re-issue)** *RCA SF 5078*	14	10 wks
10 Sep	77		**ELVIS' GOLDEN RECORDS VOL. 2 (re-issue)**		
			RCA SF 8151	27	4 wks
10 Sep	77		**HITS OF THE 70'S** *RCA LPLI 7527*	30	4 wks
10 Sep	77		**BLUE HAWAII (re-issue)** *RCA SF 8145*	26	6 wks
10 Sep	77		**ELVIS' GOLDEN RECORDS VOL. 3 (re-issue)**		
			RCA SF 7630	49	2 wks
10 Sep	77		**PICTURES OF ELVIS** *RCA Starcall HY 1023*	52	1 wk
8 Oct	77		**THE SUN YEARS** *Charly SUN 1001*	31	2 wks
15 Oct	77		**LOVING YOU** *RCA PL 42358*	24	3 wks
19 Nov	77		**ELVIS IN CONCERT** *RCA PL 02578*	13	11 wks
22 Apr	78		**HE WALKS BESIDE ME** *RCA PL 12772*	37	1 wk
3 Jun	78		**THE '56 SESSIONS VOL. 1** *RCA PL 42101*	47	4 wks
2 Sep	78		**TV SPECIAL** *RCA PL 42370*	50	2 wks
11 Nov	78		**40 GREATEST HITS (re-issue)** *RCA PL 42691*	40	14 wks
3 Feb	79		**A LEGENDARY PERFORMER VOL. 3** *RCA PL 13082* ..	43	3 wks
5 May	79		**OUR MEMORIES OF ELVIS** *RCA PL 13279*	72	1 wk
24 Nov	79	●	**LOVE SONGS** *K-Tel NE 1062*	4	13 wks
21 Jun	80		**ELVIS PRESLEY SINGS LIEBER AND STOLLER**		
			RCA International 5031	32	5 wks
23 Aug	80		**ELVIS ARON PRESLEY** *RCA ELVIS 25*	21	4 wks
23 Aug	80		**PARADISE HAWAIIAN STYLE (re-issue)**		
			RCA International INTS 5037	53	2 wks
29 Nov	80	●	**INSPIRATION** *K-Tel NE 1101*	6	8 wks
14 Mar	81		**GUITAR MAN** *RCA RCALP 5010*	33	5 wks
9 May	81		**THIS IS ELVIS PRESLEY** *RCA RCALP 5029*	47	4 wks
28 Nov	81		**THE ULTIMATE PERFORMANCE** *K-Tel NE 1141*	45	6 wks
13 Feb	82		**THE SOUND OF YOUR CRY** *RCA RCALP 3060*	31	12 wks
6 Mar	82		**ELVIS PRESLEY EP PACK** *RCA EP1*	97	1 wk
21 Aug	82		**ROMANTIC ELVIS/ROCKIN' ELVIS**		
			RCA RCALP 1000/1	62	5 wks
18 Dec	82		**IT WON'T SEEM LIKE CHRISTMAS WITHOUT**		
			YOU *RCA INTS 5235*	80	1 wk
30 Apr	83		**JAILHOUSE ROCK/LOVE IN LAS VEGAS**		
			RCA RCALP 9020	40	2 wks
20 Aug	83		**I WAS THE ONE** *RCA RCALP 3105*	83	1 wk
3 Dec	83		**A LEGENDARY PERFORMER VOL. 4** *RCA PL 84848* .	91	1 wk
7 Apr	84		**I CAN HELP** *RCA PL 89287*	71	3 wks
21 Jul	84		**THE FIRST LIVE RECORDINGS**		
			RCA International PG 89387	69	2 wks
26 Jan	85		**20 GREATEST HITS VOLUME 2**		
			RCA International NL 89168	98	1 wk
25 May	85		**RECONSIDER BABY** *RCA PL 85418*	92	1 wk
12 Oct	85		**BALLADS** *Telstar STAR 2264*	23	17 wks
29 Aug	87	●	**PRESLEY – THE ALL TIME GREATEST HITS**		
			RCA PL 90100	4	20 wks
28 Jan	89		**STEREO '57 (ESSENTIAL ELVIS VOL. 2)**		
			RCA PL 90250	60	2 wks
21 Jul	90		**HITS LIKE NEVER BEFORE (VOL. 3)** *RCA PL 90486* ..	71	1 wk

255

p

1 Sep 90	THE GREAT PERFORMANCES	*RCA PL 82227*	**62**	1 wk
24 Aug 91	COLLECTORS GOLD	*RCA PL 90574*	**57**	1 wk

PRETENDERS
UK/US, male/female vocal/instrumental group   *136 wks*

19 Jan 80	★	PRETENDERS	*Real RAL 3*	**1**	35 wks
15 Aug 81	●	PRETENDERS II	*Real SRK 3572*	**7**	27 wks
21 Jan 84		LEARNING TO CRAWL	*Real WX 2*	**11**	16 wks
1 Nov 86	●	GET CLOSE	*WEA WX 64*	**6**	28 wks
7 Nov 87	●	THE SINGLES	*WEA WX 135*	**6**	25 wks
26 May 90		PACKED!	*WEA WX 346*	**19**	5 wks

PRETTY THINGS   *UK, male vocal/instrumental group*   *13 wks*

27 Mar 65	●	PRETTY THINGS	*Fontana TL 5239*	**6**	10 wks
27 Jun 70		PARACHUTE	*Harvest SHVL 774*	**43**	3 wks

Alan PRICE   *UK, male vocalist/instrumentalist – keyboards*   *10 wks*

8 Jun 74	●	BETWEEN TODAY AND YESTERDAY			
		Warner Bros. K 56032		**9**	10 wks

Charley PRIDE   *US, male vocalist*   *17 wks*

10 Apr 71		CHARLEY PRIDE SPECIAL	*RCA SF 8171*	**29**	1 wk
28 May 77		SHE'S JUST AN OLD LOVE TURNED MEMORY			
		RCA Victor PL 12261		**34**	2 wks
3 Jun 78		SOMEONE LOVES YOU HONEY	*RCA PL 12478*	**48**	2 wks
26 Jan 80	●	GOLDEN COLLECTION	*K-Tel NE 1056*	**6**	12 wks

Maxi PRIEST   *UK, male vocalist*   *34 wks*

6 Dec 86		INTENTIONS	*10 DIX 32*	**96**	1 wk
5 Dec 87		MAXI	*10 DIX 64*	**25**	15 wks
15 Jul 90		BONAFIDE	*10 DIX 92*	**11**	13 wks
9 Nov 91		BEST OF ME TEN	*DIX 111*	**23**	5 wks

PRIMAL SCREAM   *UK, male vocal/instrumental group*   *7 wks*

17 Oct 87		SONIC FLOWER GROOVE	*Elevation ELV 2*	**62**	1 wk
5 Oct 91	●	SCREAMADELICA	*Creation CRELP 076*	**8**	6 wks

PRIMITIVES   *UK, male/female vocal/instrumental group*   *13 wks*

9 Apr 88	●	LOVELY	*RCA PL 71688*	**6**	10 wks
2 Sep 89		LAZY 86–88	*Lazy 15*	**73**	1 wk
28 Oct 89		PURE	*RCA PL 74252*	**33**	2 wks

PRINCE   *US, male vocalist*   *255 wks*

21 Jul 84	●	PURPLE RAIN – MUSIC FROM THE MOTION PICTURE			
		Warner Bros. 9251101		**7**	83 wks
8 Sep 84		1999	*Warner Bros. 923720*	**30**	21 wks
4 May 85	●	AROUND THE WORLD IN A DAY	*Warner Bros. 92-5286-1*	**5**	20 wks
12 Apr 86	●	PARADE – MUSIC FROM 'UNDER THE CHERRY MOON'			
		Warner Bros. WX 39		**4**	26 wks

11 Apr	87	● SIGN 'O' THE TIMES *Paisley Park WX 88*	**4**	32 wks
21 May	88	★ LOVESEXY *Paisley Park WX 164*	**1**	30 wks
1 Jul	89	★ BATMAN *Warner Bros. WX 281*	**1**	20 wks
1 Sep	90	★ GRAFFITI BRIDGE *Paisley Park WX 361*	**1**	8 wks
24 Aug	91	GETT OFF (import) *Paisley Park 9401382*	**33**	3 wks
12 Oct	91	● DIAMONDS AND PEARLS *Paisley Park 7599253791*	**2†**	12 wks

Purple Rain, Around The World In A Day *and* Parade *credit The Revolution, US, male/female vocal/instrumental group.* Gett Off *(a 12-inch single) and* Diamonds and Pearls *credit the New Power Generation, US, male/female vocal/instrumental group.*

PRINCE CHARLES and the CITY BEAT BAND
US, male vocalist with male vocal/instrumental group   *1 wk*

30 Apr	83	STONE KILLERS *Virgin V 2271*	**84**	1 wk

PRINCESS *UK, female vocalist*   *14 wks*

17 May	86	PRINCESS *Supreme SU1*	**15**	14 wks

P.J. PROBY *US, male vocalist*   *3 wks*

27 Feb	65	I'M P.J. PROBY *Liberty LBY 1235*	**16**	3 wks

PROCLAIMERS *UK, male vocal/instrumental duo*   *48 wks*

9 May	87	THIS IS THE STORY *Chrysalis CHR 1602*	**43**	21 wks
24 Sep	88	● SUNSHINE ON LEITH *Chrysalis CHR 1668*	**6**	27 wks

PROCOL HARUM *UK, male vocal/instrumental group*   *11 wks*

19 Jul	69	A SALTY DOG *Regal Zonophone SLRZ 1009*	**27**	2 wks
27 Jun	70	HOME *Regal Zonophone SLRZ 1014*	**49**	1 wk
3 Jul	71	BROKEN BARRICADES *Island ILPS 9158*	**42**	1 wk
6 May	72	A WHITER SHADE OF PALE/A SALTY DOG (double re-issue) *Fly Double Back TOOFA 7/8*	**26**	4 wks
6 May	72	PROCOL HARUM IN CONCERT WITH THE EDMONTON SYMPHONY ORCHESTRA *Chrysalis CHR 1004*	**48**	1 wk
30 Aug	75	PROCOL'S NINTH *Chrysalis CHR 1080*	**41**	2 wks

A Whiter Shade Of Pale/A Salty Dog *is a double re-issue although* A Whiter Shade Of Pale *was not previously a hit. The Edmonton Symphony Orchestra is a Canadian orchestra.*

PROJECT D *UK, male instrumentalist*   *18 wks*

17 Feb	90	THE SYNTHESIZER ALBUM *Telstar STAR 2371*	**13**	18 wks

PROPAGANDA
Germany, male/female vocal/instrumental group   *16 wks*

13 Jul	85	A SECRET WISH *ZTT ZTTIQ 3*	**16**	12 wks
23 Nov	85	WISHFUL THINKING *ZTT ZTTIQ 20*	**82**	2 wks
9 Jun	90	1234 *Virgin V 2625*	**46**	2 wks

Dorothy PROVINE *US, female vocalist*   *49 wks*

2 Dec	61	● THE ROARING TWENTIES—SONGS FROM THE TV SERIES *Warner Bros. WM 4035*	**3**	42 wks
10 Feb	62	● VAMP OF THE ROARING TWENTIES *Warner Bros. WM 4053*	**9**	7 wks

Members of **Poison** are surrounded by fans at the Troubadour in Los Angeles.

It took a nation of fifty-five million to put **Public Enemy** into the top ten before their home country did.

PSYCHEDELIC FURS *UK, male vocal/instrumental group* *38 wks*

15 Mar 80	**PSYCHEDELIC FURS** *CBS 84084*	18	6 wks
23 May 81	**TALK TALK TALK** *CBS 84892*	30	9 wks
2 Oct 82	**FOREVER NOW** *CBS 85909*	20	6 wks
19 May 84	**MIRROR MOVES** *CBS 25950*	15	9 wks
14 Feb 87	**MIDNIGHT TO MIDNIGHT** *CBS 450 256–1*	12	4 wks
13 Aug 88	**ALL OF THIS AND NOTHING** *CBS 461101*	67	2 wks
18 Nov 89	**BOOK OF DAYS** *CBS 465982 1*	74	1 wk
13 Jul 91	**WORLD OUTSIDE** *East West WX 422*	68	1 wk

PUBLIC ENEMY *US, male rap group* *23 wks*

30 Jul 88 ●	**IT TAKES A NATION OF MILLIONS TO HOLD US BACK** *Def Jam 462415 1*	8	9 wks
28 Apr 90 ●	**FEAR OF A BLACK PLANET** *Def Jam 4662811*	4	10 wks
19 Oct 91 ●	**APOCALYPSE 91 – THE ENEMY STRIKES BLACK** *Def Jam 4687511*	8	4 wks

PUBLIC IMAGE LTD. *UK, male vocal/instrumental group* *49 wks*

23 Dec 78	**PUBLIC IMAGE** *Virgin V 2114*	22	11 wks
8 Dec 79	**METAL BOX** *Virgin METAL 1*	18	8 wks
8 Mar 80	**SECOND EDITION OF PIL** *Virgin VD 2512*	46	2 wks
22 Nov 80	**PARIS IN THE SPRING** *Virgin V 2183*	61	2 wks
18 Apr 81	**FLOWERS OF ROMANCE** *Virgin V 2189*	11	5 wks
8 Oct 83	**LIVE IN TOKYO** *Virgin VGD 3508*	28	6 wks
21 Jul 84	**THIS IS WHAT YOU WANT . . . THIS IS WHAT YOU GET** *Virgin V 2309*	56	2 wks
15 Feb 86	**ALBUM/CASSETTE** *Virgin V 2366*	14	6 wks
26 Sep 87	**HAPPY?** *Virgin V 2455*	40	2 wks
10 Jun 89	**9** *Virgin V 2588*	36	2 wks
10 Nov 90	**THE GREATEST HITS SO FAR** *Virgin V 2644*	20	3 wks

Gary PUCKETT and the UNION GAP
US, male vocalist, male vocal/instrumental group *4 wks*

29 Jun 68	**UNION GAP** *CBS 63342*	24	4 wks

259

q

q

Q-TIPS *UK, male vocal/instrumental group* *1 wk*

30 Aug 80	**Q-TIPS** *Chrysalis CHR 1255*	50	1 wk

Suzi QUATRO *US, female vocalist/instrumentalist – guitar* *13 wks*

13 Oct 73	**SUZI QUATRO** *RAK SRAK 505*	32	4 wks
26 Apr 80 ●	**SUZI QUATRO'S GREATEST HITS** *RAK EMTV 24*	4	9 wks

QUEDO BRASS – *See CHAQUITO ORCHESTRA*

QUEEN UK, male vocal/instrumental group   890 wks

23 Mar 74	● **QUEEN 2** *EMI EMA 767*	....	5	29 wks
30 Mar 74	● **QUEEN** *EMI EMC 3006*	....	24	18 wks
23 Nov 74	● **SHEER HEART ATTACK** *EMI EMC 3061*	....	2	42 wks
13 Dec 75	★ **A NIGHT AT THE OPERA** *EMI EMTC 103*	....	1	50 wks
25 Dec 76	★ **A DAY AT THE RACES** *EMI EMTC 104*	....	1	24 wks
12 Nov 77	● **NEWS OF THE WORLD** *EMI EMA 784*	....	4	20 wks
25 Nov 78	● **JAZZ** *EMI EMA 788*	....	2	27 wks
7 Jul 79	● **LIVE KILLERS** *EMI EMSP 330*	....	3	27 wks
12 Jul 80	★ **THE GAME** *EMI EMA 795*	....	1	18 wks
20 Dec 80	● **FLASH GORDON (film soundtrack)** *EMI EMC 3351*	...	10	15 wks
7 Nov 81	★ **GREATEST HITS** *EMI EMTV 30*	....	1	338 wks
15 May 82	● **HOT SPACE** *EMI EMA 797*	....	4	19 wks
10 Mar 84	● **THE WORKS** *EMI EMC 240014*	....	2	93 wks
14 Jun 86	★ **A KIND OF MAGIC** *EMI EU 3509*	....	1	63 wks
13 Dec 86	● **LIVE MAGIC** *EMI EMC 3519*	★★★★★★★★★★★★★★★★	3	43 wks
3 Jun 89	★ **THE MIRACLE** *Parlophone PCSD 107*	....	1†	32 wks
16 Dec 89	**QUEEN AT THE BEEB** *Band Of Joy BOJLP 001*	....	67	1 wk
16 Feb 91	★ **INNUENDO** *Parlophone PCSD 115*	....	1†	23 wks
9 Nov 91	★ **GREATEST HITS II** *Parlophone PMTV 2*	....	1†	8 wks

The Works *changed label number during its run to EMI WORK 1.*

QUEENSRYCHE US, male vocal/instrumental group   8 wks

29 Sep 84	**THE WARNING** *EMI America EJ 2402201*	....	100	1 wk
26 Jul 86	**RAGE FOR ORDER** *EMI America AML 3105*	....	66	1 wk
4 Jun 88	**OPERATION MINDCRIME** *Manhattan MTL 1023*	......	58	3 wks
22 Sep 90	**EMPIRE** *EMI-USA MTL 1058*	....	13	3 wks

QUIET RIOT US, male vocal/instrumental group   1 wk

4 Aug 84	**CONDITION CRITICAL** *Epic EPC 26075*	....	71	1 wk

QUINTESSENCE
UK/Australia, male vocal/instrumental group   6 wks

27 Jun 70	**QUINTESSENCE** *Island ILPS 9128*	....	22	4 wks
3 Apr 71	**DIVE DEEP** *Island ILPS 9143*	....	43	1 wk
27 May 72	**SELF** *RCA Victor SF 8273*	....	50	1 wk

QUIREBOYS UK, male vocal/instrumental group   15 wks

10 Feb 90	● **A BIT OF WHAT YOU FANCY** *Parlophone PCS 7335*	....	2	15 wks

QUIVER – *See SUTHERLAND BROTHERS and QUIVER*

r

Harry RABINOWITZ – *See ROYAL PHILHARMONIC ORCHESTRA*

RACING CARS UK, male vocal/instrumental group   6 wks

19 Feb 77	**DOWNTOWN TONIGHT** *Chrysalis CHR 1099*	....	39	6 wks

Gerry RAFFERTY *UK, male vocalist* *78 wks*

25 Feb	78	● **CITY TO CITY** *United Artists UAS 30104*	6	37 wks
2 Jun	79	● **NIGHT OWL** *United Artists UAK 30238*	9	24 wks
26 Apr	80	**SNAKES AND LADDERS** *United Artists UAK 30298*	15	9 wks
25 Sep	82	**SLEEPWALKING** *Liberty LBG 30352*	39	4 wks
21 May	88	**NORTH AND SOUTH** *London LONLP 55*	43	4 wks

RAGGA TWINS *UK, male vocal/instrumental duo* *5 wks*

1 Jun	91	**REGGAE OWES ME MONEY** *Shut Up And Dance SUADLP 2*	26	5 wks

RAH BAND *UK, male/female vocal/instrumental group* *6 wks*

6 Apr	85	**MYSTERY** *RCA PL 70640*	60	6 wks

RAILWAY CHILDREN
UK, male vocal/instrumental group *3 wks*

21 May	88	**RECURRENCE** *Virgin V 2525*	96	1 wk
16 Mar	91	**NATIVE PLACE** *Virgin V 2627*	59	2 wks

RAIN TREE CROW *UK, male vocal/instrumental group* *3 wks*

20 Apr	91	**RAIN TREE CROW** *Virgin V 2659*	24	3 wks

RAINBOW *UK, male vocal/instrumental group* *163 wks*

13 Sep	75	**RITCHIE BLACKMORE'S RAINBOW**		
		Oyster OYA 2001	11	6 wks
5 Jun	76	**RAINBOW RISING** *Polydor 2490 137*	11	33 wks
30 Jul	77	● **ON STAGE** *Polydor 2657 016*	7	10 wks
6 May	78	● **LONG LIVE ROCK 'N' ROLL** *Polydor POLD 5002*	7	12 wks
18 Aug	79	● **DOWN TO EARTH** *Polydor POLD 5023*	6	37 wks
21 Feb	81	● **DIFFICULT TO CURE** *Polydor POLD 5036*	3	22 wks
8 Aug	81	**RITCHIE BLACKMORE'S RAINBOW (re-issue)**		
		Polydor 2490 141	91	2 wks
21 Nov	81	**BEST OF RAINBOW** *Polydor POLDV 2*	14	17 wks
24 Apr	82	● **STRAIGHT BETWEEN THE EYES** *Polydor POLD 5056* .	5	14 wks
17 Sep	83	**BENT OUT OF SHAPE** *Polydor POLD 5116*	11	6 wks
8 Mar	86	**FINYL VINYL** *Polydor PODV 8*	31	4 wks

First two albums and re-issue of first album credited to Ritchie Blackmore's Rainbow.

RAIN PARADE *US, male vocal/instrumental group* *1 wk*

29 Jun	85	**BEYOND THE SUNSET** *Island IMA 17*	78	1 wk

Bonnie RAITT *US, female vocalist/instrumentalist – guitar* *8 wks*

28 Apr	90	**NICK OF TIME** *Capitol EST 2095*	51	5 wks
6 Jul	91	**LUCK OF THE DRAW** *Capitol EST 2145*	38	3 wks

RAKIM – *See Eric B. and RAKIM*

His colleagues played the top ten albums, but **Peter Powell** was the only Radio 1 DJ to make one.

Below left: Television vamp **Dorothy Provine** roared into the top ten twice in a three-month period.

The **Pretty Things** look unimpressed by their self-titled success.

The **Quireboys**: excess all areas.

City to City contained the full-length version of the classic 'Baker Street' by **Gerry Rafferty**.

RAMONES US, male vocal/instrumental group   28 wks

23 Apr 77	LEAVE HOME Philips 9103 254	45	1 wk
24 Dec 77	ROCKET TO RUSSIA Sire 9103 255	60	2 wks
7 Oct 78	ROAD TO RUIN Sire SRK 6063	32	2 wks
16 Jun 79	IT'S ALIVE Sire SRK 26074	27	8 wks
19 Jan 80	END OF THE CENTURY Sire SRK 6077	14	8 wks
26 Jan 85	TOO TOUGH TO DIE Beggars Banquet BEGA 59	63	3 wks
31 May 86	ANIMAL BOY Beggars Banquet BEGA 70	38	2 wks
10 Oct 87	HALFWAY TO SANITY Beggars Banquet BEGA 89	78	1 wk
19 Aug 89	BRAIN DRAIN Chrysalis CHR 1725	75	1 wk

RANGE – See Bruce HORNSBY and the RANGE

Shabba RANKS UK, male rapper   2 wks

| 22 Jun 91 | AS RAW AS EVER Epic 4681021 | 51 | 2 wks |

Roland RAT SUPERSTAR UK, male rat vocalist   3 wks

| 15 Dec 84 | THE CASSETTE OF THE ALBUM Rodent RATL 1001 | 67 | 3 wks |

RATT US, male vocal/instrumental group   5 wks

13 Jul 85	INVASION OF YOUR PRIVACY Atlantic 78–1257–1	50	2 wks
25 Oct 86	DANCING UNDERCOVER Atlantic 781 683–1	51	1 wk
12 Nov 88	REACH FOR THE SKY Atlantic 781929	82	1 wk
8 Sep 90	DETONATOR Atlantic 7567821271	55	1 wk

263

r

Mark RATTRAY UK, male vocalist   7 wks

| 8 Dec 90 | SONGS OF THE MUSICALS Telstar STAR 2458 | 46 | 7 wks |

RAVEN UK, male vocal/instrumental group   3 wks

| 17 Oct 81 | ROCK UNTIL YOU DROP Neat NEAT 1001 | 63 | 3 wks |

Simon RAYMOND – See Harold BUDD/Liz FRASER/Robin GUTHRIE/Simon RAYMOND

Chris REA UK, male vocalist   276 wks

28 Apr 79	DELTICS Magnet MAG 5028	54	3 wks
12 Apr 80	TENNIS Magnet MAG 5032	60	1 wk
3 Apr 82	CHRIS REA Magnet MAGL 5040	52	4 wks
18 Jun 83	WATER SIGN Magnet MAGL 5048	64	2 wks
21 Apr 84	WIRED TO THE MOON Magnet MAGL 5057	35	7 wks
25 May 85	SHAMROCK DIARIES Magnet MAGL 5062	15	14 wks
26 Apr 86	ON THE BEACH Magnet MAGL 5069	11	37 wks
26 Sep 87	● DANCING WITH STRANGERS Magnet MAGL 5071	2	46 wks
13 Aug 88	ON THE BEACH (re-issue) WEA WX 191	37	10 wks
29 Oct 88	● NEW LIGHT THROUGH OLD WINDOWS		
	WEA WX 200	5	49 wks
11 Nov 89	★ THE ROAD TO HELL WEA WX 317	1	69 wks
9 Mar 91	★ AUBERGE East West WX 407	1†	34 wks

REAL PEOPLE UK, male vocal/instrumental group   1 wk

| 18 May 91 | THE REAL PEOPLE Columbia 4680841 | 59 | 1 wk |

REAL THING *UK, male vocal/instrumental group*   *17 wks*

6 Nov 76	**REAL THING** *Pye NSPL 18507*	34	3 wks
7 Apr 79	**CAN YOU FEEL THE FORCE** *Pye NSPH 18601*	73	1 wk
10 May 80	**20 GREATEST HITS** *K-Tel NE 1073*	56	2 wks
12 Jul 86	**BEST OF THE REAL THING** *West Five NRT 1*	24	11 wks

REBEL MC *UK, male rapper*   *10 wks*

28 Apr 90	**REBEL MUSIC** *Desire LUVLP 5*	18	6 wks
13 Jul 91	**BLACK MEANING GOOD** *Desire LUVLP 12*	23	4 wks

REBEL ROUSERS – *See Cliff BENNETT and the REBEL ROUSERS*

Ivan REBROFF *USSR, male vocalist*   *4 wks*

16 Jun 90	**THE VERY BEST OF IVAN REBROFF** *BBC REB 778* ..	57	4 wks

RED BOX *UK, male vocal/instrumental duo*   *4 wks*

6 Dec 86	**THE CIRCLE AND THE SQUARE** *Sire WX 79*	73	4 wks

RED HOT CHILLI PEPPERS
US, male vocal/instrumental group   *3 wks*

12 Oct 91	**BLOOD SUGAR SEX MAGIK** *Warner Bros WX 441*	25	3 wks

RED NOISE – *See Bill NELSON*

Sharon REDD *US, female vocalist*   *5 wks*

23 Oct 82	**REDD HOTT** *Prelude PRL 25056*	59	5 wks

Otis REDDING *US, male vocalist*   *192 wks*

19 Feb 66	● **OTIS BLUE** *Atlantic ATL 5041*	6	21 wks
23 Apr 66	**SOUL BALLADS** *Atlantic ATL 5029*	30	1 wk
23 Jul 66	**SOUL ALBUM** *Atlantic 587–011*	22	9 wks
21 Jan 67	**OTIS REDDING'S DICTIONARY OF SOUL**		
	Atlantic 588–050	23	16 wks
21 Jan 67	● **OTIS BLUE (re-issue)** *Atlantic 587–036*	7	54 wks
29 Apr 67	**PAIN IN MY HEART** *Atlantic 587–042*	28	9 wks
10 Feb 68	● **HISTORY OF OTIS REDDING** *Volt S 418*	2	43 wks
30 Mar 68	**OTIS REDDING IN EUROPE** *Stax 589–016*	14	16 wks
1 Jun 68	★ **DOCK OF THE BAY** *Stax 231–001*	1	15 wks
12 Oct 68	**IMMORTAL OTIS REDDING** *Atlantic 588–113*	19	8 wks

See also Otis Redding and Carla Thomas.

Otis REDDING and Carla THOMAS
US, male/female vocal duo   *17 wks*

1 Jul 67	**KING AND QUEEN** *Atlantic 589–007*	18	17 wks

See also Otis Redding.

Helen REDDY *Australia, female vocalist* *27 wks*

8 Feb 75	FREE AND EASY *Capitol E-ST 11348*	17 9 wks
14 Feb 76 ●	THE BEST OF HELEN REDDY *Capitol E-ST 11467*	5 18 wks

REDSKINS *UK, male vocal/instrumental duo* *4 wks*

22 Mar 86	NEITHER WASHINGTON, NOR MOSCOW *Decca FLP 1*	31 4 wks

Dan REED NETWORK *US, male vocal/instrumental group* *6 wks*

4 Nov 89	SLAM *Mercury 8388681*	66 2 wks
27 Jul 91	THE HEAT *Mercury 8488551*	15 4 wks

Lou REED *US, male vocalist* *63 wks*

21 Apr 73	TRANSFORMER *RCA Victor LSP 4807*	13 25 wks
20 Oct 73 ●	BERLIN *RCA Victor RS 1002*	7 5 wks
16 Mar 74	ROCK 'N' ROLL ANIMAL *RCA Victor APL1 0472*	26 1 wk
14 Feb 76	CONEY ISLAND BABY *RCA Victor RS 1035*	52 1 wk
3 Jul 82	TRANSFORMER (re-issue) *RCA INTS 5061*	91 2 wks
9 Jun 84	NEW SENSATIONS *RCA PL 84998*	92 1 wk
24 May 86	MISTRIAL *RCA PL 87190*	69 1 wk
28 Jan 89	NEW YORK *Sire WX 246*	14 22 wks
7 Oct 89	RETRO *RCA PL 90389*	29 5 wks

See also Lou Reed and John Cale.

Lou REED and John CALE
US/UK, male vocal/instrumental duo *5 wks*

5 May 90	SONGS FOR DRELLA *Sire WX 345*	22 5 wks

See also Lou Reed.

Don REEDMAN – *See Jeff JARRATT and Don REEDMAN*

Jim REEVES *US, male vocalist* *381 wks*

28 Mar 64 ●	GOOD 'N' COUNTRY *RCA Camden CDN 5114*	10 35 wks
9 May 64 ●	GENTLEMAN JIM *RCA RD 7541*	3 23 wks
15 Aug 64 ●	A TOUCH OF VELVET *RCA RD 7521*	8 9 wks
15 Aug 64	INTERNATIONAL JIM REEVES *RCA RD 7577*	11 15 wks
22 Aug 64	HE'LL HAVE TO GO *RCA RD 27176*	16 4 wks
29 Aug 64	THE INTIMATE JIM REEVES *RCA RD 27193*	12 4 wks
29 Aug 64 ●	GOD BE WITH YOU *RCA RD 7636*	10 10 wks
5 Sep 64 ●	MOONLIGHT AND ROSES *RCA RD 7639*	2 52 wks
19 Sep 64	COUNTRY SIDE OF JIM REEVES *RCA Camden CDN 5100*	12 5 wks
26 Sep 64	WE THANK THEE *RCA RD 7637*	17 3 wks
28 Nov 64 ●	TWELVE SONGS OF CHRISTMAS *RCA RD 7663*	3 17 wks
30 Jan 65 ●	BEST OF JIM REEVES *RCA RD 7666*	3 47 wks
10 Apr 65	HAVE I TOLD YOU LATELY THAT I LOVE YOU *RCA Camden CDN 5122*	12 5 wks
22 May 65	THE JIM REEVES WAY *RCA RD 7694*	16 4 wks
5 Nov 66 ●	DISTANT DRUMS *RCA Victor RD 7814*	2 34 wks
18 Jan 69	A TOUCH OF SADNESS *RCA SF 7978*	15 5 wks
5 Jul 69 ★	ACCORDING TO MY HEART *RCA International INTS 1013*	1 14 wks
23 Aug 69	JIM REEVES AND SOME FRIENDS *RCA SF 8022*	24 4 wks
29 Nov 69	ON STAGE *RCA SF 8047*	13 4 wks
26 Dec 70	MY CATHEDRAL *RCA SF 8146*	48 2 wks

3 Jul 71 **JIM REEVES WRITES YOU A RECORD**
RCA SF 8176 .... 47 2 wks
7 Aug 71 ● **JIM REEVES' GOLDEN RECORDS**
RCA International INTS 1070 .... 9 21 wks
14 Aug 71 ● **THE INTIMATE JIM REEVES (re-issue)**
RCA International INTS 1256 .... 8 15 wks
21 Aug 71 **GIRLS I HAVE KNOWN** RCA International INTS 1140 ... 35 5 wks
27 Nov 71 ● **TWELVE SONGS OF CHRISTMAS (re-issue)**
RCA International INTS 1188 .... 3 6 wks
27 Nov 71 **A TOUCH OF VELVET (re-issue)**
RCA International INTS 1089 .... 49 2 wks
15 Apr 72 **MY FRIEND** RCA SF 8258 .... 32 5 wks
20 Sep 75 ★ **40 GOLDEN GREATS** Arcade ADEP 16 .... 1 25 wks
6 Sep 80 **COUNTRY GENTLEMAN** K-Tel NE 1088 .... 53 4 wks

Vic REEVES UK, male vocalist 7 wks

16 Nov 91 **I WILL CURE YOU** Sense SIGH 111 .... 16† 7 wks

Neil REID UK, male vocalist 18 wks

5 Feb 72 ★ **NEIL REID** Decca SKL 5122 .... 1 16 wks
2 Sep 72 **SMILE** Decca SKL 5136 .... 47 2 wks

R.E.M. US, male vocal/instrumental group 88 wks

28 Apr 84 **RECKONING** IRS A 7045 .... 91 2 wks
29 Jun 85 **FABLES OF THE RECONSTRUCTION**
IRS MIRF 1003 .... 35 3 wks
6 Sep 86 **LIFE'S RICH PAGEANT** IRS MIRG 1014 .... 43 4 wks
16 May 87 **DEAD LETTER OFFICE** IRS SP 70054 .... 60 2 wks
26 Sep 87 **DOCUMENT** MCA MIRG 1025 .... 28 3 wks
29 Oct 88 **EPONYMOUS** IRS MIRG 1038 .... 69 3 wks
19 Nov 88 **GREEN** Warner Bros. WX 234 .... 27 20 wks
23 Mar 91 ★ **OUT OF TIME** Warner Bros WX 404 .... 1† 41 wks
12 Oct 91 ● **THE BEST OF R.E.M.** IRS MIRH 1 .... 7† 10 wks

RENAISSANCE UK, male/female vocal/instrumental group 10 wks

21 Feb 70 **RENAISSANCE** Island ILPS 9114 .... 60 1 wk
19 Aug 78 **A SONG FOR ALL SEASONS** Warner Bros. K 56460 ..... 35 8 wks
2 Jun 79 **AZUR D'OR** Warner Bros. K 56633 .... 73 1 wk

RENATO Italy, male vocalist 14 wks

25 Dec 82 **SAVE YOUR LOVE** Lifestyle LEG 9 .... 26 14 wks

RENEGADE SOUNDWAVE
UK, male vocal/instrumental group 1 wk

24 Mar 90 **SOUNDCLASH** Mute STUMM 63 .... 74 1 wk

REO SPEEDWAGON
US, male vocal/instrumental group 36 wks

25 Apr 81 ● **HI INFIDELITY** Epic EPC 84700 .... 6 29 wks
17 Jul 82 **GOOD TROUBLE** Epic EPC 85789 .... 29 7 wks

REVOLUTION – *See PRINCE*

REZILLOS *UK, male/female vocal/instrumental group*   *15 wks*

5 Aug 78	CAN'T STAND THE REZILLOS *Sire WEA K 56530* ...	16	10 wks
28 Apr 79	MISSION ACCOMPLISHED BUT THE BEAT GOES ON		
	Sire SRK 6069	30	5 wks

Charlie RICH *US, male vocalist*   *28 wks*

23 Mar 74	● BEHIND CLOSED DOORS *Epic 65716*	4	26 wks
13 Jul 74	VERY SPECIAL LOVE SONGS *Epic 80031*	34	2 wks

Richie RICH *UK, male vocalist*   *1 wk*

22 Jul 89	I CAN MAKE YOU DANCE *Gee St. GEEA 3*	65	1 wk

RICH KIDS *UK, male vocal/instrumental group*   *1 wk*

7 Oct 78	GHOST OF PRINCES IN TOWERS *EMI EMC 3263* ...	51	1 wk

Cliff RICHARD *UK, male vocalist*   *717 wks*

18 Apr 59	● CLIFF *Columbia 33SX 1147*	4	31 wks
14 Nov 59	● CLIFF SINGS *Columbia 33SX 1192*	2	36 wks
15 Oct 60	● ME AND MY SHADOWS *Columbia 33SX 1261*	2	33 wks
22 Apr 61	● LISTEN TO CLIFF *Columbia 33SX 1320*	2	28 wks
21 Oct 61	★ 21 TODAY *Columbia 33SX 1368*	1	16 wks
23 Dec 61	★ THE YOUNG ONES (film soundtrack)		
	Columbia 33SX 1384	1	42 wks
29 Sep 62	● 32 MINUTES AND 17 SECONDS *Columbia 33SX 1431* ...	3	21 wks
26 Jan 63	★ SUMMER HOLIDAY (film soundtrack)		
	Columbia 33SX 1472	1	36 wks
13 Jul 63	● CLIFF'S HIT ALBUM *Columbia 33SX 1512*	2	19 wks
28 Sep 63	● WHEN IN SPAIN *Columbia 33SX 1541*	8	10 wks
11 Jul 64	● WONDERFUL LIFE (film soundtrack)		
	Columbia 33SX 1628	2	23 wks
9 Jan 65	ALADDIN (pantomime) *Columbia 33SX 1676*	13	5 wks
17 Apr 65	● CLIFF RICHARD *Columbia 33SX 1709*	9	5 wks
14 Aug 65	MORE HITS BY CLIFF *Columbia 33SX 1737*	20	1 wk
8 Jan 66	LOVE IS FOREVER *Columbia 33SX 1769*	19	1 wk
21 May 66	● KINDA LATIN *Columbia SX 6039*	9	12 wks
17 Dec 66	● FINDERS KEEPERS (film soundtrack)		
	Columbia SX 6079	6	18 wks
7 Jan 67	CINDERELLA (pantomime) *Columbia 33SCX 6103*	30	6 wks
15 Apr 67	DON'T STOP ME NOW ... *Columbia SCX 6133*	23	9 wks
11 Nov 67	GOOD NEWS *Columbia SCX 6167*	37	1 wk
1 Jun 68	CLIFF IN JAPAN *Columbia SCX 6244*	29	2 wks
16 Nov 68	ESTABLISHED 1958 *Columbia SCX 6282*	30	4 wks
12 Jul 69	● BEST OF CLIFF *Columbia SCX 6343*	5	17 wks
27 Sep 69	SINCERELY *Columbia SCX 6357*	24	3 wks
12 Dec 70	TRACKS 'N' GROOVES *Columbia SCX 6435*	37	2 wks
23 Dec 72	BEST OF CLIFF VOL. 2 *Columbia SCX 6519*	49	2 wks
19 Jan 74	TAKE ME HIGH (film soundtrack)		
	EMI EMC 3016	41	4 wks
29 May 76	● I'M NEARLY FAMOUS *EMI EMC 3122*	5	21 wks
26 Mar 77	● EVERY FACE TELLS A STORY *EMI EMC 3172*	8	10 wks
22 Oct 77	★ 40 GOLDEN GREATS *EMI EMTV 6*	1	19 wks
4 Mar 78	SMALL CORNERS *EMI EMC 3219*	33	5 wks
21 Oct 78	GREEN LIGHT *EMI EMC 3231*	25	3 wks
17 Feb 79	● THANK YOU VERY MUCH – REUNION CONCERT AT		
	THE LONDON PALLADIUM *EMI EMTV 15*	5	12 wks
15 Sep 79	● ROCK 'N' ROLL JUVENILE *EMI EMC 3307*	3	22 wks

267

r

13 Sep	80	● I'M NO HERO	EMI EMA 796	4	12 wks
4 Jul	81	★ LOVE SONGS	EMI EMTV 27	1	43 wks
26 Sep	81	● WIRED FOR SOUND	EMI EMC 3377	4	25 wks
4 Sep	82	● NOW YOU SEE ME, NOW YOU DON'T	EMI EMC 3415	4	14 wks
21 May	83	● DRESSED FOR THE OCCASION	EMI EMC 3432	7	17 wks
15 Oct	83	● SILVER	EMI EMC 1077871	7	24 wks
14 Jul	84	20 ORIGINAL GREATS	EMI CRS 1	43	6 wks
1 Dec	84	THE ROCK CONNECTION	EMI CLIF 2	43	5 wks
26 Sep	87	● ALWAYS GUARANTEED	EMI EMD 1004	5	25 wks
19 Nov	88	★ PRIVATE COLLECTION	EMI CRTV 30	1	26 wks
11 Nov	89	● STRONGER	EMI EMD 1012	7	21 wks
17 Nov	90	● FROM A DISTANCE...THE EVENT	EMI CRTV 31 ...	3	15 wks
30 Nov	91	● TOGETHER WITH CLIFF	EMI EMD 1028	10†	5 wks

The Shadows featured on all or some of the tracks of all albums up to and including Aladdin and the following subsequent albums: More Hits By Cliff, Love Is Forever, Finders Keepers, Cinderella, Established 1958, Best Of Cliff, Best Of Cliff Vol. 2, 40 Golden Greats, Thank You Very Much, Love Songs and 20 Original Greats. *Cliff credited to Cliff Richard and the Drifters, the original name used by the Shadows. See also the Shadows.*

Keith RICHARDS UK, male vocalist/instrumentalist – guitar 3 wks

15 Oct	88	TALK IS CHEAP	Virgin V 2554	37	3 wks

Lionel RICHIE US, male vocalist 293 wks

27 Nov	82	● LIONEL RICHIE	Motown STMA 8037	9	86 wks
29 Oct	83	★ CAN'T SLOW DOWN	Motown STMA 8041	1	154 wks
23 Aug	86	● DANCING ON THE CEILING	Motown ZL 72412	2	53 wks

268

r

Jonathan RICHMAN and the MODERN LOVERS
US, male vocal/instrumental group 3 wks

27 Aug	77	ROCK 'N' ROLL WITH THE MODERN LOVERS			
		Beserkeley BSERK 9	50	3 wks

RICHMOND STRINGS/MIKE SAMMES SINGERS
UK, orchestra/male/female vocal group 7 wks

19 Jan	76	MUSIC OF AMERICA	Ronco TRD 2016	18	7 wks

Sviatoslav RICHTER – See Herbert VON KARAJAN

Nelson RIDDLE ORCHESTRA – See Shirley BASSEY; Linda RONSTADT; Kiri TE KANAWA

RIDE UK, male vocal/instrumental group 5 wks

27 Oct	90	NOWHERE	Creation CRELP 074	11	5 wks

RIGHTEOUS BROTHERS US, male vocal duo 17 wks

1 Dec	90	THE VERY BEST OF THE RIGHTEOUS BROTHERS			
		Verve 8472481	11	17 wks

Mark RILEY – See MATT BIANCO

RIP RIG AND PANIC
UK/US, male/female vocal/instrumental group 3 wks

26 Jun	82	I AM GOLD	Virgin V 2228	67	3 wks

Minnie RIPERTON *US, female vocalist* 3 wks

| 17 May 75 | **PERFECT ANGEL** *Epic EPC 80426* .... | 33 | 3 wks |

Angela RIPPON *UK, female exercise instructor* 26 wks

| 17 Apr 82 | ● **SHAPE UP AND DANCE (VOL. II)** *Lifestyle LEG 2* ..... | 8 | 26 wks |

RIVER CITY PEOPLE
UK, male/female vocal/instrumental group 10 wks

| 25 Aug 90 | **SAY SOMETHING GOOD** *EMI EMCX 3561* .... | 23 | 9 wks |
| 2 Nov 91 | **THIS IS THE WORLD** *EMI EMC 3611* .... | 56 | 1 wk |

RIVER DETECTIVES *UK, male vocal/instrumental duo* 1 wk

| 23 Sep 89 | **SATURDAY NIGHT SUNDAY MORNING** *WEA WX 2955* .... | 51 | 1 wk |

David ROACH *UK, male vocalist/instrumentalist – saxophone* 1 wk

| 14 Apr 84 | **I LOVE SAX** *Nouveau Music NML 1006* ....:.. | 73 | 1 wk |

ROACHFORD *UK, male vocalist* 32 wks

| 23 Jul 88 | **ROACHFORD** *CBS 460630 1* .... | 18 | 27 wks |
| 18 May 91 | **GET READY** *Columbia 4681361* .... | 20 | 5 wks |

ROBBIE – *See SLY and ROBBIE*

Marty ROBBINS *US, male vocalist* 15 wks

| 13 Aug 60 | **GUNFIGHTER BALLADS** *Fontana TFL 5063* .... | 20 | 1 wk |
| 10 Feb 79 | ● **MARTY ROBBINS COLLECTION** *Lotus WH 5009* ..... | 5 | 14 wks |

Paddy ROBERTS *South Africa, male vocalist* 6 wks

| 26 Sep 59 | ● **STRICTLY FOR GROWN-UPS** *Decca LF 1322* .... | 8 | 5 wks |
| 17 Sep 60 | **PADDY ROBERTS TRIES AGAIN** *Decca LK 4358* ..... | 16 | 1 wk |

B.A. ROBERTSON *UK, male vocalist* 10 wks

| 29 Mar 80 | **INITIAL SUCCESS** *Asylum K 52216* .... | 32 | 8 wks |
| 4 Apr 81 | **BULLY FOR YOU** *Asylum K 52275* .... | 61 | 2 wks |

Robbie ROBERTSON *Canada, male vocalist* 14 wks

| 14 Nov 87 | **ROBBIE ROBERTSON** *Geffen WX 133* .... | 23 | 14 wks |
| 12 Oct 91 | **STORYVILLE** *Geffen GEF 24303* .... | 30 | 2 wks |

Smokey ROBINSON *US, male vocalist* 10 wks

| 20 Jun 81 | **BEING WITH YOU** *Motown STML 12151* .... | 17 | 10 wks |

See also Marvin Gaye and Smokey Robinson.

269

r

Tom ROBINSON BAND
UK, male vocal/instrumental group   *23 wks*

3 Jun	78	● **POWER IN THE DARKNESS** *EMI EMC 3226*	**4**	12 wks
24 Mar	79	**TRB2** *EMI EMC 3296*	**18**	6 wks
29 Sep	84	**HOPE AND GLORY** *Castaway ZL 70483*	**21**	5 wks

Hope And Glory credited simply to Tom Robinson.

ROCK GODDESS   *UK, female vocal/instrumental group*   *3 wks*

12 Mar	83	**ROCK GODDESS** *A&M AMLH 68554*	**65**	2 wks
29 Oct	83	**HELL HATH NO FURY** *A&M AMLX 68560*	**84**	1 wk

ROCKIN' BERRIES   *UK, male vocal/instrumental group*   *1 wk*

19 Jun	65	**IN TOWN** *Pye NPL 38013*	**15**	1 wk

ROCKPILE   *UK, male vocal/instrumental group*   *5 wks*

18 Oct	80	**SECONDS OF PLEASURE** *F-Beat XXLP 7*	**34**	5 wks

ROCKSTEADY CREW   *US, male/female vocal group*   *1 wk*

16 Jun	84	**READY FOR BATTLE** *Charisma RSC LP1*	**73**	1 wk

ROCKWELL   *US, male vocalist*   *5 wks*

25 Feb	84	**SOMEBODY'S WATCHING ME** *Motown ZL 72147*	**52**	5 wks

Clodagh RODGERS   *Ireland, female vocalist*   *1 wk*

13 Sep	69	**CLODAGH RODGERS** *RCA SF 8033*	**27**	1 wk

RODS   *US, male vocal/instrumental group*   *4 wks*

24 Jul	82	**WILD DOGS** *Arista SPART 1196*	**75**	4 wks

Kenny ROGERS   *US, male vocalist*   *93 wks*

18 Jun	77	**KENNY ROGERS** *United Artists UAS 30046*	**14**	7 wks
6 Oct	79	**THE KENNY ROGERS SINGLES ALBUM**		
		United Artists UAK 30263	**12**	22 wks
9 Feb	80	● **KENNY** *United Artists UAG 30273*	**7**	10 wks
31 Jan	81	**LADY** *Liberty LBG 30334*	**40**	5 wks
1 Oct	83	**EYES THAT SEE IN THE DARK** *RCA RCALP 6088*	**53**	19 wks
27 Oct	84	**WHAT ABOUT ME?** *RCA PL 85043*	**97**	1 wk
27 Jul	85	● **THE KENNY ROGERS STORY** *Liberty EMTV 39*	**4**	29 wks

ROLLING STONES   *UK, male vocal/instrumental group*   *688 wks*

25 Apr	64	★ **ROLLING STONES** *Decca LK 4805*	**1**	51 wks
23 Jan	65	★ **ROLLING STONES NO. 2** *Decca LK 4661*	**1**	37 wks
2 Oct	65	● **OUT OF OUR HEADS** *Decca LK 4733*	**2**	24 wks
23 Apr	66	★ **AFTERMATH** *Decca LK 4786*	**1**	28 wks
12 Nov	66	● **BIG HITS (HIGH TIDE AND GREEN GRASS)**		
		Decca TXS 101	**4**	43 wks

Date			Title		Pos	Weeks
28 Jan	67	●	**BETWEEN THE BUTTONS** *Decca SKL 4852*	3	22 wks
23 Dec	67	●	**THEIR SATANIC MAJESTIES REQUEST**		
			Decca TXS 103	3	13 wks
21 Dec	68	●	**BEGGARS BANQUET** *Decca SKL 4955*	3	12 wks
27 Sep	69	●	**THROUGH THE PAST DARKLY (BIG HITS VOL. 2)**		
			Decca SKL 5019	2	37 wks
20 Dec	69	★	**LET IT BLEED** *Decca SKL 5025*	1	29 wks
19 Sep	70	★	**'GET YOUR YA-YA'S OUT!'** *Decca SKL 5065*	1	15 wks
3 Apr	71	●	**STONE AGE** *Decca SKL 5084*	4	7 wks
8 May	71	★	**STICKY FINGERS** *Rolling Stones COC 59100*	1	25 wks
18 Sep	71		**GIMME SHELTER** *Decca SKL 5101*	19	5 wks
11 Mar	72		**MILESTONES** *Decca SKL 5098*	14	8 wks
10 Jun	72	★	**EXILE ON MAIN STREET** *Rolling Stones COC 69100*	1	16 wks
11 Nov	72		**ROCK 'N' ROLLING STONES** *Decca SKL 5149*	41	1 wk
22 Sep	73	★	**GOAT'S HEAD SOUP** *Rolling Stones COC 59101*	1	14 wks
2 Nov	74	●	**IT'S ONLY ROCK 'N' ROLL** *Rolling Stones COC 59103* ..	2	9 wks
28 Jun	75		**MADE IN THE SHADE** *Rolling Stones COC 59104*	14	12 wks
28 Jun	75		**METAMORPHOSIS** *Decca SKL 5212*	45	1 wk
29 Nov	75	●	**ROLLED GOLD – THE VERY BEST OF THE ROLLING**		
			STONES *Decca ROST 1/2*	7	50 wks
8 May	76	●	**BLACK AND BLUE** *Rolling Stones COC 59106*	2	14 wks
8 Oct	77	●	**LOVE YOU LIVE** *Rolling Stones COC 89101*	3	8 wks
5 Nov	77	●	**GET STONED** *Arcade ADEP 32*	8	15 wks
24 Jun	78	●	**SOME GIRLS** *Rolling Stones CUN 39108*	2	25 wks
5 Jul	80	★	**EMOTIONAL RESCUE** *Rolling Stones CUN 39111*	1	18 wks
12 Sep	81	●	**TATTOO YOU** *Rolling Stones CUNS 39114*	2	29 wks
12 Jun	82	●	**STILL LIFE (AMERICAN CONCERTS 1981)**		
			Rolling Stones CUN 39115	4	18 wks
31 Jul	82		**IN CONCERT** *(import) Decca (Holland) 6640 037*	94	3 wks
11 Dec	82		**STORY OF THE STONES** *K-Tel NE 1201*	24	12 wks
19 Nov	83	●	**UNDERCOVER** *Rolling Stones CUN 1654361*	3	18 wks
7 Jul	84		**REWIND 1971–1984 (THE BEST OF THE ROLLING**		
			STONES) *Rolling Stones 4501991*	23	18 wks
5 Apr	86	●	**DIRTY WORK** *Rolling Stones CUN 86321*	4	10 wks
23 Sep	89	●	**STEEL WHEELS** *CBS 4657521*	2	18 wks
7 Jul	90	●	**HOT ROCKS 1964–1971** *London 8201401*	3	16 wks
20 Apr	91	●	**FLASHPOINT** *Rolling Stones 4681351*	6	7 wks

ROMAN HOLIDAY   UK, *male vocal/instrumental group*   *3 wks*

22 Oct	83	**COOKIN' ON THE ROOF** *Jive HIP 9*	31	3 wks

RONDO VENEZIANO
UK, *male/female orchestral group*   *33 wks*

5 Nov	83	**VENICE IN PERIL** *Ferroway RON 1*	39	13 wks
10 Nov	84	**THE GENIUS OF VENICE** *Ferroway RON 2*	60	13 wks
9 Jul	88	**VENICE IN PERIL (re-issue)** *Fanfare RON 1*	34	7 wks

Mick RONSON   UK, *male vocalist/instrumentalist – guitar*   *10 wks*

16 Mar	74	●	**SLAUGHTER ON TENTH AVENUE**		
			RCA Victor APLI 0353	9	7 wks
8 Mar	75		**PLAY DON'T WORRY** *RCA Victor APLI 0681*	29	3 wks

Linda RONSTADT   US, *female vocalist*   *39 wks*

4 Sep	76	**HASTEN DOWN THE WIND** *Asylum K 53045*	32	8 wks
25 Dec	76	**GREATEST HITS** *Asylum K 53055*	37	9 wks
1 Oct	77	**SIMPLE DREAMS** *Asylum K 53065*	15	5 wks
14 Oct	78	**LIVING IN THE USA** *Asylum K 53085*	39	2 wks
8 Mar	80	**MAD LOVE** *Asylum K 52210*	65	1 wk
28 Jan	84	**WHAT'S NEW** *Asylum 96 0260*	31	5 wks
19 Jan	85	**LUSH LIFE** *Asylum 96-0387-1*	100	1 wk

11 Nov 89 **CRY LIKE A RAINSTORM – HOWL LIKE THE WIND**
Elektra EKT 76 .... **43** 8 wks

What's New and Lush Life credited to Linda Ronstadt with the Nelson Riddle Orchestra. Cry Like A Rainstorm features Aaron Neville. See also Dolly Parton/Linda Ronstadt/Emmylou Harris.

ROSE MARIE *UK, female vocalist*   *34 wks*

13 Apr 85	**ROSE MARIE SINGS JUST FOR YOU** *A1 RMTV 1*	**30** 13 wks
24 May 86	**SO LUCKY** *A1-Spartan RMLP 2*	**62** 3 wks
14 Nov 87	**SENTIMENTALLY YOURS** *Telstar STAR 2302*	**22** 11 wks
19 Nov 88	**TOGETHER AGAIN** *Telstar STAR 2333*	**52** 7 wks

ROSE ROYCE *US, male/female vocal/instrumental group*   *62 wks*

22 Oct 77	**IN FULL BLOOM** *Warner Bros. K 56394*	**18** 13 wks
30 Sep 78	● **STRIKES AGAIN** *Whitfield K 56257*	**7** 11 wks
22 Sep 79	**RAINBOW CONNECTION IV** *Atlantic K 56714*	**72** 2 wks
1 Mar 80	★ **GREATEST HITS** *Whitfield K RRTV 1*	**1** 34 wks
13 Oct 84	**MUSIC MAGIC** *Streetwave MKL 2*	**69** 2 wks

See also compilation albums – Dino.

ROSE TATTOO *Australia, male vocal/instrumental group*   *4 wks*

26 Sep 81	**ASSAULT AND BATTERY** *Carrere CAL 127*	**40** 4 wks

Diana ROSS *US, female vocalist*   *371 wks*

24 Oct 70	**DIANA ROSS** *Tamla Motown SFTML 11159*	**14** 5 wks
19 Jun 71	**EVERYTHING IS EVERYTHING**	
	Tamla Motown STML 11178	**31** 3 wks
9 Oct 71	● **I'M STILL WAITING** *Tamla Motown STML 11193*	**10** 11 wks
9 Oct 71	**DIANA** *Tamla Motown STMA 8001*	**43** 1 wk
11 Nov 72	**GREATEST HITS** *Tamla Motown STMA 8006*	**34** 10 wks
1 Sep 73	● **TOUCH ME IN THE MORNING**	
	Tamla Motown STML 11239	**7** 35 wks
27 Oct 73	**LADY SINGS THE BLUES** *Tamla Motown TMSP 1131*	**50** 1 wk
2 Mar 74	**LAST TIME I SAW HIM** *Tamla Motown STML 11255*	**41** 1 wk
8 Jun 74	**LIVE** *Tamla Motown STML 11248*	**21** 8 wks
27 Mar 76	● **DIANA ROSS** *Tamla Motown STML 12022*	**4** 26 wks
7 Aug 76	● **GREATEST HITS 2** *Tamla Motown STML 12036*	**2** 29 wks
19 Mar 77	**AN EVENING WITH DIANA ROSS**	
	Motown TMSP 6005	**52** 1 wk
4 Aug 79	**THE BOSS** *Motown STML 12118*	**52** 5 wks
17 Nov 79	● **20 GOLDEN GREATS** *Motown EMTV 21*	**2** 29 wks
21 Jun 80	**DIANA** *Motown STMA 8033*	**12** 32 wks
28 Mar 81	**TO LOVE AGAIN** *Motown STML 12152*	**26** 10 wks
7 Nov 81	**WHY DO FOOLS FALL IN LOVE** *Capitol EST 26733*	**17** 24 wks
21 Nov 81	**ALL THE GREAT HITS** *Motown STMA 8036*	**21** 31 wks
13 Feb 82	**DIANA ROSS** *Motown STML 12163*	**43** 6 wks
23 Oct 82	**SILK ELECTRIC** *Capitol EAST 27313*	**33** 12 wks
4 Dec 82	● **LOVE SONGS** *K-Tel NE 1200*	**5** 17 wks
19 Jul 83	**ROSS** *Capitol EST 1867051*	**44** 5 wks
24 Dec 83	● **PORTRAIT** *Telstar STAR 2238*	**8** 31 wks
6 Oct 84	**SWEPT AWAY** *Capitol ROSS 1*	**40** 5 wks
28 Sep 85	**EATEN ALIVE** *Capitol ROSS 2*	**11** 19 wks
30 May 87	**RED HOT RHYTHM 'N' BLUES** *EMI EMC 3532*	**47** 4 wks
27 May 89	**WORKIN' OVERTIME** *EMI EMD 1009*	**23** 4 wks
25 Nov 89	**GREATEST HITS LIVE** *EMI EMDC 1001*	**34** 6 wks
14 Dec 91	**THE FORCE BEHIND THE POWER** *EMI EMD 1023* ..	**11** 3 wks

See also Diana Ross and Marvin Gaye; Diana Ross and the Supremes with the Temptations; Diana Ross/ Michael Jackson/Gladys Knight/Stevie Wonder; Supremes. The two Diana albums and the three Diana Ross titles are all different.

Diana ROSS and Marvin GAYE

US, female/male vocal duo   45 wks

19 Jan	74	● **DIANA AND MARVIN** Tamla Motown STMA 8015	6	43 wks
29 Aug	81	**DIANA AND MARVIN (re-issue)** Motown STMS 5001 ..	78	2 wks

See also Marvin Gaye; Diana Ross.

Diana ROSS/Michael JACKSON/Gladys KNIGHT/Stevie WONDER US, female/male vocalists 10 wks

15 Nov	86	**DIANA ROSS. MICHAEL JACKSON. GLADYS KNIGHT. STEVIE WONDER. THEIR VERY BEST BACK TO BACK** PrioriTyV PTVR 2	21	10 wks

See also Diana Ross; Michael Jackson; Gladys Knight and the Pips; Stevie Wonder.

Diana ROSS and the SUPREMES with the TEMPTATIONS US, male/female vocal group 31 wks

25 Jan	69	★ **DIANA ROSS AND THE SUPREMES JOIN THE TEMPTATIONS** Tamla Motown STML 11096	1	15 wks
28 Jun	69	**TCB** Tamla Motown STML 11110	11	12 wks
14 Feb	70	**TOGETHER** Tamla Motown STML 11122	28	4 wks

See also Supremes; Temptations; Diana Ross.

ROSTAL and SCHAEFER UK, male instrumental duo 2 wks

14 Jul	79	**BEATLES CONCERTO** Parlophone PAS 10014	61	2 wks

Mstilav ROSTROPOVICH – see Herbert VON KARAJAN

David Lee ROTH US, male vocalist 30 wks

2 Mar	85	**CRAZY FROM THE HEAT** Warner Bros. 92–5222–1	91	2 wks
19 Jul	86	**EAT 'EM AND SMILE** Warner Bros. WX 56	28	9 wks
6 Feb	88	**SKYSCRAPER** Warner Bros. 925671 1	11	12 wks
26 Jan	91	● **A LITTLE AIN'T ENOUGH** Warner Bros WX 403	4	7 wks

Uli Jon ROTH and ELECTRIC SUN

Germany, male vocal/instrumental group   2 wks

23 Feb	85	**BEYOND THE ASTRAL SKIES** EMI ROTH 1	64	2 wks

Thomas ROUND – See June BRONHILL and Thomas ROUND

Demis ROUSSOS Greece, male vocalist 143 wks

22 Jun	74	● **FOREVER AND EVER** Philips 6325 021	2	68 wks
19 Apr	75	**SOUVENIRS** Philips 6325 201	25	18 wks
24 Apr	76	● **HAPPY TO BE** Philips 9101 027	4	34 wks
3 Jul	76	**MY ONLY FASCINATION** Philips 6325 094	39	6 wks
16 Apr	77	**THE MAGIC OF DEMIS ROUSSOS** Philips 9101 131	29	6 wks
28 Oct	78	**LIFE AND LOVE** Philips 9199 873	36	11 wks

ROXETTE Sweden, male/female vocal/instrumental duo 91 wks

17 Jun	89	● **LOOK SHARP!** EMI EMC 3557	4	53 wks
13 Apr	91	● **JOYRIDE** EMI EMD 1019	2†	38 wks

David Lee Roth scaled higher than his former group Van Halen.

In 1991 **Runrig** finally enjoyed some of their phenomenal Scottish success south of the border.

Roxette (Per Gessle and Marie Frederiksson) see double at the Amsterdam Rock Festival.

ROXY MUSIC UK, male vocal/instrumental group   293 wks

29 Jul	72	● ROXY MUSIC Island ILPS 9200		10	16 wks
7 Apr	73	● FOR YOUR PLEASURE Island ILPS 9232		4	27 wks
1 Dec	73	★ STRANDED Island ILPS 9252		1	17 wks
30 Nov	74	● COUNTRY LIFE Island ILPS 9303		3	10 wks
8 Nov	75	● SIREN Island ILPS 9344		4	17 wks
31 Jul	76	● VIVA ROXY MUSIC Island ILPS 9400		6	12 wks
19 Nov	77	GREATEST HITS Polydor 2302 073		20	11 wks
24 Mar	79	● MANIFESTO Polydor POLH 001		7	34 wks
31 May	80	★ FLESH AND BLOOD Polydor POLH 002		1	60 wks
5 Jun	82	★ AVALON EG EGLP 50		1	57 wks
19 Mar	83	THE HIGH ROAD (import) EG EGMLP 1		26	7 wks
12 Nov	83	ATLANTIC YEARS 1973–1980 EG EGLP 54		23	25 wks

See also Bryan Ferry and Roxy Music.

ROYAL LIVERPOOL PHILHARMONIC ORCHESTRA – *See Carl DAVIS and the ROYAL LIVERPOOL PHILHARMONIC ORCHESTRA*

ROYAL PHILHARMONIC ORCHESTRA
UK, orchestra   113 wks

23 Dec	78	CLASSIC GOLD VOL. 2 Ronco RTD 42032		31	4 wks
13 Jan	79	CLASSICAL GOLD Ronco RTV 42020		65	1 wk
19 Sep	81	● HOOKED ON CLASSICS K-Tel ONE 1146		4	43 wks
31 Jul	82	CAN'T STOP THE CLASSICS – HOOKED ON CLASSICS 2 K-Tel ONE 1173		13	26 wks
9 Apr	83	JOURNEY THROUGH THE CLASSICS – HOOKED ON CLASSICS 3 K-Tel ONE 1226		19	15 wks
8 Oct	83	LOVE CLASSICS Nouveau Music NML 1003		30	9 wks
10 Dec	83	THE BEST OF HOOKED ON CLASSICS K-Tel ONE 1266		51	6 wks
26 May	84	AS TIME GOES BY Telstar STAR 2240		95	2 wks
26 Nov	88	RHYTHM AND CLASSICS Telstar STAR 2344		96	1 wk
5 Oct	91	SERIOUSLY ORCHESTRAL Virgin RPOLP 1		31	6 wks

All albums conducted by Louis Clark, except Love Classics, by Nick Portlock, and As Time Goes By, by Harry Rabinowitz. See also Juan Martin; Andy Williams, with the Royal Philharmonic Orchestra; Sir Charles Groves; RPO & Chorus; Sarah Walker; Julian Lloyd Webber.

RUBETTES UK, male vocal/instrumental group   1 wk

10 May	75	WE CAN DO IT State ETAT 001		41	1 wk

David RUFFIN – *See Darryl HALL and John OATES*

Jimmy RUFFIN US, male vocalist   10 wks

13 May	67	THE JIMMY RUFFIN WAY Tamla Motown STML 11048		32	6 wks
1 Jun	74	GREATEST HITS Tamla Motown STML 11259		41	4 wks

RUFUS and Chaka KHAN
US, male instrumental group and female vocalist   7 wks

12 Apr	75	RUFUSIZED ABC ABCL 5063		48	2 wks
21 Apr	84	STOMPIN' AT THE SAVOY Warner Bros. 923679		64	5 wks

The first album gave Chaka Khan no separate billing. See also Chaka Khan.

RUMOUR – *See Graham PARKER and the RUMOUR*

Todd RUNDGREN US, male vocalist   9 wks

29 Jan	77	RA Bearsville K 55514		27	6 wks
6 May	78	HERMIT OF MINK HOLLOW Bearsville K 55521		42	3 wks

275

r

RUN D.M.C. US, male rap group   31 wks

| 26 Jul 86 | **RAISING HELL** Profile LONLP 21 .... | **41** | 26 wks |
| 4 Jun 88 | **TOUGHER THAN LEATHER** Profile LONLP 38 .... | **13** | 5 wks |

RUNRIG UK, male vocal/instrumental group   21 wks

26 Nov 88	**ONCE IN A LIFETIME** Chrysalis CHR 1695	**61**	2 wks
7 Oct 89	**SEARCHLIGHT** Chrysalis CHR 1713	**11**	4 wks
22 Jun 91 ●	**THE BIG WHEEL** Chrysalis CHR 1858	**4**	15 wks

RUSH Canada, male vocal/instrumental group   92 wks

8 Oct 77	**FAREWELL TO KINGS** Mercury 9100 042	**22**	4 wks
25 Nov 78	**HEMISPHERES** Mercury 9100 059	**14**	6 wks
26 Jan 80 ●	**PERMANENT WAVES** Mercury 9100 071	**3**	16 wks
21 Feb 81 ●	**MOVING PICTURES** Mercury 6337 160	**3**	11 wks
7 Nov 81 ●	**EXIT STAGE LEFT** Mercury 6619 053	**6**	14 wks
18 Sep 82 ●	**SIGNALS** Mercury 6337 243	**3**	9 wks
28 Apr 84 ●	**GRACE UNDER PRESSURE** Vertigo VERH 12	**5**	12 wks
9 Nov 85 ●	**POWER WINDOWS** Vertigo VERH 31	**9**	4 wks
21 Nov 87 ●	**HOLD YOUR FIRE** Vertigo VERH 47	**10**	4 wks
28 Jan 89	**A SHOW OF HANDS** Vertigo 836346	**12**	4 wks
9 Dec 89	**PRESTO** Atlantic WX 327	**27**	2 wks
13 Oct 90	**CHRONICLES** Vertigo CBTV 1	**42**	2 wks
14 Sep 91 ●	**ROLL THE BONES** Atlantic WX 436	**10**	4 wks

276

r

Jennifer RUSH US, female vocalist   43 wks

16 Nov 85 ●	**JENNIFER RUSH** CBS 26488	**7**	35 wks
3 May 86	**MOVIN'** CBS 26710	**32**	5 wks
18 Apr 87	**HEART OVER MIND** CBS 450 470-1	**48**	3 wks

Patrice RUSHEN US, female vocalist   17 wks

| 1 May 82 | **STRAIGHT FROM THE HEART** Elektra K 52352 ...... | **24** | 14 wks |
| 16 Jun 84 | **NOW** Elektra 960360 .... | **73** | 3 wks |

Martin RUSHENT – See LEAGUE UNLIMITED ORCHESTRA

Brenda RUSSELL US, female vocalist   4 wks

| 23 Apr 88 | **GET HERE** A&M AMA 5178 .... | **77** | 4 wks |

Leon RUSSELL US, male vocalist   1 wk

| 3 Jul 71 | **LEON RUSSELL AND THE SHELTER PEOPLE** | | |
| | A&M AMLS 65003 .... | **29** | 1 wk |

Mike RUTHERFORD
UK, male vocalist/instrumentalist – guitar   11 wks

| 23 Feb 80 | **SMALLCREEP'S DAY** Charisma CAS 1149 .... | **13** | 7 wks |
| 18 Sep 82 | **ACTING VERY STRANGE** WEA K 99249 .... | **23** | 4 wks |

See also Mike and the Mechanics.

RUTLES   UK, male vocal/instrumental group   11 wks

| 15 Apr 78 | **THE RUTLES** Warner Bros. K 56459 .... | 12 | 11 wks |

RUTS   UK, male vocal/instrumental group   10 wks

| 13 Oct 79 | **THE CRACK** Virgin V 2132 .... | 16 | 6 wks |
| 18 Oct 80 | **GRIN AND BEAR IT** Virgin V 2188 .... | 28 | 4 wks |

Second album credited to Ruts D.C.

S

S EXPRESS   UK, male/female vocal/instrumental group   9 wks

| 1 Apr 89 | ● **ORIGINAL SOUNDTRACK** Rhythm King LEFTLP 8 .... | 5 | 9 wks |

SAD CAFE   UK, male vocal/instrumental group   36 wks

1 Oct 77	**FANX TA RA** RCA PL 25101	56	1 wk
29 Apr 78	**MISPLACED IDEALS** RCA PL 25133	50	1 wk
29 Sep 79	● **FACADES** RCA PL 25249	8	23 wks
25 Oct 80	**SAD CAFE** RCA SADLP 4	46	5 wks
21 Mar 81	**LIVE** RCA SAD LP 5	37	4 wks
24 Oct 81	**OLE** Polydor POLD 5045	72	2 wks

SADE   UK, female/male vocal/instrumental group   146 wks

28 Jul 84	● **DIAMOND LIFE** Epic EPC 26044	2	98 wks
16 Nov 85	★ **PROMISE** Epic EPC 86318	1	31 wks
14 May 88	● **STRONGER THAN PRIDE** Epic 460497 1	3	17 wks

SAILOR   UK, male vocal/instrumental group   8 wks

| 7 Feb 76 | **TROUBLE** Epic EPC 69192 .... | 45 | 8 wks |

General SAINT – See Clint EASTWOOD and General SAINT

SAINT ETIENNE   UK, male/female vocal/instrumental group   3 wks

| 26 Oct 91 | **FOXBASE ALPHA** Heavenly HVNLP 1 .... | 34 | 3 wks |

ST. PAUL'S BOYS' CHOIR   UK, choir   8 wks

| 29 Nov 80 | **REJOICE** K-Tel NE 1064 .... | 36 | 8 wks |

Ryuichi SAKAMOTO
Japan, male composer/multi-instrumentalist   9 wks

| 3 Sep 83 | **MERRY CHRISTMAS MR LAWRENCE (film soundtrack)** Virgin V 2276 .... | 36 | 9 wks |

277

S

SALT 'N' PEPA US, female rap group 41 wks

6 Aug 88	**A SALT WITH A DEADLY PEPA**	FFRR FFRLP 3	19	27 wks
12 May 90	**BLACKS' MAGIC**	ffrr 8281641	70	1 wk
6 Jul 91	**A BLITZ OF SALT-N-PEPA HITS**	London 8282491	70	2 wks
19 Oct 91	● **GREATEST HITS**	ffrr 8282911	6†	11 wks

SALVATION ARMY UK, brass band 5 wks

24 Dec 77	**BY REQUEST**	Warwick WW 5038	16	5 wks

SAM and DAVE US, male vocal duo 20 wks

21 Jan 67	**HOLD ON I'M COMIN'**	Atlantic 588–045	35	7 wks
22 Apr 67	**DOUBLE DYNAMITE**	Stax 589–003	28	5 wks
23 Mar 68	**SOUL MAN**	Stax 589–015	32	8 wks

Richie SAMBORA US, male vocalist/instrumentalist – guitar 3 wks

14 Sep 91	**STRANGER IN THIS TOWN**	Mercury 8488951	20	3 wks

Mike SAMMES SINGERS – See RICHMOND STRINGS/Mike SAMMES SINGERS

SAMSON UK, male vocal/instrumental group 6 wks

26 Jul 80	**HEAD ON**	Gem GEMLP 108	34	6 wks

David SANBORN US, male instrumentalist – saxophone 1 wk

14 Mar 87	**A CHANGE OF HEART**	Warner Bros. 925 479–1	86	1 wk

SANTANA US, male vocal/instrumental group 206 wks

2 May 70	**SANTANA**	CBS 63815	26	11 wks
28 Nov 70	● **ABRAXAS**	CBS 64807	7	52 wks
13 Nov 71	● **SANTANA 3**	CBS 69015	6	14 wks
29 Nov 72	● **CARAVANSERAI**	CBS 65299	6	11 wks
8 Dec 73	● **WELCOME**	CBS 69040	8	6 wks
21 Sep 74	**GREATEST HITS**	CBS 69081	14	15 wks
30 Nov 74	**BARBOLETTA**	CBS 69084	18	5 wks
10 Apr 76	**AMIGOS**	CBS 86005	21	9 wks
8 Jan 77	**FESTIVAL**	CBS 86020	27	3 wks
5 Nov 77	● **MOONFLOWER**	CBS 88272	7	27 wks
11 Nov 78	**INNER SECRETS**	CBS 86075	17	16 wks
24 Mar 79	**ONENESS – SILVER DREAMS GOLDEN REALITY** CBS 86037		55	4 wks
27 Oct 79	**MARATHON**	CBS 86098	28	5 wks
20 Sep 80	**THE SWING OF DELIGHT**	CBS 22075	65	2 wks
18 Apr 81	**ZE BOP**	CBS 84946	33	4 wks
14 Aug 82	**SHANGO**	CBS 85914	35	7 wks
30 Apr 83	**HAVANA MOON**	CBS 25350	84	3 wks
23 Mar 85	**BEYOND APPEARANCES**	CBS 86307	58	3 wks
15 Nov 86	**VIVA! SANTANA – THE VERY BEST**	K-Tel NE 1338 ..	50	8 wks
14 Jul 90	**SPIRITS DANCING IN THE FLESH**	CBS 4669131	68	1 wk

Oneness – Silver Dreams Golden Reality, The Swing Of Delight and Havana Moon are all credited to Carlos Santana, US, male instrumentalist – guitar. See also Carlos Santana and Alice Coltrane; Carlos Santana and Mahavishnu John McLaughlin; Carlos Santana and Buddy Miles.

Carlos SANTANA and Alice COLTRANE

US, male/female instrumental duo   *1 wk*

2 Nov 74   **ILLUMINATIONS**   CBS 69063 ....   **40**   1 wk

See also Santana.

Carlos SANTANA and Mahavishnu John McLAUGHLIN *US, male instrumental duo*

     9 wks

28 Jul   73 ● **LOVE DEVOTION SURRENDER**   CBS 69037 ....   **7**   9 wks

See also Mahavishnu Orchestra; Santana.

Carlos SANTANA and Buddy MILES

US, male instrumental duo   *4 wks*

26 Aug 72   **CARLOS SANTANA AND BUDDY MILES LIVE**
          CBS 65142 ....   **29**   4 wks

See also Santana.

Peter SARSTEDT *UK, male vocalist*

     4 wks

15 Mar 69 ● **PETER SARSTEDT**   *United Artists SULP 1219* ....   **8**   4 wks

Telly SAVALAS *US, male vocalist*

     10 wks

22 Mar 75   **TELLY**   MCA MCF 2699 ....   **12**   10 wks

SAVOY BROWN *UK, male vocal/instrumental group*

     1 wk

28 Nov 70   **LOOKIN' IN**   *Decca SKL 5066* ....   **50**   1 wk

SAXON *UK, male vocal/instrumental group*

     97 wks

12 Apr 80 ● **WHEELS OF STEEL**   *Carrere CAL 115* ....   **5**   29 wks
15 Nov 80   **STRONG ARM OF THE LAW**   *Carrere CAL 120* ....   **11**   13 wks
 3 Oct 81 ● **DENIM AND LEATHER**   *Carrere CAL 128* ....   **9**   11 wks
22 May 82 ● **THE EAGLE HAS LANDED**   *Carrere CAL 157* ....   **5**   19 wks
26 Mar 83   **POWER AND THE GLORY**   *Carrere CAL 147* ....   **15**   9 wks
11 Feb 84   **CRUSADER**   *Carrere CAL 200* ....   **18**   7 wks
14 Sep 85   **INNOCENCE IS NO EXCUSE**   *Parlophone SAXON 2* ....   **36**   4 wks
27 Sep 86   **ROCK THE NATIONS**   *EMI EMC 3515* ....   **34**   3 wks
 9 Apr 88   **DESTINY**   *EMI EMC 3543* ....   **49**   2 wks

SAW DOCTORS *Ireland, male vocal/instrumental group*

     2 wks

8 Jun 91   **IF THIS IS ROCK AND ROLL I WANT MY OLD JOB**
          BACK   *Solid ROCK 7* ....   **69**   2 wks

Leo SAYER *UK, male vocalist*

     232 wks

 5 Jan 74 ● **SILVER BIRD**   *Chrysalis CHR 1050* ....   **2**   22 wks
26 Oct 74 ● **JUST A BOY**   *Chrysalis CHR 1068* ....   **4**   14 wks
20 Sep 75 ● **ANOTHER YEAR**   *Chrysalis CHR 1087* ....   **8**   9 wks
27 Nov 76 ● **ENDLESS FLIGHT**   *Chrysalis CHR 1125* ....   **4**   66 wks
22 Oct 77 ● **THUNDER IN MY HEART**   *Chrysalis CDL 1154* ....   **8**   16 wks
 2 Sep 78   **LEO SAYER**   *Chrysalis CDL 1198* ....   **15**   25 wks

31 Mar 79 ★ **THE VERY BEST OF LEO SAYER** *Chrysalis CDL 1222* ..	**1**	37 wks
13 Oct 79 **HERE** *Chrysalis CDL 1240*	**44**	4 wks
23 Aug 80 **LIVING IN A FANTASY** *Chrysalis CDL 1297*	**15**	9 wks
8 May 82 **WORLD RADIO** *Chrysalis CDL 1345*	**30**	12 wks
12 Nov 83 **HAVE YOU EVER BEEN IN LOVE** *Chrysalis LEOTV 1* ..	**15**	18 wks

Alexei SAYLE *UK, male comedian*   5 wks

17 Mar 84 **THE FISH PEOPLE TAPES** *Island IMA 9*	**62**	5 wks

Boz SCAGGS *US, male vocalist*   29 wks

12 Mar 77 **SILK DEGREES** *CBS 81193*	**37**	24 wks
17 Dec 77 **DOWN TWO, THEN LEFT** *CBS 86036*	**55**	1 wk
3 May 80 **MIDDLE MAN** *CBS 86094*	**52**	4 wks

SCARS *UK, male vocal/instrumental group*   3 wks

18 Apr 81 **AUTHOR AUTHOR** *Pre PREX 5*	**67**	3 wks

SCHAEFER – *See ROSTAL and SCHAEFER*

Michael SCHENKER GROUP
Germany/UK, male vocal/instrumental group   42 wks

6 Sep 80 ● **MICHAEL SCHENKER GROUP** *Chrysalis CHR 1302* ...	**8**	8 wks
19 Sep 81 **MICHAEL SCHENKER GROUP** (re-issue) *Chrysalis CHR 1336*	**14**	8 wks
13 Mar 82 ● **ONE NIGHT AT BUDOKAN** *Chrysalis CTY 1375*	**5**	11 wks
23 Oct 82 **ASSAULT ATTACK** *Chrysalis CHR 1393*	**19**	5 wks
10 Sep 83 **BUILT TO DESTROY** *Chrysalis CHR 1441*	**23**	5 wks
23 Jun 84 **ROCK WILL NEVER DIE** *Chrysalis CUX 1470*	**24**	5 wks

See also MSG.

SCHON – *See HAGAR, SCHON, AARONSON, SHRIEVE*

SCORPIONS *Germany, male vocal/instrumental group*   55 wks

21 Apr 79 **LOVE DRIVE** *Harvest SHSP 4097*	**36**	11 wks
3 May 80 **ANIMAL MAGNETISM** *Harvest SHSP 4113*	**23**	6 wks
10 Apr 82 **BLACKOUT** *Harvest SHVL 823*	**11**	11 wks
24 Mar 84 **LOVE AT FIRST STING** *Harvest SHSP 2400071*	**17**	6 wks
29 Jun 85 **WORLD WIDE LIVE** *Harvest SCORP 1*	**18**	8 wks
14 May 88 **SAVAGE AMUSEMENT** *Harvest SHSP 4125*	**18**	6 wks
17 Nov 90 **CRAZY WORLD** *Vertigo 8469081*	**27**	7 wks

SCOTLAND FOOTBALL WORLD CUP
SQUAD 1974 *UK, male football team vocalists*   9 wks

25 May 74 ● **EASY EASY** *Polydor 2383 282*	**3**	9 wks

Band of the SCOTS GUARDS *UK, military band*   2 wks

28 Jun 69 **BAND OF THE SCOTS GUARDS** *Fontana SFXL 54*	**25**	2 wks

Jack SCOTT *Canada, male vocalist*   12 wks

7 May 60 ● **I REMEMBER HANK WILLIAMS** *Top Rank BUY 034* ...	**7**	11 wks
3 Sep 60 **WHAT IN THE WORLD'S COME OVER YOU** *Top Rank 25/024*	**11**	1 wk

280

S

SCREAMING BLUE MESSIAHS
UK, male vocal/instrumental group   *1 wk*

| 17 May 86 | **GUN-SHY** *WEA WX 41* .... | 90 | 1 wk |

SCRITTI POLITTI *UK, male vocal/instrumental group*   *37 wks*

11 Sep 82	**SONGS TO REMEMBER** *Rough Trade ROUGH 20*	12	7 wks
22 Jun 85	● **CUPID AND PSYCHE 85** *Virgin V 2350*	5	19 wks
18 Jun 88	● **PROVISION** *Virgin V 2515*	8	11 wks

SEAL *UK, male vocalist*   *31 wks*

| 1 Jun 91 | ★ **SEAL** *ZTT ZTT 9* .... | 1† | 31 wks |

SEARCHERS *UK, male vocal/instrumental group*   *87 wks*

10 Aug 63	● **MEET THE SEARCHERS** *Pye NPL 18086*	2	44 wks
16 Nov 63	● **SUGAR AND SPICE** *Pye NPL 18089*	5	21 wks
30 May 64	● **IT'S THE SEARCHERS** *Pye NPL 18092*	4	17 wks
27 Mar 65	● **SOUNDS LIKE THE SEARCHERS** *Pye NPL 18111*	8	5 wks

Harry SECOMBE *UK, male vocalist*   *56 wks*

31 Mar 62	**SACRED SONGS** *Philips RBL 7501*	16	1 wk
22 Apr 67	● **SECOMBE'S PERSONAL CHOICE** *Philips BETS 707* ...	6	13 wks
7 Aug 71	**IF I RULED THE WORLD** *Contour 6870 501*	17	20 wks
16 Dec 78	● **20 SONGS OF JOY** *Warwick WW 5052*	8	12 wks
13 Dec 86	**HIGHWAY OF LIFE** *Telstar STAR 2289*	45	5 wks
30 Nov 91	**YOURS SINCERELY** *Philips 5107321*	46†	5 wks

See also Harry Secombe and Moira Anderson; Harry Secombe, Peter Sellers and Spike Milligan.

Harry SECOMBE and Moira ANDERSON
UK, male/female vocal duo   *5 wks*

| 5 Dec 81 | **GOLDEN MEMORIES** *Warwick WW 5107* .... | 46 | 5 wks |

See also Harry Secombe; Moira Anderson.

Harry SECOMBE, Peter SELLERS and Spike MILLIGAN *UK, male comedy group*   *1 wk*

| 18 Apr 64 | **HOW TO WIN AN ELECTION** *Philips AL 3464* .... | 20 | 1 wk |

See also Harry Secombe; Peter Sellers; Spike Milligan.

SECOND IMAGE *UK, male vocal/instrumental group*   *1 wk*

| 30 Mar 85 | **STRANGE REFLECTIONS** *MCA MCF 3255* .... | 100 | 1 wk |

SECRET AFFAIR *UK, male vocal/instrumental group*   *15 wks*

1 Dec 79	**GLORY BOYS** *I-Spy 1*	41	8 wks
20 Sep 80	**BEHIND CLOSED DOORS** *I-Spy 2*	48	4 wks
13 Mar 82	**BUSINESS AS USUAL** *I-Spy 3*	84	3 wks

281

S

Neil SEDAKA *US, male vocalist* *61 wks*

1 Sep	73	THE TRA-LA DAYS ARE OVER *MGM 2315 248*	13	10 wks
22 Jun	74	LAUGHTER IN THE RAIN *Polydor 2383 265*	17	10 wks
23 Nov	74	LIVE AT THE ROYAL FESTIVAL HALL		
		Polydor 2383 299	48	1 wk
1 Mar	75	OVERNIGHT SUCCESS *Polydor 2442 131*	31	6 wks
10 Jul	76	● LAUGHTER AND TEARS – THE BEST OF NEIL SEDAKA		
		TODAY *Polydor 2383 399*	2	25 wks
2 Nov	91	● TIMELESS – THE VERY BEST OF NEIL SEDAKA		
		Polydor 5114421	10†	9 wks

SEEKERS *Australia, male/female vocal group* *268 wks*

3 Jul	65	● A WORLD OF OUR OWN *Columbia 33SX 1722*	5	36 wks
3 Jul	65	THE SEEKERS *Decca LK 4694*	16	1 wk
19 Nov	66	● COME THE DAY *Columbia SX 6093*	3	67 wks
25 Nov	67	SEEKERS – SEEN IN GREEN *Columbia SCX 6193*	15	10 wks
14 Sep	68	● LIVE AT THE TALK OF THE TOWN *Columbia SCX 6278*	2	29 wks
16 Nov	68	★ BEST OF THE SEEKERS *Columbia SCX 6268*	1	125 wks

Bob SEGER and the SILVER BULLET BAND
US, male vocal/instrumental group *40 wks*

3 Jun	78	STRANGER IN TOWN *Capitol EAST 11698*	31	6 wks
15 Mar	80	AGAINST THE WIND *Capitol EAST 12041*	26	6 wks
26 Sep	81	NINE TONIGHT *Capitol ESTSP 23*	24	10 wks
8 Jan	83	THE DISTANCE *Capitol EST 12254*	45	10 wks
26 Apr	86	LIKE A ROCK *Capitol EST 2011*	35	6 wks
21 Sep	91	THE FIRE INSIDE *Capitol EST 2149*	54	2 wks

282

S

SELECTER *UK, male/female vocal/instrumental group* *17 wks*

23 Feb	80	● TOO MUCH PRESSURE *2-Tone CDL TT 5002*	5	13 wks
7 Mar	81	CELEBRATE THE BULLET *Chrysalis CHR 1306*	41	4 wks

Peter SELLERS *UK, male vocalist* *84 wks*

14 Feb	59	● THE BEST OF SELLERS *Parlophone PMD 1069*	3	47 wks
12 Dec	59	● SONGS FOR SWINGING SELLERS *Parlophone PMC 1111*	3	37 wks

See also Peter Sellers and Sophia Loren; Harry Secombe, Peter Sellers and Spike Milligan; Anthony Newley, Peter Sellers, Joan Collins.

Peter SELLERS and Sophia LOREN
UK/Italy, male/female vocal duo *18 wks*

3 Dec	60	● PETER AND SOPHIA *Parlophone PMC 1131*	5	18 wks

See also Peter Sellers.

SENSATIONAL ALEX HARVEY BAND
UK, male vocal/instrumental group *42 wks*

26 Oct	74	THE IMPOSSIBLE DREAM *Vertigo 6360 112*	16	4 wks
10 May	75	● TOMORROW BELONGS TO ME *Vertigo 9102 003*	9	10 wks
23 Aug	75	NEXT *Vertigo 6360 103*	37	5 wks
27 Sep	75	SENSATIONAL ALEX HARVEY BAND LIVE		
		Vertigo 6360 122	14	7 wks

| 10 Apr 76 | **PENTHOUSE TAPES** *Vertigo 9102 007* .... | **14** | 7 wks |
| 31 Jul 76 | **SAHB STORIES** *Mountain TOPS 112* .... | **11** | 9 wks |

SENSELESS THINGS UK, *male vocal/instrumental group* *1 wk*

| 26 Oct 91 | **THE FIRST OF TOO MANY** *Epic 4691571* .... | **66** | 1 wk |

SEPULTURA Brazil, *male vocal/instrumental group* *2 wks*

| 6 Apr 91 | **ARISE** *Roadracer RO 93281* .... | **40** | 2 wks |

Taja SEVELLE US, *female vocalist* *4 wks*

| 26 Mar 88 | **TAJA SEVELLE** *Paisley Park WX 165* .... | **48** | 4 wks |

SEX PISTOLS UK, *male vocal/instrumental group* *97 wks*

12 Nov 77	★ **NEVER MIND THE BOLLOCKS HERE'S THE SEX** **PISTOLS** *Virgin V 2086*	**1**	48 wks
10 Mar 79	● **THE GREAT ROCK 'N' ROLL SWINDLE** *Virgin VD 2410*	**7**	33 wks
11 Aug 79	● **SOME PRODUCT – CARRI ON SEX PISTOLS** *Virgin VR 2*	**6**	10 wks
16 Feb 80	**FLOGGING A DEAD HORSE** *Virgin V 2142*	**23**	6 wks

SHADES OF RHYTHM
UK, male/female vocal/instrumental group *1 wk*

| 17 Aug 91 | **SHADES** *ZTT ZTT 8* .... | **73** | 1 wk |

283

S

SHADOWS UK, *male instrumental group* *442 wks*

16 Sep 61	★ **THE SHADOWS** *Columbia 33SX 1374*	**1**	57 wks
13 Oct 62	★ **OUT OF THE SHADOWS** *Columbia 33SX 1458*	**1**	38 wks
22 Jun 63	● **GREATEST HITS** *Columbia 33SX 1522*	**2**	49 wks
9 May 64	● **DANCE WITH THE SHADOWS** *Columbia 33SX 1619* ...	**2**	27 wks
17 Jul 65	● **SOUND OF THE SHADOWS** *Columbia 33SX 1736*	**4**	17 wks
21 May 66	● **SHADOW MUSIC** *Columbia SX 6041*	**5**	17 wks
15 Jul 67	● **JIGSAW** *Columbia SCX 6148*	**8**	16 wks
24 Oct 70	**SHADES OF ROCK** *Columbia SCX 6420*	**30**	4 wks
13 Apr 74	**ROCKIN' WITH CURLY LEADS** *EMI EMA 762*	**45**	1 wk
11 May 74	**GREATEST HITS (re-issue)** *Columbia SCX 1522*	**48**	6 wks
29 Mar 75	**SPECS APPEAL** *EMI EMC 3066*	**30**	5 wks
12 Feb 77	★ **20 GOLDEN GREATS** *EMI EMTV 3*	**1**	38 wks
15 Sep 79	★ **STRING OF HITS** *EMI EMC 3310*	**1**	48 wks
26 Jul 80	**ANOTHER STRING OF HITS** *EMI EMC 3339*	**16**	8 wks
13 Sep 80	**CHANGE OF ADDRESS** *Polydor 2442 179*	**17**	6 wks
19 Sep 81	**HITS RIGHT UP YOUR STREET** *Polydor POLD 5046* ..	**15**	16 wks
25 Sep 82	**LIFE IN THE JUNGLE/LIVE AT ABBEY ROAD** *Polydor SHADS 1*	**24**	6 wks
22 Oct 83	**XXV** *Polydor POLD 5120*	**34**	6 wks
17 Nov 84	**GUARDIAN ANGEL** *Polydor POLD 5169*	**98**	1 wk
24 May 86	● **MOONLIGHT SHADOWS** *Polydor PROLP 8*	**6**	19 wks
24 Oct 87	**SIMPLY SHADOWS** *Polydor SHAD 1*	**11**	17 wks
20 May 89	**STEPPIN' TO THE SHADOWS** *Polydor SHAD 30*	**11**	9 wks
16 Dec 89	**AT THEIR VERY BEST** *EMI 8415201*	**12**	9 wks
13 Oct 90	● **REFLECTION** *Roll Over 8471201*	**6**	15 wks
16 Nov 91	**THEMES AND DREAMS** *Polydor 5113741*	**21†**	7 wks

See also Cliff Richard.

SHAKATAK *UK, male/female vocal/instrumental group* 73 wks

30 Jan 82	**DRIVIN' HARD** *Polydor POLS 1030*		35	17 wks
15 May 82 ●	**NIGHT BIRDS** *Polydor POLS 1059*		4	28 wks
27 Nov 82	**INVITATIONS** *Polydor POLD 5068*		30	11 wks
22 Oct 83	**OUT OF THIS WORLD** *Polydor POLD 5115*		30	4 wks
25 Aug 84	**DOWN ON THE STREET** *Polydor POLD 5148*		17	9 wks
23 Feb 85	**LIVE!** *Polydor POLH 21*		82	3 wks
22 Oct 88	**THE COOLEST CUTS** *K-Tel NE 1422*		73	1 wk

SHAKESPEAR'S SISTER
UK/US, female vocal/instrumental duo 8 wks

2 Sep 89 ●	**SACRED HEART** *London 828131 1*		9	8 wks

SHAKIN' PYRAMIDS *UK, male vocal/instrumental group* 4 wks

4 Apr 81	**SKIN 'EM UP** *Cuba Libra V 2199*		48	4 wks

SHALAMAR *US, male/female vocal/instrumental group* 121 wks

27 Mar 82 ●	**FRIENDS** *Solar K 52345*		6	72 wks
11 Sep 82	**GREATEST HITS** *Solar SOLA 3001*		71	5 wks
30 Jul 83 ●	**THE LOOK** *Solar 960239*		7	20 wks
12 Apr 86 ●	**THE GREATEST HITS** *Stylus SMR 8615*		5	24 wks

284

S

SHAM 69 *UK, male vocal/instrumental group* 27 wks

11 Mar 78	**TELL US THE TRUTH** *Polydor 2383 491*		25	8 wks
2 Dec 78	**THAT'S LIFE** *Polydor POLD 5010*		27	11 wks
29 Sep 79 ●	**THE ADVENTURES OF THE HERSHAM BOYS**			
	Polydor POLD 5025		8	8 wks

SHAMEN *UK, male vocal/instrumental duo* 12 wks

2 Nov 90	**EN-TACT** *One Little Indian TPLP 22*		31	10 wks
28 Sep 91	**PROGENY** *One Little Indian TPLP 32*		23	2 wks

Jimmy SHAND, HIS BAND AND GUESTS
UK, male instrumentalist – accordion, with male/female
vocal/instrumental dance band 2 wks

24 Dec 83	**FIFTY YEARS ON WITH JIMMY SHAND** *Ross WGR 062*	97	2 wks

SHANNON *US, female vocalist* 12 wks

10 Mar 84	**LET THE MUSIC PLAY** *Club JABL 1*		52	12 wks

Del SHANNON *US, male vocalist* 23 wks

11 May 63 ●	**HATS OFF TO DEL SHANNON** *London HAX 8071*		9	17 wks
2 Nov 63	**LITTLE TOWN FLIRT** *London HAX 8091*		15	6 wks

Helen SHAPIRO *UK, female vocalist*   *25 wks*

10 Mar 62 ● **TOPS WITH ME** *Columbia 33SX 1397* .... **2** 25 wks

Feargal SHARKEY *UK, male vocalist*   *24 wks*

23 Nov 85   **FEARGAL SHARKEY** *Virgin V 2360* .... **12** 20 wks
20 Apr 91   **SONGS FROM THE MARDI GRAS** *Virgin V 2642* ...... **27**   4 wks

SHARPE and NUMAN *UK, male vocal/instrumental duo*   *1 wk*

8 Jul 89   **AUTOMATIC** *Polydor 839520 1* .... **59** 1 wk
See also Gary Numan.

Roland SHAW – *See MANTOVANI*

Sandie SHAW *UK, female vocalist*   *13 wks*

6 Mar 65 ● **SANDIE** *Pye NPL 18110* .... **3** 13 wks

George SHEARING – *See Nat 'King' COLE and the George SHEARING QUINTET; Peggy LEE and George SHEARING*

Pete SHELLEY *UK, male vocalist*   *4 wks*

2 Jul 83   **XL-1** *Genetic XL 1* .... **42** 4 wks

SHERRICK *US, male vocalist*   *6 wks*

29 Aug 87   **SHERRICK** *Warner Bros. WX 118* .... **27** 6 wks

Brendon SHINE *Ireland, male vocalist*   *29 wks*

12 Nov 83   **THE BRENDON SHINE COLLECTION**
            Play PLAYTV 1 .... **51** 12 wks
3 Nov 84   **WITH LOVE** *Play PLAYTV 2* .... **74**   4 wks
16 Nov 85   **MEMORIES** *Play PLAYTV 3* .... **81**   7 wks
18 Nov 89   **MAGIC MOMENTS** *Stylus SMR 991* .... **62**   6 wks

SHIRLIE – *See PEPSI and SHIRLIE*

Michelle SHOCKED *US, female vocalist*   *22 wks*

10 Sep 88   **SHORT SHARP SHOCKED** *Cooking Vinyl CVLP 1* ...... **33** 19 wks
18 Nov 89   **CAPTAIN SWING** *Cooking Vinyl 838878 1* .... **31**   3 wks

SHOP ASSISTANTS
UK, male/female vocal/instrumental group   *1 wk*

29 Nov 86   **SHOP ASSISTANTS** *Blue Guitar AZLP 2* .... **100** 1 wk

SHOWADDYWADDY
UK, male vocal/instrumental group   *126 wks*

7 Dec 74 ● **SHOWADDYWADDY** *Bell BELLS 248* .... **9** 19 wks
12 Jul 75 ● **STEP TWO** *Bell BELLS 256* .... **7** 17 wks

285

S

29 May 76	**TROCADERO** Bell SYBEL 8003	**41**	3 wks
25 Dec 76 ●	**GREATEST HITS** Arista ARTY 145	**4**	26 wks
3 Dec 77	**RED STAR** Arista SPARTY 1023	**20**	10 wks
9 Dec 78 ★	**GREATEST HITS (1976–1978)** Arista ARTV 1	**1**	17 wks
10 Nov 79 ●	**CREPES AND DRAPES** Arista ARTV 3	**8**	14 wks
20 Dec 80	**BRIGHT LIGHTS** Arista SPART 1142	**54**	8 wks
7 Nov 81	**THE VERY BEST OF** Arista SPART 1178	**33**	11 wks
5 Dec 87	**THE BEST STEPS TO HEAVEN** Tiger SHTV 1	**90**	1 wk

SHRIEKBACK   UK, male vocal/instrumental group   1 wk

11 Aug 84	**JAM SCIENCE** Arista 206 416	**85**	1 wk

SHRIEVE – See HAGAR, SCHON, AARONSON, SHRIEVE

SHY   UK, male vocal/instrumental group   2 wks

11 Apr 87	**EXCESS ALL AREAS** RCA PL 71221	**74**	2 wks

Labi SIFFRE   UK, male vocalist   2 wks

24 Jul 71	**SINGER AND THE SONG** Pye NSPL 28147	**47**	1 wk
14 Oct 72	**CRYING, LAUGHING, LOVING, LYING** Pye NSPL 28163	**46**	1 wk

SILVER BULLET BAND – See Bob SEGER and the SILVER BULLET BAND

SIGUE SIGUE SPUTNIK
UK, male vocal/instrumental group   7 wks

9 Aug 86 ●	**FLAUNT IT** Parlophone PCS 7305	**10**	6 wks
15 Apr 89	**DRESS FOR EXCESS** Parlophone PCS 7328	**53**	1 wk

SILENCERS   UK, male vocal/instrumental group   2 wks

23 Mar 91	**DANCE TO THE HOLY MAN** RCA PL 74924	**39**	2 wks

SILVER BULLET   UK, male vocal/instrumental duo   2 wks

4 May 91	**BRING DOWN THE WALLS NO LIMIT SQUAD** Parlophone PCS 7350	**38**	2 wks

SILVER CONVENTION
Germany/US, female vocal group   3 wks

25 Jun 77	**SILVER CONVENTION: GREATEST HITS** Magnet MAG 6001	**34**	3 wks

Carly SIMON   US, female vocalist   61 wks

20 Jan 73 ●	**NO SECRETS** Elektra K 42127	**3**	26 wks
16 Mar 74	**HOT CAKES** Elektra K 52005	**19**	9 wks
9 May 87	**COMING AROUND AGAIN** Arista 208 140	**25**	20 wks
3 Sep 88	**GREATEST HITS LIVE** Arista 209196	**49**	6 wks

Paul SIMON *US, male vocalist* — 260 wks

26 Feb	72	★ **PAUL SIMON** CBS 69007	1	26 wks
2 Jun	73	● **THERE GOES RHYMIN' SIMON** CBS 69035	4	22 wks
1 Nov	75	● **STILL CRAZY AFTER ALL THESE YEARS** CBS 86001	6	31 wks
3 Dec	77	● **GREATEST HITS, ETC.** CBS 10007	6	15 wks
30 Aug	80	**ONE-TRICK PONY** Warner Bros. K 56846	17	12 wks
12 Nov	83	**HEARTS AND BONES** Warner Bros. 92–3942–1	34	8 wks
13 Sep	86	★ **GRACELAND** Warner Bros. WX 52	1	100 wks
24 Jan	87	**GREATEST HITS, ETC. (re-issue)** CBS 450 166–1	73	2 wks
5 Nov	88	**NEGOTIATIONS AND LOVE SONGS 1971–1986** Warner Bros. WX 223	17	15 wks
27 Oct	90	★ **RHYTHM OF THE SAINTS** Warner Bros WX 340	1	28 wks
23 Nov	91	**THE CONCERT IN THE PARK – AUGUST 15TH 1991** Warner Bros WX 448	60	1 wk

See also Simon and Garfunkel.

SIMON and GARFUNKEL *US, male vocal duo* — 1039 wks

16 Apr	66	**SOUNDS OF SILENCE** CBS 62690	13	104 wks
3 Aug	68	★ **BOOKENDS** CBS 63101	1	77 wks
31 Aug	68	**PARSLEY, SAGE, ROSEMARY AND THYME** CBS 62860	13	66 wks
26 Oct	68	● **THE GRADUATE (film soundtrack)** CBS 70042	3	71 wks
9 Nov	68	**WEDNESDAY MORNING 3 A.M.** CBS 63370	24	6 wks
21 Feb	70	★ **BRIDGE OVER TROUBLED WATER** CBS 63699	1	303 wks
22 Jul	72	● **GREATEST HITS** CBS 69003	2	283 wks
4 Apr	81	**SOUNDS OF SILENCE (re-issue)** CBS 32020	68	1 wk
21 Nov	81	● **THE SIMON AND GARFUNKEL COLLECTION** CBS 10029	4	80 wks
20 Mar	82	● **THE CONCERT IN CENTRAL PARK** Geffen GEF 96008	6	43 wks
30 Nov	91	● **THE DEFINITIVE SIMON AND GARFUNKEL** Columbia MOODCD 21	8†	5 wks

See also Paul Simon; Art Garfunkel.

Nina SIMONE *US, female vocalist* — 12 wks

24 Jul	65	**I PUT A SPELL ON YOU** Philips BL 7671	18	3 wks
15 Feb	69	**'NUFF SAID** RCS SF 7979	11	1 wk
14 Nov	87	**MY BABY JUST CARES FOR ME** Charly CR 30217	56	8 wks

SIMPLE MINDS *UK, male vocal/instrumental group* — 293 wks

5 May	79	**A LIFE IN THE DAY** Zoom ZULP 1	30	6 wks
27 Sep	80	**EMPIRES AND DANCE** Arista SPART 1140	41	3 wks
12 Sep	81	**SONS AND FASCINATIONS/SISTERS FEELINGS CALL** Virgin V 2207	11	7 wks
27 Feb	82	**CELEBRATION** Arista SPART 1183	45	7 wks
25 Sep	82	● **NEW GOLD DREAM (81, 82, 83, 84)** Virgin V 2230	3	52 wks
18 Feb	84	★ **SPARKLE IN THE RAIN** Virgin V 2300	1	57 wks
2 Nov	85	★ **ONCE UPON A TIME** Virgin V 2364	1	83 wks
6 Jun	87	★ **LIVE IN THE CITY OF LIGHT** Virgin V SMDL 1	1	26 wks
13 May	89	★ **STREET FIGHTING YEARS** Virgin MINDS 1	1	27 wks
20 Apr	91	● **REAL LIFE** Virgin V 2660	2	25 wks

SIMPLY RED *UK, male vocal/instrumental group* — 253 wks

26 Oct	85	● **PICTURE BOOK** Elektra EKT 27	2	118 wks
21 Mar	87	● **MEN AND WOMEN** WEA WX 85	2	56 wks
25 Feb	89	★ **A NEW FLAME** Elektra WX 242	1	67 wks
12 Oct	91	★ **STARS** East West WX 427	1†	12 wks

SIMPSON – *See ASHFORD and SIMPSON*

Taja Sevelle was the most successful of Prince's Paisley Park protégés. Left: **Helen Shapiro** was almost tops with everyone in 1962.

SIMPSONS   *US, male/female cartoon group*   *30 wks*

2 Feb 91	● THE SIMPSONS SING THE BLUES *Geffen 7599243081* ..	6	30 wks

Joyce SIMS   *US, female vocalist*   *25 wks*

9 Jan 88	● COME INTO MY LIFE *London LONLP 47*	5	24 wks
16 Sep 89	ALL ABOUT LOVE *London 828129 1*	64	1 wk

Frank SINATRA   *US, male vocalist*   *613 wks*

8 Nov 58	● COME FLY WITH ME *Capitol LCT 6154*	2	18 wks
15 Nov 58	● SONGS FOR SWINGING LOVERS *Capitol LCT 6106* ...	8	8 wks
29 Nov 58	● FRANK SINATRA STORY *Fontana TFL 5030*	8	1 wk
13 Dec 58	● FRANK SINATRA SINGS FOR ONLY THE LONELY *Capitol LCT 6168*	5	13 wks
16 May 59	● COME DANCE WITH ME *Capitol LCT 6179*	2	30 wks
22 Aug 59	● LOOK TO YOUR HEART *Capitol LCT 6181*	5	8 wks
11 Jun 60	● COME BACK TO SORRENTO *Fontana TFL 5082*	6	9 wks
29 Oct 60	● SWING EASY *Capitol W 587*	5	17 wks
21 Jan 61	● NICE 'N EASY *Capitol W 1417*	4	27 wks
15 Jul 61	SINATRA SOUVENIR *Fontana TFL 5138*	18	1 wk
19 Aug 61	● WHEN YOUR LOVER HAS GONE *Encore ENC 101* ..	6	10 wks
23 Sep 61	● SINATRA'S SWINGING SESSION *Capitol W 1491*	6	8 wks
28 Oct 61	● SINATRA SWINGS *Reprise R 1002*	8	8 wks
25 Nov 61	SINATRA PLUS *Fontana SET 303*	7	9 wks
16 Dec 61	● RING-A-DING-DING *Reprise R 1001*	8	9 wks
17 Feb 62	COME SWING WITH ME *Capitol W 1594*	13	4 wks
7 Apr 62	●I REMEMBER TOMMY *Reprise R 1003*	10	12 wks
9 Jun 62	● SINATRA AND STRINGS *Reprise R 1004*	6	20 wks
27 Oct 62	GREAT SONGS FROM GREAT BRITAIN *Reprise R 1006*	12	9 wks
29 Dec 62	SINATRA WITH SWINGING BRASS *Reprise R 1005* ...	14	11 wks
27 Jul 63	● CONCERT SINATRA *Reprise R 1009*	8	18 wks
5 Oct 63	● SINATRA'S SINATRA *Reprise R 1010*	9	24 wks
19 Sep 64	IT MIGHT AS WELL BE SWING *Reprise R 1012*	17	4 wks
20 Mar 65	SOFTLY AS I LEAVE YOU *Reprise R 1013*	20	1 wk
22 Jan 66	● A MAN AND HIS MUSIC *Reprise R 1016*	9	19 wks
21 May 66	MOONLIGHT SINATRA *Reprise R 1018*	18	8 wks
2 Jul 66	● STRANGERS IN THE NIGHT *Reprise R 1017*	4	18 wks
1 Oct 66	● SINATRA AT THE SANDS *Reprise RLP 1019*	7	18 wks
3 Dec 66	FRANK SINATRA SINGS SONGS FOR PLEASURE *MFP 1120*	26	2 wks
25 Feb 67	THAT'S LIFE *Reprise RSLP 1020*	22	12 wks
7 Oct 67	FRANK SINATRA *Reprise RSLP 1022*	28	5 wks
19 Oct 68	● GREATEST HITS *Reprise RSLP 1025*	8	38 wks
7 Dec 68	BEST OF FRANK SINATRA *Capitol ST 21140*	17	10 wks
7 Jun 69	● MY WAY *Reprise RSLP 1029*	2	59 wks
4 Oct 69	A MAN ALONE *Reprise RSLP 1030*	18	7 wks
9 May 70	WATERTOWN *Reprise RSLP 1031*	14	9 wks
12 Dec 70	● GREATEST HITS VOL. 2 *Reprise RSLP 1032*	6	40 wks
5 Jun 71	● SINATRA AND COMPANY *Reprise RSLP 1033*	9	9 wks
27 Nov 71	FRANK SINATRA SINGS RODGERS AND HART *Starline SRS 5083*	35	1 wk
8 Jan 72	MY WAY (re-issue) *Reprise K 44015*	35	1 wk
8 Jan 72	GREATEST HITS VOL. 2 *Reprise K 44018*	29	3 wks
1 Dec 73	OL' BLUE EYES IS BACK *Warner Bros. K 44249*	12	13 wks
17 Aug 74	SOME NICE THINGS I'VE MISSED *Reprise K 54020*	35	3 wks
15 Feb 75	THE MAIN EVENT (TV soundtrack) *Reprise K 54031*	30	2 wks
14 Jun 75	THE BEST OF OL' BLUE EYES *Reprise K 54042*	30	3 wks
19 Mar 77	★ PORTRAIT OF SINATRA *Reprise K 64039*	1	18 wks
13 May 78	● 20 GOLDEN GREATS *Capitol EMTV 10*	4	11 wks
18 Aug 84	L.A. IS MY LADY *Qwest 925145*	41	8 wks
22 Mar 86	NEW YORK NEW YORK (GREATEST HITS) *Warner Bros. WX 32*	13	12 wks

289

S

4 Oct 86   **THE FRANK SINATRA COLLECTION**
           Capitol EMTV 41 40   5 wks

See also Frank Sinatra and Count Basie.

Frank SINATRA and Count BASIE

US, male vocalist and male orchestra leader/instrumentalist – piano   *23 wks*

23 Feb 63 ● **SINATRA – BASIE** *Reprise R 1008* 2   23 wks

See also Count Basie; Frank Sinatra.

Nancy SINATRA *US, female vocalist*   *15 wks*

16 Apr 66   **BOOTS** *Reprise R 6202* 12   9 wks
18 Jun 66   **HOW DOES THAT GRAB YOU** *Reprise R 6207* 12   3 wks
10 Oct 70   **NANCY'S GREATEST HITS** *Reprise RSLP 6409* 39   3 wks

See also Nancy Sinatra and Lee Hazlewood.

Nancy SINATRA and Lee HAZLEWOOD

US, female/male vocal duo   *17 wks*

29 Jun 68   **NANCY AND LEE** *Reprise RSLP 6273* 17   12 wks
25 Sep 71   **NANCY AND LEE (re-issue)** *Reprise K 44126* 42   1 wk
29 Jan 72   **DID YOU EVER** *RCA Victor SF 8240* 31   4 wks

See also Nancy Sinatra.

290

SINITTA *US, female vocalist*   *23 wks*

S

26 Dec 87   **SINITTA!** *Fanfare BOYLP 1* 34   19 wks
9 Dec 89   **WICKED!** *Fanfare FARE 2* 52   4 wks

SINFONIA OF LONDON – *See Howard BLAKE conducting the SINFONIA OF LONDON*

SIOUXSIE and the BANSHEES

UK, female/male vocal/instrumental group   *115 wks*

2 Dec 78   **THE SCREAM** *Polydor POLD 5009* 12   11 wks
22 Sep 79   **JOIN HANDS** *Polydor POLD 5024* 13   5 wks
16 Aug 80 ● **KALEIDOSCOPE** *Polydor 2442 177* 5   6 wks
27 Jun 81 ● **JU JU** *Polydor POLS 1034* 7   17 wks
12 Dec 81   **ONCE UPON A TIME** *Polydor POLS 1056* 21   26 wks
13 Nov 82   **A KISS IN THE DREAMHOUSE** *Polydor POLD 5064* 11   11 wks
3 Dec 83   **NOCTURNE** *Wonderland SHAH 1* 29   10 wks
16 Jun 84   **HYENA** *Wonderland SHELP 2* 15   6 wks
26 Apr 86   **TINDERBOX** *Wonderland SHELP 3* 13   6 wks
14 Mar 87   **THROUGH THE LOOKING GLASS** *Wonderland SHELP 4* 15   8 wks
17 Sep 88   **PEEP SHOW** *Wonderland SHELP 5* 20   5 wks
22 Jun 91   **SUPERSTITION** *Wonderland 8477311* 25   4 wks

SISTER SLEDGE *US, female vocal group*   *50 wks*

12 May 79 ● **WE ARE FAMILY** *Atlantic K 50587* 7   39 wks
22 Jun 85   **WHEN THE BOYS MEET THE GIRLS** *Atlantic 78–1255–1*   19   11 wks

See also Chic and Sister Sledge.

SISTERHOOD *UK, male vocal/instrumental group*   *1 wk*

26 Jul 86   **GIFT** *Merciful Release SIS 020* 90   1 wk

SISTERS OF MERCY
UK, male/female vocal/instrumental duo   *32 wks*

23 Mar 85	**FIRST AND LAST AND ALWAYS**		
	Merciful Release MR 337 L	14	8 wks
28 Nov 87 ●	**FLOODLAND** *Merciful Release MR 441 L*	9	20 wks
2 Nov 90	**VISION THING** *Merciful Release*	11	4 wks

Act was a male-only group for first album.

Peter SKELLERN *UK, male vocalist*   *28 wks*

9 Sep 78	**SKELLERN** *Mercury 9109 701*	48	3 wks
8 Dec 79	**ASTAIRE** *Mercury 9102 702*	23	20 wks
4 Dec 82	**A STRING OF PEARLS** *Mercury MERL 10*	67	5 wks

SKID ROW *UK, male vocal/instrumental group*   *3 wks*

17 Oct 70	**SKID** *CBS 63965*	30	3 wks

SKID ROW *US, male vocal/instrumental group*   *25 wks*

2 Sep 89	**SKID ROW** *Atlantic 781936 1*	30	16 wks
22 Jun 91 ●	**SLAVE TO THE GRIND** *Atlantic WX 423*	5	9 wks

SKIDS *UK, male vocal/instrumental group*   *20 wks*

17 Mar 79	**SCARED TO DANCE** *Virgin V 2116*	19	10 wks
27 Oct 79	**DAYS IN EUROPA** *Virgin V 2138*	32	5 wks
27 Sep 80 ●	**THE ABSOLUTE GAME** *Virgin V 2174*	9	5 wks

SKY *UK/Australia, male instrumental group*   *202 wks*

2 Jun 79 ●	**SKY** *Ariola ARLH 5022*	9	56 wks
26 Apr 80 ★	**SKY 2** *Ariola ADSKY 2*	1	53 wks
28 Mar 81 ●	**SKY 3** *Ariola ASKY 3*	3	23 wks
3 Apr 82 ●	**SKY 4 - FORTHCOMING** *Ariola ASKY 4*	7	22 wks
22 Jan 83	**SKY FIVE LIVE** *Ariola 302 171*	14	14 wks
3 Dec 83	**CADMIUM** *Ariola 205 885*	44	10 wks
12 May 84	**MASTERPIECES – THE VERY BEST OF SKY**		
	Telstar STAR 2241	15	18 wks
13 Apr 85	**THE GREAT BALLOON RACE** *Epic EPC 26419*	63	6 wks

SKYY *US, male vocal/instrumental group*   *1 wk*

21 Jun 86	**FROM THE LEFT SIDE** *Capitol EST 2014*	85	1 wk

SLADE *UK, male vocal/instrumental group*   *207 wks*

8 Apr 72 ●	**SLADE ALIVE** *Polydor 2383 101*	2	58 wks
9 Dec 72 ★	**SLAYED?** *Polydor 2383 163*	1	34 wks
6 Oct 73 ★	**SLADEST** *Polydor 2442 119*	1	24 wks
23 Feb 74 ★	**OLD NEW BORROWED AND BLUE** *Polydor 2383 261* .	1	16 wks
14 Dec 74 ●	**SLADE IN FLAME** *Polydor 2442 126*	6	18 wks
27 Mar 76	**NOBODY'S FOOL** *Polydor 2383 377*	14	4 wks
22 Nov 80	**SLADE SMASHES** *Polydor POLTV 13*	21	15 wks
21 Mar 81	**WE'LL BRING THE HOUSE DOWN** *Cheapskate SKATE 1*	25	4 wks
28 Nov 81	**TILL DEAF US DO PART** *RCA RCALP 6021*	68	2 wks
18 Dec 82	**SLADE ON STAGE** *RCA RCALP 3107*	58	3 wks

SLAYER *US, male vocal/instrumental group* *12 wks*

Percy SLEDGE *US, male vocalist* *4 wks*

SLEIGHRIDERS *UK, male vocal/instrumental group* *1 wk*

Grace SLICK *US, female vocalist* *6 wks*

292

S

SLIK *UK, male vocal/instrumental group* *1 wk*

SLIM CHANCE – *See Ronnie LANE and the Band SLIM CHANCE*

SLITS *UK, female vocal/instrumental group* *5 wks*

SLOWDIVE *UK, male vocal/instrumental group* *2 wks*

SLY and ROBBIE *Jamaica, male vocal/instrumental duo* *5 wks*

SLY and the FAMILY STONE
US, male/female vocal/instrumental group *2 wks*

SMALL FACES *UK, male vocal/instrumental group* *66 wks*

1 Jul 67	**SMALL FACES** *Immediate IMSP 008*	12	17 wks
15 Jun 68	★ **OGDEN'S NUT GONE FLAKE** *Immediate IMLP 012*	1	19 wks

The two albums titled Small Faces *are different.*

Brian SMITH and his HAPPY PIANO
UK, male instrumentalist – piano   *1 wk*

19 Sep 81	**PLAY IT AGAIN** *Deram DS 047*	97	1 wk

Jimmy SMITH   *US, male instrumentalist – organ*   *3 wks*

18 Jun 66	**GOT MY MOJO WORKING** *Verve VLP 912*	19	3 wks

Keely SMITH   *US, female vocalist*   *9 wks*

16 Jan 65	**LENNON–McCARTNEY SONGBOOK** *Reprise R 6142* ..	12	9 wks

O.C. SMITH   *US, male vocalist*   *1 wk*

17 Aug 68	**HICKORY HOLLER REVISITED** *CBS 63362*	40	1 wk

Steven SMITH and FATHER
UK, male instrumental duo   *3 wks*

13 May 72	**STEVEN SMITH AND FATHER AND 16 GREAT SONGS** *Decca SKL 5128*	17	3 wks

293

S

SMITH and JONES   *UK, male comedy duo*   *8 wks*

15 Nov 86	**SCRATCH AND SNIFF** *10 DIX 51*	62	8 wks

Patti SMITH GROUP
US, female/male vocal/instrumental group   *21 wks*

1 Apr 78	**EASTER** *Arista SPART 1043*	16	14 wks
19 May 79	**WAVE** *Arista SPART 1086*	41	6 wks
16 Jul 88	**DREAM OF LIFE** *Arista 209172*	70	1 wks

Third album credited simply to Patti Smith.

SMITHS   *UK, male vocal/instrumental group*   *158 wks*

3 Mar 84	● **THE SMITHS** *Rough Trade ROUGH 61*	2	33 wks
24 Nov 84	● **HATFUL OF HOLLOW** *Rough Trade ROUGH 76*	7	46 wks
23 Feb 85	★ **MEAT IS MURDER** *Rough Trade ROUGH 81*	1	13 wks
28 Jun 86	● **THE QUEEN IS DEAD** *Rough Trade ROUGH 96*	2	22 wks
7 Mar 87	● **THE WORLD WON'T LISTEN** *Rough Trade ROUGH 101*	2	15 wks
30 May 87	**LOUDER THAN BOMBS** (import) *Rough Trade ROUGH 255*	38	5 wks
10 Oct 87	● **STRANGEWAYS HERE WE COME** *Rough Trade ROUGH 106*	2	17 wks
17 Sep 88	● **RANK** *Rough Trade ROUGH 126*	2	7 wks

SMOKIE   *UK, male vocal/instrumental group*   *42 wks*

1 Nov 75	**SMOKIE/CHANGING ALL THE TIME** *RAK SRAK 517* .	18	5 wks
30 Apr 77	● **GREATEST HITS** *RAK SRAK 526*	6	22 wks

4 Nov 78	**THE MONTREUX ALBUM** *RAK SRAK 6757*	**52**	2 wks
11 Oct 80	**SMOKIE'S HITS** *RAK SRAK 540*	**23**	13 wks

SMURFS – *See Father ABRAHAM and the SMURFS*

SNAP *US, male/female rap duo*   *39 wks*

26 May 90	**WORLD POWER** *Arista 210682*	**10**	39 wks

SOFT CELL *UK, male vocal/instrumental duo*   *100 wks*

5 Dec 81	● **NON-STOP EROTIC CABARET** *Some Bizzare BZLP 2* ..	**5**	46 wks
26 Jun 82	● **NON-STOP ECSTATIC DANCING**		
	Some Bizzare BZX 1012	**6**	18 wks
22 Jan 83	● **THE ART OF FALLING APART** *Some Bizzare BIZL 3* ...	**5**	9 wks
31 Mar 84	**THE LAST NIGHT IN SODOM** *Some Bizzare BIZL 6*	**12**	5 wks
20 Dec 86	**THE SINGLES ALBUM** *Some Bizzare BZLP 3*	**58**	9 wks
1 Jun 91	● **MEMORABILIA–THE SINGLES** *Mercury 8485121*	**8**	13 wks

SOFT MACHINE *UK, male vocal/instrumental group*   *8 wks*

4 Jul 70	**THIRD** *CBS 66246*	**18**	6 wks
3 Apr 71	**FOURTH** *CBS 64280*	**32**	2 wks

SOLID SENDERS *UK, male vocal/instrumental group*   *3 wks*

23 Sep 78	**SOLID SENDERS** *Virgin V 2105*	**42**	3 wks

Diane SOLOMON *UK, female vocalist*   *6 wks*

9 Aug 75	**TAKE TWO** *Philips 6308 236*	**26**	6 wks

Sir George SOLTI and DUDLEY MOORE
UK, male conductor and male narrator/instrumentalist – piano   *5 wks*

26 Jan 91	**ORCHESTRA!** *Decca 4308361*	**38**	5 wks
See also Dudley Moore.			

Jimmy SOMERVILLE *UK, male vocalist*   *40 wks*

9 Dec 89	**READ MY LIPS** *London 8281661*	**29**	14 wks
24 Nov 90	● **THE SINGLES COLLECTION 1984–1990** *London 8282261*	**4**	26 wks

SONIA *UK, female vocalist*   *12 wks*

5 May 90	● **EVERYBODY KNOWS** *Chrysalis CHR 1734*	**7**	10 wks
19 Oct 91	**SONIA** *IQ ZL 751675*	**33**	2 wks

SONIC BOOM *UK, male vocal/instrumental group*   *1 wk*

17 Mar 90	**SPECTRUM** *Silvertone ORELP 56*	**65**	1 wk

SONIC YOUTH *US, male/female vocal/instrumental group*   *4 wks*

29 Oct 88	**DAYDREAM NATION** *Blast First BFFP 34*	**99**	1 wk

7 Jul 90 **GOO** DGC 7599242971	32	2 wks
4 May 91 **DIRTY BOOTS–PLUS 5 LIVE TRACKS**		
DGC DGC 21634	69	1 wk

SONNY and CHER US, male/female vocal duo   20 wks

16 Oct 65 ● **LOOK AT US** Atlantic ATL 5036	7	13 wks
14 May 66 **THE WONDROUS WORLD OF SONNY AND CHER**		
Atlantic 587–006	15	7 wks

See also Cher.

S.O.S. BAND US, male/female vocal/instrumental group   19 wks

1 Sep 84 **JUST THE WAY YOU LIKE IT** Tabu TBU 26058	29	10 wks
17 May 86 **SANDS OF TIME** Tabu TBU 26863	15	9 wks

David SOUL US, male vocalist   51 wks

27 Nov 76 ● **DAVID SOUL** Private Stock PVLP 1012	2	28 wks
17 Sep 77 ● **PLAYING TO AN AUDIENCE OF ONE**		
Private Stock PVLP 1026	8	23 wks

SOUL CITY SYMPHONY – See Van McCOY and the SOUL CITY SYMPHONY

SOUL II SOUL
UK, male/female vocal/instrumental group and male producer   80 wks

22 Apr 89 ★ **CLUB CLASSICS VOLUME ONE** 10 DIX 82	1	60 wks
2 Jun 90 ★ **VOLUME II (A NEW DECADE)** 10 DIX 90	1	20 wks

SOUNDS ORCHESTRAL UK, orchestra   1 wk

12 Jun 65 **CAST YOUR FATE TO THE WIND**		
Piccadilly NPL 38041	17	1 wk

SOUNDTRACKS (films, TV etc) – See VARIOUS ARTISTS

SOUP DRAGONS UK, male vocal/instrumental group   16 wks

7 May 88 **THIS IS OUR ART** Sire WX 169	60	1 wk
5 May 90 ● **LOVEGOD** Raw TV SOUPLP 2	7	15 wks

SOUTH BANK ORCHESTRA UK, orchestra   6 wks

2 Dec 78 **LILLIE** Sounds MOR 516	47	6 wks

This album was conducted by Joseph Morovitz and Laurie Holloway.

SOUTHERN DEATH CULT – See CULT

SPACE France, male instrumental group   9 wks

17 Sep 77 **MAGIC FLY** Pye NSPL 28232	11	9 wks

SPACEMEN UK, male instrumental group   1 wk

9 Mar 91 **RECURRING** Fire FIRELP 23	46	1 wk

SPANDAU BALLET UK, male vocal/instrumental group   250 wks

14 Mar 81 ● **JOURNEY TO GLORY** Reformation CHR 1331	5	29 wks
20 Mar 82 **DIAMOND** Reformation CDL 1353	15	18 wks
12 Mar 83 ★ **TRUE** Reformation CDL 1403	1	90 wks
7 Jul 84 ● **PARADE** Reformation CDL 1473	2	39 wks
16 Nov 85 ● **THE SINGLES COLLECTION** Chrysalis SBTV 1	3	49 wks
29 Nov 86 ● **THROUGH THE BARRICADES**		
Reformation CBS 450 259-1	7	19 wks
30 Sep 89 **HEART LIKE A SKY** CBS 4633181	31	3 wks
28 Sep 91 **THE BEST OF SPANDAU BALLET** Chrysalis CHR 1894	44	3 wks

SPARKS US/UK, male vocal/instrumental group   42 wks

1 Jun 74 ● **KIMONO MY HOUSE** Island ILPS 9272	4	24 wks
23 Nov 74 ● **PROPAGANDA** Island ILPS 9312	9	13 wks
18 Oct 75 **INDISCREET** Island ILPS 9345	18	4 wks
8 Sep 79 **NUMBER ONE IN HEAVEN** Virgin V 2115	73	1 wk

SPEAR OF DESTINY
UK, male vocal/instrumental group   35 wks

23 Apr 83 **GRAPES OF WRATH** Epic EPC 25318	62	2 wks
28 Apr 84 **ONE EYED JACKS** Burning Rome EPC 25836	22	7 wks
7 Sep 85 **WORLD SERVICE** Burning Rome EPC 26514	11	7 wks
2 May 87 **OUTLAND** 10 DIX 59	16	13 wks
16 May 87 **S.O.D. – THE EPIC YEARS** Epic 450 872-1	53	3 wks
22 Oct 88 **THE PRICE YOU PAY** Virgin V 2549	37	3 wks

296

S

Billie Jo SPEARS US, female vocalist   28 wks

11 Sep 76 **WHAT I'VE GOT IN MIND** United Artists UAS 29955	47	2 wks
19 May 79 ● **THE BILLIE JO SPEARS SINGLES ALBUM**		
United Artists UAK 30231	7	17 wks
21 Nov 81 **COUNTRY GIRL** Warwick WW 5109	17	9 wks

SPECIALS UK, male instrumental group   79 wks

3 Nov 79 ● **SPECIALS** 2-Tone CDL TT 5001	4	45 wks
4 Oct 80 ● **MORE SPECIALS** 2-Tone CHR TT 5003	5	19 wks
23 Jun 84 **IN THE STUDIO** 2-Tone CHR TT 5008	34	6 wks
7 Sep 91 ● **THE SPECIALS SINGLES** 2-Tone CHRTT 5010	10	9 wks

Group was male only for the first two albums. Billed as Special A.K.A. on third album.

Phil SPECTOR US, male producer   29 wks

23 Dec 72 **PHIL SPECTOR'S CHRISTMAS ALBUM**		
Apple SAPCOR 24	21	3 wks
15 Oct 77 **PHIL SPECTOR'S ECHOES OF THE 60'S**		
Phil Spector International 2307 013	21	10 wks
25 Dec 82 **PHIL SPECTOR'S CHRISTMAS ALBUM (re-issue)**		
Phil Spector International/Polydor 2307 005	96	2 wks
10 Dec 83 **PHIL SPECTOR'S GREATEST HITS/PHIL SPECTOR'S**		
CHRISTMAS ALBUM (2nd re-issue)		
Impression PSLP 1/2	19	8 wks
12 Dec 87 **PHIL SPECTOR'S CHRISTMAS ALBUM (3rd re-issue)**		
Chrysalis CDL 1625	69	6 wks

SPIDER UK, male vocal/instrumental group   2 wks

23 Oct 82	ROCK 'N' ROLL GYPSIES RCA RCALP 3101	75	1 wk
7 Apr 84	ROUGH JUSTICE A & M AMLX 68563	96	1 wk

SPINNERS UK, male vocal group   24 wks

5 Sep 70	THE SPINNERS ARE IN TOWN Fontana 6309 014	40	5 wks
7 Aug 71	SPINNERS LIVE PERFORMANCE Contour 6870 502 ...	14	12 wks
13 Nov 71	THE SWINGING CITY Philips 6382 002	20	3 wks
8 Apr 72	LOVE IS TEASING Columbia SCX 6493	33	4 wks

SPIRIT US, male vocal/instrumental duo   2 wks

18 Apr 81	POTATO LAND Beggars Banquet BEGA 23	40	2 wks

SPIRITUAL COWBOYS – See Dave STEWART and the SPIRITUAL COWBOYS

SPITTING IMAGE UK, puppets   3 wks

18 Oct 86	SPIT IN YOUR EAR Virgin V 2403	55	3 wks

SPLIT ENZ New Zealand/UK, male vocal/instrumental group   9 wks

30 Aug 80	TRUE COLOURS A & M AMLH 64822	42	8 wks
8 May 82	TIME AND TIDE A & M AMLH 64894	71	1 wk

297

S

SPOTNICKS Sweden, male instrumental group   1 wk

9 Feb 63	OUT-A-SPACE Oriole PS 40036	20	1 wk

Dusty SPRINGFIELD UK, female vocalist   98 wks

25 Apr 64	● A GIRL CALLED DUSTY Philips BL 7594	6	23 wks
23 Oct 65	● EVERYTHING COMES UP DUSTY Philips RBL 1002 ..	6	12 wks
22 Oct 66	● GOLDEN HITS Philips BL 7737	2	36 wks
11 Nov 67	WHERE AM I GOING Philips SBL 7820	40	1 wk
21 Dec 68	DUSTY ... DEFINITELY Philips SBL 7864	30	6 wks
2 May 70	FROM DUSTY WITH LOVE Philips SBL 7927	35	2 wks
4 Mar 78	IT BEGINS AGAIN Mercury 9109 607	41	2 wks
30 Jan 88	DUSTY – THE SILVER COLLECTION		
	Phonogram DUSTV 1	14	10 wks
7 Jul 90	REPUTATION Parlophone PCSD 111	18	6 wks

Rick SPRINGFIELD Australia, male vocalist   8 wks

11 Feb 84	LIVING IN OZ RCA PL 84660	41	4 wks
25 May 85	TAO RCA PL 85370	68	3 wks
26 Mar 88	ROCK OF LIFE RCA PL 86620	80	1 wk

Bruce SPRINGSTEEN US, male vocalist   387 wks

1 Nov 75	BORN TO RUN CBS 69170	17	50 wks
17 Jun 78	DARKNESS ON THE EDGE OF TOWN CBS 86061	16	40 wks
25 Oct 80	● THE RIVER CBS 88510	2	88 wks
2 Oct 82	● NEBRASKA CBS 25100	3	19 wks
16 Jun 84	★ BORN IN THE USA CBS 86304	1	126 wks
15 Jun 85	THE WILD THE INNOCENT AND THE E STREET		
	SHUFFLE CBS 32363	33	12 wks
15 Jun 85	GREETINGS FROM ASBURY PARK, N.J. CBS 32210 ..	41	10 wks

22 Nov 86	● **LIVE 1975–1985** CBS 450 227–1	**4**	9 wks
17 Oct 87	★ **TUNNEL OF LOVE** CBS 460 270–1	**1**	33 wks

Live 1975–1985 *credits the E Street Band.*

SPYRO GYRA *US, male instrumental group*   *23 wks*

14 Jul 79	**MORNING DANCE** Infinity INS 2003	**11**	16 wks
23 Feb 80	**CATCHING THE SUN** MCA MCG 4009	**31**	7 wks

SQUEEZE *UK, male vocal/instrumental group*   *106 wks*

28 Apr 79	**COOL FOR CATS** A&M AMLH 68503	**45**	11 wks
16 Feb 80	**ARGYBARGY** A&M AMLH 64802	**32**	15 wks
23 May 81	**EAST SIDE STORY** A&M AMLH 64854	**19**	26 wks
15 May 82	**SWEETS FROM A STRANGER** A&M AMLH 64899 ...	**20**	7 wks
6 Nov 82	● **SINGLES–45'S AND UNDER** A&M AMLH 68552	**3**	29 wks
7 Sep 85	**COSI FAN TUTTI FRUTTI** A&M AMA 5085	**31**	7 wks
19 Sep 87	**BABYLON AND ON** A&M AMA 5161	**14**	8 wks
23 Sep 89	**FRANK** A&M AMA 5278	**58**	1 wk
7 Apr 90	**A ROUND AND A BOUT** IRS DFCLP 1	**50**	1 wk
7 Sep 91	**PLAY** Reprise WX 428	**41**	1 wk

Chris SQUIRE *UK, male vocalist/instrumentalist – bass*   *7 wks*

6 Dec 75	**FISH OUT OF WATER** Atlantic K 50203	**25**	7 wks

STAGE CAST RECORDINGS – *See VARIOUS ARTISTS*

S

Lisa STANSFIELD *UK, female vocalist*   *37 wks*

2 Dec 89	● **AFFECTION** Arista 210379	**2**	31 wks
23 Nov 91	● **REAL LOVE** Arista 212300	**4†**	6 wks

Alvin STARDUST *UK, male vocalist*   *17 wks*

16 Mar 74	● **THE UNTOUCHABLE** Magnet MAG 5001	**4**	12 wks
21 Dec 74	**ALVIN STARDUST** Magnet MAG 5004	**37**	3 wks
4 Oct 75	**ROCK WITH ALVIN** Magnet MAG 5007	**52**	2 wks

Ed STARINK *US, male instrumentalist*   *5 wks*

27 Oct 90	**SYNTHESIZER GREATEST** Arcade ARC 938101	**22**	5 wks

Freddie STARR *UK, male vocalist*   *16 wks*

18 Nov 89	● **AFTER THE LAUGHTER** Dover ADD 10	**10**	9 wks
17 Nov 90	**THE WANDERER** Dover ADD 17	**33**	7 wks

Kay STARR *US, female vocalist*   *1 wk*

26 Mar 60	**MOVIN'** Capitol T 1254	**16**	1 wk

Ringo STARR *UK, male vocalist*   *28 wks*

18 Apr 70	● **SENTIMENTAL JOURNEY** Apple PCS 7101	**7**	6 wks

8 Dec 73	● **RINGO**	*Apple PCTC 252*	**7**	20 wks
7 Dec 74	**GOODNIGHT VIENNA**	*Apple PMC 7168*	**30**	2 wks

STARSHIP *US, male/female vocal/instrumental group*   *5 wks*

18 Jul 87	**NO PROTECTION**	*Grunt FL 86413*	**26**	5 wks

See also Jefferson Airplane; Jefferson Starship.

STARSOUND *Holland, disco aggregation*   *28 wks*

16 May 81	★ **STARS ON 45**	*CBS 86132*	**1**	21 wks
19 Sep 81	**STARS ON 45 VOL. 2**	*CBS 85181*	**18**	6 wks
3 Apr 82	**STARS MEDLEY**	*CBS 85651*	**94**	1 wk

STARTRAX *UK, disco aggregation*   *7 wks*

1 Aug 81	**STARTRAX CLUB DISCO**	*Picksy KSYA 1001*	**26**	7 wks

Candi STATON *US, female vocalist*   *3 wks*

24 Jul 76	**YOUNG HEARTS RUN FREE**	*Warner Bros. K 56259*	**34**	3 wks

STATUS QUO *UK, male vocal/instrumental group*   *431 wks*

20 Jan 73	● **PILEDRIVER**	*Vertigo 6360 082*	**5**	37 wks
9 Jun 73	**THE BEST OF STATUS QUO**	*Pye NSPL 18402*	**32**	7 wks
6 Oct 73	★ **HELLO**	*Vertigo 6360 098*	**1**	28 wks
18 May 74	● **QUO**	*Vertigo 9102 001*	**2**	16 wks
1 Mar 75	★ **ON THE LEVEL**	*Vertigo 9102 002*	**1**	27 wks
8 Mar 75	**DOWN THE DUSTPIPE**	*Golden Hour CH 604*	**20**	6 wks
20 Mar 76	★ **BLUE FOR YOU**	*Vertigo 9102 006*	**1**	30 wks
12 Mar 77	● **LIVE**	*Vertigo 6641 580*	**3**	14 wks
26 Nov 77	● **ROCKIN' ALL OVER THE WORLD**	*Vertigo 9102 014* ...	**5**	15 wks
11 Nov 78	● **CAN'T STAND THE HEAT**	*Vertigo 9102 027*	**3**	14 wks
20 Oct 79	● **WHATEVER YOU WANT**	*Vertigo 9102 037*	**3**	14 wks
22 Mar 80	● **12 GOLD BARS**	*Vertigo QUO TV 1*	**3**	48 wks
25 Oct 80	● **JUST SUPPOSIN'**	*Vertigo 6302 057*	**4**	18 wks
28 Mar 81	● **NEVER TOO LATE**	*Vertigo 6302 104*	**2**	13 wks
10 Oct 81	**FRESH QUOTA**	*PRT DOW 2*	**74**	1 wk
24 Apr 82	★ **1982**	*Vertigo 6302 169*	**1**	20 wks
13 Nov 82	● **FROM THE MAKERS OF...**	*Vertigo PROLP 1*	**4**	18 wks
3 Dec 83	● **BACK TO BACK**	*Vertigo VERH 10*	**9**	22 wks
4 Aug 84	**STATUS QUO LIVE AT THE NEC** *Vertigo (Holland) 8189 471*		**83**	3 wks
1 Dec 84	**12 GOLD BARS VOLUME 2 (AND 1)** *Vertigo QUO TV 2*		**12**	18 wks
6 Sep 86	● **IN THE ARMY NOW**	*Vertigo VERH 36*	**7**	23 wks
18 Jun 88	**AIN'T COMPLAINING**	*Vertigo VERH 58*	**12**	5 wks
2 Dec 89	**PERFECT REMEDY**	*Vertigo 842098 1*	**49**	2 wks
20 Oct 90	● **ROCKING ALL OVER THE YEARS**	*Vertigo 8467971*	**2**	25 wks
5 Oct 91	● **ROCK 'TIL YOU DROP**	*Vertigo 5103411*	**10**	7 wks

STEEL PULSE *UK, male vocal/instrumental group*   *18 wks*

5 Aug 78	● **HANDSWORTH REVOLUTION**	*Island EMI ILPS 9502*	**9**	12 wks
14 Jul 79	**TRIBUTE TO MARTYRS**	*Island ILPS 9568*	**42**	6 wks

STEELEYE SPAN
UK, male/female vocal instrumental group 48 wks

10 Apr 71	**PLEASE TO SEE THE KING** *B&C CAS 1029*	45	2 wks
14 Oct 72	**BELOW THE SALT** *Chrysalis CHR 1008*	43	1 wk
28 Apr 73	**PARCEL OF ROGUES** *Chrysalis CHR 1046*	26	5 wks
23 Mar 74	**NOW WE ARE SIX** *Chrysalis CHR 1053*	13	13 wks
15 Feb 75	**COMMONER'S CROWN** *Chrysalis CHR 1071*	21	4 wks
25 Oct 75	● **ALL AROUND MY HAT** *Chrysalis CHR 1091*	7	20 wks
16 Oct 76	**ROCKET COTTAGE** *Chrysalis CHR 1123*	41	3 wks

STEELY DAN *US, male vocal/instrumental group* 77 wks

30 Mar 74	**PRETZEL LOGIC** *Probe SPBA 6282*	37	2 wks
3 May 75	**KATY LIED** *ABC ABCL 5094*	13	6 wks
20 Sep 75	**CAN'T BUY A THRILL** *ABC ABCL 5024*	38	1 wk
22 May 76	**ROYAL SCAM** *ABC ABCL 5161*	11	13 wks
8 Oct 77	● **AJA** *ABC ABCL 5225*	5	10 wks
2 Dec 78	**GREATEST HITS** *ABC BLD 616*	41	18 wks
29 Nov 80	**GAUCHO** *MCA MCF 3090*	27	12 wks
3 Jul 82	**GOLD** *MCA MCF 3145*	44	6 wks
26 Oct 85	**REELIN' IN THE YEARS – THE VERY BEST OF STEELY DAN** *MCA DANTV 1*	43	5 wks
10 Oct 87	**DO IT AGAIN – THE VERY BEST OF STEELY DAN** *Telstar STAR 2297*	64	4 wks

Wout STEENHUIS *Holland, male instrumentalist – guitar* 7 wks

21 Nov 81	**HAWAIIAN PARADISE/CHRISTMAS** *Warwick WW 5106*	28	7 wks

300

S

Jim STEINMAN *US, male vocalist* 24 wks

9 May 81	● **BAD FOR GOOD** *Epic EPC 84361*	7	24 wks

Martin STEPHENSON and the DAINTEES
UK, male vocal/instrumental group 10 wks

17 May 86	**BOAT TO BOLIVIA** *Kitchenware KWLP 5*	85	3 wks
16 Apr 88	**GLADSOME, HUMOUR AND BLUE** *Kitchenware KWLP 8*	39	4 wks
19 May 90	**SALUTATION ROAD** *Kitchenware 8281981*	35	3 wks

STEPPENWOLF *Canada/US, male vocal/instrumental group* 20 wks

28 Feb 70	**MONSTER** *Stateside SSL 5021*	43	4 wks
25 Apr 70	**STEPPENWOLF** *Stateside SSL 5020*	59	2 wks
4 Jul 70	**STEPPENWOLF LIVE** *Stateside SSL 5029*	16	14 wks

Cat STEVENS *UK, male vocalist* 255 wks

25 Mar 67	● **MATTHEW AND SON** *Deram SML 1004*	7	16 wks
11 Jul 70	**MONA BONE JAKON** *Island ILPS 9118*	63	4 wks
28 Nov 70	**TEA FOR THE TILLERMAN** *Island ILPS 9135*	20	39 wks
2 Oct 71	● **TEASER AND THE FIRECAT** *Island ILPS 9154*	3	93 wks
7 Oct 72	● **CATCH BULL AT FOUR** *Island ILPS 9206*	2	27 wks
21 Jul 73	● **FOREIGNER** *Island ILPS 9240*	3	10 wks

Thanks in part to an effective television advertising campaign, the **Stylistics** had the top album of 1975.

Only Phil Collins kept **Lisa Stansfield** out of number one with her first album.

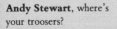

Andy Stewart, where's your troosers?

6 Apr 74	● **BUDDAH AND THE CHOCOLATE BOX**		
	Island ILPS 9274	3	15 wks
19 Jul 75	● **GREATEST HITS** *Island ILPS 9310*	2	24 wks
14 May 77	**IZITSO** *Island ILPS 9451*	18	15 wks
3 Feb 90	● **THE VERY BEST OF CAT STEVENS** *Island CATV 1* ...	4	12 wks

Ray STEVENS *US, male vocalist*   8 wks

26 Sep 70	**EVERYTHING IS BEAUTIFUL** *CBS 64074*	62	1 wk
13 Sep 75	**MISTY** *Janus 9109 401*	23	7 wks

Shakin' STEVENS *UK, male vocalist*   156 wks

15 Mar 80	**TAKE ONE** *Epic EPC 83978*	62	2 wks
4 Apr 81	● **THIS OLE HOUSE** *Epic EPC 84985*	2	28 wks
8 Aug 81	**SHAKIN' STEVENS** *Hallmark/Pickwick SHM 3065*	34	5 wks
19 Sep 81	★ **SHAKY** *Epic EPC 10027*	1	28 wks
9 Oct 82	● **GIVE ME YOUR HEART TONIGHT** *Epic EPC 10035* ...	3	18 wks
26 Nov 83	**THE BOP WON'T STOP** *Epic EPC 86301*	21	27 wks
17 Nov 84	● **GREATEST HITS** *Epic EPC 10047*	8	22 wks
16 Nov 85	**LIPSTICK POWDER AND PAINT** *Epic EPC 26646*	37	9 wks
31 Oct 87	**LET'S BOOGIE** *Epic 460 126–1*	59	7 wks
19 Nov 88	**A WHOLE LOTTA SHAKY** *Epic MOOD 5*	42	8 wks
20 Oct 90	**THERE'S TWO KINDS OF MUSIC: ROCK 'N' ROLL**		
	Telstar STAR 2454	65	2 wks

Al STEWART *UK, male vocalist*   20 wks

11 Apr 70	**ZERO SHE FLIES** *CBS 63848*	40	4 wks
5 Feb 77	**YEAR OF THE CAT** *RCA RS 1082*	38	7 wks
21 Oct 78	**TIME PASSAGES** *RCA PL 25173*	39	1 wk
6 Sep 80	**24 CARAT** *RCA PL 25306*	55	6 wks
9 Jun 84	**RUSSIANS AND AMERICANS** *RCA PL 70307*	83	2 wks

Andy STEWART *UK, male vocalist*   2 wks

3 Feb 62	**ANDY STEWART** *Top Rank 35–116*	13	2 wks

Dave STEWART and the SPIRITUAL COWBOYS *UK, male vocal/instrumental group*   7 wks

7 Apr 90	**LILY WAS HERE** *Anxious ZL 74233*	35	5 wks
15 Sep 90	**DAVE STEWART AND THE SPIRITUAL COWBOYS**		
	RCA OB 74710	38	2 wks

First album credited to David A. Stewart.

Jermaine STEWART *US, male vocalist*   12 wks

4 Oct 86	**FRANTIC ROMANTIC** *10 DIX 26*	49	4 wks
5 Mar 88	**SAY IT AGAIN** *Siren SRNLP 14*	32	8 wks

Rod STEWART *UK, male vocalist*   666 wks

3 Oct 70	**GASOLINE ALLEY** *Vertigo 6360 500*	62	1 wk
24 Jul 71	★ **EVERY PICTURE TELLS A STORY** *Mercury 6338 063* ..	1	81 wks
5 Aug 72	★ **NEVER A DULL MOMENT** *Philips 6499 153*	1	36 wks
25 Aug 73	★ **SING IT AGAIN ROD** *Mercury 6499 484*	1	30 wks
19 Oct 74	★ **SMILER** *Mercury 9104 011*	1	20 wks
30 Aug 75	★ **ATLANTIC CROSSING** *Warner Bros. K 56151*	1	88 wks

3 Jul	76	★ **A NIGHT ON THE TOWN** *Riva RVLP 1*	1	47 wks
16 Jul	77	**BEST OF ROD STEWART** *Mercury 6643 030*	18	22 wks
19 Nov	77	● **FOOT LOOSE AND FANCY FREE** *Riva RVLP 5*	3	26 wks
21 Jan	78	**ATLANTIC CROSSING (re-issue)** *Riva RVLP 4*	60	1 wk
9 Dec	78	● **BLONDES HAVE MORE FUN** *Riva RVLP 8*	3	31 wks
10 Nov	79	★ **GREATEST HITS** *Riva ROD TV 1*	1	74 wks
22 Nov	80	● **FOOLISH BEHAVIOUR** *Riva RVLP 11*	4	13 wks
14 Nov	81	● **TONIGHT I'M YOURS** *Riva RVLP 14*	8	21 wks
13 Nov	82	**ABSOLUTELY LIVE** *Riva RVLP 17*	35	5 wks
18 Jun	83	● **BODY WISHES** *Warner Bros. K 923 8771*	5	27 wks
23 Jun	84	● **CAMOUFLAGE** *Warner Bros. 925095*	8	17 wks
5 Jul	86	● **EVERY BEAT OF MY HEART** *Warner Bros. WX 53*	5	17 wks
4 Jun	88	**OUT OF ORDER** *Warner Bros. WX 152*	11	8 wks
25 Nov	89	● **THE BEST OF ROD STEWART** *Warner Bros. WX 314* ...	3	74 wks
6 Apr	91	● **VAGABOND HEART** *Warner Bros WX 408*	2	27 wks

See also the Faces. Greatest Hits changed label/number to Warner Bros. K 56744 during its chart run.

STIFF LITTLE FINGERS
UK, male vocal/instrumental group   *57 wks*

3 Mar	79	**INFLAMMABLE MATERIAL** *Rough Trade ROUGH 1*	14	19 wks
15 Mar	80	● **NOBODY'S HEROES** *Chrysalis CHR 1270*	8	10 wks
20 Sep	80	● **HANX** *Chrysalis CHR 1300*	9	5 wks
25 Apr	81	**GO FOR IT** *Chrysalis CHX 1339*	14	8 wks
2 Oct	82	**NOW THEN** *Chrysalis CHR 1400*	24	6 wks
12 Feb	83	**ALL THE BEST** *Chrysalis CTY 1414*	19	9 wks

Stephen STILLS *US, male vocalist*   *7 wks*

19 Dec	70	**STEPHEN STILLS** *Atlantic 2401 004*	30	1 wk
14 Aug	71	**STEPHEN STILLS 2** *Atlantic 2401 013*	22	3 wks
26 Jul	75	**STILLS** *CBS 69146*	31	1 wk
29 May	76	**ILLEGAL STILLS** *CBS 81330*	54	2 wks

See also Crosby, Stills and Nash; Crosby, Stills, Nash and Young; Stills–Young Band; Stephen Stills' Manassas.

Stephen STILLS' MANASSAS
US, male vocal/instrumental group   *7 wks*

20 May	72	**MANASSAS** *Atlantic K 60021*	30	5 wks
19 May	73	**DOWN THE ROAD** *Atlantic K 40440*	33	2 wks

See also Stephen Stills.

STILLS–YOUNG BAND
US/Canada, male vocal/instrumental group   *5 wks*

9 Oct	76	**LONG MAY YOU RUN** *Reprise K 54081*	12	5 wks

See also Stephen Stills; Neil Young.

STING *UK, male vocalist*   *139 wks*

29 Jun	85	● **THE DREAM OF THE BLUE TURTLES**		
		A & M DREAM 1	3	64 wks
28 Jun	86	**BRING ON THE NIGHT** *A & M BRING 1*	16	12 wks
24 Oct	87	★ **NOTHING LIKE THE SUN** *A & M AMA 6402*	1	47 wks
2 Feb	91	★ **THE SOUL CAGES** *A & M 3964051*	1	16 wks

303

S

STONE ROSES *UK, male vocal/instrumental group* 48 wks

13 May 89	**THE STONE ROSES** *Silvertone ORELP 502*	19	48 wks

STONE THE CROWS
UK, female/male vocal/instrumental group 3 wks

7 Oct 72	**ONTINUOUS PERFORMANCE** *Polydor 2391 043*	33	3 wks

STOOGES – *See Iggy POP*

STORYVILLE JAZZMEN – *See Bob WALLIS and his STORYVILLE JAZZMEN*

STRANGLERS *UK, male vocal/instrumental group* 216 wks

30 Apr 77	● **STRANGLERS IV (RATTUS NORVEGICUS)**		
	United Artists UAG 30045	4	34 wks
8 Oct 77	● **NO MORE HEROES** *United Artists UAG 30200*	2	19 wks
3 Jun 78	● **BLACK AND WHITE** *United Artists UAK 30222*	2	18 wks
10 Mar 79	● **LIVE (X CERT)** *United Artists UAG 30224*	7	10 wks
6 Oct 79	● **THE RAVEN** *United Artists UAG 30262*	4	8 wks
21 Feb 81	● **THEMENINBLACK** *Liberty LBG 30313*	8	5 wks
21 Nov 81	**LA FOLIE** *Liberty LBG 30342*	11	18 wks
25 Sep 82	**THE COLLECTION 1977–1982** *Liberty LBS 30353*	12	16 wks
22 Jan 83	● **FELINE** *Epic EPC 25237*	4	11 wks
17 Nov 84	**AURAL SCULPTURE** *Epic EPC 26220*	14	10 wks
20 Sep 86	**OFF THE BEATEN TRACK** *Liberty LBG 5001*	80	2 wks
8 Nov 86	**DREAMTIME** *Epic EPC 26648*	16	6 wks
20 Feb 88	**ALL LIVE AND ALL OF THE NIGHT** *Epic 465259*	12	6 wks
18 Feb 89	**THE SINGLES** *EMI EM 1314*	57	2 wks
17 Mar 90	**10** *Epic 4664831*	15	4 wks
1 Dec 90	● **GREATEST HITS 1977–1990** *Epic 4675411*	4	47 wks

STRAWBERRY SWITCHBLADE
UK, female vocal duo 4 wks

13 Apr 85	**STRAWBERRY SWITCHBLADE** *Korova KODE 11*	25	4 wks

STRAWBS *UK, male vocal/instrumental group* 31 wks

21 Nov 70	**JUST A COLLECTION OF ANTIQUES AND CURIOS**		
	A & M AMLS 994	27	2 wks
17 Jul 71	**FROM THE WITCHWOOD** *A & M AMLH 64304*	39	2 wks
26 Feb 72	**GRAVE NEW WORLD** *A & M AMLH 68078*	11	12 wks
24 Feb 73	● **BURSTING AT THE SEAMS** *A & M AMLH 68144*	2	12 wks
27 Apr 74	**HERO AND HEROINE** *A & M AMLH 63607*	35	3 wks

STRAY CATS *US, male vocal/instrumental group* 32 wks

28 Feb 81	● **STRAY CATS** *Arista STRAY 1*	6	22 wks
21 Nov 81	**GONNA BALL** *Arista STRAY 2*	48	4 wks
3 Sep 83	**RANT 'N' RAVE WITH THE STRAY CATS**		
	Arista STRAY 3	51	5 wks
8 Apr 89	**BLAST OFF** *EMI MTL 1040*	58	1 wk

STREETWALKERS *UK, male vocal/instrumental group* 6 wks

12 Jun 76	**RED CARD** *Vertigo 9102 010*	16	6 wks

Barbra STREISAND *US, female vocalist*   *394 wks*

22 Jan	66	● MY NAME IS BARBRA, TWO *CBS BPG 62603*	6	22 wks
4 Apr	70	GREATEST HITS *CBS 63921*	44	2 wks
17 Apr	71	STONEY END *CBS 64269*	28	2 wks
15 Jun	74	THE WAY WE WERE *CBS 69057*	49	1 wk
23 Jul	77	STREISAND SUPERMAN *CBS 86030*	32	9 wks
15 Jul	78	SONGBIRD *CBS 86060*	50	1 wk
17 Mar	79	★ BARBRA STREISAND HITS VOL. 2 *CBS 10012*	1	30 wks
17 Nov	79	WET *CBS 86104*	25	13 wks
11 Oct	80	★ GUILTY *CBS 86122*	1	82 wks
16 Jan	82	★ LOVE SONGS *CBS 10031*	1	129 wks
19 Nov	83	YENTL (original soundtrack) *CBS 86302*	21	35 wks
27 Oct	84	EMOTION *CBS 86309*	15	12 wks
18 Jan	86	● THE BROADWAY ALBUM *CBS 86322*	3	16 wks
30 May	87	ONE VOICE *CBS 450 890-1*	27	7 wks
3 Dec	88	TILL I LOVED YOU *CBS 462943 1*	29	13 wks
25 Nov	89	A COLLECTION – GREATEST HITS ... AND MORE *CBS 465845 1*	22	20 wks

STRINGS FOR PLEASURE *UK, orchestra*   *1 wk*

4 Dec	71	BEST OF BACHARACH *MFP 1334*	49	1 wk

Joe STRUMMER *UK, male vocalist*   *1 wk*

14 Oct	89	EARTHQUAKE WEATHER *Epic 465347 1*	58	1 wk

STYLE COUNCIL *UK, male vocal/instrumental duo*   *93 wks*   **305**

24 Mar	84	● CAFE BLEU *Polydor TSCLP 1*	2	38 wks
8 Jun	85	★ OUR FAVOURITE SHOP *Polydor TSCLP 2*	1	22 wks
17 May	86	● HOME AND ABROAD *Polydor TSCLP 3*	8	8 wks
14 Feb	87	● THE COST OF LOVING *Polydor TSCLP 4*	2	7 wks
2 Jul	88	CONFESSIONS OF A POP GROUP *Polydor TSCMC 5* ...	15	3 wks
18 Mar	89	● SINGULAR ADVENTURES OF THE STYLE COUNCIL *Polydor TSCTV 1*	3	15 wks

S

STYLISTICS *US, male vocal group*   *139 wks*

24 Aug	74	ROCKIN' ROLL BABY *Avco 6466 012*	42	3 wks
21 Sep	74	LET'S PUT IT ALL TOGETHER *Avco 6466 013*	26	14 wks
1 Mar	75	FROM THE MOUNTAIN *Avco 9109 002*	36	1 wk
5 Apr	75	★ THE BEST OF THE STYLISTICS *Avco 9109 003*	1	63 wks
5 Jul	75	● THANK YOU BABY *Avco 9109 005*	5	23 wks
6 Dec	75	YOU ARE BEAUTIFUL *Avco 9109 006*	26	9 wks
12 Jun	76	FABULOUS *Avco 9109 008*	21	5 wks
18 Sep	76	★ BEST OF THE STYLISTICS VOL. 2 *H & L 9109 010*	1	21 wks

STYX *US, male vocal/instrumental group*   *24 wks*

3 Nov	79	CORNERSTONE *A & M AMLK 63711*	36	8 wks
24 Jan	81	● PARADISE THEATER *A & M AMLH 63719*	8	8 wks
12 Mar	83	KILROY WAS HERE *A & M AMLX 63734*	67	6 wks
5 May	84	CAUGHT IN THE ACT *A & M AMLM 66704*	44	2 wks

SUGARCUBES *Iceland, male/female vocal/instrumental group*   *9 wks*

7 May	88	LIFE'S TOO GOOD *One Little Indian TPLP 5*	14	6 wks
14 Oct	89	HERE TODAY, TOMORROW, NEXT WEEK *One Little Indian TPLP 15*	15	3 wks

SUICIDAL TENDENCIES
UK, male vocal/instrumental group   2 wks

9 May 87	**JOIN THE ARMY** *Virgin V 2424*	81	1 wk
21 Jul 90	**LIGHTS...CAMERA...REVOLUTION** *Epic 4665691* .	59	1 wk

Donna SUMMER *US, female vocalist*   196 wks

31 Jan 76	**LOVE TO LOVE YOU BABY** *GTO GTLP 008*	16	9 wks
22 May 76	**A LOVE TRILOGY** *GTO GTLP 010*	41	10 wks
25 Jun 77 ●	**I REMEMBER YESTERDAY** *GTO GTLP 025*	3	23 wks
26 Nov 77	**ONCE UPON A TIME** *Casablanca CALD 5003*	24	13 wks
7 Jan 78 ●	**GREATEST HITS** *GTO GTLP 028*	4	18 wks
21 Oct 78	**LIVE AND MORE** *Casablanca CALD 5006*	16	16 wks
2 Jun 79	**BAD GIRLS** *Casablanca CALD 5007*	23	23 wks
10 Nov 79	**ON THE RADIO – GREATEST HITS VOLS. 1 & 2**		
	Casablanca CALD 5008	24	22 wks
1 Nov 80	**THE WANDERER** *Geffen K 99124*	55	2 wks
31 Jul 82	**DONNA SUMMER** *Warner Bros. K 99163*	13	16 wks
16 Jul 83	**SHE WORKS HARD FOR THE MONEY**		
	Mercury MERL 21	28	5 wks
15 Sep 84	**CATS WITHOUT CLAWS** *Warner Bros. 250806*	69	2 wks
25 Mar 89	**ANOTHER PLACE AND TIME** *Warner Bros. WX 219*	17	28 wks
24 Nov 90	**THE BEST OF DONNA SUMMER** *Warner Bros WX 397* ..	24	9 wks

SUNDAYS *UK, male/female vocal/instrumental group*   8 wks

27 Jan 90 ●	**READING, WRITING AND ARITHMETIC**		
	Rough Trade ROUGH 148	4	8 wks

SUNSHINE BAND – *See KC and the SUNSHINE BAND*

SUPERTRAMP *UK/US, male vocal/instrumental group*   170 wks

23 Nov 74 ●	**CRIME OF THE CENTURY** *A & M AMLS 68258*	4	22 wks
6 Dec 75	**CRISIS? WHAT CRISIS?** *A & M AMLH 68347*	20	15 wks
23 Apr 77	**EVEN IN THE QUIETEST MOMENTS**		
	A & M AMLK 64634	12	22 wks
31 Mar 79 ●	**BREAKFAST IN AMERICA** *A & M AMLK 63708* ...	3	53 wks
4 Oct 80 ●	**PARIS** *A & M AMLM 66702*	7	17 wks
6 Nov 82 ●	**FAMOUS LAST WORDS** *A & M AMLK 63732*	6	16 wks
25 May 85	**BROTHER WHERE YOU BOUND**		
	A & M AMA 5014	20	5 wks
18 Oct 86 ●	**THE AUTOBIOGRAPHY OF SUPERTRAMP**		
	A & M TRAMP 1	9	19 wks
31 Oct 87	**FREE AS A BIRD** *A & M AMA 5181*	93	1 wk

SUPREMES *US, female vocal group*   180 wks

5 Dec 64 ●	**MEET THE SUPREMES** *Stateside SL 10109*	8	6 wks
17 Dec 66	**SUPREMES A GO-GO** *Tamla Motown STML 11039*	15	21 wks
13 May 67	**SUPREMES SING MOTOWN**		
	Tamla Motown STML 11047	15	16 wks
30 Sep 67	**SUPREMES SING RODGERS AND HART**		
	Tamla Motown STML 11054	25	7 wks
20 Jan 68 ★	**GREATEST HITS** *Tamla Motown STML 11063*	1	60 wks
30 Mar 68 ●	**LIVE AT THE TALK OF THE TOWN**		
	Tamla Motown STML 11070	6	18 wks
20 Jul 68	**REFLECTIONS** *Tamla Motown STML 11073*	30	2 wks
1 Feb 69 ●	**LOVE CHILD** *Tamla Motown STML 11095*	8	6 wks
25 Sep 71	**TOUCH** *Tamla Motown STML 11189*	40	1 wk
17 Sep 77 ★	**20 GOLDEN GREATS** *Motown EMTV 5*	1	34 wks

21 Jan 89 ● **LOVE SUPREME** *Motown ZL 72701* .... **10** 9 wks

See also Diana Ross and the Supremes with the Temptations; Supremes and the Four Tops; Diana Ross. All albums beginning with Greatest Hits, *with the exception of* Touch, *are credited to Diana Ross and the Supremes.*

SUPREMES and the FOUR TOPS
US, female and male vocal groups   *11 wks*

29 May 71 ● **MAGNIFICENT SEVEN** *Tamla Motown STML 11179* ..... **6** 11 wks

See also Supremes; Four Tops.

SURVIVOR *US, male vocal/instrumental group*   *10 wks*

21 Aug 82 **EYE OF THE TIGER** *Scotti Bros SCT 85845* .... **12** 10 wks

Walter SUSSKIND – *See LONDON PHILHARMONIC CHOIR*

SUTHERLAND BROTHERS and QUIVER
UK, male vocal/instrumental group   *11 wks*

15 May 76 **REACH FOR THE SKY** *CBS 69191* .... **26** 8 wks
9 Oct 76 **SLIPSTREAM** *CBS 81593* .... **49** 3 wks

SWANS WAY *UK, male/female vocal/instrumental group*   *1 wk*

3 Nov 84 **THE FUGITIVE KIND** *Balgier SWAN 1* .... **88** 1 wk

307

S

Keith SWEAT *US, male vocalist*   *25 wks*

16 Jan 88 **MAKE IT LAST FOREVER** *Elektra 960763 1* .... **42** 21 wks
23 Jun 90 **I'LL GIVE ALL MY LOVE TO YOU** *Vintertainment EKT 60* **47** 4 wks

SWEET *UK, male vocal/instrumental group*   *8 wks*

18 May 74 **SWEET FANNY ADAMS** *RCA LPI 5038* .... **27** 2 wks
22 Sep 84 **SWEET 16 – IT'S ... IT'S ... SWEET'S HITS**
         Anagram GRAM 16 .... **49** 6 wks

SWERVEDRIVER *UK, male vocal/instrumental group*   *1 wk*

12 Oct 91 **RAISE** *Creation CRELP 093* .... **44** 1 wk

SWINGLE SINGERS *US/France, male/female vocal group*   *18 wks*

1 Feb 64 **JAZZ SEBASTIAN BACH** *Philips BL 7572* .... **13** 18 wks

SWING OUT SISTER
UK, male/female vocal/instrumental group   *32 wks*

23 May 87 ★ **IT'S BETTER TO TRAVEL** *Mercury OUTLP 1* .... **1** 21 wks
20 May 89 ● **KALEIDOSCOPE WORLD** *Fontana 838293 1* .... **3** 11 wks

SYBIL *US, female vocalist*   *6 wks*

5 Sep 87 **LET YOURSELF GO** *Champion CHAMP 1009* .... **92** 1 wk

During the 60s the **Supremes** (left) and Martha and the Vandellas accounted for eight hit albums. Unfortunately for Miss Reeves, they all belonged to Miss Ross's group.

Mark Hollis (front) was the lead singer of **Talk Talk**.

24 Feb 90   **WALK ON BY**   *PWL HF 10*   **21**   5 wks

SYLVESTER   *US, male vocalist*   *3 wks*

23 Jun 79   **MIGHTY REAL**   *Fantasy FTA 3009* .... **62**   3 wks

David SYLVIAN   *UK, male vocalist*   *21 wks*

7 Jul 84 ● **BRILLIANT TREES**   *Virgin V 2290* .... **4**   14 wks
13 Sep 86   **GONE TO EARTH**   *Virgin VDL 1* .... **24**   5 wks
7 Nov 87   **SECRETS OF THE BEEHIVE**   *Virgin V 2471* .... **37**   2 wks
See also David Sylvian and Holgar Czukay.

David SYLVIAN and Holgar CZUKAY
UK/Germany, male vocal/instrumental duo   *1 wk*

2 Apr 88   **PLIGHT AND PREMONITION**   *Virgin VE 11* .... **71**   1 wk
See also David Sylvian.

SYNTHPHONIC VARIATIONS
UK, session musicians   *1 wk*

1 Nov 86   **SEASONS**   *CBS 450 149–1* .... **84**   1 wk

309

t

t

TALK TALK   *UK, male vocal/instrumental group*   *84 wks*

24 Jul 82   **THE PARTY'S OVER**   *EMI EMC 3431* .... **21**   25 wks
25 Feb 84   **IT'S MY LIFE**   *EMI EMC 2400021* .... **35**   8 wks
1 Mar 86 ● **THE COLOUR OF SPRING**   *EMI EMC 3506* .... **8**   21 wks
24 Sep 88   **SPIRIT OF EDEN**   *Parlophone PCSD 105* .... **19**   5 wks
9 Jun 90 ● **THE VERY BEST OF TALK TALK – NATURAL HISTORY**
         Parlophone PCSD 109 .... **3**   21 wks
6 Apr 91   **HISTORY REVISITED**   *Parlophone PCS 7349* .... **35**   2 wks
28 Sep 91   **LAUGHING STOCK**   *Verve 8477171* .... **26**   2 wks

TALKING HEADS
US/UK, male/female vocal/instrumental group   *213 wks*

25 Feb 78   **TALKING HEADS '77**   *Sire 9103 328* .... **60**   1 wk
29 Jul 78   **MORE SONGS ABOUT BUILDINGS AND FOOD**
         Sire K 56531 .... **21**   3 wks
15 Sep 79   **FEAR OF MUSIC**   *Sire SRK 6076* .... **33**   5 wks
1 Nov 80   **REMAIN IN LIGHT**   *Sire SRK 6095* .... **21**   17 wks
10 Apr 82   **THE NAME OF THIS BAND IS TALKING HEADS**
         Sire SRK 23590 .... **22**   5 wks
18 Jun 83   **SPEAKING IN TONGUES**   *Sire K 923 8831* .... **21**   12 wks
27 Oct 84   **STOP MAKING SENSE**   *EMI TAH 1* .... **37**   81 wks
29 Jun 85 ● **LITTLE CREATURES**   *EMI TAH 2* .... **10**   65 wks
27 Sep 86 ● **TRUE STORIES**   *EMI EU 3511* .... **7**   9 wks
26 Mar 88 ● **NAKED**   *EMI EMD 1005* .... **3**   15 wks

TANGERINE DREAM
Germany, male instrumental group   *77 wks*

20 Apr 74	**PHAEDRA** *Virgin V 2010*	**15**	15 wks
5 Apr 75	**RUBYCON** *Virgin V 2025*	**12**	14 wks
20 Dec 75	**RICOCHET** *Virgin V 2044*	**40**	2 wks
13 Nov 76	**STRATOSFEAR** *Virgin V 2068*	**39**	4 wks
23 Jul 77	**SORCERER (film soundtrack)** *MCA MCF 2806*	**25**	7 wks
19 Nov 77	**ENCORE** *Virgin VD 2506*	**55**	1 wk
1 Apr 78	**CYCLONE** *Virgin V 2097*	**37**	4 wks
17 Feb 79	**FORCE MAJEURE** *Virgin V 2111*	**26**	7 wks
7 Jun 80	**TANGRAM** *Virgin V 2147*	**36**	5 wks
18 Apr 81	**THIEF (film soundtrack)** *Virgin V 2198*	**43**	3 wks
19 Sep 81	**EXIT** *Virgin V 2212*	**43**	5 wks
10 Apr 82	**WHITE EAGLE** *Virgin V 2226*	**57**	5 wks
5 Nov 83	**HYPERBOREA** *Virgin V 2292*	**45**	2 wks
10 Nov 84	**POLAND** *Jive Electro HIP 22*	**90**	1 wk
26 Jul 86	**UNDERWATER SUNLIGHT** *Jive Electro HIP 40*	**97**	1 wk
27 Jun 87	**TYGER** *Jive Electro HIP 47*	**88**	1 wk

TANK *UK, male vocal/instrumental group*   *5 wks*

13 Mar 82	**FILTH HOUNDS OF HADES** *Kamaflage KAMLP 1*	**33**	5 wks

TASTE *Ireland, male vocal/instrumental group*   *12 wks*

7 Feb 70	**ON THE BOARDS** *Polydor 583–083*	**18**	11 wks
9 Sep 72	**TASTE LIVE AT THE ISLE OF WIGHT** *Polydor 2383 120*	**41**	1 wk

Jeffrey TATE – *See Nigel KENNEDY*

TAVARES *US, male vocal group*   *15 wks*

21 Aug 76	**SKY HIGH** *Capitol EST 11533*	**22**	13 wks
1 Apr 78	**THE BEST OF TAVARES** *Capitol EST 11701*	**39**	2 wks

Andy TAYLOR *UK, male vocalist/instrumentalist – guitar*   *1 wk*

30 May 87	**THUNDER** *MCA MCG 6018*	**61**	1 wk

James TAYLOR *US, male vocalist*   *111 wks*

21 Nov 70	● **SWEET BABY JAMES** *Warner Bros. ES 1843*	**7**	53 wks
29 May 71	● **MUD SLIDE SLIM AND THE BLUE HORIZON** *Warner Bros. WS 2561*	**4**	41 wks
8 Jan 72	**SWEET BABY JAMES (re-issue)** *Warner Bros. K 46043*	**34**	6 wks
18 Mar 72	**MUD SLIDE SLIM AND THE BLUE HORIZON (re-issue)** *Warner Bros. K 46085*	**49**	1 wk
9 Dec 72	**ONE MAN DOG** *Warner Bros. K 46185*	**27**	5 wks
4 Apr 87	**CLASSIC SONGS** *CBS/WEA JTV 1*	**53**	5 wks

Roger TAYLOR *UK, male vocalist/instrumentalist – drums*   *9 wks*

18 Apr 81	**FUN IN SPACE** *EMI EMC 3369*	**18**	5 wks
7 Jul 84	**STRANGE FRONTIER** *EMI RTA 1*	**30**	4 wks

Kiri TE KANAWA *New Zealand, female vocalist*   37 wks

2 Apr 83	**CHANTS D'AUVERGNE VOL. 1** *Decca SXDL 7604*	57	1 wk
26 Oct 85	**BLUE SKIES** *London KTKT 1*	40	29 wks
13 Dec 86	**CHRISTMAS WITH KIRI** *Decca PROLP 12*	47	4 wks
17 Dec 88	**KIRI** *K-Tel NE 1424*	70	3 wks

Chants d'Auvergne Vol. 1 credits the English Chamber Orchestra. Blue Skies credits the Nelson Riddle Orchestra.

TEARDROP EXPLODES
UK, male vocal/instrumental group   42 wks

18 Oct 80	**KILIMANJARO** *Mercury 6359 035*	24	35 wks
5 Dec 81	**WILDER** *Mercury 6359 056*	29	6 wks
14 Apr 90	**EVERYBODY WANTS TO SHAG THE TEARDROP EXPLODES** *Fontana 8424391 72*	72	1 wk

TEARS FOR FEARS *UK, male vocal/instrumental duo*   176 wks

19 Mar 83	★ **THE HURTING** *Mercury MERS 17*	1	65 wks
9 Mar 85	● **SONGS FROM THE BIG CHAIR** *Mercury MERH 58*	2	81 wks
7 Oct 89	★ **THE SEEDS OF LOVE** *Fontana 838730 1*	1	30 wks

TECHNOTRONIC *Belgium/UK/Zaïre, male/female*
vocal/instrumental group   62 wks

6 Jan 90	● **PUMP UP THE JAM** *Swanyard SYRLP 1*	2	44 wks
2 Nov 90	● **TRIP ON THIS – REMIXES** *Telstar STAR 2461*	7	14 wks
15 Jun 91	**BODY TO BODY** *ARS 4683421*	27	4 wks

TEENAGE FANCLUB *UK, male vocal/instrumental group*   2 wks

7 Sep 91	**KING** *Creation CRELP 096*	53	2 wks
16 Nov 91	**BANDWAGONESQUE** *Creation CRELP 106*	22	2 wks

TELEVISION *US, male vocal/instrumental group*   17 wks

26 Mar 77	**MARQUEE MOON** *Elektra K 52046*	28	13 wks
29 Apr 78	● **ADVENTURE** *Elektra K 52072*	7	4 wks

TEMPERANCE SEVEN *UK, male vocal/instrumental group* 10 wks

13 May 61	**TEMPERANCE SEVEN PLUS ONE** *Argo RG 11*	19	1 wk
25 Nov 61	**TEMPERANCE SEVEN 1961** *Parlophone PMC 1152*	11	9 wks

TEMPLE CHURCH CHOIR
UK, male vocal/instrumental group   3 wks

16 Dec 61	● **CHRISTMAS CAROLS** *HMV CLP 1309*	8	3 wks

TEMPTATIONS *US, male vocal group*   99 wks

24 Dec 66	**GETTING READY** *Tamla Motown STML 11035*	40	2 wks
11 Feb 67	**TEMPTATIONS GREATEST HITS** *Tamla Motown STML 11042*	26	40 wks
22 Jul 67	**TEMPTATIONS LIVE** *Tamla Motown STML 11053*	20	4 wks

18 Nov 67	**TEMPTATIONS WITH A LOT OF SOUL**			
	Tamla Motown STML 11057	**19**	18 wks
20 Sep 69	**CLOUD NINE** *Tamla Motown STML 11109*	**32**	1 wk
14 Feb 70	**PUZZLE PEOPLE** *Tamla Motown STML 11133*	**20**	4 wks
11 Jul 70	**PSYCHEDELIC SHACK** *Tamla Motown STML 11147*	**56**	1 wk
26 Dec 70	**GREATEST HITS VOL. 2** *Tamla Motown STML 11170*	**35**	12 wks
29 Apr 72	**SOLID ROCK** *Tamla Motown STML 11202*	**34**	2 wks
20 Jan 73	**ALL DIRECTIONS** *Tamla Motown STML 11218*	**19**	7 wks
7 Jul 73	**MASTERPIECE** *Tamla Motown STML 11229*	**28**	3 wks
8 Dec 84	**TRULY FOR YOU** *Motown ZL 72342*	**75**	5 wks

See also Diana Ross and the Supremes with the Temptations.

10 C.C. *UK, male vocal/instrumental group* 197 wks

1 Sep 73	**10 C.C.** *UK UKAL 1005*	**36**	5 wks
15 Jun 74	● **SHEET MUSIC** *UK UKAL 1007*	**9**	24 wks
22 Mar 75	● **THE ORIGINAL SOUNDTRACK** *Mercury 9102 50Q*	**4**	40 wks
7 Jun 75	● **GREATEST HITS OF 10 C.C.** *Decca UKAL 1012*	**9**	18 wks
31 Jan 76	● **HOW DARE YOU?** *Mercury 9102 501*	**5**	31 wks
14 May 77	● **DECEPTIVE BENDS** *Mercury 9102 502*	**3**	21 wks
10 Dec 77	**LIVE AND LET LIVE** *Mercury 6641 698*	**14**	15 wks
23 Sep 78	● **BLOODY TOURISTS** *Mercury 9102 503*	**3**	15 wks
6 Oct 79	● **GREATEST HITS 1972–1978** *Mercury 9102 504*	**5**	21 wks
5 Apr 80	**LOOK HERE** *Mercury 9102 505*	**35**	5 wks
15 Oct 83	**WINDOW IN THE JUNGLE** *Mercury MERL 28*	**70**	2 wks

See also 10 C.C. and Godley and Creme.

10 C.C. and GODLEY AND CREME

UK, male vocal/instrumental group and instrumental duo 18 wks

29 Aug 87	● **CHANGING FACES – THE VERY BEST OF 10 C.C. AND GODLEY AND CREME** *ProTV TGCLP 1*	**4**	18 wks

See also 10 C.C; Godley and Creme.

TEN CITY *US, male vocal/instrumental group* 12 wks

18 Feb 89	**FOUNDATION** *Atlantic WX 249*	**22**	12 wks

TEN POLE TUDOR *UK, male vocal/instrumental group* 8 wks

9 May 81	**EDDIE, OLD BOB, DICK & GARRY** *Stiff SEEZ 31*	**44**	8 wks

10,000 MANIACS *US, male/female vocal/instrumental group* 8 wks

27 May 89	**BLIND MAN'S ZOO** *Elektra EKT 57*	**18**	8 wks

TEN YEARS AFTER *UK, male vocal/instrumental group* 73 wks

21 Sep 68	**UNDEAD** *Deram SML 1023*	**26**	7 wks
22 Feb 69	● **STONEDHENGE** *Deram SML 1029*	**6**	5 wks
4 Oct 69	● **SSSSH** *Deram SML 1052*	**4**	18 wks
2 May 70	● **CRICKLEWOOD GREEN** *Deram SML 1065*	**4**	27 wks
9 Jan 71	● **WATT** *Deram SML 1078*	**5**	12 wks
13 Nov 71	**SPACE IN TIME** *Chrysalis CHR 1001*	**36**	1 wk
7 Oct 72	**ROCK AND ROLL** *Chrysalis CHR 1009*	**27**	1 wk
28 Jul 73	**RECORDED LIVE** *Chrysalis CHR 1049*	**36**	2 wks

TENNILLE – *See CAPTAIN and TENNILLE*

TERRAPLANE UK, male vocal/instrumental group   1 wk

| 25 Jan 86 | **BLACK AND WHITE** Epic EPC 26439 .... | 74 | 1 wk |

Tammi TERRELL – See Marvin GAYE and Tammi TERRELL

TESLA US, male vocal/instrumental group   5 wks

11 Feb 89	**THE GREAT RADIO CONTROVERSY** Geffen WX 244	34	2 wks
2 Mar 91	**FIVE MAN ACOUSTICAL JAM** Geffen 9243111	59	1 wk
21 Sep 91	**PSYCHOTIC SUPPER** Geffen GEF 24424	44	2 wks

TESTAMENT US, male vocal/instrumental group   5 wks

28 May 88	**THE NEW ORDER** Megaforce 781849 1	81	1 wk
19 Aug 89	**PRACTICE WHAT YOU PREACH** Atlantic WX 297	40	2 wks
6 Oct 90	**SOULS OF BLACK** Megaforce 7567821431	35	2 wks

TEXAS UK, male/female vocal/instrumental group   31 wks

| 25 Mar 89 ● | **SOUTHSIDE** Mercury 838171 1 .... | 3 | 27 wks |
| 5 Oct 91 | **MOTHER'S HEAVEN** Mercury 8485781 .... | 32 | 4 wks |

THAT PETROL EMOTION
UK, male vocal/instrumental group   8 wks   **313**

10 May 86	**MANIC POP THRILL** Demon FIEND 70	84	2 wks
23 May 87	**BABBLE** Polydor TPE LP 1	30	3 wks
24 Sep 88	**END OF MILLENNIUM PSYCHOSIS BLUES**		
	Virgin V 2550	53	2 wks
21 Apr 90	**CHEMICRAZY** Virgin V 2618	62	1 wk

t

The THE UK, male vocal/instrumental group   46 wks

29 Oct 83	**SOUL MINING** Some Bizzare EPC 25525	27	5 wks
29 Nov 86	**INFECTED** Some Bizzare EPC 26770	14	30 wks
27 May 89 ●	**MIND BOMB** Epic 463319 1	4	9 wks

Matt Johnson leads The The which is an informal group of his studio guests and friends.

THEATRE OF HATE UK, male vocal/instrumental group   9 wks

| 13 Mar 82 | **WESTWORLD** Burning Rome TOH 1 .... | 17 | 6 wks |
| 18 Aug 84 | **REVOLUTION** Burning Rome TOH 2 .... | 67 | 3 wks |

THEN JERICO UK, male vocal/instrumental group   24 wks

| 3 Oct 87 | **FIRST (THE SOUND OF MUSIC)** London LONLP 26 ... | 35 | 7 wks |
| 4 Mar 89 ● | **THE BIG AREA** London 828122 1 .... | 4 | 17 wks |

THEY MIGHT BE GIANTS
US, male vocal/instrumental duo   12 wks

| 7 Apr 90 | **FLOOD** Elektra EKT 68 .... | 14 | 12 wks |

THIN LIZZY
Ireland/UK/US, male vocal/instrumental group — 228 wks

27 Sep 75	FIGHTING *Vertigo 6360 121*		60	1 wk
10 Apr 76	● JAILBREAK *Vertigo 9102 008*		10	50 wks
6 Nov 76	JOHNNY THE FOX *Vertigo 9102 012*		11	24 wks
1 Oct 77	● BAD REPUTATION *Vertigo 9102 016*		4	9 wks
17 Jun 78	● LIVE AND DANGEROUS *Vertigo 6641 807*		2	62 wks
5 May 79	● BLACK ROSE (A ROCK LEGEND) *Vertigo 9102 032*		2	21 wks
18 Oct 80	● CHINA TOWN *Vertigo 6359 030*		7	7 wks
11 Apr 81	● ADVENTURES OF THIN LIZZY *Vertigo LIZTV 1*		6	13 wks
5 Dec 81	RENEGADE *Vertigo 6359 083*		38	8 wks
12 Mar 83	● THUNDER AND LIGHTNING *Vertigo VERL 3*		4	11 wks
26 Nov 83	LIFE *Vertigo VERD 6*		29	6 wks
16 Feb 91	● DEDICATION – THE BEST OF THIN LIZZY *Vertigo 8481921*		8	16 wks

See also Phil Lynott and Thin Lizzy.

3RD BASS
US, male rap group — 1 wk

20 Jul 91	DERELICTS OF DIALECT *Def Jam 4683171*		46	1 wk

THIRD EAR BAND
UK, male instrumental group — 2 wks

27 Jun 70	AIR, EARTH, FIRE, WATER *Harvest SHVL 773*		49	2 wks

t

THIRD WORLD
Jamaica, male vocal/instrumental group — 18 wks

21 Oct 78	JOURNEY TO ADDIS *Island ILPS 9554*		30	6 wks
11 Jul 81	ROCKS THE WORLD *CBS 85027*		37	9 wks
15 May 82	YOU'VE GOT THE POWER *CBS 85563*		87	3 wks

THIS MORTAL COIL
UK, male/female instrumental group — 10 wks

20 Oct 84	IT'LL END IN TEARS *4AD CAD 411*		38	4 wks
11 Oct 86	FILIGREE AND SHADOW *4AD DAD 609*		53	3 wks
4 May 91	BLOOD *4AD DAD 1005*		65	3 wks

Carla THOMAS – *See Otis REDDING and Carla THOMAS*

Kenny THOMAS
UK, male vocalist — 10 wks

26 Oct 91	● VOICES *Cooltempo CTLP 24*		3†	10 wks

Lillo THOMAS
US, male vocalist — 7 wks

2 May 87	LILLO *Capitol EST 2031*		43	7 wks

Ray THOMAS
UK, male vocalist — 3 wks

26 Jul 75	FROM MIGHTY OAKS *Threshold THS 16*		23	3 wks

Richard THOMPSON
UK, male vocalist/instrumentalist – guitar   *7 wks*

27 Apr 85	**ACROSS A CROWDED ROOM** *Polydor POLD 5175*	80	2 wks
18 Oct 86	**DARING ADVENTURES** *Polydor POLD 5202*	92	1 wk
29 Oct 88	**AMNESIA** *Capitol EST 2075*	89	1 wk
25 May 91	**RUMOUR AND SIGH** *Capitol EST 2142*	32	3 wks

THOMPSON TWINS
UK/New Zealand, male/female vocal/instrumental group   *128 wks*

13 M., 82	**SET** *Tee TELP 2*	48	3 wks
26 Feb 83	● **QUICK STEP AND SIDE KICK** *Arista 204 924*	2	56 wks
25 Feb 84	★ **INTO THE GAP** *Arista 205 971*	1	51 wks
28 Sep 85	● **HERE'S TO FUTURE DAYS** *Arista 207 164*	5	9 wks
2 May 87	**CLOSE TO THE BONE** *Arista 208 143*	90	1 wk
10 Mar 90	**GREATEST HITS** *Stylus SMR 92*	27	8 wks

George THOROGOOD and the DESTROYERS
US, male vocal/instrumental group   *1 wk*

2 Dec 78	**GEORGE THOROGOOD AND THE DESTROYERS** *Sonet SNTF 781*	67	1 wk

THREE DEGREES *US, female vocal group*   *91 wks*

315

t

10 Aug 74	**THREE DEGREES** *Philadelphia International 65858*	12	22 wks
17 May 75	● **TAKE GOOD CARE OF YOURSELF** *Philadelphia International PIR 69137*	6	16 wks
24 Feb 79	**NEW DIMENSIONS** *Ariola ARLH 5012*	34	13 wks
3 Mar 79	● **A COLLECTION OF THEIR 20 GREATEST HITS** *Epic EPC 10013*	8	18 wks
15 Dec 79	**3D** *Ariola 3D 1*	61	7 wks
27 Sep 80	● **GOLD** *Ariola 3D 2*	9	15 wks

THROWING MUSES
US/UK, male/female vocal/instrumental group   *5 wks*

4 Feb 89	**HUNKPAPA** *4AD CAD 901*	59	1 wk
2 Mar 91	**THE REAL RAMONA** *4AD CAD 1002*	26	4 wks

THUNDER *UK/US, male vocal/instrumental group*   *16 wks*

17 Mar 90	**BACKSTREET SYMPHONY** *EMI EMC 3570*	21	16 wks

TICH – *See Dave DEE, DOZY, BEAKY, MICK and TICH*

TIFFANY *US, female vocalist*   *27 wks*

27 Feb 88	● **TIFFANY** *MCA MCF 3415*	5	21 wks
17 Dec 88	**HOLD AN OLD FRIEND'S HAND** *MCA MCF 3437*	56	6 wks

TIGERTAILZ *US, male vocal/instrumental group*   *2 wks*

7 Apr 90	**BEZERK** *Music For Nations MFN 96*	36	2 wks

TIGHT FIT *UK, male/female vocal group* *6 wks*

26 Sep 81	**BACK TO THE SIXTIES** *Jive HIP 1*	**38**	4 wks
4 Sep 82	**TIGHT FIT** *Jive HIP 2*	**87**	2 wks

TIJUANA BRASS – *See Herb ALPERT and the TIJUANA BRASS*

TIK and TOK *UK, male vocal/instrumental duo* *2 wks*

4 Aug 84	**INTOLERANCE** *Survival SUR LP 008*	**89**	2 wks

Tanita TIKARAM *UK, female vocalist* *59 wks*

24 Sep 88	● **ANCIENT HEART** *WEA WX 210*	**3**	48 wks
10 Feb 90	● **THE SWEET KEEPER** *East West WX 330*	**3**	7 wks
16 Feb 91	● **EVERYBODY'S ANGEL** *East West WX 401*	**19**	4 wks

TILBROOK – *See DIFFORD and TILBROOK*

TIMBUK THREE *US, male/female vocal/instrumental duo* *4 wks*

14 Feb 87	**GREETINGS FROM TIMBUK THREE** *IRS MIRF 1015* .	**51**	4 wks

TIME *US, male vocal/instrumental group* *1 wk*

28 Jul 90	**PANDEMONIUM** *Paisley Park WX 336*	**66**	1 wk

316

t

TIN MACHINE *US/UK, male vocal/instrumental group* *12 wks*

3 Jun 89	● **TIN MACHINE** *EMI-USA MTLS 1044*	**3**	9 wks
14 Sep 91	**TIN MACHINE II** *London 8282721*	**23**	3 wks

TOM TOM CLUB *US, female/male vocal/instrumental group* *1 wk*

24 Oct 81	**TOM TOM CLUB** *Island ILPS 9686*	**78**	1 wk

TOMITA *Japan, male instrumentalist – synthesizer* *33 wks*

7 Jun 75	**SNOWFLAKES ARE DANCING**		
	RCA Red Seal ARL 1 0488	**17**	20 wks
16 Aug 75	**PICTURES AT AN EXHIBITION**		
	RCA Red Seal ARL 1 0838	**42**	5 wks
7 May 77	**HOLST: THE PLANETS** *RCA Red Seal RL 11919*	**41**	6 wks
9 Feb 80	**TOMITA'S GREATEST HITS** *RCA Red Seal RL 43076* ...	**66**	2 wks

TONGUE 'N' CHEEK
UK, male/female vocal/instrumental group *3 wks*

22 Sep 90	**THIS IS TONGUE 'N' CHEEK** *Syncopate SYLP 6006*	**45**	3 wks

TOPOL *Israel, male vocalist* *1 wk*

11 May 85	**TOPOL'S ISRAEL** *BBC REH 529*	**80**	1 wk

Bernie TORME   UK, male vocalist/instrumentalist – guitar   3 wks

3 Jul 82	TURN OUT THE LIGHTS Kamaflage KAMLP 2	50	3 wks

Peter TOSH   Jamaica, male vocalist   1 wk

25 Sep 76	LEGALIZE IT Virgin V 2061	54	1 wk

TOTAL CONTRAST   UK, male vocal/instrumental duo   3 wks

8 Mar 86	TOTAL CONTRAST London LONLP 15	66	3 wks

TOTO   US, male vocal/instrumental group   39 wks

31 Mar 79	TOTO CBS 83148	37	5 wks
26 Feb 83 ●	TOTO IV CBS 85529	4	30 wks
17 Nov 84	ISOLATION CBS 86305	67	2 wks
20 Sep 86	FAHRENHEIT CBS 57091	99	1 wk
9 Apr 88	THE SEVENTH ONE CBS 460465 1	73	1 wk

TOURISTS   UK, male/female vocal/instrumental group   18 wks

14 Jul 79	THE TOURISTS Logo GO 1018	72	1 wk
3 Nov 79	REALITY EFFECT Logo GO 1019	23	16 wks
22 Nov 80	LUMINOUS BASEMENT RCA RCALP 5001	75	1 wk

317

t

Pete TOWNSHEND
UK, male vocalist/instrumentalist – guitar   25 wks

21 Oct 72	WHO CAME FIRST Track 2408 201	30	2 wks
3 May 80	EMPTY GLASS Atco K 50699	11	14 wks
3 Jul 82	ALL THE BEST COWBOYS HAVE CHINESE EYES		
	Atco K 50889	32	8 wks
30 Nov 85	WHITE CITY Atco 25-2392-1	70	1 wk

See also Pete Townshend and Ronnie Lane.

Pete TOWNSHEND and Ronnie LANE
UK, male vocal/instrumental duo   3 wks

15 Oct 77	ROUGH MIX Polydor 2442 147	44	3 wks

See also Pete Townshend; Ronnie Lane and the Band Slim Chance.

TOYAH   UK, female vocalist   97 wks

14 Jun 80	THE BLUE MEANING Safari IEYA 666	40	4 wks
17 Jan 81	TOYAH TOYAH TOYAH Safari LIVE 2	22	14 wks
30 May 81 ●	ANTHEM Safari VOOR 1	2	46 wks
19 Jun 82 ●	THE CHANGELING Safari VOOR 9	6	12 wks
13 Nov 82	WARRIOR ROCK – TOYAH ON TOUR Safari TNT 1	20	6 wks
5 Nov 83	LOVE IS THE LAW Safari VOOR 10	28	7 wks
25 Feb 84	TOYAH! TOYAH! TOYAH! K-Tel NE 1268	43	4 wks
3 Aug 85	MINX Portrait PRT 26415	24	4 wks

TOY DOLLS *UK, male vocal/instrumental group* — *1 wk*

25 May 85	**A FAR OUT DISC** *Volume VOLP 2*	....	71	1 wk

T'PAU *UK, female/male vocal/instrumental group* — *83 wks*

26 Sep 87	★ **BRIDGE OF SPIES** *Siren SIRENLP 8*	....	1	59 wks
5 Nov 88	● **RAGE** *Siren SRNLP 20*	....	4	17 wks
22 Jun 91	● **THE PROMISE** *Siren SRNLP 32*	....	10	7 wks

TRACIE *UK, female vocalist* — *2 wks*

30 Jun 84	**FAR FROM THE HURTING KIND** *Respond RRL 502*	...	64	2 wks

TRAFFIC *UK, male vocal/instrumental group* — *37 wks*

30 Dec 67	● **MR. FANTASY** *Island ILP 9061*	....	8	16 wks
26 Oct 68	● **TRAFFIC** *Island ILPS 9081 T*	....	9	8 wks
8 Aug 70	**JOHN BARLEYCORN MUST DIE** *Island ILPS 9116*	....	11	9 wks
24 Nov 73	**ON THE ROAD** *Island ISLD 2*	....	40	3 wks
28 Sep 74	**WHEN THE EAGLE FLIES** *Island ILPS 9273*	....	31	1 wk

TRANSVISION VAMP
UK, male/female vocal/instrumental group — *58 wks*

15 Oct 88	● **POP ART** *MCA MCF 3421*	....	4	32 wks
8 Jul 89	★ **VELVETEEN** *MCA MCG 6050*	....	1	26 wks

TRASH CAN SINATRAS
UK, male vocal/instrumental group — *1 wk*

7 Jul 90	**CAKE** *Go! Discs 82820211*	....	74	1 wk

TRAVELING WILBURYS
US/UK, male vocal/instrumental group — *44 wks*

5 Nov 88	**THE TRAVELING WILBURYS VOLUME 1** *Wilbury WX 224*	....	16	35 wks
10 Nov 90	**THE TRAVELING WILBURYS VOLUME 3** *Wilbury WX 384*	....	14	9 wks

Pat TRAVERS *US, male instrumentalist – guitar* — *3 wks*

2 Apr 77	**MAKIN' MAGIC** *Polydor 2383 436*	....	40	3 wks

Randy TRAVIS *US, male vocalist* — *2 wks*

6 Aug 88	**OLD 8 x 10** *Warner Bros. WX 162*	....	64	2 wks

John TRAVOLTA *US, male vocalist* — *6 wks*

23 Dec 78	**SANDY** *Polydor POLD 5014*	....	40	6 wks

The **Travelling Wilburys**: (left to right, back) Jeff Lynne, Bob
Dylan, George Harrison, (front) Tom Petty and Roy Orbison.

TREMELOES *UK, male vocal/instrumental group*   *7 wks*

3 Jun 67	**HERE COME THE TREMELOES**		
	CBS SBPG 63017	15	7 wks

Ralph TRESVANT *US, male vocalist*   *3 wks*

23 Feb 91	**RALPH TRESVANT** MCA MCG 6120	37	3 wks

T. REX *UK, male vocal/instrumental group*   *214 wks*

13 Jul 68	**MY PEOPLE WERE FAIR AND HAD SKY IN THEIR HAIR BUT NOW THEY'RE CONTENT TO WEAR STARS ON THEIR BROWS** *Regal Zonophone SLRZ 1003*	15	9 wks
7 Jun 69	**UNICORN** *Regal Zonophone S 1007*	12	3 wks
14 Mar 70	**A BEARD OF STARS** *Regal Zonophone SLRZ 1013*	21	6 wks
16 Jan 71	**T. REX** *Fly HIFLY 2*	13	24 wks
7 Aug 71	**THE BEST OF T. REX** *Flyback TON 2*	21	7 wks
9 Oct 71	★ **ELECTRIC WARRIOR** *Fly HIFLY 6*	1	44 wks
29 Mar 72	★ **PROPHETS, SEERS AND SAGES THE ANGELS OF THE AGES/MY PEOPLE WERE FAIR . . .** *Fly Doubleback 0037 TOOFA 3/4*	1	12 wks
20 May 72	★ **BOLAN BOOGIE** *Fly HIFLY 8*	1	19 wks
5 Aug 72	● **THE SLIDER** *EMI BLN 5001*	4	18 wks
9 Dec 72	**A BEARD OF STARS/UNICORN** *Cube TOOFA 9/10*	44	2 wks
31 Mar 73	● **TANX** *EMI BLN 5002*	4	12 wks
10 Nov 73	**GREAT HITS** *EMI BLN 5003*	32	3 wks
16 Mar 74	**ZINC ALLOY AND THE HIDDEN RIDERS OF TOMORROW** *EMI BLNA 7751*	12	3 wks
21 Feb 76	**FUTURISTIC DRAGON** *EMI BLN 5004*	50	1 wk
9 Apr 77	**DANDY IN THE UNDERWORLD** *EMI BLN 5005*	26	3 wks
30 Jun 79	**SOLID GOLD** *EMI NUT 5*	51	3 wks
12 Sep 81	**T. REX IN CONCERT** *Marc ABOLAN 1*	35	6 wks
7 Nov 81	**YOU SCARE ME TO DEATH** *Cherry Red ERED 20*	88	1 wk
24 Sep 83	**DANCE IN THE MIDNIGHT** *Marc On Wax MARCL 501*	83	3 wks
4 May 85	● **BEST OF THE 20TH CENTURY BOY** *K-Tel NE 1297*	5	21 wks
28 Sep 91	● **THE ULTIMATE COLLECTION** *Telstar STAR 2539*	4†	14 wks

Prophets . . ./My People . . . *is a double re-issue although* Prophets *had not previously been a hit.* Beard Of Stars/Unicorn *is a double re-issue. The first three albums and the two double re-issues are credited to* Tyrannosaurus Rex. Zinc Alloy . . . *and* Best Of The 20th Century Boy *are credited to* Marc Bolan and T. Rex. You Scare Me To Death *and* Dance In The Midnight *are credited to* Marc Bolan. *The* Ultimate Collection *credited to* Marc Bolan and T. Rex.

A TRIBE CALLED QUEST *US, male rap group*   *3 wks*

19 May 90	**PEOPLE'S INSTINCTIVE TRAVELS** *Jive HIP 96*	54	2 wks
12 Oct 91	**LOW END THEORY** *Jive HIP 117*	58	1 wk

TRIFFIDS *New Zealand, male vocal/instrumental group*   *1 wk*

22 Apr 89	**THE BLACK SWAN** *Island ILPS 9928*	63	1 wk

TRIUMPH *Canada, male vocal/instrumental group*   *8 wks*

10 May 80	**PROGRESSIONS OF POWER** *RCA PL 13524*	61	5 wks
3 Oct 81	**ALLIED FORCES** *RCA RCALP 6002*	64	3 wks

TROGGS *UK, male vocal/instrumental group*   *32 wks*

30 Jul 66	● **FROM NOWHERE . . . THE TROGGS** *Fontana TL 5355*	6	16 wks

25 Feb 67 ●	**TROGGLODYNAMITE** *Page One POL 001*	10	11 wks
5 Aug 67	**BEST OF THE TROGGS** *Page One FOR 001*	24	5 wks

TROUBADOURS DU ROI BAUDOUIN

Zaire, male/female vocal group **1 wk**

22 May 76	**MISSA LUBA** *Philips SBL 7592*	59	1 wk

TROUBLE FUNK *US, male vocal/instrumental group* **4 wks**

8 Nov 86	**SAY WHAT!** *Fourth & Broadway DCLP 101*	75	2 wks
5 Sep 87	**TROUBLE OVER HERE, TROUBLE OVER THERE**		
	Fourth & Broadway BRLP 513	54	2 wks

Robin TROWER *UK, male instrumentalist – guitar* **16 wks**

1 Mar 75	**FOR EARTH BELOW** *Chrysalis CHR 1073*	26	4 wks
13 Mar 76	**LIVE** *Chrysalis CHR 1089*	15	6 wks
30 Oct 76	**LONG MISTY DAYS** *Chrysalis CHR 1107*	31	1 wk
29 Oct 77	**IN CITY DREAMS** *Chrysalis CHR 1148*	58	1 wk
16 Feb 80	**VICTIMS OF THE FURY** *Chrysalis CHR 1215*	61	4 wks

TUBES *US, male vocal/instrumental group* **7 wks**

4 Mar 78	**WHAT DO YOU WANT FROM LIFE** *A & M AMS 68460*	38	1 wk
2 Jun 79	**REMOTE CONTROL** *A & M AMLH 64751*	40	5 wks
4 Jun 83	**OUTSIDE INSIDE** *Capitol EST 12260*	77	1 wk

TUBEWAY ARMY – *See Gary Numan*

Ike and Tina TURNER

US, male instrumentalist – guitar and female vocalist **1 wk**

1 Oct 66	**RIVER DEEP – MOUNTAIN HIGH** *London HAU 8298* .	27	1 wk

See also Tina Turner.

Ruby TURNER *UK, female vocalist* **19 wks**

18 Oct 86	**WOMEN HOLD UP HALF THE SKY** *Jive HIP 36*	47	11 wks
8 Oct 88	**THE MOTOWN SONGBOOK** *Jive HIP 58*	22	6 wks
17 Feb 90	**PARADISE** *Jive HIP 89*	74	2 wks

Tina TURNER *US, female vocalist* **299 wks**

30 Jun 84 ●	**PRIVATE DANCER** *Capitol TINA 1*	2	147 wks
20 Sep 86 ●	**BREAK EVERY RULE** *Capitol EST 2018*	2	49 wks
2 Apr 88 ●	**LIVE IN EUROPE** *Capitol ESTD 1*	8	13 wks
30 Sep 89 ★	**FOREIGN AFFAIR** *Capitol ESTU 2103*	1	78 wks
12 Oct 91 ●	**SIMPLY THE BEST** *Capitol ESTV 1*	2†	12 wks

See also Ike and Tina Turner.

TURTLES *US, male vocal/instrumental group* **9 wks**

22 Jul 67	**HAPPY TOGETHER** *London HAU 8330*	18	9 wks

321

t

Private Dancer was The Best in terms of weeks on chart, but *Foreign Affair* was the first number one for **Tina Turner**.

TWELFTH NIGHT *UK, male vocal/instrumental group* *2 wks*

| 27 Oct 84 | **ART AND ILLUSION** *Music For Nations MFN 36* | 83 | 2 wks |

TWENTY 4 SEVEN
US/Holland/Germany/Italy, male/female vocal/instrumental group *2 wks*

| 19 Jan 91 | **STREET MOVES** *BCM BCM 3124* .... | 69 | 2 wks |

TWIGGY *UK, female vocalist* *11 wks*

| 21 Aug 76 | **TWIGGY** *Mercury 9102 600* .... | 33 | 8 wks |
| 30 Apr 77 | **PLEASE GET MY NAME RIGHT** *Mercury 9102 601* ..... | 35 | 3 wks |

TWISTED SISTER *US, male vocal/instrumental group* *20 wks*

25 Sep 82	**UNDER THE BLADE** *Secret SECX 9*	70	3 wks
7 May 83	**YOU CAN'T STOP ROCK 'N' ROLL** *Atlantic A 0074* ...	14	9 wks
16 Jun 84	**STAY HUNGRY** *Atlantic 780156*	34	5 wks
14 Dec 85	**COME OUT AND PLAY** *Atlantic 78–1275–1*	95	1 wk
25 Jul 87	**LOVE IS FOR SUCKERS** *Atlantic WX 120*	57	2 wks

Tommy TYCHO – *See David GRAY and Tommy TYCHO*

323

t

TYGERS OF PAN TANG
UK, male vocal/instrumental group *20 wks*

30 Aug 80	**WILD CAT** *MCA MCF 3075*	18	5 wks
18 Apr 81	**SPELLBOUND** *MCA MCF 3104*	33	4 wks
21 Nov 81	**CRAZY NIGHTS** *MCA MCF 3123*	51	3 wks
28 Aug 82	**THE CAGE** *MCA MCF 3150*	13	8 wks

Bonnie TYLER *UK, female vocalist* *75 wks*

16 Apr 83	★ **FASTER THAN THE SPEED OF NIGHT** *CBS 25304*	1	45 wks
17 May 86	**SECRET DREAMS AND FORBIDDEN FIRE** *CBS 86319*	24	12 wks
29 Nov 86	**THE GREATEST HITS** *Telstar STAR 2291*	24	17 wks
21 May 88	**HIDE YOUR HEART** *CBS 460125 1*	78	1 wk

Judie TZUKE *UK, female vocalist* *61 wks*

4 Aug 79	**WELCOME TO THE CRUISE** *Rocket TRAIN 7*	14	17 wks
10 May 80	● **SPORTS CAR** *Rocket TRAIN 9*	7	11 wks
16 May 81	**I AM PHOENIX** *Rocket TRAIN 15*	17	10 wks
17 Apr 82	**SHOOT THE MOON** *Chrysalis CDL 1382*	19	10 wks
30 Oct 82	**ROAD NOISE – THE OFFICIAL BOOTLEG** *Chrysalis CTY 1405*	39	4 wks
1 Oct 83	**RITMO** *Chrysalis CDL 1442*	26	5 wks
15 Jun 85	**THE CAT IS OUT** *Legacy LLP 102*	35	3 wks
29 Apr 89	**TURNING STONES** *Polydor 839087 1*	57	1 wk

u

UB 40 *UK, male vocal/instrumental group*   442 wks

6 Sep 80 ●	**SIGNING OFF** *Graduate GRAD LP 2*	2	71 wks
6 Jun 81 ●	**PRESENT ARMS** *DEP International LP DEP 1*	2	38 wks
10 Oct 81	**PRESENT ARMS IN DUB**		
	DEP International LPS DEP 2	38	7 wks
28 Aug 82	**THE SINGLES ALBUM** *Graduate GRADLSP 3*	17	8 wks
9 Oct 82 ●	**UB 44** *DEP International LP DEP 3*	4	8 wks
26 Feb 83	**UB 40 LIVE** *DEP International LP DEP 4*	44	5 wks
24 Sep 83 ★	**LABOUR OF LOVE** *DEP International LP DEP 5*	1	76 wks
20 Oct 84 ●	**GEFFREY MORGAN** *DEP International DEP 6*	3	14 wks
14 Sep 85	**BAGGARADDIM** *DEP International LP DEP 10*	14	23 wks
9 Aug 86 ●	**RAT IN THE KITCHEN** *DEP International LP DEP 11* ...	8	20 wks
7 Nov 87 ●	**THE BEST OF UB 40 VOL. 1** *Virgin UBTV 1*	3	91 wks
23 Jul 88	**UB40** *DEP International LPDEP 13*	12	12 wks
9 Dec 89 ●	**LABOUR OF LOVE II** *DEP International LPDEP 14*	3	69 wks

UFO *UK, male vocal/instrumental group*   48 wks

4 Jun 77	**LIGHTS OUT** *Chrysalis CHR 1127*	54	2 wks
15 Jul 78	**OBSESSION** *Chrysalis CDL 1182*	26	7 wks
10 Feb 79 ●	**STRANGERS IN THE NIGHT** *Chrysalis CJT 5*	8	11 wks
19 Jan 80	**NO PLACE TO RUN** *Chrysalis CDL 1239*	11	7 wks
24 Jan 81	**THE WILD THE WILLING AND THE INNOCENT**		
	Chrysalis CHR 1307	19	5 wks
20 Feb 82 ●	**MECHANIX** *Chrysalis CHR 1360*	8	6 wks
12 Feb 83	**MAKING CONTACT** *Chrysalis CHR 1402*	32	4 wks
3 Sep 83	**HEADSTONE – THE BEST OF UFO**		
	Chrysalis CTY 1437	39	4 wks
16 Nov 85	**MISDEMEANOUR** *Chrysalis CHR 1518*	74	2 wks

u

U.K. *UK, male vocal/instrumental group*   3 wks

27 May 78	**U.K.** *Polydor 2302 080*	43	3 wks

U.K. SUBS *UK, male vocal/instrumental group*   26 wks

13 Oct 79	**ANOTHER KIND OF BLUES** *Gem GEMLP 100*	21	6 wks
19 Apr 80	**BRAND NEW AGE** *Gem GEMLP 106*	18	9 wks
27 Sep 80 ●	**CRASH COURSE** *Gem GEMLP 111*	8	6 wks
21 Feb 81	**DIMINISHED RESPONSIBILITY** *Gem GEMLP 112*	18	5 wks

Tracey ULLMAN *UK, female vocalist*   22 wks

3 Dec 83	**YOU BROKE MY HEART IN 17 PLACES** *Stiff SEEZ 51*	14	20 wks
8 Dec 84	**YOU CAUGHT ME OUT** *Stiff SEEZ 56*	92	2 wks

ULTRA VIVID SCENE *US, male vocalist*   1 wk

19 May 90	**JOY 1967–1990** *4AD CAD 005*	58	1 wk

ULTRAVOX UK/Canada, male vocal/instrumental group   225 wks

19 Jul	80	● **VIENNA** Chrysalis CHR 1296		**3**	72 wks
19 Sep	81	● **RAGE IN EDEN** Chrysalis CDL 1338		**4**	23 wks
23 Oct	82	● **QUARTET** Chrysalis CDL 1394		**6**	30 wks
22 Oct	83	● **MONUMENT – THE SOUNDTRACK** Chrysalis CUX 1452		**9**	15 wks
14 Apr	84	● **LAMENT** Chrysalis CDL 1459		**8**	26 wks
10 Nov	84	● **THE COLLECTION** Chrysalis UTV 1		**2**	53 wks
25 Oct	86	● **U-VOX** Chrysalis CDL 1545		**9**	6 wks

UNDERTONES UK, male vocal/instrumental group   47 wks

19 May	79	**THE UNDERTONES** Sire SRK 6071		**13**	21 wks
26 Apr	80	● **HYPNOTISED** Sire SRK 6088		**6**	10 wks
16 May	81	**POSITIVE TOUCH** Ardeck ARD 103		**17**	6 wks
19 Mar	83	**THE SIN OF PRIDE** Ardeck ARD 104		**43**	5 wks
10 Dec	83	**ALL WRAPPED UP** Ardeck ARD 1654281/3		**67**	4 wks
14 Jun	86	**CHER O'BOWLIES: PICK OF UNDERTONES** Ardeck EMS 1172		**96**	1 wk

UNION UK, male instrumental group   6 wks

26 Oct	91	**WORLD IN UNION** Columbia 4690471		**17**	6 wks

UNION GAP – See Gary PUCKETT and the UNION GAP

UNTOUCHABLES US, male vocal/instrumental group   7 wks

13 Jul	85	**WILD CHILD** Stiff SEEZ 57		**51**	7 wks

325

u

Midge URE UK, male vocalist   20 wks

19 Oct	85	● **THE GIFT** Chrysalis CHR 1508		**2**	15 wks
10 Sep	88	**ANSWERS TO NOTHING** Chrysalis CHR 1649		**30**	3 wks
28 Sep	91	**PURE** Arista 211922		**36**	2 wks

URIAH HEEP UK, male vocal/instrumental group   51 wks

13 Nov	71	**LOOK AT YOURSELF** Island ILPS 9169		**39**	1 wk
10 Jun	72	**DEMONS AND WIZARDS** Bronze ILPS 9193		**20**	11 wks
2 Dec	72	**THE MAGICIAN'S BIRTHDAY** Bronze ILPS 9213		**28**	3 wks
19 May	73	**LIVE** Island ISLD 1		**23**	8 wks
29 Sep	73	**SWEET FREEDOM** Island ILPS 9245		**18**	3 wks
29 Jun	74	**WONDERWORLD** Bronze ILPS 9280		**23**	3 wks
5 Jul	75	● **RETURN TO FANTASY** Bronze ILPS 9335		**7**	6 wks
12 Jun	76	**HIGH AND MIGHTY** Island ILPS 9384		**55**	1 wk
22 Mar	80	**CONQUEST** Bronze BRON 524		**37**	3 wks
17 Apr	82	**ABOMINOG** Bronze BRON 538		**34**	6 wks
18 Jun	83	**HEAD FIRST** Bronze BRON 545		**46**	4 wks
6 Apr	85	**EQUATOR** Portrait PRT 261414		**79**	2 wks

USA FOR AFRICA
US, male/female vocal/instrumental group   5 wks

25 May	85	**WE ARE THE WORLD** CBS USAID F1		**31**	5 wks

This album contains tracks by various artists in addition to the title track.

U.T.F.O. US, male vocal group   1 wk

16 Mar	85	**ROXANNE ROXANNE (6 track version)** Streetwave 6 TRACK X KHAN 506		**72**	1 wk

UTOPIA *UK, male vocal/instrumental group*   3 wks

1 Oct 77	**OOPS SORRY WRONG PLANET** *Bearsville K 53517* ...	59	1 wk
16 Feb 80	**ADVENTURES IN UTOPIA** *Island ILPS 9602*	57	2 wks

U 2 *Ireland, male vocal/instrumental group*   725 wks

29 Aug 81	**BOY** *Island ILPS 9646*	52	31 wks
24 Oct 81	**OCTOBER** *Island ILPS 9680*	11	41 wks
12 Mar 83	★ **WAR** *Island ILPS 9733*	1	143 wks
3 Dec 83	● **U2 LIVE: UNDER A BLOOD RED SKY** *Island IMA 3* ...	2	201 wks
13 Oct 84	★ **THE UNFORGETTABLE FIRE** *Island U2 5*	1	127 wks
27 Jul 85	**WIDE AWAKE IN AMERICA** (import) *Island 902791A* ...	11	16 wks
21 Mar 87	★ **THE JOSHUA TREE** *Island U2 6*	1	113 wks
20 Feb 88	**THE JOSHUA TREE SINGLES** *Island U2 PK 1*	100	1 wk
22 Oct 88	★ **RATTLE AND HUM** *Island U2 7*	1	47 wks
30 Nov 91	● **ACHTUNG BABY** *Island U 28*	2†	5 wks

V

Steve VAI *UK, male vocalist*   10 wks

2 Jun 90	● **PASSION AND WARFARE** *Food For Thought GRUB 17* ..	8	10 wks

326

Frankie **VALLI** – *See FOUR SEASONS*

v

VAN DE GRAAFF GENERATOR
UK, male vocal/instrumental group   2 wks

25 Apr 70	**THE LEAST WE CAN DO IS WAVE TO EACH OTHER** *Charisma CAS 1007*	47	2 wks

VAN HALEN *US/Holland, male vocal/instrumental group*   92 wks

27 May 78	**VAN HALEN** *Warner Bros. K 56470*	34	11 wks
14 Apr 79	**VAN HALEN II** *Warner Bros. K 566116*	23	7 wks
5 Apr 80	**WOMEN AND CHILDREN FIRST** *Warner Bros. K 56793*	15	7 wks
23 May 81	**FAIR WARNING** *Warner Bros. K 56899*	49	4 wks
1 May 82	**DIVER DOWN** *Warner Bros. K 57003*	36	5 wks
4 Feb 84	**1984** *Warner Bros. 92–3985*	15	23 wks
5 Apr 86	**5150** *Warner Bros. WS 5150*	16	18 wks
4 Jun 88	**OU812** *Warner Bros. WX 177*	16	12 wks
29 Jun 91	**FOR UNLAWFUL CARNAL KNOWLEDGE** *Warner Brothers WX 420*	12	5 wks

Luther VANDROSS *US, male vocalist*   221 wks

21 Jan 84	**BUSY BODY** *Epic EPC 25608*	42	8 wks
6 Apr 85	**THE NIGHT I FELL IN LOVE** *Epic EPC 26387*	19	10 wks
1 Nov 86	● **GIVE ME THE REASON** *Epic EPC 450134–1*	3	99 wks
21 Feb 87	**NEVER TOO MUCH** *Epic EPC 32807*	41	30 wks
4 Jul 87	**FOREVER, FOR ALWAYS, FOR LOVE** *Epic EPC 25013*	23	16 wks
16 Apr 88	**BUSY BODY (re-issue)** *Epic 460183 1*	78	4 wks
29 Oct 88	● **ANY LOVE** *Epic 462908 1*	3	22 wks
11 Nov 89	**BEST OF LUTHER VANDROSS – BEST OF LOVE** *Epic 465801 1*	14	23 wks
25 May 91	● **POWER OF LOVE** *Epic 4680121*	9	9 wks

VANGELIS *Greece, male instrumentalist – keyboards* *139 wks*

10 Jan	76	**HEAVEN AND HELL** *RCA Victor RS 1025*		31	7 wks
9 Oct	76	**ALBEDO 0.39** *RCA Victor RS 1080*		18	6 wks
18 Apr	81	● **CHARIOTS OF FIRE** (film soundtrack)			
		Polydor POLS 1026		5	97 wks
5 May	84	**CHARIOTS OF FIRE (re-issue)** *Polydor POLD 5160*		39	10 wks
13 Oct	84	**SOIL FESTIVITIES** *Polydor POLH 11*		55	4 wks
30 Mar	85	**MASK** *Polydor POLH 19*		69	2 wks
22 Jul	89	**THEMES** *Polydor VGTV 1*		11	13 wks

See also Jon and Vangelis.

VANILLA ICE *US, male rapper* *23 wks*

15 Dec	90	● **TO THE EXTREME** *SBK SBKLP 9*		4	20 wks
6 Jul	91	**EXTREMELY LIVE** *SBK SBKLP 12*		35	3 wks

VANILLA FUDGE *US, male vocal/instrumental group* *3 wks*

4 Nov	67	**VANILLA FUDGE** *Atlantic 588–086*		31	3 wks

VAPORS *UK, male vocal/instrumental group* *6 wks*

7 Jun	80	**NEW CLEAR DAYS** *United Artists UAG 30300*		44	6 wks

VARDIS *UK, male vocal/instrumental group* *1 wk*

1 Nov	80	**100 MPH** *Logo MOGO 4012*		52	1 wk

Frankie VAUGHAN *UK, male vocalist* *20 wks*

5 Sep	59	● **FRANKIE VAUGHAN AT THE LONDON PALLADIUM**			
		Philips BDL 7330		6	2 wks
4 Nov	67	**FRANKIE VAUGHAN SONGBOOK** *Philips DBL 001* ...		40	1 wk
25 Nov	67	**THERE MUST BE A WAY** *Columbia SCX 6200*		22	8 wks
12 Nov	77	**100 GOLDEN GREATS** *Ronco RTDX 2021*		24	9 wks

Sarah VAUGHAN *US, female vocalist* *1 wk*

20 Mar	60	**NO COUNT – SARAH** *Mercury MMC 14021*		19	1 wk

Stevie Ray VAUGHAN and DOUBLE TROUBLE
US, male vocal/instrumental group *1 wk*

15 Jul	89	**IN STEP** *Epic 463395 1*		63	1 wk

VAUGHAN BROTHERS *US, male vocal/instrumental group* *1 wk*

20 Oct	90	**FAMILY STYLE** *Epic 4670141*		63	1 wk

Bobby VEE *US, male vocalist* *46 wks*

24 Feb	62	● **TAKE GOOD CARE OF MY BABY** *London HAG 2428* ...		7	8 wks
31 Mar	62	**HITS OF THE ROCKIN' 50'S** *London HAG 2406*		20	1 wk
12 Jan	63	● **A BOBBY VEE RECORDING SESSION** *Liberty LBY 1084*		10	11 wks
20 Apr	63	● **BOBBY VEE'S GOLDEN GREATS** *Liberty LBY 1112* ...		10	14 wks

5 Oct 63	**THE NIGHT HAS A THOUSAND EYES** *Liberty LIB 1139*	**15**	2 wks
19 Apr 80	● **THE BOBBY VEE SINGLES ALBUM**		
	United Artists UAG 30253	**5**	10 wks

See also Bobby Vee and the Crickets.

Bobby VEE and the CRICKETS
US, male vocalist and male vocal/instrumental group　　　　　　*27 wks*

27 Oct 62	● **BOBBY VEE MEETS THE CRICKETS** *Liberty LBY 1086* .	**2**	27 wks

See also Bobby Vee; Crickets.

Suzanne VEGA　*US, female vocalist*　　　　　　*116 wks*

19 Oct 85	**SUZANNE VEGA** *A & M AMA 5072*	**11**	71 wks
9 May 87	● **SOLITUDE STANDING** *A & M SUZLP 2*	**2**	39 wks
28 Apr 90	● **DAYS OF OPEN HAND** *A & M 3952931*	**7**	6 wks

Rosie VELA　*US, female vocalist*　　　　　　*11 wks*

31 Jan 87	**ZAZU** *A & M AMA 5016*	**20**	11 wks

VELVET UNDERGROUND
US, male/female vocal/instrumental group　　　　　　*4 wks*

23 Feb 85	**V.U.** *Polydor POLD 5167*	**47**	4 wks

328

v

VENOM　*UK, male vocal/instrumental group*　　　　　　*2 wks*

21 Apr 84	**AT WAR WITH SATAN** *Neat NEAT 1015*	**64**	1 wk
13 Apr 85	**POSSESSED** *Neat NEAT 1024*	**99**	1 wk

Anthony VENTURA ORCHESTRA
Switzerland, orchestra　　　　　　*4 wks*

20 Jan 79	**DREAM LOVER** *Lotus WH 5007*	**44**	4 wks

Tom VERLAINE　*US, male vocalist*　　　　　　*1 wk*

14 Mar 87	**FLASH LIGHT** *Fontana SFLP 1*	**99**	1 wk

VIBRATORS　*UK, male vocal/instrumental group*　　　　　　*7 wks*

25 Jun 77	**THE VIBRATORS** *Epic EPC 82907*	**49**	5 wks
29 Apr 78	**V2** *Epic EPC 82495*	**33**	2 wks

VICE SQUAD　*UK, male/female vocal/instrumental group*　　　　　　*10 wks*

24 Oct 81	**NO CAUSE FOR CONCERN** *Zonophone ZEM 103*	**32**	5 wks
22 May 82	**STAND STRONG STAND PROUD** *Zonophone ZEM 104*	**47**	5 wks

Sid VICIOUS　*UK, male vocalist*　　　　　　*8 wks*

15 Dec 79	**SID SINGS** *Virgin V 2144*	**30**	8 wks

VIENNA PHILHARMONIC ORCHESTRA – *See Aram KHATCHATURIAN/VIENNA PHILHARMONIC ORCHESTRA*

VIENNA SYMPHONY ORCHESTRA
Austria, orchestra   *4 wks*

4 Apr 87	**SYMPHONIC ROCK WITH THE VIENNA SYMPHONY ORCHESTRA** *Stylus SMR 730*	**43**	4 wks

VILLAGE PEOPLE *US, male vocal group*   *28 wks*

27 Jan 79	**CRUISIN'** *Mercury 9109 614*	**24**	9 wks
12 May 79	**GO WEST** *Mercury 9109 621*	**14**	19 wks

Gene VINCENT *US, male vocalist*   *2 wks*

16 Jul 60	**CRAZY TIMES** *Capitol T 1342*	**12**	2 wks

Vinnie VINCENT *US, male vocalist/instrumentalist – guitar*   *2 wks*

28 May 88	**ALL SYSTEMS GO** *Chrysalis CHR 1626*	**51**	2 wks

Bobby VINTON *US, male vocalist*   *2 wks*

17 Nov 90	**BLUE VELVET** *Epic 4675701*	**67**	2 wks

VIOLENT FEMMES
US, male/female vocal/instrumental group   *1 wk*

1 Mar 86	**THE BLIND LEADING THE NAKED** *Slash SLAP 10* ...	**81**	1 wk

VIOLINSKI *UK, male instrumental group*   *1 wk*

26 May 79	**NO CAUSE FOR ALARM** *Jet JETLU 219*	**49**	1 wk

VISAGE *UK, male vocal/instrumental group*   *58 wks*

24 Jan 81	**VISAGE** *Polydor 2490 157*	**13**	29 wks
3 Apr 82 ●	**THE ANVIL** *Polydor POLD 5050*	**6**	16 wks
19 Nov 83	**FADE TO GREY – THE SINGLES COLLECTION** *Polydor POLD 5117*	**38**	11 wks
3 Nov 84	**BEAT BOY** *Polydor POLH 12*	**79**	2 wks

VIXEN *US, female vocal/instrumental group*   *5 wks*

8 Oct 88	**VIXEN** *Manhattan MTL 1028*	**66**	1 wk
18 Aug 90	**REV IT UP** *EMI USA MTL 1054*	**20**	4 wks

VOICE OF THE BEEHIVE
UK/US, male/female vocal/instrumental group   *23 wks*

2 Jul 88	**LET IT BEE** *London LONLP 57*	**13**	13 wks
24 Aug 91	**HONEY LINGERS** *London 8282591*	**17**	10 wks

Herbert VON KARAJAN *Germany, male conductor*   *9 wks*

26 Sep 70	**BEETHOVEN TRIPLE CONCERTO** *HMV ASD 2582* ..	51	2 wks
16 Apr 88	**THE ESSENTIAL KARAJAN**		
	Deutsche Grammophon HVKTV 1	51	5 wks
3 Aug 91	**HOLST: THE PLANETS** *Deutsche Grammophon 4352891* ...	52	2 wks

On the Beethoven concerto, the soloists were David Oistrakh (violin), Mstislav Rostropovich (cello) and Sviatoslav Richter (piano) with the Berlin Philharmonic Orchestra – Germany, orchestra.

VOW WOW *Japan/US, male vocal/instrumental group*   *1 wk*

18 Mar 89	**HELTER SKELTER** *Arista 209691*	75	1 wk

VOYAGE *UK/France, disco aggregation*   *1 wk*

9 Sep 78	**VOYAGE** *GTO GTLP 030*	59	1 wk

W

330

WAH! – *See MIGHTY WAH!*

W

John WAITE *UK, male vocalist*   *3 wks*

10 Nov 84	**NO BREAKS** *EMI America WAIT 1*	64	3 wks

Tom WAITS *US, male vocalist*   *14 wks*

8 Oct 83	**SWORDFISHTROMBONE** *Island ILPS 9762*	62	3 wks
19 Oct 85	**RAIN DOGS** *Island ILPS 9803*	29	5 wks
5 Sep 87	**FRANK'S WILD YEARS** *Island ITW 3*	20	5 wks
8 Oct 88	**BIG TIME** *Island ITW 4*	84	1 wk

WAILERS – *See Bob MARLEY and the WAILERS*

Rick WAKEMAN *UK, male instrumentalist – keyboards*   *123 wks*

24 Feb 73	● **THE SIX WIVES OF HENRY VIII**		
	A & M AMLH 64361	7	22 wks
18 May 74	★ **JOURNEY TO THE CENTRE OF THE EARTH**		
	A & M AMLH 63621	1	30 wks
12 Apr 75	● **THE MYTHS AND LEGENDS OF KING ARTHUR AND**		
	THE KNIGHTS OF THE ROUND TABLE		
	A & M AMLH 64515 0022	2	28 wks
24 Apr 76	● **NO EARTHLY CONNECTION** *A & M AMLK 64583*	9	9 wks
12 Feb 77	**WHITE ROCK** *A & M AMLH 64614*	14	9 wks
3 Dec 77	**CRIMINAL RECORD** *A & M AMLK 64660*	25	5 wks
2 Jun 79	**RHAPSODIES** *A & M AMLX 68508*	25	10 wks
27 Jun 81	**1984** *Charisma CDS 4022*	24	9 wks
16 May 87	**THE GOSPELS** *Stylus SMR 729*	94	1 wk

See also Kevin Peek and Rick Wakeman; Anderson Bruford Wakeman Howe.

Sarah WALKER – *See Sir Charles GROVES, RPO & CHORUS, Sarah WALKER*

Top left: Their extended psychedelic version of the Supremes' 'You Keep Me Hanging On' gave **Vanilla Fudge** a 1967 hit.

Top right: Two **Geno Washington** sets stomped into the top ten in 1967.

Above: Steve Strange (right) was the face of **Visage**.

Left: **Steve Winwood** was back in the high chart life in the 80s.

Scott WALKER   *US, male vocalist*   44 wks

16 Sep	67	● SCOTT *Philips SBL 7816*	3	17 wks
20 Apr	68	★ SCOTT 2 *Philips SBL 7840*	1	18 wks
5 Apr	69	● SCOTT 3 *Philips S 7882*	3	4 wks
5 Jul	69	● SONGS FROM HIS TV SERIES *Philips SBL 7900*	7	3 wks
31 Mar	84	CLIMATE OF HUNTER *Virgin V 2303*	60	2 wks

See also Walker Brothers.

WALKER BROTHERS   *US, male vocal group*   96 wks

18 Dec	65	● TAKE IT EASY *Philips BL 7691*	3	36 wks
3 Sep	66	● PORTRAIT *Philips BL 7691*	3	23 wks
18 Mar	67	● IMAGES *Philips SBL 7770*	6	15 wks
16 Sep	67	● WALKER BROTHERS' STORY *Philips DBL 002*	9	19 wks
21 Feb	76	NO REGRETS *GTO GTLP 007*	49	3 wks

See also Scott Walker.

Bob WALLIS and his STORYVILLE JAZZMEN
UK, male vocal/instrumental group   1 wk

11 Jun	60	EVERYBODY LOVES SATURDAY NIGHT		
		Top Rank BUY 023	20	1 wk

332

w

Joe WALSH   *US, male vocalist*   20 wks

17 Apr	76	YOU CAN'T ARGUE WITH A SICK MIND		
		Anchor ABCL 5156	28	3 wks
10 Jan	78	BUT SERIOUSLY FOLKS *Asylum K 53081*	16	17 wks

WANG CHUNG   *UK, male vocal/instrumental group*   5 wks

21 Apr	84	POINTS ON THE CURVE *Geffen GEF 25589*	34	5 wks

WAR – *See Eric BURDON and WAR*

Clifford T. WARD   *UK, male vocalist*   5 wks

21 Jul	73	HOME THOUGHTS *Charisma CAS 1066*	40	3 wks
16 Feb	74	MANTLE PIECES *Charisma CAS 1077*	42	2 wks

Michael WARD   *UK, male vocalist*   3 wks

5 Jan	74	INTRODUCING MICHAEL WARD *Philips 6308 189* ...	26	3 wks

WARLOCK   *Germany, male/female vocal/instrumental group*   2 wks

14 Nov	87	TRIUMPH AND AGONY *Vertigo VERH 50*	54	2 wks

Jennifer WARNES   *US, female vocalist*   12 wks

18 Jul	87	FAMOUS BLUE RAINCOAT *RCA PL 90048*	33	12 wks

Dionne WARWICK   *US, female vocalist*   *144 wks*

23 May 64	PRESENTING DIONNE WARWICK *Pye NPL 28037* ..	14	10 wks
7 May 66	● BEST OF DIONNE WARWICK *Pye NPL 28078*	8	11 wks
4 Feb 67	HERE WHERE THERE IS LOVE *Pye NPL 28096*	39	2 wks
18 May 68	● VALLEY OF THE DOLLS *Pye NSPL 28114*	10	13 wks
23 May 70	GREATEST HITS VOL. 1 *Wand WNS 1*	31	26 wks
6 Jun 70	GREATEST HITS VOL. 2 *Wand WNS 2*	28	14 wks
30 Oct 82	● HEARTBREAKER *Arista 204 974*	3	33 wks
21 May 83	THE COLLECTION *Arista 205 DIONE 1*	11	17 wks
29 Oct 83	SO AMAZING *Arista 205 755*	60	3 wks
23 Feb 85	WITHOUT YOUR LOVE *Arista 206 571*	86	2 wks
6 Jan 90	● LOVE SONGS *Arista 410441*	6	13 wks

See also Stevie Wonder.

WAS (NOT WAS)   *US, male vocal/instrumental group*   *12 wks*

| 9 Apr 88 | WHAT UP DOG?   *Fontana SFLP 4* .... | 47 | 6 wks |
| 21 Jul 90 | ARE YOU OKAY?   *Fontana 8463511* .... | 35 | 6 wks |

Geno WASHINGTON   *UK, male vocalist*   *51 wks*

| 10 Dec 66 | ● HAND CLAPPIN' – FOOT STOMPIN' – FUNKY BUTT – LIVE!   *Piccadilly NPL 38026* .... | 5 | 38 wks |
| 23 Sep 67 | ● HIPSTERS, FLIPSTERS, AND FINGER POPPIN' DADDIES   *Piccadilly NSPL 38032* .... | 8 | 13 wks |

Grover WASHINGTON Jr
US, male instrumentalist – saxophone   *10 wks*

| 9 May 81 | WINELIGHT   *Elektra K 52262* .... | 34 | 9 wks |
| 19 Dec 81 | COME MORNING   *Elektra K 52337* .... | 98 | 1 wk |

W.A.S.P.   *US, male vocal/instrumental group*   *20 wks*

8 Sep 84	W.A.S.P. *Capitol EJ 2401951*	51	2 wks
9 Nov 85	THE LAST COMMAND *Capitol WASP 2*	48	1 wk
8 Nov 86	INSIDE THE ELECTRIC CIRCUS *Capitol EST 2025*	53	3 wks
26 Sep 87	LIVE IN THE RAW *Capitol EST 2040*	23	4 wks
15 Apr 89	● THE HEADLESS CHILDREN *Capitol EST 2087*	8	10 wks

WATERBOYS   *UK, male vocal/instrumental group*   *59 wks*

16 Jun 84	A PAGAN PLACE *Ensign ENCL 3*	100	1 wk
28 Sep 85	THIS IS THE SEA *Ensign ENCL 5*	37	17 wks
29 Oct 88	FISHERMAN'S BLUES *Ensign CHEN 5*	13	19 wks
22 Sep 90	● ROOM TO ROAM *Ensign CHEN 16*	5	6 wks
11 May 91	● BEST OF THE WATERBOYS '81–'91 *Ensign CHEN 19* ..	2	16 wks

WATERFRONT   *UK, male vocal/instrumental duo*   *3 wks*

| 12 Aug 89 | WATERFRONT   *Polydor 837970 1* .... | 45 | 3 wks |

Roger WATERS   *UK, male vocalist/instrumentalist – bass*   *21 wks*

| 12 May 84 | THE PROS AND CONS OF HITCH-HIKING   *Harvest SHVL 240105* .... | 13 | 11 wks |

333

w

27 Jun 87	**RADIO K.A.O.S.** *EMI KAOS 1*	**25**	7 wks
22 Sep 90	**THE WALL – LIVE IN BERLIN** *Mercury 8466111*	**27**	3 wks

Jody WATLEY *US, female vocalist*   4 wks

5 Sep 87	**JODY WATLEY** *MCA MCG 6024*	**62**	2 wks
27 May 89	**LARGER THAN LIFE** *MCA MCG 6044*	**39**	2 wks

WAVES – *See KATRINA and the WAVES*

WAX *UK/US, male vocal/instrumental duo*   3 wks

12 Sep 87	**AMERICAN ENGLISH** *RCA PL 71430*	**59**	3 wks

Jeff WAYNE *US/UK, orchestra and cast*   232 wks

1 Jul 78	● **WAR OF THE WORLDS** *CBS 96000*	**5**	232 wks

This album featured various artists but is commonly credited to Jeff Wayne, its creator and producer. See also Kevin Peek and Rick Wakeman.

WAYSTED *UK, male vocal/instrumental group*   5 wks

8 Oct 83	**VICES** *Chrysalis CHR 1438*	**78**	3 wks
22 Sep 84	**WAYSTED** *Music For Nations MFN 31*	**73**	2 wks

334

w

WEATHER PROPHETS
UK, male vocal/instrumental group   2 wks

9 May 87	**MAYFLOWER** *Elevation ELV 1*	**67**	2 wks

WEATHER REPORT *US, male instrumental group*   12 wks

23 Apr 77	**HEAVY WEATHER** *CBS 81775*	**43**	6 wks
11 Nov 78	**MR. GONE** *CBS 82775*	**47**	3 wks
27 Feb 82	**WEATHER REPORT** *CBS 85326*	**88**	2 wks
24 Mar 84	**DOMINO THEORY** *CBS 25839*	**54**	1 wk

Marti WEBB *UK, female vocalist*   32 wks

16 Feb 80	● **TELL ME ON A SUNDAY** *Polydor POLD 5031*	**2**	23 wks
28 Sep 85	**ENCORE** *Starblend BLEND 1*	**55**	4 wks
6 Dec 86	**ALWAYS THERE** *BBC REB 619*	**65**	5 wks

Ben WEBSTER – *See Gerry MULLIGAN and Ben WEBSTER*

WEDDING PRESENT
UK, male vocal/instrumental group   14 wks

24 Oct 87	**GEORGE BEST** *Reception LEEDS 001*	**47**	2 wks
23 Jul 88	**TOMMY** *Reception LEEDS 2*	**42**	3 wks
29 Apr 89	**UKRAINSKI VISTUIP V JOHNA PEELA**		
	RCA PL 74104	**22**	3 wks
4 Nov 89	**BIZZARO** *RCA PL 74302*	**22**	3 wks
8 Jun 91	**SEA MONSTERS** *RCA PL 75012*	**13**	3 wks

WEE PAPA GIRL RAPPERS
UK, female vocal duo   *3 wks*

5 Nov 88	THE BEAT, THE RHYME AND THE NOISE *Jive HIP 67*	39	3 wks

Bert WEEDON *UK, male instrumentalist – guitar*   *26 wks*

| 16 Jul 60 | KING SIZE GUITAR *Top Rank BUY 026* .... | 18 | 1 wk |
| 23 Oct 76 | ★ 22 GOLDEN GUITAR GREATS *Warwick WW 5019* ..... | 1 | 25 wks |

WELCH – *See MARVIN, WELCH and FARRAR*

WENDY and LISA *US, female vocal duo*   *7 wks*

10 Oct 87	WENDY AND LISA *Virgin V 2444*	84	2 wks
28 Mar 89	FRUIT AT THE BOTTOM *Virgin V 2580*	45	2 wks
4 Aug 90	EROICA *Virgin V 2633*	33	3 wks

WESTWORLD
UK/US, male/female vocal/instrumental group   *2 wks*

| 5 Sep 87 | WHERE THE ACTION IS *RCA PL 71429* .... | 49 | 2 wks |

WET WET WET *UK, male vocal/instrumental group*   *110 wks*

3 Oct 87	★ POPPED IN SOULED OUT *Precious JWWWL 1*	1	71 wks
19 Nov 88	● THE MEMPHIS SESSIONS *Precious JWWWL 2*	3	13 wks
11 Nov 89	● HOLDING BACK THE RIVER *Precious 842011 1*	2	26 wks

335

w

WE'VE GOT A FUZZBOX AND WE'RE GONNA USE IT
UK, female vocal/instrumental group   *6 wks*

| 26 Aug 89 | ● BIG BANG *WEA WX 282* .... | 5 | 6 wks |

WHAM! *UK, male/female vocal/instrumental duo*   *233 wks*

9 Jul 83	★ FANTASTIC *Inner Vision IVL 25328*	1	116 wks
17 Nov 84	★ MAKE IT BIG *Epic EPC 86311*	1	72 wks
19 Jul 86	● THE FINAL *Epic EPC 88681*	2	45 wks

CARON WHEELER *UK, female vocalist*   *5 wks*

| 13 Oct 90 | UK BLAK *RCA PL 74751* .... | 14 | 5 wks |

WHISPERS *US, male vocal group*   *9 wks*

| 14 Mar 81 | IMAGINATION *Solar SOLA 7* .... | 42 | 5 wks |
| 6 Jun 87 | JUST GETS BETTER WITH TIME *Solar MCF 3381* ..... | 63 | 4 wks |

Alan WHITE *UK, male instrumentalist – drums*   *4 wks*

| 13 Mar 76 | RAMSHACKLED *Atlantic K 50217* .... | 41 | 4 wks |

Barry WHITE US, male vocalist   144 wks

9 Mar 74	STONE GON' Pye NSPL 28186	18	17 wks
6 Apr 74	RHAPSODY IN WHITE Pye NSPL 28191	50	1 wk
2 Nov 74 ●	CAN'T GET ENOUGH 20th Century BT 444	4	34 wks
26 Apr 75	JUST ANOTHER WAY TO SAY I LOVE YOU		
	20th Century BT 466	12	15 wks
22 Nov 75	GREATEST HITS 20th Century BTH 8000	18	12 wks
21 Feb 76	LET THE MUSIC PLAY 20th Century BT 502	22	14 wks
9 Apr 77	BARRY WHITE'S GREATEST HITS VOL. 2		
	20th Century BTH 8001	17	7 wks
10 Feb 79	THE MAN 20th Century BT 571	46	4 wks
21 Dec 85	HEART AND SOUL K-Tel NE 1316	34	10 wks
17 Oct 87	THE RIGHT NIGHT AND BARRY WHITE		
	Breakout AMA 5154	74	6 wks
2 Jul 88 ●	THE COLLECTION Mercury BWTV 1	5	24 wks

Karyn WHITE US, female vocalist   30 wks

11 Mar 89	KARYN WHITE Warner Bros. WX 235	20	27 wks
21 Sep 91	RITUAL OF LOVE Warner Bros WX 411	31	3 wks

Snowy WHITE UK, male vocalist/instrumentalist – guitar   5 wks

11 Feb 84	WHITE FLAMES Towerbell TOWLP 3	21	4 wks
9 Feb 85	SNOWY WHITE Towerbell TOWLP 8	88	1 wk

336

w

Tony Joe WHITE US, male vocalist   1 wk

26 Sep 70	TONY JOE CBS 63800	63	1 wk

WHITE LION US, male vocal/instrumental group   3 wks

1 Jul 89	BIG GAME Atlantic WX 277	47	1 wk
20 Apr 91	MANE ATTRACTION Atlantic WX 415	31	2 wks

WHITESNAKE UK, male vocal/instrumental group   143 wks

18 Nov 78	TROUBLE EMI International INS 3022	50	2 wks
13 Oct 79	LOVE HUNTER United Artists UAG 30264	29	7 wks
7 Jun 80 ●	READY AND WILLING United Artists UAG 30302	6	15 wks
8 Nov 80 ●	LIVE IN THE HEART OF THE CITY		
	United Artists SNAKE 1	5	15 wks
18 Apr 81 ●	COME AND GET IT Liberty LBG 30327	2	23 wks
27 Nov 82 ●	SAINTS 'N' SINNERS Liberty LBG 30354	9	9 wks
11 Feb 84 ●	SLIDE IT IN Liberty LBG 2400001	9	7 wks
11 Apr 87 ●	WHITESNAKE 1987 EMI EMC 3528	8	57 wks
25 Nov 89 ●	SLIP OF THE TONGUE EMI EMD 1013	10	8 wks

Slim WHITMAN US, male vocalist   59 wks

14 Dec 74	HAPPY ANNIVERSARY United Artists UAS 29670	44	2 wks
31 Jan 76 ★	THE VERY BEST OF SLIM WHITMAN		
	United Artists UAS 29898	1	17 wks
15 Jan 77 ★	RED RIVER VALLEY United Artists UAS 29993	1	14 wks
15 Oct 77 ●	HOME ON THE RANGE United Artists UATV 30102	2	13 wks
13 Jan 79	GHOST RIDERS IN THE SKY United Artists UATV 30202	27	6 wks
22 Dec 79	SLIM WHITMAN'S 20 GREATEST LOVE SONGS		
	United Artists UAG 30270	18	7 wks

Roger WHITTAKER   *Kenya, male vocalist*   *110 wks*

28 Jun 70	I DON'T BELIEVE IN IF ANYMORE		
	Columbia SCX 6404	23	1 wk
3 Apr 71	NEW WORLD IN THE MORNING *Columbia SCX 6456* .	45	2 wks
6 Sep 75 ●	THE VERY BEST OF ROGER WHITTAKER		
	Columbia SCX 6560	5	42 wks
15 May 76	THE SECOND ALBUM OF THE VERY BEST OF ROGER		
	WHITTAKER *EMI EMC 3117*	27	7 wks
9 Dec 78	ROGER WHITTAKER SINGS THE HITS		
	Columbia SCX 6601	52	5 wks
4 Aug 79	20 ALL TIME GREATS *Polydor POLTV 8*	24	9 wks
7 Feb 81	THE ROGER WHITTAKER ALBUM *K-Tel NE 1105* ...	18	14 wks
27 Dec 86	SKYE BOAT SONG AND OTHER GREAT SONGS		
	Tembo TMB 113	89	1 wk
23 May 87	HIS FINEST COLLECTION *Tembo RWTV 1*	15	19 wks
23 Sep 89	HOME LOVIN' MAN *Tembo RWTV 2*	20	10 wks

WHO   *UK, male vocal/instrumental group*   *203 wks*

25 Dec 65 ●	MY GENERATION *Brunswick LAT 8616*	5	11 wks
17 Dec 66 ●	A QUICK ONE *Reaction 593–002*	4	17 wks
13 Jan 68	THE WHO SELL-OUT *Track 613–002*	13	11 wks
7 Jun 69 ●	TOMMY *Track 613–013/4*	2	9 wks
6 Jun 70 ●	LIVE AT LEEDS *Track 2406–001*	3	21 wks
11 Sep 71 ★	WHO'S NEXT *Track 2408–102*	1	13 wks
18 Dec 71 ●	MEATY, BEATY, BIG AND BOUNCY *Track 2406–006* ..	9	8 wks
17 Nov 73 ●	QUADROPHENIA *Track 2647–013*	2	13 wks
26 Oct 74 ●	ODDS AND SODS *Track 2406–116*	10	4 wks
23 Aug 75	TOMMY (film soundtrack version) *Track 2657–007*	30	2 wks
18 Oct 75 ●	THE WHO BY NUMBERS *Polydor 2490–129*	7	6 wks
9 Oct 76 ●	THE STORY OF THE WHO *Polydor 2683–069*	2	18 wks
9 Sep 78 ●	WHO ARE YOU *Polydor WHOD 5004*	6	9 wks
30 Jun 79	THE KIDS ARE ALRIGHT *Polydor 2675 174*	26	13 wks
25 Oct 80	MY GENERATION (re-issue) *Virgin V 2179*	20	7 wks
28 Mar 81 ●	FACE DANCES *Polydor WHOD 5037*	2	9 wks
11 Sep 82	IT'S HARD *Polydor WHOD 5066*	11	6 wks
17 Nov 84	WHO'S LAST *MCA WHO 1*	48	4 wks
12 Oct 85	THE WHO COLLECTION *Impression IMDP 4*	44	6 wks
19 Mar 88 ●	WHO'S BETTER WHO'S BEST *Polydor WTV 1*	10	11 wks
19 Nov 88	THE WHO COLLECTION *Stylus SMR 570*	71	4 wks
24 Mar 90	JOIN TOGETHER *Virgin VDT 102*	59	1 wk

The two albums titled The Who Collection *are different.*

337

w

Jane WIEDLIN   *US, female vocalist*   *3 wks*

24 Sep 88	FUR *Manhattan MTL 1029*	48	3 wks

WILD HORSES   *UK, male vocal/instrumental group*   *4 wks*

26 Apr 80	WILD HORSES *EMI EMC 3324*	38	4 wks

Eugene WILDE   *US, male vocalist*   *4 wks*

8 Dec 84	EUGENE WILDE *Fourth & Broadway BRLP 502*	67	4 wks

Kim WILDE   *UK, female vocalist*   *78 wks*

11 Jul 81 ●	KIM WILDE *RAK SRAK 544*	3	14 wks
22 May 82	SELECT *RAK SRAK 548*	19	11 wks
26 Nov 83	CATCH AS CATCH CAN *RAK SRAK 165408*	90	1 wk

17 Nov 84	**TEASES AND DARES** MCA MCF 3250	66	2 wks
18 May 85	**THE VERY BEST OF KIM WILDE** RAK WILDE 1	78	4 wks
15 Nov 86	**ANOTHER STEP** MCA MCF 3339	73	5 wks
25 Jun 88	● **CLOSE** MCA MCG 6030	8	38 wks
26 May 90	**LOVE MOVES** MCA MCG 6088	37	3 wks

Another Step *changed label number during its chart run to MCA KIML 1.*

Colm WILKINSON   *Ireland, male vocalist*   *6 wks*

10 Jun 89	**STAGE HEROES** RCA BL 74105	27	6 wks

Alyson WILLIAMS   *US, female vocalist*   *21 wks*

25 Mar 89	**RAW** Def Jam 463293 1	29	21 wks

Andy WILLIAMS   *US, male vocalist*   *439 wks*

26 Jun 65	● **ALMOST THERE** CBS BPG 62533	4	46 wks
7 Aug 65	**CAN'T GET USED TO LOSING YOU** CBS BPG 62146 .	16	1 wk
19 Mar 66	**MAY EACH DAY** CBS BPG 62658	11	6 wks
30 Apr 66	**GREAT SONGS FROM MY FAIR LADY** CBS BPG 62430	30	1 wk
23 Jul 66	**SHADOW OF YOUR SMILE** CBS 62633	24	4 wks
29 Jul 67	**BORN FREE** CBS SBPG 63027	22	11 wks
11 May 68	★ **LOVE ANDY** CBS 63167	1	22 wks
6 Jul 68	● **HONEY** CBS 63311	4	17 wks
26 Jul 69	**HAPPY HEART** CBS 63614	22	9 wks
27 Dec 69	**GET TOGETHER WITH ANDY WILLIAMS** CBS 63800	13	12 wks
24 Jan 70	**ANDY WILLIAMS' SOUND OF MUSIC** CBS 63920	22	10 wks
11 Apr 70	★ **GREATEST HITS** CBS 63920	1	116 wks
20 Jun 70	● **CAN'T HELP FALLING IN LOVE** CBS 64067	7	48 wks
5 Dec 70	● **ANDY WILLIAMS SHOW** CBS 64127	10	6 wks
3 Apr 71	★ **HOME LOVING MAN** CBS 64286	1	25 wks
31 Jul 71	**LOVE STORY** CBS 64467	11	11 wks
29 Apr 72	**THE IMPOSSIBLE DREAM** CBS 67236	26	3 wks
29 Jul 72	**LOVE THEME FROM 'THE GODFATHER'** CBS 64869	11	16 wks
16 Dec 72	**GREATEST HITS VOL. 2** CBS 65151	23	10 wks
22 Dec 73	● **SOLITAIRE** CBS 65638	3	26 wks
15 Jun 74	● **THE WAY WE WERE** CBS 80152	7	11 wks
11 Oct 75	**THE OTHER SIDE OF ME** CBS 69152	60	1 wk
28 Jan 78	● **REFLECTIONS** CBS 10006	2	17 wks
27 Oct 84	**GREATEST LOVE CLASSICS** EMI ANDY 1	22	10 wks

Greatest Love Classics *also credits the Royal Philharmonic Orchestra. See also Royal Philharmonic Orchestra.*

Deniece WILLIAMS   *US, female vocalist*   *12 wks*

21 May 77	**THIS IS NIECEY** CBS 81869	31	12 wks

See also Johnny Mathis and Deniece Williams.

Don WILLIAMS   *US, male vocalist*   *136 wks*

10 Jul 76	**GREATEST HITS VOL. 1** ABC ABCL 5147	29	15 wks
19 Feb 77	**VISIONS** ABC ABCL 5200	13	20 wks
15 Oct 77	**COUNTRY BOY** ABC ABCL 5233	27	5 wks
5 Aug 78	● **IMAGES** K-Tel NE 1033	2	38 wks
5 Aug 78	**YOU'RE MY BEST FRIEND** ABC ABCD 5127	58	1 wk
4 Nov 78	**EXPRESSIONS** ABC ABCL 5253	28	8 wks
22 Sep 79	**NEW HORIZONS** K-Tel NE 1048	29	12 wks
15 Dec 79	**PORTRAIT** MCA MCS 3045	58	4 wks
6 Sep 80	**I BELIEVE IN YOU** MCA MCF 3077	36	5 wks
18 Jul 81	**ESPECIALLY FOR YOU** MCA MCF 3114	33	7 wks
17 Apr 82	**LISTEN TO THE RADIO** MCA MCF 3135	69	3 wks
23 Apr 83	**YELLOW MOON** MCA MCF 3159	52	1 wk

338

w

15 Oct 83	**LOVE STORIES** *K-Tel NE 1252*		22	13 wks
26 May 84	**CAFE CAROLINA** *MCA MCF 3225*		65	4 wks

Iris WILLIAMS *UK, female vocalist*   *4 wks*

22 Dec 79	**HE WAS BEAUTIFUL** *Columbia SCX 6627*		69	4 wks

John WILLIAMS *UK, male instrumentalist – guitar*   *31 wks*

3 Oct 70	**PLAYS SPANISH MUSIC** *CBS 72860*		46	1 wk
17 Jun 78	**TRAVELLING** *Cube HIFLY 27*		23	5 wks
30 Jun 79 ●	**BRIDGES** *Lotus WH 5015*		5	22 wks
4 Aug 79	**CAVATINA** *Cube HIFLY 32*		64	3 wks

See also John Williams with the English Chamber Orchestra conducted by Daniel Barenboim; Cleo Laine and John Williams.

John WILLIAMS *US, male conductor*   *10 wks*

25 Dec 82	**ET – THE EXTRATERRESTRIAL** *MCA MCF 3160*		47	10 wks

John WILLIAMS with the ENGLISH CHAMBER ORCHESTRA conducted by Daniel BARENBOIM
UK, male instrumentalist – guitar, with orchestra and male conductor   *9 wks*

8 Feb 76	**RODRIGO: CONCERTO DE ARANJUEZ** *CBS 79369* ..		20	9 wks

See also John Williams (UK).

Wendy O. WILLIAMS *US, female vocalist*   *1 wk*

30 Jun 84	**W.O.W.** *Music For Nations MFN 24*		100	1 wk

Ann WILLIAMSON *UK, female vocalist*   *13 wks*

15 Feb 86	**PRECIOUS MEMORIES** *Emerald Gem ERTV 1*		16	9 wks
6 Feb 88	**COUNT YOUR BLESSINGS** *Emerald Gem ERTV 2*		58	4 wks

Sonny Boy WILLIAMSON
US, male vocalist/instrumentalist – guitar   *1 wk*

20 Jun 64	**DOWN AND OUT BLUES** *Pye NPL 28036*		20	1 wk

Bruce WILLIS *US, male vocalist*   *28 wks*

18 Apr 87 ●	**THE RETURN OF BRUNO** *Motown ZL 72571*		4	28 wks

Mari WILSON *UK, female vocalist*   *9 wks*

26 Feb 83	**SHOW PEOPLE** *Compact COMP 2*		24	9 wks

Show People credits Mari Wilson with the Wilsations.

WILSON PHILLIPS *US, female vocal group*   *32 wks*

30 Jun 90 ●	**WILSON PHILLIPS** *SBK SBKLP 5*		7	32 wks

WIN *UK, male/female vocal/instrumental group* 1 wk

25 Apr 87 **UH! TEARS BABY** *Swampland LONLP 31* . . . . 51 1 wk

WINCHESTER CATHEDRAL CHOIR – *See Andrew Lloyd Webber*

WINDJAMMER *US, male vocal/instrumental group* 1 wk

25 Aug 84 **WINDJAMMER II** *MCA MCF 3231* . . . . 82 1 wk

WINGS – *See Paul McCartney*

Johnny WINTER *US, male/vocal instrumental group* 12 wks

16 May 70 **SECOND WINTER** *CBS 66321* . . . . 59 2 wks
31 Oct 70 **JOHNNY WINTER AND . . .** *CBS 64117* . . . . 29 4 wks
15 May 71 **JOHNNY WINTER AND LIVE** *CBS 64289* . . . . 20 6 wks

Ruby WINTERS *US, female vocalist* 16 wks

10 Jun 78 **RUBY WINTERS** *Creole CRLP 512* . . . . 27 7 wks
23 Jun 79 **SONGBIRD** *K-Tel NE 1045* . . . . 31 9 wks

Steve WINWOOD *UK, male vocalist* 120 wks

9 Jul 77 **STEVE WINWOOD** *Island ILPS 9494* . . . . 12 9 wks
10 Jan 81 **ARC OF A DIVER** *Island ILPS 9576* . . . . 13 20 wks
14 Aug 82 ● **TALKING BACK TO THE NIGHT** *Island ILPS 9777* . . . . 6 13 wks
12 Jul 86 ● **BACK IN THE HIGH LIFE** *Island ILPS 9844* . . . . 8 42 wks
7 Nov 87 **CHRONICLES** *Island SSW 1* . . . . 12 17 wks
2 Jul 88 ● **ROLL WITH IT** *Virgin V 2532* . . . . 4 16 wks
17 Nov 90 **REFUGEES OF THE HEART** *Virgin V 2650* . . . . 26 3 wks

WIRE *UK, male vocal/instrumental group* 3 wks

7 Oct 78 **CHAIRS MISSING** *Harvest SHSP 4093* . . . . 48 1 wk
13 Oct 79 **154** *Harvest SHSP 4105* . . . . 39 1 wk
9 May 87 **THE IDEAL COPY** *Mute STUMM 42* . . . . 87 1 wk

WISHBONE ASH *UK, male vocal/instrumental group* 75 wks

23 Jan 71 **WISHBONE ASH** *MCA MKPS 2014* . . . . 34 2 wks
9 Oct 71 **PILGRIMAGE** *MCA MDKS 8004* . . . . 14 9 wks
20 May 72 ● **ARGUS** *MCA MDKS 8006* . . . . 3 20 wks
26 May 73 **WISHBONE FOUR** *MCA MDKS 8011* . . . . 12 10 wks
30 Nov 74 **THERE'S THE RUB** *MCA MCF 2585* . . . . 16 5 wks
3 Apr 76 **LOCKED IN** *MCA MCF 2750* . . . . 36 2 wks
27 Nov 76 **NEW ENGLAND** *MCA MCG 3523* . . . . 22 3 wks
29 Oct 77 **FRONT PAGE NEWS** *MCA MCG 3524* . . . . 31 4 wks
28 Oct 78 **NO SMOKE WITHOUT FIRE** *MCA MCG 3528* . . . . 43 3 wks
2 Feb 80 **JUST TESTING** *MCA MCF 3052* . . . . 41 4 wks
1 Nov 80 **LIVE DATES II** *MCA MCG 4012* . . . . 40 3 wks
25 Apr 81 **NUMBER THE BRAVE** *MCA MCF 3103* . . . . 61 5 wks
16 Oct 82 **BOTH BARRELS BURNING** *A&M ASH 1* . . . . 22 5 wks

Bill WITHERS *US, male vocalist* 10 wks

11 Feb 78 **MENAGERIE** *CBS 82265* . . . . 27 5 wks

15 Jun 85	**WATCHING YOU, WATCHING ME** *CBS 26200*	60	1 wk
17 Sep 88	**GREATEST HITS** *CBS 32343*	90	4 wks

WIZZARD *UK, male vocal/instrumental group*   *11 wks*

19 May 73	**WIZZARD BREW** *Harvest SHSP 4025*	29	7 wks
17 Aug 74	**INTRODUCING EDDY AND THE FALCONS**		
	Warner Bros. K 52029	19	4 wks

WOLFSBANE *US, male vocal/instrumental group*   *3 wks*

5 Aug 89	**LIVE FAST DIE FAST** *Def American 838486 1*	48	1 wk
20 Oct 90	**ALL HELL'S BREAKING LOOSE** *Def American 8469671* ..	48	1 wk
19 Oct 91	**DOWN FALL THE GOOD GUYS** *Def American 5104131* ..	53	1 wk

Bobby WOMACK *US, male vocalist*   *15 wks*

28 Apr 84	**THE POET II** *Motown ZL 72205*	31	8 wks
28 Sep 85	**SO MANY RIVERS** *MCA MCF 3282*	28	7 wks

See also Wilton Felder.

WOMACK and WOMACK *US, male/female vocal duo*   *52 wks*

21 Apr 84	**LOVE WARS** *Elektra 960293*	45	13 wks
22 Jun 85	**RADIO M.U.S.I.C. MAN** *Elektra EKT 6*	56	2 wks
27 Aug 88	● **CONSCIENCE** *Fourth & Broadway BRLP 519*	4	37 wks

341

WOMBLES
UK, male vocalist/arranger/producer, Mike Batt under group name   *55 wks*

w

2 Mar 74	**WOMBLING SONGS** *CBS 65803*	19	17 wks
13 Jul 74	**REMEMBER YOU'RE A WOMBLE** *CBS 80191*	18	31 wks
21 Dec 74	**KEEP ON WOMBLING** *CBS 80526*	17	6 wks
8 Jan 77	**20 WOMBLING GREATS** *Warwick PR 5022*	29	1 wk

Stevie WONDER *US, male vocalist/multi-instrumentalist*   *326 wks*

7 Sep 68	**STEVIE WONDER'S GREATEST HITS**		
	Tamla Motown STML 11075	25	10 wks
13 Dec 69	**MY CHERIE AMOUR** *Tamla Motown STML 11128*	17	2 wks
12 Feb 72	**GREATEST HITS VOL. 2** *Tamla Motown STML 11196*	30	4 wks
3 Feb 73	**TALKING BOOK** *Tamla Motown STMA 8007*	16	48 wks
1 Sep 73	● **INNERVISIONS** *Tamla Motown STMA 8011*	8	55 wks
17 Aug 74	● **FULFILLINGNESS' FIRST FINALE**		
	Tamla Motown STMA 8019	5	16 wks
16 Oct 76	● **SONGS IN THE KEY OF LIFE** *Tamla Motown TMSP 6002* .	2	54 wks
10 Nov 79	● **JOURNEY THROUGH THE SECRET LIFE OF PLANTS**		
	Motown TMSP 6009	8	15 wks
8 Nov 80	● **HOTTER THAN JULY** *Motown STMA 8035*	2	55 wks
22 May 82	● **ORIGINAL MUSIQUARIUM 1** *Motown TMSP 6012*	8	17 wks
22 Sep 84	● **WOMAN IN RED – SELECTIONS FROM ORIGINAL**		
	MOTION PICTURE SOUNDTRACK		
	Motown ZL 72285	2	19 wks
24 Nov 84	**LOVE SONGS – 16 CLASSIC HITS**		
	Telstar STAR 2251	20	10 wks
28 Sep 85	● **IN SQUARE CIRCLE** *Motown ZL 72005*	5	16 wks
28 Nov 87	**CHARACTERS** *RCA ZL 72001*	33	4 wks
8 Jun 91	**JUNGLE FEVER (film soundtrack)** *Motown ZL 71750* ...	56	1 wk

The Woman In Red *also features Dionne Warwick. See also Dionne Warwick; Diana Ross/Michael Jackson/ Gladys Knight/Stevie Wonder.*

WONDER STUFF *UK, male vocal/instrumental group* *31 wks*

27 Aug 88	**THE EIGHT LEGGED GROOVE MACHINE**		
	Polydor GONLP 1	18	7 wks
14 Oct 89 ● **HUP** *Polydor 841187 1*		5	8 wks
8 Jun 91 ● **NEVER LOVED ELVIS** *Polydor 8472521*		3	16 wks

Roy WOOD *UK, male vocalist/multi-instrumentalist* *14 wks*

18 Aug 73	**BOULDERS** *Harvest SHVL 803*	15	8 wks
24 Jul 82	**THE SINGLES** *Speed SPEED 1000*	37	6 wks

WOODENTOPS *UK, male vocal/instrumental group* *6 wks*

12 Jul 86	**GIANT** *Rough Trade ROUGH 87*	35	4 wks
5 Mar 88	**WOODENFOOT COPS ON THE HIGHWAY**		
	Rough Trade ROUGH 127	48	2 wks

Edward WOODWARD *UK, male vocalist* *12 wks*

6 Jun 70	**THIS MAN ALONE** *DJM DJLPS 405*	53	2 wks
19 Aug 72	**THE EDWARD WOODWARD ALBUM** *Jam JAL 103* ..	20	10 wks

WORKING WEEK
UK, male/female vocal/instrumental group *10 wks*

6 Apr 85	**WORKING NIGHTS** *Virgin V 2343*	23	9 wks
27 Sep 86	**COMPANEROS** *Virgin V 2397*	72	1 wk

w

WORLD OF TWIST *UK, male vocal/instrumental group* *1 wk*

9 Nov 91	**QUALITY STREET** *Circa CIRCA 17*	50	1 wk

WORLD PARTY *Ireland/UK, male vocal/instrumental group* *14 wks*

21 Mar 87	**PRIVATE REVOLUTION** *Chrysalis CHEN 4*	56	4 wks
19 May 90	**GOODBYE JUMBO** *Ensign CHEN 10*	36	10 wks

WORLD'S FAMOUS SUPREME TEAM – *See Malcolm McLAREN*

WRECKLESS ERIC *UK, male vocalist* *5 wks*

1 Apr 78	**WRECKLESS ERIC** *Stiff SEEZ 6*	46	1 wk
8 Mar 80	**BIG SMASH** *Stiff SEEZ 21*	30	4 wks

Klaus WUNDERLICH
Germany, male instrumentalist – organ *19 wks*

30 Aug 75	**THE HIT WORLD OF KLAUS WUNDERLICH**		
	Decca SPA 434	27	8 wks
20 May 78	**THE UNIQUE KLAUS WUNDERLICH SOUND**		
	Decca DBC 5/5	28	4 wks
26 May 79	**THE FANTASTIC SOUND OF KLAUS WUNDERLICH**		
	Lotus LH 5013	43	5 wks
17 Mar 84	**ON THE SUNNY SIDE OF THE STREET**		
	Polydor POLD 5133	81	2 wks

WURZELS *UK, male vocal/instrumental group* *25 wks*

3 Jul	76	**COMBINE HARVESTER** *One-Up OU 2138*	15	20 wks
2 Apr	77	**GOLDEN DELICIOUS** *EMI Note NTS 122*	32	5 wks

See also Adge Cutler and the Wurzels.

Bill WYMAN *UK, male vocalist/instrumentalist – bass* *7 wks*

8 Jun	74	**MONKEY GRIP** *Rolling Stones COC 59102*	39	1 wk
10 Apr	82	**BILL WYMAN** *A & M AMLH 68540*	55	6 wks

Tammy WYNETTE *US, female vocalist* *49 wks*

17 May	75	● **THE BEST OF TAMMY WYNETTE** *Epic EPC 63578*	4	23 wks
21 Jun	75	**STAND BY YOUR MAN** *Epic EPC 69141*	13	7 wks
17 Dec	77	● **20 COUNTRY CLASSICS** *CBS PR 5040*	3	11 wks
4 Feb	78	**COUNTRY GIRL MEETS COUNTRY BOY**		
		Warwick PR 5039	43	3 wks
6 Jun	87	**ANNIVERSARY – 20 YEARS OF HITS** *Epic 450 393–1* ..	45	5 wks

343

x

X

X MAL DEUTSCHLAND
UK/Germany, male/female vocal/instrumental group *1 wk*

7 Jul	84	**TOCSIN** *4AD CAD 407*	86	1 wk

X-RAY SPEX *UK, male/female vocal/instrumental group* *14 wks*

9 Dec	78	**GERM FREE ADOLESCENTS**		
		EMI International INS 3023	30	14 wks

XTC *UK, male vocal/instrumental group* *45 wks*

11 Feb	78	**WHITE MUSIC** *Virgin V 2095*	38	4 wks
28 Oct	78	**GO 2** *Virgin V 2108*	21	3 wks
1 Sep	79	**DRUMS AND WIRES** *Virgin V 2129*	34	7 wks
20 Sep	80	**BLACK SEA** *Virgin V 2173*	16	7 wks
20 Feb	82	● **ENGLISH SETTLEMENT** *Virgin V 2223*	5	11 wks
13 Nov	82	**WAXWORKS – SOME SINGLES (1977–82)**		
		Virgin V 2251	54	3 wks
10 Sep	83	**MUMMER** *Virgin V 2264*	51	4 wks
27 Oct	84	**THE BIG EXPRESS** *Virgin V 2325*	38	2 wks
8 Nov	86	**SKYLARKING** *Virgin V 2399*	90	1 wk
11 Mar	89	**ORANGES AND LEMONS** *Virgin V 2581*	28	3 wks

γ

YARDBIRDS UK, male vocal/instrumental group — 8 wks

| 23 Jul | 66 | **YARDBIRDS** Columbia SX 6063 | 20 | 8 wks |

YAZOO UK, female/male vocal/instrumental duo — 83 wks

| 4 Sep | 82 | ● **UPSTAIRS AT ERIC'S** Mute STUMM 7 | 2 | 63 wks |
| 16 Jul | 83 | ★ **YOU AND ME BOTH** Mute STUMM 12 | 1 | 20 wks |

YAZZ UK, female vocalist — 32 wks

| 26 Nov | 88 | ● **WANTED** Big Life YAZZLP 1 | 3 | 32 wks |

YELLO Switzerland, male vocal/instrumental duo — 15 wks

21 May	83	**YOU GOTTA SAY YES TO ANOTHER EXCESS** Stiff SEEZ 48	65	2 wks
6 Apr	85	**STELLA** Elektra EKT 1	92	1 wk
4 Jul	87	**ONE SECOND** Mercury MERH 100	48	3 wks
10 Dec	88	**FLAG** Mercury 836778 1	56	7 wks
29 Jun	91	**BABY** Mercury 8487911	37	2 wks

Bryn YEMM UK, male vocalist — 14 wks

9 Jun	84	**HOW DO I LOVE THEE** Lifestyle LEG 17	57	2 wks
7 Jul	84	**HOW GREAT THOU ART** Lifestyle LEG 15	67	8 wks
22 Dec	84	**THE BRYN YEMM CHRISTMAS COLLECTION** Bay BAY 104	95	2 wks
26 Oct	85	**MY TRIBUTE – BRYN YEMM INSPIRATIONAL ALBUM** Word WSTR 9665	85	2 wks

My Tribute . . . also credits the Gwent Chorale.

YES UK, male vocal/instrumental group — 206 wks

1 Aug	70	**TIME AND A WORD** Atlantic 2400–006	45	3 wks
3 Apr	71	● **THE YES ALBUM** Atlantic 2400–101	7	29 wks
4 Dec	71	● **FRAGILE** Atlantic 2409–019	7	17 wks
23 Sep	72	● **CLOSE TO THE EDGE** Atlantic K 50012	4	13 wks
26 May	73	● **YESSONGS** Atlantic K 60045	7	13 wks
22 Dec	73	★ **TALES FROM TOPOGRAPHIC OCEANS** Atlantic K 80001	1	15 wks
21 Dec	74	● **RELAYER** Atlantic K 50096	4	11 wks
29 Mar	75	**YESTERDAYS** Atlantic K 50048	27	7 wks
30 Jul	77	★ **GOING FOR THE ONE** Atlantic K 50379	1	28 wks
7 Oct	78	● **TORMATO** Atlantic K 50518	8	11 wks
30 Aug	80	● **DRAMA** Atlantic K 50736	2	8 wks
10 Jan	81	**YESSHOWS** Atlantic K 60142	22	9 wks
26 Nov	83	**90125** Atco 790125	16	28 wks
29 Mar	86	**9012 LIVE: THE SOLOS** Atco 790 474–1	44	3 wks
10 Oct	87	**BIG GENERATOR** Atco WEX 70	17	5 wks
11 May	91	● **UNION** Arista 211558	7	6 wks

Paul Young had four visits to the top spot with *No Parlez*, the same as *Thriller*, in the same twelve-month period.

Dwight YOAKAM *US, male vocalist/instrumentalist – guitar* *4 wks*

9 May 87	**HILLBILLY DELUXE** *Reprise WX 106*	51	3 wks
13 Aug 88	**BUENAS NOCHES FROM A LONELY ROOM**		
	Reprise WX 193	87	1 wk

Faron YOUNG *US, male vocalist* *5 wks*

28 Oct 72	**IT'S FOUR IN THE MORNING** *Mercury 6338 095*	27	5 wks

Neil YOUNG *Canada, male vocalist* *175 wks*

31 Oct 70	● **AFTER THE GOLDRUSH** *Reprise RSLP 6383*	7	68 wks
4 Mar 72	★ **HARVEST** *Reprise K 54005*	1	33 wks
27 Oct 73	**TIME FADES AWAY** *Warner Bros. K 54010*	20	2 wks
10 Aug 74	**ON THE BEACH** *Reprise K 54014*	42	2 wks
5 Jul 75	**TONIGHT'S THE NIGHT** *Reprise K 54040*	48	1 wk
27 Dec 75	**ZUMA** *Reprise K 54057*	44	2 wks
9 Jul 77	**AMERICAN STARS'N'BARS** *Reprise K 54088*	17	8 wks
17 Dec 77	**DECADE** *Reprise K 64037*	46	4 wks
28 Oct 78	**COMES A TIME** *Reprise K 54099*	42	3 wks
14 Jul 79	**RUST NEVER SLEEPS** *Reprise K 54105*	13	13 wks
1 Dec 79	**LIVE RUST** *Reprise K 64041*	55	3 wks
15 Nov 80	**HAWKS AND DOVES** *Reprise K 54109*	34	3 wks
14 Nov 81	**RE-AC-TOR** *Reprise K 54116*	69	3 wks
5 Feb 83	**TRANS** *Geffen GEF 25019*	29	5 wks
3 Sep 83	**EVERYBODY'S ROCKIN'** *Geffen GEF 25590*	50	3 wks
14 Sep 85	**OLD WAYS** *Geffen GEF 26377*	39	3 wks
2 Aug 86	**LANDING ON WATER** *Geffen 924 109–1*	52	2 wks
4 Jul 87	**LIFE** *Geffen WX 109*	71	1 wk
30 Apr 88	**THIS NOTE'S FOR YOU** *WEA WX 168*	56	3 wks
21 Oct 89	**FREEDOM** *Reprise WX 257*	17	5 wks
22 Sep 90	**RAGGED GLORY** *Reprise WX 374*	15	5 wks
2 Nov 91	**WELD** *Reprise 7599266711*	20	3 wks

Rust Never Sleeps, Live Rust, Re-ac-tor, Life, Ragged Glory *and* Weld *credited to Neil Young and Crazy Horse.* Everybody's Rockin' *credited to Neil Young and the Shocking Pinks.* This Note's For You *credits the Blue Notes. See also Stills–Young Band; Crosby, Stills, Nash and Young.*

Paul YOUNG *UK, male vocalist* *212 wks*

30 Jul 83	★ **NO PARLEZ** *CBS 25521*	1	119 wks
6 Apr 85	★ **THE SECRET OF ASSOCIATION** *CBS 26234*	1	49 wks
1 Nov 86	● **BETWEEN TWO FIRES** *CBS 450 150–1*	4	17 wks
16 Jun 90	● **OTHER VOICES** *CBS 4669171*	4	11 wks
14 Sep 91	★ **FROM TIME TO TIME – THE SINGLES COLLECTION**		
	Columbia 4688251	1†	16 wks

YOUNG DISCIPLES
UK, male/female vocal/instrumental group *5 wks*

31 Aug 91	**ROAD TO FREEDOM** *Talking Loud 5100971*	21	5 wks

Sydney YOUNGBLOOD *US, male vocalist* *17 wks*

28 Oct 89	**FEELING FREE** *Circa CIRCA 9*	23	17 wks

Y&T *US, male vocal/instrumental group* *15 wks*

11 Sep 82	**BLACK TIGER** *A&M AMLH 64910*	53	8 wks

346

γ

10 Sep 83	**MEAN STREAK** *A & M AMLX 64960*	35	4 wks
18 Aug 84	**IN ROCK WE TRUST** *A & M AMLX 65007*	33	3 wks

Frank ZAPPA *US, male vocalist/multi-instrumentalist*   *55 wks*

28 Feb 70 ●	**HOT RATS** *Reprise RSLP 6356*	9	27 wks
19 Dec 70	**CHUNGA'S REVENGE** *Reprise RSLP 2030*	43	1 wk
6 May 78	**ZAPPA IN NEW YORK** *Discreet K 69204*	55	1 wk
10 Mar 79	**SHEIK YERBOUTI** *CBS 88339*	32	7 wks
13 Oct 79	**JOE'S GARAGE ACT 1** *CBS 86101*	62	3 wks
19 Jan 80	**JOE'S GARAGE ACTS 2 & 3** *CBS 88475*	75	1 wk
16 May 81	**TINSEL TOWN REBELLION** *CBS 88516*	55	4 wks
24 Oct 81	**YOU ARE WHAT YOU IS** *CBS 88560*	51	2 wks
19 Jun 82	**SHIP ARRIVING TOO LATE TO SAVE A DROWNING**		
	WITCH *CBS 85804*	61	4 wks
18 Jun 83	**THE MAN FROM UTOPIA** *CBS 25251*	87	1 wk
27 Oct 84	**THEM OR US** *EMI FZD 1*	53	2 wks
30 Apr 88	**GUITAR** *Zappa ZAPPA 6*	82	2 wks

Lena ZAVARONI *UK, female vocalist*   *5 wks*

23 Mar 74 ●	**MA** *Philips 6308 201*	8	5 wks

ZOE *UK, female vocalist*   *1 wk*

7 Dec 91	**SCARLET RED AND BLUE** *M & G 5114431*	67	1 wk

ZUCCHERO *Italy, male vocalist*   *4 wks*

18 May 91	**ZUCCHERO** *A & M EVERY 1*	29	4 wks

Z.Z. TOP *US, male vocal/instrumental group*   *185 wks*

12 Jul 75	**FANDANGO** *London SHU 8482*	60	1 wk
8 Aug 81	**EL LOCO** *Warner Bros. K 56929*	88	2 wks
30 Apr 83 ●	**ELIMINATOR** *Warner Bros. W 3774*	3	135 wks
9 Nov 85 ●	**AFTERBURNER** *Warner Bros. WX 27*	2	40 wks
27 Oct 90 ●	**RECYCLER** *War.er Brothers WX 390*	8	7 wks

Various Artists

Compilation albums are listed alphabetically by label, for each label that has produced at least three hit compilations. Other hit compilations are listed together at the end of this section. Multi-artist Film Soundtracks, TV Spin-offs and Radio Soundtracks, Stage and Studio Cast Recordings, Anonymous Cover Versions and Miscellaneous Albums are then listed separately.

On 14 January 1989, the Compilation Albums chart was established and all entries on this chart are listed in this section. A dotted line in each label section indicates when the new chart began. Some albums will have entries both above and below the line, indicating that they appeared in the main chart before 14 January 1989, and the Compilations chart thereafter.

COMPILATIONS

A & M

2 May 87	**PRINCE'S TRUST TENTH ANNIVERSARY BIRTHDAY PARTY** *A & M AMA 3906*	76	3 wks
22 Aug 87	**THE PRINCE'S TRUST CONCERT 1987** *A & M PTA 1987*	44	3 wks
5 Dec 87	**SPECIAL OLYMPICS – A VERY SPECIAL CHRISTMAS** *A & M AMA 3911*	40	5 wks
23 Dec 89	**SPECIAL OLYMPICS – A VERY SPECIAL CHRISTMAS** *A & M AMA 3911*	19	1 wk
29 Sep 90	★ **SLAMMIN'** *A & M SLAMM 1*	1	6 wks
20 Apr 91	**RAGE – MAKE SOME NOISE VOL 1** *A & M AMTV 1*	12	3 wks
29 Jun 91	★ **WINGS OF LOVE** *A & M A & M 8455061*	1	19 wks

Arcade

29 Jul 72	★ **20 FANTASTIC HITS** *Arcade 2891 001*	1	24 wks
29 Nov 72	● **20 FANTASTIC HITS VOL. 2** *Arcade 2891 002*	2	14 wks
7 Apr 73	● **40 FANTASTIC HITS FROM THE 50'S AND 60'S** *Arcade ADEP 3/4*	2	15 wks
26 May 73	● **20 FANTASTIC HITS VOL. 3** *Arcade ADEP 5*	3	8 wks
15 Nov 75	● **DISCO HITS '75** *Arcade ADEP 18*	5	11 wks
26 Mar 77	**ROCK ON** *Arcade ADEP 27*	16	10 wks
2 Jun 77	**RULE BRITANNIA** *Arcade ADEP 29*	56	1 wk
23 Feb 80	**FIRST LOVE** *Arcade ADEP 41*	58	2 wks
12 Jan 91	**POP CLASSICS – 28 CLASSIC TRACKS** *Arcade ARC 94421*	19	2 wks
30 Mar 91	● **SOFT METAL BALLADS** *Arcade ARC 933501*	5	10 wks
8 Jun 91	● **IT STARTED WITH A KISS** *Arcade ARC 910301*	9	8 wks
13 Jul 91	● **THE HEAT IS ON** *Arcade ARC 925401*	4	9 wks
31 Aug 91	● **DANCE CLASSICS VOL 1** *Arcade ARC 925501*	8	4 wks
31 Aug 91	● **DANCE CLASSICS VOL 2** *Arcade ARC 925511*	7	5 wks
21 Sep 91	★ **GROOVY GHETTO** *Arcade ARC 925601*	1	6 wks
2 Nov 91	**GROOVY GHETTO – ALL THE RAGE** *Arcade ARC 925701*	15	2 wks
14 Dec 91	**CHRISTMAS LOVE SONGS** *Arcade ARC 948201*	11†	3 wks

Atlantic

2 Apr 66	**SOLID GOLD SOUL** *Atlantic ATL 5048*	12	27 wks
5 Nov 66	**MIDNIGHT SOUL** *Atlantic 587–021*	22	19 wks
14 Jun 69	**THIS IS SOUL** *Atlantic 643–301*	16	15 wks
25 Mar 72	**THE NEW AGE OF ATLANTIC** *Atlantic K 20024*	25	1 wk
22 Jun 74	**ATLANTIC BLACK GOLD** *Atlantic K 40550*	23	7 wks
3 Apr 76	**BY INVITATION ONLY** *Atlantic K 60112*	17	6 wks
11 Apr 81	**CONCERTS FOR THE PEOPLE OF KAMPUCHEA** *Atlantic K 60153*	39	2 wks
2 Feb 85	**THIS IS SOUL** *Atlantic SOUL 1*	78	7 wks

6 Jun 87 ● **ATLANTIC SOUL CLASSICS** *Atlantic WX 105*	9	23 wks
18 Jun 88 **ATLANTIC SOUL BALLADS** *Atlantic WX 98*	84	2 wks

Beggars Banquet

21 Nov 81 **SLIP STREAM** *Beggars Banquet BEGA 31*	72	3 wks
15 May 82 **SEX SWEAT AND BLOOD** *Beggars Banquet BEGA 34*	88	1 wk
11 Sep 82 **THE BEST OF BRITISH JAZZ FUNK VOLUME 2**		
Beggars Banquet BEGA 41	44	4 wks

CBS/Columbia

20 May 67 **THRILL TO THE SENSATIONAL SOUNDS OF SUPER**		
STEREO *CBS PR 5*	20	30 wks
28 Jun 69 **THE ROCK MACHINE TURNS YOU ON** *CBS SPR 22* .	18	7 wks
28 Jun 69 **ROCK MACHINE I LOVE YOU** *CBS SPR 26*	15	5 wks
20 May 72 ● **THE MUSIC PEOPLE** *CBS 66315*	10	9 wks
21 Oct 78 **SATIN CITY** *CBS 10010*	10	11 wks
2 Jun 79 **THIS IS IT** *CBS 10014*	6	12 wks
19 Apr 80 **FIRST LADIES OF COUNTRY** *CBS 10018*	37	6 wks
21 Jun 80 **KILLER WATTS** *CBS KW1*	27	6 wks
4 Apr 81 **BITTER SUITE** *CBS 22082*	55	3 wks
16 Oct 82 ● **REFLECTIONS** *CBS 10034*	4	91 wks
22 Oct 83 **IMAGINATIONS** *CBS 10044*	15	21 wks
20 Apr 85 **CLUB CLASSICS VOLUME 2** *CBS VAULT 2*	90	2 wks
14 Mar 87 ● **MOVE CLOSER** *CBS MOOD 1*	4	19 wks
27 Jun 87 **THE HOLIDAY ALBUM** *CBS MOOD 2*	13	9 wks
30 Apr 88 ★ **NITE FLITE** *CBS MOOD 4*	1	26 wks
4 Mar 89 ● **CHEEK TO CHEEK** *CBS MOOD 6*	2	32 wks
13 May 89 ★ **NITE FLITE 2** *CBS MOOD 8*	1	26 wks
30 Dec 89 **LAMBADA** *CBS 466055 1*	15	7 wks
24 Mar 90 ★ **JUST THE TWO OF US** *CBS MOOD 11*	1	37 wks
9 Jun 90 ● **NITE FLITE 3 – BEING WITH YOU** *CBS MOOD 14* ...	3	10 wks
2 Feb 91 ● **THINKING OF YOU** *Columbia MOOD 15*	1	23 wks
2 Feb 91 ● **THE TREE AND THE BIRD** *Columbia 4678801*	9	3 wks
30 Mar 91 **EVERYBODY DANCE NOW** *Columbia 468501*	12	3 wks
20 Apr 91 ● **FREE SPIRIT – 17 CLASSIC ROCK BALLADS**		
Columbia MOODS 16	4	23 wks
20 Apr 91 ● **YOU'RE THE INSPIRATION** *Columbia MOOD 17*	10	5 wks
10 Aug 91 ● **SIMPLY . . . LOVE** *Columbia MOOD 17*	3	10 wks
17 Aug 91 ★ **THE SOUND OF THE SUBURBS** *Columbia MOOD 18* ..	1	15 wks

349

Champion

8 Nov 86 **ULTIMATE TRAX VOLUME 1** *Champion CHAMP 103* ..	66	2 wks
7 Mar 87 **ULTIMATE TRAX VOLUME 2** *Champion CHAMP 1005* .	50	2 wks
18 Jul 87 **ULTIMATE TRAX 3 – BATTLE OF THE D.J.s**		
Champion CHAMP 1008	69	2 wks

Decca

8 Feb 64 **READY STEADY GO** *Decca LK 4577*	20	1 wk
28 Jun 69 **THE WORLD OF BLUES POWER** *Decca SPA 14*	24	6 wks
5 Jul 69 **THE WORLD OF BRASS BANDS** *Decca SPA 20*	13	11 wks
6 Sep 69 ● **THE WORLD OF HITS VOL. 2** *Decca SPA 35*	7	5 wks
20 Sep 69 **THE WORLD OF PROGRESSIVE MUSIC (WOWIE**		
ZOWIE) *Decca SPA 34*	17	2 wks
20 Sep 69 **THE WORLD OF PHASE 4 STEREO** *Decca SPA 32*	29	2 wks
7 Aug 71 ● **THE WORLD OF YOUR 100 BEST TUNES**		
Decca SPA 112	10	22 wks
9 Oct 71 ● **THE WORLD OF YOUR 100 BEST TUNES VOL. 2**		
Decca SPA 155	9	13 wks
27 Sep 75 **THE WORLD OF YOUR 100 BEST TUNES VOL. 10**		
Decca SPA 400	41	4 wks
13 Dec 75 **THE TOP 25 FROM YOUR 100 BEST TUNES**		
Decca HBT 1112	21	5 wks
26 Nov 83 ● **FORMULA 30** *Decca PROLP 4*	6	17 wks
1 Jun 91 ★ **THE ESSENTIAL MOZART** *Decca 4333231*	1	22 wks
16 Nov 91 ● **ESSENTIAL OPERA** *Decca 4338221*	2†	7 wks

Deep Heat

4 Mar 89	★ **DEEP HEAT** *Telstar STAR 2345*	1	15 wks
22 Apr 89	● **DEEP HEAT – THE SECOND BURN** *Telstar STAR 2356*	2	13 wks
22 Jul 89	● **DEEP HEAT 3 – THE THIRD DEGREE** *Telstar STAR 2364*	2	13 wks
23 Sep 89	★ **DEEP HEAT 4 – PLAY WITH FIRE** *Telstar STAR 2388* ..	1	11 wks
25 Nov 89	● **DEEP HEAT 1989 – FIGHT THE FLAME** *Telstar STAR 2380*	4	17 wks
3 Feb 90	● **DEEP HEAT 5 – FEED THE FEVER** *Telstar STAR 2411* ..	1	11 wks
31 Mar 90	★ **DEEP HEAT 6 – THE SIXTH SENSE** *Telstar STAR 2412*	1	14 wks
7 Jul 90	★ **DEEP HEAT 7 – SEVENTH HEAVEN** *Telstar STAR 2422*	1	9 wks
27 Oct 90	● **DEEP HEAT 8 – THE HAND OF FATE** *Telstar STAR 2447*	3	5 wks
24 Nov 90	● **DEEP HEAT 90** *Telstar STAR 2438*	3	12 wks
26 Jan 91	★ **DEEP HEAT 9 – NINTH LIFE** *Telstar STAR 2470*	1	7 wks
1 Jun 91	● **DEEP HEAT 10 – THE AWAKENING** *Telstar STAR 2490* .	2	7 wks
21 Dec 91	● **DEEP HEAT 11 – SPIRIT OF ECSTASY** *Telstar STAR 2555*	7†	2 wks

Dino

2 Dec 89	**THAT LOVING FEELING** *Dino DINTV 5*	11	11 wks
3 Mar 90	● **THAT LOVING FEELING VOL 2** *Dino DINTV 7*	5	21 wks
23 Jun 90	● **LEATHER AND LACE** *Dino DINTV 9*	3	8 wks
11 Aug 90	● **THE SUMMER OF LOVE** *Dino DINTV 10*	9	9 wks
6 Oct 90	★ **THAT LOVING FEELING VOL 3** *Dino DINTV 11*	1	23 wks
10 Nov 90	**LEATHER AND LACE – THE SECOND CHAPTER** *Dino DINTV 12*	14	4 wks
24 Nov 90	● **ROCK 'N' ROLL LOVE SONGS** *Dino DINTV 13*	4	19 wks
29 Dec 90	**BACHARACH AND DAVID – THEY WRITE THE SONGS** *Dino DINTV 16*	16	3 wks
9 Feb 91	● **SMOKEY ROBINSON – WRITER AND PERFORMER** *Dino DINTV 17*	6	7 wks
30 Mar 91	● **HARDCORE UPROAR** *Dino DINTV 20*	2	9 wks
6 Apr 91	● **THAT LOVING FEELING VOL 4** *Dino DINTV 18*	3	10 wks
1 Jun 91	● **LOVE SUPREME** *Dino DINTV 19*	4	5 wks
15 Jun 91	★ **THE RHYTHM DIVINE** *Dino DINTV 22*	1	15 wks
13 Jul 91	● **HARDCORE DANCEFLOOR** *Dino DINTV 24*	2	10 wks
27 Jul 91	● **CHIC AND ROSE ROYCE – THEIR GREATEST HITS SIDE BY SIDE** *Dino DINTV 23*	8	6 wks
3 Aug 91	● **LA FREEWAY** *Dino DINTV 25*	6	7 wks
12 Oct 91	● **WE WILL ROCK YOU** *Dino DINTV 26*	3	6 wks
19 Oct 91	● **THAT LOVING FEELING VOL 5** *Dino DINTV 28*	2	6 wks
2 Nov 91	★ **HARDCORE ECSTASY** *Dino DINTV 29*	1†	9 wks
2 Nov 91	● **THE RHYTHM DIVINE VOL 2** *Dino DINTV 27*	6	5 wks
23 Nov 91	● **MORE ROCK 'N' ROLL LOVE SONGS** *Dino DINTV 30*	8	6 wks
7 Dec 91	● **PARTY MIX** *Dino DINTV 32*	8†	4 wks
28 Dec 91	● **ESSENTIAL HARDCORE** *Dino DINTV 33*	2†	1 wk

DJ International

20 Sep 86	**THE HOUSE SOUND OF CHICAGO** *DJ International LONLP 22*	52	12 wks
18 Apr 87	**THE HOUSE OF SOUND OF CHICAGO VOLUME 2** *DJ International LONLP 32*	38	7 wks
31 Oct 87	**JACKMASTER VOLUME 1** *DJ International JACKLP 501*	36	4 wks
13 Feb 88	**JACKMASTER VOLUME 2** *DJ International JACKLP 502*	38	3 wks

Dover

26 Mar 88	**THE CHART SHOW – ROCK THE NATION** *Dover ADD 2*	16	8 wks
14 Jan 89	**SMASH HITS PARTY '88** *Dover ADD 5*	12	5 wks
4 Mar 89	● **AND ALL BECAUSE THE LADY LOVES...** *Dover ADD 6*	2	10 wks
20 May 89	● **THE CHART SHOW – ROCK THE NATION 2** *Dover ADD 4*	8	4 wks
3 Jun 89	● **THE CHART SHOW – DANCE MASTERS** *Dover ADD 7*	4	7 wks
28 Oct 89	★ **SMASH HITS PARTY '89** *Dover ADD 8*	1	14 wks
10 Feb 90	● **ALL BY MYSELF** *Dover ADD 12*	2	15 wks
14 Jul 90	● **SMASH HITS – RAVE!** *Dover ADD 14*	1	10 wks
22 Sep 90	● **JUST SEVENTEEN – GET KICKIN'** *Dover ADD 16*	2	6 wks

3 Nov 90	● SMASH HITS 1990 *Dover ADD 18*	2	14 wks
24 Nov 90	● A TON OF HITS *Dover ADD 19*	7	8 wks
20 Apr 91	● RED HOT METAL – 18 ROCK CLASSICS *Dover ADD 21*	4	6 wks
25 May 91	★ SMASH HITS – MASSIVE! *Dover ADD 24*	1	9 wks
8 Jun 91	ALL BY MYSELF 2 *Dover ADD 23*	13	5 wks
14 Sep 91	● MOMENTS IN SOUL *Dover ADD 25*	2	7 wks
26 Oct 91	● SMASH HITS 1991 *Dover ADD 28*	3†	10 wks

EMI

21 Jun 69	IMPACT *EMI STWO 2*	15	14 wks
2 Jun 73	★ PURE GOLD *EMI EMK 251*	1	11 wks
18 Nov 78	★ DON'T WALK BOOGIE *EMI EMTV 13*	1	23 wks
21 Apr 79	● COUNTRY LIFE *EMI EMTV 16*	2	14 wks
2 Jun 79	KNUCKLE SANDWICH *EMI International EMYV 18*	19	6 wks
15 Dec 79	ALL ABOARD *EMI EMTX 101*	13	8 wks
23 Feb 80	METAL FOR MUTHAS *EMI EMC 3318*	16	7 wks
14 Jun 80	METAL FOR MUTHAS VOL. 2 *EMI EMC 3337*	58	1 wk
13 Mar 82	20 WITH A BULLET *EMI EMTV 32*	11	8 wks
26 May 84	● THEN CAME ROCK 'N' ROLL *EMI THEN 1*	5	15 wks
5 Mar 88	● UNFORGETTABLE *EMI EMTV 44*	5	21 wks
22 Oct 88	THE CLASSIC EXPERIENCE *EMI EMTVD 45*	27	12 wks
3 Dec 88	HELLO CHILDREN...EVERYWHERE *EMI EM 1307*	59	5 wks
14 Jan 89	● THE CLASSIC EXPERIENCE *EMI EMTVD 45*	8	57 wks
28 Jan 89	UNFORGETTABLE *EMI EMTV 44*	18	1 wk
18 Mar 89	★ UNFORGETTABLE 2 *EMI EMTV 46*	1	15 wks
30 Sep 89	● IS THIS LOVE *EMI EMTV 47*	2	10 wks
18 Nov 89	★ THE 80'S – ALBUM OF THE DECADE *EMI EMTVD 48* .	1	12 wks
9 Dec 89	● IT'S CHRISTMAS *EMI EMTV 49*	2	15 wks
26 May 90	★ THE CLASSIC EXPERIENCE II *EMI EMTVD 50*	1	32 wks
4 Aug 90	● THE WILD ONE *EMI EMTV 52*	8	7 wks
20 Oct 90	★ MISSING YOU – AN ALBUM OF LOVE *EMI EMTV 53* .	1	18 wks
17 Nov 90	● TRULY UNFORGETTABLE *EMI EMTVD 55*	6	9 wks
1 Dec 90	THE BEST FROM THE MGM MUSICALS *EMI EMTV 56*	12	4 wks
16 Feb 91	● MISSING YOU 2 – AN ALBUM OF LOVE *EMI EMTV 57*	2	11 wks
11 May 91	● THE CLASSIC EXPERIENCE III *EMI EMTVD 59*	3	14 wks
26 Oct 91	● SEXUAL HEALING *EMI EMTV 60*	7	6 wks
30 Nov 91	A CLASSICAL CHRISTMAS *EMI EMTV 62*	14†	5 wks

Epic

2 Jul 83	DANCE MIX – DANCE HITS VOL. 1 *Epic EPC 25564* ...	85	2 wks
24 Sep 83	DANCE MIX – DANCE HITS VOL. 2 *Epic DM 2*	51	3 wks
3 Mar 84	DANCE MIX – DANCE HITS VOL. 3 *Epic DM 3*	70	1 wk
3 Mar 84	ELECTRO SHOCK VOLTAGE *Epic VOLT 1*	73	1 wk
16 Jun 84	● AMERICAN HEARTBEAT *Epic EPC 10045*	4	22 wks
16 Jun 84	DANCE MIX – DANCE HITS VOL. 4 *Epic DM 4*	99	1 wk
8 Mar 86	● HITS FOR LOVERS *Epic EPC 10050*	2	14 wks
9 Nov 91	MELLOW MADNESS *Epic MOOD 20*	14	2 wks

FFRR

30 Jan 88	THE HOUSE SOUND OF CHICAGO VOLUME 3 *FFRR FFRLP 1*	40	4 wks
27 Aug 88	THE HOUSE SOUND OF LONDON VOLUME 4 *FFRR FFRDP 4*	70	7 wks
1 Oct 88	BALEARIC BEATS VOLUME 1 *FFRR FFRLP 5*	58	2 wks

Greatest Hits

16 Nov 85	★ THE GREATEST HITS OF 1985 *Telstar STAR 2269*	1	17 wks
8 Nov 86	● THE GREATEST HITS OF 1986 *Telstar STAR 2286*	8	13 wks
21 Nov 87	● THE GREATEST HITS OF 1987 *Telstar STAR 2309*	12	11 wks
19 Nov 88	● THE GREATEST HITS OF 1988 *Telstar STAR 2334*	11	8 wks
14 Jan 89	● THE GREATEST HITS OF 1988 *Telstar STAR 2334*	8	8 wks
18 Nov 89	● THE GREATEST HITS OF 1989 *Telstar STAR 2389*	4	12 wks
18 Nov 89	● THE GREATEST HITS OF THE 80s *Telstar STAR 2382* ..	2	18 wks
17 Nov 90	● THE GREATEST HITS OF 1990 *Telstar STAR 2439*	4	14 wks
16 Nov 91	● THE GREATEST HITS OF 1991 *Telstar STAR 2536*	4†	7 wks

351

Greatest Love

26 Dec 87		**THE GREATEST LOVE** *Telstar STAR 2316*	**11**	40 wks
31 Dec 88		**THE GREATEST LOVE 2** *Telstar STAR 2352*	**37**	2 wks
14 Jan 89	●	**THE GREATEST LOVE 2** *Telstar STAR 2352*	**3**	23 wks
14 Jan 89	●	**THE GREATEST LOVE** *Telstar STAR 2316*	**7**	31 wks
11 Oct 89	●	**THE GREATEST LOVE 3** *Telstar STAR 2384*	**4**	18 wks
27 Oct 90	●	**THE GREATEST LOVE 4** *Telstar STAR 2400*	**4**	19 wks
8 Dec 90	●	**THE VERY BEST OF THE GREATEST LOVE** *Telstar STAR 2443*	**5**	17 wks
19 Oct 91	●	**IN LOVE – GREATEST LOVE 5** *Telstar STAR 2510*	**5**	8 wks

Hits

1 Dec 84	★	**THE HITS ALBUM** *CBS/WEA HITS 1*	**1**	36 wks
13 Apr 85	★	**HITS 2** *CBS/WEA HITS 2*	**1**	21 wks
7 Dec 85	●	**HITS 3** *CBS/WEA HITS 3*	**2**	21 wks
29 Mar 86	★	**HITS 4** *CBS/WEA/RCA/Arista HITS 4*	**1**	21 wks
22 Nov 86	★	**HITS 5** *CBS/WEA/RCA/Arista HITS 5*	**1**	25 wks
25 Jul 87	★	**HITS 6** *CBS/WEA/BMG HITS 6*	**1**	19 wks
5 Dec 87	●	**HITS 7** *CBS/WEA/BMG HITS 7*	**2**	17 wks
30 Jul 88	●	**HITS 8** *CBS/WEA/BMG HITS 8*	**2**	13 wks
17 Dec 88	●	**THE HITS ALBUM** *CBS/WEA/BMG HITS 9*	**5**	4 wks
14 Jan 89	●	**THE HITS ALBUM** *CBS/WEA/BMG HITS 9*	**4**	7 wks
3 Jun 89	★	**HITS 10** *CBS/WEA/BMG HITS 10*	**1**	13 wks
2 Dec 89	●	**MONSTER HITS** *CBS/WEA/BMG HITS 11*	**2**	14 wks
11 Aug 90	●	**SNAP IT UP – MONSTER HITS 2** *CBS/WEA/BMG HITS 12*	**2**	10 wks
29 Dec 90	●	**THE HIT PACK** *CBS/WEA/BMG COMPC 1*	**2**	8 wks
10 Aug 91	★	**THE HITS ALBUM** *CBS/WEA/BMG HITS 15*	**1**	9 wks

Impression

16 Oct 82	**BEST FRIENDS** *Impression LP IMP 1*	**28**	21 wks
3 Sep 83	**SUNNY AFTERNOON** *Impression LP IMP 2*	**13**	8 wks
26 Nov 83	**PRECIOUS MOMENTS** *Impression LP IMP 3*	**77**	5 wks
7 Apr 84	**ALWAYS AND FOREVER – THE COLLECTION** *Impression LP IMP 4*	**24**	12 wks
21 Jul 84	**WIPEOUT – 20 INSTRUMENTAL GREATS** *Impression LP IMP 5*	**37**	3 wks
28 Jul 84	**SUNNY AFTERNOON VOLUME TWO** *Impression LP IMP 7*	**90**	1 wk
22 Dec 84	**FRIENDS AGAIN** *Impression LP IMP 8*	**91**	1 wk

Island

26 Aug 67		**CLUB SKA '67** *Island ILP 956*	**37**	19 wks
14 Jun 69		**YOU CAN ALL JOIN IN** *Island IWPS 2*	**18**	10 wks
29 Mar 80		**CLUB SKA '67 (re-issue)** *Island IRSP 4*	**53**	6 wks
16 Jun 84		**CREW CUTS** *Island IMA 11*	**71**	4 wks
27 Oct 84		**CREW CUTS – LESSON 2** *Island IMA 14*	**95**	2 wks
18 Jul 87	●	**THE ISLAND STORY** *Island ISL 25*	**9**	10 wks
3 Nov 90	●	**HAPPY DAZE VOLUME 1** *Island ILPTV 1*	**7**	4 wks
6 Apr 91		**HAPPY DAZE VOLUME 2** *Island ILPTV 3*	**17**	2 wks

Jack Trax

18 Jul 87	**JACK TRAX – THE FIRST ALBUM** *Jack Trax JTRAX 1* ..	**83**	2 wks
3 Oct 87	**JACK TRAX – THE SECOND ALBUM** *Jack Trax JTRAX 2*	**61**	2 wks
5 Mar 88	**JACK TRAX – THE FOURTH ALBUM** *Jack Trax JTRAX 4*	**49**	4 wks

Jetstar

30 Mar 85		**REGGAE HITS VOLUME 1** *Jetstar JETLP 1001*	**32**	11 wks
26 Oct 85		**REGGAE HITS VOLUME 2** *Jetstar JETLP 1002*	**86**	2 wks
4 Jun 88		**REGGAE HITS VOLUME 4** *Jetstar JETLP 1004*	**56**	7 wks
17 Dec 88		**REGGAE HITS VOLUME 5** *Jetstar JETLP 1005*	**96**	1 wk
5 Aug 89		**REGGAE HITS VOLUME 6** *Jetstar JETLP 1006*	**13**	6 wks
23 Dec 89		**REGGAE HITS VOLUME 7** *Jetstar JETLP 1007*	**13**	6 wks
30 Jun 90	●	**REGGAE HITS VOLUME 8** *Jetstar JETLP 1008*	**7**	5 wks
20 Jul 91	●	**REGGAE HITS VOLUME 10** *Jetstar JETLP 1010*	**6**	7 wks

K-Tel

Date		Title	Catalogue	Pos	Wks
10 Jun 72	★	**20 DYNAMIC HITS** *K-Tel TE 292*		1	28 wks
7 Oct 72	★	**20 ALL TIME HITS OF THE 50'S** *K-Tel NE 490*		1	22 wks
29 Nov 72	●	**25 DYNAMIC HITS VOL. 2** *K-Tel TE 291*		2	12 wks
2 Dec 72	★	**25 ROCKIN' & ROLLIN' GREATS** *K-Tel NE 493*		1	18 wks
31 Mar 73	★	**20 FLASHBACK GREATS OF THE SIXTIES** *K-Tel NE 494*		1	11 wks
21 Apr 73	●	**BELIEVE IN MUSIC** *K-Tel TE 294*		2	8 wks
8 Nov 75		**GOOFY GREATS** *K-Tel NE 707*		19	7 wks
13 Dec 75	●	**40 SUPER GREATS** *K-Tel NE 708*		9	8 wks
31 Jan 76	●	**MUSIC EXPRESS** *K-Tel TE 702*		3	10 wks
10 Apr 76	●	**JUKE BOX JIVE** *K-Tel NE 709*		3	13 wks
17 Apr 76		**GREAT ITALIAN LOVE SONGS** *K-Tel NE 303*		17	14 wks
15 May 76	●	**HIT MACHINE** *K-Tel TE 713*		4	10 wks
5 Jun 76		**EUROVISION FAVOURITES** *K-Tel NE 712*		44	1 wk
2 Oct 76		**SUMMER CRUISING** *K-Tel NE 918*		30	1 wk
16 Oct 76		**COUNTRY COMFORT** *K-Tel NE 294*		8	12 wks
16 Oct 76	★	**SOUL MOTION** *K-Tel NE 930*		1	14 wks
4 Dec 76	●	**DISCO ROCKET** *K-Tel NE 948*		3	14 wks
11 Dec 76		**44 SUPERSTARS** *K-Tel NE 939*		14	10 wks
12 Feb 77	●	**HEARTBREAKERS** *K-Tel NE 954*		2	18 wks
19 Feb 77	●	**DANCE TO THE MUSIC** *K-Tel NE 957*		5	9 wks
7 May 77		**HIT ACTION** *K-Tel NE 993*		15	9 wks
29 Oct 77		**SOUL CITY** *K-Tel NE 1003*		12	7 wks
12 Nov 77	●	**FEELINGS** *K-Tel NE 1006*		3	24 wks
26 Nov 77	★	**DISCO FEVER** *K-Tel NE 1014*		1	20 wks
21 Jan 78		**40 NUMBER ONE HTIS** *K-Tel NE 1008*		15	7 wks
4 Mar 78	●	**DISCO STARS** *K-Tel NE 1022*		6	8 wks
10 Jun 78	●	**DISCO DOUBLE** *K-Tel NE 1024*		10	6 wks
8 Jul 78		**ROCK RULES** *K-Tel RL 001*		12	11 wks
8 Jul 78		**THE WORLD'S WORST RECORD SHOW** *Yuk/K-Tel NE 1023*		47	2 wks
19 Aug 78		**STAR PARTY** *K-Tel NE 1034*		4	9 wks
4 Nov 78	●	**EMOTIONS** *K-Tel NE 1035*		2	17 wks
25 Nov 78	●	**MIDNIGHT HUSTLE** *K-Tel NE 1037*		2	13 wks
20 Jan 79	★	**ACTION REPLAY** *K-Tel NE 1040*		1	14 wks
7 Apr 79		**DISCO INFERNO** *K-Tel NE 1043*		11	9 wks
5 May 79		**HI ENERGY** *K-Tel NE 1044*		17	7 wks
22 Sep 79		**HOT TRACKS** *K-Tel NE 1049*		31	8 wks
24 Nov 79	●	**NIGHT MOVES** *K-Tel NE 1065*		10	10 wks
24 Nov 79		**TOGETHER** *K-Tel NE 1053*		35	8 wks
12 Jan 80	●	**VIDEO STARS** *K-Tel NE 1066*		5	10 wks
26 Jan 80		**THE SUMMIT** *K-Tel NE 1067*		17	5 wks
29 Mar 80	●	**STAR TRACKS** *K-Tel NE 1070*		6	8 wks
26 Apr 80		**GOOD MORNING AMERICA** *K-Tel NE 1072*		15	12 wks
17 May 80		**HAPPY DAYS** *K-Tel ONE 1076*		32	6 wks
17 May 80	●	**MAGIC REGGAE** *K-Tel NE 1074*		9	17 wks
14 Jun 80	●	**HOT WAX** *K-Tel NE 1082*		3	10 wks
27 Sep 80	●	**MOUNTING EXCITEMENT** *K-Tel NE 1091*		2	8 wks
11 Oct 80	●	**THE LOVE ALBUM** *K-Tel NE 1062*		6	16 wks
25 Oct 80		**AXE ATTACK** *K-Tel NE 1100*		15	14 wks
15 Nov 80	●	**CHART EXPLOSION** *K-Tel NE 1103*		6	17 wks
3 Jan 81		**NIGHTLIFE** *K-Tel NE 1107*		25	9 wks
14 Feb 81		**HIT MACHINE** *K-Tel NE 1113*		17	6 wks
21 Mar 81		**RHYTHM 'N' REGGAE** *K-Tel NE 1115*		42	4 wks
25 Apr 81	●	**CHARTBUSTERS 81** *K-Tel NE 1118*		3	9 wks
2 May 81		**AXE ATTACK 2** *K-Tel NE 1120*		31	6 wks
23 May 81	●	**THEMES** *K-Tel NE 1122*		6	15 wks
29 Aug 81		**CALIFORNIA DREAMING** *K-Tel NE 1126*		27	11 wks
19 Sep 81		**DANCE DANCE DANCE** *K-Tel NE 1143*		29	4 wks
3 Oct 81		**THE PLATINUM ALBUM** *K-Tel NE 1134*		32	11 wks
10 Oct 81	●	**LOVE IS . . .** *K-Tel NE 1129*		10	15 wks
21 Nov 81	★	**CHART HITS 81** *K-Tel NE 1142*		1	17 wks
9 Jan 82	●	**MODERN DANCE** *K-Tel NE 1156*		6	10 wks
6 Feb 82	●	**DREAMING** *K-Tel NE 1159*		2	12 wks
6 Mar 82	●	**ACTION TRAX** *K-Tel NE 1162*		2	12 wks
1 May 82		**MIDNIGHT HOUR** *K-Tel NE 1157*		98	1 wk
3 Jul 82		**TURBO TRAX** *K-Tel NE 1176*		17	7 wks
4 Sep 82		**THE NO 1 SOUNDS OF THE SEVENTIES** *K-Tel NE 1172*		83	1 wk
11 Sep 82	●	**CHARTBEAT/CHARTHEAT** *K-Tel NE 1180*		2	14 wks

30 Oct	82		THE LOVE SONGS ALBUM *K-Tel NE 1179*	28	8 wks
6 Nov	82		CHART HITS '82 *K-Tel NE 1195*	11	17 wks
6 Nov	82		DISCO DANCER *K-Tel NE 1190*	26	8 wks
18 Dec	82		STREETSCENE *K-Tel NE 1183*	42	6 wks
15 Jan	83	●	VISIONS *K-Tel ONE 1199*	5	21 wks
12 Feb	83		HEAVY *K-Tel NE 1203*	46	12 wks
5 Mar	83	●	HOTLINE *K-Tel NE 1207*	3	9 wks
11 Jun	83	●	CHART STARS *K-Tel NE 1225*	7	9 wks
20 Aug	83		COOL HEAT *K-Tel NE 1231*	79	3 wks
10 Sep	83	●	HEADLINE HITS *K-Tel NE 1253*	5	6 wks
8 Oct	83	●	THE TWO OF US *K-Tel NE 1222*	3	16 wks
8 Oct	83		IMAGES *K-Tel ONE 1254*	33	6 wks
12 Nov	83		CHART HITS '83 VOLS 1 AND 2 *K-Tel NE 1256*	6	11 wks
24 Mar	84		NIGHT MOVES *K-tel NE 1255*	15	11 wks
26 May	84	●	HUNGRY FOR HITS *K-Tel NE 1272*	4	11 wks
23 Jun	84		THE THEMES ALBUM *K-Tel ONE 1257*	43	3 wks
28 Jul	84		BREAKDANCE, YOU CAN DO IT *K-Tel ONE 1276*	18	12 wks
12 Sep	84	●	ALL BY MYSELF *K-Tel NE 1273*	7	16 wks
1 Dec	84		HOOKED ON NUMBER ONES – 100 NON-STOP HITS *K-Tel ONE 1285*	25	15 wks
2 Feb	85		FOUR STAR COUNTRY *K-Tel NE 1278*	52	6 wks
2 Mar	85		MODERN LOVE *K-Tel NE 1286*	13	7 wks
5 Oct	85		EXPRESSIONS *K-Tel NE 1307*	11	8 wks
9 Nov	85	●	ROCK ANTHEMS *K-Tel NE 1309*	10	11 wks
9 Nov	85		OVATION – THE BEST OF ANDREW LLOYD WEBBER *K-Tel ONE 1311*	34	12 wks
12 Apr	86	●	HEART TO HEART *K-Tel NE 1318*	8	15 wks
19 Apr	86		ROCK ANTHEMS – VOLUME TWO *K-Tel NE 1319*	43	9 wks
5 Jul	86		RAP IT UP – RAP'S GREATEST HITS *K-Tel NE 1324*	50	4 wks
19 Jul	86		DRIVE TIME USA *K-Tel NE 1321*	20	8 wks
18 Oct	86		DANCE HITS '86 *K-Tel NE 1344*	35	7 wks
1 Nov	86		TOGETHER *K-Tel NE 1345*	20	10 wks
7 Feb	87		IMPRESSIONS *K-Tel NE 1346*	15	14 wks
21 Mar	87		RHYTHM OF THE NIGHT *K-Tel NE 1348*	36	7 wks
21 Mar	87		HITS REVIVAL *K-Tel (Holland) KTLP 2351*	63	1 wk
13 Jun	87	●	FRIENDS AND LOVERS *K-Tel NE 1352*	10	10 wks
27 Jun	87	●	HITS REVIVAL *K-Tel NE 1363*	10	9 wks
17 Oct	87		TRUE LOVE *K-Tel NE 1359*	38	5 wks
31 Oct	87	●	FROM MOTOWN WITH LOVE *K-Tel NE 1381*	9	9 wks
14 Nov	87		ALWAYS *K-Tel NE 1377*	65	5 wks
19 Dec	87		WOW WHAT A PARTY *K-Tel NE 1388*	97	2 wks
5 Mar	88		HORIZONS *K-Tel NE 1360*	13	10 wks
30 Apr	88		HITS REVIVAL 2: REPLAY *K-Tel NE 1405*	45	3 wks
14 May	88		TSOP – THE SOUND OF PHILADELPHIA *K-Tel NE 1406*	26	9 wks
11 Jun	88		THE HITS OF HOUSE ARE HERE *K-Tel NE 1419*	12	12 wks
15 Oct	88		MOTOWN IN MOTION *K-Tel NE 1410*	28	13 wks
15 Oct	88		THE RETURN OF SUPERBAD *K-Tel NE 1421*	83	4 wks
5 Nov	88		THE LOVERS *K-Tel NE 1426*	50	5 wks
26 Nov	88		RAPPIN' UP THE HOUSE *K-Tel NE 1428*	43	7 wks

....

14 Jan	89		RAPPIN' UP THE HOUSE *K-Tel NE 1428*	19	1 wk
4 Feb	89	●	FROM MOTOWN WITH LOVE *K-Tel NE 1381*	6	7 wks
25 Mar	89	●	HIP HOUSE – THE DEEPEST BEATS IN TOWN *K-Tel NE 1430*	10	5 wks
29 Jul	89	●	GLAM SLAM *K-Tel NE 1434*	5	8 wks
23 Sep	89	●	LOVE HOUSE *K-Tel NE 1446*	5	7 wks
30 Sep	89	●	ETERNAL LOVE *K-Tel NE 1447*	5	7 wks
21 Oct	89	●	RAP ATTACK *K-Tel NE 1450*	6	7 wks
25 Nov	89		SEDUCTION *K-Tel NE 1451*	15	4 wks
10 Mar	90		CAN U FEEL IT? -- THE CHAMPION LEGEND *K-Tel ONE 1452*	12	3 wks
21 Apr	90	●	HOOKED ON COUNTRY *K-Tel NE 1459*	6	12 wks

354

London

10 Jun	89	●	FFRR – SILVER ON BLACK *London 8281551*	8	5 wks
11 Nov	89	●	DANCE DECADE – DANCE HITS OF THE 80's *London DDTV 1*	8	7 wks
16 Jun	90	●	THE NORTHERN BEAT *London 8409681*	4	8 wks
7 Jul	90		MASSIVE 4 *London 8282101*	20	2 wks

VARIOUS ARTISTS

Mercury
26 Nov 83 ● **FORMULA 30** *Mercury PROLP 4*	6	17 wks
14 Jun 86 **BEAT RUNS WILD** *Mercury WILD 1*	70	2 wks
1 Nov 86 **FORMULA 30 2** *Mercury PROLP 9*	80	3 wks

Needle
4 Jul 87 **DANCE MANIA VOLUME 1** *Needle DAMA 1*	46	4 wks
20 Feb 88 **MAD ON HOUSE VOLUME 1** *Needle MADD 1*	81	2 wks
14 May 88 **HOUSE HITS** *Needle HOHI 88*	25	8 wks

Nouveau Music
24 Sep 83 **CLASSIC THEMES** *Nouveau Music NML 1001*	61	2 wks
2 Jun 84 **ESSENTIAL DISCO AND DANCE** *Nouveau Music NML 1010*	96	1 wk
30 Mar 85 **DREAM MELODIES** *Nouveau Music NML 1013*	91	1 wk

Now!
10 Dec 83 ★ **NOW THAT'S WHAT I CALL MUSIC** *EMI/Virgin NOW 1*	1	50 wks
7 Apr 84 ★ **NOW THAT'S WHAT I CALL MUSIC 2** *EMI/Virgin NOW 2*	1	38 wks
11 Aug 84 ★ **NOW THAT'S WHAT I CALL MUSIC 3** *EMI/Virgin NOW 3*	1	30 wks
8 Dec 84 ● **NOW THAT'S WHAT I CALL MUSIC 4** *EMI/Virgin NOW 4*	2	43 wks
1 Jun 85 ● **NOW DANCE** *EMI/Virgin NOD 1*	3	14 wks
17 Aug 85 ★ **NOW THAT'S WHAT I CALL MUSIC 5** *EMI/Virgin NOW 5*	1	21 wks
30 Nov 85 ★ **NOW – THE CHRISTMAS ALBUM** *EMI/Virgin NOX 1*	1	22 wks
7 Dec 85 ★ **NOW THAT'S WHAT I CALL MUSIC 6** *EMI/Virgin NOW 6*	1	40 wks
19 Jul 86 ● **NOW – THE SUMMER ALBUM** *EMI/Virgin SUMMER 1*	7	9 wks
23 Aug 86 ★ **NOW THAT'S WHAT I CALL MUSIC 7** *EMI/Virgin NOW 7*	1	21 wks
8 Nov 86 ● **NOW DANCE '86** *EMI/Virgin NOD 2*	2	13 wks
29 Nov 86 **NOW THAT'S WHAT I CALL MUSIC '86** *EMI/Virgin/PolyGram CDNOW 86*	65	4 wks
6 Dec 86 ★ **NOW THAT'S WHAT I CALL MUSIC 8** *EMI/Virgin/PolyGram NOW 8*	1	23 wks
4 Apr 87 ★ **NOW THAT'S WHAT I CALL MUSIC 9** *EMI/Virgin/PolyGram NOW 9*	1	26 wks
3 Oct 87 ● **NOW! SMASH HITS** *EMI/Virgin/PolyGram NOSH 1*	5	10 wks
5 Dec 87 ★ **NOW THAT'S WHAT I CALL MUSIC 10** *EMI/Virgin/PolyGram NOW 10*	1	21 wks
2 Apr 88 ★ **NOW THAT'S WHAT I CALL MUSIC 11** *EMI/Virgin/PolyGram NOW 11*	1	17 wks
23 Jul 88 ★ **NOW THAT'S WHAT I CALL MUSIC 12** *EMI/Virgin/PolyGram NOW 12*	1	17 wks
3 Dec 88 ★ **NOW THAT'S WHAT I CALL MUSIC 13** *EMI/Virgin/PolyGram NOW 13*	1	6 wks

....

14 Jan 89 ★ **NOW THAT'S WHAT I CALL MUSIC 13** *EMI/Virgin/PolyGram NOW 13*	1	15 wks
1 Apr 89 ★ **NOW THAT'S WHAT I CALL MUSIC 14** *EMI/Virgin/PolyGram NOW 14*	1	18 wks
15 Jul 89 ★ **NOW DANCE '89** *EMI/Virgin NOD 3*	1	14 wks
26 Aug 89 ★ **NOW THAT'S WHAT I CALL MUSIC 15** *EMI/Virgin/PolyGram NOW 15*	1	13 wks
2 Dec 89 ★ **NOW THAT'S WHAT I CALL MUSIC 16** *EMI/Virgin/PolyGram NOW 16*	1	15 wks
10 Mar 90 ★ **NOW DANCE 901** *EMI/Virgin/PolyGram NOD 4*	1	14 wks
5 May 90 ★ **NOW THAT'S WHAT I CALL MUSIC 17** *EMI/Virgin/PolyGram NOW 17*	1	15 wks
28 Jul 90 ★ **NOW DANCE 902** *EMI/Virgin/PolyGram NOD 5*	1	13 wks
10 Nov 90 ★ **NOW DANCE 903** *EMI/Virgin/PolyGram NOD 6*	1	9 wks
1 Dec 90 ★ **NOW THAT'S WHAT I CALL MUSIC 18** *EMI/Virgin/PolyGram NOW 18*	1	18 wks
6 Apr 91 ★ **NOW THAT'S WHAT I CALL MUSIC 19** *EMI/Virgin/PolyGram NOW 19*	1	16 wks

5 Oct 91	★ NOW DANCE 91 *EMI/Virgin/PolyGram NOD 7*	1	9 wks
30 Nov 91	★ NOW THAT'S WHAT I CALL MUSIC 20		
	EMI/Virgin/PolyGram NOW 20	1†	5wks

Philips

9 Mar 63	● ALL STAR FESTIVAL *Philips DL 99500*	4	19 wks
2 Jun 73	● 20 ORIGINAL CHART HITS *Philips TV 1*	9	11 wks
2 Jun 73	NICE 'N' EASY *Philips 6441 076*	36	1 wk
6 Aug 77	NEW WAVE *Philips 5300 902*	11	12 wks

Polydor

10 Dec 66	STEREO MUSICALE SHOWCASE *Polydor 104450*	26	2 wks
9 Oct 71	THE A–Z OF EASY LISTENING *Polydor 2661 005*	24	4 wks
24 Feb 79	20 OF ANOTHER KIND *Polydor POLS 1006*	45	3 wks
19 May 79	BOOGIE BUS *Polydor 9198 174*	23	11 wks
3 May 80	● CHAMPAGNE AND ROSES *Polydor ROSTV 1*	7	14 wks
30 Aug 80	I AM WOMAN *Polydor WOMTV 1*	11	13 wks
11 Oct 80	COUNTRY ROUND UP *Polydor KOWTV 1*	64	3 wks
18 Oct 80	MONSTERS OF ROCK *Polydor 2488 810*	16	5 wks
6 Dec 80	THE HITMAKERS *Polydor HOPTV 1*	45	10 wks
4 Apr 81	● ROLL ON *Polydor REDTV 1*	3	13 wks
17 Oct 81	MONSTER TRACKS *Polydor HOPTV 2*	20	8 wks
12 Jan 85	BREAKDANCE 2 – ELECTRIC BOOGALOO		
	Polydor POLD 5168	34	20 wks
12 Nov 88	● THE PREMIER COLLECTION *Polydor ALWTV 1*	3	9 wks
14 Jan 89	★ THE PREMIER COLLECTION *Polydor ALWTV 1*	1	51 wks
4 Feb 89	★ THE MARQUEE – 30 LEGENDARY YEARS		
	Polydor MOTV 1	1	21 wks
31 Mar 90	● SKINBEAT – THE FIRST TOUCH *Polydor SKINL 101* ..	6	8 wks
18 Aug 90	★ KNEBWORTH – THE ALBUM *Polydor 843912*	1	10 wks
5 Oct 91	● ABSOLUTION – ROCK THE ALTERNATIVE WAY		
	Polydor 8457471	6	5 wks

356

Pye

9 May 59	● CURTAIN UP *Pye Nixa BRTH 0059*	4	13 wks
23 Jun 62	HONEY HIT PARADE *Pye Golden Guinea GGL 0129*	13	7 wks
30 Nov 62	ALL THE HITS BY ALL THE STARS		
	Pye Golden Guinea GGL 0162	19	2 wks
7 Sep 63	HITSVILLE *Pye Golden Guinea GGL 0202*	11	6 wks
14 Sep 63	THE BEST OF RADIO LUXEMBOURG		
	Pye Golden Guinea GGL 0208	14	2 wks
23 Nov 63	HITSVILLE VOL 2 *Pye Golden Guinea GGL 0233*	20	1 wk
4 Jan 64	THE BLUES VOL 1 *Pye NPL 28030*	15	3 wks
22 Feb 64	FOLK FESTIVAL OF THE BLUES (LIVE RECORDING)		
	Pye NPL 28033	16	4 wks
30 May 64	THE BLUES VOL 2 *Pye NPL 28035*	16	3 wks
10 Feb 68	STARS OF '68 *Marble Arch MAL 762*	23	3 wks
16 Oct 71	PYE CHARTBUSTERS *Pye PCB 15000*	36	1 wk
18 Dec 71	PYE CHARTBUSTERS VOL 2 *Pye PCB 15001*	29	3 wks

Ronco

21 Oct 72	● 20 STAR TRACKS *Ronco PP 2001*	2	13 wks
23 Jun 73	★ THAT'LL BE THE DAY *Ronco MR 2002/3*	1	8 wks
8 Nov 75	BLAZING BULLETS *Ronco RTI 2012*	17	8 wks
6 Dec 75	GREATEST HITS OF WALT DISNEY *Ronco RTD 2013* .	11	12 wks
13 Dec 75	A CHRISTMAS GIFT *Ronco P 12430*	39	5 wks
24 Jan 76	● STAR TRACKIN' 76 *Ronco RTL 2014*	9	5 wks
8 Jan 77	CLASSICAL GOLD *Ronco RTD 42020*	24	12 wks
16 Jul 77	SUPERGROUPS *Ronco RTL 2023*	57	1 wk
26 Nov 77	BLACK JOY *Ronco RTL 2025*	26	13 wks
18 Mar 78	● BOOGIE NIGHTS *Ronco RTL 2027*	5	7 wks
18 Nov 78	BOOGIE FEVER *Ronco RTL 2034*	15	11 wks
9 Jun 79	ROCK LEGENDS *Ronco RTL 2037*	54	3 wks
3 Nov 79	● ROCK 'N' ROLLER DISCO *Ronco RTL 2040*	3	11 wks
8 Dec 79	● PEACE IN THE VALLEY *Ronco RTL 2043*	6	18 wks
22 Dec 79	MILITARY GOLD *Ronco RTD 42042*	62	3 wks
25 Oct 80	STREET LEVEL *Ronco RTL 2048*	29	5 wks
8 Nov 80	● COUNTRY LEGENDS *Ronco RTL 2050*	9	12 wks
15 Nov 80	RADIOACTIVE *Ronco RTL 2049*	13	9 wks

29 Nov 80	SPACE INVADERS *Ronco RTL 2051*	47	3 wks
6 Dec 80	THE LEGENDARY BIG BANDS *Ronco RTL 2047*	24	6 wks
9 May 81	★ DISCO DAZE AND DISCO NITES *Ronco RTL 2056 A/B*	1	23 wks
19 Sep 81	● SUPER HITS 1 & 2 *Ronco RTL 2058 A/B*	2	17 wks
24 Oct 81	COUNTRY SUNRISE/COUNTRY SUNSET		
	Ronco RTL 2059 A/B	27	11 wks
14 Nov 81	ROCK HOUSE *Ronco RTL 2061*	44	4 wks
12 Dec 81	MISTY MORNINGS *Ronco RTL 2066*	44	5 wks
12 Dec 81	MEMORIES ARE MADE OF THIS *Ronco RTL 2062*	84	4 wks
26 Dec 81	● HITS HITS HITS *Ronco RTL 2063*	2	10 wks
24 Apr 82	● DISCO UK & DISCO USA *Ronco RTL 2073*	7	10 wks
15 May 82	● CHARTBUSTERS *Ronco RTL 2074*	3	10 wks
3 Jul 82	● OVERLOAD *Ronco RTL 2079*	10	8 wks
28 Aug 82	SOUL DAZE/SOUL NITES *Ronco RTL 2080*	25	10 wks
11 Sep 82	● BREAKOUT *Ronco RTL 2081*	4	8 wks
30 Oct 82	MUSIC FOR THE SEASONS *Ronco RTL 2075*	41	10 wks
27 Nov 82	CHART WARS *Ronco RTL 2086*	30	7 wks
27 Nov 82	THE GREAT COUNTRY MUSIC SHOW *Ronco RTD 2083*	38	7 wks
18 Dec 82	THE BEST OF BEETHOVEN/STRAUSS/		
	TCHAIKOWSKY/MOZART (4 LPs) *Ronco RTL 2084* .	49	10 wks
25 Dec 82	★ RAIDERS OF THE POP CHARTS *Ronco RTL 2088*	1	17 wks
19 Mar 83	● CHART RUNNERS *Ronco RTL 2090*	4	13 wks
21 May 83	● CHART ENCOUNTERS OF THE HIT KIND		
	Ronco RTL 2091	5	10 wks
18 Jun 83	LOVERS ONLY *Ronco RTL 2093*	12	13 wks
16 Jul 83	HITS ON FIRE *Ronco RTL 2095*	11	10 wks
17 Sep 83	● THE HIT SQUAD – CHART TRACKING		
	Ronco RON LP 1	4	9 wks
17 Sep 83	THE HIT SQUAD – NIGHT CLUBBING		
	Ronco RON LP 2	28	7 wks
12 Nov 83	HIT SQUAD – HITS OF '83 *Ronco RON LP 4*	12	11 wks
17 Dec 83	● GREEN VELVET *Ronco RON LP 6*	6	17 wks
7 Jan 84	CHART TREK VOLS. 1 & 2 *Ronco RON LP 8*	20	9 wks
21 Jan 84	● SOMETIMES WHEN WE TOUCH *Ronco RON LP 9* ...	8	14 wks
24 Mar 84	BABY LOVE *Ronco RON LP 11*	47	6 wks
7 Apr 84	DREAMS AND THEMES *Ronco RON LP 10*	75	2 wks

Green Velvet *was re-issued on Telstar STAR 2252.*

Serious

7 Jun 86	UPFRONT 1 *Serious UPFT 1*	17	10 wks
23 Aug 86	UPFRONT 2 *Serious UPFT 2*	27	6 wks
1 Nov 86	UPFRONT 3 *Serious UPFT 3*	37	5 wks
31 Jan 87	UPFRONT 4 *Serious UPFT 4*	21	5 wks
28 Mar 87	SERIOUS HIP-HOP 2 *Serious SHOP 2*	95	1 wk
28 Mar 87	UPFRONT 5 *Serious UPFT 5*	21	6 wks
23 May 87	UPFRONT 6 *Serious UPFT 6*	22	6 wks
4 Jul 87	BEST OF HOUSE VOLUME 1 *Serious BEHO 1*	55	12 wks
15 Aug 87	UPFRONT 7 *Serious UPFT 7*	31	4 wks
12 Sep 87	BEST OF HOUSE VOLUME 2 *Serious BEHO 2*	30	7 wks
17 Oct 87	HIP-HOP '87 *Serious HHOP 87*	81	1 wk
17 Oct 87	UPFRONT 8 *Serious UPFT 8*	22	6 wks
14 Nov 87	BEST OF HOUSE VOLUME 3 *Serious BEHO 3*	61	3 wks
12 Dec 87	BEST OF HOUSE MEGAMIX *Serious BOIT 1*	77	4 wks
19 Dec 87	UPFRONT 9 *Serious UPFT 9*	92	1 wk
20 Feb 88	DANCE MANIA VOLUME 2 *Serious DAMA 2*	59	2 wks
12 Mar 88	BEST OF HOUSE VOLUME 4 *Serious BEHO 4*	27	8 wks
9 Apr 88	UPFRONT 10 *Serious UPFT 10*	45	5 wks
14 May 88	BEST OF HOUSE MEGAMIX VOLUME 2 *Serious BOIT 2*	73	2 wks
29 Oct 88	ACID TRAX MEGAMIX VOLUME 1 *Serious DUIX 1*	93	1 wk
18 Feb 89	UPFRONT '89 *Serious UPFT 89*	15	1 wk

Starblend

12 Nov 83	IN TOUCH *Starblend STD 9*	89	2 wks
23 Jun 84	BROKEN DREAMS *Starblend SLTD 1*	48	7 wks
27 Apr 85	12 X 12 MEGA MIXES *Starblend INCH 1*	77	2 wks
3 Aug 85	AMERICAN DREAMS *Starblend SLTD 12*	43	8 wks
21 Dec 85	CHRISTMAS AT THE COUNTRY STORE		
	Starblend NOEL 1	94	1 wk

12 Jul 86	**DISCOVER COUNTRY/DISCOVER NEW COUNTRY**			
	Starblend DNC 1	60	3 wks
16 Aug 86	**HEARTBREAKERS** *Starblend BLEND 3*	38	8 wks
20 Sep 86	**ABSOLUTE ROCK 'N' ROLL** *Starblend SLTD 15*	88	1 wk

Street Sounds

19 Feb 83	**STREET SOUNDS EDITION 2** *Street Sounds STSND 002*	35	6 wks
23 Apr 83	**STREET SOUNDS EDITION 3** *Street Sounds STSND 003*	21	5 wks
25 Jun 83	**STREET SOUNDS EDITION 4** *Street Sounds STSND 004*	14	8 wks
13 Aug 83	**STREET SOUNDS EDITION 5** *Street Sounds STSND 005*	16	8 wks
8 Oct 83	**STREET SOUNDS EDITION 6** *Street Sounds STSND 006*	23	5 wks
22 Oct 83	**STREET SOUNDS ELECTRO 1** *Street Sounds ELCST 1* ..	18	8 wks
17 Dec 83	**STREET SOUNDS EDITION 7** *Street Sounds STSND 007*	48	4 wks
7 Jan 84	**STREET SOUNDS ELECTRO 2** *Street Sounds ELCST 2* ..	49	7 wks
3 Mar 84	**STREET SOUNDS HI ENERGY 1** *Street Sounds HINRG 16*	71	1 wk
10 Mar 84	**STREET SOUNDS CRUCIAL ELECTRO**		
	Street Sounds ELCST 999	24	10 wks
10 Mar 84	**STREET SOUNDS EDITION 8** *Street Sounds STSND 008*	22	7 wks
7 Apr 84	**STREET SOUNDS ELECTRO 3** *Street Sounds ELCST 3* ..	25	9 wks
12 May 84	**STREET SOUNDS EDITION 9** *Street Sounds STSND 009*	22	5 wks
9 Jun 84	**STREET SOUNDS ELECTRO 4** *Street Sounds ELCST 4* ..	25	9 wks
30 Jun 84	**STREET SOUNDS UK ELECTRO**		
	Street Sounds ELCST 1984	60	4 wks
21 Jul 84	**LET THE MUSIC SCRATCH** *Street Sounds MKL 1*	91	3 wks
11 Aug 84	**STREET SOUNDS CRUCIAL ELECTRO 2**		
	Street Sounds ELCST 1000	35	6 wks
18 Aug 84	**STREET SOUNDS EDITION 10** *Street Sounds STSND 010*	24	6 wks
6 Oct 84	**STREET SOUNDS ELECTRO 5** *Street Sounds ELCST 5* ..	17	6 wks
10 Nov 84	**STREET SOUNDS EDITION 11** *Street Sounds STSND 011*	48	4 wks
9 Mar 85	**STREET SOUNDS ELECTRO 6** *Street Sounds ELCST 6* ..	24	10 wks
9 Mar 85	**THE ARTISTS VOLUME 1** *Street Sounds ARTIS 1*	65	4 wks
18 May 85	**STREET SOUNDS ELECTRO 7** *Street Sounds ELCST 7* ..	12	7 wks
18 May 85	**STREET SOUNDS EDITION 12** *Street Sounds STSND 12*	23	4 wks
13 Jul 85	**STREET SOUNDS ELECTRO 8** *Street Sounds ELCST 8* ..	23	5 wks
13 Jul 85	**THE ARTISTS VOLUME 2** *Street Sounds ARTIS 2*	45	4 wks
17 Aug 85	**STREET SOUNDS EDITION 13** *Street Sounds STSND 13*	19	9 wks
17 Aug 85	**STREET SOUNDS NY VS LA BEATS**		
	Street Sounds ELCST 1001	65	4 wks
5 Oct 85	**STREET SOUNDS ELECTRO 9** *Street Sounds ELCST 9* ..	18	6 wks
12 Oct 85	**THE ARTISTS VOLUME 3** *Street Sounds ARTIS 3*	87	2 wks
16 Nov 85	**STREET SOUNDS EDITION 14** *Street Sounds STSND 14*	43	3 wks
21 Dec 85	**STREET SOUNDS ELECTRO 10** *Street Sounds ELCST 10*	72	6 wks
21 Dec 85	**STREET SOUNDS EDITION 15** *Street Sounds STSND 15*	58	8 wks
29 Mar 86	**STREET SOUNDS HIP-HOP ELECTRO 11**		
	Street Sounds ELCST 11	19	5 wks
5 Apr 86	**STREET SOUNDS EDITION 16** *Street Sounds STSND 16*	17	7 wks
21 Jun 86	**JAZZ JUICE 2** *Street Sounds SOUND 4*	96	1 wk
28 Jun 86	**STREET SOUNDS HIP-HOP ELECTRO 12**		
	Street Sounds ELCST 12	28	4 wks
19 Jul 86	**STREET SOUNDS EDITION 17** *Street Sounds STSND 17*	35	5 wks
6 Sep 86	**STREET SOUNDS HIP-HOP ELECTRO 13**		
	Street Sounds ELCST 13	23	5 wks
11 Oct 86	**STREET SOUNDS EDITION 18** *Street Sounds STSND 18*	20	5 wks
11 Oct 86	**JAZZ JUICE 3** *Street Sounds SOUND 5*	88	1 wk
11 Oct 86	**STREET SOUNDS HIP-HOP ELECTRO 14**		
	Street Sounds ELCST 14	40	3 wks
15 Nov 86	**STREET SOUNDS HIP-HOP ELECTRO 15**		
	Street Sounds ELCST 15	46	2 wks
6 Dec 86	**STREET SOUNDS EDITION 19** *Street Sounds STSND 19*	61	3 wks
24 Jan 87	**STREET SOUNDS ELECTRO 3** *Street Sounds ELCST 1002*	41	3 wks
7 Feb 87	**STREET SOUNDS ANTHEMS VOLUME 1**		
	Street Sounds MUSIC 5	61	3 wks
14 Feb 87	**STREET SOUNDS EDITION 20** *Street Sounds STSND 20*	25	4 wks
13 Jun 87	**STREET SOUNDS HIP-HOP ELECTRO 16**		
	Street Sounds ELCST 16	40	3 wks
4 Jul 87	**STREET SOUNDS DANCE MUSIC '87**		
	Street Sounds STSND 871	40	5 wks

358

15 Aug 87	**STREET SOUNDS HIP-HOP 17** *Street Sounds ELCST 17*	38	3 wks
15 Aug 87	**JAZZ JUICE 5** *Street Sounds SOUND 8*	97	1 wk
12 Sep 87	**BEST OF WEST COAST HIP HOP** *Street Sounds MACA 1*	80	2 wks
12 Sep 87	**STREET SOUNDS '87 VOLUME 2**		
	Street Sounds STSND 872	47	3 wks
24 Oct 87	**STREET SOUNDS HIP-HOP 18** *Street Sounds ELCST 18*	67	1 wk
12 Mar 88	**STREET SOUNDS HIP-HOP 20** *Street Sounds ELCST 20*	39	4 wks
19 Mar 88	**STREET SOUNDS 88–1** *Street Sounds STSND 881*	73	2 wks
4 Jun 88	**STREET SOUNDS HIP-HOP 21** *Street Sounds ELCST 21*	87	1 wk

Studio Two

21 Oct 67	● **BREAKTHROUGH** *Studio Two STWO 1*	2	11 wks
4 Sep 71	**TOTAL SOUND** *Studio Two STWO 4*	39	4 wks
30 Oct 71	**STUDIO TWO CLASSICS** *Studio Two STWO 6*	16	4 wks

Stylus

3 Aug 85	**THE MAGIC OF TORVILL AND DEAN** *Stylus SMR 8502*	35	9 wks
17 Aug 85	**NIGHT BEAT** *Stylus SMR 8501*	15	8 wks
24 Aug 85	**DISCO BEACH PARTY** *Stylus SMR 8503*	29	10 wks
14 Dec 85	**VELVET WATERS** *Stylus SMR 8507*	54	4 wks
28 Dec 85	**CHOICES OF THE HEART** *Stylus SMR 8511*	87	2 wks
8 Mar 86	● **NIGHT BEAT 2** *Stylus SMR 8613*	7	9 wks
17 May 86	**LET'S HEAR IT FROM THE GIRLS** *Stylus SMR 8614*	17	10 wks
1 Nov 86	**BLACK MAGIC** *Stylus SMR 619*	26	9 wks
8 Nov 86	● **HIT MIX '86** *Stylus SMR 624*	10	14 wks
22 Nov 86	**CLASSICS BY CANDLELIGHT** *Stylus SMR 620*	74	4 wks
14 Mar 87	**BANDS OF GOLD – THE SWINGING SIXTIES**		
	Stylus SMR 726	48	6 wks
21 Mar 87	**BANDS OF GOLD – THE SENSATIONAL SEVENTIES**		
	Stylus SMR 727	75	4 wks
28 Mar 87	**BANDS OF GOLD – THE ELECTRIC EIGHTIES**		
	Stylus SMR 728	82	1 wk
11 Jul 87	● **SIXTIES MIX** *Stylus SMR 733*	3	44 wks
24 Oct 87	**HIT FACTORY** *Stylus SMR 740*	18	17 wks
21 Nov 87	**HIT MIX – HITS OF THE YEAR** *Stylus SMR 744*	29	11 wks
2 Apr 88	● **HIP HOP AND RAPPING IN THE HOUSE**		
	Stylus SMR 852	5	13 wks
30 Apr 88	**THE WORLDS OF FOSTER AND ALLEN**		
	Stylus SMR 861	21	15 wks
7 May 88	**SIXTIES MIX 2** *Stylus SMR 855*	14	20 wks
4 Jun 88	**BACK ON THE ROAD** *Stylus SMR 854*	29	11 wks
30 Jul 88	● **THE GREATEST EVER ROCK 'N' ROLL MIX**		
	Stylus SMR 858	8	15 wks
3 Sep 88	● **RAP TRAX** *Stylus SMR 859*	3	13 wks
1 Oct 88	**RARE GROOVE MIX** *Stylus SMR 863*	20	10 wks
17 Oct 88	**THE GREATEST HITS OF HOUSE** *Stylus SMR 867*	26	4 wks
22 Oct 88	● **SOFT METAL** *Stylus SMR 862*	7	12 wks
26 Nov 88	**HIT MIX '88** *Stylus SMR 865*	48	7 wks
14 Jan 89	● **THE GREATEST HITS OF HOUSE** *Stylus SMR 867*	5	9 wks
14 Jan 89	● **SOFT METAL** *Stylus SMR 862*	7	26 wks
14 Jan 89	**HIT MIX '88** *Stylus SMR 865*	15	2 wks
14 Jan 89	**THE WORLDS OF FOSTER AND ALLEN**		
	Stylus SMR 861	16	3 wks
18 Feb 89	● **BEAT THIS – 20 HITS OF RHYTHM KING**		
	Stylus SMR 973	9	8 wks
11 Mar 89	**NEW ROOTS** *Stylus SMR 972*	18	1 wk
25 Mar 89	● **HIP HOUSE** *Stylus SMR 974*	3	8 wks
22 Apr 89	● **THE SINGER AND THE SONG** *Stylus SMR 975*	5	11 wks
27 May 89	● **PRECIOUS METAL** *Stylus SMR 976*	2	29 wks
24 Jun 89	● **DON'T STOP THE MUSIC** *Stylus SMR 977*	7	6 wks
15 Jul 89	● **HOT SUMMER NIGHTS** *Stylus SMR 980*	4	11 wks
19 Aug 89	● **SUNSHINE MIX** *Stylus SMP 986*	9	7 wks
26 Aug 89	● **THE GREATEST EVER ROCK 'N' ROLL MIX**		
	Stylus SMR 858	5	9 wks
2 Sep 89	● **MIDNIGHT LOVE** *Stylus SMR 981*	7	6 wks
16 Sep 89	● **LEGENDS AND HEROES** *Stylus SMR 987*	6	10 wks
21 Oct 89	● **THE RIGHT STUFF – REMIX '89** *Stylus SMR 990*	2	11 wks

359

25 Nov 89		**JUKE BOX JIVE MIX – ROCK 'N' ROLL GREATS**			
		Stylus SMR 993	13	8 wks
30 Dec 89		**WARE'S THE HOUSE** *Stylus SMR 997*	15	1 wk
13 Jan 90	★	**PURE SOFT METAL** *Stylus SMR 996*	1	23 wks
10 Mar 90	●	**RIGHT STUFF 2 – NOTHING BUT A HOUSEPARTY**		
		Stylus SMR 998	2	15 wks
26 May 90	●	**SIXTIES MIX 3** *Stylus SMR 021*	4	9 wks
22 Oct 90	●	**MOMENTS IN SOUL** *Stylus SMR 023*	9	2 wks

Tamla Motown

3 Apr 65		**A COLLECTION OF TAMLA MOTOWN HITS**		
		Tamla Motown TML 11001	16	4 wks
4 Mar 67		**16 ORIGINAL BIG HITS – VOL. 4**		
		Tamla Motown TML 11043	33	3 wks
17 Jun 67		**TAMLA MOTOWN HITS VOL. 5**		
		Tamla Motown TML 11050	11	40 wks
21 Oct 67	●	**BRITISH MOTOWN CHARTBUSTERS**		
		Tamla Motown TML 11055	2	54 wks
10 Feb 68		**MOTOWN MEMORIES** *Tamla Motown TML 11064*	21	13 wks
24 Aug 68		**TAMLA MOTOWN HITS VOL. 6**		
		Tamla Motown STML 11074	32	2 wks
30 Nov 68	●	**BRITISH MOTOWN CHARTBUSTERS VOL. 2**		
		Tamla Motown STML 11082	8	11 wks
25 Oct 69	★	**BRITISH MOTOWN CHARTBUSTERS VOL. 3**		
		Tamla Motown STML 11121	1	93 wks
21 Feb 70		**COLLECTION OF BIG HITS VOL. 8**		
		Tamla Motown STML 11130	56	1 wk
24 Oct 70	★	**MOTOWN CHARTBUSTERS VOL. 4**		
		Tamla Motown STML 11162	1	40 wks
17 Apr 71	★	**MOTOWN CHARTBUSTERS VOL. 5**		
		Tamla Motown STML 11181	1	36 wks
23 Oct 71	●	**MOTOWN CHARTBUSTERS VOL. 6**		
		Tamla Motown STML 11191	2	36 wks
26 Feb 72		**MOTOWN MEMORIES** *Tamla Motown STML 11200*	22	4 wks
18 Mar 72		**MOTOWN STORY** *Tamla Motown TMSP 1130*	21	8 wks
29 Nov 72	●	**MOTOWN CHARTBUSTERS VOL. 7**		
		Tamla Motown STML 11215	9	16 wks
3 Nov 73	●	**MOTOWN CHARTBUSTERS VOL. 8**		
		Tamla Motown STML 11246	9	15 wks
26 Oct 74		**MOTOWN CHARTBUSTERS VOL. 9**		
		Tamla Motown STML 11270	14	15 wks
1 Nov 75	●	**MOTOWN GOLD** *Tamla Motown STML 12003*	8	35 wks
5 Nov 77		**MOTOWN GOLD VOL. 2** *Motown STML 12070*	28	4 wks
7 Oct 78	●	**BIG WHEELS OF MOTOWN** *Motown EMTV 12*	2	18 wks
2 Feb 80	★	**THE LAST DANCE** *Motown EMTV 20*	1	23 wks
2 Aug 80		**THE 20TH ANNIVERSARY ALBUM** *Motown TMSP 6010*	53	2 wks
21 May 88	●	**MOTOWN DANCE PARTY** *Motown ZC 72700*	3	18 wks
19 May 90	●	**MOTOWN DANCE PARTY 2** *Motown ZL 72703*	10	7 wks
6 Oct 90	●	**SOUL DECADE: THE SIXTIES** *Mowtown ZL 74816*	3	10 wks

360

Telstar

16 Oct 82	●	**CHART ATTACK** *Telstar STAR 2221*	7	6 wks
6 Nov 82		**MIDNIGHT IN MOTOWN** *Telstar STAR 2222*	34	16 wks
18 Dec 82		**DIRECT HITS** *Telstar STAR 2226*	89	1 wk
8 Jan 83		**DANCIN' – 20 ORIGINAL MOTOWN MOVERS**		
		Telstar STAR 2225	97	1 wk
5 Feb 83		**INSTRUMENTAL MAGIC** *Telstar STAR 2227*	68	5 wks
30 Apr 83		**20 GREAT ITALIAN LOVE SONGS** *Telstar STAR 2230* ..	28	6 wks
4 Jun 83		**IN THE GROOVE – THE 12 INCH DISCO PARTY**		
		Telstar STAR 2228	20	12 wks
12 Nov 83		**ROOTS REGGAE 'N' REGGAE ROCK** *Telstar STAR 2233*	34	6 wks
19 Nov 83		**SUPERCHART '83** *Telstar STAR 2236*	22	9 wks
4 Feb 84	●	**THE VERY BEST OF MOTOWN LOVE SONGS**		
		Telstar STAR 2239	10	22 wks
26 May 84		**DON'T STOP DANCING** *Telstar STAR 2242*	11	12 wks

Date	Title	Pos	Weeks
13 Oct 84	● HITS HITS HITS – 18 SMASH ORIGINALS		
	Telstar STAR 2243	6	9 wks
8 Dec 84	LOVE SONGS – 16 CLASSIC LOVE SONGS		
	Telstar STAR 2246	20	12 wks
15 Dec 84	● GREEN VELVET Telstar STAR 2252	10	10 wks
7 Sep 85	OPEN TOP CARS AND GIRLS IN T-SHIRTS		
	Telstar STAR 2257	13	9 wks
16 Nov 85	● THE LOVE ALBUM Telstar STAR 2268	7	18 wks
30 Nov 85	THE PRINCE'S TRUST COLLECTION Telstar STAR 2275	64	5 wks
7 Dec 85	PERFORMANCE – THE VERY BEST OF TIM RICE AND		
	ANDREW LLOYD WEBBER Telstar STAR 2262	33	7 wks
7 Dec 85	MORE GREEN VELVET Telstar STAR 2267	42	5 wks
18 Dec 86	● THE CHART Telstar STAR 2278	6	12 wks
1 Nov 86	ROCK LEGENDS Telstar STAR 2290	54	7 wks
8 Nov 86	LOVERS Telstar STAR 2279	14	16 wks
22 Nov 86	SIXTIES MANIA Telstar STAR 2287	19	22 wks
6 Dec 86	MOTOWN CHARTBUSTERS Telstar STAR 2283	25	12 wks
28 Mar 87	THE DANCE CHART Telstar STAR 2285	23	8 wks
3 Oct 87	TRACKS OF MY TEARS Telstar STAR 2295	27	7 wks
31 Oct 87	LOVE SONGS Telstar STAR 2298	12	24 wks
28 Nov 87	DANCE MIX '87 Telstar STAR 2314	39	10 wks
28 Nov 87	ALWAYS AND FOREVER Telstar STAR 2301	41	10 wks
28 Nov 87	SIXTIES PARTY MEGAMIX ALBUM Telstar STAR 2307	46	7 wks
26 Dec 87	● LIFE IN THE FAST LANE Telstar STAR 2315	10	12 wks
1 Oct 88	…AND THE BEAT GOES ON Telstar STAR 2338	12	8 wks
5 Nov 88	THE HEART AND SOUL OF ROCK 'N' ROLL		
	Telstar STAR 2351	60	6 wks
12 Nov 88	THE LOVE ALBUM '88 Telstar STAR 2332	51	9 wks
19 Nov 88	BEST OF HOUSE '88 Telstar STAR 2347	33	8 wks
19 Nov 88	INSTRUMENTAL GREATS Telstar STAR 2341	79	5 wks
3 Dec 88	HYPERACTIVE Telsta STAR 2328	78	4 wks
3 Dec 88	BACK TO THE SIXTIES Telstar STAR 2348	47	6 wks
17 Dec 88	MORNING HAS BROKEN Telstar STAR 2337	88	2 wks
14 Jan 89	BEST OF HOUSE 1988 Telstar STAR 2347	11	5 wks
14 Jan 89	BACK TO THE SIXTIES Telstar STAR 2348	14	4 wks
14 Jan 89	LOVE SONGS Telstar STAR 2298	18	2 wks
25 Feb 89	★ THE AWARDS Telstar STAR 2346	1	8 wks
15 Jul 89	● PROTECT THE INNOCENT Telstar STAR 2363	9	9 wks
15 Jul 89	● RHYTHM OF THE SUN Telstar STAR 2362	12	4 wks
22 Jul 89	● THIS IS SKA Telstar STAR 2366	6	10 wks
14 Oct 89	● MOTOWN HEARTBREAKERS Telstar STAR 2343	4	10 wks
18 Nov 89	● NUMBER ONES OF THE EIGHTIES Telstar STAR 2382	2	7 wks
25 Nov 89	● HEAVEN AND HELL Telstar STAR 2361	15	12 wks
9 Dec 89	SOFT ROCK Telstar STAR 2397	15	5 wks
3 Feb 90	NEW TRADITIONS Telstar STAR 2399	13	4 wks
10 Feb 90	● MILESTONES – 20 ROCK OPERAS Telstar STAR 2379	6	11 wks
24 Feb 90	● THE AWARDS 1990 Telstar STAR 2368	3	10 wks
17 Mar 90	PRODUCT 2378 Telstar STAR 2378	16	3 wks
12 May 90	★ GET ON THIS! – 30 DANCE HITS VOLUME 1		
	Telstar STAR 22420	1	12 wks
19 May 90	● A NIGHT AT THE OPERA Telstar STAR 2414	2	12 wks
18 Aug 90	★ MEGABASS Telstar STAR 2425	1	12 wks
25 Aug 90	MOLTEN METAL Telstar STAR 2429	13	5 wks
25 Aug 90	● GET ON THIS!!! 2 Telstar STAR 2424	3	9 wks
15 Sep 90	● COUNTRY'S GREATEST HITS Telstar STAR 2433	9	7 wks
27 Oct 90	● FINAL COUNTDOWN – BEST OF SOFT METAL		
	Telstar STAR 2431	9	6 wks
3 Nov 90	● RAVE Telstar STAR 2453	10	4 wks
24 Nov 90	● THE MOTOWN COLLECTION Telstar STAR 2375	8	12 wks
1 Dec 90	● 60 NUMBER ONES OF THE SIXTIES Telstar STAR 2432	7	11 wks
8 Dec 90	● MEGABASS 2 Telstar STAR 2448	6	8 wks
23 Feb 91	● UNCHAINED MELODIES Telstar STAR 2480	6	20 wks
23 Mar 91	DON'T STOP – DOO-WOP Telstar STAR 2485	15	4 wks
30 Mar 91	● THIN ICE – THE FIRST STEP Telstar STAR 2500	2	9 wks
13 Apr 91	AFTER THE DANCE Telstar STAR 2501	16	3 wks
11 May 91	● MASSIVE HITS Telstar STAR 2505	2	6 wks
18 May 91	● UNCHAINED MELODIES II Telstar STAR 2515	3	8 wks
8 Jun 91	● MEGABASS 3 Telstar STAR 2483	3	8 wks
22 Jun 91	● FAST FORWARD Telstar STAR 2502	4	8 wks

361

3 Aug	91	★ **THIN ICE 2 – THE SECOND SHIVER** *Telstar STAR 2535* .	1	9 wks
14 Sep	91	● **Q – THE ALBUM VOL 1** *Telstar STAR 2522*	10	4 wks
28 Sep	91	● **MAKE YOU SWEAT** *Telstar STAR 2542*	4	6 wks
12 Oct	91	● **BORN TO BE WILD** *Telstar STAR 2524*	8	5 wks
2 Nov	91	● **BURNING HEARTS** *Telstar STAR 2492*	7	7 wks
9 Nov	91	● **BEST OF DANCE 91** *Telstar STAR 2537*	2†	8 wks
23 Nov	91	● **LOVE AT THE MOVIES** *Telstar STAR 2545*	6†	6 wks
23 Nov	91	**PUNK AND DISORDERLY – NEW WAVE**		
		Telstar STAR 2520	18	2 wks
30 Nov	91	**CLASSICAL MASTERS** *Telstar STAR 2549*	13†	5 wks
7 Dec	91	**LEGENDS OF SOUL – A WHOLE STACK OF SOUL**		
		Telstar STAR 2489	16†	4 wks

Green Velvet *was a re-issue of Ronco RON LP 6.*

Towerbell

28 Sep	85	**THE TV HITS ALBUM** *Towerbell TVLP 3*	26	13 wks
8 Feb	86	● **THE DANCE HITS ALBUM** *Towerbell TVLP 8*	10	11 wks
15 Mar	86	**THE CINEMA HITS ALBUM** *Towerbell TVLP 9*	44	9 wks
12 Apr	86	**THE TV HITS ALBUM TWO** *Towerbell TVLP 10*	19	7 wks
17 May	86	**SISTERS ARE DOIN' IT** *Towerbell TVLP 11*	27	9 wks
7 Jun	86	**TWO'S COMPANY** *Towerbell TVLP 12*	51	5 wks
28 Jun	86	**DANCE HITS II** *Towerbell TVLP 13*	25	8 wks
2 Aug	86	**THE ORIGINALS** *Towerbell TBDLP 14*	15	9 wks
9 Aug	86	**YOU'VE GOT TO LAUGH** *Towerbell TVLP 15*	51	3 wks

Trax

17 Dec	88	**NOEL – CHRISTMAS SONGS AND CAROLS**		
		Trax TRXLP 701	89	2 wks
22 Jul	89	**DREAMS OF IRELAND** *Trax MODEM 1035*	19	1 wk
17 Feb	90	● **ROCK OF AMERICA** *Trax MODEM 1036*	7	7 wks
19 May	90	● **FREEDOM TO PARTY – FIRST LEGAL RAVE**		
		Trax MODEM 1048	4	10 wks
28 Jul	90	● **SUMMER CHART PARTY** *Trax BWTX 1*	9	6 wks
3 Nov	90	**FREEDOM 2 – THE ULTIMATE RAVE** *Trax BWTX 4* ..	16	2 wks
17 Nov	90	**KARAOKE PARTY** *Trax BETX 5*	20	1 wk
16 Mar	91	● **KARAOKE PARTY II** *Trax TXTV 1*	7	9 wks

Trojan

7 Aug	71	**TIGHTEN UP VOLUME 4** *Trojan TBL 163*	20	7 wks
21 Aug	71	**CLUB REGGAE** *Trojan TBL 159*	25	4 wks
16 Jun	84	**20 REGGAE CLASSICS** *Trojan TRLS 222*	89	1 wk

TV

2 Oct	82	**MODERN HEROES** *TV TVA 1*	24	7 wks
9 Oct	82	**ENDLESS LOVE** *TV TV 2*	26	8 wks
6 Nov	82	**FLASH TRACKS** *TV PTVL 1*	19	7 wks
25 Dec	82	**PARTY FEVER/DISCO MANIA** *TV TVA 5*	71	3 wks

Urban

14 Nov	87	**URBAN CLASSICS** *Urban URBLP 4*	96	1 wk
24 Sep	88	**URBAN ACID** *Urban URBLP 15*	51	8 wks
8 Oct	88	**ACID JAZZ AND OTHER ILLICIT GROOVES**		
		Urban URBLP 16	86	3 wks

Vertigo

21 Jun	86	**HEAR 'N' AID** *Vertigo VERH 35*	50	2 wks
27 Aug	88	★ **HOT CITY NIGHTS** *Vertigo PROVTV 15*	1	14 wks
4 Nov	89	● **ROCK CITY NIGHTS** *Vertigo RCNTV 1*	3	14 wks

Virgin

22 Nov	80	**CASH COWS** *Virgin MILK 1*	49	1 wk
17 Apr	82	**MUSIC OF QUALITY AND DISTINCTION (VOLUME 1)**		
		Virgin V 2219	25	6 wks
1 Jun	85	**MASSIVE** *Virgin V 2346*	61	3 wks

Warwick

29 Nov	75	**ALL-TIME PARTY HITS** *Warwick WW 5001*	21	8 wks
17 Apr	76	● **INSTRUMENTAL GOLD** *Warwick WW 5012*	3	24 wks

29 May 76	HAMILTON'S HOT SHOTS *Warwick WW 5014*	15	5 wks
8 Jan 77	SONGS OF PRAISE *Warwick WW 5020*	31	2 wks
29 Jan 77	HIT SCENE *Warwick PR 5023*	19	5 wks
11 Mar 78 ●	FONZIE'S FAVOURITES *Warwick WW 5037*	8	16 wks
25 Nov 78	LOVE SONGS *Warwick WW 5046*	47	7 wks
2 Dec 78	BLACK VELVET *Warwick WW 5047*	72	3 wks
31 Mar 79	LEMON POPSICLE *Warwick WW 5050*	42	6 wks
7 Apr 79	COUNTRY PORTRAITS *Warwick WW 5057*	14	10 wks
10 Nov 79	20 SMASH DISCO HITS (THE BITCH) *Warwick WW 5061*	42	5 wks
16 Feb 80	COUNTRY GUITAR *Warwick WW 5070*	46	3 wks
14 Nov 81	DISCO EROTICA *Warwick WW 5108*	35	8 wks
10 Apr 82	PS I LOVE YOU *Warwick WW 5121*	68	3 wks
6 Nov 82	HITS OF THE SCREAMING 60'S *Warwick WW 5124*	24	10 wks
22 Dec 84	MERRY CHRISTMAS TO YOU *Warwick WW 5141*	64	2 wks

———————— *Other Compilation Albums* ————————

10 Mar 62	GREAT MOTION PICTURE THEMES *HMV CLP 1508* .	19	1 wk
24 Aug 63	THE MERSEY BEAT VOLUME 1 *Oriole PS 40047*	17	5 wks
16 May 64	OUT CAME THE BLUES *Ace of Hearts AH 72*	19	1 wk
11 Sep 66	STARS CHARITY FANTASIA SAVE THE CHILDREN FUND *SCF PL 145*	6	16 wks
8 Apr 67 ●	HIT THE ROAD STAX *Stax 589005*	10	16 wks
11 May 68	BLUES ANYTIME *Immediate IMLP 014*	40	1 wk
4 Dec 71	BREAKTHROUGH *MFP 1334*	49	1 wk
22 Jan 72 ★	CONCERT FOR BANGLADESH *Apple STCX 3385*	1	13 wks
15 Mar 75	SOLID SOUL SENSATIONS *Disco Diamond DDLP 5001* ..	30	1 wk
16 Aug 75	NEVER TOO YOUNG TO ROCK *GTO GTLP 004*	30	5 wks
6 Dec 75	SUPERSONIC *Stallion SSM 001*	21	6 wks
31 Jan 76	REGGAE CHARTBUSTERS 75 *Cactus CTLP 114*	53	1 wk
22 May 76 ●	A TOUCH OF COUNTRY *Topaz TOC 1976*	7	7 wks
3 Jul 76	GOLDEN FIDDLE AWARDS 1976 *Mountain TOPC 5002* .	45	2 wks
3 Jul 76	A TOUCH OF CLASS *Topaz TOC 1976*	57	1 wk
27 Nov 76	ALL THIS AND WORLD WAR II *Riva RVLP 2*	23	7 wks
16 Jul 77	THE ROXY LONDON WC 2 *Harvest SHSP 4069*	24	5 wks
11 Mar 78	STIFF'S LIVE STIFFS *Stiff GET 1*	28	7 wks
25 Mar 78	HOPE AND ANCHOR FRONT ROW FESTIVAL *Warner Bros. K 66077*	28	3 wks
28 Oct 78	ECSTASY *Lotus WH 5003*	24	6 wks
9 Dec 78	STARS ON SUNDAY BY REQUEST *Curzon Sounds CSL 0081*	65	3 wks
26 May 79	A MONUMENT TO BRITISH ROCK *Harvest EMTV 17* .	13	12 wks
9 Jun 79	THAT SUMMER *Arista SPART 1088*	36	8 wks
21 Jul 79 ★	THE BEST DISCO ALBUM IN THE WORLD *Warner Bros. K 58062*	1	17 wks
3 Nov 79	MODS MAYDAY 79 *Arista FOUR 1*	75	1 wk
24 May 80	PRECIOUS METAL *MCA MCF 3069*	60	2 wks
14 Mar 81	THE SOME BIZARRE ALBUM *Some Bizzare BZLP 1*	58	1 wk
4 Apr 81	REMIXTURE *Champagne CHAMP 1*	32	5 wks
30 May 81	STRENGTH THROUGH OI! *Skin SKIN 1*	51	5 wks
31 Oct 81	CARRY ON OI! *Secret SEC 2*	60	4 wks
12 Dec 81	LIVE AND HEAVY *NEMS NEL 6020*	100	2 wks
19 Dec 81	WE ARE MOST AMUSED *Ronco/Charisma RTD 2067*	30	9 wks
27 Mar 82 ●	JAMES BOND'S GREATEST HITS *Liberty EMTV 007* ...	4	13 wks
27 Mar 82	PUNK AND DISORDERLY *Abstract AABT 100*	48	8 wks
14 Aug 82	SOWETO *Rough Trade ROUGH 37*	66	3 wks
4 Sep 82	PUNK AND DISORDERLY – FURTHER CHARGES *Anagram GRAM 001*	91	2 wks
25 Sep 82	OI OI THAT'S YOUR LOT *Secret SEC 5*	54	4 wks
23 Oct 82	STREET NOISE VOLUME 1 *Streetware STR 32234*	51	4 wks
14 May 83	THE LAUGHTER AND TEARS COLLECTION *WEA LTC 1*	19	16 wks
18 Jun 83	TEARDROPS *Ritz RITZSP 399*	37	6 wks
2 Jul 83	WIRED FOR CLUBS (CLUB TRACKS VOLUME 1) *Club CLUBL 1001*	58	4 wks
3 Sep 83	COME WITH CLUB (CLUB TRACKS VOLUME 2) *Club CLUBL 002*	55	2 wks
15 Oct 83	RESPOND PACKAGE – LOVE THE REASON *Respond RRL 501*	50	3 wks

363

Date	Title	Pos	Wks
26 Nov 83	**THIS ARE TWO TONE** *Two Tone CHRTT 5007*	51	9 wks
26 Nov 83	**TWELVE INCHES OF PLEASURE** *Proto PROTO 1*	100	1 wk
16 Jun 84 ●	**EMERALD CLASSICS** *Stoic SRTV 1*	10	14 wks
21 Jul 84	**ROCKABILLY PSYCHOSIS AND THE GARAGE DISEASE**		
	Big Beat WIK 18	88	3 wks
11 Aug 84	**CHUNKS OF FUNK** *Loose End CHUNK 1*	46	5 wks
8 Sep 84	**RECORD SHACK PRESENTS – VOLUME ONE**		
	Record Shack RSTV 1	41	4 wks
8 Dec 84	**THE CHRISTMAS CAROL COLLECTION**		
	Fame WHS 413000	75	3 wks
16 Feb 85	**STARGAZERS** *Kasino KTV 1*	69	3 wks
6 Apr 85	**TOMMY BOY GREATEST BEATS** *Tommy Boy ILPS 9825*	44	6 wks
25 May 85 ●	**OUT NOW!** *Chrysalis/MCA OUTV 1*	2	16 wks
13 Jul 85	**KERRANG! KOMPILATION** *EMI/Virgin KER 1*	84	2 wks
24 Aug 85	**20 HOLIDAY HITS** *Creole CTV 1*	48	6 wks
19 Oct 85	**IQ6: ZANG TUMB TUUM SAMPLED** *ZTT IQ 6*	40	3 wks
26 Oct 85 ●	**OUT NOW! 2** *Chrysalis/MCA OUTV 2*	3	12 wks
16 Aug 86 ●	**THE HEAT IS ON** *Portrait PRT 10051*	9	12 wks
16 Aug 86	**SUMMER DAYS, BOOGIE NIGHTS** *Portrait PRT 10052* .	40	6 wks
18 Oct 86	**THE POWER OF LOVE** *West Five WEF 4*	33	7 wks
28 Mar 87	**HEART OF SOUL VOLUME 1** *Mastersound HASL 001* ...	96	1 wk
30 May 87	**THE SOLAR SYSTEM** *Solar MCG 3338*	70	1 wk
6 Jun 87	**CHICAGO JACKBEAT VOLUME 2** *Rhythm King LEFTLP 2*	67	2 wks
11 Jul 87	**LONELY IS AN EYESORE** *4AD CAD 703*	53	2 wks
1 Aug 87	**FIERCE** *Cooltempo CTLP 4*	37	6 wks
8 Aug 87	**KICK IT! – THE DEF JAM SAMPLER ALBUM**		
	Def Jam KICKIT 1	19	7 wks
24 Oct 87	**THE WORD** *Zomba HOP 217*	86	1 wk
26 Mar 88	**THE WORD VOLUME 2** *Jive HOP 220*	70	2 wks
9 Apr 88	**SERGEANT PEPPER KNEW MY FATHER**		
	NME PELP 100	37	8 wks
3 Sep 88	**HOUSE HALLUCINATIONS (PUMP UP LONDON)**		
	Breakout HOSA 9002	90	2 wks
8 Oct 88	**BROTHERS IN RHYTHM** *Ariola 303374*	35	5 wks
12 Nov 88	**THE HIT FACTORY VOLUME 2** *Fanfare/PWL HF 4*	16	9 wks
24 Dec 88	**THE BEIDERBECKE COLLECTION** *Dormouse DM 20* ..	89	2 wks
14 Jan 89	**THE HIT FACTORY VOLUME 2** *Fanfare/PWL HF 4*	13	3 wks
14 Jan 89	**THE BEIDERBECKE COLLECTION** *Dormouse DM 20* ..	14	5 wks
18 Feb 89	**CAPITOL CLASSICS VOLUME 1** *Capitol EMS 1316*	16	2 wks
15 Apr 89	**THE SONGS OF BOB DYLAN** *Start STDL 20*	13	5 wks
1 Jul 89	**THIS IS GARAGE** *Cooltempo CTLP 12*	18	2 wks
15 Jul 89 ●	**THE HIT FACTORY VOLUME 3** *Fanfare/PWL HF 8*	3	10 wks
5 Aug 89	**THE 2 TONE STORY** *2 Tone CHRTT 5009*	16	5 wks
19 Aug 89 ●	**HEART AND SOUL** *Heart & Soul HASTV 1*	2	12 wks
16 Sep 89	**WAREHOUSE RAVES** *Rumour RUMLD 101*	15	4 wks
23 Sep 82 ●	**JUST SEVENTEEN – HEARTBEATS** *Fanfare FARE 1* ..	3	6 wks
14 Oct 89 ●	**ITALIA – DANCE MUSIC FROM ITALY**		
	deConstruction 64289	4	6 wks
17 Feb 90 ●	**BODY AND SOUL – HEART AND SOUL II**		
	Heart & Soul 8407761	2	14 wks
24 Mar 90	**EMERALD CLASSICS VOLUMES I & 11**		
	Westmoor WMTV 1	14	2 wks
31 Mar 90	**WAREHOUSE RAVES 3** *Rumour RUMLD 103*	12	5 wks
7 Apr 90	**LET'S DANCE – SOUND OF THE SIXTIES PART 1**		
	Old Gold OG 1702	18	1 wk
21 Apr 90	**PURE LOVERS VOLUME 1** *Charm CLP 101*	14	4 wks
21 Apr 90 ●	**THE EARTHQUAKE ALBUM**		
	Live Aid Armenia AIDLP 001	3	10 wks
16 Jun 90	**LOVERS FOR LOVERS VOLUME 3** *Business WBRLP 903*	18	1 wk
7 Jul 90 ●	**THE ULTIMATE 60s COLLECTION** *Castle Communications*	4	11 wks
28 Jul 90	**NOTHING COMPARES TO THIS** *Parkfield PMLP 5020* .	13	2 wks
4 Aug 90 ●	**HEART AND SOUL III – HEART FULL OF SOUL**		
	Heart & Soul 8450091	4	9 wks
4 Aug 90	**NOBODY'S CHILD – ROMANIAN ANGEL APPEAL**		
	Warner Bros. WX 353	18	2 wks
22 Sep 90	**PURE LOVERS VOLUME 2** *Charm CLP 102*	12	3 wks
29 Sep 90	**WAREHOUSE RAVES 4** *Rumour RUMLD 104*	13	3 wks
13 Oct 90 ●	**ESSENTIAL CLASSICS** *Deutsche Grammophon 4315411*	6	9 wks
3 Nov 90 ●	**RED HOT AND BLUE** *Chrysalis CHR 1799*	6	3 wks

22 Dec 90	**CHRISTMAS GREATEST HITS** *Legends In LELP 501*	16	1 wk
12 Jan 91	**THE ULTIMATE BLUES COLLECTION**		
	Castle Communications CTVLP 206	14	6 wks
19 Jan 91	**DANCE ENERGY** *Virgin Television VTDLP 3*	20	2 wks
16 Feb 91 ●	**SOUL REFLECTION** *Heart And Soul 8453341*	2	12 wks
23 Feb 91 ★	**AWESOME!** *EMI/Virgin/PolyGram EMTV 58*	1	12 wks
16 Mar 91 ●	**SONG FROM THE HEART** *Mawson And Wareham PHMC 2*	10	1 wk
6 Apr 91	**PURE LOVERS VOLUME 3** *Charm CLP 103*	16	2 wks
4 May 91 ●	**MARQUEE METAL** *Marquee 8454171*	5	6 wks
11 May 91 ●	**THE BEST OF INDIE TOP 20** *Beechwood BOTT 1*	10	3 wks
11 May 91 ●	**WAREHOUSE RAVES 5** *Rumour RUMLD 105*	18	1 wk
18 May 91	**SOUTHERN KNIGHTS** *Knight KTVLP 1*	13	2 wks
1 Jun 91 ●	**DANCE ENERGY VOLUME 2** *Virgin Television VTLP 4* ..	6	5 wks
22 Jun 91 ●	**IT'S COOL** *Parlophone PCSTV 1*	3	7 wks
22 Jun 91	**REACTIVATE VOLUME 1: BELGIAN TECHNO ANTHEMS**		
	React REACTLP	1	4 wks
13 Jul 91 ★	**PURPLE RAINBOWS** *Polydor/EMI 8455341*	1	13 wks
20 Jul 91	**BREAKS BASS AND BLEEPS** *Rumour RAID 504*	20	1 wk
5 Sep 91 ●	**XL RECORDINGS – THE SECOND CHAPTER**		
	Quest XL LP 108	5	9 wks
28 Sep 91 ●	**THE POWER AND THE GLORY** *Vertigo 5103601*	2	9 wks
28 Sep 91	**CLASSIC MELLOW MASTERCUTS**		
	Mastercuts CUTSLP 3	18	2 wks
5 Oct 91 ●	**REACTIVATE VOLUME 2: PHASERS ON FULL**		
	React REACTLP 2	9	4 wks
12 Oct 91	**I'M YOUR FAN – THE SONGS OF LEONARD COHEN**		
	East West WX 444	16	2 wks
19 Oct 91 ●	**MOODS** *Virgin Television VTLP 5*	2†	11 wks
26 Oct 91 ★	**TWO ROOMS – ELTON JOHN AND BERNIE TAUPIN**		
	Mercury 8457491	1†	10 wks
2 Nov 91	**PURE LOVERS VOLUME 4** *Charm CLP 104*	19	1 wk
2 Nov 91 ●	**AWESOME! 2** *EMI/Virgin/PolyGram EVP 1*	2	8 wks
9 Nov 91	**RAVE** *Reachin' REMULP 01*	18	2 wks
16 Nov 91	**R & S RECORDS – ORDER TO DANCE** *R & S RSLP 1* .	18	1 wk
30 Nov 91 ●	**DANCE ENERGY VOLUME 3** *Virgin Television VTLP 6* ..	10	4 wks
14 Dec 91 ●	**STEAMIN' – HARDCORE 92** *Cookie Jar JARTV 1*	3†	3 wks

365

FILM SOUNDTRACKS

8 Nov 58 ★	**SOUTH PACIFIC** *RCA RB 16065*	1	286 wks
8 Nov 58 ●	**THE KING AND I** *Capitol LCT 6108*	4	103 wks
8 Nov 58 ●	**OKLAHOMA** *Capitol LCT 6100*	4	90 wks
6 Dec 58 ●	**CAROUSEL** *Capitol LCT 6105*	8	15 wks
31 Jan 59 ●	**GIGI** *MGM C 770*	2	88 wks
10 Oct 59 ●	**PORGY AND BESS** *Philips ABL 3282*	7	5 wks
23 Jan 60 ●	**THE FIVE PENNIES** *London HAU 2189*	2	15 wks
7 May 60 ●	**CAN CAN** *Capitol W 1301*	2	31 wks
28 May 60	**PAL JOEY** *Capitol LCT 6148*	20	1 wk
23 Jul 60	**HIGH SOCIETY** *Capitol LCT 6116*	16	1 wk
5 Nov 60	**BEN HUR** *MGM C 802*	15	3 wks
21 Jan 61	**NEVER ON SUNDAY** *London HAT 2309*	17	1 wk
18 Feb 61 ●	**SONG WITHOUT END** *Pye GGL 30169*	9	10 wks
29 Apr 61 ●	**SEVEN BRIDES FOR SEVEN BROTHERS** *MGM C 853*	6	22 wks
3 Jun 61	**EXODUS** *RCA RD 27210*	17	1 wk
11 Nov 61	**GLENN MILLER STORY** *Ace Of Hearts AH 12*	12	7 wks
24 Mar 62 ★	**WEST SIDE STORY** *Philips BBL 7530*	1	175 wks
28 Apr 62 ●	**IT'S TRAD DAD** *Columbia 33SX 1412*	3	21 wks
22 Sep 62	**THE MUSIC MAN** *Warner Bros. WB 4066*	14	9 wks
3 Nov 62	**PORGY AND BESS** *CBS APG 60002*	14	7 wks
15 Jun 63	**JUST FOR FUN** *Decca LK 4524*	20	2 wks
31 Oct 64 ●	**MY FAIR LADY** *CBS BPG 72237*	9	51 wks
31 Oct 64	**GOLDFINGER** *United Artists ULP 1076*	14	5 wks
16 Jan 65 ●	**MARY POPPINS** *HMV CLP 1794*	2	82 wks
10 Apr 65 ★	**SOUND OF MUSIC** *RCA RB 6616*	1	381 wks
30 Apr 66	**FUNNY GIRL** *Capitol W 2059*	19	3 wks
11 Sep 66 ●	**DR ZHIVAGO** *MGM C 8007*	3	106 wks
22 Jul 67	**CASINO ROYALE** *RCA Victor SF 7874*	35	1 wk
29 Jul 67	**A MAN AND A WOMAN** *United Artists SULP 1155*	31	11 wks

28 Oct 67	●	**THOROUGHLY MODERN MILLIE** *Brunswick STA 8685*	9	19 wks
9 Mar 68	●	**THE JUNGLE BOOK** *Disney ST 3948*	5	51 wks
21 Sep 68		**STAR** *Stateside SSL 10233*	36	1 wk
12 Oct 68	●	**THE GOOD, THE BAD AND THE UGLY**		
		United Artists SULP 1197	2	18 wks
23 Nov 68	●	**OLIVER** *RCA Victor SB 6777*	4	107 wks
23 Nov 68		**CAMELOT** *Warner Bros. WS 1712*	37	1 wk
8 Feb 69	●	**CHITTY CHITTY BANG BANG** *United Artists SULP 1200*	10	4 wks
10 May 69		**FUNNY GIRL** *CBS 70044*	11	22 wks
14 Jun 69	●	**2001 – A SPACE ODYSSEY** *MGM CS 8078*	3	67 wks
20 Dec 69	●	**EASY RIDER** *Stateside SSL 5018*	2	67 wks
24 Jan 70		**JUNGLE BOOK (re-issue)** *Disney BVS 4041*	25	26 wks
7 Feb 70	●	**PAINT YOUR WAGON** *Paramount SPFL 257*	2	102 wks
14 Mar 70		**HELLO DOLLY** *Stateside SSL 10292*	45	2 wks
18 Jul 70		**WOODSTOCK** *Atlantic 2662 001*	35	19 wks
24 Apr 71	●	**LOVE STORY** *Paramount SPFL 267*	10	33 wks
12 Feb 72	●	**CLOCKWORK ORANGE** *Warner Bros. K 46127*	4	46 wks
8 Apr 72		**FIDDLER ON THE ROOF** *United Artists UAD 60011/2*	26	2 wks
13 May 72		**2001 – A SPACE ODYSSEY (re-issue)** *MGM 2315 034*	20	2 wks
29 Nov 72		**SOUTH PACIFIC (re-issue)** *RCA Victor SB 2011*	25	2 wks
31 Mar 73		**CABARET** *Probe SPB 1052*	13	22 wks
14 Apr 73		**LOST HORIZON** *Bell SYBEL 8000*	36	3 wks
22 Sep 73		**JESUS CHRIST SUPERSTAR** *MCA MDKS 8012/3*	23	18 wks
23 Mar 74	●	**THE STING** *MCA MCF 2537*	7	35 wks
27 Apr 74		**AMERICAN GRAFFITI** *MCA MCSP 253*	37	1 wk
8 Jun 74		**A TOUCH OF CLASS** *Philips 6612 040*	32	1 wk
5 Oct 74		**SUNSHINE** *MCA MCF 2566*	47	3 wks
5 Apr 75		**TOMMY** *Polydor 2657 014*	21	9 wks
31 Jan 76		**JAWS** *MCA MCF 2716*	55	1 wk
5 Mar 77		**MOSES** *Pye 28503*	43	2 wks
9 Apr 77	★	**A STAR IS BORN** *CBS 86021*	1	54 wks
2 Jul 77		**THE BEST OF CAR WASH** *MCA MCF 2799*	59	1 wk
11 Mar 78	★	**SATURDAY NIGHT FEVER** *RSO 2658 123*	1	65 wks
22 Apr 78	●	**THE STUD** *Ronco RTD 2029*	2	19 wks
29 Apr 78		**CLOSE ENCOUNTERS OF THE THIRD KIND**		
		Arista DLART 2001	40	6 wks
6 May 78		**THE LAST WALTZ** *Warner Bros. K 66076*	39	4 wks
20 May 78		**THANK GOD IT'S FRIDAY** *Casablanca TGIF 100*	40	5 wks
27 May 78		**FM** *MCA MCSP 284*	37	7 wks
8 Jul 78	★	**GREASE** *RSO RSD 2001*	1	47 wks
12 Aug 78		**SGT PEPPER'S LONELY HEARTS CLUB BAND**		
		A & M AMLZ 66600	38	2 wks
7 Oct 78		**CONVOY** *Capitol EST 24590*	52	1 wk
30 Jun 79		**THE WORLD IS FULL OF MARRIED MEN**		
		Ronco RTD 2038	25	9 wks
14 Jul 79		**THE WARRIORS** *A & M AMLH 64761*	53	7 wks
6 Oct 79		**QUADROPHENIA** *Polydor 2625 037*	23	16 wks
5 Jan 80		**THE SECRET POLICEMAN'S BALL** *Island ILPS 9601*	33	6 wks
9 Feb 80		**SUNBURN** *Warwick RTL 2044*	45	7 wks
16 Feb 80		**GOING STEADY** *Warwick WW 5078*	25	10 wks
8 Mar 80		**THE ROSE** *Atlantic K 50681*	68	1 wk
7 Jun 80		**THE GREAT ROCK 'N' ROLL SWINDLE** *Virgin V 2168*	16	11 wks
19 Jul 80	●	**XANADU** *Jet JET LX 526*	2	17 wks
16 Aug 80	●	**CAN'T STOP THE MUSIC** *Mercury 6399 051*	9	8 wks
6 Sep 80	★	**FAME** *RSO 2479 253*	1	25 wks
14 Feb 81	●	**DANCE CRAZE** *2-Tone CHRTT 5004*	5	15 wks
12 Dec 81		**THE SECRET POLICEMAN'S OTHER BALL**		
		Springtime HAHA 6003	69	4 wks
20 Mar 82		**THE SECRET POLICEMAN'S OTHER BALL (THE**		
		MUSIC) *Springtime HAHA 6004*	29	5 wks
17 Jul 82		**THE SOUND OF MUSIC (re-issue)** *RCA Ints 5134*	98	1 wk
4 Sep 82		**ROCKY III** *Liberty LBG 30351*	42	7 wks
4 Sep 82		**ANNIE** *CBS 70219*	83	2 wks
11 Sep 82		**BRIMSTONE AND TREACLE** *A & M AMLH 64915*	67	3 wks
12 Feb 83		**AN OFFICER AND A GENTLEMAN** *Island ISTA 3*	40	14 wks
25 Jun 83		**RETURN OF THE JEDI** *RSO RSD 5023*	85	5 wks
2 Jul 83	●	**FLASHDANCE** *Casablanca CANH 5*	9	30 wks
1 Oct 83		**STAYING ALIVE** *RSO RSBG 3*	14	8 wks
21 Apr 84	●	**FOOTLOOSE** *CBS 70246*	7	25 wks
21 Apr 84		**AGAINST ALL ODDS** *Virgin V 2313*	29	10 wks

Date		Title	Pos	Weeks
16 Jun	84	● **BREAKDANCE** *Polydor POLD 5147*	6	29 wks
7 Jul	84	**BEAT STREET** *Atlantic 780154*	30	13 wks
18 Aug	84	**ELECTRIC DREAMS** *Virgin V 2318*	46	7 wks
29 Sep	84	**GHOSTBUSTERS** *Arista 206 559*	24	25 wks
16 Feb	85	**BEVERLY HILLS COP** *MCA MCF 3253*	24	32 wks
22 Jun	85	**A VIEW TO A KILL** *Parlophone BOND 1*	81	1 wk
11 Jan	86	**BACK TO THE FUTURE** *MCA MCF 3285*	66	8 wks
1 Feb	86	**MISTRAL'S DAUGHTER** *Carrere CAL 221*	53	3 wks
1 Feb	86	● **ROCKY IV** *Scotti Brothers SCT 70272*	3	22 wks
5 Apr	86	**ABSOLUTE BEGINNERS** *Virgin V 2386*	19	9 wks
26 Apr	86	**OUT OF AFRICA** *MCA MCF 3310*	81	2 wks
5 Jul	86	**LABYRINTH** *EMI America AML 3104*	38	2 wks
11 Oct	86	● **TOP GUN** *CBS 70296*	4	46 wks
11 Apr	87	**THE BLUES BROTHERS** *Atlantic K 50715*	59	26 wks
2 May	87	**PLATOON** *WEA WX 95*	90	2 wks
18 Jul	87	**BEVERLY HILLS COP 2** *MCA MCF 3383*	71	5 wks
1 Aug	87	**THE LIVING DAYLIGHTS** *Warner Bros. WX 111*	57	6 wks
1 Aug	87	● **WHO'S THAT GIRL** *Sire WX 102*	4	25 wks
22 Aug	87	**LA BAMBA** *London LONLP 36*	24	15 wks
3 Oct	87	**FULL METAL JACKET** *Warner Bros. 925 613-1*	60	4 wks
31 Oct	87	● **DIRTY DANCING** *RCA BL 86408*	4	63 wks
16 Jan	88	**FLASHDANCE (re-issue)** *Mercury PRICE 111*	93	2 wks
20 Feb	88	**CRY FREEDOM** *MCA MCG 6029*	73	2 wks
14 May	88	● **MORE DIRTY DANCING** *RCA BL 86965*	3	27 wks
24 Sep	88	● **BUSTER** *Virgin V 2544*	6	16 wks
22 Oct	88	**GOOD MORNING VIETNAM** *A&M AMA 3913*	50	9 wks
14 Jan	89	● **BUSTER** *Virgin V 2544*	2	36 wks
14 Jan	89	★ **DIRTY DANCING** *RCA BL 86408*	1	137 wks
21 Jan	89	● **GOOD MORNING VIETNAM** *A&M AMA 3913*	7	28 wks
21 Jan	89	● **THE BLUES BROTHERS** *Atlantic K 50715*	4	73 wks
28 Jan	89	★ **THE LOST BOYS** *Atlantic 7817671*	1	51 wks
4 Feb	89	● **COCKTAIL** *Elektra EKT 54*	2	15 wks
4 Feb	89	**MORE DIRTY DANCING** *RCA BL 86965*	14	17 wks
18 Mar	89	**SCANDAL** *Parlophone PCS 7331*	13	3 wks
22 Apr	89	● **TOP GUN** *CBS 70296*	4	31 wks
13 May	89	**DIRTY DANCING – LIVE IN CONCERT** *RCA BL 90336*	19	2 wks
15 Jul	89	**LICENCE TO KILL** *MCA MCG 6051*	17	2 wks
22 Jul	89	**GHOSTBUSTERS 2** *MCA MCG 6056*	15	4 wks
10 Mar	90	**THE DELINQUENTS** *PWL HF 11*	16	1 wk
26 May	90	● **PRETTY WOMAN** *EMI USA MTL 1052*	2	66 wks
23 Jun	90	● **TEENAGE MUTANT NINJA TURTLES** *SBK SBKLP 6*	6	18 wks
11 Aug	90	● **DAYS OF THUNDER** *Epic 4671591*	4	15 wks
27 Oct	90	**GHOST** *Milan A 620*	15	4 wks
2 Feb	91	● **ROCKY V** *Capitol EST 2137*	9	9 wks
2 Mar	91	● **GREASE** *Polydor 8179981*	8	9 wks
23 Mar	91	**THE GODFATHER III** *Columbia 4678131*	19	1 wk
27 Apr	91	**NEW JACK CITY** *Giant 7599244091*	16	5 wks
1 Jun	91	● **MERMAIDS** *Epic 467874*	6	15 wks
27 Jul	91	● **ROBIN HOOD – PRINCE OF THIEVES** *Polydor 5110502*	3	14 wks

The West Side Story *album on Philips BBL 7530 during its chart run changed label and number to CBS BPG 62058.*

STAGE CAST RECORDINGS

These albums still qualify for inclusion on the main chart, not the Compilation Albums chart.

Date		Title	Pos	Weeks
8 Nov	58	● **MY FAIR LADY (BROADWAY)** *Philips RBL 1000*	2	129 wks
24 Jan	59	● **WEST SIDE STORY (BROADWAY)** *Philips BBL 7277*	3	27 wks
26 Mar	60	● **AT THE DROP OF A HAT (LONDON)** *Parlophone PMC 1033*	9	1 wk
26 Mar	60	● **FINGS AIN'T WOT THEY USED TO BE (LONDON)** *Decca LK 4346*	5	11 wks
2 Apr	60	● **FLOWER DRUM SONG (BROADWAY)** *Philips ABL 3302*	2	27 wks
7 May	60	● **FOLLOW THAT GIRL (LONDON)** *HMV CLP 1366*	5	9 wks

21 May 60	● MOST HAPPY FELLA (BROADWAY)	*Philips BBL 7374* .	6	13 wks
21 May 60	MAKE ME AN OFFER (LONDON)	*HMV CLP 1333*	18	1 wk
28 May 60	● FLOWER DRUM SONG (LONDON)	*HMV CLP 1359* ..	10	3 wks
9 Jul 60	MOST HAPPY FELLA (LONDON)	*HMV CLP 1365*	19	1 wk
30 Jul 60	WEST SIDE STORY (BROADWAY)	*Philips SBBL 504* ..	14	1 wk
10 Sep 60	● OLIVER (LONDON)	*Decca LK 4359*	4	91 wks
11 Mar 61	KING KONG (SOUTH AFRICA)	*Decca LK 4392*	12	8 wks
6 May 61	● MUSIC MAN (LONDON)	*JMH CLP 1444*	8	13 wks
24 Jun 61	● SOUND OF MUSIC (BROADWAY)	*Philips ABL 3370* ...	4	19 wks
22 Jul 61	BYE-BYE BIRDIE (LONDON)	*Philips ABL 3385*	17	3 wks
22 Jul 61	BEYOND THE FRINGE (LONDON)	*Parlophone PMC 1145*	13	17 wks
29 Jul 61	● SOUND OF MUSIC (LONDON)	*HMV CLP 1453*	4	68 wks
9 Sep 61	● STOP THE WORLD I WANT TO GET OFF (LONDON)			
		Decca LK 4408	8	14 wks
14 Jul 62	● BLITZ (LONDON)	*HMV CLP 1569*	7	21 wks
18 May 63	HALF A SIXPENCE (LONDON)	*Decca LK 4521*	20	2 wks
3 Aug 63	PICKWICK (LONDON)	*Philips AL 3431*	12	10 wks
4 Jan 64	MY FAIR LADY (BROADWAY)	*CBS BPG 68001*	19	1 wk
22 Feb 64	AT THE DROP OF ANOTHER HAT (LONDON)			
		Parlophone PMC 1216	12	11 wks
3 Oct 64	● CAMELOT (BROADWAY)	*CBS APG 60001*	10	12 wks
16 Jan 65	CAMELOT (LONDON)	*HMV CLP 1756*	19	1 wk
11 Mar 67	● FIDDLER ON THE ROOF (LONDON)	*CBS SBPG 70030*	4	50 wks
28 Dec 68	● HAIR (LONDON)	*Polydor 583–043*	3	94 wks
30 Aug 69	OLIVER (LONDON) (re-issue)	*Decca SPA 30*	23	4 wks
6 Sep 69	HAIR (BROADWAY)	*RCA SF 7959*	29	3 wks
19 Feb 72	GODSPELL (LONDON)	*Bell BELLS 203*	25	17 wks
18 Nov 78	EVITA (LONDON)	*MCA MCF 3257*	24	18 wks
1 Aug 81	● CATS (LONDON)	*Polydor CATX 001*	6	26 wks
6 Nov 82	MACK AND MABEL (BROADWAY)	*MCA MCL 1728* ..	38	7 wks
7 Aug 84	STARLIGHT EXPRESS (LONDON)			
		Starlight/Polydor LNER 1	21	9 wks
15 Feb 86	LES MISERABLES (LONDON)			
		First Night ENCORE 1 ..	72	4 wks
21 Feb 87	★ THE PHANTOM OF THE OPERA (LONDON)			
		Polydor PODV 9/Really Useful PODV 3	1†	126 wks
16 Sep 89	★ ASPECTS OF LOVE (LONDON)	*Polydor 841126 1*	1	16 wks
29 Jun 91	FIVE GUYS NAMED MOE (LONDON)			
		First Night CAST 23	59	1 wk
31 Aug 91	★ JOSEPH AND THE AMAZING TECHNICOLOUR DREAMCOAT (LONDON)	*Really Useful 511301*	1†	18 wks

Really Useful given label credit midway through 'The Phantom of the Opera' chart run.

STUDIO CAST RECORDINGS

25 Jun 60	SHOWBOAT	*HMV CLP 1310*	12	1 wk
8 Feb 72	● JESUS CHRIST SUPERSTAR	*MCA MKPS 2011/2*	6	20 wks
22 Jan 77	● EVITA	*MCA MCX 503*	4	35 wks
17 Jun 78	WHITE MANSIONS	*A&M AMLX 64691*	51	3 wks
10 Nov 84	● CHESS	*RCA PL 70500*	10	16 wks
18 May 85	WEST SIDE STORY	*Deutsche Grammophon 41525*	11	32 wks
2 Nov 85	CHESS PIECES	*Telstar STAR 2274*	87	3 wks
10 May 86	WEST SIDE STORY – HIGHLIGHTS			
		Deutsche Grammophon 45963	72	6 wks
17 May 86	DAVE CLARK'S 'TIME'	*EMI AMPH 1*	21	6 wks
11 Oct 86	● SOUTH PACIFIC	*CBS SM 42205*	5	24 wks
27 Jun 87	MATADOR	*Epic VIVA 1*	26	5 wks
21 Nov 87	MY FAIR LADY	*DECCA MFL 1*	41	12 wks

TV and RADIO SOUNDTRACKS and SPIN-OFFS

13 Dec 58	● OH BOY!	*Parlophone PMC 1072*	9	14 wks
4 Mar 61	● HUCKLEBERRY HOUND	*Pye GGL 004*	10	12 wks
28 Feb 63	THAT WAS THE WEEK THAT WAS			
		Parlophone PMC 1197	11	9 wks

28 Mar 64	**STARS FROM STARS AND GARTERS** *Pye GGL 0252*	17	2 wks
4 Nov 72	**THE BBC 1922–1972 (TV AND RADIO EXTRACTS)**		
	BBC 50	16	7 wks
4 Jan 75	**BBC TV'S BEST OF TOP OF THE POPS**		
	Super Beeb BELP 001	21	5 wks
10 Apr 76	★ **ROCK FOLLIES** *Island ILPS 9362*	1	15 wks
22 Oct 77	**10 YEARS OF HITS – RADIO ONE** *Super Beeb BEDP 002*	39	3 wks
8 Apr 78	● **PENNIES FROM HEAVEN** *World Records SH 266*	10	17 wks
1 Jul 78	**MORE PENNIES FROM HEAVEN** *World Records SH 267* .	31	4 wks
15 Dec 79	**FAWLTY TOWERS** *BBC REB 377*	25	10 wks
7 Feb 81	**FAWLTY TOWERS VOLUME 2** *BBC REB 405*	26	7 wks
14 Feb 81	**HITCHHIKERS GUIDE TO THE GALAXY VOLUME 2**		
	Original ORA 54	47	4 wks
1 Aug 81	**MUSIC OF COSMOS** *RCA RCALP 5032*	43	10 wks
21 Nov 81	**BRIDESHEAD REVISITED** *Chrysalis CDL 1367*	50	12 wks
23 Oct 82	**ON THE AIR – 60 YEARS OF BBC THEME MUSIC**		
	BBC REF 454	85	3 wks
26 Nov 83	**REILLY ACE OF THEMES** *Red Bus BUSLP 1004*	54	6 wks
4 Feb 84	**AUF WIEDERSEHEN PET** *Towerbell AUF 1*	21	6 wks
18 Feb 84	**THE TUBE** *K-Tel NE 1261*	30	6 wks
8 Sep 84	**SONG AND DANCE** *RCA BL 70480*	46	4 wks
18 May 85	**VICTORY IN EUROPE – BROADCASTS FROM BBC**		
	CORRESPONDENTS *BBC REC 562*	61	1 wk
28 Sep 85	**THE TV HITS ALBUM** *Towerbell TVLP 3*	26	13 wks
26 Oct 85	**MIAMI VICE** *BBC/MCA REMV 584*	11	9 wks
16 Nov 85	**THE EASTENDERS SING-A-LONG ALBUM**		
	BBC REB 586	33	10 wks
23 Nov 85	**TELLY HITS – 16 TOP TV THEMES** *Stylus BBSR 508* ...	34	6 wks
15 Feb 86	● **JONATHAN KING'S ENTERTAINMENT U.S.A.**		
	Stylus SMR 6812	6	11 wks
12 Apr 86	**THE TV HITS ALBUM TWO** *Towerbell TVLP 10*	19	7 wks
5 Jul 86	**TELLY HITS 2** *Stylus BBSR 616*	68	2 wks
18 Oct 86	**THE VERY BEST OF ENTERTAINMENT U.S.A.**		
	VOLUME 2 *Priority UPTVR 1*	44	4 wks
1 Nov 86	**SIMON BATES – OUR TUNE** *Rolydor PROLP 10*	58	5 wks
26 Dec 86	● **THE SINGING DETECTIVE** *BBC REN 608*	10	24 wks
27 Jun 87	**THE ROCK 'N' ROLL YEARS 1956–59** *BBR REN 631* ..	80	2 wks
27 Jun 87	**THE ROCK 'N' ROLL YEARS 1960–63** *BBC REN 632* ..	84	1 wk
27 Jun 87	**THE ROCK 'N' ROLL YEARS 1964–67** *BBC REN 633* ..	71	2 wks
27 Jun 87	**THE ROCK 'N' ROLL YEARS 1968–71** *BBC REN 634* ..	77	1 wk
3 Oct 87	**MOONLIGHTING** *MCA MCF 3386*	50	6 wks
17 Oct 87	**MIAMI VICE 2** *MCA MCG 6019*	71	4 wks
28 Nov 87	**THE CHART SHOW – DANCE HITS '87** *Chrysalis ADD 1*	39	6wks
1 Oct 88	● **MOONLIGHTING 2** *WEA WX 202*	5	9 wks
1 Oct 88	**MIAMI VICE 3** *MCA MCG 6033*	95	1 wk
8 Oct 88	● **ONES ON 1** *BBC REF 693*	10	7 wks
17 Jun 89	● **RAY MOORE – A PERSONAL CHOICE** *BBC STAR 2352*	7	4 wks
23 Sep 89	**TV TUNES** *K-Tel NE 1429*	17	3 wks
17 Feb 90	● **PENNIES FROM HEAVEN** *BBC REF 768*	8	13 wks
16 Feb 91	● **BRITS 1991 – THE MAGIC OF BRITISH MUSIC**		
	Telstar/BPI STAR 2481	7	6 wks
21 Sep 91	**THE OLD GREY WHISTLE TEST – BEST OF THE TEST**		
	Windsong International OGWTLP 1	13	3 wks

369

ANONYMOUS COVER VERSIONS

29 Feb 64	**BEATLEMANIA** *Top Six TSL 1*	19	1 wk
7 Aug 71	**HOT HITS 5** *MFP 5208*	48	1 wk
7 Aug 71	★ **HOT HITS 6** *MFP 5214*	1	7 wks
7 Aug 71	**TOP OF THE POPS VOL. 17** *Hallmark SHM 740*	16	3 wks
7 Aug 71	★ **TOP OF THE POPS VOL. 18** *Hallmark SHM 745* ..	1	12 wks
7 Aug 71	**MILLION SELLER HITS** *MFP 5203*	46	2 wks
21 Aug 71	**SMASH HITS SUPREMES STYLE** *MFP 5184*	36	3 wks
2 Oct 71	● **TOP OF THE POPS VOL. 19** *Hallmark SHM 750* ..	3	9 wks
23 Oct 71	● **HOT HITS 7** *MFP 5236*	3	9 wks
6 Nov 71	**SMASH HITS COUNTRY STYLE** *MFP 5228*	38	1 wk

VARIOUS ARTISTS

13 Nov 71	★ **TOP OF THE POPS VOL. 20** *Hallmark SHM 739*	1	8 wks
27 Nov 71	**NON STOP 20 VOL. 4** *Plexium PXMS 1006*	35	2 wks
4 Dec 71	**SMASH HITS 71** *MFP 5229*	21	3 wks
11 Dec 71	● **HOT HITS 8** *MFP 5243*	2	4 wks
27 Sep 75	**40 SINGALONG PUB SONGS** *K-Tel NE 509*	21	7 wks
6 Nov 76	**FORTY MANIA** *Ronco RDT 2018*	21	6 wks

MISCELLANEOUS

12 Sep 70	**EDINBURGH MILITARY TATTOO 1970** *Waverley SZLP 2121*	34	4 wks
18 Sep 71	**EDINBURGH MILITARY TATTOO 1971** *Waverley SZLP 2128*	44	1 wk
11 Dec 71	**ELECTRONIC ORGANS TODAY** *Ad-Rhythm ADBS 1*	48	1 wk
8 Dec 73	● **MUSIC FOR A ROYAL WEDDING** *BBC REW 163*	7	6 wks
27 Dec 75	**STRINGS OF SCOTLAND** *Philips 6382 108*	50	1 wk
8 Aug 81	★ **THE OFFICIAL BBC ALBUM OF THE ROYAL WEDDING** *BBC REP 413*	1	11 wks
3 Jul 82	**JOHN PAUL II – THE PILGRIM POPE** *BBC REB 445*	71	4 wks
9 Aug 86	**ROYAL WEDDING** *BBC REP 596*	55	1 wk
28 Dec 91	**TRIVIAL PURSUIT – THE MUSIC MASTER GAME** *Telstar STAC 2550*	20†	1 wk

FACTS
AND
FEATS

Luciano Pavarotti, the first classical artist to top the album chart.

MOST WEEKS ON CHART

The following table lists the 146 recording acts that have spent 150 weeks or more on the British albums chart from the first chart on 8 Nov 1958 up to and including the chart of 28 Dec 1991. It is, of course, possible for an act to be credited with two or more chart weeks in the same week if the act has more than one album on the chart in any one week.

Beatles	1082
Simon & Garfunkel	1039
Dire Straits	1030
Elvis Presley	1026
Queen	890
David Bowie	869
Fleetwood Mac	765
Pink Floyd	746
Phil Collins	730
U2	725
Cliff Richard	717
Elton John	709
Rolling Stones	688
Rod Stewart	666
Frank Sinatra	613

(plus 23 weeks with Count Basie)

Bob Dylan	560

(plus 3 with the Grateful Dead)

Meatloaf	548
Beach Boys	547
Carpenters	546
Michael Jackson	538

(plus 58 weeks with Jackson Five, 10 weeks with Diana Ross, Gladys Knight and Stevie Wonder, and 24 weeks with Diana Ross)

Paul McCartney/Wings	516
Madonna	514
Abba	506
Neil Diamond	481
Mike Oldfield	473
Shadows	442
UB40	442
Andy Williams	439
Led Zeppelin	432
Status Quo	431

Tom Jones	415
Barbra Streisand	394
Bruce Springsteen	387
James Last	386

(plus 8 weeks with Richard Clayderman)

Genesis	385
The Sound of Music (Original Soundtrack)	382
Jim Reeves	381
Diana Ross	371

(plus 45 weeks with Marvin Gaye, 31 weeks with the Supremes and the Temptations, 10 weeks with Michael Jackson, Gladys Knight and Stevie Wonder, and 24 weeks with Michael Jackson)

Electric Light Orchestra	370
Eurythmics	367
Duran Duran	345
Police	328
Stevie Wonder	326

(plus 10 weeks with Diana Ross, Gladys Knight and Michael Jackson)

Barry Manilow	321
Buddy Holly and the Crickets	319

(Crickets plus 7 alone; plus 27 with Bobby Vee)

Herb Alpert	312
Moody Blues	310
Madness	300
Tina Turner	299

(plus 1 week with Ike and Tina Turner)

John Lennon	297
Bob Marley and the Wailers	294
Lionel Richie	293
Roxy Music	293

(plus 104 weeks with Bryan Ferry)

Simple Minds	293
Billy Joel	289
South Pacific (Original Soundtrack)	288
Johnny Cash	285
Eagles	284
Chris Rea	276
Pet Shop Boys	273
Deep Purple	271
Seekers	268
Blondie	266

(plus 26 with Debbie Harry)

Shirley Bassey	266
George Benson	262

(plus 6 weeks with Earl Klugh)

Paul Simon 260
(plus 1039 weeks with Simon &
Garfunkel)
Prince 255
Cat Stevens 255
Kate Bush 253
Simply Red 253
Erasure 250
Spandau Ballet 250
Whitney Houston 249
Eric Clapton 240
(plus 96 weeks with Cream, 17 weeks
with John Mayall, and 1 week as
Derek and the Dominoes)
George Mitchell Minstrels 240
Four Tops 239
(plus 11 weeks with the Supremes)
Chris De Burgh 238
AC/DC 236
Engelbert Humperdinck 233
Wham! 233
Leo Sayer 232
Jeff Wayne's War of the
Worlds 232
Jethro Tull 229
Thin Lizzy 228
(plus 10 weeks with Phil Lynott)
Ultravox 225
Level 42 223
Luther Vandross 221
Roy Orbison 218
Jean-Michel Jarre 216
Stranglers 216
Marc Bolan/T. Rex/
Tyrannosaurus Rex 214
Bee Gees 213
Talking Heads 213
Paul Young 212
Orchestral Manoeuvres in the
Dark 211
Black Sabbath 209
Jimi Hendrix 209
(plus 2 weeks with Curtis Knight)
Elkie Brooks 208
Nana Mouskouri 208
Slade 207
Santana 206
Yes 206
John Denver 204
(plus 21 weeks with Placido Domingo)
Who 203
Sky 202

10 C.C. 197
(plus 18 weeks with Godley & Creme)
Donna Summer 196
Gilbert O'Sullivan 195
Johnny Mathis 193
(plus 16 weeks with Natalie Cole, 11
weeks with Deniece Williams and 8
weeks with Henry Mancini)
Otis Redding 192
(plus 17 weeks with Carla Thomas)
Perry Como 191
Joan Armatrading 187
ZZ Top 185
Glen Campbell 183
(plus 1 week with Bobbie Gentry)
Elvis Costello 182
Cream 182
(plus 96 weeks with Eric Clapton)
Human League 181
Richard Clayderman 180
(plus 8 weeks with James Last)
Supremes 180
(plus 31 weeks with the Temptations,
and 11 weeks with the Four Tops)
Bread 179
Max Bygraves 176
Cure 176
Tears For Fears 176
Neil Young 175
(plus 79 weeks with Crosby, Stills,
Nash and Young, and 5 weeks with
Stills-Young Band)
West Side Story (Original
Soundtrack) 175
London Symphony Orchestra . . 173
(plus 24 weeks with various soloists)
Val Doonican 170
Iron Maiden 170
Supertramp 170
Peter Gabriel 169
Peters and Lee 166
INXS 164
Rainbow 163
Deacon Blue 162
Jam 162
Smiths 158
Guns N' Roses 157
Bryan Adams 156
Shakin' Stevens 156
Earth Wind and Fire 154
Gloria Estefan/Miami Sound
Machine 154

373

Bryan Ferry 154
(plus 104 weeks with Roxy Music)
Five Star 153
Cher. 151
(plus 20 weeks with Sonny & Cher)
Mantovani 151
Marillion 151

Donny Osmond has racked up 104 weeks as a solo act, 103 as part of the Osmonds, and 19 with his sister Marie, a total of **226** weeks.

Alison Moyet has been on the chart for 142 weeks as a soloist and 83 as half of Yazoo, a total of **225** weeks.

Steve Winwood has clocked up 120 weeks on the chart as a solo act, 47 weeks as a member of the Spencer Davis Group, 37 playing in Traffic and 10 as part of Blind Faith, a total of **214** weeks.

Graham Nash has had 8 weeks on the chart as a soloist, 5 weeks as half of a duo with David Crosby,14 weeks as one third of Crosby Stills and Nash, 79 weeks as one quarter of Crosby, Stills, Nash and Young and 106 weeks as one fifth of the Hollies, a total of **212** weeks.

Luciano Pavarotti has been on the charts for 137 weeks as a soloist, 63 weeks with Jose Carreras and Placido Domingo and 1 week with Henry Mancini, a total of **201** weeks.

Vangelis has 138 weeks of chart life as a soloist and 53 more as half of Jon and Vangelis, a total of **191** weeks.

Jon Bon Jovi has been on the charts for 23 weeks as a soloist, and for 148 more with his band Bon Jovi, a total of **171** weeks.

Dionne Warwick has 144 solo chart weeks, and 19 more on Stevie Wonder's soundtrack album, *Woman In Red*. This is a total of **163** weeks.

374

Mr. Acker Bilk has scored 76 weeks as a soloist and with his Paramount Jazz Band, a further 61 weeks with Chris Barber, and 24 weeks with Kenny Ball and Chris Barber, a total of **161** weeks.

David Sylvian has 21 weeks on the chart, 1 in partnership with Holgar Czukay and 136 as a member of Japan, a total of **158** weeks.

Marvin Gaye has spent 98 solo weeks on the chart, 45 with Diana Ross, 9 with Smokey Robinson and 4 with Tammi Terrell, a total of **156** weeks.

Placido Domingo has clocked up 52 chart weeks as a soloist, 63 with José Carreras and Luciano Pavarotti, 21 with John Denver and 18 on Andrew Lloyd Webber's *Requiem*, a total of **154** weeks.

Boy George has 6 solo weeks to his credit and 144 more as lead vocalist with Culture Club, a total of **150** weeks.

Daryl Hall enjoyed 5 weeks of solo chart life in 1986 to go with 145 weeks in partnership with John Oates, total **150** weeks.

There are ten people who have been on the albums charts in total for over 1000 weeks, if we count their solo albums and albums by groups of which they were fully paid up members. They are, in order:

Paul McCartney . . . . . . 1598 weeks
John Lennon . . . . 1379 weeks
Paul Simon . . . . 1299 weeks
George Harrison . . . . . . 1215 weeks
Phil Collins . . . . 1167 weeks
Ringo Starr . . . . 1110 weeks
Art Garfunkel . . . . 1097 weeks
Mark Knopfler . . . . 1064 weeks
John Illsley . . . . 1030 weeks
Elvis Presley . . . . 1026 weeks

MOST WEEKS ON CHART
IN A YEAR

There have been 50 instances of one act clocking up 100 or more chart weeks in one year, although this feat has not been achieved since 1988. Dire Straits' record score in 1986 is the equivalent of four albums on the chart every week throughout the year.

217	Dire Straits	1986
198	David Bowie	1983
182	David Bowie	1973
177	Bruce Springsteen	1985
168	U2	1985
167	Simon and Garfunkel	1970
158	Dire Straits	1985
135	Tom Jones	1968
131	Phil Collins	1985
127	Madonna	1987
126	U2	1987
125	Johnny Cash	1970
125	Madonna	1986
122	Beatles	1970
121	Otis Redding	1968
117	Queen	1987
116	Beach Boys	1968
116	Police	1980
116	Dire Straits	1984
115	Jim Reeves	1964
115	Moody Blues	1970
114	Michael Jackson	1988
113	Phil Collins	1986
112	Bob Dylan	1965
112	Abba	1978
112	Electric Light Orchestra	1979
111	Andy Williams	1971
109	George Mitchell Minstrels	1962
108	Pink Floyd	1977
107	David Bowie	1974
107	Dire Straits	1983
107	Michael Jackson	1984
107	Queen	1986
107	Fleetwood Mac	1988
106	Carpenters	1974
106	Abba	1977
105	Elton John	1975
105	Duran Duran	1983
104	Beatles	1964
104	Simon and Garfunkel	1973
104	Beatles	1974
103	Four Tops	1968
102	Led Zeppelin	1970
102	Simon and Garfunkel	1971
101	Herb Alpert	1967
101	Simon and Garfunkel	1974
100	Simon and Garfunkel	1975
100	Blondie	1979
100	U2	1984
100	Pet Shop Boys	1988

Simon and Garfunkel have racked up 100 chart weeks in a year five times. Dire Straits have done it four times, in consecutive years (1983 to 1986 inclusive). The Beatles, David Bowie and U2 have topped the century in three years, while Abba, Phil Collins, Madonna, Michael Jackson and Queen have done it twice.

375

MOST WEEKS ON CHART
IN EACH CHART YEAR

1958	Elvis Presley	16*
1959	Frank Sinatra	56*
1960	Elvis Presley	51
1961	Elvis Presley	91*
1962	George Mitchell Minstrels	109*
1963	Cliff Richard	72
1964	Jim Reeves	115*
1965	Bob Dylan	112
1966	Beach Boys	95
1967	Herb Alpert	101
1968	Tom Jones	135*
1969	Seekers	66
1970	Simon and Garfunkel	167*
1971	Andy Williams	111
1972	Cat Stevens	89
1973	David Bowie	182*
1974	David Bowie	107
1975	Elton John	105
1976	Demis Roussos	84

1977	Pink Floyd	108
1978	Abba	112
1979	Electric Light Orchestra	112
1980	Police	116
1981	Barry Manilow	92
1982	Japan	85
1983	David Bowie	198*
1984	Dire Straits	116
1985	Bruce Springsteen	177
1986	Dire Straits	217*
1987	Madonna	127
1988	Michael Jackson	114
1989	Guns N' Roses	85
1990	Phil Collins	85
1991	Michael Bolton	63

(*denotes record annual total at the time)

In 1960, the soundtrack album *South Pacific* was on the charts for all 53 chart weeks of the year, a greater total than that of the year's individual champion, Elvis Presley.

376

Elvis Presley and David Bowie have each been the year's chart champions three times, and Dire Straits have won twice. No other act has been chart champion more than once.

Only three acts have chart careers featuring newly recorded hit albums over more than 30 years. They are Cliff Richard (1959 to 1991), the Shadows (1961 to 1991) and Shirley Bassey (1961 to 1991). Sir Harry Secombe first hit the albums chart in 1959 as a member of the Goons, and had a hit album on the chart at the end of 1991, but his solo chart career stretches only 29 years and nine months.

MOST WEEKS ON CHART
IN 1990

85	Phil Collins
78	UB40
76	New Kids On The Block
66	Nigel Kennedy
57	Carpenters
53	Madonna
	Technotronic
	Tina Turner
48	Sinead O'Connor
47	Michael Bolton
	Chris Rea

(*Luciano Pavarotti had 43 weeks solo, plus 18 with José Carreras and Placido Domingo, a total of 61 weeks*)

MOST WEEKS ON CHART
IN 1991

63	Michael Bolton
62	Roxette
61	Rod Stewart
57	Chris Rea
55	Elton John
53	Phil Collins
	Doors
52	Madonna
	Luciano Pavarotti
	(*plus 45 weeks with José Carreras and Placido Domingo*)
51	R.E.M.

(*José Carreras had 12 weeks solo and 45 with Luciano Pavarotti and Placido Domingo, a total of 57 weeks. Placido Domingo had 10 weeks solo and 45 with Pavarotti and Carreras, a total of 55 weeks*)

MOST WEEKS ON CHART
BY ONE ALBUM

This is a list of all the albums that have spent a total of 100 weeks or more
on the chart to the end of 1991. Re-releases and re-issues are counted,
provided that the re-issue is identical to the original release.

Rumours *Fleetwood Mac* 443
Bat Out Of Hell *Meat Loaf* 416
The Sound Of Music *Original Film Soundtrack* 382
Greatest Hits *Queen* 338
Bridge Over Troubled Water *Simon and Garfunkel* 303
Dark Side Of The Moon *Pink Floyd* 301
South Pacific *Original Film Soundtrack* 288
Greatest Hits *Simon and Garfunkel* 283
Face Value *Phil Collins* 274
Tubular Bells *Mike Oldfield* 264
Makin' Movies *Dire Straits* 249
Jeff Wayne's War Of The Worlds *Various* 232
U2 Live: Under A Blood Red Sky *U2* 201
Love Over Gold *Dire Straits* 198
Brothers in Arms *Dire Straits* 195
No Jacket Required *Phil Collins* 176
West Side Story *Original Film Soundtrack* 175
Off the Wall *Michael Jackson* 173
The Rise And Fall Of Ziggy Stardust And The Spiders From Mars
  David Bowie 172
Thriller *Michael Jackson* 168
Hello I Must Be Going *Phil Collins* 164
Sergeant Pepper's Lonely Hearts Club Band *Beatles* 164
Alchemy – Dire Straits Live *Dire Straits* 163
The Buddy Holly Story *Buddy Holly* 156
Can't Slow Down *Lionel Richie* 154
Like A Virgin *Madonna* 152
Manilow Magic *Barry Manilow* 151
The Beatles 1962–1966 *Beatles* 148
Private Dancer *Tina Turner* 147
War *U2* 143
Best Of The Beach Boys *Beach Boys* 142
Going Places *Herb Alpert* 138
Led Zeppelin II *Led Zeppelin* 138
Eliminator *ZZ Top* 135
Greatest Hits *Abba* 130
Dire Straits *Dire Straits* 130
Legend *Bob Marley and the Wailers* 129
Love Songs *Barbra Streisand* 129
My Fair Lady *Original Broadway Cast* 129
The Unforgettable Fire *U2* 127
Born In The USA *Bruce Springsteen* 126
Phantom Of The Opera *Original London Cast* 126
The Best Of The Seekers *Seekers* 125
The Singles 1969–1973 *Carpenters* 125

377

Only one of these albums, Queen's **Greatest Hits**, was still on the chart at the end of 1991.

Five of the eight Dire Straits albums released to the end of 1991 are in this list. Three albums each by the Beatles, Phil Collins, Simon and Garfunkel, Michael Jackson and U2 have spent over 100 weeks on the chart, as well as two each by David Bowie, Duran Duran, Electric Light Orchestra, Whitney Houston, and Madonna. Paul Simon, John Lennon and Paul McCartney each feature in four albums which have enjoyed at least 100 weeks of chart life.

The sales of a record are not necessarily reflected in the length of its chart run. *Off The Wall* and *Thriller* have both had longer chart runs than Michael Jackson's best seller in Britain, *Bad*, while Dire Straits' biggest seller, *Brothers in Arms*, still has some way to go before its chart life overtakes that of *Makin' Movies*.

Dirty Dancing *Original Film Sountrack* spent 63 weeks on the main chart up to the beginning of 1989, and a further 137 weeks on the compilations chart to the end of 1991, a total of 200 weeks of chart action. No other album has totalled over 100 weeks on the Compilation Album charts, nor by a combination of appearances on the two charts. The leading performers on the Compilation Albums Chart in its first three years of existence are:

Dirty Dancing *Original Film Soundtrack*	137
The Blues Brothers *Original Film Soundtrack*	73
Pretty Woman *Original Film Soundtrack*	66
The Classic Experience *Various Artists*	57
The Lost Boys *Original Film Soundtrack*	51

MOST HIT ALBUMS

An album is a hit if it spends only one week at number 100. Double, treble and quadruple albums count as only one hit. Re-issues do not count as a new hit.

95   Elvis Presley
55   James Last
(plus 1 with Richard Clayderman)
49   Frank Sinatra
(plus 1 with Count Basie)
47   Cliff Richard
37   Rolling Stones
34   Bob Dylan
(plus 1 with Grateful Dead)
30   Elton John
29   Shirley Bassey
29   Diana Ross
(plus 3 with the Supremes and the Temptations, plus 2 with Marvin Gaye, and 1 with Gladys Knight, Stevie Wonder & Michael Jackson)
27   David Bowie
26   Beach Boys
26   Neil Diamond
26   Jim Reeves
25   Beatles
25   Shadows

25   Status Quo
24   Johnny Mathis
(plus 1 with Natalie Cole, 1 with Deniece Williams and 1 with Henry Mancini)
24   Andy Williams
23   Jethro Tull
22   Tom Jones
22   Paul McCartney/Wings
22   Neil Young
(plus 1 with Stills-Young Band and 3 with Crosby, Stills, Nash and Young)
21   Who
20   Marc Bolan/T. Rex/ Tyrannosaurus Rex
20   Deep Purple
20   Hawkwind
(includes 1 as Hawklords)
20   Gary Numan/Tubeway Army
(plus 1 with Sharpe and Numan)
20   Santana
(Carlos Santana 3 more with various other partners)
20   Rod Stewart
(plus 1 with the Faces)
19   Jimi Hendrix
(plus 1 with Curtis Knight)
19   Iron Maiden
19   Queen
18   Black Sabbath
18   Van Morrison

18 Roy Orbison
17 Eric Clapton
   (plus 1 with John Mayall and
   1 with Cream)
17 Mike Oldfield
16 Herb Alpert
16 Carpenters
16 Johnny Cash
16 Alice Cooper
16 Genesis
16 Barry Manilow
16 Moody Blues
16 Pink Floyd
16 Slade
16 Stranglers
16 Barbra Streisand
16 Tangerine Dream
16 Yes
15 Elvis Costello
   (includes 1 as the Costello
   Show)
15 David Essex
15 Stevie Wonder
   (plus 1 with Diana Ross,
   Gladys Knight and Michael
   Jackson)
14 Cure
14 John Denver
   (plus 1 with Placido Domingo)
14 Fleetwood Mac
14 Kiss
14 Motorhead
14 Donna Summer
14 Don Williams
13 Bee Gees
13 Foster and Allen
13 Michael Jackson
   (plus 1 with Diana Ross, Gladys
   Knight and Stevie Wonder,
   1 with Jackson Five)
13 London Symphony Orchestra
13 Joni Mitchell
13 Rush
13 UB40
13 Wishbone Ash
12 Abba
12 Joan Armatrading
12 George Benson
   (plus 1 with Earl Klugh)
12 Max Bygraves
12 Electric Light Orchestra
12 Hollies

12 Jacksons
   (4 as Jackson Five including one
   with Michael Jackson, 8 as Jacksons)
12 Jean-Michel Jarre
12 Billy Joel
12 Judas Priest
12 Led Zeppelin
12 John Lennon/Plastic Ono Band
12 Mantovani
12 John Mayall
   (plus 1 with Eric Clapton)
12 Roxy Music
   (plus 2 with Bryan Ferry)
12 Siouxsie and the Banshees
12 Temptations
   (plus 3 with Diana Ross and the
   Supremes)
12 Thin Lizzy
   (plus 1 with Phil Lynott)
12 Uriah Heep
12 Frank Zappa

Elkie Brooks

11 AC/DC
11 Elkie Brooks
11 Ray Conniff
11 Barbara Dickson
11 Val Doonican
11 Doors
11 Everly Brothers
   (Phil Everly 1 more solo)
11 Hall and Oates
   (Daryl Hall 1 more solo)
11 Engelbert Humperdinck
11 Joe Jackson
11 Kinks
11 Level 42
11 Bob Marley and the Wailers
11 George Mitchell Minstrels
11 Public Image Ltd

11	Chris Rea
11	Leo Sayer
11	Shakin' Stevens
11	Supremes *(plus 1 with Four Tops, 3 with Diana Ross and the Temptations)*
11	10 C.C. *(plus 1 with Godley and Creme)*
11	Dionne Warwick
11	Barry White
10	Barclay James Harvest
10	Byrds
10	Richard Clayderman *(plus 1 with James Last)*
10	Chris De Burgh
10	Fall
10	Four Tops *(plus 1 with Supremes)*
10	Rory Gallagher
10	Buddy Holly and the Crickets *(Crickets plus 1 with Bobby Vee and 1 solo)*
10	Bert Kaempfert
10	King Crimson
10	Nana Mouskouri
10	Olivia Newton-John
10	Alan Parsons Project
10	Gene Pitney
10	Prince
10	Rainbow
10	Showaddywaddy
10	Paul Simon
10	Simon and Garfunkel *(Art Garfunkel 6 more solo; Paul Simon 10 more solo)*
10	Simple Minds
10	Squeeze
10	Cat Stevens
10	Talking Heads
10	U2
10	Roger Whittaker

Marc Almond has six solo hit albums to his credit, six more as vocalist with Soft Cell and two as Marc and the Mambas, a total of 14.

Ginger Baker has had one hit as leader of Ginger Baker's Air Force, one as co-general in the Baker-Gurvitz Army, eight as drummer

with Cream and one more as part of the *Cream of Eric Clapton*, a total of 11.

Mr Acker Bilk has had nine hit albums either solo or with his Paramount Jazz Band, as well as two more with Chris Barber and one with Kenny Ball and Chris Barber, a total of 12.

Jack Bruce has one solo hit album, eight as bassist with Cream and one more as part of the *Cream of Eric Clapton*, a total of ten.

David Cassidy has had six hit albums and four more as part of the Partridge Family, a total of ten.

Nat 'King' Cole had eight hit albums on his own, plus one with Dean Martin and one with George Shearing, a total of ten.

David Crosby has had one solo hit album, one as half of Graham Nash and David Crosby, two as one third of Crosby Stills and Nash, three as one quarter of Crosby Stills Nash and Young, and six more as part of the Byrds, a total of 12 hit albums.

381

Placido Domingo has seven solo hit albums, one with John Denver, one with Luciano Pavarotti and José Carreras and one more as a principal singer on Andrew Lloyd Webber's *Requiem*, a total of ten.

Emerson Lake and Palmer have had nine hit albums, Emerson Lake and Powell one more, and Greg Lake one on his own.

The Four Tops have nine hit albums, plus one more with the Supremes, a total of ten.

Marvin Gaye has nine hit albums to his credit and one each with Tammi Terrell, Diana Ross and Smokey Robinson, a total of 12.

Deborah (Debbie) Harry has had three solo hit albums, seven as lead vocalist of Blondie and two more billed as Deborah Harry and Blondie, totalling 12.

Don Henley has two solo hit albums to go with eight as a member of the Eagles, a total of ten.

Mark Knopfler has had two solo hit albums to go with eight Dire Straits hits, one Notting Hillbillies good time and a duet with Chet Atkins, total 12.

Manfred Mann have had six hit albums, and Manfred Mann's Earth Band four more, a total of ten.

Morrissey has had three solo hit albums and eight as vocalist with the Smiths, total 11.

Graham Nash has had one solo hit album, one with David Crosby, two with Crosby Stills and Nash, three with Crosby Stills Nash and Young, and was one of the Hollies on eight of their hit albums, a total of 15.

382

Donny Osmond has had six solo hit albums, three more with Marie Osmond and seven as one of the Osmonds, a total of 17.

Otis Redding has had nine hit albums and one more with Carla Thomas, a total of ten.

Lionel Richie has three solo hit albums, and features as lead vocalist on eight of the Commodores' hit albums, a total of 11.

David Stewart has had eight hit albums as a Eurythmic, three as a Tourist and two more leading his Spiritual Cowboys, a total of 13.

Stephen Stills has four solo hit albums, two as leader of Stephen Stills' Manassas, two as part of Crosby Stills and Nash, three as one quarter of Crosby Stills Nash and Young, and one as half of the Stills-Young Band, giving him a share in 12 hit albums.

Midge Ure has had three solo hit albums, one as a member of Slik, seven as part of Ultravox and four involved with Visage, a total of 15.

Vangelis has amassed six solo hit albums, plus four more with Jon Anderson, making ten hit albums in all.

Rick Wakeman has hit the charts nine times, plus once more with Kevin Peek and again with Anderson Bruford Wakeman Howe, a total of 11 hit albums. He was also part of Yes for nine of their hit albums.

Scott Walker has had five solo hit albums and five more as part of the Walker Brothers, a total of ten.

Steve Winwood has had seven solo hit albums, three more as lead vocalist of the Spencer Davis Group, five with Traffic and one with Blind Faith, a total of 16.

MOST TOP TEN HIT ALBUMS

The rules for this category are the same as for Most Hit Albums, except that the album must have mde the Top Ten for at least one week.

36	Elvis Presley
31	Cliff Richard
29	Rolling Stones
27	Frank Sinatra
	(plus 1 with Count Basie)
24	Bob Dylan
19	David Bowie
18	Beatles
18	Paul McCartney/Wings
18	Status Quo
17	Elton John
17	Queen
16	Iron Maiden

16 Rod Stewart
    (plus 1 with the Faces)
14 Beach Boys
13 Genesis
13 Pink Floyd
13 Who
12 Jim Reeves
11 Elvis Costello
11 Tom Jones
11 Led Zeppelin
11 Shadows
    (plus 16 with Cliff Richard)
10 Andy Williams
10 Yes
 9 Black Sabbath
 9 Deep Purple
 9 Depeche Mode
 9 Fleetwood Mac
 9 Jimi Hendrix
 9 Roxy Music
    (plus 2 with Bryan Ferry)
 8 Abba
 8 Bee Gees
 8 Carpenters
 8 Cure
 8 Dire Straits
 8 Buddy Holly and the Crickets
    (Crickets plus 1 with Bobby Vee)
 8 Johnny Mathis
    (plus 1 with Natalie Cole)
 8 Moody Blues
 8 Prince
 8 Rush
 8 Stranglers
 8 Thin Lizzy
 8 UB40
 8 Stevie Wonder
 7 AC/DC
 7 Blondie
    (includes one listed as Deborah Harry and Blondie; Debbie Harry one more solo)
 7 Marc Bolan/T. Rex/Tyrannosaurus Rex
 7 Kate Bush
 7 Cream
    (plus 1 with Eric Clapton)
 7 Electric Light Orchestra
 7 Emerson Lake and Palmer
 7 Eurythmics
 7 Jam

 7 John Lennon/Plastic Ono Band
 7 Madonna
 7 George Mitchell Minstrels
 7 Diana Ross
    (plus 1 with Marvin Gaye)
 7 Simon and Garfunkel
    (Paul Simon 6 more solo, Art Garfunkel 2 more solo)
 7 Smiths
    (Morrissey 3 more solo)
 7 Cat Stevens
 7 10 C.C.
    (plus 1 with Godley and Creme)
 7 Ultravox
 7 Whitesnake
 6 Shirley Bassey
 6 Eric Clapton
    (plus 1 with Cream)
 6 Russ Conway
 6 Neil Diamond
 6 Duran Duran
 6 Free
 6 Peter Gabriel
 6 Hollies
 6 Engelbert Humperdinck
 6 Jethro Tull
 6 Level 42
 6 Madness
 6 Barry Manilow
 6 Mantovani
 6 Marillion
 6 Gary Numan/Tubeway Army
 6 Roy Orbison
 6 Orchestral Manoeuvres In The Dark
 6 Police
 6 Leo Sayer
 6 Paul Simon
    (plus 6 with Simon and Garfunkel)
 6 Simple Minds
 6 Supremes
    (plus 1 with the Four Tops, 1 with Diana Ross and the Temptations)
 6 U2
 5 Herb Alpert
 5 Joan Armatrading
 5 Big Country
 5 Max Bygraves
 5 Johnny Cash
 5 Phil Collins
 5 Culture Club

383

5 John Denver
5 Val Doonican
5 Eagles
5 Echo and the Bunnymen
5 Duane Eddy
5 Everly Brothers
5 Bryan Ferry
  (plus 2 with Roxy Music)
5 Michael Jackson
  (plus 2 with Jacksons)
5 Jean-Michel Jarre
5 Billy Joel
5 Jack Jones
5 Kinks
5 James Last
5 Bob Marley and the Wailers
5 Meatloaf
5 New Order
5 Mike Oldfield
5 Pet Shop Boys
5 Rainbow
5 Santana
  (plus 1 with Mahavishnu John McLaughlin)

5 Showaddywaddy
5 Slade
5 Spandau Ballet
5 Bruce Springsteen
5 Barbra Streisand
5 Style Council
5 Supertramp
5 Tina Turner
5 Paul Young

Since the failure of Led Zeppelin's boxed CD set *Led Zeppelin* to make the Top Ten in 1990, no act has hit the chart ten times or more and taken every hit into the Top Ten. **Led Zeppelin** have now scored eleven Top Tens out of twelve tries. **Depeche Mode** have a 100% Top Ten album record, with nine out of nine, and **Dire Straits** have hit the Top Ten with each one of their eight albums.

Led Zeppelin

MOST HITS
WITHOUT A TOP TEN HIT

Only seven acts have had ten or more hit albums without ever reaching the Top Ten. They are **Tangerine Dream** (16 hits), **Foster and Allen** (13 hits), **Doors** (11 hits), **Public Image Ltd.** (11 hits), **Barclay James Harvest** (10 hits), **Fall** (10 hits) and **Alan Parsons Project** (10 hits). The Alan Parsons Project has never even hit the Top Twenty, their most successful album being their eighth hit, *Ammonia Avenue*, which reached number 24 in 1984.

James Last has hit the Top Ten only five times out of 55 chart entries, a hit-making career which includes a run of 31 consecutive hit albums (his second to 32nd hits inclusive) which all missed the Top Ten. **Neil Young** has so far clocked up 20 hit albums since his last Top Ten hit and **Hawkwind** have hit the charts 17 times since their last brief taste of Top Ten glory.

There were 57 compilation albums on the **Street Sounds** label totalling 269 weeks on the charts, but the highest placing for any of them was 12 by *Street Sounds Electro 7* in March 1985.

385

MOST HITS
WITHOUT A NUMBER ONE HIT

55	James Last (*who has had one no. 2 hit*)
29	Shirley Bassey (*who has had one no. 2 hit*)
29	Diana Ross (*who has had two no. 2 hits, and has hit number one twice with the Supremes and once with the Supremes and Temptations*)
26	Neil Diamond (*who has had one no. 2 hit*)
20	Hawkwind (*who have had one no. 9 hit*)
20	Santana (*who have had two no. 6 hits; Carlos Santana has made three hit albums with other partners, none of which hit the top*)
19	Jimi Hendrix (*who has had two no. 2 hits*)
18	Van Morrison (*whose biggest hit has reached no. 5*)
17	Eric Clapton (*who has had three no. 3 hits, but has hit number one as part of both of both Cream and Blind Faith*)
16	Herb Alpert (*who has had one no. 2 hit*)
16	Johnny Cash (*who has had one no. 2 hit*)
16	Stranglers (*who have had two no. 2 hits*)
16	Tangerine Dream (*whose biggest hit reached no. 12*)
15	Elvis Costello (*who has had two no. 2 hits*)
15	David Essex (*who has had one no. 2 hit*)
15	Stevie Wonder (*who has hit no. 2 three times*)

MOST ALBUMS ON THE CHART
IN ONE WEEK

Dire Straits' record total of 217 weeks on the chart in one year (1986) is the equivalent of an average of four albums in the Top 100 in every week of the year. Only four artists in the history of the albums chart have charted seven albums in one week, as follows:

14 albums in a chart of 60 . . . . Elvis Presley . . . . 10 Sep 1977
12 albums in a chart of 60 . . . . Elvis Presley . . . . 17 Sep 1977
11 albums in a chart of 60 . . . . Elvis Presley . . . . 1 Oct 1977
11 albums in a chart of 60 . . . . Elvis Presley . . . . 8 Oct 1977
10 albums in a chart of 100 . . . . David Bowie . . . . 16 July 1983
 9 albums in a chart of 60 . . . . Elvis Presley . . . . 24 Sep 1977
 9 albums in a chart of 100 . . . . David Bowie . . . . 11 Jun 1983
 9 albums in a chart of 100 . . . . David Bowie . . . . 9 Jul 1983
 8 albums in a chart of 20 . . . . Jim Reeves . . . . 26 Sep 1964
 8 albums in a chart of 100 . . . . David Bowie . . . . 27 Aug 1983
 7 albums in a chart of 20 . . . . Jim Reeves . . . . 29 Aug 1964
 7 albums in a chart of 20 . . . . Jim Reeves . . . . 5 Sep 1964
 7 albums in a chart of 20 . . . . Jim Reeves . . . . 3 Oct 1964
 7 albums in a chart of 20 . . . . Jim Reeves . . . . 10 Oct 1964
 7 albums in a chart of 60 . . . . Elvis Presley . . . . 15 Oct 1977
 7 albums in a chart of 100 . . . . David Bowie . . . . 14 May 1983
 7 albums in a chart of 100 . . . . David Bowie . . . . 21 May 1983
 7 albums in a chart of 100 . . . . David Bowie . . . . 28 May 1983
 7 albums in a chart of 100 . . . . David Bowie . . . . 4 Jun 1983
 7 albums in a chart of 100 . . . . David Bowie . . . . 18 Jun 1983
 7 albums in a chart of 100 . . . . David Bowie . . . . 30 Jul 1983
 7 albums in a chart of 100 . . . . David Bowie . . . . 20 Aug 1983
 7 albums in a chart of 100 . . . . Bruce Springsteen . . . . 15 Jun 1985
                         (nine consecutive weeks) to 10 Aug 1985

Of all these instances, only Elvis Presley on 10 September 1977 and Bruce Springsteen for four weeks from 6 July 1985 held the top spot. The most complete chart domination was by Jim Reeves on 26 September 1964, when he accounted for 40% of the albums chart. Bruce Springsteen's achievement in the summer of 1985 is the only example of an artist who has released as many as seven albums charting *all* his albums at once. In 1986, Dire Straits charted all six of their albums (one of which was a double album) for a total of twelve weeks. For seven of those weeks they held the number one spot.

LEAST SUCCESSFUL CHART ACT

Between 8 August 1981 and 14 January 1989, when the chart was a Top 100, eight acts achieved the minor distinction of a chart career consisting of only one week at no. 100. These acts, in chronological order, were:

17 Oct 81	Ronnie Laws	*Solid Ground*
17 Dec 83	Sleighriders	*A Very Merry Disco*
11 Feb 84	Europeans	*Live*
30 Jun 84	Wendy O. Williams	*WOW*
30 Mar 85	Second Image	*Strange Reflections*
12 Oct 85	Alien Sex Fiend	*Maximum Security*
29 Nov 86	Shop Assistants	*Shop Assistants*
3 Oct 87	Bolshoi	*Lindy's Party*

There is also a compilation album which lasted at no. 100 for just 1 week:

26 Nov 83	Various Artists	*Twelve Inches Of Pleasure*

Before 8 August 1981 and since 14 January 1989, 20 acts achieved the slightly less negative ultimate of one week of chart life on the bottom rung of a smaller chart:

			Chart Size
11 Jun 60	Bob Wallis and his Storyville Jazzmen	*Everybody Loves Saturday Night*	20
18 Jun 60	Shelley Manne	*My Fair Lady*	20
25 Jun 60	Knightsbridge Strings	*String Sway*	20
17 Dec 60	Big Ben Banjo Band	*More Minstrel Melodies*	20
24 Dec 60	New World Theatre Orchestra	*Let's Dance To The Hits Of The 30s and 40s*	20
14 Jul 62	Erroll Garner	*Close Up In Swing*	20
9 Feb 63	Spotnicks	*Out-A-Space*	20
18 Apr 64	Harry Secombe, Peter Sellers & Spike Milligan	*How To Win An Election*	20
20 Jun 64	Sonny Boy Williamson	*Down And Out Blues*	20
29 Jul 67	Manitas de Plata	*Flamenco Guitar*	40
22 Jun 68	Solomon King	*She Wears My Ring*	40
17 Aug 68	O.C. Smith	*Hickory Holler Revisited*	40
28 Feb 70	Bobbie Gentry & Glen Campbell	*Bobbie Gentry And Glen Campbell*	50
20 Jun 70	Moira Anderson	*These Are My Songs*	50
28 Nov 70	Savoy Brown	*Lookin' In*	50
13 Apr 74	Deke Leonard	*Kamikaze*	50
1 Apr 78	Culture	*Two Sevens Clash*	60
30 Sep 78	Cerrone	*Supernature*	60
18 Mar 89	Vow Wow	*Helter Skelter*	75
16 Jul 91	Fishbone	*The Reality Of My Surroundings*	75

Nine compilation albums have also spent just one week at the bottom of the smaller charts, as follows:

28 May 60	*'Pal Joey' Original Film Soundtrack*	20

23 Nov 63	....	*Hitsville Volume 2*	20
8 Feb 64	....	*Ready Steady Go!*	20
11 May 68	....	*Blues Anytime*	40
3 Nov 79	....	*Mods Mayday 79*	75
23 Dec 89	....	*Reggae Hits Volume 7*	20
17 Nov 90	....	*Karaoke Party*	20
20 Jul 91	....	*Breaks Bass and Bleeps*	20
28 Dec 91	....	*Trivial Pursuit – The Music Master Game*	20

(The last four albums were listed on the compilation chart only)

The ADICTS spent one week at number 99 with their only hit album, *The Sound of Music*, and one week on the bottom rung, number 75, with their only hit single, *Bad Boy*. This is the nearest to the ultimate least successful chart double so far.

Moira Anderson

THE NUMBER ONE ALBUMS
8 NOVEMBER 1958 TO 28 DECEMBER 1991

There have been 426 albums which have topped the charts in the 33 years since it was first compiled. In the first ten years of the albums charts, only 44 albums headed the lists, but over the past ten years there have been more number one albums than singles. The full list is as follows:

		Weeks
8 Nov 58	South Pacific *Film Soundtrack (RCA)*	70
12 Mar 60	The Explosive Freddy Cannon *Freddy Cannon (Top Rank)*	1
19 Mar 60	South Pacific *Film Soundtrack (RCA)*	19
30 Jul 60	Elvis Is Back *Elvis Presley (RCA)*	1
6 Aug 60	South Pacific *Film Soundtrack (RCA)*	5
10 Sep 60	Down Drury Lane To Memory Lane *101 Strings (Pye)*	5
15 Oct 60	South Pacific *Film Soundtrack (RCA)*	13
14 Jan 61	GI Blues *Elvis Presley (RCA)*	7
4 Mar 61	South Pacific *Film Soundtrack (RCA)*	1
11 Mar 61	GI Blues *Elvis Presley (RCA)*	3
1 Apr 61	South Pacific *Film Soundtrack (RCA)*	1
8 Apr 61	GI Blues *Elvis Presley (RCA)*	12
1 Jul 61	South Pacific *Film Soundtrack (RCA)*	4
29 Jul 61	Black And White Minstrel Show *George Mitchell Minstrels (HMV)*	4
26 Aug 61	South Pacific *Film Soundtrack (RCA)*	1
2 Sep 61	Black and White Minstrel Show *George Mitchell Minstrels (HMV)*	1
9 Sep 61	South Pacific *Film Soundtrack (RCA)*	1
16 Sep 61	Black And White Minstrel Show *George Mitchell Minstrels (HMV)*	1
23 Sep 61	The Shadows *Shadows (Columbia)*	4
21 Oct 61	Black And White Minstrel Show *George Mitchell Minstrels (HMV)*	1
28 Oct 61	The Shadows *Shadows (Columbia)*	1
4 Nov 61	21 Today *Cliff Richard (Columbia)*	1
11 Nov 61	Another Black And White Minstrel Show *George Mitchell Minstrels (HMV)*	8
6 Jan 62	Blue Hawaii *Elvis Presley (RCA)*	1
13 Jan 62	The Young Ones *Cliff Richard (Columbia)*	6
24 Feb 62	Blue Hawaii *Elvis Presley (RCA)*	17
23 Jun 62	West Side Story *Film Soundtrack (Philips/CBS)*	5
28 Jul 62	Pot Luck *Elvis Presley (RCA)*	5
1 Sep 62	West Side Story *Film Soundtrack (CBS)*	1
8 Sep 62	Pot Luck *Elvis Presley (RCA)*	1
15 Sep 62	West Side Story *Film Soundtrack (CBS)*	1
22 Sep 62	The Best Of Ball, Barber and Bilk *Kenny Ball, Chris Barber and Acker Bilk (Pye)*	1
29 Sep 62	West Side Story *Film Soundtrack (CBS)*	3

389

20 Oct 62 The Best Of Ball, Barber and Bilk
           Kenny Ball, Chris Barber and Acker Bilk (Pye) 1
27 Oct 62 Out Of The Shadows *Shadows (Columbia)* 3
17 Nov 62 West Side Story *Film Soundtrack (CBS)* 1
24 Nov 62 Out Of The Shadows *Shadows (Columbia)* 1
 1 Dec 62 On Stage With The Black And White Minstrels
           George Mitchell Minstrels (HMV) 2
15 Dec 62 West Side Story *Film Soundtrack (CBS)* 1
22 Dec 62 Out Of The Shadows *Shadows (Columbia)* 1
29 Dec 62 Black And White Minstrel Show
           George Mitchell Minstrels (HMV) 2

12 Jan 63 West Side Story *Film Soundtrack (CBS)* 1
19 Jan 63 Out Of The Shadows *Shadows (Columbia)* 2
 2 Feb 63 Summer Holiday *Cliff Richard and the Shadows (Columbia)* 14
11 May 63 Please Please Me *Beatles (Parlophone)* 30
 7 Dec 63 With The Beatles *Beatles (Parlophone)* 21

 2 May 64 Rolling Stones *Rolling Stones (Decca)* 12
25 Jul 64 A Hard Day's Night *Beatles (Parlophone)* 21
19 Dec 64 Beatles For Sale *Beatles (Parlophone)* 7

 6 Feb 65 Rolling Stones No. 2 *Rolling Stones (Decca)* 3
27 Feb 65 Beatles For Sale *Beatles (Parlophone)* 1
 6 Mar 65 Rolling Stones No. 2 *Rolling Stones (Decca)* 6
17 Apr 65 Freewheelin' Bob Dylan *Bob Dylan (CBS)* 1
24 Apr 65 Rolling Stones No. 2 *Rolling Stones (Decca)* 1
 1 May 65 Beatles For Sale *Beatles (Parlophone)* 3
22 May 65 Freewheelin' Bob Dylan *Bob Dylan (CBS)* 1
29 May 65 Bringing It All Back Home *Bob Dylan (CBS)* 1
 5 Jun 65 The Sound Of Music *Soundtrack (RCA)* 10
14 Aug 65 Help *Beatles (Parlophone)* 9
16 Oct 65 The Sound Of Music *Soundtrack (RCA)* 10
25 Dec 65 Rubber Soul *Beatles (Parlophone)* 9

19 Feb 66 The Sound Of Music *Soundtrack (RCA)* 10
30 Apr 66 Aftermath *Rolling Stones (Decca)* 8
25 Jun 66 The Sound Of Music *Soundtrack (RCA)* 7
13 Aug 66 Revolver *Beatles (Parlophone)* 7
 1 Oct 66 The Sound Of Music *Soundtrack (RCA)* 18

 4 Feb 67 Monkees *Monkees (RCA)* 7
25 Mar 67 The Sound Of Music *Soundtrack (RCA)* 7
13 May 67 More Of The Monkees *Monkees (RCA)* 1
20 May 67 The Sound Of Music *Soundtrack (RCA)* 1
27 May 67 More Of The Monkees *Monkees (RCA)* 1
 3 Jun 67 The Sound Of Music *Soundtrack (RCA)* 1
10 Jun 67 Sergeant Pepper's Lonely Hearts Club Band
           Beatles (Parlophone) 23
18 Nov 67 The Sound Of Music *Soundtrack (RCA)* 1
25 Nov 67 Sergeant Pepper's Lonely Hearts Club Band
           Beatles (Parlophone) 1
 2 Dec 67 The Sound Of Music *Soundtrack (RCA)* 3

The Beatles

Jethro Tull

24 Oct 70   Atom Heart Mother   *Pink Floyd (Harvest)* 1
31 Oct 70   Motown Chartbusters Vol. 4   *Various (Tamla Motown)* 1
7 Nov 70   Led Zeppelin 3   *Led Zeppelin (Atlantic)* 3
28 Nov 70   New Morning   *Bob Dylan (CBS)* 1
5 Dec 70   Greatest Hits   *Andy Williams (CBS)* 1
12 Dec 70   Led Zeppelin 3   *Led Zeppelin (Atlantic)* 1
19 Dec 70   Greatest Hits   *Andy Williams (CBS)* 4

16 Jan 71†   Bridge Over Troubled Water   *Simon and Garfunkel (CBS)* . . . 11
3 Apr 71   Home Loving Man   *Andy Williams (CBS)* 2
17 Apr 71   Motown Chartbusters Vol. 5   *Various (Tamla Motown)* 3
8 May 71   Sticky Fingers   *Rolling Stones (Rolling Stones)* 4
5 Jun 71   Ram   *Paul and Linda McCartney (Apple)* 2
19 Jun 71   Sticky Fingers   *Rolling Stones (Rolling Stones)* 1
26 Jun 71   Tarkus   *Emerson, Lake and Palmer (Island)* 1
3 Jul 71   Bridge Over Troubled Water   *Simon and Garfunkel (CBS)* 5
7 Aug 71   Hot Hits 6   *Various (MFP)* 1
14 Aug 71   Every Good Boy Deserves Favour   *Moody Blues (Threshold)* 1
21 Aug 71   Top Of The Pops Vol. 18   *Various (Hallmark)* 3
11 Sep 71   Bridge Over Troubled Water   *Simon and Garfunkel (CBS)* 1
18 Sep 71   Who's Next   *Who (Track)* 1
25 Sep 71   Fireball   *Deep Purple (Harvest)* 1
2 Oct 71   Every Picture Tells A Story   *Rod Stewart (Mercury)* 4
30 Oct 71   Imagine   *John Lennon/Plastic Ono Band (Apple)* 2
13 Nov 71   Every Picture Tells A Story   *Rod Stewart (Mercury)* 2
27 Nov 71   Top Of The Pops Vol. 20   *Various (Hallmark)* 1
4 Dec 71   Four Symbols   *Led Zeppelin (Atlantic)* 2
18 Dec 71   Electric Warrior   *T. Rex (Fly)* 6

29 Jan 72   Concert For Bangladesh   *Various (Apple)* 1
5 Feb 72   Electric Warrior   *T. Rex (Fly)* 2
19 Feb 72   Neil Reid   *(Decca)* 3
11 Mar 72   Harvest   *Neil Young (Reprise)* 1
18 Mar 72   Paul Simon   *Paul Simon (CBS)* 1
25 Mar 72   Fog On The Tyne   *Lindisfarne (Charisma)* 4
22 Apr 72   Machine Head   *Deep Purple (Purple)* 2
6 May 72   Prophets, Seers And Sages And The Angels Of The Ages/
               My People Were Fair And Had Sky In Their Hair But Now
               They're Content To Wear Stars On Their Brows
               Tyrannosaurus Rex (Fly Double Back) 1
13 May 72   Machine Head   *Deep Purple (Purple)* 1
20 May 72   Bolan Boogie   *T. Rex (Fly)* 3
10 Jun 72   Exile On Main Street   *Rolling Stones (Rolling Stones)* 1
17 Jun 72   20 Dynamic Hits   *Various (K-Tel)* 8
12 Aug 72   20 Fantastic Hits   *Various (Arcade)* 5
16 Sep 72   Never A Dull Moment   *Rod Stewart (Philips)* 2
30 Sep 72   20 Fantastic Hits   *Various (Arcade)* 1
7 Oct 72   20 All Time Hits Of The Fifties   *Various (K-Tel)* 8
2 Dec 72   25 Rockin' And Rollin' Greats   *Various (K-Tel)* 3
23 Dec 72   20 All Time Hits Of The Fifties   *Various (K-Tel)* 3

† This includes 8 weeks at number one when charts were not published due to a
postal strike.

13 Jan 73 Slayed? *Slade (Polydor)* 1
20 Jan 73 Back To Front *Gilbert O'Sullivan (MAM)* 1
27 Jan 73 Slayed? *Slade (Polydor)* 2
10 Feb 73 Don't Shoot Me, I'm Only The Piano Player*Elton John (DJM)* . . 6
24 Mar 73 Billion Dollar Babies *Alice Cooper (Warner Bros.)* 1
31 Mar 73 20 Flashback Great Hits Of The Sixties *Various (K-Tel)* 2
14 Apr 73 Houses Of The Holy *Led Zeppelin (Atlantic)* 2
28 Apr 73 Ooh La La *Faces (Warner Bros.)* 1
5 May 73 Aladdin Sane *David Bowie (RCA Victor)* 5
9 Jun 73 Pure Gold *Various (EMI)* 3
30 Jun 73 That'll Be The Day *Various (Ronco)* 7
18 Aug 73 We Can Make It *Peters and Lee (Philips)* 2
1 Sep 73 Sing It Again *Rod Stewart (Mercury)* 3
22 Sep 73 Goat's Head Soup *Rolling Stones (Rolling Stones)* 2
6 Oct 73 Sladest *Slade (Polydor)* *3*
27 Oct 73 Hello *Status Quo (Vertigo)* 1
3 Nov 73 Pin Ups *David Bowie (RCA)* 5
8 Dec 73 Stranded *Roxy Music (Island)* 1
15 Dec 73 Dreams Are Nothin' More Than Wishes
  David Cassidy (Bell) 1
22 Dec 73 Goodbye Yellow Brick Road *Elton John (DJM)* 2

5 Jan 74 Tales From Topographic Oceans *Yes (Atlantic)* 2
19 Jan 74 Sladest *Slade (Polydor)* 1
26 Jan 74 And I Love You So *Perry Como (RCA)* 1
2 Feb 74 The Singles 1969–73 *Carpenters (A & M)* 4
2 Mar 74 Old, New, Borrowed And Blue *Slade (Polydor)* 1
9 Mar 74 The Singles 1969–73 *Carpenters (A & M)* 11
25 May 74 Journey To The Centre Of The Earth
  Rick Wakeman (A & M) 1
1 Jun 74 The Singles 1969–73 *Carpenters (A & M)* 1
8 Jun 74 Diamond Dogs *David Bowie (RCA)* 4
6 Jul 74 The Singles 1969–73 *Carpenters (A & M)* 1
13 Jul 74 Caribou *Elton John (DJM)* 2
27 Jul 74 Band On The Run *Wings (Apple)* 7
14 Sep 74 Hergest Ridge *Mike Oldfield (Virgin)* 3
5 Oct 74 Tubular Bells *Mike Oldfield (Virgin)* 1
12 Oct 74 Rollin' *Bay City Rollers (Bell)* 1
19 Oct 74 Smiler *Rod Stewart (Mercury)* 1
26 Oct 74 Rollin' *Bay City Rollers (Bell)* 1
2 Nov 74 Smiler *Rod Stewart (Mercury)* 1
9 Nov 74 Rollin' *Bay City Rollers (Bell)* 2
23 Nov 74 Elton John's Greatest Hits *Elton John (DJM)* 11

8 Feb 75 His Greatest Hits *Engelbert Humperdinck (Decca)* 3
1 Mar 75 On The Level *Status Quo (Vertigo)* 2
15 Mar 75 Physical Graffiti *Led Zeppelin (Swansong)* 1
22 Mar 75 20 Greatest Hits *Tom Jones (Decca)* 4
19 Apr 75 The Best Of The Stylistics *Stylistics (Avco)* 2
3 May 75 Once Upon A Star *Bay City Rollers (Bell)* 3
24 May 75 The Best Of The Stylistics *Stylistics (Avco)* 5
28 Jun 75 Venus And Mars *Wings (Apple)* 1

395

Leo Sayer

30 Oct 76 Soul Motion *Various (K-Tel)* 2
13 Nov 76 The Song Remains The Same *Led Zeppelin (Swansong)* 1
20 Nov 76 22 Golden Guitar Greats *Bert Weedon (Warwick)* 1
27 Nov 76 20 Golden Greats *Glen Campbell (Capitol)* 6

8 Jan 77 Day At The Races *Queen (EMI)* 1
15 Jan 77 Arrival *Abba (Epic)* 1
22 Jan 77 Red River Valley *Slim Whitman (United Artists)* 4
19 Feb 77 20 Golden Greats *Shadows (EMI)* 6
2 Apr 77 Portrait *Frank Sinatra (Reprise)* 2
16 Apr 77 Arrival *Abba (Epic)* 9
18 Jun 77 Live At The Hollywood Bowl *Beatles (Parlophone)* 1
25 Jun 77 The Muppet Show *Muppets (Pye)* 1
2 Jul 77 A Star Is Born *Soundtrack (CBS)* 2
16 Jul 77 Johnny Mathis Collection *Johnny Mathis (CBS)* 4
13 Aug 77 Going For The One *Yes (Atlantic)* 2
27 Aug 77 20 All Time Greats *Connie Francis (Polydor)* 2
10 Sep 77 Elvis Presley's 40 Greatest Hits *Elvis Presley (Arcade)* 1
17 Sep 77 20 Golden Greats
           Diana Ross and the Supremes (Tamla Motown) 7
5 Nov 77 40 Golden Greats *Cliff Richard (EMI)* 1
12 Nov 77 Never Mind The Bollocks Here's The Sex Pistols
           Sex Pistols (Virgin) 2
26 Nov 77 Sound Of Bread *Bread (Elektra)* 2
10 Dec 77 Disco Fever *Various (K-Tel)* 6

396

21 Jan 78 The Sound Of Bread *Bread (Elektra)* 1
28 Jan 78 Rumours *Fleetwood Mac (Warner Bros.)* 1
4 Feb 78 The Album *Abba (Epic)* 7
25 Mar 78 20 Golden Greats *Buddy Holly/Crickets (MCA)* 3
15 Apr 78 20 Golden Greats *Nat King Cole (Capitol)* 3
6 May 78 Saturday Night Fever *Various (RSO)* 18
9 Sep 78 Night Flight To Venus *Boney M (Atlantic/Hansa)* 4
7 Oct 78 Grease *Soundtrack (RSO)* 13

6 Jan 79 Greatest Hits *Showaddywaddy (Arista)* 2
26 Jan 79 Don't Walk – Boogie *Various (EMI)* 3
10 Feb 79 Action Replay *Various (K-Tel)* 1
17 Feb 79 Parallel Lines *Blondie (Chrysalis)* 4
17 Mar 79 Spirits Having Flown *Bee Gees (RSO)* 2
31 Mar 79 Greatest Hits Vol. 2 *Barbra Streisand (CBS)* 4
28 Apr 79 The Very Best Of Leo Sayer *Leo Sayer (Chrysalis)* 3
19 May 79 Voulez-Vous *Abba (Epic)* 4
16 Jun 79 Discovery *Electric Light Orchestra (Jet)* 5
21 Jul 79 Replicas *Tubeway Army (Beggars Banquet)* 1
28 Jul 79 The Best Disco Album In The World *Various (Warner Bros.)* . . . 6
8 Sep 79 In Through The Out Door *Led Zeppelin (Swansong)* 2
22 Sep 79 The Pleasure Principle *Gary Numan (Beggars Banquet)* 1
29 Sep 79 Oceans Of Fantasy *Boney M (Atlantic/Hansa)* 1
6 Oct 79 The Pleasure Principle *Gary Numan (Beggars Banquet)* 1
13 Oct 79* Eat To The Beat *Blondie (Chrysalis)* 1
13 Oct 79* Reggatta De Blanc *Police (A & M)* 4

* Two charts published this week because of a change in chart collation.

10 Nov 79 Tusk *Fleetwood Mac (Warner Bros.)* 1
17 Nov 79 Greatest Hits Vol. 2 *Abba (Epic)* 3
8 Dec 79 Greatest Hits *Rod Stewart (Riva)* 5

12 Jan 80 Greatest Hits Vol. 2 *Abba (Epic)* 1
19 Jan 80 Pretenders *Pretenders (Real)* 4
16 Feb 80 The Last Dance *Various (Motown)* 2
1 Mar 80 String Of Hits *Shadows (EMI)* 3
22 Mar 80 Tears And Laughter *Johnny Mathis (CBS)* 2
5 Apr 80 Duke *Genesis (Charisma)* 2
19 Apr 80 Greatest Hits *Rose Royce (Whitfield)* 2
3 May 80 Sky 2 *Sky (Ariola)* 2
17 May 80 The Magic Of Boney M *Boney M (Atlantic/Hansa)* 2
31 May 80 McCartney II *Paul McCartney (Parlophone)* 2
14 Jun 80 Peter Gabriel *Peter Gabriel (Charisma)* 2
28 Jun 80 Flesh And Blood *Roxy Music (Polydor)* 1
5 Jul 80 Emotional Rescue *Rolling Stones (Rolling Stones)* 2
19 Jul 80 The Game *Queen (EMI)* 2
2 Aug 80 Deepest Purple *Deep Purple (Harvest)* 1
9 Aug 80 Back In Black *AC/DC (Atlantic)* 2
23 Aug 80 Flesh And Blood *Roxy Music (Polydor)* 3
13 Sep 80 Telekon *Gary Numan (Beggars Banquet)* 1
20 Sep 80 Never For Ever *Kate Bush (EMI)* 1
27 Sep 80 Scary Monsters And Supercreeps *David Bowie (RCA)* 2
11 Oct 80 Zenyatta Mondatta *Police (A & M)* 4
8 Nov 80 Guilty *Barbra Streisand (CBS)* 2
22 Nov 80 Super Trouper *Abba (Epic)* 9

397

24 Jan 81 Kings Of The Wild Frontier *Adam and the Ants (CBS)* 2
7 Feb 81 Double Fantasy *John Lennon (Geffen)* 2
21 Feb 81 Face Value *Phil Collins (Virgin)* 3
14 Mar 81 Kings Of The Wild Frontier *Adam and the Ants (CBS)* 10
23 May 81 Stars On 45 *Starsound (CBS)* 5
27 Jun 81 No Sleep Til Hammersmith *Motorhead (Bronze)* 1
4 Jul 81 Disco Daze & Disco Nites *Various (Ronco)* 1
11 Jul 81 Love Songs *Cliff Richard (EMI)* 5
15 Aug 81 The Official BBC Album Of The Royal Wedding
           Soundtrack *(BBC)*. 2
29 Aug 81 Time *Electric Light Orchestra (Jet)* 2
12 Sep 81 Dead Ringer *Meat Loaf (Epic)* 2
26 Sep 81 Abacab *Genesis (Charisma)* 2
10 Oct 81 Ghost In The Machine *Police (A & M)* 3
31 Oct 81 Dare *Human League (Virgin)* 1
7 Nov 81 Shaky *Shakin' Stevens (Epic)* 1
14 Nov 81 Greatest Hits *Queen (EMI)* 4
12 Dec 81 Chart Hits '81 *Various (K-Tel)* 1
19 Dec 81 The Visitors *Abba (Epic)* 3

9 Jan 82 Dare *Human League (Virgin)* 3
30 Jan 82 Love Songs *Barbra Streisand (CBS)* 7
20 Mar 82 The Gift *Jam (Polydor)* 1
27 Mar 82 Love Songs *Barbra Streisand (CBS)* 2

Howard Jones

Date	Title	Artist	Weeks
10 Apr 82	The Number Of The Beast *Iron Maiden (EMI)*		2
24 Apr 82	1982 *Status Quo (Vertigo)*		1
1 May 82	Barry Live In Britain *Barry Manilow (Arista)*		1
8 May 82	Tug Of War *Paul McCartney (Parlophone)*		2
22 May 82	Complete Madness *Madness (Stiff)*		2
5 Jun 82	Avalon *Roxy Music (Polydor)*		1
12 Jun 82	Complete Madness *Madness (Stiff)*		1
19 Jun 82	Avalon *Roxy Music (Polydor)*		2
3 Jul 82	The Lexicon Of Love *ABC (Neutron)*		3
24 Jul 82	=The Lexicon Of Love *ABC (Neutron)*		1
	=Fame *Original Soundtrack (RSO)*		1
31 Jul 82	Fame *Original Soundtrack (RSO)*		1
7 Aug 82	Kids From Fame *Kids from Fame (BBC)*		8
2 Oct 82	Love Over Gold *Dire Straits (Vertigo)*		4
30 Oct 82	Kids From Fame *Kids from Fame (BBC)*		4
27 Nov 82	The Singles—The First Ten Years *Abba (Epic)*		1
4 Dec 82	The John Lennon Collection *John Lennon (Parlophone)*		6
15 Jan 83	Raiders Of The Pop Charts *Various Artists (Ronco)*		2
29 Jan 83	Business As Usual *Men At Work (Epic)*		5
5 Mar 83	Thriller *Michael Jackson (Epic)*		1
12 Mar 83	War *U2 (Island)*		1
19 Mar 83	Thriller *Michael Jackson (Epic)*		1
26 Mar 83	The Hurting *Tears For Fears (Mercury)*		1
2 Apr 83	The Final Cut *Pink Floyd (Harvest)*		2
16 Apr 83	Faster Than The Speed Of Night *Bonnie Tyler (CBS)*		1
23 Apr 83	Let's Dance *David Bowie (EMI America)*		3
14 May 83	True *Spandau Ballet (Reformation)*		1
21 May 83	Thriller *Michael Jackson (Epic)*		5
25 Jun 83	Synchronicity *Police (A & M)*		2
9 Jul 83	Fantastic! *Wham! (Inner Vision)*		2
23 Jul 83	You And Me Both *Yazoo (Mute)*		2

6 Aug 83 The Very Best Of The Beach Boys *Beach Boys (Capitol)* 2
20 Aug 83 18 Greatest Hits *Michael Jackson plus the Jackson Five (Telstar)* . . . 3
10 Sep 83 The Very Best Of The Beach Boys *Beach Boys (Capitol)* 1
17 Sep 83 No Parlez *Paul Young (CBS)* 1
24 Sep 83 Labour Of Love *UB 40 (DEP International)* 1
1 Oct 83 No Parlez *Paul Young (CBS)* 2
15 Oct 83 Genesis *Genesis (Charisma/Virgin)* 1
22 Oct 83 Colour By Numbers *Culture Club (Virgin)* 3
12 Nov 83 Can't Slow Down *Lionel Richie (Motown)* 1
19 Nov 83 Colour By Numbers *Culture Club (Virgin)* 2
3 Dec 83 Seven And The Ragged Tiger *Duran Duran (EMI)* 1
10 Dec 83 No Parlez *Paul Young (CBS)* 1
17 Dec 83 Now! That's What I Call Music *Various Artists (EMI/Virgin)* . . 4

14 Jan 84 No Parlez *Paul Young (CBS)* 1
21 Jan 84 Now! That's What I Call Music *Various Artists (EMI/Virgin)* . . 1
28 Jan 84 Thriller *Michael Jackson (Epic)* 1
4 Feb 84 Touch *Eurythmics (RCA)* 2
18 Feb 84 Sparkle In The Rain *Simple Minds (Virgin)* 1
25 Feb 84 Into The Gap *Thompson Twins (Arista)* 3
17 Mar 84 Human's Lib *Howard Jones (WEA)* 2
31 Mar 84 Can't Slow Down *Lionel Richie (Motown)* 2
14 Apr 84 Now! That's What I Call Music 2
　　　　　Various Artists (EMI/Virgin) 5
19 May 84 Legend *Bob Marley and the Wailers (Island)* 12
11 Aug 84 Now! That's What I Call Music 3
　　　　　Various Artists (EMI/Virgin) 8
6 Oct 84 Tonight *David Bowie (EMI America)* 1
13 Oct 84 The Unforgettable Fire *U2 (Island)* 2
27 Oct 84 Steeltown *Big Country (Mercury)* 1
3 Nov 84 Give My Regards To Broad Street
　　　　　Paul McCartney (Parlophone) 1
10 Nov 84 Welcome To The Pleasure Dome
　　　　　Frankie Goes To Hollywood (ZTT) 1
17 Nov 84 Make It Big *Wham! (Epic)* 2
1 Dec 84 The Hits Album/The Hits Tape
　　　　　Various Artists (CBS/WEA) 7

19 Jan 85 Alf *Alison Moyet (CBS)* 1
26 Jan 85 Agent Provocateur *Foreigner (Atlantic)* 3
16 Feb 85 Born In The U.S.A. *Bruce Springsteen (CBS)* 1
23 Feb 85 Meat Is Murder *Smiths (Rough Trade)* 1
2 Mar 85 No Jacket Required *Phil Collins (Virgin)* 5
6 Apr 85 The Secret Of Association *Paul Young (CBS)* 1
13 Apr 85 The Hits Album 2/The Hits Tape 2
　　　　　Various Artists (CBS/WEA) 6
25 May 85 Brothers In Arms *Dire Straits (Vertigo)* 2
8 Jun 85 Our Favourite Shop *Style Council (Polydor)* 1
15 Jun 85 Boys And Girls *Bryan Ferry (EG)* 2
29 Jun 85 Misplaced Childhood *Marillion (EMI)* 1
6 Jul 85 Born In The U.S.A. *Bruce Springsteen (CBS)* 4
3 Aug 85 Brothers In Arms *Dire Straits (Vertigo)* 2

399

17 Aug 85 Now! That's What I Call Music 5
Various Artists (EMI/Virgin) 5
21 Sep 85 Like A Virgin *Madonna (Sire)* 1
28 Sep 85 Hounds Of Love *Kate Bush (EMI)* 2
12 Oct 85 Like A Virgin *Madonna (Sire)* 1
19 Oct 85 Hounds Of Love *Kate Bush (EMI)* 1
26 Oct 85 The Love Songs *George Benson (K-Tel)* 1
2 Nov 85 Once Upon A Time *Simple Minds (Virgin)* 1
9 Nov 85 The Love Songs *George Benson (K-Tel)* 1
16 Nov 85 Promise *Sade (Epic)* 2
30 Nov 85 The Greatest Hits Of 1985 *Various Artists (Telstar)* 1
7 Dec 85 Now! That's What I Call Music 6
Various Artists (EMI/Virgin) 2
21 Dec 85 Now! – The Christmas Album *Various Artists (EMI/Virgin)* . . . 2

4 Jan 86 Now! That's What I Call Music 6
Various Artists (EMI/Virgin) 2
18 Jan 86 Brothers In Arms *Dire Straits (Vertigo)* 10
29 Mar 86 Hits 4 *Various Artists (CBS/WEA/RCA Ariola)* 4
26 Apr 86 Street Life – 20 Great Hits *Bryan Ferry/Roxy Music (EG)* 5
31 May 86 So *Peter Gabriel (Virgin)* 2
14 Jun 86 A Kind Of Magic *Queen (EMI)* 1
21 Jun 86 Invisible Touch *Genesis (Charisma)* 3
12 Jul 86 True Blue *Madonna (Sire)* 6
23 Aug 86 Now! That's What I Call Music 7
Various Artists (EMI/Virgin) 5
27 Sep 86 Silk And Steel *Five Star (Tent)* 1
4 Oct 86 Graceland *Paul Simon (Warner Bros.)* 5
8 Nov 86 Every Breath You Take – The Singles *Police (A & M)* 2
22 Nov 86 Hits 5 *Various Artists (CBS/WEA/RCA Ariola)* 2
6 Dec 86 Now! That's What I Call Music 8
Various Artists (EMI/Virgin) 6

17 Jan 87 The Whole Story *Kate Bush (EMI)* 2
31 Jan 87 Graceland *Paul Simon (Warner Bros.)* 3
21 Feb 87 Phantom Of The Opera *Original London Cast (Polydor)* 3
14 Mar 87 The Very Best Of Hot Chocolate *Hot Chocolate (RAK)* 1
21 Mar 87 The Joshua Tree *U2 (Island)* 2
4 Apr 87 Now! That's What I Call Music 9
Various Artists (EMI/Virgin/Phonogram) 5
9 May 87 Keep Your Distance *Curiosity Killed The Cat (Mercury)* 2
23 May 87 It's Better To Travel *Swing Out Sister (Mercury)* 2
6 Jun 87 Live In The City Of Light *Simple Minds (Virgin)* 1
13 Jun 87 Whitney *Whitney Houston (Arista)* 6
25 Jul 87 Introducing The Hardline According To Terence Trent
D'Arby *Terence Trent D'Arby (CBS)* 1
1 Aug 87 Hits 6 *Various Artists (CBS/WEA/BMG)* 4
29 Aug 87 Hysteria *Def Leppard (Bludgeon Riffola)* 1
5 Sep 87 Hits 6 *Various Artists (CBS/WEA/BMG)* 1
12 Sep 87 Bad *Michael Jackson (Epic)* 5
17 Oct 87 Tunnel Of Love *Bruce Springsteen (CBS)* 1
24 Oct 87 Nothing Like The Sun *Sting (A & M)* 1
31 Oct 87 Tango In The Night *Fleetwood Mac (Warner Bros.)* 2

400

Deacon Blue

401

7 Jan 89 Now! That's What I Call Music 13
   Various Artists (EMI/Virgin/Polygram) 1

(From 14 January 1989, compilation albums were excluded from the main chart)

14 Jan 89 The Innocents *Erasure (Mute)* 1

21 Jan 89 The Legendary Roy Orbison *Roy Orbison (Telstar)* 3

11 Feb 89 Technique *New Order (Factory)* 1

18 Feb 89 The Raw And The Cooked *Fine Young Cannibals (London)* 1

25 Feb 89 A New Flame *Simply Red (Elektra)* 4

25 Mar 89 Anything For You
   Gloria Estefan and Miami Sound Machine (Epic) 1

1 Apr 89 Like A Prayer *Madonna (Sire)* 2

15 Apr 89 When The World Knows Your Name *Deacon Blue (CBS)* 2

29 Apr 89 A New Flame *Simply Red (Elektra)* 1

6 May 89 Blast *Holly Johnson (MCA)* 1

13 May 89 Street Fighting Years *Simple Minds (Virgin)* 1

20 May 89 Ten Good Reasons *Jason Donovan (PWL)* 2

3 Jun 89 The Miracle *Queen (Parlophone)* 1

10 Jun 89 Ten Good Reasons *Jason Donovan (PWL)* 2

24 Jun 89 Flowers In The Dirt *Paul McCartney (Parlophone)* 1

1 Jul 89 Batman *Prince (Warner Bros.)* 1

8 Jul 89 Velveteen *Transvision Vamp (MCA)* 1

15 Jul 89 Club Classics Volume One *Soul II Soul (10)* 1

22 Jul 89 A New Flame *Simply Red (Elektra)* 2

5 Aug 89 Cuts Both Ways *Gloria Estefan (Epic)* 6

16 Sep 89 Aspects Of Love *Original London Cast (Polydor)* 1

23 Sep 89 We Too Are One *Eurythmics (RCA)* 1

30 Sep 89 Foreign Affair *Tina Turner (Capitol)* 1

7 Oct 89 The Seeds Of Love *Tears For Fears (Fontana)* 1

14 Oct 89 Crossroads *Tracy Chapman (Elektra)* 1

21 Oct 89 Enjoy Yourself *Kylie Minogue (PWL)* 1

28 Oct 89 Wild! *Erasure (Mute)* 2

11 Nov 89 The Road To Hell *Chris Rea (WEA)* 3

2 Dec 89 ... But Seriously *Phil Collins (Virgin)* 8

27 Jan 90 Colour *Christians (Island)* 1

3 Feb 90 ... But Seriously *Phil Collins (Virgin)* 7

24 Mar 90 I Do Not Want What I Haven't Got
   Sinead O'Connor (Ensign) 1

31 Mar 90 Changesbowie *David Bowie (EMI)* 1

7 Apr 90 Only Yesterday *Carpenters (A & M)* 2

21 Apr 90 Behind The Mask *Fleetwood Mac (Warner Brothers)* 1

28 Apr 90 Only Yesterday *Carpenters (A & M)* 5

2 Jun 90 Vol II (1990 A New Decade) *Soul II Soul (10)* 3

23 Jun 90 The Essential Pavarotti *Luciano Pavarotti (Decca)* 1

30 Jun 90 Step By Step *New Kids On The Block (CBS)* 1

7 Jul 90 The Essential Pavarotti *Luciano Pavarotti (Decca)* 3

28 Jul 90 Sleeping With The Past *Elton John (Rocket)* 5

1 Sep 90 Graffiti Bridge *Prince (Paisley Park)* 1

8 Sep 90 In Concert *Luciano Pavarotti, Placido Domingo and
   José Carreras (Decca)* 1

15 Sep 90 Listen Without Prejudice Vol. 1 *George Michael (Epic)* 1

22 Sep 90	In Concert *Luciano Pavarotti, Placido Domingo and José Carreras (Decca)*	4
20 Oct 90	Some Friendly *Charlatans (Situation Two)*	1
27 Oct 90	The Rhythm Of The Saints *Paul Simon (Warner Brothers)*	2
10 Nov 90	The Very Best Of Elton John *Elton John (Rocket)*	2
24 Nov 90	The Immaculate Collection *Madonna (Sire)*	9
26 Jan 91	MCMXC AD *Enigma (Virgin International)*	1
2 Feb 91	The Soul Cages *Sting (A & M)*	1
9 Feb 90	Doubt *Jesus Jones (Food)*	1
16 Feb 91	Innuendo *Queen (Parlophone)*	2
2 Mar 91	Circle Of One *Oleta Adams (Fontana)*	1
9 Mar 91	Auberge *Chris Rea (East West)*	1
16 Mar 91	Spartacus *Farm (Produce)*	1
23 Mar 91	Out Of Time *R.E.M. (Warner Brothers)*	1
30 Mar 91	Greatest Hits *Eurythmics (RCA)*	9
1 Jun 91	Seal *Seal (ZTT)*	3
22 Jun 91	Greatest Hits *Eurythmics (RCA)*	1
29 Jun 91	Love Hurts *Cher (Geffen)*	6
10 Aug 91	The Essential Pavarotti II *Luciano Pavarotti (Decca)*	2
24 Aug 91	Metallica *Metallica (Vertigo)*	1
31 Aug 91	Joseph And The Amazing Technicolour Dreamcoat *Jason Donovan/Original London Cast (Really Useful)*	2
14 Sep 91	From Time To Time – The Singles Collection *Paul Young (Columbia)*	1
21 Sep 91	On Every Street *Dire Straits (Vertigo)*	1
28 Sep 91	Use Your Illusion II *Guns N' Roses (Geffen)*	1
5 Oct 91	Waking Up The Neighbours *Bryan Adams (A & M)*	1
12 Oct 91	Stars *Simply Red (East West)*	2
26 Oct 91	Chorus *Erasure (Mute)*	1
2 Nov 91	Stars *Simply Red (East West)*	1
9 Nov 91	Greatest Hits II *Queen (Parlophone)*	1
16 Nov 91	Shepherd Moons *Enya (WEA)*	1
23 Nov 91	We Can't Dance *Genesis (Virgin)*	1
30 Nov 91	Dangerous *Michael Jackson (Epic)*	1
7 Dec 91	Greatest Hits II *Queen (Parlophone)*	4

403

Since 14 January 1989, the albums charts have been split into a Top 75 'Artist Albums' and a Top 20 'Compilation Albums'. The 52 number one hits on the Compilation Albums are as follows:

14 Jan 89	Now! That's What I Call Music 13 *(EMI/Virgin/Polygram)*	1
21 Jan 89	The Premiere Collection *(Really Useful/Polydor)*	2
4 Feb 89	The Marquee – Thirty Legendary Years *(Polydor)*	4
4 Mar 89	The Awards *(Telstar)*	1
11 Mar 89	The Premiere Collection *(Really Useful/Polydor)*	1
18 Mar 89	Deep Heat *(Telstar)*	1
25 Mar 89	Unforgettable 2 *(EMI)*	1
1 Apr 89	Now! That's What I Call Music 14 *(EMI/Virgin/Polygram)*	7
20 May 89	Nite Flite 2 *(CBS)*	2
3 Jun 89	The Hits Album 10 *(CBS/WEA/BMG)*	6
15 Jul 89	Now! Dance '89 *(EMI/Virgin)*	6

26 Aug 89 Now! That's What I Call Music 15 *(EMI/Virgin/Polygram)* 5
30 Sep 89 Deep Heat 4 – Play With Fire *(Telstar)* 5
4 Nov 89 Smash Hits Party '89 *(Dover)* 3
25 Nov 89 The 80s – The Album Of The Decade *(EMI)* 1
2 Dec 89 Now! That's What I Call Music 16 *(EMI/Virgin/Polygram)* 7

20 Jan 90 Pure Soft Metal *(Stylus)* 2
3 Feb 90 Deep Heat 5 – Feed the Fever *(Telstar)* 2
17 Feb 90 Pure Soft Metal *(Stylus)* 3
10 Mar 90 Now Dance 901 *(EMI/Virgin/Polygram)* 4
7 Apr 90 Deep Heat 6 –The Sixth Sense *(Telstar)* 2
21 Apr 90 Just The Two Of Us *(CBS)* 2
5 May 90 Now That's What I Call Music 17 *(EMI/Virgin/Polygram)* 5
9 Jun 90 The Classic Experience II *(EMI)* 4
7 Jul 90 Deep Heat 7 – Seventh Heaven *(Telstar)* 1
14 Jul 90 Smash Hits – Rave! *(Dover)* 2
28 Jul 90 Now Dance 902 *(EMI/Virgin/Polygram)* 3
18 Aug 90 Knebworth –The Album *(Polydor)* 2
1 Sep 90 Megabass *(Telstar)* 4
29 Sep 90 Slammin' *(A & M)* 1
6 Oct 90 That Loving Feeling Vol. 3 *(Dino)* 3
27 Oct 90 Missing You – An Album Of Love *(EMI)* 3
17 Nov 90 Now Dance 903 *(EMI/Virgin/Polygram)* 2
1 Dec 90 Now That's What I Call Music 18 *(EMI/Virgin/Polygram)* 7

19 Jan 91 Dirty Dancing *(Original Soundtrack) (RCA)* 2
2 Feb 91 Deep Heat – The Ninth Life *(Telstar)* 2
16 Feb 91 The Lost Boys *(Original Soundtrack) (Atlantic)* 1
23 Feb 91 Awesome!! *(EMI)* 3
16 Mar 91 Unchained Melodies *(Telstar)* 3
6 Apr 91 Now That's What I Call Music 19 *(EMI/Virgin/Polygram)* 5
11 May 91 Thinking Of You *(Columbia)* 2
25 May 91 Smash Hits – Massive *(Dover)* 2
8 Jun 91 The Essential Mozart *(Decca)* 1
15 Jun 91 The Rhythm Divine *(Dino)* 1
22 Jun 91 The Essential Mozart *(Decca)* 1
29 Jun 91 Wings Of Love *(A & M)* 5
3 Aug 91 Thin Ice 2– The Second Shiver *(Telstar)* 1
10 Aug 91 Purple Rainbows *(Polydor)* 1
17 Aug 91 The Hits Album *(Sony/BMG)* 2
31 Aug 91 The Sound Of The Suburbs *(Columbia)* 3
21 Sep 91 Groovy Ghetto *(Arcade)* 2
5 Oct 91 Now Dance 91 *(EMI/Virgin/Polygram)* 3
26 Oct 91 Two Rooms – Elton John & Bernie Taupin *(Mercury)* 1
2 Nov 91 Hardcore Ecstasy *(Dino)* 4
30 Nov 91 Now That's What I Call Music 20 *(EMI/Virgin/Polygram)* . . . 5+

All albums were, of course, credited to 'Various Artists'.

MOST NUMBER ONE ALBUMS

12	Beatles
9	Rolling Stones
8	Abba
8	Led Zeppelin
8	Queen
7	David Bowie
7	Paul McCartney/Wings
7	Rod Stewart
6	Bob Dylan
6	Elton John
6	Elvis Presley
6	Cliff Richard
5	Genesis
5	Police
4	Dire Straits
4	Fleetwood Mac
4	Madonna
4	Roxy Music *(1 with Bryan Ferry)*
4	Shadows
4	Simple Minds
4	Status Quo
4	U2
3	Boney M
3	Kate Bush
3	Carpenters
3	Phil Collins
3	Deep Purple
3	Erasure
3	Eurythmics
3	Michael Jackson *(plus 1 with Jacksons)*
3	John Lennon
3	George Mitchell Minstrels
3	Moody Blues
3	Gary Numan/Tubeway Army
3	Pink Floyd
3	Prince
3	Paul Simon *(plus 2 with Simon and Garfunkel)*
3	Slade
3	Barbra Streisand
3	T. Rex
3	Andy Williams
3	Paul Young

Diana Ross and the Supremes have had two number ones and one more with the Temptations.

Bryan Ferry has one solo number one to go with the four Roxy Music chart toppers, on all of which he sang lead and on one of which he was given equal billing with Roxy Music as it also featured several solo Ferry tracks.

Sting has two solo number one albums as well as five as lead singer of the Police.

George Michael has two solo chart-topping albums and 2 more as half of Wham!

Luciano Pavarotti has had two number one albums as a soloist plus one in collaboration with José Carreras and Placido Domingo.

MOST WEEKS AT NUMBER ONE

163	Beatles
115	Cast of *South Pacific* Film Soundtrack
70	Cast of *The Sound of Music* Film Soundtrack
49	Abba
49	Elvis Presley
48	Simon and Garfunkel
43	Rolling Stones
29	Carpenters
29	Cliff Richard
28	Elton John
27	Rod Stewart
23	Phil Collins
22	Dire Straits
22	Bob Dylan
21	David Bowie
21	Shadows *(plus 22 weeks backing Cliff Richard)*
20	Queen
19	Madonna

19 George Mitchell Minstrels
18 Cast of *Saturday Night Fever* Film Soundtrack
16 Paul McCartney/Wings
15 Police
15 Barbra Streisand
14 Michael Jackson
  (plus 3 with Jackson Five)
14 Led Zeppelin
13 Beach Boys
13 Cast of *Grease* Film Soundtrack
13 Broadway cast of *West Side Story*
13 Eurythmics
13 Roxy Music
12 Adam and the Ants
12 Kids from 'Fame'
12 Bob Marley and the Wailers
12 T. Rex

11 Paul Simon
10 John Lennon
10 Diana Ross and the Supremes
  (plus 4 with the Temptations)
10 Simply Red
10 Stylistics
10 Slim Whitman

List excludes individual appearances on compilations and soundtracks, except where the soundtrack is credited to one artist, for example Elvis Presley's Blue Hawaii.

Luciano Pavarotti has enjoyed six solo weeks at number one, plus five more with Placido Domingo and José Carreras.

Grease

MOST WEEKS AT NUMBER ONE
IN A CALENDAR YEAR

Only five acts have spent more than 20 weeks on top of the charts in any one year. Two of these were film soundtrack casts. The feat has not been achieved since 1970.

52	*Cast of* South Pacific	1959
45	*Cast of* South Pacific	1960
40	Beatles	1964
34	Beatles	1963
30	*Cast of* The Sound Of Music	1966
26	Beatles	1967
24	Elvis Presley	1962
	Simon and Garfunkel	1970
22	Elvis Presley	1961
20	*Cast of* The Sound Of Music	1965

407

MOST NUMBER ONE ALBUMS
IN A CALENDAR YEAR

Only two acts have achieved the feat of getting three albums to number one in one year. They are:

1965   Beatles *(Beatles For Sale, Help, Rubber Soul)*
1972   T. Rex *(Electric Warrior, Prophets Seers . . ./My People Were Fair . . . , Bolan Boogie*

The second of T. Tex's three number ones was a re-issued double album of Tyrannosaurus Rex material, so Marc Bolan's achievement could be considered even better than the Beatles, whose chart-topping albums were all single discs.

Sixteen acts have had two number one hits in a year, as follows:

5 times	Beatles	(1963, 1964, 1965, 1969, 1970)
4 times	Abba	(1979, 1980, 1981, 1982)
3 times	Elton John	(1973, 1974, 1990)
2 times	Bob Dylan	(1965, 1970)
	Led Zeppelin	(1970, 1976)
	George Mitchell Minstrels	(1961, 1962)
Once	David Bowie	(1973)
	Erasure	(1989)
	Monkees	(1967)

Gary Numan/Tubeway Army . . . . (1979)
Mike Oldfield . . . . (1974)
Elvis Presley . . . . (1962)
Queen . . . . (1991)
Slade . . . . (1973)
T. Rex . . . . (1972)
Andy Williams . . . . (1971)

In 1981, Phil Collins had number one hits as a soloist and as part of Genesis. In 1983 Michael Jackson hit the top with *Thriller* and also with a Greatest Hits package featuring tracks by the Jackson Five as well as some solo tracks by Michael. In 1990 Luciano Pavarotti was on top of the charts with *The Essential Pavarotti* and, seven weeks later, *In Concert* with José Carreras and Placido Domingo.

SELF-REPLACEMENT AT THE TOP

Only three acts have ever knocked themselves off the top of the charts. They

are:

BEATLES *With The Beatles* replaced *Please Please Me* on 7 Dec 63
BEATLES *Beatles for Sale* replaced *A Hard Day's Night* on 19 Dec 64
BOB DYLAN *Bringing It All Back Home* replaced *Freewheelin' Bob Dylan* on 29 May 65
MIKE OLDFIELD *Tubular Bells* replaced *Hergest Ridge* on 5 Oct 74

On 7 Aug 82 *Kids From Fame* replaced *Fame* at the top, but the TV spin-off featured an entirely different cast from the album sound-track.

Hergest Ridge was released after *Tubular Bells* but got to number one first. Bob Dylan had two Top Ten hit albums released between *Freewheelin'* and *Bringing It All Back Home*.

Mike Oldfield

MOST WEEKS AT NUMBER ONE
BY AN ALBUM IN TOTAL

115	South Pacific	*Film Soundtrack*
70	The Sound Of Music	*Film Soundtrack*
41	Bridge Over Troubled Water	*Simon and Garfunkel*
30	Please Please Me	*Beatles*
27	Sergeant Pepper's Lonely Hearts Club Band	*Beatles*
22	GI Blues	*Elvis Presley (Film Soundtrack)*
21	With The Beatles	*Beatles*
21	A Hard Day's Night	*Beatles (Film Soundtrack)*
18	Blue Hawaii	*Elvis Presley (Film Soundtrack)*
18	Saturday Night Fever	*Film Soundtrack*
17	Abbey Road	*Beatles*
17	The Singles 1969–1973	*Carpenters*
15	... But Seriously	*Phil Collins*
14	Brothers In Arms	*Dire Straits*
14	Summer Holiday	*(Cliff Richard and the Shadows (Film Soundtrack)*
13	John Wesley Harding	*Bob Dylan*
13	Grease	*Film Soundtrack*
13	West Side Story	*Film Soundtrack*
12	Kings Of The Wild Frontier	*Adam and the Ants*
12	The Kids From 'Fame'	*Kids From Fame*
12	Legend	*Bob Marley and the Wailers*
12	The Rolling Stones	*Rolling Stones*
11	Greatest Hits	*Abba*
11	Beatles For Sale	*Beatles*
11	Elton John's Greatest Hits	*Elton John*
11	20 All Time Hits Of The Fifties	*Various Artists*
10	Arrival	*Abba*
10	20 Golden Greats	*Beach Boys*
10	Greatest Hits	*Eurythmics*
10	Rolling Stones No. 2	*Rolling Stones*

No disc has spent more than 7 weeks at number one on the Compilation Albums chart. That total has been achieved by three of the **Now! That's What I Call Music** series, numbers 14, 16 and 18.

MOST CONSECUTIVE WEEKS AT NUMBER ONE
BY ONE ALBUM

70	South Pacific *Film Soundtrack*	from 8 Nov 58
30	Please Please Me *Beatles*	from 11 May 63
23	Sergeant Pepper's Lonely Hearts Club Band *Beatles*	from 10 Jun 67
21	With The Beatles *Beatles*	from 7 Dec 63
21	A Hard Day's Night *Beatles*	from 25 Jul 64
19	South Pacific *Film Soundtrack*	from 19 Mar 60
18	The Sound Of Music *Film Soundtrack*	from 1 Oct 66

18	Saturday Night Fever *Film Soundtrack*	from 6 May 78
17	Blue Hawaii *Elvis Presley*	from 24 Feb 62
14	Summer Holiday *Cliff Richard and the Shadows*	from 2 Feb 63
13	South Pacific *Film Soundtrack*	from 15 Oct 60
13	Bridge Over Troubled Water *Simon and Garfunkel*	from 21 Feb 70
13	Grease *Film Soundtrack*	from 7 Oct 78
12	GI Blues *Elvis Presley*	from 8 Apr 61
12	Rolling Stones *Rolling Stones*	from 2 May 64
12	Legend *Bob Marley and the Wailers*	from 19 May 84
11	Abbey Road *Beatles*	from 4 Oct 69
11	Bridge Over Troubled Water *Simon and Garfunkel*	from 16 Jan 71
11	The Singles 1969–1973 *Carpenters*	from 9 Mar 74
11	Elton John's Greatest Hits *Elton John*	from 23 Nov 74
10	The Sound Of Music *Film Soundtrack*	from 5 Jun 65
10	The Sound Of Music *Film Soundtrack*	from 16 Oct 65
10	The Sound Of Music *Film Soundtrack*	from 19 Feb 66
10	John Wesley Harding *Bob Dylan*	from 9 Mar 68
10	20 Golden Greats *Beach Boys*	from 24 Jul 76
10	Kings Of The Wild Frontier *Adam and the Ants*	from 14 Mar 81
10	Brothers In Arms *Dire Straits*	from 18 Jan 86

The run of 11 weeks by *Bridge Over Troubled Water* includes 8 weeks at number one when charts were not published because of a postal strike.

LONGEST CLIMB TO NUMBER ONE

Four albums have taken more than one year from their original date of chart entry to climb to the number one position on the regular chart, as follows:

3 years 298 days
Tyrannosaurus Rex

(from 13 Jul 68 to 6 May 72)
My People Were Fair And Had Sky In Their Hair, But Now They're Content To Wear Stars On Their Brows

2 years 67 days
Elvis Presley

(from 5 Jul 75 to 10 Sep 77)
40 Greatest Hits

1 year 321 days
Original Soundtrack

(from 6 Sep 80 to 24 Jul 82)
Fame

1 year 83 days
Mike Oldfield

(from 14 Jul 73 to 5 Oct 74)
Tubular Bells

Ten other albums have taken 30 weeks or more to reach the top, as follows:

| *Rumours* | Fleetwood Mac | **49 weeks** |
| *The Freewheelin' Bob Dylan* | Bob Dylan | **48 weeks** |

Sleeping With The Past	Elton John	**44 weeks**
Like A Virgin	Madonna	**44 weeks**
Circle Of One	Oleta Adams	**40 weeks**
Black And White Minstrel Show	George Mitchell Minstrells	**36 weeks**
Born In The USA	Bruce Springsteen	**36 weeks**
Greatest Hits	Andy Williams	**35 weeks**
Band On The Run	Wings	**33 weeks**
And I Love You So	Perry Como	**30 weeks**

Tyrannosaurus Rex hit number one with the longest titled album ever to hit the top only after it was re-released in 1972 as a double album with *Prophets, Seers, Sages And The Angels Of The Ages*. Presley's album hit the top in the period immediately following his death. *Tubular Bells* spent 11 weeks at number two before replacing its follow-up at the very top, and *Rumours* remained 32 weeks in the Top Ten before hitting the number one slot. *The Freewheelin' Bob Dylan* climbed to the top during its seventh chart run. Oleta Adams became the first chart act ever to re-enter the charts at number one, 38 weeks after an original 2 week run for *Circle Of One*, during which it peaked at number 49.

The Soundtrack album of the film *Dirty Dancing* came on to the main chart on 31 October 1987, before the formation of the Compilation Albums chart. It spent 63 weeks on the main chart without ever climbing higher than number four, before being switched to the Compilations Chart on 14 January 1989. On 19 January 1991, 3 years and 80 days after its first entry on the main chart and 2 years and 5 days after it first came on to the Compilations Chart, it topped the Compilation Albums chart for the first time.

411

Perry Como

MOST CONSECUTIVE NUMBER ONE
HIT ALBUMS

Twenty-two different acts have hit the very top of the albums chart with three or more consecutive official album releases, as follows:

11 Beatles (From *Please Please Me* in 1963 to *Let It Be* in 1970. All the Beatles albums made while they were actively recording hit number one. During this run *A Collection Of Beatles Oldies, Magical Mystery Tour* (import) and *Yellow Submarine* all hit the charts, but only the *Oldies* album could be considered even vaguely as part of the official sequence of Beatles albums. If it is considered an official album release, then the Beatles have a best consecutive run of 7 number ones, and a smaller run of four)

8 Abba (From 1976 to 1982: *Greatest Hits* to *The Singles – The First Ten Years* inclusive)

8 Led Zeppelin (From 1970 to 1979: *Led Zeppelin 2* to *In Through The Out Door* inclusive)

6 Rod Stewart (From 1971 to 1976: *Every Picture Tells A Story* to *A Night On The Town* inclusive)

5 Police (From 1979 to 1986: *Reggatta De Blanc* to *Every Breath You Take – The Singles* inclusive. These were their final five albums)

5 Rolling Stones (From 1969 to 1973: *Let It Bleed* to *Goat's Head Soup*. Their last two official releases on Decca and their first three on Rolling Stones Records)

4 Bob Dylan (From 1968 to 1970: *John Wesley Harding* to *New Morning* inclusive)

4 Elton John (From 1973 to 1975: *Don't Shoot Me, I'm Only The Piano Player* to *Elton John's Greatest Hits* inclusive)

4 Simple Minds (From 1984 to 1989: *Sparkle In The Rain* to *Street Fighting Years* inclusive. Each album spent only one week at the top of the charts)

3 Boney M (From 1978 to 1980: *Night Flight To Venus, Oceans Of Fantasy* and *The Magic Of Boney M*)

3 David Bowie. (From 1973 to 1974: *Aladdin Sane, Pin-Ups* and *Diamond Dogs*)

3 Dire Straits (From 1985 to 1991: *Brothers In Arms, Money For Nothing* and *On Every Street*)

3 Erasure (From 1988 to 1991: *The Innocents, Wild!* and *Circus*)

3 Genesis (From 1983 to 1991: *Genesis, Invisible Touch* and *We Can't Dance*. These were three consecutive official releases, although their 1970 album *Trespass* charted for the first time between the success of *Genesis* and *Invisible Touch*)

3 Michael Jackson (From 1982 to 1991: *Thriller, Bad* and *Dangerous*. No fewer than five other albums under the Jackson name hit the charts during this hat-trick, but there is no doubt that these were three consecutive official releases by Jacko)

3 George Mitchell Minstrels (From 1961 to 1963, the first album chart hat-trick: *The Black And White Minstrel Show, Another Black And White Minstrel Show* and *On Stage With The George Mitchell Minstrels*)

3 **Gary Numan** (From 1979 to 1980: *Replicas, The Pleasure Principle* and *Telekon. Tubeway Army* was released before *Replicas*, even though it hit the charts later)

3 **Prince** (From 1988 to 1991: *Lovesexy, Batman* and *Graffiti Bridge*)

3 **Queen** (From 1989 to 1991: *Miracle, Innuendo* and *Greatest Hits Vol. 2*)

3 **Slade** (From 1973 to 1974: *Slayed?, Sladest* and *Old New Borrowed And Blue.*)

3 **T. Rex** (From 1971 to 1972: *Electric Warrior, Prophets Seers And Sages The Angels Of The Ages/My People Were Fair And Had Sky In Their Hair But Now They're Content To Wear Stars On Their Brows* and *Bolan Boogie.* The second of the three was a double album reissue, but it had never been issued in that format, and one half of the double album had never been a hit before)

3 **U2** (From 1984 to 1988: *The Unforgettable Fire, The Joshua Tree* and *Rattle And Hum*)

Prince

STRAIGHT IN AT NUMBER ONE

After the first chart on 8 November 1958, no album made its chart debut at number one until the Beatles' fifth album, *Help*, did so on 14 August 1965. However, it is now a routine event in the albums charts, so much so that of 24 number one hit albums in 1991, 22 came on to the charts at number one. Eighteen acts have achieved this feat at least three times, as follows:

7   DAVID BOWIE

6   ROLLING STONES

5   BEATLES
    GENESIS
    LED ZEPPELIN
    POLICE

4   ABBA
    DIRE STRAITS
    ELTON JOHN
    PAUL McCARTNEY
    QUEEN
    SIMPLE MINDS
    U2

3   PHIL COLLINS
    ERASURE
    MADONNA
    PRINCE
    STATUS QUO

Paul McCartney has therefore achieved the feat nine times, five times with the Beatles and four times solo. Phil Collins has done it eight times, five times with Genesis and three times solo.

413

THE TOP TWENTY ALBUMS ACTS

A table showing the comparative achievements of the twenty most charted album acts of all time.

Act	Year First Charted	Total Weeks	Total Hits	Top Ten	No. Ones	Most Charted Album
Beatles	1963	1082	25	18	12	*Sgt. Pepper's Lonely Hearts Club Band*: 164 wks
Simon and Garfunkel	1966	1039	10	7	2	*Bridge Over Troubled Water*: 303 wks
Dire Straits	1978	1030	8	8	4	*Makin' Movies*: 249 wks
Elvis Presley	1958	1026	95	36	6	*Blue Hawaii*: 65 wks
Queen	1974	890	19	17	8	*Greatest Hits*: 338 wks
David Bowie	1972	869	27	19	7	*The Rise And Fall Of Ziggy Stardust And The Spiders From Mars*: 172 wks
Fleetwood Mac	1968	765	14	9	4	*Rumours*: 443 wks
Pink Floyd	1967	746	16	13	3	*Dark Side Of The Moon*: 301 wks
Phil Collins	1981	730	5	5	3	*Face Value*: 274 wks
U2	1981	725	10	6	4	*Live Under A Blood Red Sky*: 201 wks
Cliff Richard	1959	717	47	31	6	*Love Songs*: 43 wks
Elton John	1970	709	30	17	6	*Greatest Hits* and *Goodbye Yellow Brick Road*: 84 wks
Rolling Stones	1964	688	37	29	9	*Rolling Stones*: 51 wks
Rod Stewart	1970	666	20	16	7	*Atlantic Crossing*: 88 wks
Frank Sinatra	1958	613	49	27	1	*My Way*: 59 wks
Bob Dylan	1964	560	34	24	6	*Greatest Hits*: 83 wks
Meat Loaf	1978	548	7	5	1	*Bat Out Of Hell*: 416 wks
Beach Boys	1965	547	26	14	2	*Best Of The Beach Boys*: 142 wks
Carpenters	1971	546	16	8	3	*Singles 1969–1973*: 125 wks
Michael Jackson	1972	538	13	5	3	*Off The Wall*: 173 wks

Over the past two years since *British Hit Albums 4* was published, the Carpenters have climbed back into the Top 20 acts, at the expense of Abba, who slip to number 23. All the top acts except for the Beatles and Frank Sinatra have appeared in the charts over the past two years. Phil Collins has added most to his total in 1990 and 1991, a further 138 weeks, which moved him up from 14th to 9th on the overall weeks on chart listing. No other acts in the top 20 added 100 weeks over the past two years.

Nobody apart from Phil Collins has climbed even two places within the Top 20 since the end of 1989, but Michael Jackson has fallen three places, while the Rolling Stones and Frank Sinatra have each slipped two rungs.

Both Elvis Presley and Frank Sinatra featured in the very first albums chart. The most recent arrival to the charts of any of the Top 20 acts is by U2, whose first album chart action came in the week ending 29 Aug 1981.

Of the 20 leading acts, ten are British, eight are American, one is a transatlantic mixture (Fleetwood Mac), and one is Irish. There are nine male solo acts, but no female soloists. Christine McVie and Stevie Nicks of Fleetwood Mac, and Karen Carpenter make the only dent in the male supremacy of the albums charts, although the highest ranked female soloist, Madonna, can expect to crash the Top Twenty in time for the sixth edition of *British Hit Albums*. She is currently at number 22.

If we look at the top acts on the basis of the average number of weeks each album has spent in the charts (i.e. Total Weeks divided by Total Hits), six acts prove to have spent an average of more than one year on the charts with each album:

Phil Collins	146.0 weeks on chart per album
Dire Straits	128.8 weeks on chart per album
Simon and Garfunkel	103.9 weeks on chart per album
Meat Loaf	78.3 weeks on chart per album
U2	72.5 weeks on chart per album
Fleetwood Mac	54.6 weeks on chart per album

415

At the other end of the scale, each album hit by Elvis Presley has lasted on average only 10.8 weeks on the chart, each Frank Sinatra hit lasts only 12.5 weeks, and each Cliff Richard album hangs around for no more than 15.3 weeks. Bob Dylan (16.5 weeks) and the Rolling Stones (18.6 weeks) are the only other acts to average fewer than 20 weeks of chart action per hit.

Ranking acts purely on the basis of weeks on chart is not a perfect solution, but in the case of the albums charts, overall success equates far more closely with chart life than on the singles charts. Long-running chart successes are what both the performers and their record companies are looking for. This chart is not meant to reflect total sales, but merely the relative chart success of the biggest album acts in British chart history.

If the occasional typographical error were to be allowed, we could say that **Paul Gambaccini** spent part of the last two years *Sleeping With The Pest*, musing about *The Existential Pavarotti* as *The Soul Ages*. To be strictly accurate, Gambaccini changed radio stations, changed television networks, and even changed the airline for which he does in-flight entertainment. Thank heavens *Hit Albums* and *Hit Singles* have remained constant parts of his life. Paul is not yet *Out of Tim*.

Tim Rice's latest album venture is *Tycoon*, his translation and adaptation of the Michel Berger/Luc Plamondon French hit musical *Starmania*. The album features tracks by Kim Carnes, Celine Dion, Matt and Luke Goss, Nina Hagen, Tom Jones, Peter Kingsbury, Cyndi Lauper, Kevin Robinson, Ronnie Spector and Willy de Ville. He is currently writing songs for two forthcoming Walt Disney animated feature films, *Aladdin* and *King of the Jungle*. He took 7 for 27 for Heartaches CC against Mullion in September 1991.

Jonathan Rice has had a busy two years since the last *British Hit Albums* hit the bookstalls, despite the absence of outstandingly brilliant new albums to listen to, apart from Runrig's *The Big Wheel*. He has written books on bridge (the card game, not the Sydney Harbour type), doing business in Japan and cricket pavilions. He has also invented a business game and acquired a copy of *Des O'Connor's Greatest Hits*, which for some reason he has not yet got round to listening to. Another tragedy in his life has been the death of Kevin the goldfish (aged 6).